THE PICTURE HISTORY OF THE BOSTON CELTICS

"Wait, I've got it—the Celtics. *We'll call them the* Boston Celtics!

"The name has a great basketball tradition. And Boston is full of Irishmen.

"Yes, that's it. We'll put them in green uniforms and call them the Boston Celtics."

—Founder Walter Brown
during a conversation
with team publicist
J. Howard McHugh in
Summer 1946.

Boston Garden, as it was when the Celtics were born in 1946.

Boston Garden, as it is now.

GEORGE SULLIVAN

THE PICTURE HISTORY OF THE BOSTON CELTICS

The Bobbs-Merrill Company, Inc.
Indianapolis/New York

Books by George Sullivan

The Picture History of the Boston Celtics
The Picture History of the Boston Red Sox
Yankees: An Illustrated History (with John Powers)
The Flying Fisherman (with R.V. "Gadabout" Gaddis)

Jacket photo by Dick Raphael
Published by The Bobbs-Merrill Co., Inc.
Indianapolis/New York
Manufactured in the United States of America
Revised edition
First Paperback Printing
Designed by J. Tschantre Graphic Services, Ltd.

Library of Congress Cataloging in Publication Data
Sullivan, George, 1933-
The picture history of the Boston Celtics.

Includes index.
1. Boston Celtics (Basketball team)–History.
I. Title.
GV885.52.B67S92 1982 796.32′364′0974461 82-4129
1980-81 ISBN 0-672-52728-6 AACR2

For my sisters and brother:
Mary, Catherine, Anne, Eleanor and James
—like the Celtics, a championship quintet

ACKNOWLEDGMENTS

My boxscore has a long assist column.

Particular thanks go to Joe Fitzgerald, Sam Brogna and Tom Henshaw. All three newsmen gave generous and exceptional help.

Fitzgerald, a *Boston Herald American* columnist, compiled a treasury of material while authoring two major books on the Celtics and gave me complete access to those riches.

Brogna, another *Boston Herald American* veteran, covered the Celtics' birth in 1946 and has been at courtside ever since. His Celtic knowledge is vintage, and he let me borrow abundantly from both his memory and files.

Henshaw, former Associated Press and *Boston Herald Traveler* writer, now a prolific freelancer, is another young old pro who allowed me to probe his memories and files, both copious.

Other sportswriting colleagues who helped in a variety of ways—all important—include: Bob Duffy, John Powers, Bob Ryan and Tom D'Angelo of the *Boston Globe* and Kevin Dupont, Hugh Wheelwright, David Cataneo and Tom Melville of the *Boston Herald American.* So did Ken Meyer of WBZ radio in Boston.

The Naismith Memorial Basketball Hall of Fame at Springfield, Massachusetts, was a bonanza. No request stumped executive director Lee Williams and librarian June Harrison Steitz as they cheerfully provided a fountain of facts and artwork, including many photographs from the Hall's invaluable William G. "Bill" Mokray Collection.

The Hall of Fame was just one source of the illustrations that enhance this book.

The *Boston Globe* and *Boston Herald American* also furnished some notable photographs, as did the Associated Press and United Press International. So did the skilled lenses of Frank O'Brien, Dick Raphael, George Kalinsky, John Fredrickson, Steve Lipofsky, Art Illman, Ted Fitzgerald, Ray Foley, Steve Carter and John Moxley.

Other valuable artwork came from the collections of Bob Remer, Sam Cohen, Tim Cohane, Tom Feenan and Peter Shaw, along with those of former Celtics Chuck Cooper, Bob Cousy, Tom Heinsohn, Ed Macauley, Saul Marsch (formerly Mariaschin) and Tom (Satch) Sanders. They scoured attics and cellars, and produced some masterpieces.

And a wealth of photos was provided by the Celtics' organization. Red Auerbach and his front-office team could not have been more cooperative in response to my requests and questions. The majority was fielded by an all-pro tandem: publicist Howie McHugh and public relations director Tod Rosensweig. McHugh was the midwife at the Celtics' birth in 1946, and has been fussing over them (and the media) ever since while becoming a Boston and NBA institution. And Jeff Twiss and John Creed were always ready with an assist.

Special thanks go to Jeff Cohen, longtime Celtic vice president, now vice president of the football Boston Breakers. It was he who suggested and encouraged me to do a book on the Celtics more than a dozen years ago, and now knows I was listening after all. Also always accommodating and in unfailing good humor through all the good years, and the few poor ones, have been Mary Faherty, secretary to Auerbach, and Jan Volk, the team's general counsel and vice president.

For my second Bobbs-Merrill book in a row, my appreciation to editors Gene Rachlis and Barbara Lagowski for their advice and patience, and to Kevin Connors for his interest and enthusiasm. Thanks also to the Jim Tschantre Graphics squad for its expertise.

A major assist also goes to Mary Sullivan Ford, who maintained both her berth as all-star typist and her pedestal in the Big Sister Hall of Fame.

And, finally, I am grateful to my home team—Betty and our Lisa, George and Sean—for not blowing the whistle as I went one-on-one with a typewriter through what must have seemed quadruple overtime.

GEORGE SULLIVAN
Belmont, Massachusetts
September 1982

Table of Contents

BOSTON CELTICS
1966
WORLD
CHAMPIONS
BOSTON CELTICS
1962
WORLD
CHAMPIONS
BOSTON CELTICS
1961
WORLD
CHAMPIONS
BOSTON CELTICS
1965
WORLD
CHAMPIONS
BOSTON CELTICS
1960
WORLD
CHAMPIONS
BOSTON CELTICS
1959
WORLD
CHAMPIONS
BOSTON CELTICS
1957
WORLD
CHAMPIONS

THE TRADITION

"The Celtics aren't a team. They're a way of life."

Arnold (Red) Auerbach

The Boston Celtics are the greatest team in basketball history, and by many yardsticks the most successful in *any* professional sport.

They don't have as many world championships as baseball's New York Yankees (22 World Series rings in 78 years) or hockey's Montreal Canadians (22 Stanley Cup inscriptions in 72 years). But at half the age, the Celtics have a better title ratio, collecting 13 National Basketball Association crowns in 35 years. And their eight consecutive world championships from 1959 through 1966 far surpass the five straight won by the 1949-53 Yankees and 1956-60 Canadians. Nor can any other team approach the Celtics' procession of nine championships in 10 years and 11 titles in 13 seasons.

When that dynasty ended in 1969, the tradition was passed on to another Celtic generation that quickly produced two more 9-feet-by-15, green-and-white banners to hang from the Boston Garden rafters with all the others. And by decade's end the tradition was passed on to still another Celtic generation that forged the most stunning turnaround in league history and is now on the threshold of what could be another championship era.

It is a tradition that continues with each passing season and has carved a record that has become a legend.

So is the lineup of Celtics that has paraded across the antique Garden's parquet floor over the years:

. . . Easy Ed Macauley, Bob Cousy, Bill Sharman, Frank Ramsey, Jungle Jim Loscutoff, Tom Heinsohn, Bill Russell, Sam Jones, K.C. Jones, Tom (Satch) Sanders, John Havlicek, Larry Siegfried, Don Nelson, Don Chaney, Jo Jo White, Dave Cowens, Paul Silas, Charlie Scott, Nate (Tiny) Archibald, Larry Bird. . . .

And the drum major twirling the baton for that parade, of course, is *Arnold (Red) Auerbach*. It is Auerbach who has sculpted that Celtic tradition, after founder Walter Brown had laid the cornerstone, and has given it continuity over the decades—first as coach, then as general manager and president.

It is Auerbach who transformed the team from doormat to champion, who convinced a galaxy of stars that the only important statistic is winning, who implemented the world's most devasting fastbreak, who installed a system that with rare exception has made Basketball Celtics Style roundball at its exciting best and raised the artistic level of the sport. It is Auerbach who has made the Celtics the most copied team in basketball history and the team that has influenced the sport more than any other.

It also was Auerbach who was overseer of another imprint left on sports history by the Celtics. A triple imprint, really.

The Celtics made history by breaking the NBA's color line in 1950 when they drafted Chuck Cooper, the league's first black. The Celtics made history during the 1963-64 season when they became the first NBA team to dare put five blacks on the court at the same time (when Willie Naulls would sub for starter Tom Heinsohn and team with Bill Russell, Satch Sanders and the Jones boys). And the Celtics made history in 1966 by becoming the first major league team in *any sport* to be directed by a black, when Auerbach turned over the coaching reins to Russell.

It is part of the overall fabric that has made the Celtics a name filled with mystique and magic. The green jersey is to basketball what the Yankee pinstripe is to baseball. And so while the Celtics represent Boston and New England, they also are a national team, a team known around the world.

Yet it is a team that was a stepchild on the Boston sports scene, born in a city that was hockey hotbed during the Wintertime and considered basketball a game for giraffes running around in their underwear. It is a team so bad in those early days that it was only half-jokingly called Smeltics. And it is a team that, despite all its success on the court, not too long ago was the league's most unstable franchise as it bounced from one owner to another—buffeted by a dozen ownership changes (including a bizarre franchise swap) in the 15 years between Walter Brown's death in 1964 and Harry Mangurian taking over sole ownership in 1979 to finally provide financial stability.

It is an unlikely success story. This is that story in words and pictures.

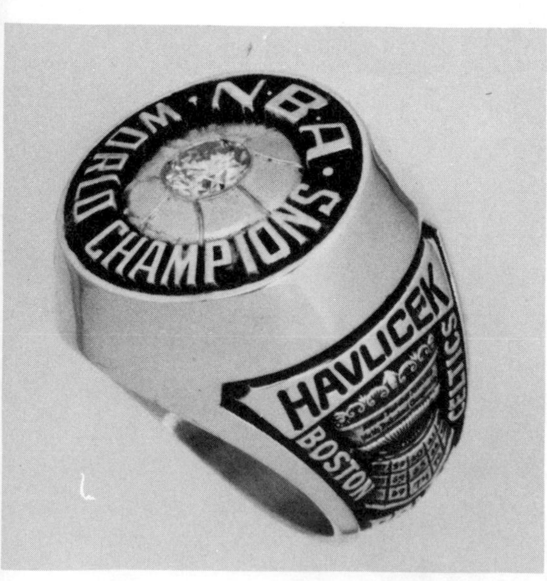

THE SEASONS

"Ladies and gentlemen, here come the world champion Boston Celtics!"

Boston Garden public address announcers have thundered that introduction 532 times over the years as Celtic defending champions jogged onto the court for pregame warmups and organist John Kiley pumped out "It's a Great Day Tonight for the Irish!"

1946–47

Boston's Newest Sports Thrill

MAJOR LEAGUE Basketball

TONIGHT

BOSTON CELTICS vs. CHICAGO

TIME 8:30 P.M.

RESERVED SEATS $2.75, $2.00, $1.25 TAX INC.

BOSTON ARENA

The Celtics were a *smash* in their Boston debut on November 5, 1946. A two-handed setshot by Kevin (Chuck) Connors shattered the glass backboard at the west end of Boston Arena, and the unveiling of professional basketball in Boston was delayed an hour beyond the scheduled 8:30 tapoff between the Celtics and Chicago Stags.

Glass backboards were a novelty then, the latest in basketball hardware, and the Arena had no replacement. A truck was dispatched across town for one at Boston Garden, where Gene Autry's Rodeo was playing to a packed house.

A backboard was discovered stored behind the Brahma bull's pen. So quick-thinking Celtic publicist Howie McHugh bribed a couple of tipsy cowboys to fetch it—and be careful not to break the glass, please. (The delicate maneuver produced some high drama and the thought that if the unsteady wranglers failed in their mission, Boston's first major league basketball game would be a halfcourt affair.)

"I never saw two guys sober up so fast in my life," recalls McHugh, now the league's elder statesman, the only fulltime employee to have served with unbroken service since that first season.

Meanwhile, back at the Arena, the 4,329 first-nighters who had paid $1.25, $2 and $2.75 to sit in on history this Election Tuesday were kept entertained by John Kiley's organ music and a variety of shooting contests (at the east end) featuring Boston's newest team.

The Celtics sported white T-shirts and shorts with green trim and lettering, a shamrock on each hip, white knee socks ringed by four green stripes at the top, black leather knee guards and high white sneakers.

John (Honey) Russell's starting lineup averaged 6 feet 1½, an inch shorter than the squad's overall average, and included the league's tiniest player in 5-6 Mel Hirsch.

The backboard smashed by Connors—whose sense of timing and flair for the dramatic would be appreciated more in Hollywood than in Boston—may have been a sign.

The Celtics would lose that home opener in a 57-55 thriller (their second defeat, having already gotten off on the wrong sneaker in a road game, flattened by the Providence Steamrollers, 59-53). And that was just the start. The Celts hit the road and lost all three games on the trip, including their first overtime game that was a van Gogh in frustration at St. Louis.

Boston frittered away a halftime lead by scoring only one field goal in the third period, but still should have won in regulation. Instead, the Celtics folded in one of the more imaginative ways to lose a basketball game.

Kevin (Chuck) Connors, who would become famous as a television sharpshooter called "The Rifleman," smashed the glass backboard with a warmup shot, delaying the Celtics' Boston debut an hour.

With less than a minute remaining in the fourth quarter, Russell sent Al Brightman into the game to protect a dwindling lead. The eager forward reported to the St. Louis radio announcer at courtside, mistaking him for the official scorer. That breach of rules cost Boston a technical foul, and the Bombers made the free throw.

Even then the Celtics should have won. They had the lead and the basketball with five seconds left. But an overanxious Celtic, not identified in the reports of the game, fell while dribbling and lost the ball to an opponent whose desperation shot tied the game.

Boston then lost in overtime, 64-62. Still bristling over the technical for Brightman's lapse, the Celtics filed the first protest in their history. Which, of course, they also lost.

Front row (left to right): Jack (Dutch) Garfinkel, Chuck Hoefer, coach John (Honey) Russell, Johnny Simmons and Wyndol Gray. Back row: trainer Harvey Cohn, Al Brightman, Art Spector, Harold Kottman, Connie Simmons, Jerry Kelly and assistant coach Danny Silva.

It was that sort of first season for the Celtics, and the parade of setbacks and disappointments had started not long after the Basketball Association of America was born on June 6.

The league was formed by the Arena Managers Association of America during their meeting in New York, and the idea was to create tenants that would fill empty dates in their buildings.

The arena operators felt pro basketball was a game whose time had come. The sport hadn't caught on for decades, unable to shake its fly-by-night image of playing in dingy gyms and dancehalls dating back to the twenties. Now the time seemed right. With World War II just ended, restrictions were off, bigger crowds than ever were flocking to sports events seeking entertainment, dollars were plentiful, an abundance of athletic talent was marching home—and something called television was on the horizon.

Walter Brown, the sportsman who headed the Boston Garden-Arena Corporation, and Cleveland Arena operator Al Sutphin were the pistons behind the new league that embraced 11 franchises in two divisions. Boston, Providence, New York, Philadelphia, Pittsburgh and Washington comprised the East, Cleveland, Detroit, Toronto, Chicago and St. Louis the West. (Only Boston, New York and Philadelphia would survive five years.)

Not coincidentally, except for Washington, there was a National or American Hockey League team housed in each arena where the bas-

Celtics founder Walter Brown was a hockey man who fell in love with basketball.

John (Honey) Russell, the Celtics' first coach.

Little Chuck Hoefer, a 5-foot-9, 158-pound backcourtman, was acquired from Toronto for Mike (Red) Wallace over New Year's in the second trade in Celtic history, three weeks after the Kappen-Becker deal.

ketball teams would play. The arena operators were hockey people, and so the basketball league was founded largely by hockey people. That included Brown, an international hockey pioneer and president of the Boston Bruins, a man who uniquely would be elected to both the hockey and basketball halls of fame.

The person chosen to head the league also came from hockey—AHL president Maurice Podoloff, a New Haven lawyer, banker and realtor. At 5-2, it was noted that the league with the tallest players had the shortest president.

Actually, there were two other pro basketball leagues, but neither was generally considered truly major league—the American (basically a weekend league in Eastern cities) and the National (mostly in smaller cities in upper-state New York and the Midwest). The new league was on firmer foundation because it had the important backing of the big arenas in major cities.

A name was a bit of a problem, though. With American and National taken, the new league adopted the cumbersome title of Basketball Association of America (a matter the BAA would rectify by the end of the forties, absorbing the National League and becoming the National Basketball Association).

The naming of the Celtics was less of a problem. The name grew out of a conversation between Brown and McHugh, captain and star goaltender of Dartmouth's 1934 Ivy hockey champions who now was on the Garden publicity staff and assigned to handle the new basketball team owned by the Garden.

Brown and McHugh batted around a number of nicknames, including Whirlwinds, Unicorns and Olympics.

"Wait, I've got it—the *Celtics,*" Brown said suddenly. "We'll call them the *Boston Celtics!*

"The name has a great basketball tradition from the old Original Celtics in New York. And Boston is full of Irishmen.

"Yes, that's it. We'll put them in green uniforms and call them the *Boston Celtics.*"

McHugh tried to dissuade Brown.

"I told him no team with an Irish name had ever won a damned thing in Boston, including a pro football team named the Shamrocks that had fallen flat," McHugh recalls. "But Walter's mind was made up, and when his mind was made up on something, that was that.

"I sometimes think back on that and wonder what would have happened if I'd been able to talk Walter out of that name Celtics. Do you think Boston Unicorns would be a household name around the world today?"

So Boston's basketball baby was christened the Celtics, but the name didn't have much immediate luck o' the Irish. The first in a succession of obstacles popped up when Brown lost the coach he thought he'd long since lined up. That was Frank Keaney, whose Rhode Island team had been one-point losers to Kentucky in that Spring's NIT while featuring tourney MVP Ernie Calverley and Keaney's "firehouse" style of basketball that was a forerunner of the fastbreak.

Brown had to scramble for a replacement and came up with John Davis Russell, onetime defensive star of the legendary Original Celtics and a top college coach at Seton Hall and Manhattan. The previous season, at age 42, he had coached Manhattan to a 15-8 record while concluding his 3,200-game pro playing career as player-coach of Trenton in the American League.

"Honey Russell gives us the best of both worlds," Brown said, noting that most BAA coaches had college or pro backgrounds, not both.

Russell took over the Celtic reins at a disadvantage. Most teams had long before named coaches, coaches who ever since had been busy signing talent. With no college draft that first season, each club was on its own acquiring players. The only restrictions set by the league were that each player be paid within $3,000–$10,000 salary limits (few would make more than $6,000) and that squad payrolls not exceed $55,000.

Russell had to scrape for what was left in uncommitted talent and assemble a squad for the October 1 start of training camp. But the disadvantages of Boston basketball weren't a surprise to Russell, having played in the hockey town a number of times with touring pro teams.

"The first time I played in Boston was at the Arena," he told writers. "When we walked onto the court a half-hour before tapoff, the place was ice cold from the ice beneath the floor, the lighting was terrible—and the baskets were installed *upside down*."

All of which was a clue to the basketball IQ and interest of Bostonians, most of whom were addicted to hockey despite basketball having been invented only 90 miles away in Springfield, Massachusetts, 55 years earlier. And those who preferred basketball would be difficult to pry away from the college game, particularly as played by Holy Cross and Rhode Island. College doubleheaders were catching on at the Garden, among the reasons Brown was optimistic the pro game would succeed, too.

"I realize we have a tough row to hoe," he said. "We may have nobody here all year.

"But when I started with college basketball I was prepared to stay with it five years before it paid off. Within two seasons it was making its own way.

"Basketball is a great game that's been kicked around brutally for 50 years. It never had a chance as it was operated on the professional level. We'll profit from the mistakes of others.

"Two things sold me on our league. One is that more people play and see basketball than any other sport. The other is that nobody in our league knows anything about the game. We're promoters. We'll *promote* the game.

"And we're ready to go. We're ready."

Coach Honey Russell recruited the only brother combination in Celtic history—Connie (left) and Johnny (right) Simmons.

Celtics' Hoop Ace Seeks Dodger Job

Seeks Two Goals

Star Garden Bout

Greb-Desmarais Title Manchester Go Tues.

$5000 HOLIDAY 'CAP AT ROCK

Ex-NHL Players Join Coast Teams

Tulane Tackle Served Army, Navy

Durfee Jinx Perils Coyle

Third Streak On Spot Tomorrow as Foes Clash

CELTICS' FIRST GAME

November 2, 1946, at Providence
(Rhode Island Auditorium)

CELTICS (53)

	FG	FT	Pts.
Kappen, F	0	2	2
J. Simmons, F	1	2	4
Gray, F	2	1	5
Wallace, F	4	1	9
Connors, C	3	1	7
C. Simmons, C	3	0	6
Fenley, G	3	2	8
Hirsch, G	0	0	0
Vaughn, G	3	2	8
Brightman, G	1	0	2
Spector, G	1	0	2
Totals	21	11	53

PROVIDENCE STEAMROLLERS (59)

	FG	FT	Pts.
Martin, F	7	4	18
Shannon, F	6	3	15
Callahan, F	2	3	7
Calverley, C	2	1	5
Mearns, G	2	3	7
Shea, G	1	0	2
Goodwin, G	1	3	5
Totals	21	17	59

Score by periods:	1	2	3	4
Steamrollers:	14	12	12	21–59
Celtics:	10	16	14	13–53

Referees: Eddie Boyle and Johnny Nucatola.
Attendance: 4,406.

FIRST VICTORY

November 16, 1946, at Boston Garden

CELTICS (55)

	FG	FT	Pts.
Gray, LF	3	7	13
Hirsch	0	0	0
Kappen, RF	0	3	3
Wallace	0	0	0
Fenley	1	1	3
Connors, C	4	3	11
Kottman	4	1	9
C. Simmons, LG	4	1	9
Spector	1	1	3
J. Simmons, RG	1	0	2
Vaughn	0	0	0
Totals	18	17	.53

TORONTO HUSKIES (49)

	FG	FT	Pts.
D. Fitzgerald, LF	1	0	2
Miller	0	0	0
Fucarino, RF	0	0	0
Hurley	2	2	6
Nostrand, C	4	4	12
Sadowski	5	4	14
McCarron, LG	2	1	5
Wertis	0	2	2
Hoefer	0	1	1
B. Fitzgerald, RG	2	3	7
Totals	16	17	49

Attendance: 5,176

Art Spector:

"It was a survival situation for the Celtics that first season, and we were a little frightened we weren't going to make it—that the team might not make it in Boston, or that the league might fall apart.

"So we did a lot of pioneering—speaking engagements and clinics, everything we could to promote professional basketball in the Boston area. We did as much talking as possible, every chance we could.

"Our crowds at the Garden and Arena were pretty lean generally, but the people who did come out were real fans, and we felt that if we could survive that first season the sport would catch on. Which it eventually did, although not until Bob Cousy came along to turn the franchise around.

"But there wouldn't be a Boston Celtics if it weren't for Walter Brown. The Garden had severe reservations about losing money and paying halfway decent salaries to us. But Walter believed in the Celtics and went into great personal debt to keep the team alive.

"Walter was without a doubt the finest gentleman I've ever known. He was Boston's most valuable asset—a truly great, great human being."

So were the 20 candidates who reported to the first Celtic workout at the Arena Annex on October 1, 32 days before the season opener at Providence. The squad worked out on the second-floor gym by day, slept on cots downstairs by night—an arrangement necessitated by the post-war housing shortage that drew no complaints from Celtic accountants.

The annex was connected to the main Arena, where the Celtics would play seven of their 30 home games when the Garden was booked. But the team couldn't practice at the Arena during the preseason because it was being used mostly for hockey and skating. And because the league allowed no exhibition games that first preseason, there was no need to set up the Arena's new $11,000 parquet floor (ingeniously constructed of scraps because of wartime shortages) that has since been shifted to the Garden and become a Celtic landmark and relic.

So the new floor and glass backboards weren't installed at the Arena until just before the ill-fated opener—not long after Russell trimmed his squad to the maximum 12 players.

Wyndol Gray was the best known to Bostonians. The 6-1 forward had captained Harvard's 20-3 NCAA Tournament team the previous season.

There was a set of brothers (the only one in Celtic history)—6-8 foward-center Connie Simmons, a 21-year-old non-collegian fresh out of the Army, and Johnny Simmons, a 6-1 guard who later would play a season of big league baseball as a Washington Senators outfielder.

Connors, the 6-7 starting pivotman nicknamed Li'l Abner by teammates, also would play in the majors—67 games as a first baseman with the Brooklyn Dodgers and Chicago Cubs.

Others on that first squad were Brightman (6-2), Art Spector (6-4), Virgil Vaughn (6-4), Warren Fenley (6-3), Mike (Red) Wallace (6-1), Tony Kappen (5-10), and the Mutt & Jeff duet of 6-8 reserve center Harold Kottman and 5-6 Hirsch.

By season's end, 20 players would wear Celtic Green, including two NFL players who dropped by to watch practice and were pressed into service—Boston Yanks receivers Hal Crisler for four games, Don Eliason for one.

It was that kind of season as the Celtics went 0-5 before winning (in their first game at the Garden), then 1-10, 5-20 and finally 22-38 to tie the Toronto Huskies for last place in the East—27 games behind Red Auerbach's Washington Capitols powerhouse.

Those Caps had provided the highpoint of the Boston season. The Celtics upset them, 47-38, to spoil their brash 29-year-old coach's first visit to the Garden in mid-January, not long after Washington had completed a 17-victory streak (still tied with one by the '59-'60 Celtics as the NBA's longest).

Still, as Connors recalls of the Celtics' first edition, "We weren't much of a basketball team. We were the *worst*."

Well, almost.

There were no Boston names among the league's Top 20 scorers. Connie Simmons was the only Celtic in double figures, averaging 10.3 points. He also led the team in field-goal percentage with .320, free-throw percentage with .677 and assists with 62 in 60 games (assists were awarded far more conservatively then).

The Celtics were decent enough on defense, ranking No. 3 with a 65 points-allowed average. But they had the league's weakest offense, dead last at 60.1.

All of which left the Celtics less than a red-hot attraction as Walter Brown tried to push his new product. The Celtics drew 108,240 in 30 home dates, a 3,608 average that was about half what college doubleheaders were averaging at the Garden. And whereas Holy Cross would jam the building, the Celtics never half-filled it—6,327 their top home crowd.

It added up to a Celtic bath of about $125,000 that first season, and the question around Boston was how long the team would survive. All three fellow doormats of the league—Detroit, Pittsburgh and Toronto—had dropped out at season's end. Would the Celtics be next?

FIRST HOME GAME

November 5, 1946, at Boston Arena

CELTICS (55)

	FG	*FT*	*Pts.*
Gray, LF	6	0	12
Kappen	1	1	3
Wallace, RF	3	0	6
Hirsch	0	0	0
Connors, C	2	4	8
C. Simmons	0	0	0
Kottman	0	0	0
Fenley, LG	2	1	5
Brightman	0	0	0
Spector, RG	2	0	4
J. Simmons	6	1	13
Vaughn	1	2	4
Totals	23	9	55

CHICAGO STAGS (57)

	FG	*FT*	*Pts.*
Zaslofsky, LF	13	2	28
Duffy	1	0	2
Baker	0	0	0
Jaros, RF	1	2	4
Parrack	1	1	3
Halbert, C	3	3	9
Gilmer	0	0	0
Rottner, LG	3	0	6
Kautz	1	0	2
Davis, RG	1	1	3
Seminoff	0	0	0
Carlson	0	0	0
Totals	24	9	57

Score by periods:	1	2	3	4
Stags:	15	12	19	11–57
Celtics:	13	20	13	9–55

Referees: Pat Kennedy and James Biersdorfer.
Attendance: 4,329.

This photograph appeared in the old *Boston Traveler* the night of the first Celtic home game (left to right): Harold Kottman, Kevin (Chuck) Connors, coach John (Honey) Russell, Wyndol Gray, Warren Fenley and Tony Kappen. Kappen would go down in history as the first Celtic traded, shipped to Pittsburgh in early December for Moe Becker.

1947–48

CELTICS' FIRST PLAYOFF GAME

March 28, 1948, at Boston Garden

CELTICS (72)

	FG	FT	Pts.
Mariaschin, LF	3	3	9
Stump	0	0	0
Riebe, RF	8	6	22
Munroe	1	0	2
Sadowski, C	5	12	22
Garfinkel, LG	3	2	8
Noszka	0	0	0
Bloom, RG	3	1	7
Spector	1	0	2
Totals	24	24	72

CHICAGO STAGS (79)

	FG	FT	Pts.
Gilmur, LF	3	4	10
Huston	0	2	2
Zaslofsky, RF	5	8	18
Phillip	5	2	12
Miasek, C	6	4	16
Rottner	1	0	2
Vance, LG	3	2	8
Schadler	0	0	0
Seminoff, RG	4	3	11
Rock	0	0	0
Totals	27	25	79

Attendance: 2,842 (smallest of season).

The Celtics' top two draft choices in 1947 were Purdue's Eddie Ehlers and DePaul's Gene Stump, a couple of all-America types on and off the court.

The second day of training camp at Boston Arena, the two rookies bumped into Walter Brown.

"How's it going, fellas?" the Celtic owner asked.

"Well, Mr. Brown, pro basketball isn't quite what we expected," said Ehlers, who received a $10,000 bonus from the New York Yankees in baseball and was a draft pick of the Chicago Bears besides being the Celtics' No. 1 selection. "We're not sure it's for us."

"Why not?" asked the surprised Brown. "What's the problem?"

"Well," said Stump, "when we came out on the court this morning, there was Ed Sadowski in uniform practicing his hookshot—with a big cigar in his mouth."

Ed Sadowski was the Celtics' new attraction, their first star. He looked like a Prussian general—a strapping 6-foot-5, 240-pounder with a half-shaved head. And teammates said he had a Prussian general's attitude to match, a bossy, self-centered pivotman.

Howie McHugh:

"Sadowski was a pip. Once, during a game in Boston, he wasn't getting the ball often enough to suit him. So he called a timeout.

"'See those people up there?' he asked in the huddle, gesturing toward the stands. 'Those people came to see Big Ed score. But Big Ed can't score if Big Ed doesn't shoot the ball. And Big Ed can't shoot the ball if Big Ed doesn't have the ball. So let's pass the goddam ball to Big Ed!'"

At age 30, Sadowski was a pro veteran, having broken into the old National League in 1940. He was awarded to the Celtics from the collapsed Cleveland franchise, where he had been the team's leading scorer with a 15.9 average. In fact, Big Ed, as he liked to be called, had been with two teams the previous season. He was Toronto's original coach—a player-coach—but lasted only 12 games; Coach Sadowski was fired, Player Sadowski traded to Cleveland.

Sadowski replaced Kevin (Chuck) Connors in the Boston pivot. Coincidentally, both had played college ball at Seton Hall under Celtic coach John (Honey) Russell.

Top draft choices Eddie Ehlers (right) and Gene Stump (second right) huddle with veteran Art Spector (second left) and coach Honey Russell. Ehlers was the first player ever drafted by the Celtics, Stump the second.

From left: Mel Riebe, Art Spector, Ed Sadowski, Jack (Dutch) Garfinkel, Saul Mariaschin.

Front row (left to right): Saul Mariaschin, George Munroe, Cecil Hankins, coach John (Honey) Russell, Jack (Dutch) Garfinkel, Mel Riebe and Chuck Hoefer. Back row: trainer Harvey Cohn, Gene Stump, Eddie Ehlers, Art Spector, Connie Simmons, Ed Sadowski, Kevin (Chuck) Connors and John Janisch.

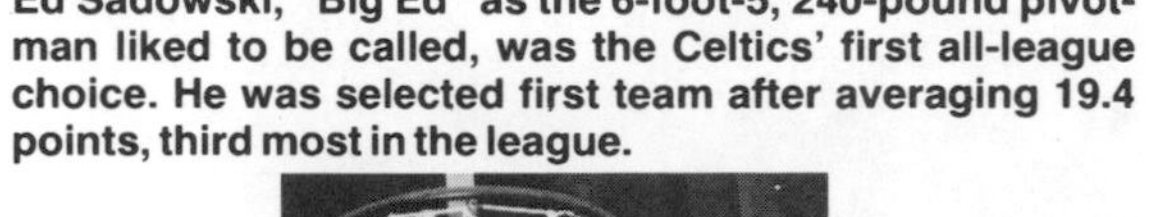

Ed Sadowski, "Big Ed" as the 6-foot-5, 240-pound pivotman liked to be called, was the Celtics' first all-league choice. He was selected first team after averaging 19.4 points, third most in the league.

George Munroe attended Harvard Law School while playing for the Celtics. The Dartmouth graduate is the only Rhodes Scholar in Celtic history.

Sadowski went on to more than quadruple Connors' 1946-47 average, placing third in the league with a 19.4 figure. And at season's end Big Ed was named first-team all-league—the first Celtic to earn that honor.

Saul Mariaschin, a published songwriter from Brooklyn, was a runnerup for Rookie of the Year. The playmaking former Harvard captain was among the league's Top 10 in assists with a 1.4 average under the then ultra-conservative formula for awarding assists.

Still, the Celtics' record didn't improve appreciably. At 20-28 they were saved from another last-place finish only by the near-total collapse of Providence's 6-42 Steamrollers. And although the Celts did make the playoffs, they were erased by Chicago in three games, 1-2, even though they had home advantage in all three games because the Stags' court was unavailable.

And when Russell was out at season's end, so was Sadowski—gone to the Philadelphia Warriors. But in one season Big Ed had carved his name in Celtic legend as a character as well as the franchise's first major scorer and all-league selection.

Saul Mariaschin, a published songwriter from Harvard, was a Rookie of the Year runnerup. A tireless runner and clever playmaker, he was among the league's Top 10 in assists and the Celtics' No. 3 scorer.

1948–49

Art Spector, a rebounder and digger, was called the "Original Celtic," the player from Boston's first squad in 1946-47 to play longest with the team—four years.

Dermie O'Connell (left) and George Kaftan joined the Celtics in mid-season after graduating from Holy Cross in January.

Coach Doggie Julian strikes a familiar pose of frustration in front of the bench.

In 1948, the Celtics were not the darlings of New England basketball. That distinction went to Holy Cross' Cinderella team, dubbed the "Fancy Pants A.C."

The small Jesuit school from Worcester, an hour's drive from Boston, captured the 1947 NCAA basketball championship, winning its last 23 games. It is the only New England college ever to win that title. And Alvin (Doggie) Julian's Crusaders came close to repeating in 1948, stringing together 18 victories in succession at one stretch before being derailed by eventual NCAA champion Kentucky in the Eastern finals.

Holy Cross was filling Boston Garden to its 13,909 brim (and then some) most times it played there. In marked contrast, the most the Celtics had attracted for any home game in their two seasons was 6,239, and that was almost double their home average.

To capitalize on Holy Cross' popularity, Walter Brown hired Julian as the Celtics' coach for 1948-49. And when Crusader stars George Kaftan and Dermie O'Connell graduated in January, they went directly from Holy Cross Purple to Celtic Green in midseason. Predictably, a crowd of 10,691 greeted the pair's pro debut at Boston Garden.

And Celtic fans weren't disappointed. Kaftan in particular ran up some impressive figures the remainder of the season. After getting 10 points in his debut, Kaftan scored 21 in his next game and went on to average 14.5 in 21 games, the only Celtic to average more than 10 points.

By season's end, Celtic home attendance was up more than 30 percent to an average of nearly 5,000. But the team still was losing money as well as games (escaping last place but missing the playoffs). Confronted by another loss of about $100,000—for a three-year total estimated at $350,000—Boston Garden-Arena stockholders were suggesting to Walter Brown that it was time to give up on a bad investment. In reply, the Garden-Arena president was asking the stockholders to try it one more year.

And after that one more year—another bath in red ink estimated at $100,000 more—the stockholders would have enough. Following the 1949-50 season they would dump the franchise, selling it to Brown. He would bring in a partner from Providence named Lou Pieri to help shoulder the financial burden. Brown would also hock his home and securities to keep his dream alive.

Marjorie Brown:

"So many of our friends were begging Walter to give it up. And I wanted him to give it up, too.

"We had just finished paying off our house when the Celtics came along. Walter owned stock in the Ice Capades, and we had used the dividends to pay off our mortgage.

"By 1950 Walter had sold most of the stock and re-mortgaged the house. Almost everything we owned was locked up in the Celtics. All I could think of was, 'What will happen to us if it's all lost?' I was worried.

"But Walter loved that team. I've heard people say that he hung on because he was stubborn, or because he was too proud to admit failure. That wasn't it at all. The Celtics were Walter's idea from the very beginning, and he just never stopped believing in them."

Johnny Bach went on to more fame as a coach than he attracted with a 3.5-point average during his one pro season with the Celtics. He coached alma mater Fordham (18 seasons, .576) and Penn State (10 seasons, .504) before returning to pro basketball on Golden State's staff.

Front row (left to right): Art Spector, Eddie Ehlers, George Kaftan, coach Alvin (Doggie) Julian, Dermie O'Connell, Gene Stump and Jim Seminoff. Back row: Phil Farbman, Bob Doll, George Nostrand, Bob Kinney and John Ezersky.

CELTICS SCORE 100 POINTS FOR FIRST TIME

February 25, 1949, at Boston Arena

CELTICS (102)	FG	FT	Pts.
Ehlers, LF	2	1	5
Ezersky	3	7	13
Farbman	2	2	6
Kaftan, RF	6	2	14
Stump	0	0	0
Kinney, C	5	4	14
Nostrand	8	3	19
Seminoff, LG	3	3	9
Spector	2	1	5
O'Connell, RG	7	0	14
Doll	1	1	3
Totals	39	24	102

ST. LOUIS BOMBERS (83)	FG	FT	Pts.
Maugham, LF	4	3	11
Gunther	0	3	3
Smawley, RF	12	3	27
Putnam	1	1	3
Parham	2	5	9
Roberts, C	3	0	6
Logan, LG	5	7	17
Miller	0	0	0
Schnellbacher, RG	3	1	7
Wilcutt	0	0	0
Totals	30	23	83

Referee: Eddie Boyle.
Attendance: 4,428.

Mel Riebe

John Ezersky

George Nostrand

Chick Halbert

1949–50

Tony Lavelli entertained the Boston Garden audience with his accordian at halftime (above), then made the mighty Lakers face his basketball music in the second half (below) as he tuned in with 23 of his 26 points to key a stunning upset by the Celtics.

At halftime of a Celtics-Lakers game at Boston Garden, a stool and a microphone are brought to midcourt and the crowd cheers as a familiar figure wearing a green sateen sweatsuit trots onto the court with an accordian slung from his shoulders.

Top draft choice Tony Lavelli, in his 13th game as a Celtic, is about to entertain the 5,206 customers with a one-man concert as eight news photographers jockey for position nearby.

Lavelli was a local boy made good on two fronts. He was an accomplished accordianist who had done coast-to-coast concerts at age 12, was on NBC radio (long before network television) at 13 and had played New York's Roxy Theater by 19. As a youngster in the Boston suburb of Somerville, he had spent hour after hour seven days a week practicing as a prodigy in *two* areas—music (specializing in the accordian) and basketball (specializing in the hookshot).

That hookshot made Lavelli a legend—first at Somerville High, then at Yale. His heroics helped make his high school team state champions, so popular that the Tech Tourney had to be moved into Boston Garden, where it quickly became a Massachusetts institution. And at Yale, Tony made Helms' All-America as a *freshman*. By his senior season, he was a consensus All-America—and top draftee of the struggling Celtics, who were desperate for a gate attraction.

"Walter Brown begged me to sign," recalls Lavelli, who was mulling his musical future and an opportunity to go to Hollywood. After missing the 1949-50 season's first three weeks, Lavelli finally joined the Celtics.

A special arrangement with the league allowed Lavelli to play a little music with his basketball. The NBA paid him $125 each for a minimum of 25 halftime concerts around the league, at least one in each city.

And that's what Lavelli was doing this December 1949 night at Boston Garden while his Celtic teammates were relaxing in the locker room. Lavelli didn't seem to miss the breather. While he had come off the bench to score 3 points in the first half, the 6-foot-3, 185-pound forward drummed home 23 points in the second half for a total of 26 (topping opponent George Mikan's 21) to spark the Celtics' stunning 87-69 upset of the defending champion Lakers, who had led by 15 points in the first half.

The next morning's *Boston Herald* headlined twin rave reviews of the versatile Lavelli's doubleheader. Basketball writer Joe Looney lauded Tony's contribution to the Celts' "most convincing triumph since the pro game became established here little more than three years ago." And music critic Rudolph Elie praised Tony's accordian interpretations of "Lady of Spain" and selections from "William Tell."

Former Ivy League rivals Tony Lavelli (right) and Ed Leede became teammates as Celtics rookies. Lavelli had captained Yale, Leede Dartmouth.

Former Holy Cross captain and star playmaker Joe Mullaney (left) is reunited with his college coach, Doggie Julian (center), as he signs a Celtic contract with owner Walter Brown. Mullaney would be used little as a Celtic but went on to coaching fame with nine teams, most notably Providence College and the Los Angeles Lakers.

Joe Mullaney:

"I was a benchwarmer on that '49-'50 club. We were the worst team the Celtics ever had. Just awful.

"Tony Lavelli? I've never seen anyone whose hookshot could compare with his. Absolutely nobody. And I've been around basketball a little.

"Tony had unbelievable precision with that hook, drilling one after another from as far out as 16-17 feet in practice. I marveled at that precision—like Bill Sharman's, only with the hook. It was something to see.

"Lavelli was total precision, and that ended up working against him. When he got muscled and shoved, it would throw off his shot the identical distance he had been moved. So he got pushed around quite a bit.

"Tony could function with that hookshot in the college game, where they didn't allow much physical contact. But in the pros you could get more physical, and that threw off his shot.

"Lavelli was a delicate sort of guy, and I think he lacked the aggressiveness you had to have in the pros. But, brother, he had some kind of hookshot. The very best."

Lavelli would top his 26 points against the Lakers with a pair of 28-point games against the Knicks in March. But such performances were few by any Celtic, and Bob Kinney led Boston's scorers with a 11.1-point average (Lavelli finished at 8.8). And the team tumbled to last place a dismal 22-46, a .324 percentage that still ranks as the Celtics' worst ever. Accordingly, the playoffs were missed again and home attendance shrunk to a likely inflated 4,252 average—not counting the "home" game at Providence against the Warriors that drew exactly 216.

At season's end, Alvin (Doggie) Julian unexpectedly resigned. And although Tony Lavelli didn't know it, he had played his last game as a Celtic. A new Celtic coach soon would make it clear that he was cleaning house and that popular native son Lavelli didn't fit into his plans.

"He's gone," brash Arnold (Red) Auerbach would say. "He's not tough enough to play pro ball, and I've got no time for sentiment."

Ernie Calverley never wore this Celtic uniform in anything but a preseason game. Walter Brown purchased the defunct Providence franchise to get rights to the former Rhode Island State star, MVP of the 1946 NIT and a 1947 second-team all-league choice as a Steamroller rookie. So Brown was stunned when Doggie Julian cut Calverley just before the season opener.

CELTICS UPSET MIGHTY LAKERS

December 22, 1949, at Boston Garden

CELTICS (87)	FG	FT	Pts.
Hertzberg, LF	1	0	2
O'Connell	9	1	19
Kaftan, RF	1	2	4
Shannon	5	2	12
Kinney, C	2	5	9
Englund	1	1	3
Doll, LG	1	1	3
Walker	0	0	0
Lavelli	9	8	26
Leede, RG	3	1	7
Seminoff	0	2	2
Totals	32	23	87

MINNEAPOLIS LAKERS (69)	FG	FT	Pts.
Pollard, LF	5	1	11
Ferrin, RF	6	0	12
Mikan, C	7	7	21
Carlson	0	0	0
Jaros, LG	0	0	0
Mikkelsen	3	3	9
Hassett	2	0	4
Schaefer, RG	2	3	7
Martin	1	1	3
Harrison	1	0	2
Totals	27	15	69

Score by periods:	1	2	3	4	
Celtics	12	22	23	30	—87
Lakers	19	18	12	20	—69

Free Throws Missed: Boston (8)—Kinney 3, Lavelli 3, O'Connell, Shannon. Minneapolis (7)—Mikan 3, Mikkelsen 3, Hassett.
Referees: Johnny Nucatola and Bunny Hearn.
Attendance: 5,206.

1950–51

Bob Cousy drives between George Mikan (99) and Bob Harrison (16) for a basket against the Minneapolis Lakers. Cousy would replace Mikan as the NBA's No. 1 player, and the Celtics would replace the Lakers as the league's perennial champion.

Red Auerbach greets the Celtics' three top rookies (left to right): Chuck Cooper, Bob Cousy and Bob Donham.

More than 30 years after being the first black drafted in the NBA, Chuck Cooper still has in his Pittsburgh home a letter from Celtics founder Walter Brown. "It's dated May 10, 1950, and welcomes me to the Celtics," Cooper says. "Typical of Mr. Brown, it adds: 'Keep at those books. Remember, nobody can ever take an education away from you.'"

And in the Celtic archives, there's a telegram from Cooper to Brown: "Thank you for having the courage to offer me a contract in pro basketball. I hope I'll never give you the chance to regret it. [Signed] Chuck Cooper."

The Celtics stunned the NBA draft meeting at Chicago on April 25, 1950, when Walter Brown, leading off the second round, selected Duquesne All-America Chuck Cooper, a black.

Another owner finally broke the silence by asking, "Walter, don't you know he's a colored boy?"

"I don't give a damn if he's striped or polka dot or plaid," Brown roared. "Boston takes Charles Cooper of Duquesne."

The NBA's color line had been shattered.

If that weren't enough to shock the sports world, the Celtics had already dumbfounded—and angered—New England fans earlier in the day. Picking first in the entire draft, they chose Bowling Green's little-under-7-foot Charlie Share instead of Holy Cross' little-over-6-foot Bob Cousy, who was taken three picks later by someplace called Tri-Cities. That the Celtics were desperate for a big man to build around didn't satisfy New Englanders, who idolized the flashy Cousy, celebrated as the "Houdini of the Hardwoods."

Ironically, Share became expendable later in the day when Boston got Easy Ed Macauley, the league's second-best big man next to the great George Mikan. During a special lottery to find homes for personnel from the defunct St. Louis Bomber and Anderson (Indiana) Packer franchises, the Celtics got top prize Macauley, who as a rookie the previous season was second-team all-league while placing fifth in scoring with a 16.1 average.

These were only the first in a chain of major moves that would add up to a pivotal year for the Celtics and transform them from a weak also-ran into an exciting contender—and save the franchise.

Two days after the college draft, Arnold (Red) Auerbach was named coach at a salary of $10,000. The 32-year-old former Washington Caps and Tri-Cities Hawks coach promptly gave a sample of the explosiveness that would be a trademark of his often-stormy Celtic career by stirring up the 50 or so members of the Boston media attending his coming-out luncheon.

Pressed on why the Celtics had ignored Cousy in the draft, Auerbach turned in irritation to Brown. "Walter," he snapped, "am I suppose to win or am I suppose to worry about the local yokels and please these guys?"

While the writers and broadcasters were mulling that instantly immortal line, Auerbach added: "I don't give a damn for sentiment or names. That goes for Cousy and everybody else. The only thing that counts with me is ability, and Cousy hasn't proven to me he's got that ability. I'm not interested in someone just because he happens to be a local yokel. That won't bring more than a dozen extra fans into the building on a regular basis. What will bring fans in is a winning team, and that's what I aim to have."

No sooner had the fuss over Cousy begun to fade when it erupted again six months later. The Celtics passed up another chance at getting him, making it clear they wanted The Cooz no more in October than they had in April.

Cousy's rights had been traded by Tri-Cities to Chicago, and then the Chicago franchise folded. At a meeting to dispose of the Stags' players less than a month before the season's opener, the NBA owners couldn't decide which teams should get the top three players: sharpshooter Max Zaslofsky, playmaker Andy Phillip and Cousy. Boston, New York and Philadelphia all wanted Zaslofsky and, to lesser extent, Phillip and Cousy.

Front row (left to right): Ken Sailors, Bob Donham, Sidney (Sonny) Hertzberg, Bob Cousy, Ed Leede and Red Auerbach. Back row: Ed Stanczak, Chuck Cooper, Harry Boykoff, Andy Duncan, Brady Walker, John Mahnken and Ed Macauley.

After wrangling much of the day, President Maurice Podoloff, with Solomon-like wisdom, put three names in Syracuse owner Danny Biasone's hat. He affixed price tags of $15,000 on Zaslofsky, $10,000 on Phillip and $8,500 on Cousy.

Walter Brown graciously (if foolishly) declined first pick, saying he had that privilege (as the surviving team with the poorest record) in both the college and St. Louis-Anderson drafts. So the Knicks' Ned Irish went first and drew Zaslofsky's name. Then the Warriors' Eddie Gottlieb picked Phillips' name. That left the Celtics with Cousy—stuck with the player who would revolutionize the sport and be known as the "Babe Ruth of basketball."

Three weeks later, the Celtic debuts of Cousy, Macauley, Cooper and Auerbach were spoiled by a 107-84 walloping at Fort Wayne. The Celts went on to lose their first three games under Auerbach, and Boston fans were wondering if the team would ever be a winner—with or without Cousy.

The Celtics then won their next seven, and 10 of 12, to become a contender that challenged Philadelphia for first place the remainder of the season. The Celts concluded their first winning season at 39-30, in second place 2½ games out, and Macauley became the first Celtic to average 20 points for a season, placing third in the league at 20.4.

The Celtics were bounced from the playoffs in two straight by the Knicks. But the tide had been reversed. The Celtics were on their way.

Ed Macauley:

"That's when the Celtics' winning tradition started.

"We weren't the powerhouse that the Celtics later became. But we were a contender, an appealing club, a colorful team featuring great shooters and Cooz' fantastic ballhandling.

"We changed the Boston fans' image of pro basketball. They began to appreciate the sport in general and the team in particular."

Brash Arnold (Red) Auerbach was named the Celtics' new coach at age 32. Despite some combustion which got him off to a bad start with the media and public, Auerbach transformed the team into an immediate contender.

COUSY, AUERBACH, COOPER, MACAULEY MAKE CELTIC DEBUTS

November 1, 1950, at Fort Wayne, Indiana

CELTICS (84)

	FGA	*FGM*	*FTA*	*FTM*	*Reb.*	*Ast.*	*PF*	*Pts.*
Cooper	6	3	3	3	2	0	4	9
Mahnken	7	3	0	0	3	0	3	6
Leede	8	2	4	4	2	1	4	8
Hertzberg	7	1	3	2	3	3	1	4
Walker	1	0	0	0	5	0	0	0
Macauley	5	3	6	3	4	1	3	9
Duncan	2	1	4	3	3	0	2	5
Stanczak	6	1	9	7	5	0	4	9
Sailors	7	2	5	5	1	0	2	9
Donham	7	4	6	1	5	0	4	9
Cousy	10	4	8	8	7	0	3	16
Totals	66	24	48	36	40	5	30	84

FORT WAYNE PISTONS (107)

	FGA	*FGM*	*FTA*	*FTM*	*Reb.*	*Ast.*	*PF*	*Pts.*
Schaus	8	3	10	8	5	4	5	14
Foust	12	7	7	5	13	0	3	19
Kerris	7	4	6	6	10	2	4	14
Klueh	11	5	6	5	8	2	2	15
Oldman	9	5	4	1	6	1	6	11
Riffey	5	4	0	0	1	1	3	8
Johnson	17	5	4	2	3	5	5	12
Carpenter	2	0	2	2	0	0	0	2
Burris	6	3	0	0	6	5	5	6
Hargis	5	2	3	2	2	0	3	6
Totals	82	38	42	31	54	20	36	107

Score by periods:	1	2	3	4
Pistons	26	21	30	30—107
Celtics	21	24	16	23—84

Field Goal Percentage: Celtics .364, Pistons .463.
Free Throw Percentage: Celtics .750, Pistons .738.
Referees: Pat Kennedy and Max Tabbacci.

1951–52

Bill Sharman (right) joined Bob Cousy to give the Celtics basketball's finest backcourt combination of the fifties, perhaps of all time, en route to pedestals in the Basketball Hall of Fame.

The pieces of Red Auerbach's jigsaw puzzle were falling into place. First, Bob Cousy and Ed Macauley fit into place in 1950-51. Now, in Fall 1951, along came Bill Sharman to complete the Celtics' Big Three.

A month earlier, Sharman had been on the Brooklyn Dodgers' bench at the Polo Grounds when Bobby Thompson hit his "homerun heard around the world" that gave the New York Giants the most dramatic pennant in National League history.

Sharman, trying to crack Brooklyn's celebrated Carl Furillo-Duke Snider-Andy Pafko outfield, had been summoned from St. Paul for the last month of the season. "You'll play as soon as we clinch the pennant," he was told, and it didn't seem that would take long as the Dodgers still had much of their 13½-game lead of August.

In a classic collapse, the Dodgers never clinched—and Sharman never got into a major league baseball game.

It was while on a late-season trip with the Dodgers, though, that the trail led Sharman to Boston.

Through some shrewd dealing by Red Auerbach, the Celtics had acquired NBA rights to Sharman, a gifted athlete out of USC who had broken Hank Luisetti's Pacific Coast Conference scoring record before signing a bonus contract with the Dodgers.

The previous season Auerbach had traded Charlie Share's rights to the Fort Wayne Pistons for Bob (Gabby) Harris, $10,000 and a player to be named. With the $10,000 Auerbach purchased burly Bob Brannum from Sheboygan for some much-needed muscle. And at season's end the player to be named turned out to be Sharman, who had played for Washington that year.

The Capitols had folded at mid-season, and Fort Wayne was awarded the sweetshooting rookie who led the Caps in scoring with a 12.2-point average. But instead of reporting to the Pistons, Sharman decided to get an early jump on the baseball season and play Winter ball before reporting to the Dodger camp.

Sharman had always made it clear that baseball was his main sports interest and that basketball was something to help keep himself in shape while picking up some extra money until he made the grade with the Dodgers. The Pistons didn't know if Sharman would ever play basketball again, so had no objection when Auerbach asked for him as the "player to be named" to complete the Share deal.

Then came that day in late September when Sharman and Dodger teammate Clyde King, in town for a series against the Boston Braves, dropped by a Celtic workout at Boston Arena. Before long, Sharman had his sports jacket and shoes off and was popping in baskets from all over the court.

Bob Cousy:

"Sharman was perpetual motion out there. He never stopped moving without the ball. For a passer like me, this was ideal because I could always pick him out. And once Willie got the ball, of course, he was the greatest shooter who's ever come along."

Afterward, Auerbach had some persuading to do. He had to convince Sharman that basketball wasn't such a bad sport after all—particularly if it paid $14,000, one of the sport's top salaries. Auerbach had to assure Walter Brown that Sharman was worth $14,000, especially to a franchise flirting with bankruptcy.

Bob Cousy and Dick McGuire of the Knicks battled head to head seven seasons, always an interesting matchup.

Five weeks later, in the Celtics' season-opener, Sharman was in the Boston lineup. He scored 19 points to go along with Bob Cousy's 25 during a 97-65 victory over the Indianapolis Olympians at Boston—the Celtics' first opening-game victory ever. In the next game, Cousy scored 24 and Sharman 22, and the pair was literally off and running in establishing Boston's dynamic duo as the NBA's best backcourt tandem of the fifties—and perhaps of all time—en route to pedestals in the Basketball Hall of Fame.

Red Auerbach:

"That was the season that Cousy started coming into his own—still a little rough around the edges, but he had all his confidence and was beginning to take charge out there. And now he had the ideal partner to feed, Bill Sharman.

"With Bill, it didn't matter how Bob threw the ball—over his head or behind his back or what. Sharman was going to catch it and put up his jump shot. Bill was the best pure shooter I ever saw.

"Sharman and Cousy were some combination. A great combination."

That combination helped make the Celtics into a genuine threat as they narrowly missed the NBA East title, finishing one game behind Syracuse. Named first-team all-league for the first of 10 straight times, Cousy was third in NBA scoring at 21.7, Macauley was fourth at 19.2. And Sharman was the Celtics' third high scorer at 10.7, a hint of his sharpshooting to come.

Bill Sharman:

"It worked out so well for me. Cooz was a magician. I knew if I kept moving he'd put the ball into my hands somehow. And he did, time after time after time."

Sharman would soon forget about baseball as he quickly established himself a two-way NBA star—a fierce competitor whose one-hand jumpshot was almost unstoppable, whose foul shooting ranks among the best in basketball history and whose defense was dogged.

Sharman's first Celtic season ended in frustration, though. After the Celtics defeated the New York Knicks in the playoff opener, Sharman was knocked out of the best-of-three series by illness. And without him, Boston lost the next two games—including the double-overtime finale that ended in a major controversy and had the Boston press hollering for a Congressional investigation. (See March 26, 1952 in "Dates" chapter.)

Sharman's illness? Chicken pox.

"For heaven's sake, Willie," Cousy needled his embarrassed partner, "couldn't you at least have gotten an *adult's* disease?"

Bob Cousy came out dribbling in the NBA All-Star Game again hosted by Walter Brown at Boston Garden. The showcase attracted another crowd of more than 10,000 to become an annual league fixture.

Chuck Cooper (left) and Ed Macauley

COUSY, SHARMAN FORM NEW BACKCOURT DUET

November 4, 1951, at Boston Arena

CELTICS (97)	FG	FT	Reb.	Pts.	INDIANAPOLIS OLYMPIANS (65)	FG	FT	Reb.	Pts.
McKinney, LF	2	0	3	4	Jones, LF	1	0	1	2
Brannum	1	8	12	10	Holland	1	1	1	3
Cooper, RF	4	3	10	11	Barnhorst, RF	6	2	2	14
Harris	2	0	5	4	Walther	0	0	7	0
Macauley, C	7	2	4	16	Lavoy, C	0	2	1	2
Mahnken	2	0	5	4	Lofgran	5	4	12	14
Donham, LG	1	0	4	2	Tosheff, LG	5	6	4	16
Sharman	9	1	2	19	Crocker	0	0	0	0
Cousy, RG	9	7	11	25	O'Brien, RG	3	3	2	9
Dickey	1	0	3	2	Graboski	2	1	10	5
Totals	38	21	59	97	*Totals*	23	19	40	65

Score by periods:	1	2	3	4
Celtics	18	19	25	35—97
Olympians	17	19	13	16—65

Attendance: 3,012.

Front row (left to right): Ed Macauley, co-owner Lou Pieri, coach Red Auerbach, co-owner Walter Brown and Horace (Bones) McKinney. Back row: Dick Dickey, Bill Sharman, Bon Donham, Chuck Cooper, John Mahnken, Bob (Gabby) Harris, Bob Brannum, Bob Cousy and trainer Harvey Cohn.

1952–53

Bob Cousy scored 50 points in the Celtics' four-overtime playoff victory over Syracuse. By game's end, Paul Seymour (right) would be playing on a painfully sprained ankle and Bob Brannum (18) and Dolph Schayes (4) would be long gone, banished for a fistfight that nearly sparked a riot.

Nearly 30 years later, it remains one of the classic games in basketball history, a wild playoff megathriller that's now part of NBA legend.

Saturday afternoon, March 21, 1953, at Boston Garden: Celtics 111, Syracuse Nationals 105 in *four* overtime periods.

Bob Cousy, playing *66* of the game's 68 minutes despite a thigh pull that has him limping, scores *50* points, *25* of them in overtime. In all, he converts *30* of 32 free throws, including 18 in a row (most of those at the end, when the game hangs in the balance).

Fourteen of the game's 20 players are disqualified. Twelve foul out, two others (Dolph Schayes and Bob Brannum) are thrown out for fighting. But three disqualified Nats and one disqualified Celtic are allowed to remain in the game so each team can field five players—the opposition awarded an extra free throw when a disqualified player commits another foul.

By game's end, the 11,058 spectators are limp from an emotional rollercoaster that has transported them through 3 hours and 11 minutes of melodramatic peaks and valleys.

The overtime hysteria is too much for two Celtic officials, a pair who have been with the team since its birth—in fact, who collaborated to name the team in 1946.

Midway through those frenzied overtimes, publicist Howie McHugh is overcome in the pressbox by headaches so severe that he passes out. At about the same time, in another part of the Garden, owner Walter Brown leaves his seat and paces the lobby the remainder of the game.

"It was just too much for me," Brown would say. He had been unable to escape the roar of the crowd, though, and it lured him to frequently peek through a fire door to check the big scoreboard suspended over midcourt.

It was a day of delirium at the Garden, and it started early. Fans were in an uproar from early in the second period when the

Red Auerbach is suited up, too, as he greets his squad for the opening of training camp at Boston Arena. Candidates include (left to right) Bob Cousy, Bob Donham, Bob Brannum, Bob Harris, Don Rehfeldt, John Mahnken and Ed Macauley. Rehfeldt, a former Baltimore Bullet and Milwaukee Hawk, didn't make the squad.

Schayes-Brannum fisticuffs nearly triggered a riot as Syracuse's Paul Seymour and Billy Gabor tried to take on a squad of Boston police who had come onto the floor. And the frenzy continued throughout as the lead swung back and forth like a pendulum.

It was, Jack Barry wrote in his *Boston Globe* lead the next morning, a game "defying description." And an eight-column banner headline splashed across the page: *Cousy Does Everything in Victory but Take Tickets.*

"It has to rank as one of the most exciting games ever, although not the most artistic," recalls McHugh, who has missed only "four or five" Celtic home games ever. "There were an awful lot of whistles (107 of them for 130 free throws, of which 108 were made).

"What a thriller, though. Cooz' performance has to be the most incredible I've ever seen by one guy. He was just unbelievable, putting in the ball from everywhere including midcourt.

"And it wasn't just 50 points; it was 50 *pressure* points. Of his last 3 points in regulation and the 25 he got in overtime, all except the final couple were *crucial.* If he doesn't make them, we lose.

"It was the greatest clutch performance I've ever seen."

The 24-year-old Cousy had led the league in assists (7.7) and was third in scoring (19.8) that season as the 46-25 Celtics, the NBA's top offensive team (88.1), finish a close third in the East—1 game behind Syracuse, 1½ behind New York.

In just his third pro season, the 6-foot-1 Cousy already had established himself as the patron saint of average-size basketball players everywhere. As Red Auerbach has said, "Cooz was doing things with a basketball that no one had ever seen before."

Bob Brannum (18) was the Celtics' strongman, as he displays here with the help of Ken Rollins (left) and John Mahnken (right).

Bob Cousy dribbles ball away from Rochester's Bobby Wanzer.

Front row (left to right): Ken Rollins, Bob Donham, trainer Harvey Cohn, coach Red Auerbach, Bob Cousy and Bill Sharman. Back row: Bob Brannum, John Mahnken, Ed Macauley, president Walter Brown, Gene Conley, Bob Harris and Chuck Cooper.

Gene Conley (center) pitched for both the Boston Braves and their Milwaukee farm in 1952, and at Summer's end was summoned by Red Auerbach for a Celtic tryout on Bill Sharman's recommendation. Despite having been away from basketball, the rugged 6-foot-9 rebounder earned a contract from Walter Brown (left) here—becoming one of only three Celtics to make the majors in baseball as well as basketball. (Chuck Connors and Johnny Simmons were the others; Sharman sat on the Dodgers' bench for a month but never got into a game.) After one season with the Celtics, the Braves paid Conley extra to give up basketball and concentrate on baseball—which he did for five years before returning to play on the 1958-59 World Champion Celtics.

On this day, despite a heavy cold and a wobbly right leg that might buckle at any time, Cousy wove a new chapter as the Celtics advanced to the Eastern finals for the first time ever by eliminating Syracuse, 2-0.

Sample these heroics:

End of regulation: Cousy sinks three free throws, the last with two seconds remaining, to tie the game at 77.

First overtime: Cousy scores 6 of Boston's 8 points, including a free throw with one second left to tie the game at 86.

Second overtime: With both teams playing a period of slowdown, each totals only 4 points. Cousy drives for 2 of Boston's 4 in the final seconds to tie the game at 90.

Third overtime: Celtics get the ball with 13 seconds to go and trailing by 5 points. Cousy, who will score 8 of Boston's 9 points this period, couples a basket and free throw for a 3-point play with 5 seconds left. Syracuse's pass-in goes deep into Celtic territory and is batted around. Out of the pack comes Cousy. Seeing time running out as he crosses midcourt, he lets go a running one-hander—a desperation 30-footer—and beats the buzzer to tie the game at 99.

Fourth overtime: Syracuse quickly builds another 5-point lead, 104-99. But Cousy answers with a free throw, two baskets sandwiched around a crucial steal, and four more free throws for 9 of Boston's 12 points in the period. And the Celtics finally prevail, 111-105, as the Garden boils over and the crowd mobs Cousy.

"He's the guy who did it, just that one kid," admired Al Cervi, Syracuse's player-coach. "What a player. He's the best."

Cousy, who had labored the last two overtime periods under the cloud of five fouls and had to be careful he didn't foul out, said he was lucky.

"There was a prayer going with every shot, and I certainly needed them," said the exhausted star, hunched over in his seat and fighting back tears. "I don't want to have to play another game like that again. Boy, it's too much. I was lucky."

COUSY SCORES 50 IN 4-OVERTIME VICTORY

March 21, 1953, at Boston Garden

CELTICS (111)	FG	FT	PF	Pts.	SYRACUSE NATIONALS (105)	FG	FT	PF	Pts.
Donham	1	0	6	2	*Schayes	2	4	2	8
Harris	4	6	6	14	Gabor	3	3	6	9
Cooper	2	5	7	9	Lochmueller	1	1	6	3
*Brannum	3	0	1	6	Osterkorn	1	0	6	2
Mahnken	0	1	5	1	Lloyd	4	5	5	13
Macauley	4	10	6	18	Rocha	5	9	6	19
Mahoney	0	0	5	0	Jorgenson	2	4	6	8
Cousy	10	30	5	50	King	4	8	6	16
Sharman	3	3	6	9	Cervi	0	9	7	9
Rollins	0	2	5	2	Seymour	5	8	5	18
Totals	27	57	52	111	*Totals*	27	51	55	105

Score by periods:	1	2	3	4	O1	O2	O3	O4
Celtics	21	19	22	15	9	4	9	12—111
Syracuse	22	20	17	18	9	4	9	6—105

Free Throws Missed: Syracuse (14)—Rocha 3, Lochmueller 2, Lloyd 2, Gabor 2, Cervi 2, Jorgensen, King, Seymour. Boston (8)—Donham 3, Cousy 2, Mahoney, Cooper, Rollins.

*Brannum and Schayes banished in 2d period, the first players ever ejected from NBA playoff game for fighting.

Referees: Arnie Heft and Charlie Eckman.
Attendance: 11,058.

Battle of the boards between Celtics and Knicks pits (left to right) Sherwin Raiken, Chuck Cooper, Bob Harris and Ernie Vandeweghe.

"People said we couldn't win the big ones, that we haven't got it when the chips are down," he added. "Beating Syracuse twice has to dispel that talk for good."

Well, at least for a week—until the Celtics were starched by the Knicks, 3-1, in the Eastern finals. But that couldn't diminish the brilliance of Cousy's four-overtime masterpiece.

His 50 points shattered the NBA playoff scoring record (47, set the previous year by George Mikan) and the Garden's all-time mark (46, set 15 days earlier by Ed Macauley). Nearly 30 years later, Cousy's 32 free throws, 30 conversions, 18 in a row all are still NBA playoff highs.

In all, it remains the greatest clutch performance in overtime in NBA history—in the league's longest playoff game.

Red Auerbach:

"Nobody who saw the game will ever forget either the game or Cooz. He was fabulous, just fabulous."

1953–54

Bob Cousy flips an over-the-shoulder pass to trailer Bob Donham as Laker Jim Pollard watches.

Jack Nichols worked his way through Tufts Dental School playing for the Celtics. He's now the Seattle SuperSonics' team dentist.

Red Auerbach:

"Walter was getting a bit panicky around this time because his dough was running thin and we still weren't taking in that much at the gate. He wasn't like some owners who had a lot of money or wealthy buildings like Madison Square Garden to back them up. He was on his own.

"There was one whole year Walter owed me $6,000. I never asked him for it because I knew he didn't have it. A few times the players had to wait for paychecks, and one time he had to hold off giving them their playoff money so we could meet operating expenses.

"We never complained about it. We knew Walter was staking his life on the success of the Celtics, and every time we lost it tore him apart. So he often let an aching heart do his talking for him.

"As well as being our biggest fan and best friend, he was our worst critic whenever he let his famous temper get loose. Walter had a beautiful Irish temper and a very sharp tongue to go with it.

"But that was the way he was, and you had to love him in spite of it. We understood him and knew he didn't mean a lot of the things he said in his blowoffs. After a while it got to the point where the writers stopped quoting his outbursts because they knew by the time the newspapers hit the streets Walter would have apologized and forgotten about it.

"The man had no capacity for anger. He couldn't stay mad.

"Walter just said what he had on his mind. He said it in simple English, and he usually said it in public for all to hear. He never pulled any punches. He'd usually end up taking it back, but he never denied saying it. He was totally honest. Walter and I had occasional differences, but he was a magnificent human being who personified everything good in sports.

"And he was a man for all sports, associated with a lot of them, particularly hockey. But the more Walter came to understand basketball, the more he appreciated it. He became obsessed with the Celtics. And the more the team struggled, the more determined he was to see it survive. He loved the team.

"And that love was returned. The players truly loved him. They certainly didn't love him for his money; everyone knew he was broke most of the time. They loved him because he was Walter Brown, and so did I."

Walter Brown's Irish temper was boiling as he addressed the basketball writers' weekly luncheon at Boston's Hotel Lenox.

"I have three players getting more money than the entire Philadelphia team, but all they're doing is reading their press clippings," he said, eyes flashing.

"I don't care a thing about statistics, figures or three leading scorers. I've had all that for three years and it hasn't won me a thing. I want to win. If we don't, a great many of the boys are going to play for less salary—from us or from some other teams.

"I have the most expensive team in the league and it's in the second division. I can lose just as easily with a cheap ballclub."

The Celtics had dropped three of their first four games, including a 78-72 loss to the Philadelphia Warriors the previous day at Boston

Walter Brown did some finger-pointing this season, although it just looks that way here. Listening are (left to right) Chuck Cooper, Bob Harris, Bill Sharman, Bob Donham, Ernie Barrett, Red Auerbach, Bob Brannum (face partially hidden), Ed Mikan and Ed Macauley.

Garden before a capacity crowd that included one very frustrated owner.

Brown hadn't cooled off over night and, never one to hold back, now was erupting at the Monday noon press luncheon.

Catching the brunt of his wrath was his high-priced Big Three of Bob Cousy, Ed Macauley and Bill Sharman, each getting around $15,000 a year. Of the NBA's 110 players that season, only Minneapolis Laker superstar George Mikan was being paid more.

Cousy, Macauley and Sharman would have company in the frying pan this day. Red Auerbach made it a double-barreled blast by roasting every Celtic.

"Cousy is back where he was three years ago," the coach said. "He has been trying too much of that behind-the-back razzle-dazzle. He makes a spectacular play but we lose the ball. Cooz can make this team or he can kill it."

Auerbach continued his critique on down the lineup: Macauley, Sharman, Brannum, Barksdale, Nichols. "I didn't leave out anyone," he recalls.

Ernie Barrett, teaming here with Bob Cousy, was the reason for a rare spat between Red Auerbach and Walter Brown. Auerbach didn't use the rookie during a road trip on which the Celtics lost all four games, and Brown complained to Auerbach: "What am I paying 10 men for if you're going to lose with eight? I might as well save myself two salaries." The two friends began yelling at each other but made up a few days later.

Celtics engage in basketball ballet during training camp (clockwise): Bob Brannum (18), Bob Harris (13), Bob Cousy (14), Ed Macauley (22), Bill Sharman (21), Ernie Barrett (23), Bob Donham (part of his No. 12 showing) and Chuck Cooper (11).

Front row (left to right): Bill Sharman, Bob Cousy, coach Red Auerbach, Bob Donham and Ernie Barrett. Back row: trainer Harvey Cohn, Bob Brannum, Bob Harris, Ed Macauley, Jack Nichols, Don Barksdale, Chuck Cooper and president Walter Brown.

No sooner had Auerbach and Brown spoken than Cousy's telephone began ringing as the media sought his reaction. And the more the sensitive Cousy heard, the more he sizzled. He got so upset he asked to go on a Worcester radio show and did some talking of his own.

"I don't understand why these statements about me were made at the luncheon today," he said on the air. "And I don't understand this trade talk. I'm pretty upset about it. If the Celtics aren't satisfied with my playing, *I* want to be traded."

Cousy didn't sleep much that night, he would say later.

"I was still angry at Walter and Red," he would recall. "Yet I was worried about them wanting to deal me off and was sore at myself for making such a foolish remark. I kept thinking of how happy I'd been when I'd joined the Celtics, and the more I thought about it the more I kicked myself for talking as though I wanted to leave."

Cousy and Auerbach huddled the next day.

"Look, nobody wants to trade you," Auerbach said. "I hope you've got that straight."

"Good," Cousy said. "I don't want to go anywhere. If the Celtics traded me, I'd quit."

Meanwhile, Brown was talking to the press and apologizing for his remarks.

COUSY CELEBRATES WORCESTER HOMECOMING

February 22, 1954, at Worcester Auditorium

CELTICS (111)	FG	FT	Pts.	BALTIMORE BULLETS (110)	FG	FT	Pts.
Donham	2	0	4	Houbregs	8	13	29
Brannum	5	0	10	Miller	3	6	12
Cooper	0	0	0	Fritsche	0	0	0
Barksdale	3	1	7	Felix	12	5	29
Nichols	2	0	4	Hoffman	7	2	16
Macauley	5	2	12	Hans	7	5	19
Harris	1	1	3	Smyth	2	1	5
Sharman	7	9	23				
Cousy	17	8	42				
Barrett	3	0	6				
Totals	45	21	111	*Totals*	39	32	110

Score: After regulation—88-88.
After 1st overtime—94-94.
After 2d overtime—100-100.
After 3d overtime—Boston 111, Baltimore 110.

Attendance: 3,800 (capacity).

Air travel was coming into vogue (along with hats) as the Celtics arrive unhappily home after losing a playoff game at Syracuse. Coming down the stairs (from top) are Ernie Barrett, Bob Donham, Bob Brannum, Don Barksdale, Bob Harris and Jack Nichols. Across the front (from right) are Ed Macauley, Chuck Cooper, Red Auerbach and Bill Sharman.

Celtics' playoff frustration of the early- and mid-fifties is mirrored in this here-we-go-again cameo the day after dropping the opening game of the Eastern finals to Syracuse. The Celtics went on to lose the next day to be ousted, 0-2. Huddling around Red Auerbach are (left to right) Bob Brannum, Jack Nichols, Don Barksdale, Bill Sharman (face partially hidden), Ed Macauley, Bob Harris, Ernie Barrett, Chuck Cooper, trainer Harvey Cohn and Bob Donham.

"Maybe I ought to fire myself," he said. "I'm so eager to have a winner that I'm more a fan than an executive. I get upset when we lose games. I'm going to keep my big mouth shut, and I've asked Red to keep his mouth shut, too."

Neither would succeed, but one of the few publicly aired family squabbles of the Brown Era was over.

The Celtics soon were untracked and contending again.

Cousy again led the league in assists (7.2 average) and was runnerup in scoring (19.2), followed by Macauley (18.9) third and Sharman (16.0) seventh. Macauley (.486) and Sharman (.450) were 1-2 in field-goal percentage, and Sharman (.844) led in free-throw percentage. And for the third straight season, the Celtics were the NBA's highest scoring team (averaging 87.7 points).

But in the end it was the same story: another second-place finish (tied with Syracuse, 2 games behind New York), another wipe out from the playoffs (this time by Syracuse 2-0, in the Eastern finals).

So the season ended as it had started—with frustration.

1954–55

Bob Cousy twists an acrobatic pass to Bill Sharman when challenged by Knick star Nat (Sweetwater) Clifton.

The Celtics celebrate after eliminating the Knicks in the Eastern semifinals. Then Boston fell to Syracuse in the Eastern finals. Enjoying the fun while it lasts (front row, left to right): Ed Macauley, Red Auerbach, Frank Ramsey and Jack Nichols; (back row) Red Morrison, Togo Palazzi, Don Barksdale, Bob Brannum, Fred Scolari, Bill Sharman, Bob Cousy and trainer Harvey Cohn.

The Celtics made history in their season opener at Rochester, a nationally televised Saturday afternoon game on October 30, 1954.

It was the first game played to the tick of the NBA's new 24-second clock, which would revolutionize pro basketball.

"The 24-second rule was a milestone," Red Auerbach says, "because it killed the freeze and resulting fouling that would turn games into free-for-alls the last few minutes."

It also saved the league from probable self-destruction.

The new rule speeded up games, providing 48 minutes of action. A team failing to take a shot within 24 seconds counted by an electronic clock would lose possession. That eliminated stallball and, in turn, substantially reduced fouling.

No longer could a team with the lead freeze the ball or slow its game to a walk while setting up a sure shot. No longer would the trailing team have to deliberately foul to get the ball back. No longer would the leading team then foul right back in a trading of fouls that made the game a travesty as opponents paraded from one end of the court to the other for what became foul-shooting contests.

The "old" game often had left spectators either napping from boredom or fuming from irritation.

The Celtics had engaged in exactly such burlesque the previous March 20 during a 78-79 playoff victory over the Knicks at Boston, a three-hour-plus marathon of fouls and squabbles seen on national television. That game was Exhibit A in a trend among teams that was earning the NBA a "bush league" reputation.

That national embarrassment between the Celtics and Knicks helped prod NBA owners into action the following month at the league meetings. So did a pending contract with NBC for 1954-55, the league's first substantial television package. Stallball and intentional fouls might be sound basketball strategy, but they could also turn off viewers who, in turn, could turn off their TV sets.

So the NBA made two key rule changes.

First, Syracuse owner Danny Biasone's proposal for a 24-second clock was adopted. In concert with that, a rule limiting fouls was passed. Now a team could commit only six in a quarter before being slapped with an extra penalty. Additional fouls each cost an extra free-throw. If a one-shot foul, the shooter would get another shot for an extra point; if a two-shot foul, the shooter would get there chances to make two points.

That combination of new rules proved a success from the start, cutting the chorus of whistles that had continually interrupted the flow of what was supposed to be a game of movement.

Now it was an action sport, bad only for teams with set offenses—slow and deliberate teams like Minneapolis. The Lakers had been devastating by taking all the time necessary to set up 6-foot-10 George Mikan, basketball's dominating force who had been almost unstoppable wheeling for hookshots before retiring the previous Spring.

Instead, the "new" game was tailor-made for a running team, a fastbreak team—a team like the Celtics.

Boston had been a run-and-shoot team since the coming of Auerbach and Cousy in 1950. That had been Auerbach's style throughout his coaching career, and Cousy, of course, was the master at quarterbacking the fastbreak. "Cooz was the best guard who ever lived when it came to executing the fastbreak," Auerbach says.

And in Sharman and Macauley, Cousy had teammates with the speed and quick-shooting ability to make it work. Well, almost. One key ingredient was missing: The big rebounder to (1) get the ball and trigger the fastbreak, and at the same time (2) prevent the enemy from getting second and third shots.

Ed Macauley:

"Most players have 'x' number of things they can do. They can shoot, pass, rebound, handle the ball, play defense and so on. And the most you can expect of an individual is to be proficient is in perhaps three, maybe three and a half, of those categories. You develop great teams when you blend your strength, my strength, someone else's strength and come up with the exact combination you're looking for.

"Our problem was that Cousy, Sharman and I were all great runners and shooters, but I wasn't big enough physically to do the job under the boards. I just didn't have the muscle to compete with a Mikan, a Pollard or a Mikkelsen.

"And by playoff time I'd be at a bigger disadvantage than ever, because the type of running game we played takes its toll toward the end of a season. The fatigue begins to set in."

Red Auerbach wasn't always so happy on the bench as his Celtics slipped to a .500 record.

Even so, the speeded-up game suited the Celtics well. After losing their first two games, Boston defeated Syracuse 107-84. The Celtics would top the 100-point mark 46 more times that season—compared to just 10 times the previous season.

The Celtics would lead the league with a 101.4-point average—nearly 14 points per game more than their NBA-high average of 87.7 in 1953-54, typical of the 13.6 increase throughout the league. But the Celts also led the NBA in an even more telltale statistic: points *allowed.* Almost incredibly, by surrendering an average of 101.5 per game, they were giving up more points than they were getting despite scoring the most points in basketball.

And so by season's end, the Celtics had tumbled to their worst record under Auerbach—barely reaching .500 by winning their final game to finish at 36-36. That was six victories fewer than 1953-54, 10 less than 1952-53, as the team appeared to be going in the wrong direction.

Third-place Boston came to life briefly in the playoffs, ousting second-place New York, 2-1. But eventual NBA champion Syracuse made quick work of the Celtics in the Eastern finals, 3-1, by outrebounding them.

That underlined something everyone already knew from painful repetition all season: In 24-second basketball, with more shots to be retrieved and more fastbreaks to be ignited, the Celtics needed a rebounder more than ever.

24-SECOND CLOCK USED FOR 1st TIME

October 30, 1954, at Rochester

CELTICS (95)	*FG*	*FT*	*PF*	*Pts.*	ROCHESTER ROYALS (98)	*FG*	*FT*	*PF*	*Pts.*
Barksdale	0	0	0	0	Coleman	3	1	2	7
Nichols	5	4	4	14	Marshall	4	2	4	10
Brannum	0	2	4	2	Christensen	1	3	1	5
Macauley	5	11	4	21	Nachamkin	3	5	2	11
Cousy	4	10	1	18	Spoelstra	1	2	6	14
Morrison	0	1	2	1	Risen	5	7	6	17
Sharman	10	4	4	24	Wanzer	11	3	5	25
Ramsey	3	9	5	15	McMahon	3	0	2	6
Scolari	0	0	2	0	Davies	3	7	3	13
Totals	27	41	26	95	*Totals*	34	30	31	98

Score by periods:	1	2	3	4
Celtics	17	25	29	24—95
Royals	27	28	11	32—98

Free Throws Missed: Celtics (6)—Sharman 3, Ramsey 2, Macauley. Royals (7)—Coleman, Marshall, Christensen, Nachamkin, Risen, Wanzer, McMahon.

Frustrated Syracuse defender George King tackles dribbling Bob Cousy as the Nats' John (Red) Kerr (dark uniform) and the Celtics' Bill Sharman (No. 21, white uniform) move in.

1955–56

Front row (left to right): Jim Loscutoff, Jack Nichols, president Walter Brown, coach Red Auerbach, Ed Macauley and Arnie Risen. Second row: trainer Harvey Cohn, Bill Sharman, Ernie Barrett, Dwight (Red) Morrison, Dick Hemric, Togo Palazzi and Bob Cousy.

Bob Cousy is embraced by Ernie Barrett (left) after scoring 29 points as the Celtics defeated Syracuse in the playoff opener. But the Nats would win the next two games to oust Boston for the third straight year, ending another Celtic season in frustration. That's veteran Arnie Risen (second right) and rookie Jim Loscutoff (right).

It was the same old Celtic story: another second-place finish, another quick exit from the playoffs. More disappointment, more frustration.

Bob Cousy:

"Willie Sharman, Ed Macauley and I would bust our fannies into exhaustion and then come up with no appreciable results when the season was over.

"We'd usually end up second and never got beyond the Eastern finals, and we got that far only three times. It was tremendously frustrating.

"Red took the brunt of the blame, but it wasn't his fault. There's no question in my mind that Arnold got the most out of his material during those seasons. He brought us as far as we could possibly go. We simply didn't have the horses to go all the way.

"We could shoot like hell, we could pass extremely well, we could run very well, and we played pretty fair defense for a running team and without a big guy backing us up. We had everything except the big rebounder."

As usual, the Celtics led the league in scoring (fifth straight season) with a 106-point average, an NBA record. As usual, Bob Cousy led the league in assists (fourth straight season) with an 8.9 average, an NBA record. As usual, Bill Sharman led the league in free-throw percentage (fourth straight season) with 87 percent. As usual, the Big Three of Sharman (19.9), Cousy (18.8) and Ed Macauley (17.5) were among the league's scoring leaders.

And as usual, after being NBA East bridesmaid again (6 games behind eventual league championship Philadelphia), the Celtics were bounced from the playoffs by Syracuse again (third straight season)—this time in the opening round.

There had been hope in Boston that these playoffs would be different. In the opener, the Celtics roared from behind on the thrust of Cousy's 29 points and thumped the defending champion Nationals, 110-93. But Syracuse won the next two games to oust the Celtics, a familiar ending.

It would be the last time the Celtics ever would be given the bum's rush in an opening round, but there was no way of knowing that then. After his team had been eliminated, Red Auerbach spelled out his frustration for *Boston Globe* sports editor/columnist Jerry Nason.

"Damn it," Auerbach fretted. "With the talent we've got, if we can just come up with a big man who'll get us the rebounds, we'll win everything in sight!"

Celtic newcomers Arnie Risen (left) and Jim Loscutoff.

Red Auerbach:
"Those years were frustrating as hell. But we weren't going anywhere until we solved the little matter of controlling the basketball. And that's where Mr. Russell would come in the next season."

Surrounded by Pistons, Bill Sharman still gets a pass away.

AN OLD STORY—MORE PLAYOFF FRUSTRATION

March 17, 1956, at Boston Garden

CELTICS (110)	FG	FT	Pts.	SYRACUSE NATIONALS (93)	FG	FT	Pts.
Nichols	4	1	9	Conlin	9	3	21
Macauley	5	2	12	Schayes	3	12	18
Loscutoff	7	2	16	Tucker	2	0	4
Hemric	3	0	6	Lloyd	2	0	4
Risen	3	3	9	Kerr	7	0	14
Morrison	2	0	4	King	4	1	9
Sharman	7	6	20	Rocha	3	2	8
Cousy	11	7	29	Seymour	1	1	3
Barrett	1	1	3	Kenville	2	0	4
Palazzi	1	0	2	Farley	3	2	8
Totals	44	22	110	*Totals*	36	21	93

Score by periods:	1	2	3	4	
Celtics	25	26	29	30	—110
Nationals	22	19	31	21	—93

Attendance: 5,446.

March 19, 1956, at Syracuse

CELTICS (98)	FG	FT	Pts.	SYRACUSE	FG	FT	Pts.
Sharman	3	2	8	Schayes	3	9	15
Barrett	3	2	8	Conlin	3	0	6
Cousy	9	10	28	Rocha	4	6	14
Hemric	2	6	10	Kerr	10	3	23
Risen	5	4	14	Lloyd	3	4	10
Morrison	0	0	0	King	6	6	18
Nichols	7	4	18	Farley	2	1	5
Loscutoff	3	3	9	Seymour	3	4	10
Macauley	1	1	3	Kenville	0	0	0
Palazzi	0	0	0				
Totals	33	32	98	*Totals*	34	33	101

Score by periods:	1	2	3	4	
Celtics	21	29	20	28	—98
Nationals	21	32	28	20	—101

March 21, 1956, at Boston Garden

CELTICS (97)	FG	FT	Pts.	SYRACUSE NATIONALS (102)	FG	FT	Pts.
Sharman	8	8	24	Rocha	2	0	4
Barrett	0	0	0	Conlin	1	2	4
Cousy	8	6	22	Schayes	10	7	27
Hemric	0	3	3	Kerr	2	3	7
Risen	4	6	14	Lloyd	2	1	5
Morrison	0	0	0	King	6	2	14
Nichols	5	4	14	Kenville	1	0	2
Loscutoff	1	2	4	Seymour	7	7	21
Macauley	6	4	16	Farley	8	2	18
Totals	32	33	97	*Totals*	39	24	102

Score by periods:	1	2	3	4	
Celtics	22	23	31	21	—97
Nationals	21	36	21	24	—102

Attendance: 11,669.

1956–57

It was the Season the Celtics Blossomed, the turning point that transformed them from also-rans to champions.

It began with Red Auerbach scheming to acquire the player who in 1980 would be voted the greatest player in NBA history. It concluded with a storybook ending that was one of the great games in basketball history.

Sandwiched in between was the Celtics' first championship season as Walter Brown finally collected the grail he had been pursuing more than a decade. And that was just the start. Although no one could know it then, that 1956-57 season launched sports' greatest dynasty—one that would sputter only twice in 13 years.

The story of that season began in a New York hotel the previous Spring—on April 20, 1956—when the Celtics finally acquired their missing link by drafting William Fenton Russell.

"He was the guy we desperately needed," Auerbach says now. "And he turned out to be all I expected and more—the greatest of them all, the best basketball player who ever lived."

"Russ revolutionized basketball and was the man who made us go," Bob Cousy says. "Without him we wouldn't have won a championship."

The Celtics landed Russell on a two-part maneuver by Auerbach. First he traded veteran Ed Macauley and rookie-to-be Cliff Hagan to St. Louis for the Hawks' first-round pick, the second overall choice in the draft. Auerbach then used that ticket to claim Russell, the 6-foot-10 backbone of the University of San Francisco team that had swept 55 games in a row and back-to-back national championships.

Before pulling it off, Auerbach had left little to chance and cleared the way:

(1) He made reasonably sure that Rochester, which had first pick overall, wouldn't take Russell.

Russell had helped make up the Royals' mind. Hoping to be drafted by the Lakers to fill retired George Mikan's sneakers, he purposely scared off Rochester owner Les Harrison by saying he wanted at least $25,000. Harrison decided he had enough rebounding in 6-7 forward Maurice Stokes, who had led the league with a 16.3 rebound average that season as the NBA's Rookie of the Year. So Harrison assured Brown that he would opt for backcourt help instead and draft Sihugo Green.

(2) Auerbach fenced with crafty Hawks owner Ben Kerner, his old boss at Tri-Cities.

At first Auerbach offered only Macauley, who wanted to return to his St. Louis hometown because his son had taken seriously ill that Spring. Macauley was a favorite in St. Louis after starring there as a schoolboy and collegian, and Kerner was looking for a local hero as a drawing card to help root the team in St. Louis after shifting the club from Milwaukee the previous year.

And Macauley's rebounding deficiency wouldn't be as acute with the Hawks, who already had a 6-11 center in Chuck Share and could move slick-shooting Easy Ed to forward.

Another likely factor in Kerner's decision was Russell's color. It wasn't yet time for a black to be comfortable in St. Louis. The NBA had only about a dozen blacks (Russell would be the Celtics' only one his first season, with Chuck Cooper and Don Barksdale gone), and they found themselves the object of racial taunts in the league's southernmost city.

And, finally, Kerner couldn't afford the $25,000 any more than Harrison.

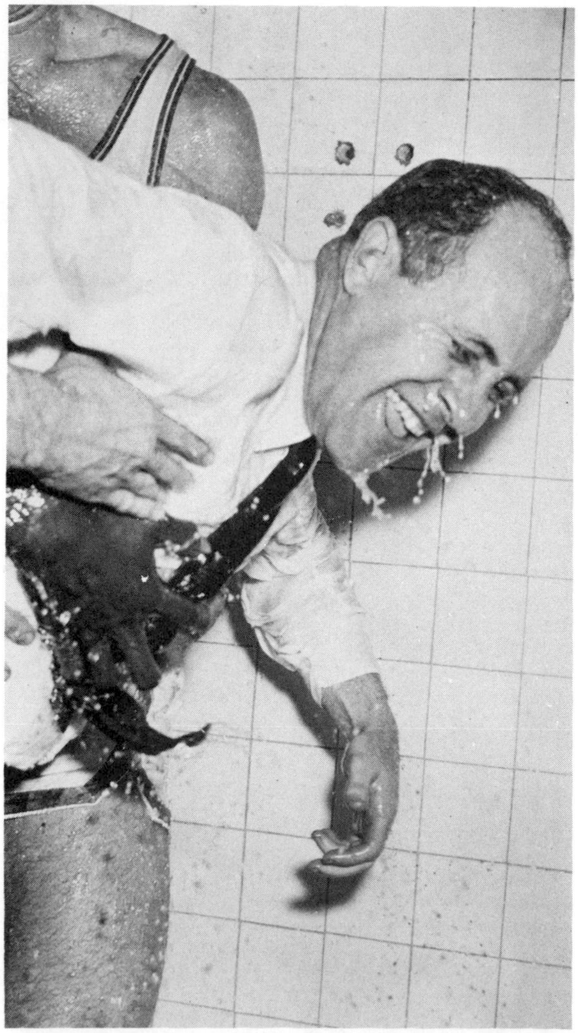

The Celtics are champions at last, and Red Auerbach happily pays the price—a dunking in the shower. His clothes soaked, the coach had to don an old sweatsuit for the drive across downtown Boston to his hotel.

Still, Kerner realized Auerbach coveted Russell. So he insisted that, besides Macauley, he get Hagan, one of three Kentucky stars Boston had drafted three years earlier even though they had another college season and faced two years in the Army after that. Auerbach surrendered Hagan with reluctance, but he knew he had another promising rookie forward in the wings—Tommy Heinsohn. The Celtics would claim the Holy Cross All-America as a territorial choice with their own pick in the first round.

(3) Auerbach cleared the last Russell hurdle by getting a waiver on the NBA rule that forbade a team from trading its No. 1 draft choice.

League officials and owners consented, confident the trade would benefit both teams, which it did.

Three other considerations likely influenced both Rochester and St. Louis in passing on Russell.

One was that he was intent upon playing in the Olympics at Melbourne, and that meant he would miss the season's first two months. Since Australia's seasons are reversed, the Summer competition would be held in November and early December. Could the Royals and Hawks, with 1955-56's worst records, afford to wait until nearly midseason for help?

Also, the prize choice would be wasted if Russell signed with the Globetrotters, who reportedly were offering him $50,000 (but in reality were talking only $17,000 tops).

And, finally, there was some suspicion that Russell couldn't succeed in the pros.

"There's no question Red was the first to realize what Russell could mean," Warriors founder Eddie Gottlieb once told *Boston Herald American* columnist and author Joe Fitzgerald. "Russell was not a scorer in college, and that made him a question mark when he came into our league. A lot of people said, 'He can't shoot, he can't score, so what good is he?'

"But Red recognized a way he could take advantage of Russell's defense and rebounding and get big results.

"So you've got to give the man credit. He was the first to spot Russell's real greatness. He saw things nobody else saw back then."

And what Boston Garden fans saw when Russell returned with his Olympic gold medal and played his first NBA game—a 95-93 victory over St. Louis on Saturday afternoon national TV on December 22—was a messiah.

He used a kangaroo leap and octopus reach to reap a harvest of rebounds and blocked shots to unfurl the fastbreak, demoralizing and wearing out opponents while delighting Celtic fans. He had signed for $19,500 and quickly proved worth every penny as he perfectly complemented the talents of his teammates.

The Celtics were in first place when Russell joined them, managing a 16-8 record (including a 10-game winning streak) by using the aging Arnie Risen and Jack Nichols in the pivot, even moving Heinsohn in there at times from forward.

Now, with Russell aboard and Frank Ramsey back from his Army hitch on January 4, there would be no catching the Celtics. They ran off an eight-victory streak in late January to build their record to 31-14.

Bob Cousy greeted Bill Russell when the rookie reported to the Celtics in December after winning Olympic gold at Melbourne. The pair would collaborate seven seasons as the trigger to the Celtics' textbook fastbreak—and 25 years later they would be chosen to the NBA's all-time team.

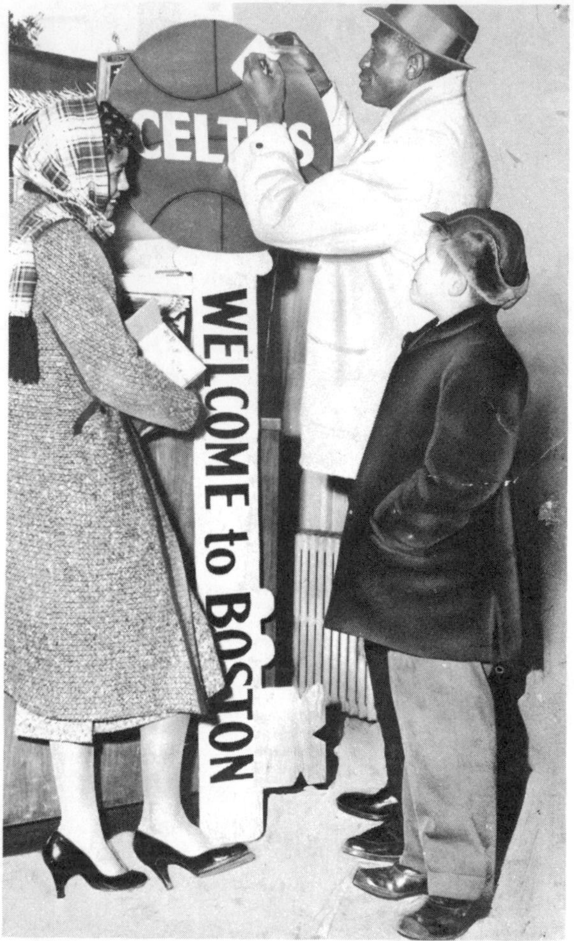

Bill Russell signs an autograph for 10-year-old Dennis Brogna as the new Celtic and bride Rose arrive at Boston's Logan Airport from a quick honeymoon following the Olympics at Melbourne. It was Russell's first autograph in Boston—and one of the few during his 13 years as a Celtic, generally refusing even teammates.

"This club at full strength is the answer to a coach's dreams," Auerbach was saying, suddenly finding coaching life easier at age 39. "We've got the same great backcourt strength we've always had. We're stronger than ever up front. And we've got good depth everywhere.

"Russell is going to be the best center in the business, if he isn't already. I've never seen anyone do what he did—come in at mid-season with no experience, no training and no knowledge of the league and take right over.

"Naturally, I'm keeping my fingers crossed, but barring injuries, we might just go all the way."

It *was* all over in the East as the Celtics coasted home with a best-in-league 44-28 record for their first division crown by six games over Syracuse.

With Russell, Heinsohn and Jim Loscutoff under the boards, opponents found that rebounds, once easy pickings against Boston, now were scarce. And besides dominating the boards with a 19.6 rebound average, Russell had proven an effective hub on offense—not only scoring more than predicted (14.7), but feeding Heinsohn (16.2, including a 41-point performance) in the corner and Sharman (21.6) and Cousy (20.6) in the backcourt. That gave the Celtics three scorers in the NBA's Top 12 and for the first time two scorers in the 20s. And Cousy again led the league in assists (7.7), Sharman in free-throw percentage (.905, including a league record 55-in-a-row streak).

The Celtics continued to roll in the playoffs, wiping out Syracuse in three straight—swift revenge against the team that had knocked them out of the previous three playoffs.

Then came the championship series against St. Louis in a fitting match of the teams that had made the previous Spring's supertrade.

The agony . . .
Star of the game Tom Heinsohn, fouled out after contributing 37 points and 23 rebounds, hides his tears beneath a warmup jacket in the final minute of double overtime as the Celtics scheme to defend their thin lead in Game 7 of the NBA finals.

Front row (left to right): Lou Tsioropoulos, Andy Phillip, Frank Ramsey, coach Red Auerbach, Bob Cousy, Bill Sharman and Jim Loscutoff. Back row: president Walter Brown, Dick Hemric, Jack Nichols, Bill Russell, Arnie Risen, Tom Heinsohn, trainer Harvey Cohn and vice president Lou Pieri.

After breaking a tie moments earlier with a free throw, Frank Ramsey scores the deciding basket with 72 seconds remaining in the second overtime period of the finals' seventh game. Those last 72 seconds on the clock would take 10 minutes to complete before the Celtics wrapped up a 125-123 victory over St. Louis for Boston's first NBA championship.

. . . and the ecstacy
And moments later, Heinsohn is mobbed by ecstatic Boston Garden fans and carried off the floor as the Celtics are world champions for the first time.

The Celtics had beaten the Hawks in seven of nine games during the season, but St. Louis had improved after two midseason changes—acquiring old Laker Slater (Dugie) Martin to bolster the backcourt and making Alex Hannum player-coach. Martin and Jack McMahon gave the Hawks two of the NBA's top five assistmen, and they had plenty of sharpshooters to feed. Bob Pettit was the best cornerman in the league, its No. 2 scorer (24.7) and rebounder (14.6). Macauley had clocked the most minutes of any Hawk while averaging 16.5 points, ninth best in the league. Jack Coleman and Share also were in double figures, and Hagan was developing into stardom up front.

The series would be a tense and furious one, a sizzler.

Game 1 in Boston set the tone, an overtime shootout won by the Hawks, 125-123, as Pettit scored 37 points, Sharman 36. But the Celtics won Game 2 by 20 points to send the series to St. Louis tied.

Veterans Arnie Risen (left) and Jack Nichols (right) kept the Celtics' pivot warm for Bill Russell while he missed the first 24 games because of the Olympics.

Bill Sharman averaged 20 points for the first time, 21.1 to be exact, seventh best in the league—a notch ahead of Bob Cousy at 20.6.

Tension had been mounting in the series, and tempers were taut before Game 3. Auerbach was growling that his team had been given old and ragged basketballs for warmups. Then some of the Celtics told him that the basket seemed too high. Flushed with anger, Auerbach demanded that the referees measure the basket's height—which they did on a stepladder as the crowd jeered and Kerner steamed.

And the volatile Hawk owner boiled over when the officials ruled the basket's height was the regulation 10 feet. He and Auerbach engaged in a lively courtside conversation, cut short when the Boston coach charged from 12 feet away and punched Kerner squarely in the mouth, swelling his lip (and later costing Auerbach a $300 league fine).

Red Auerbach:
"The first championship is always the sweetest, so there will never be another one for me like '57.

"I'll always remember that series for another reason, too. For losing my head and punching Ben Kerner. I'll always regret that punch because Ben was one of the class guys in our league going way back.

"Other than that, it was one hell of a year."

"He cussed me out," Auerbach told the press. "What he called me isn't printable. I wasn't going to take that."

"Aw, all I called him was a busher. He's a big sorehead," Kerner said. "That stuff he was pulling was bush. With all the talent he has, he still has to pull tricks like that."

The teams went on to split the next four games, and the series came down to a seventh-game showdown on a Saturday afternoon at Boston before an overflowing Garden and a national television audience.

It was a classic with an unexpected twist for the Celtics. Their proven marksmen, Sharman and Cousy (who would be named first-team all-league again) proved human by going ice cold and the rookies saved the day. Sharman (a .416 shooter that season) hit just three of 20 from the floor, Cousy (.378 that season) only two of 20 (although dealing 11 assists). But Heinsohn mustered 37 points and 23 rebounds before tearfully fouling out and Russell 32 rebounds and 19 points.

Russell also blocked five shots and dazzled fans during a spectacular and pivotal four-second span midway through the final minute of regulation. With Coleman driving for a layup that could have given St. Louis a 3-point lead, Russell swooped in from midcourt and swatted away the ball, then sprinted to the other end and scored a basket that gave Boston the lead—having dramatically bossed both boards within four seconds.

Pettit, who would score 39 points and add 19 rebounds despite a wrist broken earlier in the series, sent the game into overtime with two free throws with three seconds remaining. And a jumper by Coleman with nine seconds left in the first overtime spelled double-OT when Sharman's answering shot clanged off the rim.

After Heinsohn fouled out with two minutes to go, Ramsey's 20-footer gave the Celtics the lead as the clock wound down—*slowly,* the final 72 seconds on the clock taking 10 minutes to complete. And after Loscutoff made a free throw, it was Boston 125, St. Louis 123—with one second left.

Bill Russell is fouled by St. Louis' Bob Pettit (9) in the Celtic rookie's pro debut, a nationally televised 95-93 victory over the Hawks at Boston Garden. Russell played 21 minutes, collecting 16 rebounds and 6 points.

Hannum, who two minutes earlier put himself into his first game in three weeks, called time out and designed a play around the fact that the clock doesn't start until a player on the court touches the ball.

Inbounding the ball at his own end, Hannum hurled it the length of the floor off the Boston backboard and into the waiting hands of Pettit in the foul lane. Pettit rebounded the ball and flipped it back up in the same motion, and the rushed shot skidded off the rim as the buzzer sounded and Russell nearly went into orbit jumping with joy.

The Celtics finally were world champions, and seemingly half of Boston poured onto the floor and mobbed its heroes. Russell and Loscutoff beat the fans to Auerbach, hoisting him to their shoulders before he could light his sweetest victory cigar. The coach fared better than Heinsohn, who was paraded high above the crowd—until unceremoniously dropped, bloodying his knee.

Heinsohn's wound didn't prevent him and Auerbach from grabbing Russell in the locker room and shaving off his goatee—the beard that had caused some controversy around the league among fans used to clean-shaven athletes.

"Well, there it is, boys—I mean, there it *isn't*," Russell laughed, emerging from the shower room. "It's gone down the drain. I promised they could do it if we won the title, and now nobody can ask me about the thing any more.

"If we'd lost I was going to keep it on until we won the championship—no matter how many years it took."

Russell was celebrating his third title within 13 months—NCAA, Olympic and NBA.

"This one scared hell out of me," he said. "I never was so scared in my life. I was shaking all over. Did you see my legs when it was over? I felt like jumping all night I was so happy."

So was Heinsohn, the center of attraction.

"Jeepers, of course I feel pressure, like anyone else," the NBA's Rookie of the Year told reporters. "But if a shot's there, take it. So I took them. What the deuce is a guy suppose to do with the ball, eat it?"

"What a show Tommy put on," Sharman marveled. "I never saw anyone play like that under such pressure, let alone a rookie."

"The kid's the greatest," admired Cousy, voted the playoff's MVP by a point over Pettit. "What pressure. And how he played under it."

And it paid off to the tune of $1,681.81 per Celtic after splitting up the $18,500 prize money. It wasn't enough to acquire a champagne taste yet, so they celebrated with beer—drinking it, spraying it, showering each other with it.

"We've been chasing this thing seven years," the drenched Auerbach said, peeling off his soaked clothes before donning an old sweatshirt for the drive across town to his hotel. "My nervous system is shot."

"Yes, we've been trying to get to the top for seven years, and now we're finally here," Cousy said. "People are calling us great. But now we've got to do it again, just to show we are the greatest. And it won't be easy."

Easy Ed Macauley came back to Boston wearing an enemy uniform.

CELTICS WIN THEIR FIRST CHAMPIONSHIP

April 13, 1957, at Boston Garden

CELTICS (125)

	Min.	*FGA*	*FGM*	*FTA*	*FTM*	*Reb.*	*Ast.*	*PF*	*Pts.*
Heinsohn	45	33	17	11	3	23	2	6	37
Risen	20	12	6	8	4	10	0	6	16
Loscutoff	18	4	0	3	3	2	0	5	3
Ramsey	28	13	6	7	4	8	1	2	16
Russell	54	17	7	10	5	32	2	5	19
Nichols	9	7	4	0	0	1	0	3	8
Cousy	58	20	2	10	8	3	11	4	12
Sharman	48	20	3	3	3	1	3	3	9
Phillip	10	2	2	2	1	1	3	3	5
Totals	290	128	47	54	31	84	22	37	125

ST. LOUIS HAWKS (123)

	Min.	*FGA*	*FGM*	*FTA*	*FTM*	*Reb.*	*Ast.*	*PF*	*Pts.*
Coleman	36	12	4	5	2	5	7	6	10
Share	21	6	0	8	5	6	0	4	5
Hagan	40	15	7	14	10	16	0	6	24
Macauley	21	3	2	8	5	8	1	6	9
Pettit	56	34	14	13	11	19	3	4	39
Hannum	2	1	0	0	0	0	0	1	0
McMahon	37	10	3	0	0	5	5	6	6
Park	21	5	3	2	1	4	1	1	7
Martin	56	16	6	12	11	8	7	3	23
Totals	290	102	39	62	45	77	23	37	123

Score by periods:	1	2	3	4	O1	O2
Celtics:	26	25	32	20	10	12–125
Hawks:	28	25	24	26	10	10–123

Field Goal Percentage: Celtics .367, Hawks .382.
Free Throw Percentage: Celtics .574, Hawks .726.
Team Rebounds: Celtics 3, Hawks 6.
Referees: Sid Borgia and Mendy Rudolph.
Attendance: 13,909.

1957–58

Top draft choice Sam Jones was among rookies reporting to Red Auerbach for early training camp at Northeastern University.

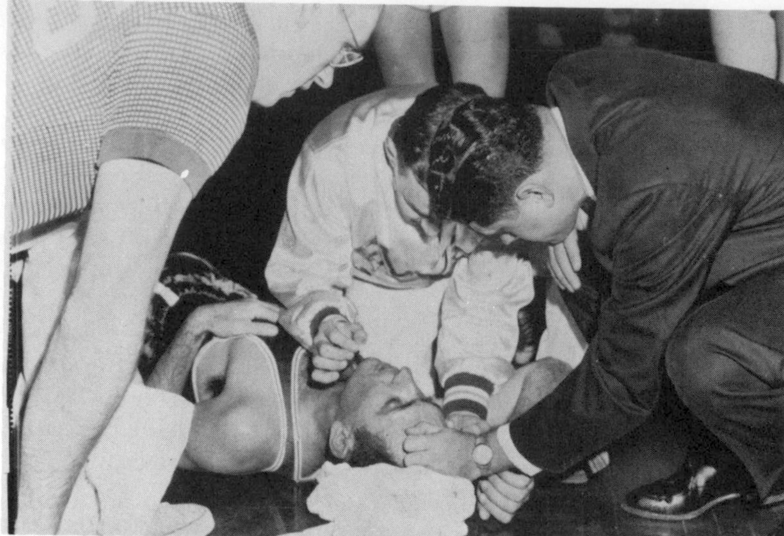

Bill Russell, who suffered a severe ankle sprain and chip fracture, wasn't the only Celtic hobbled during the finals with the Hawks. Bob Cousy played in agony with a pulled instep tendon, and he was shaken up when fouled by Med Park in Game 4 at St. Louis. Cousy and Russell both took intensive treatment twice a day throughout the series. Cousy didn't miss a game, and Russell returned for Game 6. But it was no use, and the ankle gave out completely. The Celtics went on to lose the game, 110-109—and their championship.

Frank Ramsey is sandwiched between two Rochester Royals while pursuing a rebound. With Jim Loscutoff sidelined most of the season, Ramsey stepped out of his sixth-man role and played forward almost exclusively as the Celtics won their second straight Eastern Division title.

There was cobra-quick Bill Russell, in a cameo of basketball ballet, soaring to block a Bob Pettit shot.

There was Russell, the NBA's Most Valuable Player that season, landing heavily on the outside of his left foot, the ankle buckling beneath him.

And there was Russell crashing to the floor in a heap—and, as if the pain didn't hurt enough, there was a whistle being blown in his direction for goaltending.

The date is engraved darkly in Celtic history: April 2, 1958. The place: Kiel Auditorium, the 10,000-seat snakepit in St. Louis.

It is the third minute of the third period of the third game of the NBA finals between the Celtics and Hawks—the title series tied at one victory apiece—in a rematch of last year's finalists.

Nobody knows it yet, but Russell has severely sprained the ankle—and suffered a chip fracture, something not revealed until after the series.

Nobody knows it yet, but Russell is essentially through for the series as he hobbles off the court assisted by teammate Arnie Risen and Buddy LeRoux, in his first game as a Celtic trainer. "I was finished," Russell would recall years later, "and I knew it."

Nobody else did, though, and so nobody knows that the Celtics are dead despite an assortment of heroics in the next three and a half games. With one NBA championship in the trophy case, the Celtics are about to be dethroned.

In defense of their title the Celtics had won their first 14 games and gone on to total 49 victories, their most in a season—five more than the season before. That was the most wins in the league—only two NBA teams had ever won more—as Boston wrapped up its second straight Eastern title.

Russell had smashed NBA records by collecting 1,564 rebounds, hundreds more than anyone ever had in a season, for a 22.7 average. Bob Cousy had led the league in assists for the sixth straight year,

Front row (left to right): Frank Ramsey, Andy Phillip, president Walter Brown, coach Red Auerbach, vice president Lou Pieri. Bob Cousy and Bill Sharman. Back row: Lou Tsioropoulos, Jim Loscutoff, Jack Nichols, Bill Russell, Arnie Risen, Tom Heinsohn, Sam Jones and trainer Harvey Cohn.

averaging 7.1. And Bill Sharman had what would prove his best scoring season, averaging 22.3 points.

Jim Loscutoff missed all but five early season games because of knee surgery, so Frank Ramsey played forward most of the time. The fourth backcourt man was a rookie named Sam Jones. He was the No. 1 draft choice from little North Carolina College recommended by Celt alumnus Horace (Bones) McKinney, the Wake Forest coach who advised Red Auerbach: "This guy can shoot. Get him if you can."

The playoffs had begun as an extension of Boston's regular-season success. The Celtics swept past Philadelphia, 4-1—a good Warriors team: Paul Arizin, Neil Johnston, Woody Sauldsberry, Tom Gola, Joe Graboski, and Jack George.

St. Louis would prove more of a challenge, intent upon finally capturing the prize that had so narrowly eluded them the previous Spring. Back for another try were old rivals Pettit, Ed Macauley, Cliff Hagan, Slater Martin, Chuck Share, Jack McMahon, Jack Coleman.

After a split of the first two games in Boston, the series shifted to St. Louis.

Then came Russell's injury. His ankle swollen and aching, Russell returned to the game briefly but had to retire for good a few minutes later and went to a hospital for X-rays.

LeRoux would attend to Russell around the clock the next 10 days. Russell's cranky ankles had been troubling him even before the injury, so a few days earlier Auerbach had "borrowed" LeRoux from the Boston Bruins, Walter Brown's other team, to work on the superstar. Now, with Russell's left ankle a disaster area, LeRoux was needed more than ever—and, incidentally, would never return to hockey. Instead, he would replace aging Harvey Cohn as the Celtics' head trainer the following season.

The Celtics didn't quit without their defensive backbone. Instead, they seemed to pull together more to compensate.

"With Russ on the floor we have a bad tendency to relax off the boards," Cousy explained after Russell's injury. "We sort of figure he's coming down with any rebounds and so we've been getting sloppy. We've been going out there lately with pretty much individual effort.

"Well, when Russ got hurt, the rest of the guys sensed they had to help each other out—and they did. They were passing the ball setting up blocks and crashing for those rebounds."

Tom Heinsohn hooks a shot over the Knicks' Art Spoelstra.

Jim Loscutoff was sidelined all but five early season games because of knee surgery. He was missed particularly in the playoffs, when Bill Russell was out—meaning the Celtics were without two of the previous season's top 10 NBA rebounders.

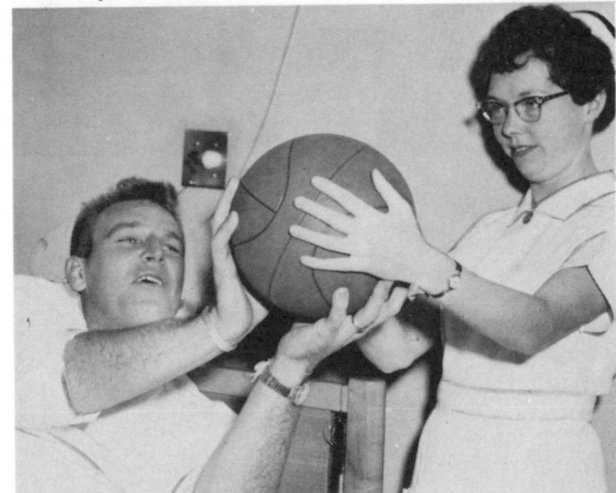

RUSSELL HURT . . .

April 2, 1958, at St. Louis

CELTICS (108)

	FG	FT	PF	Pts.
Russell	4	6	2	14
Cousy	3	5	4	11
Heinsohn	4	3	6	11
Nichols	1	1	1	3
Phillip	0	0	0	0
Risen	2	4	5	8
Sharman	8	5	2	21
Ramsey	10	9	6	29
Jones	2	4	2	8
Tsioropoulos	1	1	4	3
Totals	35	38	32	108

ST. LOUIS HAWKS (111)

	FG	FT	PF	Pts.
Pettit	10	12	4	32
Coleman	6	0	4	12
Davis	3	1	4	7
Share	3	1	4	7
Wilfong	1	1	2	3
Hagan	7	4	6	18
Park	1	0	3	2
Macauley	1	3	0	5
McMahon	3	2	4	8
Martin	3	11	3	17
Totals	38	35	34	111

Score by periods:	1	2	3	4
Celtics:	25	24	26	33–108
Hawks:	23	26	34	28–111

Referees: Mendy Rudolph and Arnie Heft.
Attendance: 10,148.

Bob Cousy drives between a pair of St. Louis defenders—forever the basketball small man operating in a forest of taller men.

That had been evident as soon as Russell departed Game 3. The Celtics promptly fought back from a 12-point deficit—a surge led by Frank Ramsey. He'd score 29 points before fouling out with 46 seconds remaining and the Celtics trailing by 2. But in the end, poor foul shooting (missing 22 of 60 free throws as wads of paper often were hurled to distract the shooter) did in the Celtics, 111-108.

There was talk of Russell coming back for the next game three days later at St. Louis. He was taking intensive therapy twice a day at a hospital there with Cousy, who had pulled an instep tendon that would have him in agony the remainder of the series.

But Russell's ankle was too tender to tape for Game 4. And, once again, the Celtics rallied together in his absence. They evened the series, 109-98, as Auerbach abandoned the fastbreak and went to a slow, deliberate pace while shuffling Risen, Tom Heinsohn, Jack Nichols and even Cousy into the pivot.

"Loscy's absence really hurts," Auerbach said. "We could really use him hitting those boards now."

Instead, a glum Loscutoff was back in Boston—as a *Boston Globe* photograph showed—listening to the game on the radio with wife Lynn at his side.

With Loscutoff and Russell out, the Celtics were missing their top two rebounders of the previous season, two of the NBA's top 10. It left the 6-foot-9 Risen, 6-foot-7 Nichols and 6-foot-7 Heinsohn outsized by St. Louis' front line of the 6-foot-11 Share, 6-foot-9 Pettit and 6-foot-8 Macauley.

The Celtics couldn't hold off the Hawks in the next game as St. Louis squeezed out a 102-100 victory at Boston. That put the Hawks ahead, 3-2, and sent the series back to St. Louis, where they could wrap up their first NBA title before the home folks—and not risk a seventh game back in Boston that would give Russell more time to heal.

With the Celtics facing elimination, Russell discards his crutches and plays in Game 6. His ankle heavily wrapped, he enters in the early minutes with Boston leading, 7-4. And he scores 8 points while

Former Bostonian Ed Macauley points out the Garden to roommate Slater Martin before the opener of the Celtics-Hawks rematch in the finals.

struggling through 20 minutes of action. But it's no use. He is only a shadow of his usual efficiency, and the ankle finally gives out completely and he is assisted off the floor.

Once again the Celtics play furiously in Russell's absence and lead by a point with four minutes left in a tug-of-war thriller. But every Celtic burst is answered with a clutch basket by Pettit, who is playing the game of his life. With no Russell to harrass him, he overpowers Heinsohn and scores a playoff record 50 points—including 19 of St. Louis' final 21, and adds 19 rebounds.

Boston trails by only a point with a minute to play, but St. Louis draws ahead by 3 on a Pettit tap-in before allowing a harmless basket by Sharman, the last of his 26 points this night.

And when the buzzer sounds—Hawks 110, Celtics 109—teammates and fans mob Pettit, a hero who has averaged 29.2 points for the series, and carry him off the court.

Afterward, in the Celtic locker room, Auerbach puts a hand on Russell's shoulder and whispers: "There will be other seasons, Russ."

Red Auerbach:

"Russell's absence wasn't the reason we lost in '58. We were beaten by a great team. They deserved the title."

Ed Macauley:

"If Russell hadn't been hurt, we wouldn't have beaten the Celtics."

. . . CELTICS DETHRONED

April 12, 1958, at St. Louis

CELTICS (109)

	FG	FT	PF	Pts.
Heinsohn	5	13	5	23
Tsioropoulos	4	6	1	14
Ramsey	3	2	6	8
Risen	4	4	3	12
Nichols	0	0	0	0
Russell	2	4	4	8
Cousy	4	7	3	15
Sharman	10	6	4	26
Jones	1	1	0	3
Phillip	0	0	4	0
Totals	33	43	30	109

ST. LOUIS HAWKS (110)

	FG	FT	PF	Pts.
Pettit	19	12	1	50
Hagan	5	5	6	15
Macauley	0	2	5	2
Davis	2	1	2	5
Share	3	2	6	8
Coleman	3	2	3	8
Martin	0	4	4	4
Park	1	3	1	5
McMahon	4	1	5	9
Wilfong	1	2	1	4
Totals	38	34	34	110

Score by periods:	1	2	3	4
Celtics:	18	34	25	32–109
Hawks:	22	35	21	32–110

Referees: Arnie Heft and Mendy Rudolph.
Attendance: 10,216.

Bill Russell was the league's MVP as he smashed rebounding records, averaging 22.7 and grabbing hundreds more than anyone ever had in an NBA season. The swooping Russell got the ball even when surrounded, as he is here by four Knicks.

Bob Pettit

1958–59

Walter Brown accepts the NBA championship trophy from league president Maurice Podoloff after the Celtics regained their crown by sweeping the Lakers, 4-0, in the finals—an NBA first. Brown had blasted Podoloff at midseason and called for his removal, but both now were smiling—at least for the camera.

Red Auerbach stood, soaking wet in the Celtics' dressing room at the Minneapolis Armory, trying to draw on a soggy cigar.

"We set a lot of records this season, and some may be broken some day," the coach hoarsely told the writers, half-shouting to be heard above the celebration. "But one won't be—winning the championship in four straight games.

"It's never been done in basketball before. And it's only what these guys deserve. People have been talking about them being the greatest basketball team of all time. Well, they proved it, didn't they, sweeping through four games? What a bunch!"

They were a bunch who had chafed all season, determined to regain their lost NBA championship. Now it was theirs again after the stunning 4-0 blitz of the Lakers in the finals.

Minutes earlier, two floors above, the Celtics had clinched the title with a 118-113 victory, dashed off the court carrying their coach and piled into a waiting elevator for the ride down to their locker room. And they were singing—actually *singing*—as they squeezed aboard.

But the packed elevator wouldn't budge. So the Celtics abandoned it, eager to begin the championship ritual. They found a small shower room at that level and pounced on their first two victims—Auerbach and trainer Buddy LeRoux—to start the traditional dunkings. Then, laughing and hollering, they all danced down two flights of stairs to their dressing room to get on with some serious celebrating.

Red Auerbach:

"Sweeping the Lakers was a great achievement and one of my big memories. It was the first time it had been done in the finals, and it wouldn't be done again for a dozen years.

"I recall something else very clearly about that series. Walter Brown had been having tough financial sledding keeping the Celtics alive all those years. So, after we'd wiped out the Lakers a couple of games, a lot of people were actually urging Walter to 'let it go five or six games and get some of your money back.'

"He was absolutely furious and shut those people up real good."

Walter Brown was there, making a rare road appearance. So was Chuck Cooper, the Celtic alumnus who had broken the NBA's color line and now was earning a master's degree in social work at the University of Minnesota.

Brown went from player to player shaking hands.

"Sorry you had to play so much," the owner said to Bill Russell, who had ripped down 30 rebounds, including five in the final moments to preserve the victory.

"I'm not sorry, I enjoyed it!" Russell replied. "Anytime you're on a great team like this you enjoy staying on the floor."

Russell and the other veterans were saying, yes, this title was special, but in a different way from the 1957 championship. That had been a thrill because it was their first; this was a thrill because it was regaining something lost—and doing it in a record four straight.

Which was the better Celtic team, '57 or '59?

"This is a great team—yes, better than the '57 club," Bob Cousy said. "It can do more things. This team had everything. It exploded on offense and played defense, too."

Front row (left to right): vice president Lou Pieri (inset), Gene Conley, Bob Cousy, coach Red Auerbach, president Walter Brown, Bill Sharman and Bill Russell. Back row: trainer Buddy LeRoux, K.C. Jones, Lou Tsioropoulos, Tom Heinsohn, Ben Swain, Jim Loscutoff, Sam Jones and Frank Ramsey.

The Celtics had proven that all season while winning their third straight Eastern crown in a runaway. They set a league record for most victories while hammering out a 52-20 record to win the division by a dozen games.

Their most-ever 116.4-point average was over 6 points a game more than any other team as the Celtics were a scoring machine that shredded NBA records all season. And none of those peaks was more flabbergasting than a 173-139 victory over the Lakers that would be probed by the league president and still remains the highest-scoring game in NBA history.

It was played on a Friday afternoon in February, a game scheduled primarily for schoolchildren on Winter vacation. As an added attraction, Marques Haynes and the Harlem Magicians performed in the preliminary game, and it would be difficult to tell where the Magicians left off and the Celtics began.

Adding a dash of humorous irony, that morning Auerbach had emphasized the importance of defense to 4,000 coaches and youngsters at a basketball clinic in the Garden. Proving they didn't always practice what their coach preached—especially with Bill Russell sidelined by a leg injury—the Celtics went out and put on a performance that, depending on your point of view, either set the sport 10 years ahead or 10 years behind.

The crowd of 6,183 was agog at the display of awesome offense and awful defense as the Celtics shattered a half-dozen NBA team records and one individual mark—28 assists by Cousy, including 19 in a half and 12 in a quarter.

It was the assist matter that had gotten the Celtics record-minded early. Informed in the second period that Cousy had a chance at erasing Richie Guerin's mark of 21 assists in a game, Auerbach sent his captain back into the game. Cooz tied the record with a pass to Sam Jones off a 2-on-1 break in the sixth minute of the final period, and surpassed it two minutes later on a flip to Jim Loscutoff. Cousy added six more before game's end for the record 28 that would stand 19 years.

"That man Cousy is too much," opponent Hot Rod Hundley would admire afterward. "He's the greatest ever!"

Meanwhile, the record-hungry fans were goading the Celtics on to smash one mark after another. Entering the final quarter, the Celts needed only 26 points to set a single-game high by one team.

CELTICS REGAIN CHAMPIONSHIP

April 9, 1959, at Minneapolis

CELTICS (118)

	FG	*FT*	*PF*	*Pts.*
Heinsohn	9	5	4	23
Loscutoff	2	0	5	4
Ramsey	10	4	4	24
Russell	5	5	1	15
Conley	3	4	5	10
Sharman	14	1	3	29
Sam Jones	0	2	0	2
K.C. Jones	0	0	0	0
Totals	46	26	24	118

MINNEAPOLIS LAKERS (113)

	FG	*FT*	*PF*	*Pts.*
Baylor	12	6	4	30
Mikkelsen	7	6	3	20
Ellis	1	0	1	2
Hamilton	0	2	1	2
Foust	2	0	4	4
Krebs	6	1	5	13
Garmaker	6	4	4	16
Leonard	9	5	2	23
Fleming	1	1	2	3
Hundley	0	0	2	0
Totals	44	25	28	113

Score by periods:	1	2	3	4
Celtics:	34	30	24	30–118
Lakers:	34	28	25	26–113

Free Throws Missed: Celtics (14)—Russell 5, Cousy 3, Conley 2, Ramsey 2, Sharman, Heinsohn. Lakers (6)—Mikkelsen 3, Baylor 2, Leonard.
Referees: Arnie Heft and Mendy Rudolph.
Attendance: 8,124.

HIGHEST–SCORING GAME IN NBA HISTORY

February 27, 1959, at Boston Garden

CELTICS (173)

	Min.	FGA	FGM	FTA	FTM	Reb.	Ast.	PF	Pts.
Heinsohn	36	28	18	12	7	11	2	3	43
Sam Jones	12	15	4	0	0	9	2	1	8
Loscutoff	35	18	5	2	1	9	2	6	11
Ramsey	26	18	8	5	4	13	2	2	20
Conley	29	12	7	0	0	11	3	5	14
Swain	15	3	1	3	3	6	0	6	5
Sharman	29	25	13	3	3	5	3	2	29
K.C. Jones	13	6	6	0	0	4	1	3	12
Cousy	45	18	10	12	11	5	28	3	31
Totals	240	143	72	37	29	80*	43	31	173

MINNEAPOLIS LAKERS (139)

	Min.	FGA	FGM	FTA	FTM	Reb.	Ast.	PF	Pts.
Baylor	40	24	7	14	14	20	4	4	28
Foust	15	5	0	12	8	8	0	2	8
Mikkelsen	32	18	10	5	5	9	0	3	25
Hamilton	15	11	4	0	0	6	0	1	8
Krebs	16	7	2	1	1	5	0	2	5
Ellis	17	9	4	6	4	9	0	2	12
Garmaker	31	3	1	2	1	1	3	4	3
Fleming	18	11	5	4	3	4	3	2	13
Hundley	35	23	9	5	3	14	3	5	21
Leonard	21	13	5	9	6	5	2	4	16
Totals	240	124	47	58	145	89*	15	29	139

Score by periods:	1	2	3	4
Celtics:	40	43	38	52–173
Lakers:	30	34	31	44–139

* *Includes Team Rebounds:* Celtics 7, Lakers 8.
Field Goal Percentage: Celtics .504, Lakers .379.
Free Throw Percentage: Celtics .784, Lakers .776.
Referees: Mendy Rudolph and Jim Weston.
Attendance: 6,183.

Taking no chances, they machine-gunned 52 for the 173 record that still endures two decades later, a plateau even Wilt Chamberlain's clubs never scaled.

In all, seven players scored 20 or more points: Tom Heinsohn 43, Cousy 31, Bill Sharman 29 and Frank Ramsey 20 for Boston, Elgin Baylor 28, Vern Mikkelsen 25 and Hundley 21 for Minneapolis.

"There was little we could do about their phenomenal shooting," numbed Laker coach Johnny Kundla said of the Celtics' marksmanship—.504 (72 of 143) from the floor, .784 (29 of 37) from the free-throw line.

The barrage stunned Auerbach, too. "I've never seen anything like it," he said, "in my 13 years in professional basketball."

Neither had Maurice Podoloff, calling the score "unbelievable," and the NBA president was quoted by the wire services as saying he planned an investigation to make sure the players weren't "goofing off" on defense.

Podoloff later denied the quote, but Walter Brown said he didn't believe him and called for his removal.

"I telephoned Podoloff today and blasted him," the angry owner told the Celtics' weekly press luncheon the following Monday. "He shouldn't have been raising doubts about the integrity of the game with absurd statements. We'd be sitting ducks for the reformers, especially since the (college) scandals of several years ago."

Reminded that he had been an avid sponsor when Podoloff was named to head the league in 1946, Brown nodded, "When I make a mistake, I make a beaut." He added: "Podoloff has had no use for Red Auerbach. He hasn't had any use for Bob Cousy. Well, I guess he'll have to include me on his pet hate list, too."

None of which hindered the Celtics as they collected another divisional title.

Arnie Risen, Jack Nichols and Andy Phillip had retired. But Loscutoff was back from knee surgery. Providing additional muscle, Gene Conley returned from a five-year leave while pursuing a baseball career; after pitching for the Braves in their 1957 World Series triumph over the Yankees, the 6-foot-9, 230-pound ironman now would become the first to wear world championship rings in two sports.

Also signing aboard, after an Army stint and brief fling as a defensive back with the Rams, was a rookie with pickpocket-quick hands. His name was K.C. Jones, a tenacious 6-footer who had teamed with Russell as the University of San Francisco had won back-to-back NCAA titles.

The newcomers made their contributions in supporting roles as Cousy, Russell, Sharman and Heinsohn again were among league leaders.

Four Celtics were among the Top 15 scorers: Sharman (8th, 20.4), Cousy (9th, 20.0), Heinsohn (13th, 18.8) and Russell (15th, 16.7). For the second year, Russell led in rebounds, this time with a record average of 23. Cousy had most assists for the eighth straight year, averaging 8.6. And Sharman won his sixth free-throw crown in seven years with a .932 figure that's still the Celtic record. (And he would go nearly the full playoffs without missing a foul shot, making a still NBA record 56 in a row before missing one late in the final game—exceeding his old mark of 55.)

The regular season over, the Celtics' biggest test would come in the Eastern playoff finals against a Syracuse team strengthened by the midseason addition of George Yardley, the league's 1958 scoring leader for Detroit. Nats coach Paul Seymour had pried the balding jumpshooter loose in a trade, teaming him with Dolph Schayes and John (Red) Kerr up front, with Larry Costello and prize rookie Hal Greer in the backcourt.

Boston and Syracuse split the series' first six games, each winning at home alternately and setting up the finale at the Garden.

"Red gave the greatest pep talk I've ever heard before that game," Buddy LeRoux once told *Boston Herald American* columnist Joe Fitzgerald. "My eyes were wet when I left that room, and I've heard a thousand pep talks in my lifetime. But nothing like that one."

Garden fans groaned as Syracuse piled up a 16-point lead in the second quarter before the Celtics narrowed their deficit to 68-60 at halftime. Boston continued to nibble at the Nats' lead until midway through the last quarter when the Celts took the lead and built it to 115-108. Syracuse then ran off 10 points in a row, but the Celtics retrieved the lead on a Cousy push shot that beat the 24-second clock and a Russell 3-pointer with little more than two minutes remaining.

But with 1:58 left, Russell fouled out, joining the disqualified Ramsey who had scored 28 points despite an index finger in a cast. Conley took over in the pivot and pulled down three crucial rebounds to ward off the storming Nats, and forever after Auerbach would credit him with saving that '59 title.

But it was Cousy, with 25 points, who was carried off the floor by the fans when the buzzer sounded: Boston 130, Syracuse 125.

"That's the greatest basketball game I've ever seen," bubbled Sharman.

Bill Russell rejects a Laker shot.

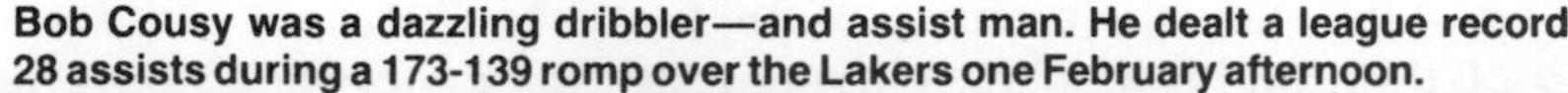

Bob Cousy was a dazzling dribbler—and assist man. He dealt a league record 28 assists during a 173-139 romp over the Lakers one February afternoon.

K.C. Jones (right) and Bill Russell, who had led the University of San Francisco to two national championships, were reunited when the tenacious guard with the pickpocket-quick hands completed an Army hitch and preseason stint as a Los Angeles Ram defensive back. Football's loss was basketball's gain as K.C. would become a model of defensive excellence for backcourtmen.

Bob Cousy scored 25 points in the seventh game thriller against Syracuse.

Then, in what loomed an anticlimax, came the NBA finals against Minneapolis in a series pitting the league's two most successful coaches at that time, Auerbach and Kundla.

Kundla created a little stir in Boston that season when asked to compare the Celtics to his legendary Laker teams of the late-forties and early-fifties featuring George Mikan. "The Celtics are a great team," he said, "But not quite as great as my old Lakers—because of George Mikan. His physical strength, clutch playing and constant hustle put him over Bill Russell, as great as Russell is."

Bostonians argued that the fast and agile Russell would have run the lumbering Mikan into the floor—particularly in the 24-second clock era.

In any case, Mikan had long since retired and the Lakers were still trying to recover. In that direction they now had the NBA's Rookie of the Year in exciting Elgin Baylor (fourth in scoring with 24.9, third in rebounding with 14), who had sparked them from the cellar to a second-place finish and then to an upset of St. Louis in the Western finals.

Baylor or not, the Celtics were 5-1 favorites. Minneapolis hadn't beaten Boston in more than two years—22 consecutive losses since March 1, 1957. Still, no one was predicting a sweep—not in a championship series.

Yet that's exactly what happened as the Celtics were never really pressed.

The sweep was the Lakers' last gasp in Twin Cities. They slumped to a disappointing 25-50 the next season, and then they were gone—off to Los Angeles, following the baseball Dodgers, as the NBA joined the jet age and became a coast-to-coast league.

But that was more than a year away as the Celtics celebrated this night at the Minneapolis Armory, their dynasty taking root. And across the way, in the Laker room, Kundla was announcing his resignation to become coach at the University of Minnesota—at a reported pay cut from $13,500 to $12,000.

And he'd take the memory of the powerhouse Celtics with him. "If they stay healthy," he told reporters, "it's going to be a long time before that team gets beaten."

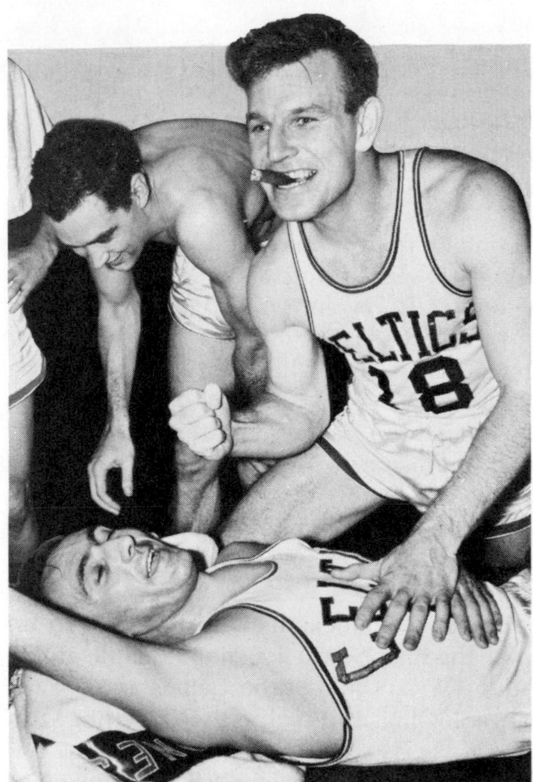

Jim Loscutoff smokes a victory cigar as he and fellow muscleman Gene Conley (left) celebrate with exhausted Bob Cousy after eliminating Syracuse to advance to the championship series.

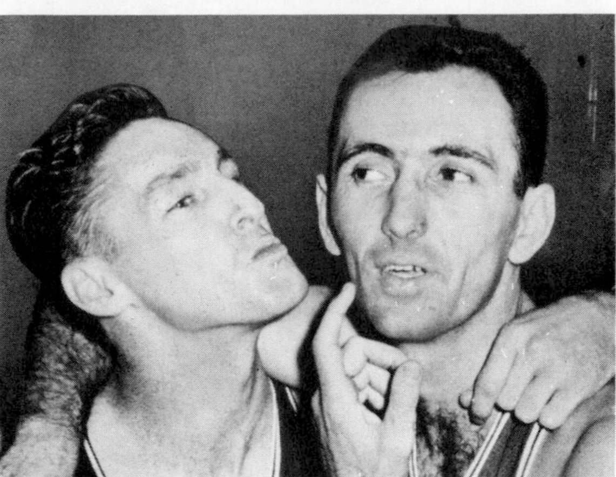

Bill Sharman puckers up to pin a championship kiss on Bob Cousy after the Celtics had regained the NBA title.

1959–60

Bill Russell and Wilt Chamberlain pose for photographers before their long-awaited first confrontation at Boston Garden in November.

Walter Brown tore up Bob Cousy's contract and awarded him a new one that could exceed the one signed by Wilt Chamberlain. The idea was to maintain the Celtic captain's distinction as the NBA's highest-paid player.

It was billed as the Great Basketball Matchup:

The classic Unstoppable Force vs. the Immovable Object.

Offensive Superman vs. Defensive Superman.

Goliath vs. Goliath (although Boston's Goliath was 3 to 6 inches shorter than Philadelphia's Goliath).

Wilt Chamberlain vs. Bill Russell.

The long-awaited confrontation pitted the Celtic who had revolutionized defense in his three pro seasons and a Philadelphia Warrior rookie who most predicted would revolutionize offense—and perhaps destroy basketball in the process.

If anyone could stop Wilt (The Stilt) Chamberlain it would be William Felton Russell.

So the encounter was heralded as the greatest man-to-man combat between giants in the history of sports. Accordingly, their measurements were compared like those of prize fighters: Chamberlain listed at 7-foot-1 1/16th (but opponents insisting he was 1 to 3 inches taller) and Russell listed at 6-foot-10 (but puckishly insisting he was "only 6-9 13/16ths").

Media from around the country flocked to Boston Garden on November 7, 1959, to cover the historic duel against a battle-of-the-undefeated backdrop—the Warriors at 5-0, the Celtics at 3-0. Fans jammed the building to overflowing, and scalpers were getting $10 a ticket, four times face value.

And when the Warriors came onto the floor for warmups, fans ringed the court and *oohed* and *aahed* as Chamberlain stuffed the ball through the basket, seemingly ramming his arms down through the hoop to his elbows.

Wilt had popularized the dunk, and, with 280 pounds of velocity behind it, it appeared unstoppable. And the other weapon in his arsenal, the fallaway jumper from 10-15 feet, seemed only slightly less lethal.

"He's Babe Ruth all over again," promised Warriors owner Eddie Gottlieb, an NBA founder who had used all his influence to get territorial rights to the onetime Philadelphia schoolboy sensation even though Chamberlain went to college at Kansas.

Such superlatives were nothing new to Chamberlain. When he chose Kansas over more than 200 other colleges, coach Phog Allen gushed: "With him we'll never lose a game. We could win the national championship with Wilt, two sorority girls and two Phi Beta Kappas."

Not quite. As a sophomore, Chamberlain did take Kansas to the NCAA finals, but the Jayhawks didn't even win the Big Eight Conference his junior year. And the next season Wilt was gone, touring a year with the Globetrotters for which he received somewhere between $45,000-$65,000, according to varying reports.

Now Chamberlain was a Warrior, and the estimates of his salary ranged between $30,000-$65,000.

Even the lowest figure topped what Bob Cousy had been receiving as the NBA's top-paid player. So Walter Brown tore up his superstar's contract worth about $25,000 and awarded him a new one with bonus clauses that could earn Cousy as much as $41,000 a year.

Russell vs. Chamberlain over the years

Bob Cousy drives on Phil Jordan as the Celtics' NBA record-equaling victory streak is snapped at 17 by last-place Cincinnati during a New Year's doubleheader at Detroit. The Celts then coasted to a league-record 59-16 finish, 10 games ahead of runnerup Philadelphia in the East. And the Celtics' 124.5-point season's scoring average still ranks as their all-time high.

Not only was Chamberlain getting the fattest guaranteed contract before even playing a league game, and not only were many experts already handing the title to Philadelphia, but before Wilt had stuffed his first NBA basket Jimmy Breslin wrote a magazine article headlined *Can Basketball Survive Chamberlain?*

The Celtics survived Chamberlain this night, jumping to a 22-7 lead and easing to a 115-105 victory. Chamberlain outscored Russell, 30-22 (taking twice as many shots, Bostonians argued), but Russell had more rebounds, 35-28. And the crowd was ecstatic when Russell climbed an invisible stepladder to block one of his taller foe's shots.

"I don't think I was nervous, but I was tense," Chamberlain said afterward. "Russell didn't play me the way I expected. I thought he'd guard me tighter. But he played off me and moved in on my jumper."

Years later, Wilt would add: "I was a little nervous, and I guess it showed in the game. Still, I thought I played pretty well for a rookie going against a guy who was supposed to be the greatest defensive player in history—and playing in a madhouse like Boston Garden at that."

Russell was impressed.

"I've played against men as big, but never against anyone that good *and* big," Russell said afterward. "You can't relax a second against him. He's the best rookie I've ever seen. I wish I was that good when I started."

Years later, Russell would add: "Wilt made me a believer the first five minutes I played against him. Both of us grabbed a loose ball at the same time, and I tried to yank it away from him. Did you ever try to bend a lamppost with your bare hands? That's how strong Wilt's arms were.

"Then he began to pull on me. I actually felt my feet leaving the floor. *I'm going to look awfully silly,* I thought, *if he stuffs the ball and me through the hoop.* Fortunately, the referee blew the whistle for a jump ball."

It was the beginning of a classic rivalry that would continue through the 1960s. (And at decade's end, Russell would bury Chamberlain by a 3-1 landslide in a vote for NBA Player of the Sixties.)

Let them eat cake, Red Auerbach may have been telling his players as (left to right) Frank Ramsey, Bill Sharman and Gene Conley dig into one after eliminating St. Louis in Game 7 for the Celtics' second straight world championship.

While that first Russell-Chamberlain duel was spectacular enough, a forgotten star stole the show, according to *Sports Illustrated*, which reported in its next issue:

"... the occasion was turned into a double feature by Boston's Bob Cousy, who evidently had not been told what the big attraction was supposed to be. In any event, he dominated the game as he has so often done in recent years—though without adequate recognition, simply because we have all come to take this incredible athlete for granted.

"Last Saturday, after nine years as a professional, Cousy displayed a dozen sleight-of-hand tricks with the basketball that no one had ever seen before. He set up his teammates for scores all night and made 24 points.

"'The hardest thing about playing against Cousy,' the veteran Slater Martin has said, 'is to resist the temptation to stand around and watch him.' From the stands, happily, no one is obliged to resist."

Cousy would average a career-high 9.5 assists that season, leading the league for the eighth straight time, and became the first NBA player to chalk up more than 5,000 career assists. And Russell snared an NBA record 51 rebounds (and scored 23 points) during a February game against Syracuse at Boston.

But while Celtic stars were setting records by ones and twos, Chamberlain was smashing them by the dozen. He rewrote a litany of NBA scoring marks—including a 37.6-point average (first league leader in the 30s) and 2,707 total points (602 more than Bob Pettit's record high the previous season). He scored 50 more points seven times, including twice against Boston. He also led the league in rebounds (averaging 27 to Russell's 24).

Overall, Chamberlain was the major reason that league attendance was up 23 per cent, nearly a half-million tickets.

CELTICS ADD ANOTHER CROWN

April 9, 1960, at Boston Garden

CELTICS (122)

	Min.	*FGM*	*FGA*	*FTM*	*FTA*	*Reb.*	*Ast.*	*PF*	*Pts.*
Heinsohn	28	10	17	2	2	8	2	5	22
Conley	17	2	6	1	2	7	1	6	5
Ramsey	43	11	20	2	3	13	0	5	24
Guarilia	1	0	2	0	0	1	1	0	0
Russell	47	7	15	8	10	35	4	2	22
Richter	9	0	0	0	1	0	0	4	0
Sharman	22	4	15	3	3	4	2	1	11
Sam Jones	25	8	14	2	2	4	2	1	18
Cousy	47	8	25	3	4	6	14	1	19
K.C. Jones	1	0	0	1	2	0	1	0	1
Totals	240	50	114	22	29	83	27	25	122

ST. LOUIS HAWKS (103)

	Min.	*FGM*	*FGA*	*FTM*	*FTA*	*Reb.*	*Ast.*	*PF*	*Pts.*
Pettit	43	8	18	6	13	14	4	4	22
Piontek	19	3	7	5	6	6	2	2	11
Hagan	39	7	17	5	5	5	0	4	19
Lovellette	41	8	19	2	3	7	4	4	18
Ferry	3	0	0	0	0	0	0	1	0
Green	45	7	14	3	6	5	5	4	17
McCarthy	40	7	11	2	2	1	2	4	16
Ferrari	10	0	1	0	0	1	1	0	0
Totals	240	40	87	23	35	47	18	23	103

Score by Periods:	1	2	3	4
Celtics	29	41	26	26—122
Hawks	30	23	25	25—103

Field Goal Percentage: Celtics .438, Hawks .459.
Free Throw Percentage: Celtics .758, Hawks .657.
Team Rebounds: Celtics 5, Hawks 8.
Referees: Mendy Rudolph and Jim Duffy.
Attendance: 13,909.

In the NBA finals, old nemesis Slater Martin (22) shadowed Bob Cousy like—well, like a Hawk, and Cooz reacted with hookshots among other maneuvers.

Tom Heinsohn draws a foul from Guy Rodgers in the sixth game of the Eastern playoffs. Warrior Paul Arizin is on the left.

There was plenty of anxiety for Red Auerbach and his Celtics during and after Game 6 as St. Louis tied the series, forcing another seventh-game showdown at Boston for the NBA title.

While Chamberlain was dominating statistics, the Celtics were ruling the victory column. They won 11 of their first 12 games before running off a record-equaling 17-victory streak that left them 30-4 by New Year's—rolling on to an NBA record 59-16 finish, 10 games ahead of runnerup Philadelphia in the East. The Celtics' 124.5-point scoring averge that season still ranks as their all-time best.

And it was more Russell vs. Chamberlain in the playoffs as Boston and Philadelphia collided in the Eastern finals.

The series was spiced by brief but resounding fisticuffs between Chamberlain and Tom Heinsohn during a rough Game 2 at Philadelphia which also featured a skirmish between Auerbach and a customer. The main bout came to an abrupt halt when a roundhouse right by Wilt, intended for Heinsohn's jaw, struck peacemaker Tom Gola. Heinsohn recalls Chamberlain's fist hitting the back of Gola's head; Wilt says it struck his teammate's arm. Whichever, Chamberlain's shooting hand was at the least severely bruised and some claimed broken.

Doctors suggested Chamberlain sit out Game 3, but he played with his sore hand heavily wrapped the next two games and performed far below par as the Celtics won both for a 3-1 lead. ("We might have won that series if I hadn't been injured," Wilt would say.) But Chamberlain erupted in Game 5, scoring a Boston Garden record 50 points (including 22 field goals) as Philadelphia won, 129-107.

Two nights later, the Celtics put the Warriors away—but it wasn't easy. With 11 seconds remaining and the score tied, Guy Rodgers, seeking to improve his game-high 31 points, missed two free throws. The Celtics called time out and set up a final shot for Bill Sharman. He missed, but Heinsohn outleaped the Warriors beneath the basket for a tip-in at the buzzer that stilled the Convention Hall crowd, ousted the Warriors and sent Wilt into temporary retirement.

In the locker room, the disheartened Chamberlain revealed he was quitting. He said he was fed up with being manhandled in the NBA and, besides, he had "achieved everything a man can achieve in pro basketball."

Predictably, Chamberlain would change his mind. Equally predictably, his words had not been generally received with sympathy.

"He's quitting?" Cousy was quoted. "Good. Now we can get back to playing basketball."

The NBA finals were almost anticlimactic, although they seesawed the full seven-game distance. For the third championship series in four years, the Celtics faced the St. Louis Hawks now coached by old friend Easy Ed Macauley. He had the league's tallest regular 1-2 punch in Bob Pettit and Clyde Lovellette, both 6-foot-9, along with Cliff Hagan in a corner and Johnny McCarthy and Sihugo Green in the backcourt.

After the series went 1-1, 2-2 and 3-3, the Celtics broke open the finale with a 41-23 second period for a 70-53 halftime lead, and it was all over as Russell triggered one fastbreak after another.

Frank Ramsey had contributed a game-high 24 points and 13 rebounds, Heinsohn scored 22 points and Cousy 19 points and 14 assists. But Russell had been devastating with 35 rebounds and 22 points.

"He played one of the truly great games of all time," Pettit said afterward. "He never did anything wrong.

"I'm not much for talking about other players, but I'll take my hat off to Bill Russell as a basketball player and as a man anytime."

Red Auerbach:

"Chamberlain was a giant among giants. I'll never take that away from him. I don't expect to see anybody like Wilt again in my lifetime.

"But if you're asking who was better—Chamberlain or Russell—it isn't even close. Russell was better because he played with his head and he had a bigger heart. He was a winner. And I think Russ was a better athlete, too.

"If you think I'm being too parochial, believe me when I say there wasn't a player in the league who wouldn't have preferred having Russell on his team instead of Chamberlain."

Bill Russell:

"Wilt Chamberlain was supposed to put me into total eclipse when he came into the league that year. I think he had the opposite effect—in one sense, magnifying my importance to the team.

"I did have a big challenge on my hands from the moment I first stepped onto the court against Wilt, though. His physical power was awesome. He could jump higher from a crouch than anyone in the league. And he was a good shooter with that fallaway jumper. He was a great one.

"That first year he was starting center for the East and MVP in the All Star Game. He was first-team all-league. And he was both the NBA's MVP and Rookie of the Year. He also had very good players starting with him in that Philadelphia lineup: Arizin, Sauldsberry, Gola and Rodgers. But the Celtics were champions.

"Wilt was my greatest challenge and toughest competition. He won his awards. I won mine. To me, the greatest awards were championships."

Wilt Chamberlain:

"The press started the Russell vs. Chamberlain thing that very first time we played each other. That was the beginning of my battles with Russell, battles I always seemed to lose—at least that's how the sportswriters and most fans came to look at it.

"I guess sportswriters are human and have their favorites like everyone else. Their favorite, especially after I came into the league, was Bill Russell. I think most fans and sportswriters subconsciously resented my ability to do so many things well. I could shoot, rebound, pass, run and block shots. That made me seem almost inhuman. There was no way anyone could identify with me.

"Russell, on the other hand, was a great rebounder and shot-blocker but a horrible shooter. Early in his career everyone acknowledged that he was a horrible shooter. But as his legend grew, people started saying he probably could score more but 'chose' to concentrate on defense.' That was bull, and Bill knew it. That's why he worked so hard on defense and rebounding; he knew he couldn't score."

The Eastern finals against Philadelphia had many tense moments.

1960–61

Red Auerbach hugs Jim Loscutoff as the Celtics eliminate St. Louis at Boston Garden to win their third straight NBA championship.

Another Spring, another championship.

And once again, there in the eye of the locker room celebration was a sopping wet Red Auerbach surrounded by the media.

"This is the greatest team ever assembled," he said after the Celtics had won their third consecutive NBA title by eliminating the St. Louis Hawks at Boston Garden. "And there are two reasons for it.

"One is the way these guys get along together and play as a unit. On some teams the players get into each other's hair over a long schedule. That doesn't happen here.

"And the other reason we're so damned good is the quality of our people. We've always got somebody ready to explode. Any one of them can tear you apart. One night it's Heinsohn. The next night it's Cousy. Then Sharman. Or maybe it's Ramsey or Sam. And, of course, there's Russell. Somebody's always picking up the slack for us.

"With most teams you can win if you stop one man. Stop Chamberlain and you win. Stop a Pettit, a Baylor, a Schayes and you win. But you can't stop the Celtics that way. That's why we're the best."

Auerbach's modesty was questionable but not his facts.

The Celtics had won their division by 11 games with a best-in-NBA 57-22 record to annex their fifth straight Eastern title. Then they had thumped Syracuse and St. Louis, each with 4-1 dispatch, to hoist their fourth NBA flag in five years.

Two decades later, the 1961 championship still ranks as the Celtics' easiest ever.

And that lineup *was* something special, a balanced blend of young and old talent that was, well, unbeatable.

Significantly, the Celtics didn't have a scorer in the league's top dozen, and only Tom Heinsohn (21.3) reached the 20-point plateau. But six Celtics averaged in double figures.

At 27, Bill Russell was in his prime as supreme chairman of the boards and the NBA's Most Valuable Player for the second time.

The Celtics were in a happy mood after clinching their fifth straight divisional title, this time by an 11-game margin over runnerup Philadelphia. Giving Tom Heinsohn (15) thumbs down for some reason are (left to right) Bill Sharman, Bob Cousy, K.C. Jones, Tom Sanders, Frank Ramsey, Sam Jones, Gene Conley, Jim Loscutoff, Red Auerbach and Bill Russell.

Heinsohn, at 26, was leading the team in scoring for the second straight year with his remarkable arsenal of shots including his spectacular running hook from the corner. Going on 31, Jim Loscutoff was back at the other forward setting crunching picks and crashing the boards following a back operation, the first NBA player to successfully bounce back from disc surgery.

The backcourt was showing a little age—on paper.

At 32, Cousy had to be past his peak. Yet his performance rarely reflected that. Yes, for the first time in nine years he was not the league's assist leader, supplanted by Cincinnati rookie Oscar Robertson. But Cousy still averaged 7.7 assists and 18.1 points, and enjoyed one of his finest playoff series that added to his legend.

And while Sharman would turn 35 a month after the playoffs, he led the league as usual in free-throw average (.921) and averaged 16 points despite playing much less. Auerbach had begun the changing of the guard from Sharman to Sam Jones, who at 27 was blossoming into one of the league's purest shooters. Yet Sharman, in what would be his Celtic farewell, went out in style in the playoffs—including scoring 30 and 27 points against Syracuse while hounding Hal Greer and Dick Barnett through that series.

There were those who suggested that Boston's second five would have fared well as a separate entry into the NBA. Besides Sam Jones, there were Frank Ramsey, K.C. Jones, Gene Conley and the club's No. 1 draft choice, Tom (Satch) Sanders, who was quickly establishing himself as the classic defensive forward (as Bob Pettit learned in the finals).

The sum of all those Celtic parts was a machine so proficient as to drain drama from both the regular season and playoffs. The Celts were *too* good.

It took some fireworks at Syracuse to enliven the Eastern finals. A 10-minute melee between the Celtics and customers interrupted Game 4, a nationally televised Saturday matinee.

POLICE QUELL FANS AS CELTS TOP NATS, headlined the *Boston Globe,* which reported a "near full-scale riot" and noted that "only the rugged strong-arm work of Syracuse police cooled off the uprising." Photographs splashed across the page pictured Loscutoff being restrained by a helmeted policeman and an usher, and Loscutoff and Auerbach confronting front-row taunters while being jeered by every Syracusan in sight.

For the first time in nine years, Bob Cousy wasn't the NBA assist leader, supplanted by Cincinnati rookie Oscar Robertson (No. 14, about to be picked off here by No. 15 Tom Heinsohn). But at age 32 Cousy still averaged 7.7 assists and 18.1 points.

CELTICS DOWN HAWKS FOR 3d STRAIGHT TITLE

April 11, 1961, at Boston Garden

CELTICS (121)

	Min.	FGA	FGM	FTA	FTM	Ast.	PF	Pts.
Heinsohn	23	15	8	3	3	2	5	19
Loscutoff	6	5	2	0	0	0	4	4
Ramsey	33	14	6	4	4	0	4	16
Sanders	29	7	2	1	0	4	4	4
Russell	48	17	9	17	12	3	2	30
Conley	5	4	2	0	0	0	1	4
Cousy	42	16	5	10	8	12	4	18
K.C. Jones	6	3	1	4	2	2	2	4
Sharman	12	4	2	2	2	1	1	6
Sam Jones	36	17	8	0	0	4	4	16
Totals	240	102	45	41	31	28	31	121

ST. LOUIS HAWKS (112)

	Min.	FGA	FGM	FTA	FTM	Ast.	PF	Pts.
Pettit	37	22	7	18	10	3	4	24
Sauldsberry	23	15	2	1	1	4	4	5
Hagan	45	21	11	4	4	2	2	26
Lovellette	25	17	6	3	3	1	3	15
Foust	3	1	0	0	0	0	2	0
Wilkens	18	13	6	4	4	2	5	16
Green	26	11	5	3	2	1	4	12
McCarthy	41	5	2	2	0	6	3	4
Ferrari	22	8	4	4	2	3	2	10
Totals	240	113	43	39	26	22	29	112

Score by periods:	1	2	3	4	
Celtics:	33	29	37	22	–121
Hawks:	39	22	23	28	–112

Rebounds: Celtics 89, Hawks 61.
Rebound Leaders: Celtics—Russell 38, Sanders 10; Hawks—Pettit 11, Sauldsberry 11.
Field Goal Percentage: Celtics .441, Hawks .381.
Free Throw Percentage: Celtics .756, Hawks .667.
Referees: Mendy Rudolph and Earl Strom.
Attendance: 13,909.

Larry Costello (left) and Dolph Schayes (right) all but tackle Bob Cousy as the frustrated Nats were destroyed in the Eastern finals, 4-1.

Front row (left to right): vice president Lou Pieri (inset), K.C. Jones, Bob Cousy, coach Red Auerbach, president Walter Brown, Bill Sharman and Frank Ramsey. Back row: trainer Buddy LeRoux, Tom (Satch) Sanders, Tom Heinsohn, Gene Conley, Bill Russell, Gene Guarilia, Jim Loscutoff and Sam Jones.

All of which was not unusual at the aptly named Onondaga *War* Memorial. "Syracuse fans felt when they bought a ticket it made them *participants,"* recalls broadcaster Johnny Most. "So when you went into that building it was 10 against 7,500. Those people were part of the team, and everybody took part and did something to try to beat the visiting team."

Having no wish to return and face those odds again, the Celtics wrapped up the series against the Nats the following afternoon in Boston as Russell scored 25 points, swept 33 rebounds and blocked six shots.

"I put Bill Russell in another world as a basketball player," Syracuse coach Alex Hannum said afterward. "There's nobody like him. Nobody."

Those anticipating another Boston–St. Louis classic in the championship series were disappointed. The Hawks proved no more of a test than the Nats despite new coach Paul Seymour having run them all the way to a 51-28 record, St. Louis' most victories ever, and then to a 4-3 victory in the Western finals over the Lakers, now Los Angeles residents.

Boston destroyed St. Louis by 34 points in the opener, 129-95, with seven Celtics scoring in double figures, and the series was essentially over.

Some combustion enlivened that series, too. As at Syracuse, it also flared up in Game 4 on the road during a Boston victory. Cousy, in the process of contributing 22 points, 11 assists and some hypnotic dribbling, and the frustrated Seymour nearly came to blows—in the same Kiel Auditorium where Auerbach had punched Hawks owner

---

Ben Kerner:

"For sheer excellence, you couldn't beat those great Celtic teams. The way they'd run and move the ball was something to see. It was thrilling to watch, even while they were beating you. No other team played that way."

Bill Russell collected 38 rebounds and 30 points in the championship finale against the befuddled Hawks.

Bill Russell was voted the NBA's MVP a second time while averaging 16.9 points and 23.9 rebounds—contributing to those statistics here against Detroit as Piston Don Ohl watches.

Jim Loscutoff became the first NBA player to successfully come back from disc surgery. Trainer Buddy LeRoux pronounces Loscy fit.

Ben Kerner in the finals four years earlier. And in a curious exchange of roles, Loscutoff was credited as peacemaker in the Cousy-Seymour near bout.

Two days later, the Celtics rang up another world championship with a 121-112 victory over the befuddled Hawks as Russell collected 38 rebounds and 30 points.

"Russell never stopped," Seymour said afterward. "Every time I looked, he was dunking shots, blocking shots, playing every guy on the floor at one time or another, just to let them know who he was.

"It's the same old story: He's a big man in a big game."

Opposing center Clyde Lovellette said he knew exactly how big Russell was.

"He doesn't have very wide shoulders," Lovellette said of his future Celtic teammate, "but he's great enough to put four men on his back and carry them."

Jim Loscutoff is restrained by a policeman and usher at Syracuse during a 10-minute melee between the Celtics and fans during the Eastern finals.

1961–62

SELVY MISSES SHOT, CELTICS CHAMPS AGAIN

April 18, 1962, at Boston Garden

CELTICS (110)

	Min.	*FGA*	*FGM*	*FTA*	*FTM*	*Reb.*	*Ast.*	*PF*	*Pts.*
Braun	4	3	0	0	0	0	0	1	0
Cousy	44	13	3	10	2	7	9	4	8
Guarilia	4	1	0	0	0	1	1	1	0
Heinsohn	22	13	3	3	2	3	2	6	8
K.C. Jones	20	4	1	0	0	3	0	2	2
Sam Jones	47	31	12	4	3	8	3	2	27
Loscutoff	11	8	3	0	0	8	0	6	6
Ramsey	33	11	4	16	15	5	2	6	23
Russell	53	18	8	17	14	40	4	2	30
Sanders	27	11	3	0	0	7	0	6	6
Totals	265	113	37	50	36	92*	21	36	110

LOS ANGELES LAKERS (107)

	Min.	*FGA*	*FGM*	*FTA*	*FTM*	*Reb.*	*Ast.*	*PF*	*Pts.*
Baylor	51	40	13	21	15	22	4	6	41
Felix	12	2	0	4	2	1	3	3	2
Hawkins	10	3	2	0	0	2	4	4	4
Hundley	4	0	0	0	0	0	1	0	0
Joliff	9	2	0	0	0	2	0	2	0
Krebs	41	11	4	0	0	13	0	6	8
LaRusso	36	10	3	3	1	11	0	6	7
Selvy	49	10	2	8	6	8	4	3	10
West	53	30	14	8	7	6	0	4	35
Totals	265	108	38	44	31	81*	16	34	107

Score by periods:	1	2	3	4	OT
Celtics	22	31	22	25	10—110
Lakers	22	25	28	25	7—107

Field Goal Percentage: Celtics .328, Lakers .352.
Free Throw Percentage: Celtics .720, Lakers .705.
**Includes Team Rebounds:* Celtics 10, Lakers 16.
Referees: Sid Borgia and Richie Powers.
Attendance: 13,909.

Another world title, another dunking for Red Auerbach—by Bob Cousy this time—as the Celtics win their fifth NBA championship in six seasons. After coasting to their sixth straight divisional title, the playoffs proved the toughest of any ever won by the Celtics—14 memorable games, including two seventh-game scares that literally went down to the last second time.

It would all come down to 5/8ths of an inch, the width of a basketball rim at Boston Garden.

The score was tied at 100, and two seconds remained on the clock in the seventh game of the NBA's first coast-to-coast championship series.

There was Los Angeles Laker Frank Selvy with the ball, open by the end line to the left of the Celtics basket.

It has been generally reported that Selvy was no more than 8 feet from the basket. Bob Cousy, who had been covering Selvy but was picked off from play, recalls the distance "15 to 18 feet." Selvy remembers it being more like 20 feet.

Whichever, it is a fork in the road of Celtic history. If Selvy makes the shot, the dynasty will end at three. If Selvy misses, the Celtics are still alive with an overtime chance at a fourth straight world title. No NBA team had ever won that many in a row, not even the Minneapolis Lakers' Mikan era teams.

It all depends on an uncontested but hurried putt by a shooter who twice was the nation's top collegiate scorer and once scored 100 points in a game as an All-America at Furman.

Selvy, nicknamed Pops at age 29, was the Lakers' "other" guard, teaming in the Los Angeles backcourt with sensational sophomore Jerry West. Although Selvy had a 14.7-point average this season, scoring wasn't his primary role; his job was to bring the ball upcourt and feed sharpshooters Elgin Baylor (38.2) and Jerry West (30.8).

"But Frank is an excellent shooter," Cousy has said. "Give him room and he'll hit a jumper 9 times out of 10."

Selvy had proven that in the last minute by scoring two clutch baskets to bring the Lakers back from a 4-point deficit. And with five seconds left, Los Angeles had called time out to set up a championship-winning shot.

That shot figured to be taken by West or Baylor. And if you had to guess one, it would probably be Baylor. Besides his near 40-point average that season, he had scored a playoff record 61 points on this same Garden floor in Game 5 to backbone a Laker victory that forced the Celtics into the back-to-the-wall position of having to sweep the series' final two games.

So for the crucial last seconds, Red Auerbach has put Bill Russell on Baylor. And he had K.C. Jones on West, Tom (Satch) Sanders on Rudy LaRusso, Cousy on Selvy, and Frank Ramsey on Hot Rod Hundley, who has just been inserted into the Los Angeles lineup as the best ballhandler by coach Fred Schaus.

"It was a madhouse when we were in the huddle," Hundley recalls. "Then the buzzer blew and that great crowd was hushed.

"Oh, my God, here we go. I hadn't played much in the series and was scared to death. We had it in our hands. One basket and we're the champs. Five seconds—a lifetime."

Baylor and LaRusso were to come out of the corners to set screens for the two guards. Hundley would get it to the free men, West or Selvy, who'd shoot off the screen.

Selvy's inbounds pass for Hundley is deflected out of bounds by the leaping Cousy. On his second try, Selvy times Cousy's jump and gets the ball to Hundley at the top of the key.

"Baylor and LaRusso threw up their screens," Hundley says. "I looked to West's side, K.C. was on top of him. There was no way I could get the ball to Jerry.

"It passed through my mind to shoot. Hell, there it was, the one shot. Oh, my God, wouldn't I have been the hero? All my life I'd never wanted it more. But I couldn't do it. I mean it wasn't right. I hadn't been playing, I wasn't sharp.

"I still think about it at night, when I'm alone. Sometimes I think I would have made it. I was meant to take a shot like that. Maybe I would have made it. I like to think so.

"It wasn't my shot, though. West or Selvy. West was covered. If Selvy was, too, I'd shoot. I looked to Pops. He was wide open and I flipped the ball to him."

With the clock running out, Selvy hurries his jumper. The ball hits the front rim, skips across the open hole, strikes the back rim—and *falls off.*

Frank Selvy:

"It was a fairly tough shot. I was almost on the baseline, so far I couldn't bank the ball.

"I thought the shot was good. It hit the front rim, the back. But all the time I thought it was good.

"I would trade all my points for that one last basket."

"I thought it was going in," Schaus would say.

So did Baylor. He would have had a chance at the rebound, he said afterward, "but I pulled my hand away because I though the ball was going in."

Russell was in orbit, pouncing on the rebound, wrapping both arms around the ball and hugging it as the buzzer sounds.

"I nearly had a heart attack watching Selvy's shot," Russell recalls. "Everything was riding on it. When it bounced off the rim I just grabbed it and hung on for dear life."

Hot Rod Hundley:

"Poor Pops. He'll never forget that miss. No one will let him forget it.

"He shot the ball and he missed. All-time hero, all-time goat. That thin line.

"The dressing room was like a morgue. It was up to ol' Hot Rod to cheer 'em up, especially Selvy. His head was between his knees. I touched him, he looked up, and I said, 'Pops, don't worry, man. Don't feel bad. You only cost us about 30 grand.'"

The dynasty is still alive—at least for a five-minute overtime.

This was the Celtics' second consecutive playoff series to come down to the final second of the seventh game at Boston. So had the Eastern finale against the Philadelphia Warriors two weeks earlier.

The Celtics had won a record 60 victories while running away with the division title again—by 11 games over runnerup Philadelphia for the second year in a row.

They had done it without Bill Sharman (retired to coach the Los Angeles Jets in the rival ABA, replaced in the Boston lineup by Sam Jones). And they had done it despite awesome Wilt Chamberlain, who that season *averaged* 50.4 points and scored 100 during a March game against the New York Knicks at Hershey, Pennsylvania. Under orders from new Warrior coach Frank McGuire to assault the basket, Wilt also had poured in 78, 73, 67 twice and 65 twice (and a Boston Garden record 62 against the Celtics) as he forged the greatest scoring season of his career.

Frank Ramsey was hobbled throughout the playoffs by a crippling thigh pull that had him warming up beneath the stands during games. Yet he scored 23 points, including 15 of 16 free throws, in finals against the Lakers.

Wilt Chamberlain averaged a record 50.4 points, including 100 in one game against the Knicks, but Bill Russell was voted the league's MVP for the second straight year.

Six-foot-ten Bill Russell leans on six-foot Philadelphian Guy Rodgers while setting a pick for Bob Cousy in Game 5 of the Eastern finals—not long before the brawling started and Boston Garden patrons were screaming for Rodgers' blood.

SAM JONES' SHOT OUSTS WARRIORS

April 5, 1962, at Boston Garden

CELTICS (109)

	Min.	*FGA*	*FGM*	*FTA*	*FTM*	*Ast.*	*PF*	*Pts.*
Cousy	40	21	8	5	5	8	4	21
Heinsohn	39	22	9	7	7	2	5	25
K.C. Jones	29	4	1	3	2	10	4	4
Sam Jones	43	29	12	4	4	2	2	28
Loscutoff	9	5	1	1	0	1	6	2
Ramsey	3	2	1	2	2	0	0	4
Russell	48	14	7	5	5	3	3	19
Sanders	29	8	2	3	2	1	6	6
Totals	240	105	41	30	27	27	30	109

PHILADELPHIA WARRIORS (107)

	Min.	*FGA*	*FGM*	*FTA*	*FTM*	*Ast.*	*PF*	*Pts.*
Attles	23	4	0	0	0	1	4	0
Arizin	38	22	4	11	11	1	4	19
Chamberlain	48	15	7	9	8	3	3	22
Conlin	2	0	0	0	0	0	1	0
Meschery	48	19	10	13	12	2	3	32
Rodgers	43	15	6	8	6	6	6	18
Gola	38	14	7	2	2	2	2	16
Totals	240	89	34	43	39	15	23	107

Score by periods:	1	2	3	4
Celtics	34	18	28	29—109
Warriors	23	33	25	26—107

Rebounds: Celtics 66 (Russell 22),
Warriors 60 (Chamberlain 22).
Field Goal Percentage: Celtics .391, Warriors .382.
Free Throw Percentage: Celtics .900, Warriors .907.
Referees: Sid Borgia and Mendy Rudolph.
Attendance: 13,909.

Still, it was Chamberlain's archrival Russell who would be voted Most Valuable Player by NBA players for the second straight year, the third time in all.

While the Celtics had stormed to a record victory total during the regular season, the playoffs would prove the toughest of any they have ever won—14 memorable games including the two series-deciders that remain classics in Celtic history.

Also notable in Celtic annals was a wild Game 5 at Boston, which produced a succession of confrontations that resembled hockey more than basketball.

Pairings featured Chamberlain vs. Sam Jones, Jim Loscutoff vs. Guy Rodgers, Tom Heinsohn vs. Ted Luckenbill. Dwarfed by their adversaries, Jones and Rodgers picked up photographer stools at courtside as equalizers—Rodgers while on the run from an enraged Loscutoff. Earlier, Rodgers had scorned Jones for grabbing a stool against Chamberlain. Sam, a David challenging the Goliath Wilt, explained his logic afterward: "If I'm going to fight him, I'm not going to fight him fair."

Garden fans got into the act, too. After Rodgers had bloodied Carl Braun's mouth with a sucker punch, the Warrior guard took off—and ran smack into a group of fans, who began pummeling him before police rescued him.

All of which enlivened a series already brimming with excitement as each team won at home while splitting the first six games.

Then, in Game 7, with two seconds remaining, Sam Jones' 18-foot fallaway shot from the left of the key gave Boston a 109-107 lead.

"It seemed like someone, maybe the good Lord, grabbed Sam's shot and guided it into the basket," Loscutoff would say.

After a Warrior timeout, Ed Conlin in-bounded the ball from mid-court and arched a high pass for Chamberlain, who was jousting with Russell beneath the Boston basket. Both leaped, an Russell batted the ball away to Sam Jones as the buzzer sounded.

The Lakers had watched that game, seated in the first row after arriving early for a championship series that might not be played in Boston, and West was quoted as labeling the game "the greatest I've ever seen."

Now West, in the process of scoring 35 points in the seventh game of the NBA finals, is involved in a title game even more dramatic.

"As we huddled before overtime," he has recalled, "I remember seeing Russell sitting on a stool near the Celtic bench. His body seemed limp, his head was hung, and sweat was pouring off him. I figured he had nothing left."

Overtime begins and Russell is everywhere, continuing the exhaustless perpetual motion that is making him the Celtics' playoff leader in scoring (22.4 average) as well as rebounds (26.4).

"I'm better in the playoffs," Russell once said, "because they're shorter and mean more."

In the opening minute, Frank Ramsey becomes the fourth Celtic to foul out trying to cover Baylor, joining Heinsohn, Sanders and Loscutoff on the sidelines. Gene Guarilia, a little-used forward, is sent into the game by Auerbach.

"I remember when Red walked down the bench looking for someone to guard Baylor after Ramsey fouled out," Guarilia says in recalling the four minutes that would highlight his four-season

Celtic career. "He pointed to me and said, 'All I'm telling you is hold him and grab him, but don't give him any 3-point plays or cheap fouls. And when we get the ball, hustle your ass downcourt."

Guarilia does the job. He deflects a couple of Baylor shots. ("I have long arms and he wasn't getting off his feet that well because he was tired. Each time he shot I managed to tip the ball.") He also feeds Russell for a resounding stuff, collects a rebound and, with two minutes remaining, harrasses Baylor into a disqualifying sixth foul.

Baylor receives a thundering ovation usually reserved for Celtic heroes as he walks back to the Laker bench, his season ended with a 41-point, 22-rebound performance.

With Baylor goes Los Angeles' last hope. The Celtics have a 5-point advantage—the lead having changed hands for the 13th and final time—and hold off the Lakers. Cousy dribbles out the last 20 seconds and it's all over: *Boston 110, Los Angeles 107.*

After two seventh-game scares, the winners—and still champions—the Boston Celtics.

The Garden erupts in its annual Spring ritual.

"I remember ducking under the scorer's table to protect myself," Cousy recalls. "The fans poured onto the court as if they had been keeping everything inside them for too long."

They mob Sam Jones, who scored 5 of his 27 points in overtime (bouncing back from a 1-for-10 start to make 11 of his last 21). They mob Frank Ramsey, who scored 23 points (including 15 of 16 free throws) despite a throbbing thigh pull that had him taped like a mummy and warming up with sprints in the Garden corridors during the game.

And they mob Russell, who has played every second of the game's 53 minutes while totaling 40 rebounds (25 in one half) and 30 points (4 in overtime and, overall, 14 of 17 free throws) to set or tie a variety of NBA and club records. Tears are rolling down Russell's cheeks.

In the locker room, he sits in a corner, the tears still coming. "Well," he says finally, "I'm glad *that's* over."

Bill Russell rang up 40 rebounds and 30 points in the NBA title game.

Jim Loscutoff chases Philadelphia's Guy Rodgers around the Boston Garden court in April during the Celtics' victory in Game 5 of the Eastern finals. Rodgers picked up a stool moments after this photograph was taken as he eluded the enraged Loscutoff, who fumed afterward: "I don't know what I'd have done if I'd gotten my hands on him. I might have broken him in two." Rodgers escaped from Loscutoff, but not Garden fans following another another skirmish, and they pummeled him before police rescued him. Other bouts included Tom Heinsohn–Ted Luckenbill and Wilt Chamberlain–Sam Jones, with Sam also picking up a photographer's stool as an equalizer in his mismatch.

Old foes Tom Heinsohn and Laker Rudy LaRusso compete for the basketball in Game 5 of the finals. Heinsohn scored 30 points to lead the Celtics to victory and a 3-2 series advantage.

1962–63

Front row (left to right): K.C. Jones, Bill Russell, president Walter Brown, coach Red Auerbach, vice president Lou Pieri, Bob Cousy and Sam Jones. Back row: Frank Ramsey, Gene Guarilia, Tom (Satch) Sanders, Tom Heinsohn, Clyde Lovellette, John Havlicek, Jim Loscutoff, Dan Swartz and trainer Buddy LeRoux.

Bob Cousy bids an emotional farewell to Celtic fans on "Cousy Day," which afterward would be labeled the "Boston Tear Party." As Cousy tried to compose himself during his halftime goodbye, a fan in Boston Garden's upper balcony relieved an awkward silence by hollering the instantly classic "We love ya, Cooz!" That's Cousy's daughter Patricia looking up at her father.

From beginning to end, it was the Year of The Cooz—Bob Cousy's last hurrah.

It had been marked a special season since the previous Spring, when Cousy announced that he would play one final season before becoming basketball coach at Boston College.

So, at age 34, the magnetic Cousy was retiring as a Celtic after 13 seasons, during which he not only did more than any other player to establish professional basketball in New England but also to transform a wobbly league into a solid one.

Bob Cousy: the hypnotic dribbler, dazzling passer, inventive playmaker and deadly sharpshooter—and doing it all in a forest of tall men.

Around the league, fans poured into arenas for one last round of oohs and aahs, for one final look at the 6-foot-1 David who had become a legend in a sport of Goliaths.

Through it all, the Celtic captain had one final goal: to go out a winner.

The Celtics breezed to a seventh straight division pennant, 10 games ahead of Syracuse with a best-in-NBA record of 58-22. And that regular season was capped on the final day—St. Patrick's Day—by Bob Cousy Day at Boston Garden. It was a tearful farewell later labeled the Boston Tear Party. At one point, as Cousy tried to compose himself during the emotional halftime ceremonies, a throaty fan in the upper balcony relieved an awkward silence by hollering the instantly classic "We love ya, Cooz!"

Cousy's determination to go out a winner was obvious during the playoffs, which proved more of a struggle than the regular season.

The Cincinnati Royals, featuring Oscar Robertson and Wayne Embry, pushed the Celtics to the 7-game limit in the Eastern finals before Cousy helped fire the Celtics to a back-to-the-wall victory in the clincher with 21-point, 11-assist brilliance.

And he proved it again during what proved the final game of the NBA finals against the Lakers before a record playoff crowd of 15,521 at the Los Angeles Sports Arena and a national TV audience.

Bill Russell receives the All-Star Game's MVP trophy from NBA president Maurice Podoloff. Russell led the East to victory with 19 points and 24 rebounds to outscore the West's Wilt Chamberlain, who had 17 points and 19 rebounds.

The changing of the guard began as Bob Cousy eased the quarterbacking reigns over to K.C. Jones despite the urgings of some Rhode Island Auditorium fans.

Bob Cousy waves goodbye to Celtic fans.

COUSY RALLIES CELTS TO TITLE IN FINAL GAME

April 24, 1963, at Los Angeles

CELTICS (112)

	Min.	*FGA*	*FGM*	*FTA*	*FTM*	*Reb.*	*Ast.*	*PF*	*Pts.*
Cousy	30	16	8	2	2	3	7	4	18
Havlicek	28	20	8	3	2	2	5	2	18
Heinsohn	33	18	8	9	6	9	2	4	22
K.C. Jones	14	6	3	4	3	2	4	3	9
Sam Jones	24	10	2	3	1	3	0	3	5
Ramsey	20	8	4	3	2	1	0	2	10
Russell	48	12	5	5	2	24	9	3	12
Sanders	43	14	9	0	0	7	3	5	18
Totals	240	104	47	29	18	61*	30	26	112

LOS ANGELES LAKERS (109)

	Min.	*FGA*	*FGM*	*FTA*	*FTM*	*Reb.*	*Ast.*	*PF*	*Pts.*
Barnett	24	12	4	4	4	1	1	3	12
Baylor	47	24	11	6	6	8	8	3	28
Ellis	19	3	3	3	3	5	1	1	9
Krebs	12	3	0	0	0	2	0	3	0
LaRusso	42	14	9	1	1	5	3	4	19
Selvy	16	3	1	2	1	3	3	3	3
West	44	24	13	10	6	7	9	0	32
Wiley	36	6	3	1	0	14	1	3	6
Totals	240	89	44	27	21	58*	26	20	109

Score by periods:	1	2	3	4
Celtics:	33	33	26	20–112
Lakers:	35	17	28	29–109

* *Includes Team Rebounds:* Celtics 10, Lakers 13.
Field Goal Percentage: Celtics .452, Lakers .494.
Free Throw Percentage: Celtics .621, Lakers .778.
Referees: Earl Strom and Norm Drucker.
Attendance: 15,521.

Frank Ramsey presents Bob Cousy a gift from teammates.

Hemmed in by Lakers Rudy LaRusso (35) and Jerry West (44), Bob Cousy flips a behind-the-back pass to Tom Heinsohn.

Bob Cousy relaxes with his parents after "Cousy Day."

Ahead 3-2 in the series, the Celtics were leading by 9 points with 10:57 remaining when Cousy, who had scored 18 points, went down near midcourt with torn ligaments in his left foot. In obvious pain, Cousy was assisted off the floor—his arms draped around the shoulders of Jim Loscutoff and Buddy LeRoux—as the arena thundered with what figured to be his farewell.

While Cousy's foot was frozen and strapped by LeRoux, Los Angeles seized the momentum behind Jerry West and Elgin Baylor to cut Boston's lead to 1 point. To the crowd's amazement, Cousy returned with 4:43 left and rallied the Celtics to a 112-109 victory. Fittingly, Cousy dribbled out the final seconds before heaving the basketball to the rafters as the buzzer sounded signaling the Celtics' fifth straight NBA championship—and Cousy's last.

The Cooz had gone out a winner—and with a Hollywood touch.

Bob Cousy:

"I've always wanted to be the best. It wasn't enough to be good enough. It wasn't enough to be very good. I had to be the best, because that's what it's all about.

"So I wanted to go out with a good last game for myself, I wanted to go out on a winning game, and I wanted to go out with a world championship.

"God was good to me. He granted me my final wish."

Bob Cousy is framed by Lakers while attempting a layup in NBA finals.

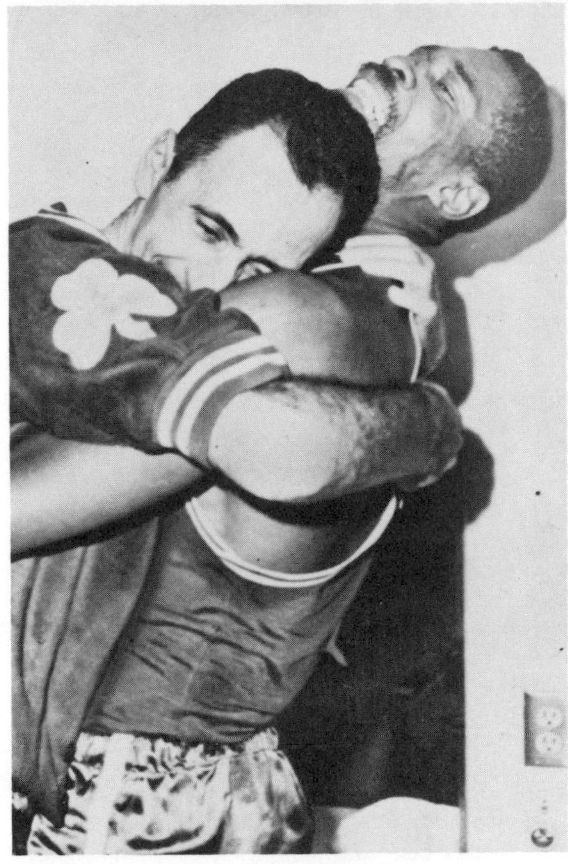

Bob Cousy and Bill Russell embrace in the Celtics' locker room after Cousy's last game.

Owner Walter Brown (center) and Red Auerbach salute Bob Cousy with a farewell toast at the squad's breakup dinner.

1963–64

The Celtics celebrate their sixth consecutive world championship, the only pro team to win that many in a row—surpassing baseball's New York Yankees and hockey's Montreal Canadiens. Clustered around Red Auerbach are (clockwise) K.C. Jones, Frank Ramsey, John Havlicek and Bill Russell.

Walter Brown called Tom Heinsohn "the No. 1 heel in my long association with sports" when the NBA Players Association came within minutes of striking the All-Star Game at Boston in January. The two men huddled privately three days later as Heinsohn, the players association president, tried to explain his case, but the meeting broke up without resolution. Brown wouldn't speak to Heinsohn for the remainder of the season—until the team's breakup dinner, when there was a happy ending to one of the rare hostilities within the Celtic family during the Brown era.

"Everyone was wondering what would happen to us without Cousy," Red Auerbach recalls. "You don't lose the greatest playmaker of all time without missing him.

"We came to camp that Fall after reading all Summer about the end of the Celtic dynasty. Some idiot had even come up to Russell on the street and said, 'You'd better hustle now that you don't have Cousy to carry the team.' That really upset Russ, who had been the league's MVP the last three seasons.

"You know, I think we'd won in 1963 because it was Cooz' last season and I think we won in 1964 because we were playing *without* Bob. We had something to prove."

"I think," agrees Tom Heinsohn, "that we all dedicated ourselves to winning without Bob to prove ourselves."

Besides proving they could win without "Mr. Basketball," the Celtics also proved that season that an NBA team could put five black players on the court at the same time and the roof wouldn't fall in. Heinsohn was the only white in the starting lineup, teaming with Tom (Satch) Sanders at forward, Bill Russell at center, and Sam and K.C. Jones in the backcourt. Newly acquired veteran Willie Naulls was a reserve forward, and when he was used in place of Heinsohn it often resulted in an all-black five.

"It was no big deal," Auerbach says now. "I didn't even think about it at the time. I just did it. No, there was no negative reaction by anyone around the league."

Typical of Celtic attitude, the players joked about it.

Tom (Satch) Sanders shows one way to stop Laker superstar Jerry West. The Celtics usually used a more conventional-but-relentless pressing defense that season. "That was easily the best defensive team we ever had—maybe the best of all time," Russell says now.

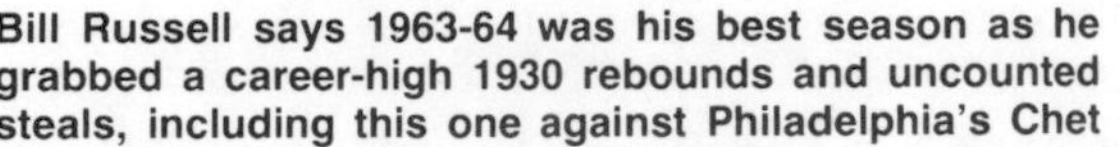

Bill Russell says 1963-64 was his best season as he grabbed a career-high 1930 rebounds and uncounted steals, including this one against Philadelphia's Chet Walker. Russell was a man with something to prove: that the Celtics could win without Bob Cousy—and that he could escape Cousy's shadow.

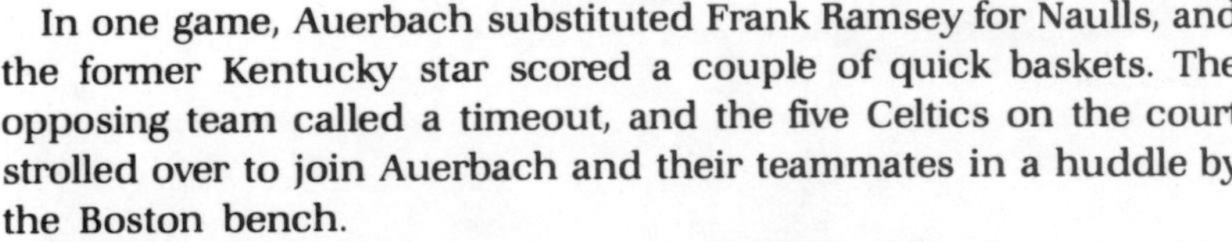

In one game, Auerbach substituted Frank Ramsey for Naulls, and the former Kentucky star scored a couple of quick baskets. The opposing team called a timeout, and the five Celtics on the court strolled over to join Auerbach and their teammates in a huddle by the Boston bench.

"Well, Red," Ramsey drawled, "it looks like ah'm the new white hope."

The Celtic huddle broke up in laughter, and Boston Garden fans wondered what was so funny in the middle of a game.

Race was never a problem on the championship-era Celtics (nor was creed, unless you count the time a Jewish dentist accused Auerbach of being anti-Semitic when the complainant's kid brother was cut in training camp).

There *was* a rare instance of hostility in the Celtic family during the 1964-65 season, though. Walter Brown became furious at Heinsohn at the NBA All-Star Game in Boston when the participants, seeking pension benefits for all league players from stalling owners, came within minutes of striking the nationally televised showcase.

That the incident occurred in Boston Garden was ironic; of all NBA owners, Brown was generous to his players, sometimes to a fault. It was just a coincidence that the long-stewing situation came to a head in Boston, and certainly wasn't intended as an affront to Brown personally. Contributing to the jigsaw of coincidences was that the Players Association president happened to be Heinsohn, who not only was a Celtic but a favorite of Brown.

Unintentional though it was, Brown was shattered. The man who had founded the All-Star Game at his own risk 13 years earlier when he could ill afford it was now a host embarrassed in his own

6TH STRAIGHT WORLD TITLE TOPS YANKEES, CANADIENS

April 26, 1964, at Boston Garden

CELTICS (105)

	Min.	*FGA*	*FGM*	*FTA*	*FTM*	*Reb.*	*Ast.*	*PF*	*Pts.*
Havlicek	31	14	6	3	2	2	4	2	14
Heinsohn	27	17	7	6	5	8	3	4	19
K.C. Jones	38	7	3	1	1	3	5	5	7
Sam Jones	37	16	7	9	4	2	5	4	18
Naulls	15	4	2	0	0	4	0	4	4
Ramsey	20	14	7	4	4	2	4	3	18
Russell	48	11	5	5	4	26	6	3	14
Sanders	34	13	5	1	1	10	0	6	11
Totals	240	96	42	29	21	72*	27	31	105

SAN FRANCISCO WARRIORS (99)

	Min.	*FGA*	*FGM*	*FTA*	*FTM*	*Reb.*	*Ast.*	*PF*	*Pts.*
Attles	32	12	4	8	3	1	2	5	11
Chamberlain	48	28	12	13	6	27	2	5	30
Hightower	31	9	2	7	6	7	0	6	10
Hill	1	0	0	0	0	0	0	0	0
Lee	19	4	3	3	3	3	0	3	9
Meschery	21	8	3	6	3	2	0	0	9
Rodgers	45	24	8	4	3	4	7	6	19
Thurmond	43	11	3	6	5	14	0	2	11
Totals	240	96	35	47	29	69*	11	27	99

Score by periods:	1	2	3	4
Celtics	22	23	29	31—105
Warriors	24	17	30	28—99

**Includes Team Rebounds:* Celtics 15, Warriors 9.
Field Goal Percentage: Celtics .438, Warriors .365
Free Throw Percentage: Celtics .724, Warriors .617
Referees: Richie Powers and Earl Strom.
Attendance: 13,909.

Veteran Willie Naulls joined the Celtics, frequently giving them an all-black lineup—an NBA first.

building. In his hurt he lashed out at Heinsohn, labeling him "the No. 1 heel in my long association with sports."

Asked if he'd trade his star forward, Brown snapped, "No, but if I had a team in Honolulu I'd ship him there."

The Celtic owner wouldn't speak to Heinsohn the remainder of the season. But at the team's breakup dinner, Brown dramatically buried the hatchet by telling the audience: "No living thing—horse, dog or human—ever gave so much competitively as Tommy contributed to the Celtics," as he pinned much of the credit for the team's latest championship on Heinsohn.

Heinsohn had plenty of company as the Celtics emphatically answered the question of whether they could continue rolling without Cousy.

Moving into the lineup in place of Cousy, K.C. Jones not only contributed stout defense as everyone expected, but he also dealt the third most assists in the league while quarterbacking the world's most famous fastbreak.

And although John Havlicek never started a game, the perpetual-motion sophomore led the team in scoring with a 19.9-point average while taking over the retiring Ramsey's role as basketball's best sixth man.

But it was a new pressing defense—made relentless by Russell, Sanders, K.C. Jones and Havlicek—that made the Celtics devastating.

"That was easily the best defensive team we ever had—and maybe the best of all time," Russell says now. "Maybe that's why it rates as my favorite team."

"We changed our game and concentrated more on defense," Auerbach explains, "figuring we'd have enough offense if we pitched in and helped Russell shut off the opposition. And it worked, the pressing defense setting up offensive opportunities.

"We won 59 games (four more than Cincinnati in NBA East), one short of our NBA record. Then in the playoffs we rolled by two pretty darn good teams—Cincinnati (Robertson, Twyman, Embry and Rookie of the Year Jerry Lucas) and San Francisco (Chamberlain, Rodgers, Meschery, Hightower). It was Ramsey's and Loscutoff's turn to go out winners."

The NBA title was the Celtics' sixth in a row as they became the first pro team to win six successive world championships—surpassing the five straight won by baseball's 1949-53 New York Yankees and hockey's 1956-60 Montreal Canadiens.

The Celtics had made their point—and none more so than Russell. Among other achievements, he averaged nearly 25 rebounds (and 15 points) a game—1,930 rebounds in all, the most of his career, while finally escaping the shadow of Cousy.

Tom Heinsohn:

"Boston pretty much considered Russell an intruder as long as Cousy was around to excite them. But I think everyone in Boston finally was convinced about Russell when we won that '64 championship without Cooz."

Although it was the only season in a five-year stretch that league players didn't select him the NBA's Most Valuable Player, Russell looks back now and says, "I consider 1964 my best year."

The numbers of Ed Macauley and Bob Cousy were retired to the Boston Garden rafters on opening night along with the 1963 Eastern and NBA pennants.

John Havlicek was joined in the NBA by two of his former Ohio State teammates—Boston's Larry Siegfried and Cincinnati's Jerry Lucas, who would be selected the league's Rookie of the Year.

Walter Brown raises Red Auerbach's hand in triumph for the Celtics' seventh world championship in eight years. It was Brown's last. He would die of a heart attack before another season rolled around.

1964–65

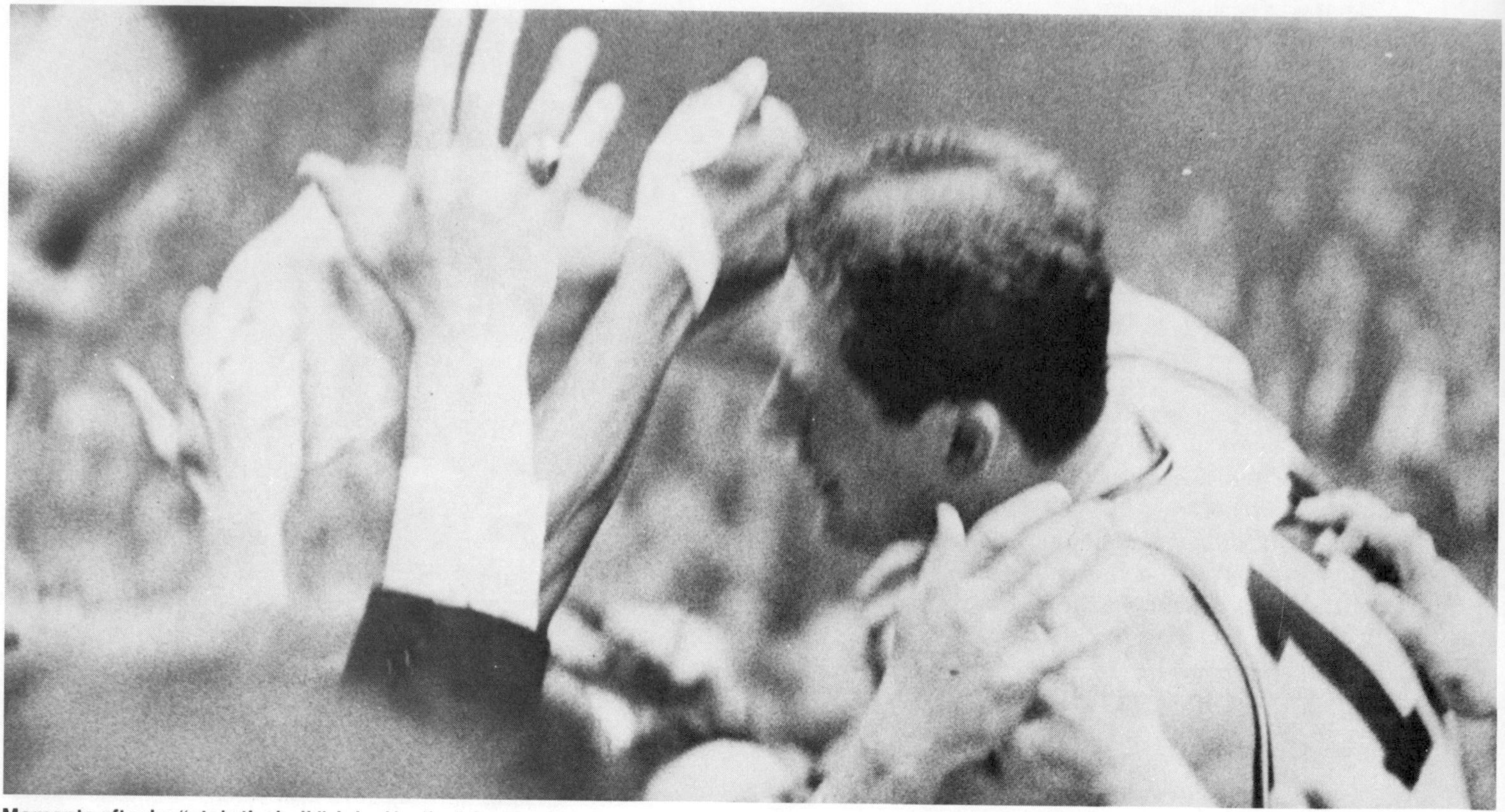

Moments after he "stole the ball," John Havlicek is swept away by fans after preserving the Celtic dynasty by intercepting Philadelphia's throw-in in the final seconds of the Eastern finals.

Johnny Most:

"I shouted myself hoarse: 'Havlicek stole the ball! Havlicek stole the ball! Havlicek stole the ball!' "

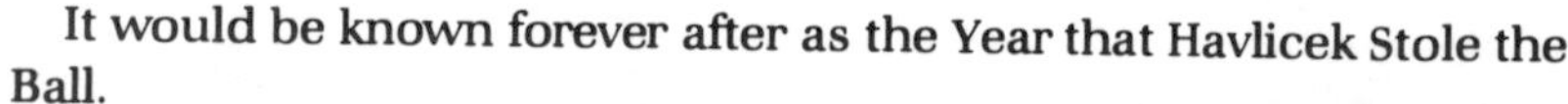

It would be known forever after as the Year that Havlicek Stole the Ball.

It was the season that the Celtics' dynasty was nearly ended, incredibly, by a guy wire that supported a backboard at Boston Garden. But the reign was preserved by the most famous play in Celtic history, immortalized by Johnny Most's rasping rhetoric.

The season was prefaced by the death of Walter Brown a few days before training camp opened. And when No. 1 was retired for the Celtic founder, raised to the Garden rafters on opening night, Bill Russell vowed, "We'll win the championship for Mr. Brown's memory."

Wearing black mourning patches sewn on their left shoulder straps, the Celtics roared to their ninth straight NBA East pennant. They made a shambles of their division, jumping to a 31-7 start by New Year's and going on to eclipse their own NBA record for most victories—winning 62 against only 18 losses. Runnerup Cincinnati trailed by *14* games.

Then came the Eastern playoff finals against old foes Wilt Chamberlain and the Philadelphia 76ers, both in new costumes. The Sixers were the old Syracuse Nationals, who moved to Philadelphia the previous season to replace the Warriors, who had shifted to San Francisco. The Warriors had taken Chamberlain to the West Coast,

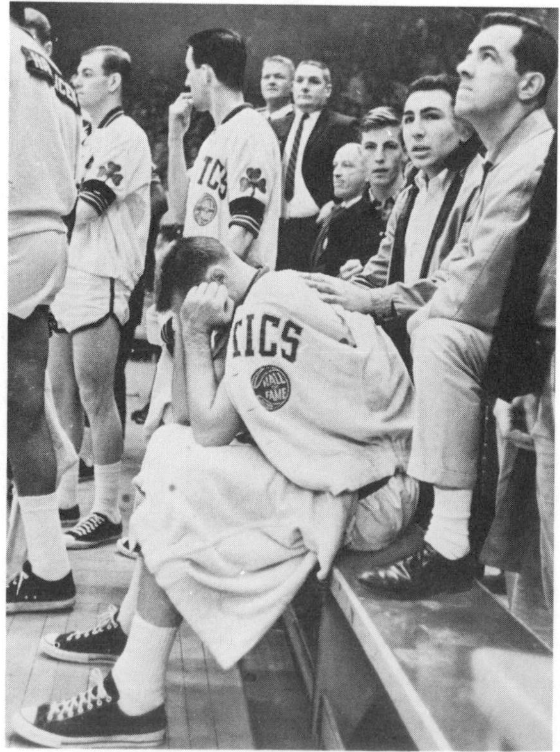

This is what the Celtics bench looked like moments before "Havlicek stole the ball" in the Eastern finals' last seconds. Tom Heinsohn apparently can't bear to look as fans swarm around the bench, including one with a friendly hand on Heinsohn's shoulder. That's Larry Siegfried biting a fingernail and rookie Ron Bonham beyond.

but during the 1965 All-Star break stunned the basketball world by sending Wilt back to his Philadelphia hometown in a deal that seemed almost a giveaway.

Chamberlain rallied the 76ers to a 40-40 finish, making them a playoff threat that quickly eliminated Cincinnati, 3-1.

Philadelphia and Boston had split 10 regular-season games, and the seesaw pattern continued in the Eastern finals. It was a sizzling series tied at 1-1, 2-2 and 3-3 as it alternated between the two cities—each team winning before its rabid home fans.

"Throwing eggs was big," John Havlicek recalls. "There got to be a contest between fans in the two cities. Who could throw more eggs, Philly or Boston?"

The intensity was heightened by controversy in the fourth game. Trailing by two points with one second remaining, the Sixers inbounded the ball to Hal Greer near midcourt. His desperation 35-footer slammed off the backboard into the basket at the buzzer, sending the Convention Hall crowd into ecstasy—and the game into overtime. The Celtics protested that the whole thing had to take longer than one second, an anger not cooled when the 76ers went on to win, 134-131.

Not surprisingly, the series came down to a seventh-game showdown at Boston. Technically, the game would decide the Eastern representative to the NBA finals; in reality, it would determine the NBA champion. Western Division champion Los Angeles clearly was no competition without Elgin Baylor, who had torn knee ligaments in the Lakers' first playoff game.

Before the tapoff at Boston Garden, the rival coaches huddled briefly to discuss the backboard-supporting guy wires. A Garden novelty, these thin cables ran overhead from each side of the backboard to the balcony facing. Their plane had been lowered for this game, and Schayes suggested that if an inbounds pass struck a wire, possession would remain with the team that had passed the ball.

Auerbach shook his head. "The rule has always been that if the ball strikes the wire, the other team gets the ball out of bounds," he said. "Why change it now?"

Bill Russell is congratulated by Red Auerbach after scoring his 10,000th Celtic point during the JFK memorial game against Baltimore.

Wilt Chamberlain returned to Philadelphia in a midseason trade and made the 76ers a playoff threat. That's Tom Sanders confronting Wilt at left, while at right Satch collides with another Sixer heavyweight, Luke Jackson.

Bill Russell kneels in pain after being scratched in the left eye by Jerry West (44) during the second-period rebound action in the title series' last game. "I couldn't see out of the eye the rest of the game," Russell recalls. "I spent the next 10 days in bed because doctors thought I might lose the sight of that eye."

The Celtics came out charging and took an 18-point lead after just eight minutes. But the Sixers rallied to take a 62-61 lead into the locker room at intermission.

Philadelphia improved that lead to 66-61 in the opening minutes of the second half before the growling Auerbach signaled for a timeout to regroup his Celtics. Whatever the coach said, the Celtics stormed out of the huddle and regained the lead, 90-82, going into the fourth period. And with Sam Jones scoring 37 and Havlicek 26, Boston still led by 7 points, 110-103, with about a minute left when Auerbach lit his victory cigar.

"We had the game locked up," he would say later. "No way we were going to lose it."

The Celtics grew cautious, trying to avoid 3-point plays, and allowed Chamberlain 6 straight points punctuated by an uncontested dunk to cut Boston's lead to 1 point with five seconds remaining.

The Sixers pressed desperately as Russell took the ball out of bounds just to the right of the Celtic basket, not far from the Boston bench. Harassed, the 6-foot-10 Russell backed up a halfstep and jumped as he tried to inbound the ball with both arms upstretched over his head.

The ball traveled only inches before striking the guy wire overhead and caroming out of bounds.

"Russell lost the ball off the support!" astonished Johnny Most screamed into his microphone in the broadcasting cage on the rim of the first balcony. "And the Celtics are claiming that Chamberlain hit him on the arm!"

Russell was still beneath the guy wire but now was kneeling on one knee, pounding the floor with his fist and repeating, "Oh, my God . . . oh, my God . . ."

A few feet away, the other Celtics stood by the bench dumbfounded—like almost everyone else in the building.

"I'll always remember Russ walking over to the huddle," Buddy LeRoux recalls. "He just looked at the others and said, 'Somebody bail me out. I blew it.' "

"Nobody knew what to do," Sanders remembers. "Russell came over shaking his head and saying, 'I don't believe it, I just don't believe it.' Nobody wanted to believe that something as simple as that could put us in that kind of position. It was like a nightmare."

If the Boston bench was in shock, the Philadelphia bench was in chaos.

"It was crazy," Schayes says now. "Everybody was trying to make up a play. Everybody was yakking and screaming and talking at once. I said, 'Hold it. We only have a few seconds left. Let me talk.' "

Philadelphia's main options were clear: (1) Get the ball to Chamberlain close to the basket for a stuff; even if fouled while shooting, he'd have three shots to make one for a tie and two for a victory; (2) Get the ball to Greer for a quick outside shot, with Wilt underneath to guide the ball in if necessary, and with 7-foot-2 Chamberlain, 6-foot-9 Jackson and 6-foot-9 Kerr crashing the boards for any rebound, or (3) Get the ball outside to Walker, who could thread the ball to Chamberlain or Greer, which ever was open, or if both were covered he could drive himself.

Schayes' first thought was Chamberlain. "Go to Wilt and let him power to the basket," he recalls. "But I knew they would have grabbed him, and he wasn't the best foul shooter."

'JOHNNY HAVLICEK STOLE THE BALL!'

April 15, 1965, at Boston Garden

CELTICS (110)

	Min.	*FGM*	*FGA*	*FTM*	*FTA*	*Reb.*	*Ast.*	*PF*	*Pts.*
Havlicek	42	10	30	6	7	11	1	5	26
Heinsohn	16	1	5	0	0	7	2	5	2
K.C. Jones	36	2	9	2	3	4	10	5	6
S. Jones	48	15	31	7	9	2	1	3	37
Naulls	4	0	0	0	0	0	0	1	0
Russell	48	7	16	1	2	29	8	3	15
Sanders	34	8	17	2	2	10	2	5	18
Siegfried	12	2	4	2	3	3	0	1	6
Totals	240	45	112	20	26	66	24	28	110

PHILADELPHIA 76ERS (109)

	Min.	*FGM*	*FGA*	*FTM*	*FTA*	*Reb.*	*Ast.*	*PF*	*Pts.*
Bianchi	24	3	11	1	1	0	0	4	7
Chamberlain	48	12	15	6	13	32	2	1	30
Costello	24	7	7	1	1	3	0	5	3
Gambee	29	6	15	13	14	6	0	6	25
Greer	48	5	12	2	2	8	9	4	12
Jackson	17	3	10	2	4	2	0	2	8
Kerr	2	0	1	0	2	0	0	0	0
Walker	48	10	19	4	5	5	1	4	24
Totals	240	46	90	29	42	56	12	26	109

Score by Periods:	1	2	3	4
Celtics	35	26	29	20—110
76ers	26	36	20	27—109

Field Goal Percentage: Celtics .402, 76ers .444.
Free Throw Percentage: Celtics .769, 76ers .690.
Referees: Richie Powers and Earl Strom.
Attendance: 13,909

"We would have mangled Wilt," Sanders says of Chamberlain, who was only 5 of 13 at the line that night and 46 percent for the season. "Anything to get him on that line."

So Schayes decided to go to Option 2. Greer would inbound the ball deep to Walker outside, Kerr would set a pick on K.C. Jones at the baseline, Greer would slip in behind the screen, take a return pass from Walker and put up a quick one-hander from the corner.

As Chamberlain and Russell jousted for position beneath the basket, Greer hesitated before finally lobbing the ball toward Walker about 25 feet away near the top of the key.

"Hal was being harassed," Schayes recalls. "The moment the ball left his hands, I knew it was gone. I knew it was going to be grabbed."

"I didn't put enough on the ball," Greer would say afterward. "That's all there is to it. I just didn't put enough on it."

"I knew he had five seconds to inbound," Havlicek remembers, "so I started counting to myself: 1,001, 1,002, 1,003. Usually something has happened by then. So by 1,003½ I started to peek a little more."

Havlicek turned his head in time to see the ball arching toward Walker. Hondo uncoiled, leaped into the air and slapped the ball away.

And from high above courtside, Johnny Most erupted:

"...and Havlicek steals it! Over to Sam Jones. Havlicek stole the ball!

"It's all over! It's alllll over!

"Johnny Havlicek is being mobbed by the fans! It's alllll over! Johnny Havlicek stole the ball!..."

Red Auerbach:

"I couldn't believe it when Havlicek broke up that pass-in. I lost my voice. I couldn't open my mouth."

Russell rushed to Havlicek, hugged him and pinned a hurried kiss on his forehead before the surging crowd swept their hero away. The fans carried him all the way down the corridor outside the locker room, where they finally put him down—clad only in his supporter, socks and sneakers, his jersey longsince torn off and shredded, his shorts pulled down around his knees.

And inside the locker room, Russell, giddy with relief, told writers: "This is one game that went right down to the wire."

◆ ◆ ◆

Screaming himself hoarse, this was Johnny Most's classic "Havlicek stole the ball!" broadcast on Boston radio station WHDH:

"Greer is putting the ball in play. He gets it out deep *and Havlicek steals it! Over to Sam Jones. Havlicek stole the ball!*

"It's all over! It's alllll over!

"Johnny Havlicek is being mobbed by the fans! It's alllll over! Johnny Havlicek stole the ball!

"Oh, boy, what a play by Havlicek at the end of this ball game! Johnny Havlicek stole the ball on the pass-in!

"Oh, my, what a play by Havlicek! A spectacular series comes to an end in spectacular fashion!

"John Havlicek is being hoisted aloft...raises his hand...Bill Russell wants to grab Havlicek! He hugs him! He squeezes John Havlicek!

"Havlicek saved this ballgame! Believe that! Johnny Havlicek saved this ball game! The Celtics win it, 110 to 109!"

◆ ◆ ◆

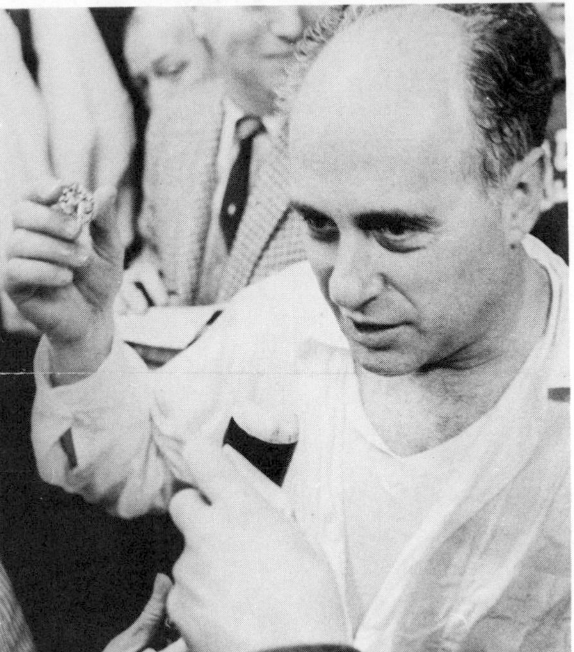

Drenched Red Auerbach displays to media, including network television, a silver St. Christopher medal amid the clubhouse celebration.

"I've never said a word about this before now," Auerbach said, "but back in September Marjorie Brown came to me and told me she wanted me to have this. She hoped it would bring us good luck.

"It was Walter's St. Christopher medal. He used to hold it in his hand at every Celtic game. And I carried it in my pocket all season. It was there in every game, in every huddle, and that's why I'm holding it up in this room right now. This was Walter's championship. We won it this year for him."

Johnny Most

1965–66

Red Auerbach goes out a champion, and pays for it with his last victory shower—administered by coaching successor Bill Russell.

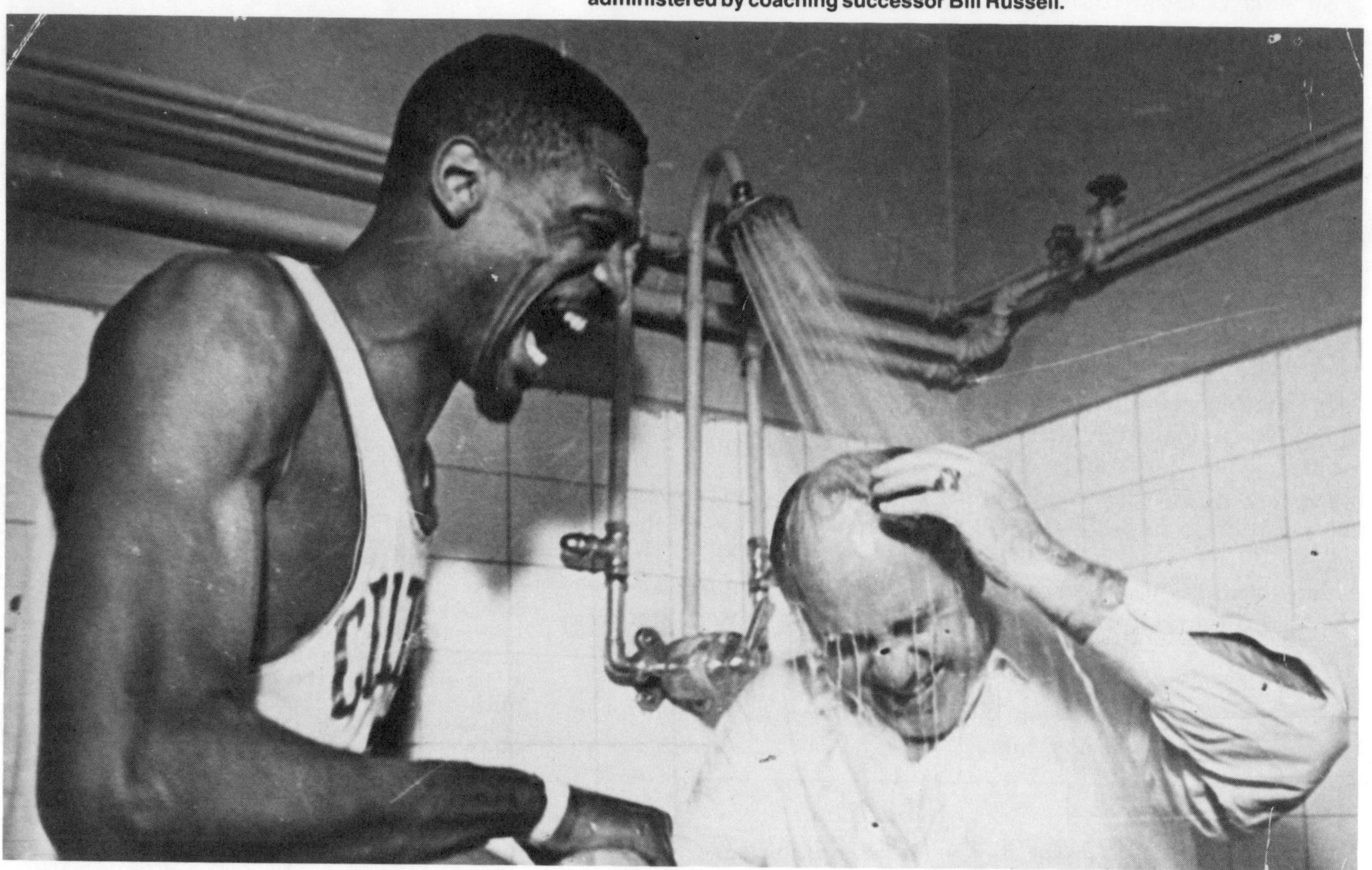

RED AUERBACH'S LAST CHAMPIONSHIP
April 28, 1966, at Boston Garden

CELTICS (95)

	Min.	*FGA*	*FGM*	*FTA*	*FTM*	*Reb.*	*Ast.*	*PF*	*Pts.*
Havlicek	48	21	6	6	4	16	2	3	16
K.C. Jones	31	9	2	1	1	2	3	5	5
Sam Jones	29	21	10	2	2	5	0	5	22
Naulls	3	1	0	0	0	1	0	3	0
Nelson	28	9	2	4	4	8	2	3	8
Russell	48	22	10	5	5	32	1	5	25
Sanders	31	9	3	1	1	4	3	5	7
Siegfried	22	13	4	5	4	2	2	4	12
Totals	240	105	37	24	21	77	13	33	95

LOS ANGELES LAKERS (93)

	Min.	*FGA*	*FGM*	*FTA*	*FTM*	*Reb.*	*Ast.*	*PF*	*Pts.*
Baylor	45	22	6	6	6	14	1	1	18
Boozer	4	0	0	0	0	2	1	1	0
Ellis	34	11	5	3	2	11	0	2	12
Goodrich	30	9	2	3	2	4	1	4	6
Hazzard	24	7	5	5	2	2	3	2	12
Imhoff	14	1	0	0	0	3	0	3	0
King	16	4	1	1	0	2	0	1	2
LaRusso	25	7	2	4	3	6	0	5	7
West	48	27	12	16	12	10	3	3	36
Totals	240	88	33	38	27	60	9	22	93

Score by Periods:	1	2	3	4
Celtics	27	26	23	19—95
Lakers	20	18	22	33—93

Field Goal Percentage: Celtics .352, Lakers .375.
Free Throw Percentage: Celtics .875, Lakers .711.
Team Rebounds: Celtics 7, Lakers 6.
Referees: Earl Strom and Mendy Rudolph.
Attendance: 13,909.

The Celtics had won "one for Cousy" and for other retiring Celtics while collecting past championships. Now it was time to win "one for Auerbach."

Arnold (Red) Auerbach was coaching one final season before retiring from the bench at age 48 to concentrate on general managing. He announced those plans before the season opened so that old rivals could take one last shot at dethroning him and his Celtics as they aimed at an eighth straight world championship, their ninth in 10 seasons—streaks that aren't likely to be equaled in any major league sport.

So 1965-66 was marked a special season from the start, and it lived up to expectations.

In one town after another, opponents and fans around the NBA made final salutes to Auerbach—often with a good-natured needle. One night in Cincinnati, for example, management distributed 5,000 free cigars to customers to celebrate the occasion—cigars to be lit when the Royals beat the Celtics. But at game's end, the only person lighting up was Auerbach, a victor once again.

The Royals nearly slipped Auerbach a loaded cigar in the playoffs, though—after Boston had finished second in the East, one game behind the 55-25 Philadelphia 76ers, the first time in 10 years the Celtics didn't win the division. Boston was on the verge of elimination from the playoffs as Cincinnati won two of the first three games in the best-of-five series. But the Celts survived the scare by winning the next two games, including the 112-103 finale as Sam Jones scored a clutch 34 points.

Next the Celtics gained revenge for Philadelphia having taken their division championship during the regular season by rolling over the 76ers, 4-1, in the Eastern finals. And, for the fourth time in five years, the NBA title series pitted Boston vs. Los Angeles, and the championship came down to a seventh-game showdown.

Bill Russell is introduced as the new Celtic coach, to succeed Red Auerbach the following season. The Celtics made history as Russell became the first black to direct a major league team in any sport. Auerbach made the announcement early in the NBA finals, ending speculation which he felt was distracting the team. Originally, Russell had turned down the job; Frank Ramsey, Bob Cousy and Tom Heinsohn also weren't interested. Auerbach reportedly was considering Alex Hannum when Russell changed his mind.

Red Auerbach:

"Everyone had figured that I'd pick my spot, that I'd quit after a season when we'd won, making sure I went out a winner.

"Emotionally and physically, I had been drained after the previous season, after the 1965 championship. In the year since Walter Brown had died, I was general manager, coach, scout, promoter—everything. I looked awful. I could have retired then and no one could have blamed me. It would have been easy.

"Yet the idea bothered me. Would people say I was quitting on top? Would they say I got out while the getting was good?

"Usually I didn't give a damn what people said or thought about me. They could call me a bastard, a poor sport, an egotist—anything they felt like calling me. But I did care about this; I didn't want to be called a quitter. That was very important to me.

"Well, they would never be able to say that about me because I would never give them a chance. I announced my retirement a year ahead of time, giving everyone one last crack at me.

"So there was absolutely no guarantee I'd go out a winner. Remember, Cousy, Sharman, Heinsohn, Ramsey and Loscutoff were gone. And we were getting old fast.

"Well, everyone had their last shot at me, everyone had their chance. And when it was over—the longest year of my life—there was a lump in my throat as I walked out of the locker room after that last game. And, yes, I did cry later. Of course.

"Yes, later there were times I considered coming back. In fact, Russell tried to talk me out of quitting and even spoke to my wife about it. 'You can't let that man retire,' he said. 'What a waste.'

"But any time I had any doubts, all I did was look at one of the pictures on my office wall—one taken at the last game. I look so worn and weary that it scares me. The 16-20 hour days seven days a week had taken an awful toll, and I made up my mind never to go back."

With the Boston Garden crowd roaring approval in crescendo, the Celtics jumped to a 10-0 start, held a 53-38 advantage at halftime, led by 19 early in the second half, and were coasting at 76-60 entering the fourth quarter. Only one drama remained—the moment Auerbach would light his final coaching cigar, his trademarked victory signal that delighted friend and infuriated foe.

The Celtics and 76ers engage in a February melee at the Garden as Boston's Woody Sauldsberry and Philadelphia's Dave Gambee exchange punches.

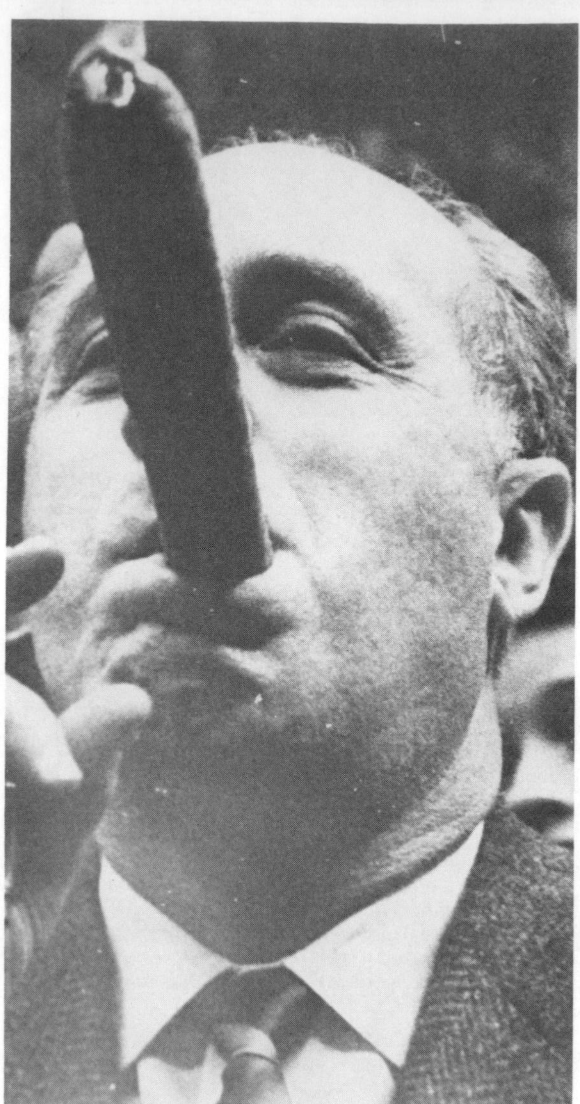

Red Auerbach puffs an oversized cigar to celebrate his 1,000th NBA coaching triumph—a January victory over Los Angeles at Boston.

With four minutes remaining, the Celtics led by 13. The turnaway crowd of 13,909 knew that Auerbach would soon unwrap his cigar. Still, they also knew that Auerbach had never made the mistake of lighting up prematurely, only to have his team collapse and be caught in the embarrassment of chewing on a victory cigar in defeat. That had almost happened during the previous year's playoffs when Red had nearly swallowed his cigar as Bill Russell hit the wire supporting the backboard against Philadelphia to nearly cost the Celtics a championship.

So Auerbach would be extra cautious about lighting up this final time, even though Massachusetts Governor John Volpe was camped next to the Celtic bench, armed with a lighter and eager to fire up The Last Cigar.

With 30 seconds remaining, Russell's spectacular stuff gave Boston a 10-point cushion—the final installment of a 25-point 32-rebound going-away present to Auerbach from his successor. Eleven days earlier, Auerbach had picked Russell as his replacement, as a player-coach, so the team could put speculation behind them and get on with the business of winning another championship.

The countdown continued.

"Thirty seconds left, and the Celtics are on the verge of their ninth championship," Johnny Most told his radio audience from high above courtside. "The crowd is going beserk!"

Hysteria *was* setting in as the crowd surrounded the court, anticipating the kill and wanting to rub elbows with history.

Jerry West scored two quick baskets, but Boston still led by 6 with 16 seconds left, and that was safe enough for Auerbach. He turned toward Volpe and allowed the future US Secretary of Transportation to light The Last Cigar.

"I never came closer to disaster," Auerbach would note later.

The sight of Auerbach lighting up ignited the crowd, and it went wild now, swarming onto the court.

"Havlicek has called time out because he can't get the ball in play. The crowd has surged down the end line," Most shouted hoarsely into his microphone. "They can't finish the ballgame. They can't get the ball in play.

"The crowd in its delirium and joy has thrown things onto the floor.

"Red Auerbach is being mobbed by fans, players...

"Officials are asking the crowd to *please* pull back. The crowd wants to get at these guys and hug 'em.

Bill Russell and Wilt Chamberlain nearly came to blows and are separated by referee John Vanak as the argument becomes more heated. The playoff incident was triggered by a fistfight between Celtic Larry Siegfried (behind Russell at left) and 76er Billy Cunningham (not shown), which started on the Boston Garden court and carried into the crowd. When Chamberlain moved in to restrain Siegfried, Russell joined the get-together. Angry words and gestures followed, but no blows were struck between the giant archrivals, who were friendly off the court and often dined at each other's home.

An eerie hush shrouds Boston Garden as the Lakers whittle the Celtics' lead to two points, 95-93, with 4 seconds left. Moments earlier the crowd had hysterically swarmed over the court in a premature celebration. Now herded back to the sidelines, Sam Jones (far right in white) puts the ball in play with a pass-in to K.C. Jones near the Celtic bench and—3, 2, 1...

"Auerbach has implored the crowd to step back and let them get the ball in play... I have never seen anything like this... the fans are on the supports of the baskets."

Shooed back by John Havlicek, Sam Jones and other Celtic players, spectators still crowded around the Celtic bench, and at times Auerbach had to jump up to see over their heads. And what he saw, unbelievably, was Celtic turnovers—*four* of them as the Boston lead dwindled to 95-91 with six seconds to go as Laker Leroy Ellis took a jump shot.

"It's *good!*" Most screamed. "Four seconds left, and the lead is down to *two points!*"

Ellis' basket pulled the plug on crowd noise, and an eerie hush fell over the Garden.

"K.C. with the ball, gets surrounded," Most rasped. "One second. *That's it! It's all over!* Havlicek got the pass and he gets *mobbed! It's alllll over!*"

And in an instant, Auerbach was hoisted onto shoulders amid a sea of bobbing heads and transported to the Celtic locker room for the traditional dunking in the showers.

"I feel drunk," the sopping-wet Auerbach yelled after his dunking, still embracing the game ball from his 885th Celtic victory and 1,037th NBA triumph, "and I haven't even had a drink!"

... Red Auerbach is swallowed up by the crowd as cameras record his last hurrah.

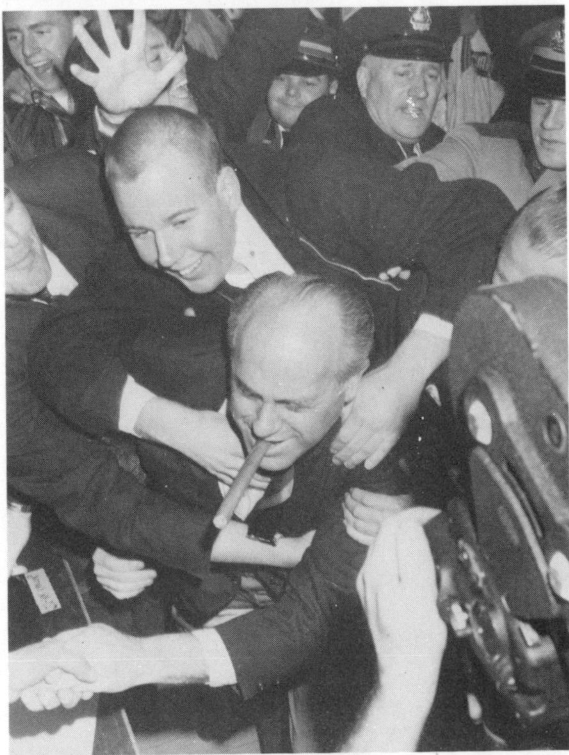

1966–67

Red Auerbach launches Bill Russell's coaching career with—of course—a cigar as the team reported in September. Russell, the first black to direct a major league team in any sport, would lead the Celtics to 60 victories in his first coaching season. Yet by regular season's end, the Celtics would be 8 games off the pace and the two men would discuss the possibility of Auerbach returning to coach during the playoffs.

It looked like another season of frustration at the hands of Bill Russell and the Celtics for Wilt Chamberlain in this December cameo during a Boston victory. But it wasn't to be. Instead, the "new" Wilt finally emerged a winner after seven frustrating years. Playing the best basketball of his career under new 76er coach Alex Hannum, Chamberlain powered Philadelphia to record 68-13 heights to finish 8 games ahead of the Celtics in the regular season and dethrone them, 4-1, in the Eastern finals. In 1980 that 1966-67 Sixer club was voted the best team in NBA history.

It was the Year the Greatest Sports Dynasty Ended. The Celtics were finally dethroned, ending their string of eight NBA championships.

It was Philadelphia's season as the "new" Wilt Chamberlain finally emerged a winner after seven frustrating seasons of being foiled by archrival Bill Russell.

It was also the year the Celtics broke another color line. They had done it first in 1950 by drafting and signing the first black in NBA history, Chuck Cooper. Now they became the first team in any major league directed by a black as Red Auerbach turned over the coaching reins to William Felton Russell.

Red Auerbach:

"Sure that was a rough season on Russ. He didn't enjoy being a player-coach. It's too much for anybody to be the team's top player, rebounder and leader, and have to worry about substitutions, too.

"Yes, we discussed my coming back—temporarily, for the playoffs. But if you make a break, you've got to stick with it. You can't walk in and say to the players, 'OK, boys, it's playoff time. Here I am, your coach again.'

"No, you've got to keep it the same and sink or swim. We sank that year, but not the next."

Bill Russell:

"Wilt and the 76ers beat us in '67 because they were better. They almost ran us off the court."

And Russell directed the Celtics to 60 victories, 6 more than under Auerbach the previous season and matching the second most of any team in Celtic history. Yet that 60-21 record left Boston *eight* games behind the 76ers, whose 68-13 was a league record that easily topped the NBA's previous best of 62-18 by the '64-'65 Celtics.

All season it had been a two-team league. Philadelphia and Boston so dominated the league that only one other of the NBA's 10 teams managed a winning record—San Francisco, under new coach Bill Sharman. But the Warriors weren't even close at 44-37, 16 victories less than Boston's 60, 24 fewer than Philadelphia's 68.

The 76ers were simply awesome under new coach Alex Hannum, the longtime Celtic adversary who had been successful handling Chamberlain at San Francisco. Now Hannum had Wilt playing the best basketball of his career, shooting less (24.1-point average) but rebounding (first in league) and passing (third in league, best ever by a big man) more. Wilt also was teamed with an impressive cast—Chet Walker, Luke Jackson and Billy Cunningham up front, Hal Greer, Wally (Wonder) Jones and a back-from-retirement Larry Costello in the backcourt.

The 76ers won 15 of their first 16 games (losing only at Boston), then skyrocketed to 46-4 (half the losses to the Celtics)—a .920 clip that was unparalleled for that many games in any major league sport. Yet, the Celtics had a 5-4 advantage over the 76ers in their regular-season series.

That gave Boston fans reason for optimism entering the playoffs despite the knowledge that the Celtics were an ageing team. Russell was 33, Sam Jones nearly 34 and K.C. Jones almost 35 as he prepared to retire at season's end. Even the Celts' two key pickups, a pair of

Philadelphia's Wally Jones (24) tries to fight through a Bill Russell pick, and Chet Walker (25) and Luke Jackson (54) close in on John Havlicek during the Eastern finals. Sam Jones (partially hidden by Russell) scored 32 points, Havlicek 31 in this lone Celtic victory of the series to escape the indignity of a sweep.

five-time All-Stars named Bailey Howell (at power forward) and Wayne Embry (as Russell's relief), had turned 30 during the season.

Wayne Embry:

"I had been in a lot of losing playoff locker rooms at Cincinnati, but this was the Celtics' first and I wondered how they'd react.

"You know what I heard in that room? 'OK, guys, let's go congratulate the winners.' There was no crying or anything like that. They just congratulated the winners. And that told me I was still among champions."

It was like old times as the Celtics rolled over the Knicks, 3-1, in the playoffs' opening round. But the Eastern finals against the 76ers were another story. The Celtics could win only one game—the fourth. With the nation watching on Sunday afternoon TV, they avoided the indignity of a sweep by squeezing out a 121-117 victory at Boston behind Sam Jones' 32 points and John Havlicek's 31 as Russell outrebounded Chamberlain, 28-22.

That only postponed the inevitable. The end came two days later at Philadelphia as Convention Hall rocked to the chant of *"Boston is dead! Boston is dead!"*

The Celtics were buried, 140-116, and as the buzzer signaled the end of their reign, many of the 13,007 fans swarmed onto the court in celebration. Russell darted through the crowd to catch up with K.C. Jones, putting an arm around his friend's shoulder as they walked off a basketball floor as teammates for the last time—ending a trail that had taken them from national championships at the University of San Francisco to Olympic gold at Melbourne to a string of Celtic crowns in Boston.

K.C. Jones was one of the few Celtic heroes of the sixties who would go out a loser.

A *loser*—that was a new label for the Celtics.

"And the best way to be a good loser," Russell told reporters afterward, "is to shut up."

The next day, though, John Havlicek had a few words at the club's annual breakup dinner, telling his teammates, "We're only dead until October."

He was right.

It was a season of frustration for new coach Bill Russell as his Celtics chased the 76ers in vain.

'WE'RE ONLY DEAD UNTIL OCTOBER'

April 11, 1967, at Philadelphia

PHILADELPHIA 76ers (140)

	Min.	*FGM*	*FGA*	*FTM*	*FTA*	*Reb.*	*Ast.*	*PF*	*Pts.*
Walker	42	9	14	8	9	12	4	0	26
Jackson	30	3	8	1	1	9	1	2	7
Chamberlain	47	10	16	9	17	36	13	1	29
Greer	47	12	28	8	11	2	4	2	32
Wally Jones	28	10	18	3	6	2	6	5	23
Cunningham	23	5	12	11	12	8	2	4	21
Guokas	23	1	7	0	0	4	5	5	2
Totals	240	50	103	40	56	79	35	20	140

CELTICS (116)

	Min.	*FGM*	*FGA*	*FTM*	*FTA*	*Reb.*	*Ast.*	*PF*	*Pts.*
Howell	26	7	14	1	1	8	0	4	15
Havlicek	48	16	36	6	8	6	2	5	38
Russell	42	2	5	0	1	21	7	5	4
Sam Jones	38	9	25	1	2	2	3	6	19
Siegfried	42	8	18	8	9	6	8	4	24
Sanders	4	0	0	0	0	1	1	2	0
Nelson	11	3	8	0	0	3	1	3	6
Embry	6	0	4	0	0	2	1	3	0
K.C. Jones	16	2	4	0	0	4	1	6	4
Barnett	7	2	4	2	2	2	0	0	6
Totals	240	49	118	18	23	64	24	38	116

Score by Periods:	1	2	3	4
Philadelphia	26	39	35	40—140
Celtics	37	33	24	22—116

Field Goal Percentage: Celtics .485, 76ers .415.
Free Throw Percentage: Celtics .714, 76ers .783.
Referees: Norm Drucker and Mendy Rudolph.
Attendance: 13,007.

1967–68

"Over and over that Summer, people kept asking, 'What happened?'" John Havlicek recalls. "It became very stale after a while, and I got sick of hearing it.

"I think we all came back determined that we weren't going to listen to that again the following summer."

With that objective, the Celtics launched the season with six victories in a row. By late November they were 14-3, by Christmas 25-7. But the Philadelphia 76ers were winning, too—proving that their 1966-67 performance hadn't been a fluke. And by schedule's end, the Sixers were 62-20, eight games ahead of the 54-28 Celtics, in second place for the third straight season.

After their 25-7 start, the Celtics had cooled off, going 29-21 the rest of the way as they faded over the long haul. Hadn't that proven what everyone was saying—that the Celtics were too old? Those reports of their demise had not been exaggerated last year, had they?

Still, entering the playoffs, there was optimism among the Celtics that they could regain their crown.

"We believed we still had more to give," Sam Jones recalls. "We had Russell, and he was the saviour. As long as he stayed healthy, I never worried about winning."

Yet winning *was* a problem for the Celtics in the playoffs' opening round against the Detroit Pistons, led by guard Dave Bing, the league's leading scorer with a 27.1-point average. After taking the opener fairly easily, the Celtics lost the next two games—and their homecourt advantage—and again began reading and hearing all the old-age and has-beens stories again.

Bill Russell then revised his lineup and made John Havlicek a starter, and the former best sixth man in basketball responded with 35-, 18- and 31-point splurges as the Celtics swept the series' final three games to oust the Pistons.

In the Cobo Arena locker room after the clincher, Russell was handed a piece of tickertape showing that the 76ers also had won their semifinal, setting up a Boston-Philadelphia showdown.

Red Auerbach did plenty of talking during training camp at Boston State College. Above, the general manager huddles with player-coach Bill Russell and captain John Havlicek. Below, he addresses the squad (clockwise): Sam Jones, Don Nelson, trainer Joe DeLauri, Wayne Embry, Havlicek, Tom Sanders, Larry Siegfried, Tom Thacker, Russell and Bailey Howell.

Philadelphia's Alex Hannum congratulates rival coach Bill Russell after the Celtics had completed their record comeback from a 3-1 series deficit and upset the 76ers.

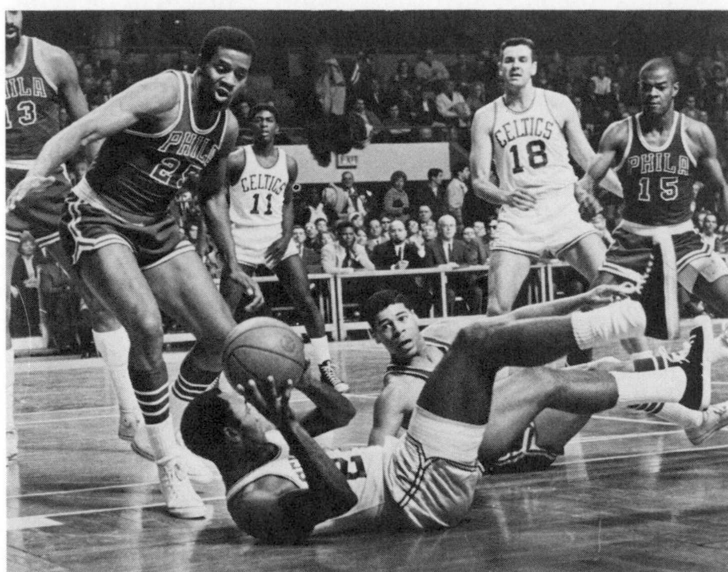

Sam Jones and Philadelphia's Wally (Wonder) Jones collide, and both take a tumble.

"Now," said Russell, one not given to rash promises, "it's going to be different."

It was time for revenge. If the Celtics were to regain their lost crown, they would have to wrench it from the head that wore it. And the Celts took a giant step in that direction in the opener of the Eastern finals at Philadelphia's new Spectrum. They upset the Sixers convincingly, 127-118, as Havlicek continued his acceleration toward superstardom with 35 points while Sam Jones added 28 and Bailey Howell 24.

The victory took place the night after Martin Luther King's assassination. After consulting with Russell and Wilt Chamberlain as team representatives, it had been decided to play the opener on schedule, since no funeral arrangements had been set, then postpone the remainder of the series for five days.

Those five days gave the 76ers a chance to regroup and mend a rash of injuries, and they stormed back to win the next three games. Now it seemed an impossible task for the old, tired and bruised Celtics to beat the mighty Sixers three straight, especially with two of those games scheduled for Philadelphia.

No NBA team had ever lost a seven-game series at any playoff level after leading 3-1.

"Before the next game," Wayne Embry recalls, "John Havlicek and I walked into the locker room and wrote 'PRIDE' on the blackboard in great big letters."

Corny? Perhaps, but as Tom (Satch) Sanders says, "The things other people laughed at, the Celtics believed in."

Bailey Howell lays ball up over Philadelphia's Luke Jackson.

Whatever the stimulus, the Celtics bounced back to humble the 76ers, 122-104, to disappoint the Philadelphians who had packed the Spectrum to witness a Celtic guillotining for the second straight year.

"I don't want this season to end," Havlicek said after contributing 29 points and 10 assists while playing all 48 minutes. "In a game like this, if all your guts fall out you just pick them up, stuff them back and keep going."

Satch Sanders and Wilt Chamberlain soar for a rebound during playoff action as the Celtics became the first NBA team ever to trail 3-1 in a series and win—dethroning the defending world champion 76ers in the Eastern finals.

Tom (Satch) Sanders:

"I'll always remember that playoff series with Philadelphia because it made me appreciate one of basketball's most simple and effective plays—the pick and roll.

"We kept running it over and over, again and again—I'd say at least 20 percent of the time—and Philadelphia just couldn't deal with it.

"It was our #2 play—very effective against man-to-man—with Russell, who always set an effective pick, simply going into a high post for a shooter—whoever was there. If Sam was there, it was Sam. If Havlicek was there, it was Havlicek.

"It forced Wilt into a switching situation, and he sort of refused. And when he did switch, he had problems with Sam or Havlicek.

"What had happened was this: When we got behind in that series, we had to sit down and see what had worked against Philadelphia in the past, then go with it. The answer was the pick and roll, and we stuck with it.

"It became our bread-and-butter play and they just couldn't stop it, so we ran it to death. Besides taking a lot of communication and agility, it took a lot of concentration and discipline to keep using it because going with the same play tends to be boring, and we were a team that could do a lot of things. But we had the discipline to stick with it, and it paid.

"Our comeback from the 3-1 deficit in that series was a very disciplined presentation of basketball."

CELTICS DETHRONE THE 76ERS

April 19, 1968, at Philadelphia

CELTICS (100)	FG	FT	Pts	PHILADELPHIA 76ERS (96)	FG	FT	Pts.
Embry	0	0	20	Green	1	2	4
Havlicek	7	7	21	Greer	8	6	22
Howell	8	1	17	Guokas	2	0	4
Sam Jones	9	4	22	Jackson	7	1	15
Nelson	5	0	10	Wally Jones	8	2	18
Russell	4	4	12	Chamberlain	4	6	14
Siegfried	7	4	18	Melchionni	0	0	0
Thacker	0	0	0	Walker	8	3	19
Totals	40	20	100	*Totals*	38	20	96

Score by periods:	1	2	3	4
Celtics	26	20	27	27—100
76ers	21	19	29	27—96

Attendance: 15,202.

Larry Siegfried aggravates his back injury and is attended to by trainer Joe DeLauri and John Havlicek.

And the Celtics kept going, winning the next two games including the 100-96 finale at Philadelphia—dethroning the Sixers in the same city where the Celts had yielded their throne the previous Spring.

"They deserved to win. They were tougher," said Wilt Chamberlain, who oddly had shot only twice during the second half in what was to be his final game as a Sixer. (He would be wearing a different uniform the following season when opposing Boston in another memorable playoff series.)

"Yes, this is the most satisfying victory of my career—so far," said Russell, his first NBA title as a coach now clearly in sight. "But we haven't won anything until we win the championship."

Standing between the Celtics and that championship were the Los Angeles Lakers. The *rested* Los Angeles Lakers. They had been relaxing six days after breezing through the Western playoffs with eight victories in nine games—while the Celtics were bone-weary after coming from behind in two pressure series.

The old rivals split the first four games. The Celtics then captured the next two—clinching decisively at Los Angeles' new Forum, 124-109, as Havlicek scored 40 points, Howell 30 and Larry Siegfried 22 (and added two of his trademarked headlong dives along the floor to recover key loose balls).

For the third straight series in these playoffs, the Celtics had clinched in the opponent's backyard to regain the title the hard way.

So, for the 10th time in 12 years, the Celtics again were world champions.

Their dynasty wasn't over after all. It had just been interrupted briefly.

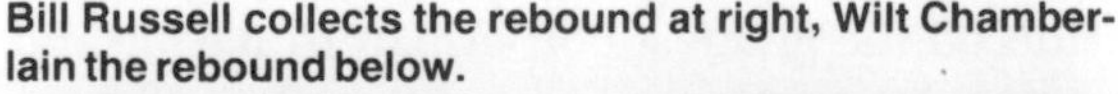

Bill Russell collects the rebound at right, Wilt Chamberlain the rebound below.

CELTICS REGAIN NBA CHAMPIONSHIP

May 2, 1968, at Los Angeles

CELTICS (124)	FG	FT	Pts.	LOS ANGELES LAKERS (109)	FG	FT	Pts.
Embry	0	0	0	Baylor	13	2	28
Havlicek	14	12	40	Clark	7	3	17
Howell	13	4	30	Counts	5	1	11
Sanders	0	0	0	Crawford	3	0	6
Nelson	2	0	4	Goodrich	5	1	11
Russell	5	2	12	Hawkins	6	0	12
Johnny Jones	1	0	2	Imhoff	1	0	2
Sam Jones	6	0	12	Mueller	0	0	0
Siegfried	7	8	22	West	8	6	22
Graham	0	0	0				
Thacker	0	0	0				
Weitzman	1	0	2				
Totals	49	26	124	*Totals*	48	13	109

Score by periods:	1	2	3	4
Celtics	35	35	24	30—124
Lakers	28	22	28	31—109

Field Goal Percentage: Celtics .505, Lakers .475.
Free Throw Percentage: Celtics .897, Lakers .500.
Referees: Norm Drucker and Earl Strom.
Attendance: 17,392.

1968–69

World champions again, the Celtics are welcomed back to Boston's Logan Airport by a crowd that includes Massachusetts Governor Francis Sargent—shaking hands with Bill Russell, who is careful not to drop his bottle of champagne.

It all came down to one final game—the seventh game of the NBA finals at Los Angeles.

The coronation of the Lakers was set after years of frustration as perennial bridesmaid to the Celtics. With three of basketball's all-time greats now in their lineup, the Lakers finally would be champions of the world.

Fittingly, the crowning would take place at home—in the gleaming neo-Roman Forum for the long-suffering Laker followers to see.

Jack Kent Cooke had made all the arrangements. Nets filled with thousands of balloons clung to the ceiling, to be cut loose at the moment of victory. The USC Trojan Marching Band was poised beneath the stands, ready to strut onto the court blaring *Happy Days Are Here Again.* A playoff record 17,568 spectators would explode in victory celebration. And cases of champagne awaited the Lakers, stacked in the hallway outside their locker room.

But a funny thing happened at the Forum that Monday night in early May. The over-the-hill Celtics jumped to a 12-point lead over Wilt Chamberlain, Jerry West, Elgin Baylor and the other Lakers, expanded it to 17 in the third period, then held on at the end for a 108-106 victory and their 11th NBA title in 13 years.

"What are they going to do with all those blankety-blank balloons now?" general manager Red Auerbach laughed as he pointed toward the rafters while running off the floor and darting beneath the stands, where the USC musicians were packing up their instruments. "Anybody want to buy some balloons cheap?"

That was Auerbach's second deflating quote of the season at Laker expense.

The first had come when Los Angeles acquired Chamberlain to give the Lakers a weapon to cope with Bill Russell for the first time. Wilt was the superstar big man they had always lacked to go along with what many considered the greatest cornerman in Baylor and the greatest backcourtman in West.

The Lakers now were labeled the "greatest basketball team ever assembled," and there were forecasts that they would run away from the rest of the league.

"Don't forget," Auerbach had responded to such talk, "you still play this game with only one basketball."

And the Lakers hadn't exactly run away from the NBA West pack, but had little difficulty winning the division by 7 games. Meanwhile, the Celtics, handicapped by old age and the injuries that went with it, struggled to fourth place, their lowest finish in 20 seasons, 9 games behind first-place Baltimore in NBA East.

Sam Jones, who had announced he'd retire at season's end, was the oldest player in the league at nearly 36. Bill Russell, who had been mulling retirement for some time and some suspected would quit after the playoffs, was 35. The Celtics could also start three others in the 30 bracket: Bailey Howell, 32, Tom (Satch) Sanders, 30, and retread newcomer Emmette Bryant, 30. And even John Havlicek, Don Nelson and Larry Siegfried all were—could it be?—29 or close to it. The average age of Boston's eight regulars was a creaky 31.

So, was there any doubt the Celtics were over the hill? Besides their fourth-place finish, wasn't the succession of injuries that wracked them all season another symptom of old age?

Well, some debated that. They claimed the wily Celtics were simply pacing old legs, playing well enough to qualify but saving their energy for the playoffs that decide the champion.

BILL RUSSELL, SAM JONES BOW OUT WITH TITLE

May 5, 1969, at Los Angeles

CELTICS (108)

	Min.	*FGA*	*FGM*	*FTA*	*FTM*	*Reb.*	*Ast.*	*PF*	*Pts.*
Havlicek	48	19	11	7	4	9	5	5	26
Bryant	42	21	9	3	2	5	3	4	20
Howell	23	11	4	2	1	4	0	4	9
Jones	32	16	10	4	4	7	2	6	24
Nelson	25	12	6	7	4	6	2	5	16
Siegfried	22	9	2	4	3	2	2	5	7
Russell	48	7	2	4	2	21	6	5	6
Totals	240	95	44	31	20	59	20	34	108

LOS ANGELES LAKERS (106)

	Min.	*FGA*	*FGM*	*FTA*	*FTM*	*Reb.*	*Ast.*	*PF*	*Pts.*
Baylor	43	22	8	5	4	15	7	4	20
Chamberlain	43	8	7	13	4	27	3	5	18
Counts	21	13	4	2	1	7	1	4	9
Egan	27	10	3	6	3	3	4	4	9
Erickson	39	11	2	3	2	7	3	6	6
Hawkins	19	4	1	0	0	2	0	4	2
West	48	29	14	18	14	13	12	2	42
Totals	240	97	39	47	28	80	30	29	106

Score by Periods:	1	2	3	4
Celtics	28	31	32	17—108
Lakers	25	31	20	30—106

Field Goal Percentage: Celtics .463, Lakers .402.
Free Throw Percentage: Celtics .645, Lakers .596.
Team Rebounds: Celtics 5, Lakers 6.
Turnovers: Celtics 11, Lakers 14.
Referees: Mendy Rudolph and Earl Strom.
Attendance: 17,568.

"No, we haven't been saving ourselves," Sam Jones said. "It's just that we haven't had the same lineup all season because of all the injuries. But now everyone's healthy for the playoffs."

There was yet another factor, and only one Celtic knew of it. "About midway through that season I decided that I was playing my last year," Russell would reveal later. "We were hoping to win a last championship for Sam. Privately, I dedicated myself to leaving just as happy as Sam at season's end."

Whatever the reasons, the Celtics breezed through the first two rounds over teams that had finished ahead of them in the standings—eliminating second-place Philadelphia, 4-1, then third-place New York (which had a 6-1 advantage over Boston during the regular season), 4-2.

Bill Russell:

"We had more material in other years. But no team ever had more guts than that one."

It also took Los Angeles only 11 games to advance to the finals.

The Celtics were defending champions, but the Lakers were favored. Besides the other reasons, there was this clincher: L.A. not only had a 4-2 edge in their regular-season series, but one of those victories had been a 108-73 rout at Boston during a nationally televised embarrassment in March, a 35-point drubbing that ranked among the worst since the Celtic franchise's early days. And, finally, there was the matter of Laker homecourt advantage if the series went to a seventh game.

And it did come down to that seventh-game showdown after the teams divided the first six games, each winning before home fans.

One of the Celtic victories had been an 89-88 thriller in the fourth game. The Lakers had the ball and a 1-point lead with 15 seconds left, but Bryant stole the ball. After a timeout with 7 seconds remaining, Howell set a pick for Sam Jones—but Sam slipped as he began to shoot, and the ball fell short. It hit the front rim, hit the back rim, teetered teasingly, then fell through for the win as Boston Garden shook.

Approaching 36, Sam Jones played one final season—as always the lethal shooter, as he is here against the Hawks.

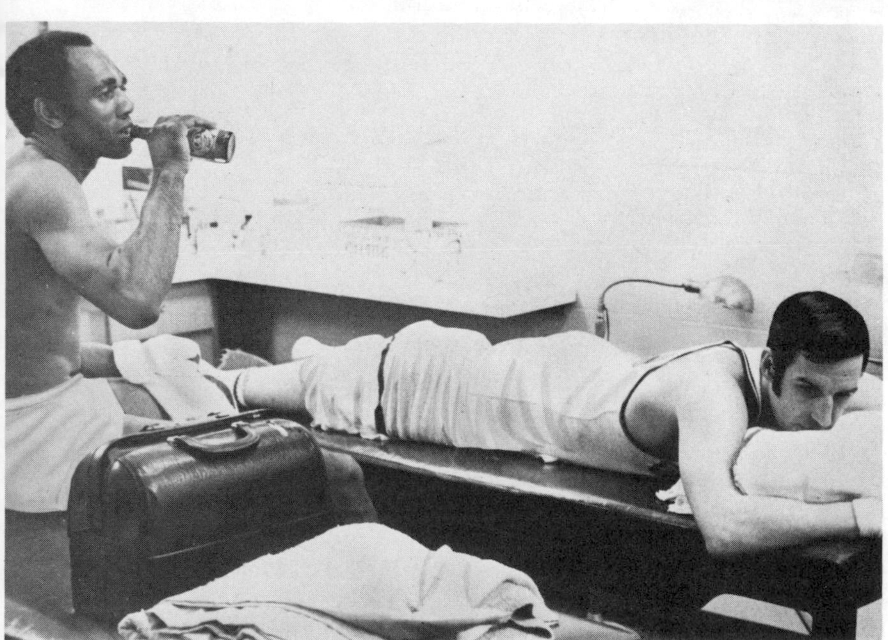

Sam Jones and Larry Siegfried enjoy a quiet toast in the trainer's room after the Celtics eliminated the Knicks, 4-2, to win the Eastern finals and advance to the NBA title series.

John Havlicek and New York's Bill Bradley shadowed each other in the Eastern finals.

Bill Russell had a memorable final season as a Celtic.

"I tried to pull the shot back, couldn't, then just wanted to hit the basket so Russ could put in the rebound," Sam explained afterward. He had forgotten that Russell wasn't in the game, having taken himself out during the timeout to get Sanders, a better foul shooter, into the game.

Now it was all down to one game at Los Angeles, and a nation watched on ABC.

Boston jumped to leads of 17-9 and 24-12. But L.A. closed to 28-25 at quarter's end. The halftime margin was the same, 59-56 Boston.

The Lakers tied the score at 60, then went cold, missing 15 shots and not scoring a point for 5 minutes and 24 seconds. The Celtics took advantage to rebuild their lead to 11, and by the final seconds of the third period Boston was up by 17, 91-74.

The Lakers nibbled away at that lead in the fourth period, but with less than 5½ minutes to go the Celtics led, 103-94. Then something happened that is still debated not only by fans but by the principals.

Chamberlain limped to the sidelines after hurting a knee while coming down with a rebound, and took himself out of the game.

Bill Russell rejects a shot by Jerry West during the NBA finals. West would be voted the playoffs' MVP as he scored a record 556 points, including 42 in the final game. But the superstar guard would be frustrated by the Celtics again—and with an ironic postscript. The color of the automobile he received as playoff MVP was—incredibly—*Celtic Green.*

(Russell later would indicate that Wilt should not have left the game for any reason less than a broken leg. The criticism ruptured a longtime friendship, creating bad feeling between the men. It also was a clue that Russell was retiring, because he never would have publicly antagonized his archrival had he intended to oppose him again on a basketball court.)

Mel Counts, the former Celtic, replaced Wilt and helped rally the Lakers to within a point, 103-102, with 3:07 remaining.

Chamberlain indicated he had sufficiently recovered to return, but coach Butch van Breda Kolff refused to put him back in (and it would help cost him his job). The pair had openly disagreed much of the season, and now were exchanging bitter words on the bench as the world championship was being decided.

Meanwhile, the Forum was vibrating in anticipation of a last-minute victory.

Eighty seconds remained, and the ageing Celtics were fading. Havlicek set for a quick shot to avoid a 24-second violation, but the ball was knocked loose—and picked up by Nelson to the right of the key. The ex-Laker's desperation 15-footer struck the back rim, bounded straight up about three feet, then dramatically dropped straight through the basket—*swish!*

"I rushed the shot to beat the clock," Nelson recalls. "It didn't 'feel' good and I didn't think it'd go in. I was just hoping it'd hit the rim in time and we'd have a chance at the rebound."

The basket gave the Celtics a three-point cushion for the final 77 seconds, and they improved it to 108-102 before allowing a couple of free throws and a meaningless basket at the buzzer: *108-106.*

The Celtic dynasty wasn't dead yet. And of all the 11 world championships, in many ways this was the Celtics' sweetest—hammered out after they had been written off as has-beens.

Red Auerbach:

"That seventh game will always be one of my favorites. Not only was most everything in the Lakers' favor, but Jack Kent Cooke got stuck with a lot of balloons in his rafters.

"And Russ and Sam went out winners."

Jerry West:

"I couldn't believe it had happened again. Not this time, not again. I had been disappointed by the Celtics before, but this was the worst. It was so hard because I felt we had the better team this time. In other years I could rationalize our setbacks, but not this one. It was almost like we weren't supposed to win.

"I just sat in the awful quiet of our locker room listening to all the noise coming through the walls from the Boston players celebrating in the next room. I couldn't stand listening to it.

"I didn't cry, but I sure wanted to."

John Havlicek shoos over-eager fans off the Boston Garden court with one second remaining in Game 4 and the Celtics leading, 89-88. The Celtics won the game to even the title series.

Usually even-tempered John Havlicek argues with Darell Garretson (33), and as the Celtic captain becomes more emphatic Ed Rush steps in with a restraining hand. Mostly, though, Havlicek played non-stop basketball and again led the team in scoring—averaging 21.6 points during the regular schedule, 25.4 in the playoffs.

1969–70

Bill Russell visited Boston Garden and took a bow a few days after being named NBA Player of the 1960s by the Associated Press. Controversially, Russell would not acknowledge an even longer ovation two years later on the day his No. 6 was retired.

Tom Heinsohn was often frustrated and sometimes angry, and his sideline histrionics invited technical fouls and sometimes the wrath of hometown fans.

Skeptics suspected Tom Heinsohn was a coaching puppet for Red Auerbach.

Bill Russell the superstar was gone. Bill Russell the coach was gone. Sam Jones the slick sharpshooter was gone.

And now Tom Heinsohn's right shoe was gone—sailing high and deep into the Boston Garden seats during a game. With form that Garo Yepremian would have admired, the Celtics' new coach had taken a kick at a towel in front of the bench, and *oops.*

Heinsohn—angry, frustrated and now embarrassed—stood there grimacing, hands on hips, one loafer on and one loafer off, as a ballboy was dispatched into the elevated loges to retrieve the shoe.

It was a cameo that summed up a season of embarrassment, anger and frustration for Heinsohn as he began rebuilding the depleted Celtics to respectability.

Havlicek, Nelson, Sanders and Howell were back at forward, and Siegfried and Bryant had returned at guard. But Howell and Sanders not only were a year older but sometimes ailing, and Siegfried and Bryant soon were feuding with Heinsohn.

Most of all, Heinsohn had to find a center. Jim (Bad News) Barnes, Russell's 6-foot-8 backup the previous season, wasn't the answer. Nor was 6-foot-9 Rich Johnson, who had played only 168 minutes in 1968-69 as the team's third-round draftee. Nor was 7-foot Rich Niemann in six games after being acquired on waivers from Milwaukee early in the season.

The new center would be a 7-footer named Hank Finkel, promptly dubbed "High Henry" by Johnny Most, the master of alliteration. Purchased from San Diego, the former Dayton All-America had only limited experience in three pro seasons. But he was willing and intelligent, and he had a good shot, both inside and out.

Unfortunately, Finkel also appeared to be a gentle giant, his genuine nice-guy manner showing through. He also had the impossible job of following the graceful and immense Russell in the Celtic pivot, probably the toughest act to follow in NBA history. The comparison was as inevitable as it was unfair, and it left Finkel looking clumsy.

The result was predictable. Although later in his six-season Celtic career he would become immensely popular as a reserve, almost a folk hero, that first year Finkel was an immediate (and unmistakably large) target for Boston boo birds. He and Heinsohn would absorb the brunt of the fans' hostility as the team struggled through its rebirth.

The Celtics lost the opener to Cincinnati, 110-108, in a return of two natives to Boston Garden—new Royals coach Bob Cousy facing longtime Celt teammate and carpoolmate Heinsohn in a matchup of rookie pro coaches.

The Celtics went on to drop their first four games and 11 of 14 to sink to the bottom of NBA East. And as they tumbled, so did attendance. Six times fewer than 5,000 showed up at the Garden, including only 3,944 for the Lakers in early December.

But those who did show up were vocal, scorching Heinsohn and Finkel with jeers and taunts.

"They're only frustrated," shrugged the good-natured Finkel. "Their frustration is aimed at me because Russell was so great and I can't do the things he did."

Heinsohn was maligned for different reasons, a variety of them.

John Havlicek:

"In the last few years we had kept winning because we were so good defensively. We'd just pushed everything toward Russell and let him take care of it.

"After Russ left, we still had a lot of capable people, but we had no dominating figure at center. I don't say that condemning Henry. We expected him to do a job like Russell did, and that wasn't fair.

"But the fact is, when Russ left we went from being one of the best defensive teams to one of the lesser defensive teams. And that's where games are won: defense.

"So that's where he had to improve in a hurry."

Captain John Havlicek accepts the 1969 NBA championship trophy for the defending champion Celtics on opening night from league commissioner Walter Kennedy.

Henry Finkel, the Celtics' new center, collides with Baltimore's Jack Marin at left and Los Angeles' Mel Counts at right. Finkel, a 7-footer acquired from San Diego, had the toughest act to follow in NBA history—Bill Russell.

ROOKIE JO JO COMES OF AGE

January 28, 1970, at Boston Garden

CELTICS (112)	FG	FT	Pts.	PHILADELPHIA 76ERS (100)	FG	FT	Pts.
Barnes	1	1	3	Clark	10	10	30
Bryant	0	0	0	Cunningham	9	3	21
Finkel	7	1	15	Guokas	4	0	8
Havlicek	8	6	22	Hetzel	0	2	2
Howell	4	3	11	Imhoff	4	6	14
Johnson	0	1	1	Jones	6	1	13
Kuberski	1	0	2	Ogden	0	0	0
Nelson	4	0	8	Washington	5	1	11
Sanders	6	4	16	Wilson	0	1	1
Siegfried	3	0	6				
White	12	4	28				
Totals	46	20	112	*Totals*	38	24	100

Score by periods:	1	2	3	4
Celtics	27	25	30	30—112
76ers	32	13	23	32—100

Referees: Richie Powers and John Parker.
Attendance: 5,287.

The obvious one was the fact that fans (and much of the press) still weren't convinced that Heinsohn was the coach. He had been appointed at the start of training camp as general manager Red Auerbach left the gym door open until literally the last minute in case Russell changed his mind about retirement. And even when Heinsohn got the job, there was a suspicion that he was simply a puppet for Auerbach.

Tom Heinsohn:

"It was not the easiest year to be coach of the Boston Celtics."

It was difficult for Heinsohn to shed his old image of being Auerbach's whipping boy. Would Red entrust the team to a player he so often had criticized? And even if he would, how basketball smart could Heinsohn be if Auerbach had rapped him so much as a player over the years? Both questions contributed to the skepticism that Heinsohn was really running the club. Some cynics even suggested that Auerbach was using hand signals to instruct Heinsohn from the press row, where the general manager sometimes sat, or from his box across the floor.

And, finally, there were the sideline histrionics of the demonstrative Heinsohn, basketball's man of 1,000 faces. These antics may have vented the rookie coach's frustration, but they also invited technical fouls and tended to incite the Boston crowd, sometimes against him.

Meanwhile, the team hustled and scrapped—and lost. And as it continued to lose, Heinsohn more and more began building for the future by going with the club's youngsters.

Top draftee Jo Jo White, the former Olympian who missed training camp and the first dozen games because of Marine Corps Reserve duty, was showing signs of being the playmaking guard the Celtics hoped would lead them back. He also was expected to be a scorer, an adjustment from his college role at Kansas, and by late January he was hitting in the 20s consistently, including a 28-point splurge and a couple of 26-point games.

Top draft choice Jo Jo White missed training camp and the first dozen games because of Marine Corps duty (right). Above, he makes his Celtic debut, watching the early action from the bench before going in and scoring 5 points against Baltimore at Boston.

White often teamed in the backcourt with another key to the youth movement, Don Chaney. The former University of Houston star also was a No. 1 draft choice but hadn't been used much as a rookie the previous season. He was a defensive standout who needed to cultivate his shooting to keep opponents honest.

And the new blood among the forwards was Steve Kuberski, a 6-foot-8 boardbanger who decided to forego his final season at Bradley after Boston drafted him No. 3.

"When it became clear we weren't going anywhere," Heinsohn recalls, "I turned the rest of the season over to the kids—White, Chaney and Kuberski.

"It was a season to forget anyway."

For the first time in exactly 20 years, the Celtics missed the playoffs. Their 34-48 record translated into 26 games behind the first-place Knicks in NBA East, but three games ahead of the Pistons to mercifully escape the distinction of going from the NBA championship to a division cellar in one year.

Steve Kuberski and Don Chaney were keys to Celtic rebuilding along with Jo Jo White. Kuberski, at left above with fellow forward Don Nelson, was a 6-foot-8 boardbanger who signed despite having another season of college eligibility. It was Nelson who urged Auerbach to draft Kuberski, a neighbor from Moline, Illinois. At left, Chaney, on far right with backcourt veterans Emmette Bryant (7) and Larry Siegfried (20), was a defensive standout who hadn't played much as the Celtics' top draftee the previous season.

Larry Siegfried had a busy last season as a Celtic. He and Tom Heinsohn, friendly as teammates, didn't get along in their new coach-player relationship. To the satisfaction of both, Siegfried was gone at season's end—and played two more seasons with the Rockets and Hawks.

Larry Siegfried (20) and Philadelphia's Wally Jones clash in a November brawl that brought Celtic alumnus Gene Conley galloping down from the stands as a peacemaker to pull apart the combatants.

1970–71

"Boston drafts Dave Cowens of Florida State."

Those seven words—selecting the second prominent redhead in Celtic history on the first round of the NBA's 1970 college draft—are among the more momentous ever spoken by Red Auerbach.

Cowens would prove the crucial man in the middle that coach Tom Heinsohn needed so desperately in his rebuilding scheme to go along with veterans John Havlicek, Tom (Satch) Sanders and Don Nelson and the emerging Jo Jo White, Don Chaney and Steve Kuberski.

Rookie Dave Cowens checks the fine print of his new three-year contract totaling an estimated $270,000.

Tom Heinsohn:

"With David aboard, I knew it would just be a matter of time before we'd be back on top. But Rome wasn't built in a day. We were trying to phase out one dynasty and phase in another."

"Cowens was exactly what we needed, the key missing part," Heinsohn would say years later. "The first time I saw Dave in training camp he was a 6-9 Havlicek, and he's never stopped running. All I had to do was wind him up, which is how I made Dave Cowens the new Bill Russell of the Boston Celtics."

Cowens had been scouted by Mal Graham, the onetime No. 1 draft choice out of NYU whose Celtic career had been cut short by a physical disability after just two seasons in the late-1960s.

Graham reported back to Auerbach bubbling with enthusiasm about the rugged Cowens' size, shooting, defensive abilities, mobility, speed and tireless, can-run-all-day endurance. And Graham, a black, added: "He's the best-jumping white man I've ever seen."

Auerbach took a look for himself. "Cowens scared me the first time I scouted him," he recalls. "He was so good I kept hoping he'd make a mistake. There were some scouts from other teams there, and I figured if they saw the same potential that I did, we were dead."

The only question was whether at 6-foot-8½ Cowens was big enough to play the pivot in the NBA. Even if not, he figured to be an extraordinary forward.

So Auerbach sweated out whether Cowens would be available when Boston's turn came in the draft. The Celtics were fortunate on

Red Auerbach and team president Jack Waldron congratulate each other after getting Dave Cowens in the NBA draft, held by telephonic hookup around the league. The Celtics' draft brain trust includes (at left) coach Tom Heinsohn and scout Mal Graham, a Celtic No. 1 draft choice himself in 1967, whose glowing reports on Cowens included the label of "best-jumping white man I've ever seen."

two counts. One was that they would draft fourth, their highest selection since 1950, a silver lining to last season's collapse. The other was that Florida State had been banned from NCAA tournaments the last two years because of recruiting violations, so Cowens hadn't received the national exposure usually attracted by the star of a 20-2 team, the only team to beat national runnerup Jacksonville and 7-foot-2 Artis Gilmore during the regular schedule.

Still, Auerbach held his breath as, in order, Detroit chose Bob Lanier, San Diego picked Rudy Tomjanovich and Atlanta took Pete Maravich in the draft's coast-to-coast telephone hookup among clubs.

That's when a relieved Auerbach picked up the speaker in his Boston office and spoke the seven words that changed the course of Celtic history by naming Cowens as Boston's choice.

The general manager was ecstatic, and so were other members of the Celtic family once they got to see Cowens perform with a basketball.

Sanders saw Cowens in action that summer and recalls: "All the ingredients were there. And I kept thinking how nice it was going to be working with a real horse again."

Havlicek and Nelson saw Cowens, too, and concurred.

Debate on whether Cowens was big enough to compete against 7-footers in the NBA pivot continued through training camp. When the season opened, Cowens was at forward and another 6-foot-9 rookie, Garfield Smith, was working at center with Henry Finkel.

In the opener at New York, Cowens made his NBA debut and overpowered veteran all-pro Dave DeBusschere with 16 points and 17 rebounds. And two days later at Philadelphia, in his second pro game, Cowens scored 27 points.

Heinsohn soon shifted him to center, where Cowens preferred—to be, as *Boston Herald American* columnist Joe Fitzgerald has written, Boston's David dueling everyone else's Goliath.

"I was totally fascinated by Cowens," Heinsohn recalls. "Russell revolutionized the game during my day and now I could see that David was going to do the same thing in his day. He was going to prove you don't have to be a big stud to win. Sure, Russell was only 6-9 on paper, but those tremendously long arms and super jumping ability made him, in effect, a 7-footer. Dave is nowhere near as big.

"There are two factors in playing center: size and quickness. Dave was going to prove that quickness would be just as important as size. But to do that he had to play the game with greater intensity than any other center.

"He had to make every game a test of stamina. Other centers were forced to play his style and just couldn't do it. They stayed with him in the first quarter. In the second quarter they fell a step behind. By the third quarter it was obvious they couldn't take the pace. And by the final period, they were completely unable to play their own style.

"Cowens made them play differently than anybody else did. Most teams wait for their centers to catch up on offense, but Cowens is right in the middle of the offense from the start. Nobody has to wait for David. And that means his opponent must run faster than he's used to.

"It's really noticeable in the other team's defense. Opposing centers are forced to come out after Dave, which means their teammates aren't able to play a funnel defense against us the way they did with Russell.

COWENS OUTSCORES ALCINDOR, 36-26

February 28, 1971, at Boston Garden

CELTICS (99)	FG	FT	Pts.	MILWAUKEE BUCKS (111)	FG	FT	Pts.
Cowens	16	4	36	Alcinder	9	8	26
Dinwiddie	1	0	2	Boozer	4	1	9
Finkel	0	0	0	Cunningham	1	0	2
Havlicek	9	3	21	Dandridge	7	2	16
Kuberski	1	1	3	McGlocklin	6	1	13
Nelson	3	8	14	McLemore	1	2	4
White	7	0	14	Robertson	9	6	24
Chaney	1	1	3	G. Smith	7	1	15
Williams	3	0	6	Hebb	1	0	2
Totals	41	17	99	*Totals*	45	21	111

Score by periods:	1	2	3	4
Bucks	27	23	33	28—111
Celtics	33	26	17	23—99

Referees: Richie Powers and Ken Hudson.
Attendance: 10,880.

Dave Cowens scored his season-high 36 points while going head-to-head with 7-foot-2 sophomore Lew Alcindor, who was leading Milwaukee to the NBA title.

"What's more, David takes such a toll on his opponents that they're forced to come out of the lineup more often. And when that happens, the other teams must change their entire strategy.

"Dave is a remarkable kid. He's the consummate athlete, willing to bust his fanny every night for you. And when the others see him diving all over the floor for loose balls, it makes everyone play harder, too. He's a great inspiration."

So Heinsohn took Cowens aside and told him: "David, you're going to play center like no one's ever played it before. You're going to make your man run up the floor so hard he's going to get dead tired. You're going to wear him out."

Which was fine with Cowens.

"Most of the players I go against are a lot taller, but that doesn't bother me," he said then. "I can run the 100-yard dash with anyone in the league. To be effective, I have to use my speed all the time. I've got to force the bigger guys out of their patterns and into mine.

"Bill Russell? Hey, don't compare us. Russell was Russell and I'm me. He's the best defensive player in basketball history. I don't have the physical abilities in that respect. But I'm a better offensive player than he was."

Russell was among those who said Cowens belonged in the pivot.

"Play him there. He'll do the job," Russell advised. "Forget about his height. The way he jumps he's big enough. And nobody is going to intimidate him."

Dave Cowens was a rugged competitor.

Another Celtic alumnus agreed.

"Cowens intimidates *you* with hustle," K.C. Jones said. "He blocks shots, dives for loose balls and never stops running. You don't find people his size doing that."

Nelson pointed out something else at midseason.

"I've heard one comment over and over from opponents: They're *afraid* of him," Nellie said. "They think he's a crazy man, because they know if they get in his way he'll knock them down. That's one of the many ways David makes up for what he lacks in size."

By February, Cowens was scoring 36 points while going head-to-head with a 7-foot-2 Milwaukee sophmore named Lew Alcindor and powering 28 rebounds and 22 points in a game at Philadelphia.

Still, the Celtics were consistently inconsistent as they continued to suffer from growing pains.

Dave Cowens:

"We made a lot of mistakes that season. With inexperience came inconsistency. But we tried to learn from our errors. And while we did they stuck with us. They kept us together and gave us time to learn."

The result was a rollercoaster ride. The Celtics beat the San Francisco Warriors by 30 points, lost to them by 38, then beat them by 30 again. They beat the San Diego Rockets by 30, lost to them by 24. They beat the Cincinnati Royals by 18, lost to them by 19. And they beat the Baltimore Bullets by 46, and lost to them by 19.

The erratic play left captain and perfectionist John Havlicek fuming at one point: "This is the dumbest team I ever played on!"

Havlicek was the glue that held the Celtics together, and that season averaged 28.9 points and 45.4 minutes a game—still Celtic records.

By season's end, the Celtics had won 10 more games than they had the previous year—their 44-38 record the eighth-best among the league's 17 teams. And although they didn't make the playoffs for the second straight year, the Celtics' record was better than those of three teams that did qualify from inferior divisions.

"I played OK for my first time around," reviewed Cowens, who averaged 15 points and 17 rebounds and would be voted the league's best rookie by the players and share the official Rookie of the Year award with Portland's Geoff Petrie in balloting by the media. "But we didn't make the playoffs, so I didn't play well enough."

Heinsohn had no complaints.

"We had kids on this club who didn't know what they were doing in September," he said. "They didn't know the league and had never played an 82-game schedule. And they still damn near made the playoffs in what was suppose to be a grooming year.

"There's talent here, but like a good stew it has to simmer awhile. This is going to be one very good ballclub in the very near future."

John Havlicek was the glue that held the Celtics together—averaging 28.9 points (second in the league to Lew Alcindor's 31.7) and 45.4 minutes a game, still Celtic records. Havlicek also led the team in assists with a 7.5 average, fourth best in the league.

1971–72

Tom Heinsohn preps the Celtics for their first playoffs in three years after winning their first Eastern Division title since 1965.

Tom Heinsohn liked to compare the building of his ideal basketball team to constructing a rich beef stew or a spicy spaghetti sauce. Choose good ingredients, get them bubbling and simmering together, and maybe add a dash of oregano somewhere along the line. Ultimately, everything enhances everything else.

The coach could sense that blend during the 1970-71 season when his Celtics were developing into a cohesive group of role players based around a workhorse center named Dave Cowens, a budding playmaker/shooter in Jo Jo White and a perpetual-motion marvel in John Havlicek.

Around them, the coach placed a textbook defensive forward in sly veteran Tom (Satch) Sanders, an aggressive young defensive guard in Don Chaney, a banging inside forward named Steve Kuberski and a wily old shooting forward, Don Nelson.

Together they played a full-tilt running game tied to assertive defense, forcing opponents to work 24 seconds for a basket and then getting it back in seven.

The Celtics' 44-38 record the previous season would have won the Central Division and qualified the Celtics for the playoffs. Now, with another year of development behind them, Boston expected no less. The resurrection was complete; now, the renaissance.

Yet Heinsohn had no illusions about their dramatic improvement.

"You are good because you are quick," he told his team. "You are great when you are quick and aggressive. You're not the kind of team that can win on an off-night the way the Bucks, Knicks and Lakers can. Anything you accomplish will be the result of hard work and hustle."

Those qualities, Heinsohn stressed, would bring crucial consistency. And if nothing else, the 1971-72 season brought consistency back to the Celtics.

They won 56 games (their most in five years), captured the divisional title (their first since 1965) and reached the Eastern Conference finals. More to the point, for the first time in two years the Celtics defeated every team in the league. They were the NBA's second-toughest (behind eventual champion Los Angeles) team at

Bill Russell's No. 6 is raised to the rafters at Boston Garden, empty except for a few workers and (left to right) Don Nelson, John Havlicek, Russell, Red Auerbach, Tom Heinsohn, Don Chaney and Tom Sanders. Russell had fought Auerbach's efforts to retire the number but finally consented on the condition that it be done in privacy with his former teammates before the Garden gates opened.

Dave Cowens covers his face in disgust after fouling out against the Bulls. Cowens was maturing into one of the league's top centers as a sophomore—averaging 18.8 points and 15.2 rebounds—and reducing his disqualifications from 15 to 10.

The Celtics weren't the only ones who could play the running game. So could the Knicks, quarterbacked by Walt Frazier, who quickly eliminated Boston, 4-1, in the Eastern finals—displaying a cohesiveness the young Celtics were still striving for.

home, only nine losses in 41 games, and were 21-16 on the road.

The consistency created its own winning streaks. After a 97-75 loss to Golden State in the season's opener shook them awake, the Celtics won 10 of 11 and took control of the Atlantic Division race. From mid-January to mid-February, when contenders frequently grow bored and flat, they won 14 of 16, then finished the season with 12 victories in their last 15 games.

Except for their West Coast trips (which ended 2-11), Boston slumped only once—a 4-8 stretch at the end of November which Heinsohn remedied by replacing Kuberski with Sanders at power forward. From there the Celtics won 13 of 15. Consistency.

Yet the most noticeable development was the rapid maturity of Cowens. Instead of regressing in any sophomore letdown, he grew to be a nightly force and a symbol of the New Celtics.

His exuberance hadn't been merely rookie enthusiasm. Cowens still dove headlong for loose balls, played hands-on, bumping defense and battled for rebounds.

And his mobility and stamina freed his teammates to mount the most creative and flexible offense in the league.

Instead of installing the center at the low post and funneling the ball to him, as Milwaukee did with Kareem Abdul-Jabbar and Los Angeles did with Wilt Chamberlain, the Celtics could let Cowens fire out the fast break, follow it as a trailer, and pop in soft jumpers from the top of the key.

And Cowens could play at that pace all night long. No center had ever attacked the game that way. Cowens intrigued *everybody*.

"It's not just the fans who 'ooh' and 'aah' when he's doing his thing," Sanders told *Boston Globe* writer Bob Ryan. "The other players can't help but react to somebody jumping, kicking, elbowing way up there. Those gentlemen on the bench sit and say, 'Ooh, look at that.' "

CELTICS BACK IN PLAYOFFS

March 29, 1972, at Boston Garden

CELTICS (126)

	Min.	*FGA*	*FGM*	*FTA*	*FTM*	*Reb.*	*Ast.*	*PF*	*Pts.*
Chaney	23	8	5	3	3	5	1	5	13
Cowens	40	21	10	4	3	16	3	2	23
Finkel	8	3	1	0	0	2	0	1	2
Glover	1	1	1	0	0	2	0	0	2
Havlicek	44	23	13	8	6	8	10	5	32
Kuberski	21	10	7	1	1	13	1	3	15
Morgan	1	0	0	0	0	0	0	0	0
Nelson	22	6	3	2	2	3	3	0	8
Sanders	22	6	3	0	0	3	3	3	6
Smith	1	2	0	0	0	0	0	1	0
White	36	20	12	3	1	6	5	3	25
Williams	21	6	0	0	0	4	7	5	0
Totals	240	106	55	21	16	71*	33	26	126

ATLANTA HAWKS (108)

	Min.	*FGA*	*FGM*	*FTA*	*FTM*	*Reb.*	*Ast.*	*PF*	*Pts.*
Adams	34	13	5	2	2	12	1	4	12
Bellamy	36	15	5	16	10	11	3	3	20
Christian	12	3	2	1	1	1	0	1	5
Gilliam	33	14	6	2	2	5	8	2	14
Halliburton	2	1	0	0	0	0	0	0	0
Hudson	43	28	14	1	1	2	5	2	29
Maravich	35	19	7	6	5	6	4	3	19
May	6	0	0	6	5	3	0	2	5
Trapp	2	1	0	0	0	0	0	0	0
Washington	37	9	2	0	0	6	3	3	4
Totals	240	103	41	34	26	55*	24	20	108

Score by periods:	1	2	3	4	
Celtics:	28	34	33	31	–126
Hawks:	30	23	30	25	–108

* *Includes Team Rebounds:* Celtics 9, Hawks 9.
Turnovers: Celtics 20, Hawks 20.
Field Goal Percentage: Celtics .519, Hawks .398.
Free Throw Percentage: Celtics .762, Hawks .765.
Referees: Jake O'Donnell, Jack Madden, Ken Hudson.

Attendance: 12,815.

Cowens had been the league's co-Rookie of the Year the previous season. Now he'd reduced his fouls and disqualifications dramatically, had increased his scoring average to 18.8 and rebounds to 15 a game, and was playing the NBA's best centers to a standstill while giving away four or more inches.

"He's getting smarter all the time," Heinsohn said. "He's seeing his options better on plays. Last year it was make the move or do nothing. Now he knows what's going on. By next year he's going to be some kind of player."

By January Cowens was good enough to start for the East in the All-Star Game and dominate it, scoring 14 points and grabbing 20 rebounds. "Now I know why Boston is winning," said Knick guard Walt Frazier.

With Willis Reed crippled by bad knees and 6-foot-8 power forward Jerry Lucas trying to fill in, New York never really challenged down the stretch and finished eight games behind. The Celtics clinched the divisional title by beating the sagging 76ers on St. Patrick's Day in Hershey, Pennsylvania, where they celebrated with champagne and chocolate bars.

Yet the renaissance still needed work. Though Boston's record was fourth-best in the league, the club had a losing record against opponents over .500 and split six games with the Knicks. When Kuberski was in the lineup, the Celtics started four men under 25. It was a rambunctious team that oozed with promise, but it still needed a year of seasoning and fine-tuning.

Dave Cowens is helped by Kareem Abdul-Jabbar after injuring a leg.

The warning signals came in the opening playoff series with Atlanta, which had finished 36-46 and lost all four of their regular-season games with Boston. Though the Celtics dominated all three games in Boston, they lost the first two at The Omni as Lou Hudson (41 points) and Pete Maravich (36) riddled them in turn. It took a 22-point performance by Kuberski, who had shredded the Hawks with 20 points and 10 rebounds in 21 minutes in Game 5, to close out the series in six games on the road. And the Hawks weren't the Knicks.

Reality arrived quickly. The Knicks had done a fine job of patching with Lucas in the pivot and had picked up Earl Monroe, the showman guard, in midseason from Baltimore. New York's nucleus, with Dave DeBusschere and Bill Bradley at forward, Frazier and Dick Barnett at guard, had already achieved the balance and cohesion Boston was still striving for.

From Lucas to Frazier, the Knicks shot beautifully from the outside. They passed instinctively and played a unison defense that delighted purists. They were an intellectual's team—Bradley had been a Rhodes Scholar and would ultimately serve in the U.S. Senate, Lucas could memorize telephone books.

As a team, the Knicks were too much for Boston and the Celtics knew it early. New York ripped away the homecourt advantage in Game 1 with an embarrassingly easy 116-94 triumph and went on to take the series in five games, losing only Game 3 and going on to win the finale, 111-103, at Boston after falling behind 14-0.

The Knicks had won the important Lucas vs. Cowens matchup, overpowered the Celtic bench, and played them to a standoff or better everywhere else. It was a lesson in savvy, role playing and communal effort that Boston was unlikely to forget—even after the Knicks were drubbed in five games by the Lakers for the championship.

Still, the Celtics' improvement had been extraordinary in two

Herm Gilliam glides high for a shot over John Havlicek as the Hawks proved surprisingly stubborn foes before falling in the series, 4-2.

years—22 more victories, a divisional title and a return to respectability around the league.

And in the front offices in Phoenix and Boston, an agreement was being struck that would bring the Celtics a power forward to protect the boards while Cowens was roaming. The power forward's name was Paul Silas, and he was the missing ingredient in Heinsohn's stew.

Tom Heinsohn:

"I never saw a more depressing locker room than after the Knicks won that final game at Boston. Our players were inconsolable. They had expected so much of themselves and then nothing.

"I should have been disappointed, but I wasn't. I wasn't because I saw the team growing."

1972–73

The symbol of the season was a sling, the one cradling John Havlicek's useless shooting arm as he sat on the bench in street clothes and watched the Celtics' greatest season come apart in the Eastern Conference finals while Tom Heinsohn fumed at the officials and cursed fate in a double-overtime thriller at New York.

Havlicek's right shoulder had given away in Game 3 at Boston while he was fighting his way through a Dave DeBusschere pick. The shoulder was hyperextended—a stretching of the muscles that left Havlicek in agony—and afterward a couple of writers had to help the captain peel off his jersey.

Leading by two points when Havlicek was injured early in the final period, the Knicks had quickly scored four straight baskets to break the game open. The 98-91 victory gave the Knicks a 2-1 edge, took away Boston's homecourt advantage, and sent the series back to New York for what proved one of the more memorable games in Celtic history.

As Havlicek watched from the bench at Madison Square Garden, the Celtics lost a 76-60 lead in the final 10 minutes of regulation—giving up the ball seven straight times without a shot on four bad passes, two offensive fouls and a three-second violation. Two overtime periods later, the Knicks were 117-110 victors.

New York momentum, 20,000 howling partisans and, Heinsohn insisted, the one-sided officiating of Jack Madden and Jake O'Donnell had all played a part.

"You've got to be up by 20 points going into the fourth quarter in this place, and we were only up 16," the coach raged to the press after chasing the referees to their dressing room. "We played a hell of a super ballgame and we were only up 16."

Heinsohn pointed to the lopsided free-throw column on the statistic sheet. "Knicks 38, Celtics 23," the NBA's Coach of the Year growled. "Who are they kidding?"

Tom Heinsohn:

"We were the best team for 82 games of the regular season but didn't win the championship. So we had to do it all over again."

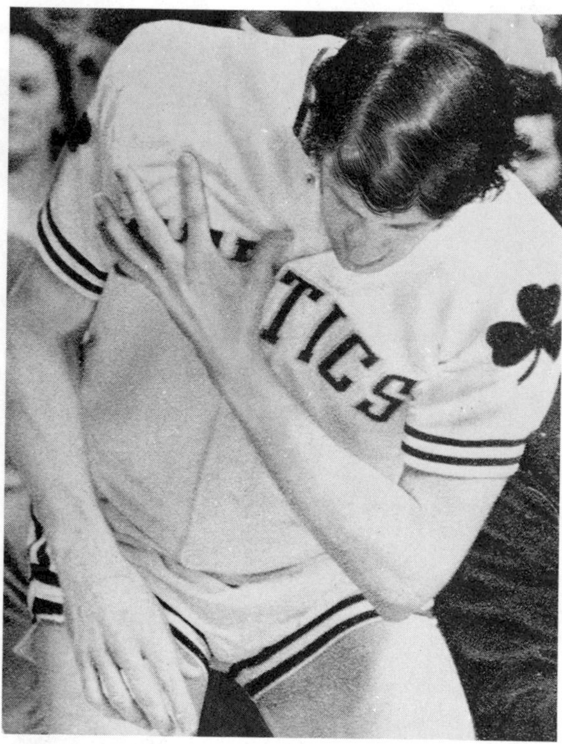

John Havlicek injured his right shoulder crucially during Game 3 of the Eastern finals while battling his way through a pick by Knick Dave DeBusschere. The injury left Havlicek in agony—and out of the memorable next game when the series returned to New York.

Tom Heinsohn and Dave Cowens swept the league's top two individual honors. Heinsohn, at age 38, was voted Coach of the Year. The 24-year-old Cowens, averaging 20.5 points and third-best-in-league 16.2 rebounds, was chosen Most Valuable Player—far ahead of John Havlicek, who was fifth in balloting with 88 points to Cowens' 444.

"It was nice of the players around the league to pick me MVP, a nice compliment of your year's work, I suppose," Cowens said later. "But I wasn't excited about it; that's not my nature. Besides, I didn't even feel I was MVP of my own team; I thought Havlicek was."

"The kid deserved it," Heinsohn said, "but it's too bad they don't give two cups instead of one. Havlicek is an MVP in my book, too."

With Havlicek returning with a virtually unmanageable arm, the Celtics scrambled back to tie the series at 3-3 and bring it back to Boston. But the Knicks won the finale easily, holding the Celtics to 78 points, their weakest playoff effort since 1954—before the 24-second clock.

The 94-78 loss ended on a downer what had been a season of uppers—a 68-14 regular-season record that was the Celtics' best ever and No. 3 on the NBA's all-time list. Dave Cowens, Jo Jo White and Havlicek all had enjoyed superb seasons and a newcomer named Paul Silas proved to be the missing link.

Boston had extracted him from Phoenix in September for NBA rights to Charlie Scott. North Carolina's star guard was headed for the ABA in 1970 when Red Auerbach shrewdly made him a throwaway draft pick (No. 7) in case Scott changed his mind. Now, two years later, Scott was jumping to the NBA for a lucrative contract with the Suns, and the Celtics had to be compensated.

To a club that needed somebody patrolling the boards while Cowens lured opposing big men from their encampments beneath the basket. Silas, at 6-foot-7 and 220 pounds was the ideal acquisition. At 29 he was a canny veteran with eight years of solid service in St. Louis, Atlanta and Phoenix.

John Havlicek welcomes Paul Silas to the Celtic family after Red Auerbach extracted him—from the Phoenix Suns. The 6-foot-7 Silas proved the final ingredient that would put the Celtics on the threshhold of another championship, patrolling the boards while Dave Cowens lured the opposing big man from beneath the basket.

"Getting Silas helped my game a lot," Cowens recalls. "I could go outside and free lance a little knowing that Paul would be inside on the boards. That took some of the burden off me." Besides grabbing more than 1,000 rebounds, Silas would average 13.3 points a game.

Celtic fans held a "day" in January for one of their all-time favorites, Tom (Satch) Sanders. After 14 seasons, Sanders was retiring to coach at Harvard. He's joined in the spotlight by his mother Luethel, daughter Simone and wife Kaaren.

Wilt Chamberlain was hitting the boards as usual in his last appearance at Boston Garden, retiring at season's end.

A stint with Weight Watchers had taken 40 pounds and left him quicker and more agile, a fine defensive forward who would grab 1,000 rebounds a year and score in double figures.

"Silas is one of the three best rebounding forwards in the NBA," former 76er Billy Cunningham said. "He's an absolute steal, and Boston will win its division easily."

Which the Celtics did. From the day training camp convened and every man weighed in under his prescribed weight, the Celts were a hungry, energetic club bent on putting distance between themselves and the rest of the Atlantic Division.

The Celtics won their first 10 games, nine more in a row at the beginning of December, and 24 of their last 26 even though the divisional race had been long since wrapped up.

"This is the most amazing team I've ever been on," Silas marveled. "They can be tired but somehow they always play hard. That's the great thing about this club. These guys come to play every night."

The Celtics' margin over the Knicks, who'd crushed them 4-1 in the 1971-72 playoffs, was a full 11 games by schedule's end, with Buffalo 47 games behind in third place and Philadelphia trailing by 59 games in fourth.

The Celtics' 32 road victories set a league record; their 33-6 mark

Newcomer Paul Silas could score as well as sweep the boards—even when surrounded by four Bucks (left to right): Lucius Allen, Bob Dandridge, Chuck Terry and Kareem Abdul-Jabbar.

at home was second only to New York's. On the West Coast, where their record had been 2-11 a year earlier, they won 9 of 10. No group of Celtics had ever been that dominant. The renaissance was complete.

"We have proven we can play any type of game against any team," said a satisfied Heinsohn. "We can play fast or slow. We have an inside game and an outside game."

At 24, Cowens had forged his best season—20.5 points a game, 1,329 rebounds and 333 assists—and earned the league's Most Valuable Player award. White, at 26, had made the transition from gunner to field general. Silas, with his 13.3-point average, 1,039 rebounds and defensive craftsmanship, was everything Boston had hoped for.

But the central figure was Havlicek who, at 33, was aging like fine champagne. He had played more minutes (3,367) than any Celtic but Cowens, led the team in scoring (23.8), free-throw percentage (.858) and assists (529) and was third in rebounds (567).

Dave Cowens held Walt Bellamy to a below-average 13.7-point average as the Celtics downed the Hawks, 4-2, in the Eastern semifinals.

John Havlicek scored 51 points—still the most in Celtic history—while setting a half-dozen team records during the Celtics' 25-point victory over Atlanta in the playoff opener. Pete Maravich (right) pistoled 37 for the Hawks in Game 4 of the series.

Dave Cowens displayed stout defense as well as offense against the Knicks in the Eastern finals.

He'd made both the NBA All-Star and All-Defense teams. He could play forward or guard, start or come off the bench, and he fouled out of only one game. If White was the ignition and Cowens the pistons, Havlicek was the flywheel, always in motion and indispensable.

When an aching knee slowed him at the beginning of February, the team lost two games in five days; otherwise it might have won 70 and set a league record. Balanced as the Celtics were, they weren't nearly as self-sufficient without their captain.

Havlicek's 54 points gave them an easy 134-109 victory over Atlanta in the opener of their playoff series, and Boston went on to take Game 2 at The Omni by 13 points.

Then, with a sweep a distinct possibility, the Celtics went flat. With Havlicek's stomach turned inside out by an intestinal bug, forward Lou Hudson scored 37 points, guards Pete Maravich and Herm Gilliam combined for 49 more and the Hawks humbled the

John Havlicek (left) and Dave Cowens were among Boston heroes in a classic playoff series with the New York Knicks that climaxed a memorable Celtic season that always will be remembered for the championship that got away.

Celtics at Boston, 118-105. Two nights later, with Maravich tossing in 37, the Hawks tied the series.

"We have to refresh our memories," Silas remarked. "We are not the greatest team that ever lived."

The Celtics struggled past the Hawks, 108-101, in Game 5, then found themselves losing in the fourth quarter of Game 6 in Atlanta. But with White pumping in three quick baskets, Boston ran off 22 straight points as the Hawks collapsed in a flurry of stolen passes, blocked shots and air balls. The final was 121-103, and within hours hundreds of fans had jammed North Station for a ticket-buying vigil. The Knicks were coming.

And in their most spectacular offensive show of the season, Boston ran them out of the building, 134-108, New York's worst beating of the year, as White scored 30 points, Havlicek 27.

Dave Cowens hooks a shot against the Knicks.

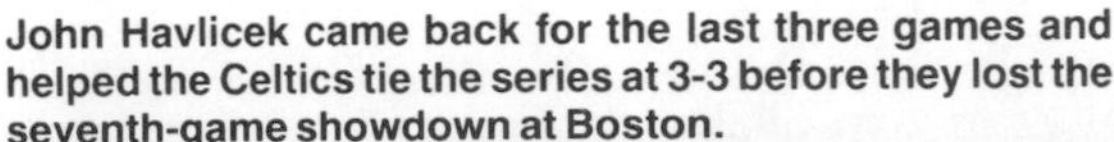

John Havlicek came back for the last three games and helped the Celtics tie the series at 3-3 before they lost the seventh-game showdown at Boston.

KNICKS BEAT CELTICS IN DOUBLE OVERTIME

April 22, 1973, at New York

CELTICS (110)

	Min.	*FGA*	*FGM*	*FTA*	*FTM*	*Reb.*	*Ast.*	*PF*	*Pts.*
Chaney	30	6	2	0	0	3	5	6	4
Cowens	55	29	14	7	5	14	2	6	33
Finkel	3	0	0	0	0	1	0	0	0
Kuberski	25	7	3	0	0	2	0	3	6
Nelson	53	14	6	4	4	5	2	5	16
Silas	49	9	2	2	1	23	5	2	5
Westphal	19	7	3	0	0	1	1	4	6
White	46	31	12	10	10	7	6	6	34
Williams	10	4	3	0	0	3	2	3	6
Totals	290	107	45	23	20	69*	23	35	110

NEW YORK KNICKS (117)

	Min.	*FGA*	*FGM*	*FTA*	*FTM*	*Reb.*	*Ast.*	*PF*	*Pts.*
Barnett	4	2	1	0	0	0	0	1	2
Bibby	14	3	1	0	0	0	0	1	2
Bradley	33	17	5	3	3	4	3	5	13
DeBusschere	51	17	8	6	6	10	3	3	22
Frazier	57	30	15	12	7	9	4	5	37
Gianelli	16	4	4	4	2	3	1	1	10
Jackson	20	4	3	4	2	4	0	1	8
Lucas	15	2	0	4	3	3	1	1	3
Meminger	38	7	4	5	2	5	7	6	10
Reed	42	11	5	0	0	9	2	6	10
Totals	290	97	46	38	25	60*	21	30	117

Score by periods:	1	2	3	4		
Celtics:	20	28	24	17	12	9–110
Knicks:	25	17	14	33	12	16–117

* *Includes Team Rebounds:* Celtics 10, Knicks 13.
Turnovers: Celtics 27, Knicks 21.
Field Goal Percentage: Celtics .421, Knicks .474.
Free Throw Percentage: Celtics .870, Knicks .658.
Referees: Jack Madden and Jake O'Donnell.
Attendance: 19,694.

Tom Heinsohn was frequently angry during Knick series.

The Knicks, who had shot 51 percent themselves, were dazzled. "Nobody," said Dave DeBusschere, "scores 134 points on us."

New York returned the favor in *its* Garden three days later, leading 60-42 at the half, 93-62 after three quarters while giggling their way to a 129-96 laugher that was Boston's worst beating of the season.

"OK, OK," Silas conceded. "Each team has had its fun. We killed them and they killed us. The party is done. The joking is over."

But the Celtics' miseries were just beginning. Game 3 left them with a 98-91 loss and without Havlicek. "I can't even make a layup," he told Heinsohn, who scratched him from the next one.

Then came the bizarre series of errors and whistles in New York, the double-overtime calamity.

"There's no way you're ever going to win down here," Heinsohn said. "They won't let you get anything going. Look at the damn stat sheet. Madden and O'Donnell should be ashamed of themselves, those bastards."

The controversy diverted attention from the heroics of White (34 points), Cowens (33 points and 14 rebounds) and Silas, who dehydrated himself while battling the boards for 49 minutes.

"He lost 20 pounds in that game," recalls Frank Challant, then the trainer. "As soon as he came into the locker room we covered him with ice towels and began wetting his lips. Anybody else would have been in the hospital for a day."

Now down 3-1, Havlicek had to play, even though assistant trainer Mark Volk had to comb his hair for him. Entering the game midway through the first half, Hondo proceeded to score 18 points, eight of them lefthanded, and hand out five assists.

And despite Boston's 1-for-19 shooting the final eight minutes, the Celtics held on, 98-97, on two Silas free throws at the end, and stayed alive.

"I don't know how Havlicek did it," Walt Frazier raved in the Knick locker room. "He was strictly a one-armed player. Yet he put in a couple with his right hand. He just went crazy."

"The man is phenomenal," said DeBusschere.

Two days later at New York, the Celtics ran away in the final four minutes to win, 110-100, and the series shifted back to Boston for the finale.

Dave Cowens appears uneasy about a Boston starting lineup—being introduced for Game 4 at New York—that didn't include John Havlicek. The captain was sitting on the bench in street clothes, a sling cradling his useless shooting arm. He'd helplessly watch one of the most memorable—and controversial—games in Celtic history.

Fans began camping in the North Station concourse during the night for the 10 a.m. opening of ticket windows. The result was the heaviest single-game sale in Celtic history—and a monumental traffic jam outside on Causeway Street that snarled that corner of Boston.

The fans were pumped up by the thought of the NBA crown returning to the Garden, and so were the Celtics.

"I've never been in a seventh game before," mused Cowens. "It should be interesting."

It wasn't. Even with the Knicks playing their worst quarter of the series (seven turnovers, 36 percent shooting), the Celtics managed only a 22-19 lead at the quarter.

"I could feel it in my bones even then," Silas would say. "We weren't playing with the old ferocity."

Havlicek had entered the game late in the first period, and the Knicks soon began exploiting the damaged captain's lack of mobility,challenging his dribbles and sagging on him. Under heavy pressure, two of his bad passes and a blocked shot gave them six points in three minutes, and New York went on to a 94-78 triumph—and, ultimately, to its second NBA title in four years after rolling over the Lakers, 4-1, in the championship series.

The Knicks weren't taking any bows after eliminating the Celtics, though.

"Hey, I'm not proud of this seven-games thing," Frazier said. "We're supposed to be the smart team, right? We're playing a team with a one-armed superstar, right? Yet we didn't exploit them until today.

"The Celtics won their last two games on sheer hustle and guts. White, Chaney—they were great. Cowens—that man is unbelievable. Wherever we went, it seemed that he was always there.

"Proud? I'm not proud. I think we were lucky, real lucky."

All of which brought no consolation to the Celtics.

"I think we had the tools to go all the way," Havlicek said. "This series was our biggest hurdle and we just didn't jump high enough. I guess it just wasn't meant to be."

Don Nelson:

"That's one championship that got away because I still feel we had the best team.

"I still feel if we had won that double-overtime game, when we lost on some very questionable calls, we'd have gone all the way."

John Havlicek's comeback earned the admiration of the Knicks, including Phil Jackson (18). "I don't know how the man did it," Walt Frazier said. "The man is phenomenal," Dave DeBusschere said.

The Celtics take the cake—if not the championship—sampled by John Havlicek and Jo Jo White during a City Hall reception.

1973–74

"We had a hell of a season last year," Tom Heinsohn mused in training camp. "We captured the imagination of the Boston public. There's a reason we didn't win, and we all know what it was."

Now, with John Havlicek's shoulder mended, the Celtics seemed a distinct favorite to overtake the aging New York Knicks in the East and proceed to the championship round that had escaped them the previous Spring.

And once Heinsohn went back to starting Don Nelson at forward and bringing Paul Silas off the bench, Boston went on a tear. The Celtics swept a dozen games at one point, and won five of six on their first West Coast trip while rolling up a 29-6 record by mid-January.

Then, on a snowy night in Kansas City, the Celtics squandered a 15-point lead and watched the Kings go on to a 109-97 victory. It didn't seem serious at the time. "It was just one of those things," Havlicek sang, emerging from the shower. But from that point the Celts struggled, going 27-20 for the remainder of the regular season.

The league is better this year, Heinsohn shrugged. "And everyone is gunning for us," the coach said. "Last year they didn't believe we were that good. Now they know. They're getting out the siege guns."

There were no 12-victory streaks down the stretch. Momentum, the fluid feeling of rolling from one week to another, playing in a groove every night, had fled. The old veterans—Havlicek, Silas, Nelson—were murmuring openly about Heinsohn and the lack of direction.

ABDUL-JABBAR SKYHOOK SINKS CELTICS IN 2d OT

May 10, 1974, at Boston Garden

MILWAUKEE BUCKS (102)

	Min.	FGA	FGM	FTA	FTM	Reb.	Ast.	PF	Pts.
Dandridge	41	16	8	4	4	4	1	5	20
Warner	23	6	2	2	1	8	1	6	5
Abdul-Jabbar	58	26	16	2	2	8	6	4	34
Robertson	58	13	8	2	2	4	10	3	18
Davis	44	6	5	3	2	8	2	2	12
Perry	34	10	3	0	0	8	2	3	6
McGlocklin	24	4	2	2	1	2	3	1	5
R. Williams	8	3	1	0	0	1	0	1	2
Totals	290	84	45	15	12	54*	25	25	102

CELTICS (101)

	Min.	FGA	FGM	FTA	FTM	Reb.	Ast.	PF	Pts.
Havlicek	58	29	14	10	8	9	4	2	36
Nelson	13	6	3	1	0	4	1	2	6
Cowens	43	19	5	4	3	8	2	6	13
White	54	21	7	5	4	4	11	2	18
Chaney	48	11	5	3	2	6	1	5	12
Finkel	15	3	2	1	1	3	1	2	5
Silas	45	7	1	4	3	9	6	1	5
Westphal	4	6	3	0	0	2	1	3	6
Totals	290	102	40	28	21	57*	27	23	101

Score by periods:	1	2	3	4	01	02
Bucks	27	20	22	17	4	12—102
Celtics	19	21	23	23	4	11—101

**Includes Team Rebounds:* Celtics 12, Bucks 11.
Turnovers: Celtics 13, Bucks 25.
Field Goal Percentage: Celtics .392, Bucks .536.
Free Throw Percentage: Celtics .750, Bucks .800.
Referees: Mendy Rudolph and Darell Garretson.
Attendance: 15,320.

The Celtics brought the NBA championship trophy back to Boston for a massive City Hall Plaza reception in May after defeating the Milwaukee Bucks in a storybook title series. The trophy—fittingly named the Walter Brown Cup—is held aloft by coach Tom Heinsohn, captain John Havlicek and general manager Red Auerbach.

Front row (left to right): Jo Jo White, Don Chaney, John Havlicek, general manager Red Auerbach, board chairman Bob Schmertz, coach Tom Heinsohn, Dave Cowens, Paul Silas and assistant coach John Killilea. Back row: assistant trainer Mark Volk, team dentist Dr. Sam Kane, Paul Westphal, Phil Hankinson, Steve Downing, Don Nelson, Henry Finkel, Steve Kuberski, Art (Hambone) Williams, team physician Dr. Tom Silva and trainer Frank Challant.

"It's like falling in and out of love with someone," Silas would say. "We have fallen out of love with Heinsohn."

All of which the coach took in stride.

"I know the players are grumbling," Heinsohn told the *Boston Globe's* Bob Ryan, "but you have to understand the situation. This is rubber room time. The players are griping at each other. They can't stand each other's smelly feet and they're looking for something to complain about. It's a tough time of the season. But we're doing it the way the Old Celtics did. Get a big lead and let them catch us."

The early burst had provided a comfortable cushion in the division race; by the end of February New York was 6 games behind, Buffalo 12½. Rest and fine-tuning for the playoffs lay ahead. But the final two games of the schedule—a defeat by the Bullets and the first loss to the 76ers since February 1971—sent up warning signals. How ready was this team?

"What I'd like to do would be to get together a few of the thinking players at somebody's house and go over the films with a six-pack," Nelson said after the Celtics had wrapped up a third straight Atlantic title. "But it's not going to happen. We won 56 games, but it was a disappointing season. There's just not the same attitude as last year."

And Buffalo, which Boston had once beaten 21 times in a row, now loomed a dangerous first-round foe. The Braves were young, fleet-footed and confident. Nobody, they felt, had as instinctive a playmaker as Ernie DiGregorio, the Rookie of the Year from Providence, or as gifted a shooter as 6-foot-9 center Bob McAdoo, the previous Rookie of the Year and now the league's top scorer (30.6).

After dividing the series' first four games, the Celtics took a 3-2 advantage in Boston before the teams returned to Buffalo and the biggest crowd ever to witness an indoor sporting event in western New York.

Dave Cowens appears on a trampoline, and he reached new heights as the league's No. 2 rebounder with a 15.7 average. He also was the Celtics' No. 2 scorer with a 19-point average.

Amid a forest of bedsheet banners and waterfalls of noise, the Braves scampered off to a 26-20 lead at the quarter and still led 70-63 in the third period, when Heinsohn decided to retool his attack. He replaced guard Paul Westphal with forward Don Nelson, moved Havlicek to the backcourt in Westphal's slot, and let Jo Jo White run wild on the slower DiGregorio. With 6:24 left to play Boston was leading 97-88, the series apparently in hand.

But as the Celtic attack bogged down, the lead shrunk to 4 points with 20 seconds left, and two turnovers allowed McAdoo to tie it at 106 with a pair of resounding stuffs. It took two free throws by White, after McAdoo had fouled him at the buzzer to end it there.

The difference had been Havlicek, who'd averaged 30 points the final four games. Now he would lead the sacking of New York, whose spiritual leader Dave DeBusschere had been slowed by a pulled stomach muscle.

As Havlicek pumped in 25 points and added a dozen assists, the Celtics breezed, 113-88, in the series opener at Boston. "That was the 26- or 27-year-old Havlicek out there today," Heinsohn whooped. "When he does that nobody can beat us."

Even without Havlicek, Boston prospered. With their captain on the bench in foul trouble, the Celtics walked away from the defending champions in the third quarter and won Game 2 by 12 points. The Knicks then managed their only victory in the series, and to do that much they had to hold off a late Boston charge after blowing a 20-point lead.

The Celtics won the next two games, finishing it at Boston Garden. As Dave Cowens fueled a 22-4 third-quarter run with two 3-point plays, Boston sprinted off to a 105-94 victory and buried a year-old ghost.

"The best team won this time," said Knick star Walt Frazier. "We just ran out of gas. And they kept coming at us."

Red Auerbach:

"That '74 championship was a turning point in our history.

"For the first time Boston fans finally realized the magnitude of our championships. Until then, the Celtics were a household name all over the country—except in our own backyard. Somehow, the impact of all those titles hadn't hit home.

"Then overnight it did. I think part of it was that people didn't realize what they'd lost until they'd lost it for a couple of years. And that double-overtime thriller with Milwaukee also had a lot to do with it.

"That game was incredible. After that heartbreaker, everyone thought we'd roll over and play dead in the seventh game at Milwaukee. Instead, we won with that big display of guts, and people have never forgotten it."

Boston welcomes the Celtics home as world champions again.

Especially Havlicek. He had scored 25, 27, 27, 36 and 33 points, had shot 41-for-70 in the last three games, and had been reborn.

"He's better than ever," Red Auerbach marveled. "He can do everything he always could and now he just takes charge of a ballgame."

Looming ahead was 7-foot-2 Kareem Abdul-Jabbar and a Milwaukee club that had rolled up the league's best record (59-23) and lost only once while ripping through playoff sets with Los Angeles and Chicago.

It was to be the classic matchup between a team of role players with a fiery, scrambling 6-foot-9 center and a team that revolved around the Big Man as all-purpose scorer, rebounder, shot-blocker and traffic cop.

The final four games would be won by the visiting team. Neither club would score 100 points in regulation until the seventh-game finale. And Game 6—Milwaukee's stirring double-overtime victory at Boston—would be witnessed by the largest television audience (38.9 million) in NBA history.

From series start, the Celtics tried to choke off the Buck attack before the ball could get to Abdul-Jabbar, pressing relentlessly fullcourt. Game 1 was easy for the Celts, a 35-19 lead at the quarter parlayed into a 98-83 triumph at Milwaukee Arena. Defense, Boston was proving again, won playoff games.

"Against Chicago, the Bucks got the ball upcourt in 4 seconds," Auerbach reasoned. "If one of their plays bogged down, they could go to something else. With us, they only have 10 or 12 seconds to start their plays and that only leaves time for one option."

"We must press this team if we're going to win," Heinsohn said. "If we stop pressing and let them get the ball into the big guy all the time, we lose. It's as simple as that."

Trailing 2-1, Milwaukee decided to relieve the pressure on its backcourt by switching 6-foot-7 Mickey Davis to guard and having wily, if aging, Oscar Robertson bring up the ball. That strategy brought a 97-89 victory at Boston and tied the series, but Heinsohn remained confident.

"They were super-careful with the ball and still had 17 turnovers," the coach said. "We're still going to win this thing."

With Silas dominating matters inside, as Cowens worked at luring Abdul-Jabbar from his lair, the Celtics spirited away Game 5, 96-87, and went back home to wrap it up.

Ernie DiGregorio was a key reason the young Braves were a dangerous first-round foe. Ernie D, the former Providence College hero, led the league in assists with an 8.2 average and was Rookie of the Year.

Tom Heinsohn gets some advice from referee Earl Strom as the playoffs opened against Buffalo.

It was another Cowens vs. Abdul-Jabbar war in the NBA finals.

Yet from the beginning the night belonged to the Bucks, who ran up leads of 27-19 and 47-40 on the way to a substantial third-quarter lead. It took a fourth-quarter comeback, climaxed by a corner jumper and diving steal by Cowens, to force an overtime.

The foes feinted their way through one 5-minute session, each team scoring only 4 points in what Havlicek would label "the finest 5 minutes of defensive basketball I've ever seen played by two teams." Then, when Cowens fouled out with 1:46 remaining in the second overtime, it was left to Havlicek to keep Boston alive (he'd score 9 of Boston's 15 overtime points).

His instinctive followup of a missed jumper (after Don Chaney had stolen the ball) had rescued the Celtics with 5 seconds left in the first overtime. Now he tricked Bobby Dandridge into a 3-point play to give them the lead. And as the second session drew to a close, Havlicek swished two bullseyes from the corner over a menacing Abdul-Jabbar, including the apparent winner with 8 seconds to go—101-100.

Years later, Havlicek would rate that last basket his finest moment as a Celtic, more memorable than his Stolen Ball nine years earlier.

"It was one of the toughest plays I ever made, especially considering the circumstances," he said. "I was in the corner and had to shoot it so high, on such an exaggerated arc over Jabbar. When he came out, the basket disappeared.

"And I was fouled on the play; Jabbar just crashed into me. I saw a picture of it later and everybody, including referee Mendy Rudolph, had his head turned watching the ball. So nobody saw the foul.

"It wouldn't have fouled Jabbar out, but it would have given us a chance at a 2-point lead and a different set of circumstances going into the final seconds."

Havlicek's heroics had put the Celtics on the threshold of the world championship, and the Garden thundered in anticipation.

Yet Abdul-Jabbar, with the clock running out and Milwaukee's last-chance play in shambles, found time and space to bring the Bucks back home. Stuck with the ball on the broken play, he lured Cowens' replacement Hank Finkel to the right corner and arched a spectacular skyhook, his hallmark, cleanly through—*swish!*—with 3 seconds remaining.

Unique view of one of the most electric moments in basketball history: Kareem Abdul-Jabbar's spectacular skyhook swishing through the basket to beat the Celtics in Game 6. Stuck with the ball on a broken play with time running out, the Bucks' star arched his clutch shot over Henry Finkel from the right corner—and it dropped through with 3 seconds left, the digital clock clicking from 4 to 3 as the ball fell through the netting.

John Havlicek and Jo Jo White embrace as the Celtics regain the world championship at Milwaukee.

There it was: Milwaukee 102, Boston 101, with the seventh game scheduled for the Bucks' 10,000-seat cockpit of an arena.

So Heinsohn, who'd worked his matchups and strategies with the thoughtful care of a chessmaster all series long, decided to go for broke. Robertson, at age 35, had played all 58 minutes less than 48 hours earlier. And Cowens was still fuming after fouling out of Game 6 with a title on the line. "You never saw a man madder at himself than Dave," said Havlicek. "He felt he had let us down."

The Celtics would sag on Abdul-Jabbar, choking off access to him, and dare the Bucks to shoot from outside. Given the stakes, it was a stunning gamble—and it worked perfectly. Sandwiched between Cowens in front and Silas in back, Abdul-Jabbar was held scoreless for nearly 18 minutes through the middle of the game as the Celtics built a 17-point lead. During that span, the exhausted Robinson shot 2-for-13, and the alternate source of supply, Curtis Perry and Cornell Warner, went 3-for-10 between them.

Meanwhile, as an irrepressible Cowens was on his way to a 28-point, 14-rebound performance, the Celtics had run away to a 63-46 lead by the time Abdul-Jabbar came up for air in the third quarter. And with 1:34 remaining and the Celtics' first NBA championship in five years (and his first as coach) assured, Heinsohn pulled his regulars and Auerbach ignited the victory cigar and watched the final touches applied to a sweet 102-87 triumph. Role players and defense, the timeless staples of basketball, had prevailed.

"I think defensively this is the best team ever to come along," alumnus Bob Cousy decided. "We used to play the same way, but I'm not sure these kids don't play it better."

And how did the Celtics feel about Heinsohn's coaching now? "I must admit that I was wrong about him," Silas would say. "The longer the season went, the better he got. Like a player, he rose to the occasion."

Kareem Abdul-Jabbar beat the Celtics in Game 6 with his clutch skyhook, but the Celtics got even with the Bucks' superstar in deciding Game 7.

1974–75

Their reign as world champions—this latest reign—lasted one day short of one year.

It had taken the Celtics five years to regain their NBA crown, and K.C. Jones' Washington Bullets six games to take it away.

As the Celtics sat, dethroned and numb, in the visitors' dressing room at Capital Centre on May 11, 1975, Don Nelson spoke for all of them. "It's something I'll remember the rest of my life," he said of the humbling.

The Celtics, who had beaten Milwaukee in 1974 on brains, poise and flexibility, had simply never been themselves this time. They used poor shot selection. They handled the ball sloppily. They lost their composure. They squandered the homecourt advantage in the first game. And they fell behind by at least 15 points in each of the three games at Capital Centre, the Bullets' turbulent, 19,000-seat cave in the middle of an old soybean field in Landover, Maryland.

"If there was one thing that surprised me it was that they didn't crack," Paul Silas said after the Bullets had applied the 98-92 clincher. "I thought we could always fight back, but when we did they kept their poise. That's the mark of a great team."

It was a stunning climax to a season in which the Celtics had won 60 games, dominated the Atlantic Division and crushed the Houston Rockets in five games in the playoffs' opening round. And then, simply, they had met their match, both competitively and stylistically.

No matter what your point of view, Kareem Abdul-Jabbar was a big problem for Dave Cowens and the Celtics.

The Celtics had spent five years rebuilding, molding a philosophy and an image, perfecting their running game, fitting their talent into roles. Suddenly, they realized they weren't unique.

The Bullets played with the same kind of switching, clutching, face-to-face defense. They could crank up the fastbreak. And they had a slot for everybody—Wes Unseld as rebounder and pick-setter, Phil Chenier as shooting guard, Kevin Porter as playmaker, Mike Riordan as defensive forward, Nick Weatherspoon as streak-shooting sixth man and Elvin Hayes as Dave Cowens—scorer, shot blocker, rebounder, intimidator.

Plus, of course, a former Celtic was head coach—old favorite K.C. Jones.

Front row (left to right): Jo Jo White, John Havlicek, general manager Red Auerbach, board chairman Bob Schmertz, coach Tom Heinsohn, Paul Silas, Don Chaney and Dave Cowens. Back row: team dentist Dr. Sam Kane, assistant trainer Mark Volk, Kevin Stacom, Glenn McDonald, Paul Westphal, Jim Ard, Henry Finkel, Don Nelson, Ben Clyde, Phil Hankinson, trainer Frank Challant and team physician Dr. Tom Silva.

"Playing them," John Havlicek said, "is like looking in the mirror."

While Boston was winning the division by 11 games over Buffalo, Washington was matching the pace game for game. The Bullets duplicated the Celtics' 60-22 record while finishing 19 games ahead of Houston in the Central Division non-race.

Still, the Bullets had been life and death with Buffalo in their playoff matchup, needing the full seven games before advancing to the Eastern finals against Boston. And this was virtually the same group of Celtics who'd won the 1974 championship—Cowens at center, Silas, Havlicek and Nelson rotating up front, and Jo Jo White, Don Chaney and Paul Westphal sharing the backcourt duties.

They had shaken off an undistinguished start (11-10 at the end of November) to win 39 of 48 games after New Year's Day and equaled their own NBA mark of 32-9 on the road. Their cool demolition of Houston in the playoffs came directly from the Heinsohn textbook.

As Cowens wore out all three Rocket centers (Kevin Kunnert, Steve Hawes, Zaid Abdul-Aziz) Boston ran Houston into a frazzle, spreading the offense among five or six people a night, everyone geting into double figures.

Buffalo's Bob McAdoo gets a piggyback ride and John Havlicek gets tagged with a foul.

Don Nelson ends up in the laps of spectators while chasing a loose ball. Nelson was more comfortable shooting the basketball as he led the league in field-goal percentage with a .539 average.

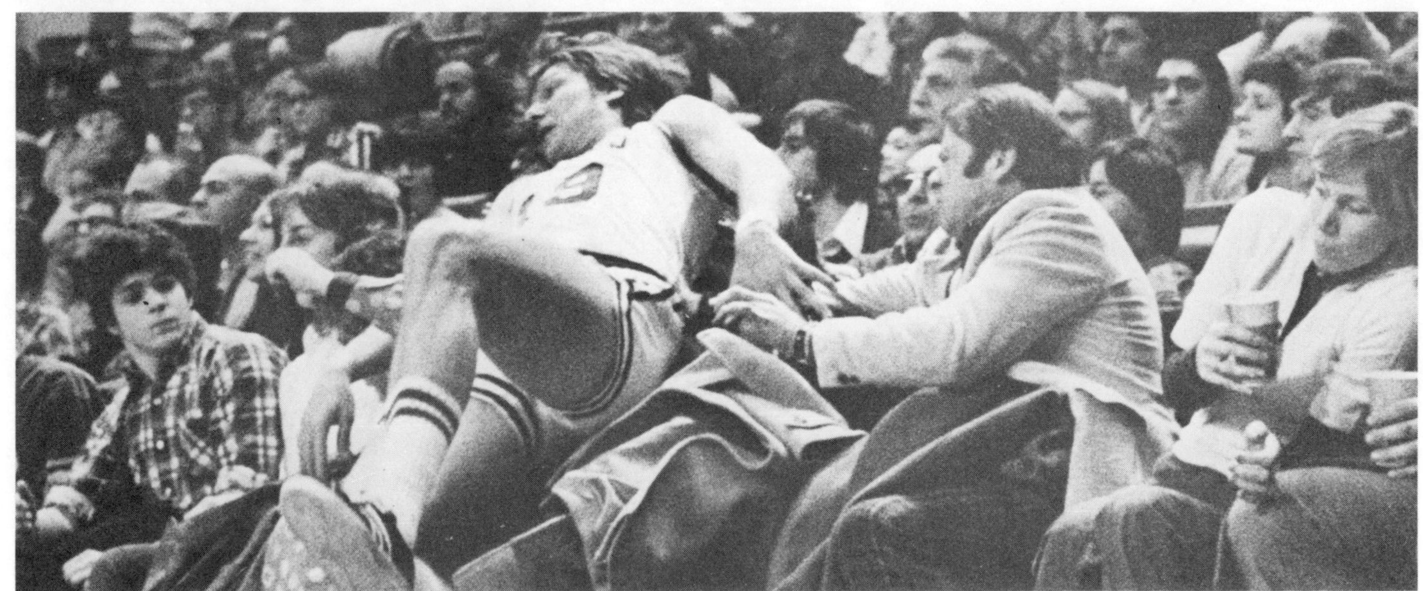

Houston's Rudy Tomjanovich couldn't get away from Dave Cowens as the Celtics demolished the Rockets, 4-1, in the playoffs' opening round.

After shrugging off a hail of debris that included ice, shoes, ballpoint pens, a golf ball and a transistor radio at The Summit ("It was a combination of Syracuse, Philadelphia and St. Louis," chuckled Havlicek), the Celtics polished off the Rockets at Boston, 128-115, with the kind of style even the Houston players appreciated.

"I didn't understand how they did it then," said guard Mike Newlin, "and I don't understand how they did it now. We knew it was coming but couldn't seem to do anything about it. Still, this is the most fun I've ever had in my life."

Yet Boston was never able to match that same crisp fluidity in the Washington series. The Celtics' dominance lasted for exactly one half in the opener at the Garden, when they took a 55-43 halftime lead into the dressing room. The Bullets came out to score 11 straight at the start of the third quarter, then knocked out the Celtics with a 20-6 run down the stretch after Boston had regained the lead at 67-60.

Tom Heinsohn couldn't watch anymore in the final moments of the Eastern finals' Game 6 as the Bullets dethroned the Celtics, 4-2.

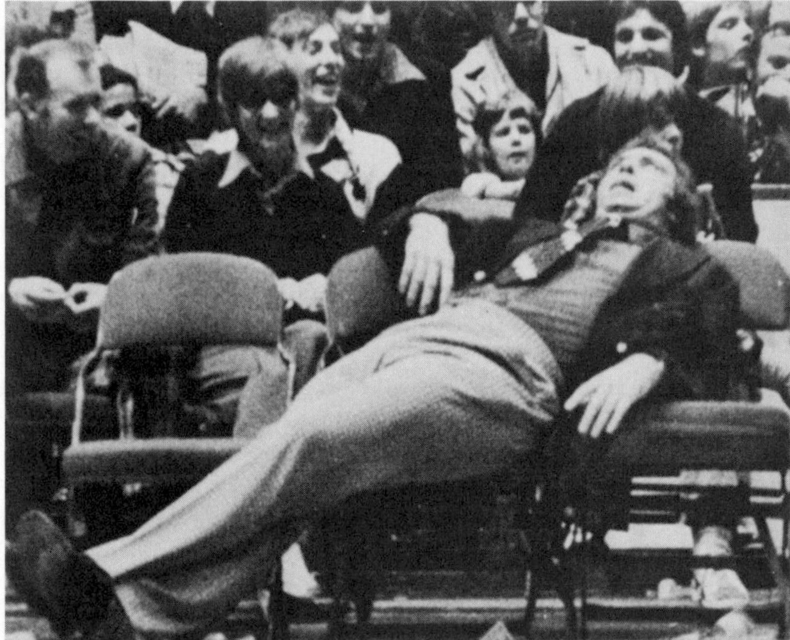

Tom Heinsohn falls back in a feigned faint of disbelief over a referee's call during a December victory at Philadelphia.

The final was 100-95, and Heinsohn was disgusted.

"We thought we were playing the Houston Rockets," the coach bristled. "You don't play 24 minutes of basketball against the Washington Bullets and win. You've got to play 48 damn hard minutes."

But the momentum was gone and the Celtics never retrieved it.

Before a booming Capital Centre crowd of 19,035 that saluted every one of Hayes' 29 points ("EEEeee!"), Washington blew the Celtics out of Game 2, 117-92. The Bullets controlled the tempo almost from the start, leaving the Celts frustrated and bewildered.

"We've got to stop worrying so much about what they're going to do," Havlicek said. "Let's do our own thing."

With Cowens and Silas playing fiercely, the Celtics won Game 3 (101-90) and 5 (103-99) at Boston, sandwiched around a 119-108 loss at Landover. The Bullets had been awesome at home all season, their 36-5 mark there the league's best.

The Celtics found themselves playing out of a deep hole in every game there. Washington would roll up a 15-point lead by the second quarter, withstand a Boston charge, and answer it with an equally skillful countersurge.

In the finale, the Bullets piled up a 53-35 advantage late in the first half and let Boston scramble and fall short again. This was a page from the Auerbach textbook. You dictated, let the opponent react, and exploited his reaction.

It was a humbling lesson, and it grew in irony when the Bullets were embarrassed by Golden State in four straight for the championship. The rest of the league had caught up.

Red Auerbach:

"It was a disappointment losing that season because we felt we had the best team. Two bad halves killed us—one in the first game, one in the last. But Washington deserved credit; they beat us."

A CHAMPIONSHIP LOST

May 11, 1975, at Landover, Md.

CELTICS (92)

	Min.	*FGA*	*FGM*	*FTA*	*FTM*	*Reb.*	*Ast.*	*Pts.*
Havlicek	40	18	7	6	5	6	4	19
Silas	48	10	3	4	2	18	1	8
Cowens	46	22	11	2	1	21	0	23
Chaney	30	8	2	0	0	2	4	4
White	40	25	7	4	4	4	6	18
Nelson	21	7	5	4	4	2	2	14
Westphal	15	8	3	0	0	3	3	6
Totals	240	98	38	20	16	66*	20	92

WASHINGTON BULLETS (98)

	Min.	*FGA*	*FGM*	*FTA*	*FTM*	*Reb.*	*Ast.*	*Pts.*
Hayes	48	19	7	2	1	11	2	15
Riordan	22	8	5	0	0	1	1	10
Unseld	47	4	4	2	2	17	2	10
Chenier	43	22	9	6	6	4	7	24
Porter	40	16	8	10	5	4	11	21
Haskins	9	3	1	2	1	0	0	3
Weatherspoon	30	11	7	1	1	5	1	15
Robinson	1	0	0	0	0	0	0	0
Totals	240	83	41	23	16	50*	24	98

Score by periods:	1	2	3	4
Celtics:	18	22	26	26—92
Bullets:	26	29	18	25—98

**Includes Team Rebounds:* Celtics 10, Bullets 8.
Turnovers: Celtics 25, Bullets 24.
Field Goal Percentage: Celtics .388, Bullets .494.
Free Throw Percentage: Celtics .800, Bullets .696.
Referees: Don Murphy and Jake O'Donnell.
Attendance: 19,035.

Don Chaney and John Havlicek were witnesses for the Boston defense against Houston.

1975–76

Tom Heinsohn gets a champagne shampoo from John Havlicek after the Celtics won Game 6 at Phoenix to wrap up their 13th world championship.

The Celtics were already in the dressing room celebrating, mobbing their captain with the numb right foot and planning on closing out a championship season within 48 hours in the Valley of the Sun.

With time running out in the second overtime, John Havlicek had made a driving, leaning, off-balance bank shot and thousands of Bostonians had sprinted past 13 policemen and swarmed onto the Garden floor.

Few of them noticed that referee Richie Powers still had two fingers held above his head, insisting that the final seconds be played out. And fewer still saw that Phoenix guard Paul Westphal, the former Celtic, was shrewdly calling an illegal timeout that would give the Suns yet another chance.

This was a muggy Friday night in June, and the Celtics, summoned from their locker room, would go on to win what is widely considered the greatest professional basketball game ever played. It lasted three overtimes, was decided by the margin of one basket, gave Boston a 3-2 lead in the title series and all but assured the Celtics a 13th—and delightfully unexpected—championship.

"That triple-overtime game was my greatest moment," Jo Jo White says now of the 128-126 thriller to which he contributed 33 points en route to the playoffs' MVP award. "Everything I put up went in, everything I did was right.

"And of all the thrills in my 10 Boston seasons, winning that '76 championship was the biggest. That was some kind of season."

On paper the Celtics were a team in transition, going through yet another changing of the guard.

Don Chaney had switched to the ABA Spirits of St. Louis before the season. Don Nelson had already announced that this was his last year. Paul Silas, bogged down in a contract dispute, also would exit at season's end, traded to Denver. Havlicek, at 36, was playing on a torn fascia in his right arch, icing it, running on it, and icing it again.

The Celtics became No. 1 again, winning their 13th world championship. Bostonians welcome them home from Phoenix following a memorable title series which included a triple-overtime masterpiece.

And a new face was playing alongside Jo Jo in the backcourt. Charlie Scott, who'd been obtained from Phoenix for Westphal, was going through his own transition from bombardier to multi-purpose guard.

Yet Boston had cruised through the schedule with the league's second-best record—54-28—and had won the Atlantic Division by eight games over Buffalo despite not having a scorer among the NBA's top 20.

The Celtics had reached the finals with large amounts of guile, tenacity and rebounding (Cowens and Silas among the league's top four) and a dash of luck.

The Celtics had wanted to avoid Philadelphia, Washington and defending champion Golden State along the playoff road; all of them could have exploited one Boston deficiency or another. So Buffalo had bounced the 76ers in overtime in their three-game mini-series, Cleveland had surprised Washington by 2 points in their seventh game, and Phoenix had stunned the Warriors in their finale at Oakland.

Still, it was a struggle. Havlicek injured his foot in the opener with Buffalo and carried a turquoise plastic wash basin under his arm for the remainder of the playoffs, immersing his arch in ice water twice as often as doctors advised.

"Two Hondo handfuls," he'd say, returning from the hotel ice bin several times a day.

"It was just a matter of self-discipline," Havlicek would say later. "It would have been easy to say 'forget about it,' to just not play. But that's where playing on this team all those years helps. I've seen so many guys play with a lot worse injuries—Frank Ramsey, K.C. Jones, Bill Russell.

"I just wanted to do as much as I could. I was just along for the ride. The other guys pulled me along... and I was glad to go."

Havlicek missed three games, then re-injured the foot against Cleveland in the Eastern finals and was limited in two more. But he played in every other contest, 15 of 18 in all, including 58 minutes in the decisive triple-overtime victory.

With Cowens and Silas teaming marvelously in the frontcourt, White having his finest stretch as a professional and Scott adapting to his new role better than anyone had anticipated, the Celtics disposed of both the Braves and Cavaliers in six games, clinching each series on the road.

On a form sheet, Phoenix seemed an unlikely finalist—a third-place team that finished just two victories over .500, trailed Golden State by 17 games in the Pacific race and needed a late-season drive to qualify for the playoffs.

The Celtics easily won the first two games in Boston, 98-87 and 105-90, but the world turned upside down when they arrived at Phoenix.

The Mean 13 (as in 13,000 zealots) at Veterans Memorial Coliseum had watched their '*Sun*derellas' defy odds for more than two months. So they were hardly surprised when Phoenix won the next two games, 105-98 and 109-107, and shifted the pressure onto the Celtics' back for Game 5.

There had never been one like it. From the beginning it belonged to the Celts, who rolled up a 42-20 edge in the second quarter and led, 92-83, with 3:49 to play. Then Westphal, who had emerged from a third-guard role as a Celtic to stardom (20.5 scoring average) at Phoenix, scored 9 of the Suns' next 11 points, including 5 in a row, to put it into overtime.

Don Nelson was playing his final season after 11 Celtic years, announcing his retirement for season's end.

Infuriated by Mike Newlin twice jumping in front of him and falling untouched to draw offensive fouls, irate Dave Cowens slams into Newlin with a double-forearm thrust that sent the Houston guard sprawling. Cowens then hollered at referee Bill Jones: "Now *that*'s a foul!" Cowens was awarded a technical foul for unnecessary roughness.

CELTICS OUTLAST SUNS IN TRIPLE-OVERTIME

June 4, 1976, at Boston Garden

CELTICS (128)

	Min.	*FGA*	*FGM*	*FTA*	*FTM*	*Reb.*	*Ast.*	*PF*	*Pts.*
Havlicek	58	19	8	7	6	5	8	2	22
Silas	44	11	8	1	1	4	4	6	17
Cowens	55	23	9	11	8	5	4	6	26
White	60	29	15	4	3	0	9	2	33
Scott	33	14	3	0	0	2	3	6	6
McDonald	13	5	3	2	2	0	3	2	8
Ard	16	6	3	2	2	1	1	1	8
Kuberski	13	5	2	0	0	3	0	1	4
Stacom	3	0	0	0	0	0	0	0	0
Nelson	20	4	1	2	2	0	1	1	4
Totals	315	116	52	29	24	28*	33	27	128

PHOENIX SUNS (126)

	Min.	*FGA*	*FGM*	*FTA*	*FTM*	*Reb*	*Ast.*	*PF*	*Pts.*
Perry	52	20	10	4	3	15	6	5	23
Heard	61	19	8	2	1	12	4	1	17
Adams	37	16	9	2	2	9	5	6	20
Sobers	41	22	11	4	3	2	6	2	25
Westphal	42	20	11	3	3	2	2	4	25
Van Arsdale	35	5	1	4	3	4	1	1	5
Erickson	4	2	0	0	0	0	1	0	0
Awtrey	23	3	2	3	3	4	0	6	7
Lumpkin	12	2	0	0	0	1	4	0	0
Hawthorne	8	3	1	2	2	4	0	3	4
Totals	315	112	53	24	20	62*	29	28	126

Score by periods:	1	2	3	4	01	02	03
Celtics	36	25	16	18	6	11	16—128
Suns	18	27	27	23	6	11	14—126

**Includes Team Rebounds:* Celtics 8, Suns 9.
Turnovers: Celtics, 25, Suns 29.
Field Goal Percentage: Celtics .448, Suns .473.
Free Throw Percentage: Celtics .828, Suns .833.
Referees: Richie Powers and Don Murphy.
Attendance: 15,320.

For more than nine minutes—virtually two full five-minute overtimes—the opponents played cautiously, looking for an opening. Then they crammed an evening's worth of dramatics into 19 seconds as Boston fans went on an emotional elevator.

A drive by White gave Boston a 109-106 lead. A jumper by Dick Van Arsdale whittled it to a point. Then Westphal stole the Celtics' inbounds pass to set up a second-rebound swish by Curtis Perry, and the Suns found themselves ahead.

The ball, and the final shot, would belong to Havlicek. His off-balance banker touched off the wild, premature Garden party which quickly turned ugly once the spectators realized that Powers, ever in control amid chaos, was insisting the game be played out. One fan slugged him; thousands more showered him with verbal abuse.

That's when Westphal had come up with the ploy that would give the Suns one final breath. Phoenix had exhausted its allotment of timeouts. By calling one, Westphal would draw a technical foul and give Boston a free throw; but the Suns would receive the ball at halfcourt instead of at their baseline. And with only two seconds left on the clock, that made all the difference in the world.

White's foul shot made it 112-110, but Phoenix forward Gar Heard had time to launch a 22-foot turnaround at the buzzer and it was tied.

The final overtime would be a war of attrition with some unlikely heroes. Cowens, Scott and Silas, along with Alvan Adams and Dennis Awtrey, the Suns' big men, either had or would foul out.

So Jim Ard, replacing Cowens, controlled a vital jump ball and later sank the two free throws that equaled the final margin. White, who scored 15 of his 33 points in overtime, added two baskets. And Glenn McDonald, who would be waived before the next regular season began, scored 6 points after coming in for Silas. Boston built a 126-120 lead and it was over—both the game and the series.

"The Suns played so hard and yet they still lost," Silas would observe. "They had to come away with an empty feeling. They couldn't have done a better job, but they have nothing to show for it."

Dave Cowens and Curtis Perry are separated in Game 5 by referee Richie Powers. It was Powers who would be slugged—by an irate customer—before the end of this wild triple-overtime game, considered by many to be the greatest basketball game ever played.

Jo Jo White's free throw is about to drop through the hoop to lengthen Boston's lead to 2 points with a second to go in the second overtime period. White was awarded the shot when Phoenix' Paul Westphal shrewdly took an illegal timeout for a technical foul that would give the Suns the ball at midcourt.

Both sides were exhausted, but the symbol was Tom Heinsohn, who slumped in the dressing room, his head buried in his arms, too drained to even speak to the press. Colitis, high blood pressure and stress had ravaged the coach; he would take medication to forestall hospitalization after the playoffs.

Thirty-nine hours later the Celtics were playing in Phoenix with the temperature 100 degrees outside. It was their 100th game of the season, and they concluded it with a 17-6 run in the final seven minutes that produced an 87-80 victory and Title No. 13.

"Here we are again," crowed Red Auerbach, his clothes drenched from the shower, smoke billowing from a victory cigar. "We won every series the same way this time: win two, lose two, win one and then win in front of their *hos*-tile crowd."

In a corner of the Boston room Havlicek gazed at his wash basin.

"I might just get it bronzed," he said. "This wasn't my championship. I've been a lot more important in other ones. This one was Jo Jo's and Dave's and Charlie's and Paul's. I just sort of moved along with them. I was just out there, doing what I could do."

Playoff MVP Jo Jo White is fed a piece of championship cake by John Havlicek at the City Hall reception.

Tom Heinsohn:

"We never had our arsenal for a playoff game. We never knew what we could expect from John. We had to adjust from game to game. We got down to the last one and everybody poured his guts out. That's the only way we won. With spunkiness. We knew what we had to do."

It had been that kind of season, that kind of championship, every man playing his role.

"This team had to scratch and claw for everything," Auerbach would say. "Never once in the playoffs did I chew them out—you know, give them a zing like I did in other years. They did the best they could."

Referee Richie Powers is in the middle of this mob scene after being slugged by a Garden customer when Powers insisted a second remained after John Havlicek's apparent game-winning basket. Powers continued in the game while his attacker was taken away by police.

1976–77

Dave Cowens' unused locker symbolizes a season in which a series of improbables riddled the Celtics. The most unlikely of all occurred eight games into the season when Cowens took an "indefinite leave of absence," saying he had "lost my enthusiasm" and walked out on an estimated $280,000 a season. But he would return in January after a 30-game absence.

After 11 years as a Celtic, Don Nelson had retired. That was not unexpected. His playing time had been halved the previous season, and with championship rings for four fingers and a thumb, he'd decided it was "time to move on and find a new gig."

But nobody had figured on the departure of Paul Silas, whose contract dispute dragged on through training camp to an impasse.

As insurance the front office had bought power forward Sidney Wicks from Portland. Then, as the Celtics were packing for the flight to Indianapolis and the season's opener, came the trade. Silas was going to Denver in a three-way deal that would bring Detroit forward Curtis Rowe, Wicks' old UCLA soulmate, to Boston.

On paper the moves seemed sound as the Celtics geared to defend their championship.

Wicks had been a marvelous college player five years earlier, dominating Jacksonville's 7-foot-2 Artis Gilmore in the NCAA championship game. At Portland, where he'd been expected to lead the franchise out of the expansion wilderness, his performance had been mercurial but frequently brilliant, the scoring average in the 20s with 800 rebounds a season.

Rowe had been solid and stable at UCLA (coach John Wooden had said that Rowe never played a bad game for him) and had been an All-Star for the Pistons. More important, general manager Red Auerbach felt, Wicks and Rowe had been winners, keystones in college basketball's most enduring dynasty. They would be comfortable as Celtics, he reasoned, familiar with a winning tradition and the responsibilities that went with it.

Yet Nelson and Silas were not easily replaced. Their contributions had largely been intangible, not found in box scores—character, perspective, poise, a sense of continuity. "Nellie, Silas," guard Kevin Stacom would muse. "They were *men.*"

Now they were gone, and eight games into the season so was Cowens. Saying he'd "lost my enthusiasm," he took an "indefinite leave of absence."

With Wicks and two reasonably competent backups in Jim Ard and Tom Boswell filling in, the Celtics were able to tread water. Then, as suddenly as he'd disappeared, Cowens returned one mid-January afternoon after a 30-game absence.

The 76ers were still within striking distance. With a newly motivated Cowens, Boston figured to take the Atlantic Division race to the wire. But less than a minute into Cowens' first game back,

Charlie Scott sits on the Celtic bench with a broken forearm, fractured in the first minute of Dave Cowens' first game back in January. Scott would miss 39 games.

Ecstatic teammates carry Jo Jo White off the court at Philadelphia's Spectrum after his corner jumpshot beat the buzzer to give the Celtics a victory in Game 1 of the Eastern semifinals, wresting the homecourt advantage from the 76ers.

against Indiana, Charlie Scott drove baseline, soared and fell heavily against the support, fracturing a forearm.

Out until April, doctors told Heinsohn. Still, behind John Havlicek, Jo Jo White, Wicks and a rejuvenated Cowens, Boston went on to win 44 games and take second place behind Philadelphia. And with Scott back in the lineup, the playoff mini-series with San Antonio was over quickly, 2-0—a resounding victory at the Garden and a chaotic one at The HemisFair.

Buoyant, the club flew directly to Philadelphia and stripped the homecourt advantage from the 76ers in the opening game as White hit a jumper from the corner at the buzzer and the Celtics danced in triumph beneath the basket.

But the Sixers won three of the next four games, and the Celtics had to scramble wildly in Game 6 at Boston to stay alive. The finale would be at the Spectrum, and the Celtics had never lost a seventh game to any Philadelphia team. Pride, tradition, the green jerseys—all of that would surely come into play.

Game 7 was close for three quarters, but the Celtics had run their veterans into the ground in Game 6. As Shue shuttled in fresh legs from the league's most versatile bench, Philadelphia seized the lead with one offensive burst—including a critical basket by bombardier/guard Lloyd Free—and the final 12 minutes were a study in exhaustion. White, the hero of Game 1, was 0-for-13 from the floor in the second half.

"And Boston calls *t-i-i-i-m-e!*" PA announcer Dave Zinkoff crowed again and again in the final minutes as Heinsohn brought his weary troops to the sidelines, hoping for a miracle. There was none, and as the last seconds ran out on an 83-77 Philadelphia victory, Free dribbled the ball lazily in the backcourt, doing a disco shimmy and waving his index finger: We're No. 1.

Dave Cowens:

"Yes, my taking that leave that season created quite a stir, but it was something I had to do. I was very tired of basketball. I was not mentally with it and had to get away.

"It wasn't a rash decision, believe me. I had given it a lot of thought. I had been on a down period, but everyone goes through down periods; so I went to training camp hoping to work my way out of it. I thought once the season started I might regain my interest and enthusiasm.

"But it didn't happen, and it got to the point where I was feeling guilty taking my salary. I wasn't making a contribution or helping the team. I had no motivation or enthusiasm, and I couldn't play this game without desire.

"Sure I thought about all the money I'd be passing up, and that didn't make my decision any easier. But I just had to do it; I had to do the right thing.

"Yes, I suppose in one sense it was selfish of me to leave the club. But it would have been selfish of me to continue playing the way I had been, too. Some suggested I also cheated the fans by leaving. Well, if I'd kept playing, the fans wouldn't have seen much of a player anyway, so they'd have been cheated in the first place.

"As it turned out, I wasn't gone that long anyway. And when I came back, my enthusiasm had returned and I was anxious to play again. I could cope again."

Julius Erving gave the Celtics a headache throughout the Eastern semifinals. The former University of Massachusetts star, already legendary as "Dr. J," was playing his first NBA season after five years in the ABA and led Philadelphia in scoring with a consistent 27-point average through both the regular-season and the playoffs.

CELTICS DETHRONED AT PHILADELPHIA

May 1, 1977, at Philadelphia

PHILADELPHIA (83)

	Min.	FGA	FGM	FTA	FTM	Reb.	Ast.	PF	Pts.
Erving	39	19	6	2	2	8	1	2	14
McGinnis	30	13	4	1	0	12	4	5	8
Jones	32	1	1	0	0	6	1	4	2
Bibby	35	9	3	2	2	9	3	3	8
Collins	35	11	3	4	4	3	1	3	10
Mix	27	1	0	8	6	8	4	3	6
Free	26	27	10	7	7	5	1	1	27
Dawkins	16	10	3	2	2	2	0	3	8
Totals	240	91	30	26	23	57*	15	24	83

CELTICS (77)

	Min.	FGA	FGM	FTA	FTM	Reb.	Ast.	PF	Pts.
Havlicek	47	19	4	5	5	6	5	5	13
Rowe	34	9	5	5	4	11	0	3	14
Cowens	46	16	5	2	1	27	1	3	11
White	47	24	7	5	3	7	2	2	17
Scott	41	14	3	8	4	7	6	5	10
Wicks	19	8	3	2	2	7	0	4	8
Boswell	2	0	0	0	0	0	0	0	0
Sanders	4	0	0	5	4	0	0	3	4
Totals	240	90	27	35	23	82*	14	25	77

Score by periods:	1	2	3	4
Celtics	19	26	18	14—77
76ers	24	26	21	12—83

* *Includes Team Rebounds:* Celtics 17, 76ers 4.
Turnovers: Celtics 27, 76ers 19.
Field Goal Percentage: Celtics .300, 76ers .330.
Free Throw Percentage: Celtics .657, 76ers .885.
Technical Fouls: Rowe, Mix, Collins, Shue (76er coach).
Referees: Jake O'Donnell and Joe Gushue.
Attendance: 18,276.

1977–78

On paper, it was a remarkable collection of talent. Seven of these Celtics had played in at least one NBA All-Star Game. And at least three seemed destined for the Hall of Fame.

There was Dave Cowens in the pivot, Sidney Wicks and Curtis Rowe in the corners, Jo Jo White and Charlie Scott in the backcourt. Dave Bing, a newly signed free agent, was third guard. And John Havlicek was sixth man.

Yet no Celtic team ever played with less cohesion and spirit, heard more catcalls from its fans or finished with a worse record (32-50).

When the 1977-78 was over, Tom Heinsohn had been fired and Scott traded, Havlicek had retired, 18 men had worn the green jersey and the Celtics had missed the playoffs for the first time since 1971.

"I used to think I knew something about basketball," a baffled Havlicek would say at one point. "Now, I don't know."

It was a year that defied logic and it began going sour in training camp, where Heinsohn had only two of his nucleus of veterans available for steady work. White's heels were bothering him. Cowens wanted certain afternoons off to work on his Nautilus machines. And both Wicks and Havlicek were unsigned.

Management wasn't worried about Havlicek; he merely wanted to rest his 37-year-old bones, work into shape at his own pace and extract a few hundred bluefish from the Cape Cod Canal adjacent to training camp at Massachusetts Maritime Academy.

But Wicks didn't sign until the afternoon of the opener at San Antonio, where the Spurs beat Boston for the first time ever. The Celtics, who had built a dynasty by answering the bell superbly conditioned and motivated, simply weren't ready to play basketball. It was an omen. Before the road trip was done, the Celtics were off to their worst start (1-5) in seven years and Heinsohn was fuming.

"I'm getting tired of hearing people in the stands saying, 'When are the Celtics going to play like the Celtics?'" he growled.

Longtime favorite John Havlicek says goodbye to Celtic fans during Havlicek Day ceremonies at Boston Garden.

Everyone was laughing when Tom Heinsohn signed a multi-year contract with Red Auerbach and team owner Irv Levin (left) before the season. But the three would not be laughing long after the Celtics opened what would prove the worst season yet in the club's history.

Except for a game here, a weekend there, they never did. Most games would slide away before the second quarter began, amid hoots from the Boston Garden balconies, leaving players frustrated and bewildered afterward.

"I'm confused," Cowens would say. "I lie awake nights thinking. I try to think back to other teams I've been on, other situations, but I've never been part of a situation like this."

Neither had Red Auerbach, and when the slump reached 1-8 with an embarrassing loss at home to the Spurs, the general manager dressed down the club, calling them quitters. No pride, he told them.

But the losing continued. By the end of November the record was 6-12, Philadelphia was eight games ahead in the division race, and Heinsohn was disgusted.

"I think a lot of people have been conditioned to rationalizing away losing," the coach said. "Some people are used to losing, but I'm not. I'm tired of making excuses. There are no excuses left."

So Heinsohn benched every starter except Cowens, put Tom Boswell and Fred Saunders (a journeyman who'd impressed him with hustle and scrap) in the corners and went with Havlicek and Bing as a 71-year-old backcourt.

Ernie DiGregorio wore a Celtic uniform for the last 27 games, including one memorable night in April when the former Providence College hero went home to Providence Civic Center and rang up 24 points, 7 rebounds and 4 assists to ignite a Celtic rally that fell just short against Washington.

Tom Heinsohn fumed in disgust on the Celtic bench with assistant coach Tom (Satch) Sanders as the Celtics reeled to a 1-8 start.

Tom Heinsohn glumly sits at home after being fired in early January after nine seasons, five division titles and two NBA championships—the first Celtic coach relieved during a season.

Tom (Satch) Sanders was a popular choice to succeed Tom Heinsohn, moving up from assistant to head coach.

It was a matter of attitude, Heinsohn felt, and that attitude was depressingly evident at the club's traditional Christmas party at the Garden. Only Havlicek and White and their families bothered to attend. At the end of the afternoon, when it was obvious there would be nobody else, Auerbach silently gathered up the unclaimed gifts and put them away.

Tom Heinsohn:

"You can't be a dictator now. The Knute Rockne era, the Vince Lombardi era, the Red Auerbach era are all dead now. You're the Henry Clays now, the Great Compromisers.

"You can't yell at these ballplayers. You can't stand up and scream like Red used to. There's nobody who walks in as a dictator. You are trying to find a way to have a workable relationship and a workable system. You devise a program, and then you present it. But sometimes it comes in conflict with what other people think ought to be done."

By now rumors were rampant. Scott was supposed to be on the trading block, and Heinsohn's job on the line. The first West Coast trip, five games in six days just before Christmas with owner Irv Levin and Auerbach on hand, was the final exam.

Before boarding the jet at Boston's Logan Airport, Heinsohn examined his ticket. "Well," he said to *Boston Globe* writer John Powers, "at least they gave me roundtrip."

Though Cowens dueled Kareem Abdul-Jabbar to a standoff, Boston lost the first game at Los Angeles. There were two semi-respectable losses at Portland and Golden State. Then Cowens was felled by the flu and the final two games were predictable routs—132-99 at Seattle, the worst beating of the season, and 129-110 at Phoenix, the 15th road loss in 16 games.

Bing, who had played for a succession of losers in Detroit, shook his head. "I've been in this situation before," he said. "I hear guys sitting around talking and I know where their heads are at, and I can see it's not right."

Levin had promised several changes if his team came up empty on the Coast, and two days after Christmas he followed through. Scott was traded to the Lakers for old Celtic Don Chaney, power forward Kermit Washington (sitting out a 60-day suspension for slugging Houston's Rudy Tomjanovich) and a first-round draft choice.

And on January 3, Heinsohn found Auerbach waiting for him at practice at Lexington Christian Academy. After nine seasons, five division titles and two NBA championships, Heinsohn was being dismissed—the first Celtic coach ever fired during a season.

"I thought we'd begun to turn this thing around, but I guess they thought it was the best time to make a change," he shrugged.

"I have a tremendous feeling of loyalty to Red," Heinsohn added. "I think he did everything he could to make it a livable situation. I think he understood what was going on—even if other people didn't."

Auerbach looked fatigued and melancholy when he met with the media later in the day at the Garden. He said this had been the toughest decision in his 32 NBA seasons.

"I love the guy," Auerbach said. "I was hoping I could stretch the

Top draftee Cedric (Cornbread) Maxwell was giving promise of being among the better No. 1 picks in Celtic history while averaging 17 minutes and 7.3 points a game. (Yes, he wore No. 30 his first two Celtic seasons before surrendering it to teammate M. L. Carr after some heavy negotiating and switching to No. 31.)

thing out as long as I could, because I was hoping and hoping these monkeys would turn it around.

"I don't know whether I could do any better," Auerbach conceded, but a change had to be made. The players, immune to Heinsohn's stereophonic booming, had tuned him out. Tom (Satch) Sanders, his old roommate and assistant coach, would take over.

"I'm looking for gentlemen who can give us consistency," Sanders said. "Every night."

Yet the season continued to slide. By the end of January the road record was 2-20, Havlicek had announced his retirement, effective at season's end, and White's 488-game ironman streak had come to an end amid aching heels and bitterness over contract negotiations.

The final 10 weeks of the season came apart amid a flurry of injuries. White underwent heel surgery in March. Boswell dislocated a finger. Rowe was having knee trouble. When the club neared the end of its second western swing, Sanders had only three reserves available—fourth guard Kevin Stacom plus free agents Ernie DiGregorio and Zaid Abdul-Azziz, both working on 10-day contracts.

Abdul-Azziz (the former Don Smith) had been working with his import-export business near Seattle and hadn't touched a basketball in 13 months, but he was the nearest available big man. He would play in two games and return to his business, never having worn Celtic Green in Boston Garden.

Mathematically, the playoffs were a possibility until April 2, and Sanders even chalked the numbers on a dressing room blackboard.

"They still think they have a chance, don't they," said Detroit coach Bob Kauffman. "They still think they're going to turn it around. Well, you bring back Russell and Cousy and Heinsohn and the Jones boys. Put a 14 on somebody and a 6 . . . and maybe the numbers will bring 'em back."

The end came officially with a week left when Indiana's Mike Flynn, the worst foul shooter on the West Conference's worst team, dropped in two free throws to beat the Celtics at Boston. Five days later, a 111-109 defeat by the Pistons at the Garden—Loss No. 49—formally made it the worst season in franchise history.

The only thing left was Havlicek's finale, a Sunday afternoon home game against Buffalo. He wanted to play all 48 minutes. "I began my career running," he told Sanders, "and I want to end it running."

"Havlicek Day" morning, the honored guest turned up in the locker room wearing a tuxedo ("you should wear special clothes on special occasions"), let an 8-minute standing ovation wash over him before the game and wept when Sanders took him out with 15 seconds remaining and a 131-114 victory assured.

He had scored 29 points, a career total of 26,395 in 1,270 Celtic games, an NBA record for longevity.

In the dressing room, Havlicek found a telegram from movie immortal John Wayne, in Boston for surgery. "Hondo is watching," it read. "Congratulations."

Dave Bing was signed as a free agent, playing the final season of his brilliant 12-year career as the Celtics' third guard and averaging 13.6 points.

HAVLICEK SCORES 29 IN HIS LAST GAME

April 9, 1978, at Boston Garden

CELTICS (131)

	Min.	*FGM*	*FGA*	*FTM*	*FTA*	*Reb.*	*Ast.*	*Pts.*
Wicks	15	5	6	3	5	7	2	13
Chaney	24	3	6	1	1	2	1	7
Cowens	39	9	16	2	3	15	3	20
Havlicek	41	11	33	7	8	5	9	29
Bing	37	9	13	6	6	4	5	24
DiGregorio	15	2	4	1	1	2	3	5
Washington	34	4	5	9	11	14	2	17
Maxwell	23	3	4	6	6	6	1	12
Boswell	12	1	4	2	2	3	1	4
Totals	240	47	91	37	43	68*	27	131

BUFFALO BRAVES (114)

	Min.	*FGM*	*FGA*	*FTM*	*FTA*	*Reb.*	*Ast.*	*Pts.*
Barnes	28	4	13	2	2	6	2	10
Willoughby	26	3	9	2	2	3	2	8
Nater	42	11	19	6	7	15	2	28
Smith	27	3	11	4	4	0	0	10
Averitt	42	7	26	6	7	4	7	20
McNeill	24	6	11	6	8	6	1	18
Glenn	27	4	11	1	1	1	5	9
Lloyd	6	1	4	1	1	1	0	3
Jones	15	2	7	0	0	2	2	4
Owens	3	1	2	2	2	2	1	4
Totals	240	42	113	30	34	57*	20	114

Score by periods:	1	2	3	4
Celtics	26	32	36	37—131
Braves	25	21	36	32—114

**Includes Team Rebounds:* Celtics 10, Braves 17.
Turnovers: Celtics 21, Braves 9.
Field Goal Percentage: Celtics .516, Braves .372.
Free Throw Percentage: Celtics .860, Braves .882.
Technical Fouls: Cowens, Smith.
Referees: Ed Rush and Jess Kersey.
Attendance: 15,276.

1978–79

While the ruins of the worst season in Celtic history were still smouldering, owner Irv Levin vowed that reconstruction would begin immediately.

John Havlicek and Dave Bing had retired. Kevin Stacom and Tom Boswell had played out their options. Charlie Scott had never really been replaced after being traded in midseason. And power forward Kermit Washington, one of the season's few bright spots, was up for renegotiation.

No effort or expense would be spared in re-creating a contender, Levin told Red Auerbach, and the general manager took the owner at his word.

The 1977-78 nightmare had been good for one thing, the sixth overall choice in the college draft, and Auerbach used it to pick Larry Bird, a magnificent power forward out of Indiana State and by any measure the best player available.

Bird was an eligible junior (he had transferred from Indiana and his class had graduated) and had the option of either signing or finishing his senior year. Every general manager hungered for him, but few wanted to risk a high draft choice on an uncertainty. Bird had decided to stay in school and most clubs wanted immediate help.

It was a gamble, but a sound one, Auerbach reasoned. If you drafted Bird you owned his rights for a year. He might change his mind in the interim. And even if he decided he'd rather play elsewhere, Auerbach could recoup his investment by dealing his rights to the club Bird wanted.

The Scott trade had also produced the Lakers' second pick in the first round, the eighth overall, which Auerbach cashed for the shooting guard Boston needed, taking Freeman Williams, the national scoring champion from Portland State.

While the draft was going on, the Celtics signed free agent Kevin Kunnert, the 7-foot Rocket refugee who would provide the backup help Dave Cowens required at center. And Washington ultimately was signed.

The refurbishing was well underway, and Levin was pleased. Everyone would be at training camp this time, the season would begin at home, and the attitude would be better all around. "I'm highly confident we'll make the playoffs," he said.

Yet within a week the franchise was in turmoil again. Levin and Buffalo owner John Y. Brown, the former Kentucky Fried Chicken mogul, had huddled at the league meetings in San Diego and decided to swap their franchises as though they were sets of Lionel trains.

Brown would keep the Celtics in Boston and run them, with partner Harry Mangurian, as an absentee owner. Levin would move the Braves to San Diego, where they'd be closer to his West Coast-based business, and rename them the Clippers.

Adding to the bizarre flavor, the exchange would involve a major trade. Washington, Williams, Kunnert and Sidney Wicks were bundled off to San Diego for forwards Marvin Barnes and Billy Knight and guard Tiny Archibald.

The sheer dizziness of it perturbed Auerbach, who hadn't been consulted. Before long, he was flying to New York and talking with Knick management about a lucrative offer—a four-year contract as club president at the highest salary ever offered an NBA executive.

"It was all so goddam flattering," he thought, and returned to Causeway Street ready to pack. Forty-two years after he'd left Brooklyn to go to college, Arnold Auerbach was going home."

Chris Havlicek raises his father's No. 17 to the Boston Garden ceiling. The ceremony was a highlight of the season as the Celtics plunged to an even more dismal record than the year before—29-53, the worst in their history, while finishing last in their division for the first time in 29 years.

Dave Cowens:

"That season was the worst year I've ever had in this game. From both my personal game and team standpoints. It was an embarrassment, a nightmare in many ways.

"And I'm talking about the entire season, not just my coaching experience, although that was a large part of it. It was a chopped-up season for me, like a guy must feel who is traded two or three times in one year.

"It wasn't that I thought I'd be a great coach or that I was on an ego trip or out to prove anything personally. I just wanted to be in a strong position to have a say in the team's future, to get things done. I wanted to help the team get back to where it belonged, to make it competitive again. So when I was offered the job, I said OK.

"It was one thing after another. Like when the team began to win, there was the McAdoo trade. There was no sense playing hard, beating your head against the wall, if someone on the outside could come in and take away everything you'd done. Emotionally, it was very hard.

"It would have been nice to have had some of the more pleasant aspects of the job, but for the most part that just wasn't the situation at the time.

"Looking back on it, no, I don't think one man can do both jobs—play and coach—at the same time real well. I'm not sorry I took the job, though. I have no regrets about the decision. It was good for me in some ways. It was a learning experience, a tremendous growing experience.

"I became a more coachable player because of it. It helped my mental discipline. I had to think about a lot more than just myself. And I've become more tuned in to things that affect other players.

"Every player should coach for a month or so to understand the job's complexities. It's constant pressure. I knew there would be a lot of planning and scouting involved, but I didn't know what it did to you emotionally.

"So I gained a lot of insight and some enjoyment from the dual role. But overall it certainly wasn't a fun year and I hope no one has to go through one like it again."

The possibility left Bostonians stunned. "Ayy, Red," a voice would growl from a truck window. "Stay." Elderly women would try to change his mind in Chinese restaurants. The shuttle pilot would poke his head through the door as Auerbach was boarding. A cabbie lectured him. Havlicek called Auerbach and told him: If you're not here, they're not retiring my number.

"You started here," his wife Dot told him. "Why do you want an intermediate stop before you quit?"

Auerbach made a final trip to New York, then called Brown. There would have to be ground rules, Auerbach told him, and he would have to be consulted on any personnel moves.

"I was afraid maybe I'd pick up the paper one day and find out I was traded," Auerbach told the *Boston Globe*'s John Powers.

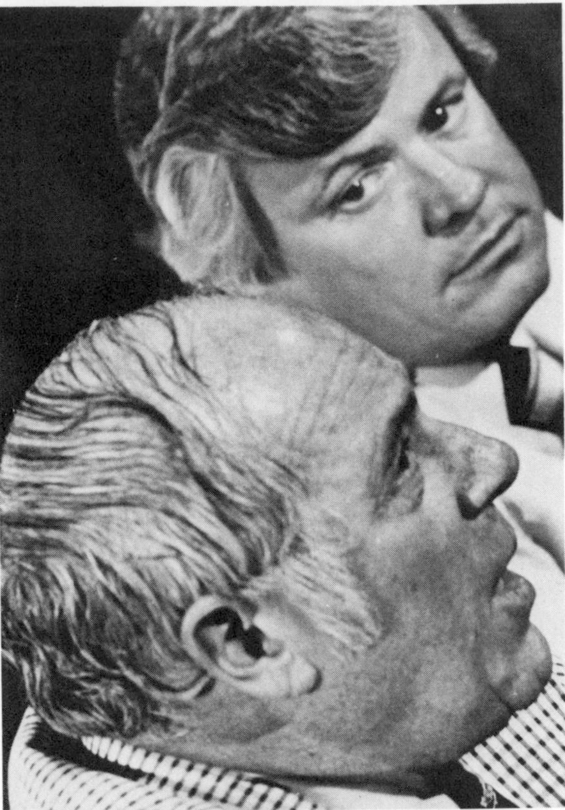

New board chairman John Y. Brown holds his first Boston press conference in July after he and Irv Levin swapped franchises. After meeting the press, Brown and Red Auerbach huddled in a discussion that reportedly was heated.

Chris Ford was obtained from Detroit for Earl Tatum in October and would average 15.6 points and 4.7 assists, tieing Tiny Archibald for the team's assist leadership.

LOWEST EBB IN CELTIC HISTORY

March 9, 1979, at Pontiac, Mich.

DETROIT PISTONS (160)

	Min.	FGA	FGM	FTA	FTM	Reb.	Ast.	Pts.
Carr	34	13	8	6	4	8	3	20
Douglas	21	10	7	3	1	0	3	15
Lanier	24	16	11	2	2	8	1	24
Long	24	14	7	2	2	3	0	16
Porter	37	18	12	8	6	3	25	30
Tyler	23	7	5	2	0	5	0	10
Tatum	20	9	5	5	4	5	4	14
Poquette	20	6	4	0	0	5	1	8
Wakefield	15	4	2	0	0	1	2	4
Brewer	11	2	2	0	0	7	0	4
Sheppard	11	8	6	7	3	2	0	15
Totals	240	108	69	35	22	57*	36	160

CELTICS (117)

	Min.	FGA	FGM	FTA	FTM	Reb.	Ast.	Pts.
McAdoo	28	20	7	7	5	5	0	19
Maxwell	31	14	9	5	4	10	4	22
Cowens	28	8	3	0	0	9	8	6
Ford	31	17	10	4	2	3	3	22
Archibald	23	12	4	5	4	0	3	12
Robey	26	5	2	0	0	5	1	4
Judkins	21	6	3	1	1	3	1	7
Rowe	21	9	4	0	0	5	0	8
Chaney	8	2	0	2	1	1	1	1
Stacom	13	9	5	0	0	2	1	10
Sanders	10	9	2	2	2	2	1	6
Totals	240	111	49	26	19	54*	23	117

Score by periods:	1	2	3	4	
Pistons:	42	36	36	46	–160
Celtics:	33	20	31	33	–117

* *Includes Team Rebounds:* Celtics 9, Pistons, 10.
Turnovers: Celtics 3, Pistons 5.
Field Goal Percentage: Celtics .441, Pistons .639.
Free Throw Percentage: Celtics .731, Pistons .629.
Referees: Joe Gushue, Bill Jones and Ken Falkner.
Attendance: 9,104.

Former Providence College star Marvin Barnes was waived in early February after 38 games in a Celtic uniform, his promise unfulfilled.

Still, it was Brown's club and trading was in his blood. The future governor of Kentucky enjoyed the idea of dreaming up a deal over breakfast and making it by lunchtime, the more Byzantine the better. Eighteen players had worn a Buffalo uniform that year, 19 the year before.

And before the 1978-79 season was done, the Boston roster also would become a revolving door, 18 players in all wearing Celtic Green.

Earl Tatum was acquired from Indiana in July and traded to Detroit for Chris Ford in October.

Dennis Awtrey, bought from Phoenix in October to replace Kunnert, was dealt to Seattle in January.

By Valentine's Day the Celtics had made six trades and signed three free agents—and done most of it within a whirlwind month from mid-January to mid-February—that left the fans reeling and the club in chaos.

Tom (Satch) Sanders:

"No, I'm not bitter about being fired as coach. But it disturbed me, no question; that's only human. I certainly didn't like it, but I understood it.

"I wasn't naive when I took the job. I knew the facts of pro coaching life. I knew the rules of the game, that 90-95 percent of coaches will be fired. It's in the stars from the day you're hired, at the end of the rainbow. It's just a question of when.

"But you should have some fair control over your coaching destiny, like picking your own players so you can sink or swim with your own people. I didn't have that opportunity, and that's what bothered me.

"First of all, when I took the head coaching job the year before, moving up to succeed Heinie at midseason, I knew it wasn't the right time to be coach of that team. But when a head coach is fired and the assistant is offered the job, the assistant really has no options.

"If he doesn't take it, the guy who does usually brings in his own assistant, which is understandable. So, knowing that's the way it works, an assistant must take the top job when it's offered whether he wants it or not—or say goodby to that team. By turning down the job you're saying you don't want to stay.

"So those were the circumstances when I replaced Tommy. Okay, we go through the remainder of the year and have plans all set for the upcoming season, good plans for the future. Then Levin and Brown get together and make their little deal as businessmen will.

"Hey, it was their teams, their money, their rights. But it put me at a large disadvantage as a coach. All our plans were down the drain, and it was back to square one with a new set of players, some of whom were not exactly overjoyed by the idea of coming to Boston.

"That was the hand I was dealt, and I had to play with it. And, predictably, it didn't play very well. We got off to a slow start. And when things aren't going well, somebody must pay the price—usually the coach. And that was me."

Knight was shipped to Indiana for center Rick Robey. Barnes was waived outright. Jo Jo White, who'd been MVP of the 1976 playoffs and a Celtic his whole career, was traded to Golden State for a draft choice at age 32.

Yet Brown saved the shocker for last.

After a Saturday night game at New York on February 10, John Y. and fiancee Phyllis George went to late dinner with Knick General Manager Eddie Donovan and Sonny Werblin. The former Miss America-turned-sportscaster had been telling her future husband how much she admired Knick center Bob McAdoo. All right, little lady—how about it, boys? How much for the Big Mac?

Two days later the deal was announced: McAdoo was a Celtic for three first-round draft choices Auerbach had been squirreling for Spring. McAdoo, of course, could not have been less complementary to Cowens in the frontcourt. He would play only 20 games as a Celtic before moving on.

Amid the confusion the Celtics plunged to their worst record ever, 29-53, and finished last in the Atlantic Division. They had lost 12 of their first 14 games, whereupon Tom (Satch) Sanders, after only 10 months on the job, was dismissed and Cowens made player-coach.

"There was turmoil in the front office," Cowens would recall. "Nobody really knew where we were going. And with most of our veterans gone, we were almost like an expansion club.

"I guess you'd call it a character builder," said Cowens, who announced his retirement as coach (but not as a player) at the team's breakup dinner the night of the final game. "Some people gutted it out the whole way, some quit."

Bob McAdoo became a Celtic in mid-February for a player to be named and three first-round draft choices that Red Auerbach had been saving for Spring to rebuild with.

Arnold Auerbach introduces Dave Cowens as the first player-coach in Celtic history——and the second coach nicknamed "Red" in Celtic history.

Phyllis George takes a closer look at fiancee John Y. Brown's Celtics. The former Miss America-turned-sportscaster told her future husband how much she admired Knick center Bob McAdoo and—*presto*—McAdoo became a Celtic even though he didn't fit into the team's scheme.

1979–80

Larry Bird signs a Celtic contract for a reported $3.25 million over five years, making him the highest-paid rookie in sports history. Looking on with delight are (left to right) new board chairman Harry Mangurian, Red Auerbach and new coach Bill Fitch—the Celtic brass who would take the wreckage of the last two seasons and rebuild it into the most stunning turnaround in NBA history.

He was given the locker between Dave Cowens and Don Chaney, the two oldest Celtics, and inside hung a fresh white jersey with No. 33 etched in green.

"This sure isn't training camp," Larry Bird sighed moments before the Celtics' 1979-80 opener with the Houston Rockets. "This is the big time."

He was about to bounce a basketball in Boston Garden for the first time, and the capacity crowd waited restlessly for a half-rookie, half-messiah.

"I'm glad the first one's at home," Bird said, "because I always feel better in front of my own fans."

And those fans gave him a standing ovation and released a dove when the Birdman was introduced, before he'd played a minute of professional basketball. After a year of speculation, while the 6-foot-9 Player of the Year finished his college career at Indiana State, he proved worth the wait—and the money, the reported $3.25 million over five years that made him the highest-paid rookie in sports history.

"We never had a corner man who can do the things he can," Red Auerbach decided, even before the season. "His intensity reminds me of Havlicek. Sanders was a great rebounder and Heinsohn a great shooter, but here's a guy who can do both of those things and is also a great passer with great hands. This kid is in their class at this point. He's in the Celtic mold as we used to know it."

And the club itself was quickly back in that role as well. The previous season had been an embarrassment, the players filing through a revolving door while loss followed loss. Now there was a new sole owner, a new coach, four new players and a revamped attitude. *No More Games,* promised the advertising campaign, showing a revitalized snarling Cowen.

John Y. Brown had sold his interest to partner Harry Mangurian (who was content to remain in the background while Auerbach handled the day-to-day affairs) and had gone off to become governor of Kentucky.

And Cowens had given up his player-coach double duty and again was concentrating on the pivot. He happily made way for Bill Fitch, who had been handling the Cleveland Cavaliers since their 1970-71 inception and was Coach of the Year in 1976 when the Celtics had won their last championship.

"I knew my relationship with Dave would be good," said Fitch, who would be voted Coach of the Year again at season's end (and Auerbach named Executive of the Year). "That's the last thing I worried about. I told him, 'You have the same rights you had as coach last season. You just don't have the responsibilities'."

The responsibilities of rebuilding from the wreckage of a 29-53 season were sobering enough. Fitch placed heavy emphasis on conditioning, preparation and pride of performance, and from the beginning the results were impressive. Boston won its first four games, 10 of 12, 20 of 26, and went on to claim the Atlantic Division title by two games over Philadelphia. The record was 61-21, the best in the league and an improvement of 32 games—the most stunning turnaround in NBA history. The 61 victories equaled the number the Celtics had mustered in the previous two seasons *combined.*

And home attendance kept pace—up 46 percent, with 30 sellouts in 39 Garden games along with two more full houses at Hartford.

Larry Bird adds a couple of rebounds to his team-leading 10.4 average, fourth best in the league.

Front row (left to right): Cedric (Cornbread) Maxwell, assistant coach K.C. Jones, board chairman Harry Mangurian, captain Dave Cowens, general manager Red Auerbach, coach Bill Fitch and Don Chaney. Back row: Gerald Henderson, M.L. Carr, Larry Bird, Rick Robey, Eric Fernsten, Jeff Judkins, Chris Ford, Nate Archibald and trainer Ray Melchiorre.

There were no empty seats from late January on, and the 14,546 average between Boston and Hartford was 1,100 a game better than the Celtics previous best and dwarfed attendance during their dynasty of the fifties and sixties.

The popularity wasn't confined to New England. Twenty-seven of the Celtics' 41 road games were sellouts, too.

The difference at the gate and on the floor was Bird, who was named Rookie of the Year and first-team all-league despite a broken index finger that hampered his shooting during the early season.

From the start he performed like a veteran, quickly shouldering the primary scoring and rebounding duties while delighting the crowd with the kind of instinctive passing that hadn't been seen around the Garden in half a dozen years—and never from a rookie forward.

"He has some skills coming into this league that a lot of guys never acquire," marveled Cowens. "He knows how to play within his game."

That game was extraordinarily well-rounded. Bird led the club in minutes (averaging 36 a game), points (21.6, 16th in league), rebounds (10.4, 10th in league) and steals (1.7), and dished out more assists (4.5) than any Celtic but playmaker Tiny Archibald (8.4), who ranked second in the NBA.

Bird's passing was unselfish—and contagious. "If you're open, he'll get you the ball," Cowens noted. "And he makes the other guys want to pass."

Overall, Bird gave Boston a dimension it had been lacking up front, providing a fine outside shot (he ranked third in the league in 3-point field goals), creating movement and opportunity with his passing, and freeing frontcourt partners Cowens and Cedric Maxwell to concentrate on their roles. Once again, there *were* roles.

Cowens, at 31, had been slowed by a succession of foot miseries, yet he was still the Celtics' "rock," as Fitch called him—intimidator, scorer, rebounder, court leader. "If he doesn't play," Fitch said, "we don't win."

Nate (Tiny) Archibald was the biggest Celtic surprise of all, the league's best comeback story. The 6-foot-1 playmaker once again was the slick ball handler and penetrator, and was second in the league in assists with an 8.4 average while averaging 14.1 points.

Cedric (Cornbread) Maxwell was the league's top marksman for the second straight season—improving his field-goal percentage to a lofty .609. That set a Celtic record as Maxwell joined Wilt Chamberlain and Kareem Abdul-Jabbar as the only players ever to shoot over .600 from the field in a season. Maxwell was the Celtics' second-leading scorer with a 16.9 average and their best offensive rebounder.

Maxwell, in his third season, had developed into a superb inside man, the team's best offensive rebounder, most frequent foul shooter, No. 2 scorer and the league's best marksman, 60.9 percent from the floor.

Chris Ford was the defensive guard with the long-range touch, second only to Seattle's Downtown Freddie Brown in 3-pointers. M.L. Carr, who'd been signed as a free agent (Bob McAdoo going to Detroit as compensation, with Boston also getting two first-round draft picks), became a loose and diligent sixth man in the Celtic tradition, banging up front or handling the ball in backcourt. Rick Robey would come off the bench and help the Celts win 21 of 27 in Cowen's absence.

Yet the most pleasant surprise of all was the re-emergence of Archibald as a playmaking force. Once again he was the ballhandler and penetrator who had revived the small man's role in the NBA. With Bird and Cowens, who'd always been a fine passer, complementing him up front, Archibald averaged 8.4 assists a game and doubled that figure 24 times.

He provided the cement that bonded the Celtics together again, and they responded by winning games in streaks—one of nine, two of seven and two of six games. Boston never lost more than two in a row and were 45-6 in games when they either had the lead or were tied at the end of the quarter.

The Celtics' 61 victories were their most since 1973, yet they could never put more than four games between themselves and the 76ers, who won 59. Head to head, the Celtics and Sixers were even—the Celts winning all three meetings in Boston, the 76ers sweeping the three in Philadelphia.

Boston's four-game sweep of Houston in the opening playoff series was merely a prelude. Philadelphia, which had upended Bos-

BIRD, CARR, FITCH MAKE CELTIC DEBUTS

October 12, 1979, at Boston Garden

CELTICS (114)

	Min.	*FGA*	*FGM*	*FTA*	*FTM*	*Reb.*	*Ast.*	*Pts.*
Maxwell	38	17	9	4	4	7	1	22
Bird	28	12	6	2	2	10	5	14
Cowens	30	13	5	1	1	13	0	11
Archibald	38	9	4	6	5	2	11	13
Ford	27	15	7**	2	2	3	2	17
Carr	30	10	6	3	3	4	3	15
Robey	16	6	4	3	3	2	1	11
Judkins	11	5	2	4	3	0	0	7
G. Henderson	9	5	1	0	0	1	2	2
Chaney	11	3	1	0	0	3	1	2
Fernstein	2	1	0	0	0	0	0	0
Totals	240	96	45	25	23	54*	26	114

HOUSTON ROCKETS (106)

	Min.	*FGA*	*FGM*	*FTA*	*FTM*	*Reb.*	*Ast.*	*Pts.*
Tomjanovich	26	9	4	1	0	5	1	8
Reid	33	10	5	3	1	4	3	11
Malone	39	17	10	14	11	16	2	31
T. Henderson	25	5	3	2	1	2	2	7
Murphy	30	15	5	3	2	1	3	12
Dunleavy	27	8	4	11	10	1	5	18
M. Jones	7	2	1	0	0	1	0	2
Barry	22	8	4**	0	0	1	0	9
White	14	0	0	2	2	2	1	2
D. Jones	17	7	3	0	0	3	0	6
Totals	240	81	39	36	27	60*	19	106

Score by periods:	1	2	3	4
Celtics	31	25	34	24—114
Rockets	29	24	27	26—106

**Includes Team Rebounds:* Celtics 9, Rockets 24.
**Ford and Barry each made one 3-point field goal.
Turnovers: Celtics 16, Rockets 22.
Field Goal Percentage: Celtics .469, Rockets .481.
Free Throw Percentage: Celtics .920, Rockets .750.
Referees: Jim Capers and Dick Bavetta.
Attendance: 15,320.

When free agent Michael Leon Carr signed with the Celtics in July, new teammate Dave Cowens dropped by to welcome him. The Celtics had to compensate the Pistons for Carr, and Red Auerbach engineered the cutest deal of his career by shipping unwanted Bob McAdoo to Detroit in payment—and extracting two first-round choices in the bargain.

ton in the Celtics' last playoff appearance three years earlier, was waiting in the wings with much the same cast.

And from the beginning the Celtics found themselves on the defensive, outmaneuvered up front and overpowered on the bench. The 76ers ripped away the homecourt advantage with a 96-93 victory in the opener and went on to eliminate Boston in five games, the Celtics' worst playoff showing since 1972.

"They stuck us in a microwave oven," Fitch would say, "stuck in the fork and then we were done."

The Sixers, who had been a high-octane, star-spangled shooting circus in 1977, had since learned to play grudging defense, and they shut down the Celtics with embarrassing efficiency, holding them to double figures in every game.

"I'd like to score 100 points some night," mused Fitch. "Just to see if that goldang scoreboard works that high."

The poise and inventiveness that had marked the Celtics' regular-season play simply never surfaced. Phladelphia knocked out Boston's frontcourt weapons one by one—Darryl Dawkins kept Cowens under wraps, Julius Erving neutralized Maxwell and Caldwell Jones, the reserve center, frustrated Bird.

It was role-playing at its purest, with 76ers coach Billy Cunningham unwrapping appropriate reserves as he needed them—Bobby Jones and Steve Mix in the frontcourt, Henry Bibby at guard. The thumping Boston took inside later prompted Fitch to trade for Golden State's 7-foot center Robert Parish and draft Minnesota's Kevin McHale, a 6-foot-11 banger. The value of a ready reserve had rarely been so obvious.

"We kept hoping that they'd take a day off," Fitch sighed. "I mean just be off one day and we'd be right back at them. But they never took off at all. They kept coming right at us."

The series turned in Game 3 at The Spectrum. With Jones shutting off access to Bird, the Celtic offense sputtered and came apart

General manager Red Auerbach salutes as the Celtics clinch the Atlantic Division title with a late-March victory over Cleveland at Boston Garden.

Coach Bill Fitch congratulates his players as the Celtics clinch the divisional title, climaxing their last-to-first comeback.

Gerald Henderson drives on Houston's Allen Leavell during the Celtics' 4-0 sweep of the Rockets in the Eastern semifinals. The rookie guard, signed as a free agent out of a minor league, was the fastest Celtic and a leaper who often teamed with M.L. Carr as the team's strongest defensive backcourt.

in a flurry of turnovers and indecision. With 17 seconds to tie the game at 99 and send it into overtime, Boston never got off a shot.

The Sixers went on to grab Game 4 and headed up to Boston to end it, 105-94. From 60-59 in the third game, the Celtics had never held the lead.

"We had the best record in the NBA," Bird fretted, "and they put us away like nothing. We never played one good game, not even the one we won."

It was baffling, and the weirdness even stalked the Celtics into their locker room, where a falling mirror opened a 14-stitch gash in Carr's back after Game 4.

It was a decidedly un-Celtic demise and there was an un-Celtic postscript to it. At their meeting to divide the playoff money, the team decided to vote trainer Ray Melchiorre only half a share. Owner Harry Mangurian would make up the missing half-share, but the incident was embarrassing and heightened the season's sour ending.

"I have to wonder at times what goes through the minds of these players who make such big money," a disappointed Auerbach would say. "But it's their decision and they'll have to live with their consciences."

Dave Cowens:

"Except for the ending, it was a very satisfying season.

"We had a new coach in Bill Fitch, and different people came in with different things to prove—me, Tiny, Bird. After a tough season, we needed to please the fans—and to please ourselves.

"We got off to a good start and things just snowballed. We surprised a lot of people; hell, we surprised ourselves. By midseason we knew we were good.

"I hadn't had so much fun in this sport in a long time."

Dave Cowens and referee Wally Rooney step in between 6-foot-6 M.L. Carr and 6-foot-11½ Darryl Dawkins in Game 5. Carr was playing with a 14-stitch gash in his back after a mirror had fallen on him in a freak locker-room accident following Game 4 at Philadelphia.

Larry Bird scores over Philadelphia's Julius Erving. Bird scored 33 points in Game 2, the Celtics' only victory in the Eastern finals.

1980–81

Larry Bird celebrates his first NBA championship with a cigar, Red Auerbach's victory trademark.

It was a classic instance of there being some very good news and some very bad news for the Celtics—with the good news prevailing.

The bad news was that Dave Cowens stunned the basketball world during the preseason by retiring just before his thirty-third birthday.

Cowens had concluded the previous season by happily stating that he "hadn't had so much fun in this sport in a long time." Now, on the threshold of a promising new season, the team leader revealed an agonizing decision in a Terre Haute, Indiana, motel as the Celtics toured the Midwest on an exhibition tour.

"It is unbelievably frustrating to remain in a rugged occupation with waning skills," he wrote in a farewell which he distributed to the media on October 1, citing "a highly weakened and worn out set of feet and ankles." (See Cowens' complete retirement statement on Pages 175-177.)

Cowens' departure (leaving Cedric Maxwell, six weeks shy of his twenty-fifth birthday, the ranking Celtic in seniority) was the second by a 10-season veteran in little more than a week. Ten days earlier Pete Maravich had quietly packed his bag a final time and left training camp at Hellenic College, saying he had lost his enthusiasm for the basketball grind—and leaving behind a void which underscored the lingering questions about the Boston backcourt.

The jolting double dose of bad news would seemingly outweigh any possible good news for the Celtics. Yet there would be overpowering good news: the Celts went on to win the NBA championship.

It was an improbability launched by vintage Auerbach maneuvering as the Celtic general manager dealt Boston's No. 1 slot in the entire draft to Golden State (so the Warriors could take Joe Barry Carroll, whom they coveted) in return for fourth-year center Robert Parish and Golden State's third spot in the first round (so the Celtics could take center-forward Kevin McHale, whom they preferred to Carroll or anyone else). The addition of the 7-foot Parish and the 6-10 McHale was clearly a master twin stroke in bolstering Boston's frontcourt when Auerbach executed it in June, but the Red-handed coup took on extraordinary import four months later when Cowens surprisingly quit.

Indeed, this would be a season replete with Celtic surprises—and revivals.

Front row (left to right): Chris Ford, Cedric Maxwell, president/general manager Red Auerback, coach Bill Fitch, board chairman Harry Mangurian, Larry Bird and Nate (Tiny) Archibald. Back row: assistant coach K. C. Jones, Wayne Kreklow, M. L. Carr, Rick Robey, Robert Parish, Kevin McHale, Eric Fernsten, Gerald Henderson, assistant coach Jimmy Rodgers and trainer Ray Melchiorre.

The first comeback came during the regular season. After falling six games behind the division-leading Philadelphia 76ers in December, the Celtics ran off a string of 25 victories in 26 games.

Comeback 1 was culminated in the regular-schedule finale, when the Celtics beat the 76ers, 98-94, at Boston Garden. The victory gave the Celts a tie for best record in the league at 62-20, the homecourt advantage throughout the playoffs, the Atlantic Division title and a reprieve from facing the 60-22 Milwaukee Bucks in the playoffs.

While Philadelphia played a mini-series against Indiana, the Celtics rested before sweeping the Chicago Bulls—who had won 10 in a row—four straight in the Eastern Conference semifinals.

The Celtics rested again as the Sixers concluded a grueling seven-game showdown with Don Nelson's Bucks to set up a Boston-Philadelphia Eastern final, the eighth time in 17 years the rivals met in post-season play.

"I've been around almost from the inception of that rivalry, and there's no love lost between the two franchises," Philadelphia coach Billy Cunningham told reporters. "I cannot imagine enjoying beating anybody more than the Boston Celtics."

Indeed, what was called the advent of the *real* NBA playoffs was destined to take on historic proportions. "It's cream against cream," advised Julius Erving, the Sixers' legend in his own time from the University of Massachusetts.

Game 1 at Boston saw Philadelphia erase a fourth-quarter Celtic rally. Riding Larry Bird's hot shooting (33 points), the Celts had bounced back from a nine-point deficit with less than three minutes remaining for a 104-103 lead with four seconds to play.

Boston's go-ahead points came on a pair of Bird free throws after a disputed Lionel Hollins foul. "I heard a whistle," Hollins said, "and when I found out the foul was on me I was so mad I decided this game wasn't over."

It wasn't. Andrew Toney drove the baseline with two seconds left and was tripped by Maxwell. Toney then coolly sank both free throws for a 105-104 Philly win.

"It was a dumb play," Maxwell said of his foul. "The most deflating thing is that I thought we had it won."

The Celtics had Game 2 won virtually from the opening tapoff. Aware that to lose the first two games of a series at home meant almost certain extinction, Boston used 34 points from Bird—23 in the first half—to fuel the series' only blowout, 118-99.

"We weren't moving our feet," Cunningham reviewed. "We were reaching and grabbing. We were completely outplayed."

The series moved to Philadelphia for Game 3, and the Celtics promptly suffered their 10th straight loss at the Spectrum, 110-100.

Bird had averaged 34 points in his previous three playoff outings, so Cunningham took Caldwell and Bobby Jones off the Celtic forward and replaced them with Erving. Bird was held to 22 points as the 76ers never trailed after the game's five-minute mark. Other testimony to Boston's offensive inadequacy was Parish's 1-for-14 performance as the Celtics as a team shot a season-low .378 from the floor.

"When people have talked about my defense, they've usually criticized it," Erving said. "It feels good to have people talking about my whole game."

Cedric Maxwell was voted MVP of the playoffs.

Versatile M. L. Carr continued to do an aggressive job on offense and defense at both forward and guard despite missing 41 early-season games with a broken bone in his right foot.

Robert Parish muscles past Philadelphia's Bobby Jones.

Nate (Tiny) Archibald drives past Philadelphia's Bobby Jones (24) as Julius Erving (6) moves in for a possible rebound during the Eastern finals.

The Celtics' losing streak in Philadelphia became known as the Spectrum Jinx after Game 4 as another late rally by Boston fell short, 107-105.

With Parish hampered by an aching back and by foul trouble, the Sixers built a 17-point halftime lead. But a 31-17 advantage in the third period pulled Boston within three, 82-79, before taking the lead once and tieing the game three times in the final quarter.

The Celtics' last gap was choked when Bobby Jones intercepted a halfcourt pass from Tiny Archibald intended for Bird with two seconds remaining. "The last seconds were chaos," Jones said. "All I could think of was Bird, all I could see was Bird as everything moved around me. I just got back there in time." And the Sixers led the series, 3-1.

Striving to be only the fourth team ever to rebound from that deficit in a seven-game NBA series, the Celtics took a giant step in that direction with a finally successful late rally in Game 5 at Boston.

The Celtics avoided elimination with a comeback that started with 1:51 to play and Philadelphia ahead, 109-103. During those last two minutes, coach Bill Fitch switched to defensive platooning to take advantage of the quickness of M. L. Carr and Gerald Henderson.

It worked. Without Maurice Cheeks, sidelined by sinus headaches, the 76ers were held scoreless in that final 1:51 as the Celtics poured in eight points for an eventual 111-109 victory.

But the game still came down to the final second. After Erving had fouled in the backcourt, Carr went to the line with that last second showing on the clock and sank the first free throw. But he intentionally missed the next two, hoping the time consumed by the rebound would end the game.

Darryl Dawkins rebounded the final miss and managed to call time, giving Philadelphia the ball at halfcourt. But Bobby Jones' inbound pass was intercepted by Parish to end it as the ancient Garden echoed in relief.

"We should have beat them," Cunningham said. "I believe very strongly that we're the better team. I think we should win."

The prospects for a Sixer win seemed likely with the Celtics coming back into the Spectrum pit for Game 6.

"Jinx? Psyched out?" Fitch responded to questions concerning his team failure to win there in two years. "Those thoughts are nowhere in my mind. Sure it would be tough to walk out of that damned building having lost again without wanting to dynamite the place. But we're not planning on bringing any dynamite."

Fitch might have longed for some explosives in the second quarter as the 76ers held a 17-point lead, which the Celtics managed to trim to nine at the half.

Then, with 8:10 remaining in the third quarter, the Celtics got their desperately needed spark. Maxwell, called for a loose-ball foul, stumbled out of bounds. On his way back inbounds, a Philadelphia fan taunted Maxwell, and the usually even-tempered Celtic plunged into the stands after his tormentor.

"It was an unfortunate incident," Maxwell said. "All I want to say is that it spurred our team on."

The result was an emotional, physical duration as the Celtics and Sixers fought with fierce determination. When Bird dumped in one three-point play, for example, five bodies including his own hit the floor.

Celtic determination was excessively fierce at times, according to Cunningham. "That was one of the poorest officiated games I've ever seen in the playoffs," the 76er coach said of the game in which referees Jack Madden and Paul Mihalak assessed 64 fouls.

With 14 seconds left, the Celtics clinched a trip back to Boston for a seventh game. Rookie Andrew Toney drove on rookie Kevin McHale, who blocked Toney's drive and recovered the ball in mid-air to seal the Celts' 100–98 win, their first at the Spectrum since January 20, 1979. "This is the most joyous occasion of my life," McHale said.

Appropriately, the rivals who had finished the regular schedule both at 62-20, splitting the regular season 3-3 and the playoffs 3-3, would decide the finale by the slimmest of margins. And—appropriately—the Celtics forged their 91-90 triumph with a comeback.

Philadelphia, which had built 11-point leads in the second and third quarters, held an 89–82 edge with 5:23 remaining in the game on an Erving reverse layup. It would be the final Sixer basket of the season.

With 4:34 left and the Celtics down by six, Fitch figured it was time for Boston's run. Bird and Parish re-entered the game, and the Celtic coach advised his bench: "We've got them right where we want them."

M. L. Carr duels Sixer Caldwell Jones on the boards during Eastern finals.

Larry Bird signals the celebration to begin at Boston Garden as the 76ers' desperate last-second attempt fails and the Celtics win the Eastern playoffs. That's Cedric Maxwell (31) and Chris Ford (42) at left, Gerald Henderson (43) at right.

CELTICS OUST 76ERS IN GAME 7

May 3, 1981, at Boston Garden

CELTICS (91)

	Min.	FGA	FGM	FTA	FTM	Reb.	Ast.	PF	Pts.
Maxwell	39	12	9	5	1	6	2	1	19
Bird	43	*17	8	7	6	11	5	1	23
Parish	30	17	7	2	2	8	0	5	16
Archibald	38	14	3	11	7	1	0	1	13
Ford	27	*10	3	2	1	4	3	2	7
Robey	14	5	1	4	2	7	1	1	4
Carr	17	6	1	0	0	3	2	2	2
McHale	15	4	0	2	1	2	2	3	1
Henderson	16	4	2	2	2	4	1	1	6
Fernsten	1	0	0	0	0	0	0	1	0
Totals	240	89	34	35	22	46	16	18	91

PHILADELPHIA 76ERS (90)

	Min.	FGA	FGM	FTA	FTM	Reb.	Ast.	PF	Pts.
Erving	37	21	11	2	1	8	5	5	23
C. Jones	47	7	6	0	0	15	2	1	12
Dawkins	27	12	7	3	2	4	0	5	16
Hollins	33	9	1	0	0	3	5	3	2
Cheeks	42	8	3	7	6	5	7	4	12
B. Jones	25	10	5	3	3	6	2	5	13
Toney	21	9	4	0	0	1	2	3	8
Mix	8	4	2	0	0	3	0	1	4
Totals	240	80	39	15	12	45	23	27	90

Score by periods:	1	2	3	4
Celtics	26	22	23	20—91
76ers	31	22	22	15—90

**3-Point Plays:* Bird 1-1, Ford 0-1.
Team Rebounds: Celtics 13, 76ers 8.
Turnovers: Celtics 13, 76ers 22.
Field Goal Percentage: Celtics .382, 76ers .488.
Free Throw Percentage: Celtics .629, 76ers .800.
Referees: Darell Garretson and Jake O'Donnell.
Attendance: 15,320.

Cedric Maxwell and Houston's Robert Reed vie for the basketball during NBA finals as (left to right) Bill Willoughby, Robert Parish and Moses Malone look on.

The Celtics completed their escape from the brink of defeat with defense, picking off passes, double-teaming the ball and rotating their defenses. "That's how you hold a team to one point in five minutes," McHale said.

The game-winner came after Dawkins missed inside. Bird stumbled out with the rebound, streaked down the left side, pulled up 17 feet from the basket, open on the break, and dropped in a banker with 1:03 on the clock.

Carr followed by intercepting another Erving pass (the Doctor would end up with six of Philly's 22 turnovers), but Gerald Henderson lost the ball to Hollins—setting up Cheeks with two shots from the free-throw line with 29 seconds left.

Carr approached Cheeks, patted him on the backside, and cautioned: "Don't choke." Cheeks could make only one shot.

Boston then ran down the clock until a Carr 22-footer deflected off the rim to Parish—who lost it to Bobby Jones with one second left.

With one last chance at redemption, the 76ers had Erving trying to slip open near the basket, but Jones' inbounds pass hit the top of the backboard. "Not even the Doctor could get that one," McHale noted. And the Celtics had their 91–90 victory.

"It is something that goes down in the annals of Celtic history," Maxwell said of the Celtics' comeback from the 1-3 deficit to earn another trip to the NBA finals. "It was the biggest thing in our lives."

"I really can't believe that Philly kept letting us back in," Bird said. "I never gave up. Too many people in life give up."

The excitement of the series with Philadelphia—which many were calling the de facto NBA final because of the weakness of the prospective Western entries—left the Celtics with the predictable letdown entering the anticlimactic championship series against the Houston Rockets, a 40–42 team that Boston had beaten 13 straight times in the previous two and a half seasons.

That flatness showed in Game 1 at Boston as the Celtics squeezed out a 98-95 victory on superior rebounding.

Bird (21 points, 18 rebounds) hit a 20-footer from the left baseline to put the Green ahead for good, 92-91, with 4:28 remaining. Boston improved that to 96-91, but a pair of Tom Henderson baskets trimmed it to 96-95. And after a Bird lay-in, Rudy Tomjanovich's three-pointer at the buzzer hit the back rim.

"We kept telling ourselves we were ready," Bird said. "But we weren't."

Boston was jolted back to reality in Game 2, as Moses Malone gathered 31 points and 15 rebounds to snap the Celtics' 14-game curse over Houston, 92-90. Despite the Celtics' overall poor play, they still had a chance to tie until Tiny Archibald's 19-foot jumper missed with two seconds left.

The team's inefficiency was enough to cause Fitch to crush a locker room blackboard at halftime, and the final score did little to improve his humor.

Game 3 was all Boston, though—94-71 at Houston—as the Celtics held the Rockets to 35 percent from the field, their lowest point total of the season and the lowest point total of any NBA finalist since 1955.

But Houston bounced back in Game 4, Rocket coach Del Harris using just six players—benching Calvin Murphy for the first time in his career—and a slow, scrappy style to even the series at 2-2 with a 91-86 victory. "If we didn't win this one," Harris said, "I felt this series was over."

As the series returned to Boston for Game 5, a verbal war developed.

"The Celtics aren't that good," Malone said. "They just get a lot of write-ups. I didn't even have that much respect for them after they beat us 14 straight times.

"I respect the old Celtics, the ones who won 13 championships. But I don't think that much of this club. I could take four guys off the streets of Petersburg (his Virginia hometown) and beat them."

The Celtics had heard enough. With Cornbread Maxwell leading the way with 28 points and 15 rebounds, Boston ran away from Houston, 109–80.

Back at the Summit for Game 6, the Celtics' 14th championship seemed iced with a 17-point lead early in the fourth quarter. But the Rockets staged one more surge, pulling within three with 2:05 to play.

But Bird (27 points), who had been shooting 29 percent for the series, took over, dumping in a baseline fade, a 20-footer and a three-pointer to put the Celtics up by six, 95-89, en route to their 102-91 coronation.

The newest generation in a bloodline of champions had won it.

"Those last few seconds, watching the clock wind down and knowing the great moment was about to happen, all I could feel was this great power rushing through my body, getting ready to explode," M.L. Carr said. "I don't think there could be another feeling in the world like this. Just call it complete happiness."

"When I saw Larry and Max slapping hands and hugging, that's when I realized with my heart what we had done," said Fitch, like his players savoring his first NBA championship. "They had all become part of that heritage that hangs in Boston Garden. They had been rewarded for hard work with a title, and there are a lot of fine players in the NBA who will never know what they feel."

Red Auerbach:

"When you think of the depths of adversity this team came from . . . And don't forget, not one guy on that court had a ring. Not one. If you had asked me two years ago about something like this, I couldn't have predicted it in a million years."

Robert Parish stuffs a basket over Houston's Robert Reed during NBA finals as Rocket Bill Willoughby (left) and Celtic Nate (Tiny) Archibald (7) move in for rebound that never came.

1981–82

Larry Bird had a ball while surpassing his brilliant sophomore season in almost all statistical categories. For the second consecutive year he was runnerup for the league's MVP trophy as he finished 10th in scoring (22.9), 7th in rebounding (10.9) and 5th in free-throw accuracy (.863) — and for the second straight season led NBA forwards in assists, averaging 5.7 per game. And frosting the cake, Bird was MVP of the NBA All-Star Game.

For the Fitch/Bird-era Celtics, it was their first taste of a task that had faced their predecessors so often—defending the NBA title.

The Celtics met the challenge during the regular season by compiling a 63-19 record, the best in the league and the second best in the club's history. It was also the first time in Celt annals (second time in league history) that a team won 60 or more games in each of three consecutive seasons.

In the course of capturing their third straight Atlantic Division title, the Celtics—seeking to be the first team since the 1967-68/1968-69 Celtics to win back-to-back NBA championships—never lost more than two consecutive games and authored a club record 18-game winning streak.

During that streak, which broke the record of 17 by the 1959-60 team, the Celtics were without Tiny Archibald for 11 games (stressed wrist ligaments), Larry Bird five games (broken cheek bone) and Chris Ford three games (back problems).

Still, the Celtics exhausted observers' superlatives during that streak, part of a strong final two months of the season that saw Boston win 25 of its last 29 games. The Celtics clinched the division crown April 9—coincidentally, the night the club hoisted alumnus Jo Jo White's No. 10 to the Garden rafters.

Some of the more dramatic regular-season moments came off the court, as the basketball world anxiously waited during the early season to see if Red Auerbach would complete yet another coup—the Celtic general manager this time was chasing Danny Ainge, Brigham Young's All-America guard.

Auerbach had surprised the league during the previous spring's draft when he selected Ainge in the second round (31st pick overall) since most had assumed that Ainge, having played two seasons in the Toronto Blue Jays' infield, had foregone basketball for a baseball career.

But after a four-month battle with the Blue Jays—including a trip to US District Court in New York which ruled that Ainge belonged to Toronto—the Celtics finally settled with the baseball team for a reported $800,000. Ainge signed with Boston November 27 for an estimated $300,000 a year for five years. He was activated December 9 as the Celtics made roster room by selling second-round pick Tracy Jackson, another guard, to the Chicago Bulls.

"Isn't it unbelievable that Red has done it again?" Paul Westphal said after Auerbach's latest maneuver. "It's like Willie Sutton walking down the street with cops all around. They know he's going to steal something, but they don't do anything about it."

M. L. Carr was happy to be back after missing 26 early-season games with a hairline fracture of his right leg. It was the second straight season that a broken bone sidlined Carr; he missed 41 games in early 1980-81 with a fractured right instep. That's Cedric Maxwell (top) with Carr as they exercise before a game.

Boston entered the Eastern Conference semifinal series against the Washington Bullets—0-6 vs. Boston during the regular season—with cautious optimism, most of the cautiousness coming from Bill Fitch.

"Washington looks as good as anybody I've seen," the coach said of the 43-39 Bullets. "Each game is going to be a doggone tough encounter."

Fitch would ultimately prove correct, but the series opener in Boston made his warning seem unnecessary. The two-week layoff since clinching the division title apparently failed to dull the Celts as they eased past the Bullets, 109-91.

In doing so, the Celtics survived a 3-for-10 showing by Bird and a 6-for-16 performance by Robert Parish—thanks in significant part to Rick Robey. The backup center replaced Parish late in the third quarter and never came out, contributing 10 points and creditable defense. "If I had a game ball to give," Fitch advised, "I'd give it to Robey."

Thoughts of an easy series evaporated during Game 2 at the Garden. Frank Johnson capped a Bullet comeback—aided by sloppy Celtic play—with a 29-foot three-point shot with three seconds left that swished through rim and strings for a 103-102 Washington victory.

The Celtics had entered the second half leading 51-44, but self-destructed during the third quarter. The Bullets, despite shooting 13 for 32, hustled and fought for second and third shots, turning 12 offensive rebounds into 20 points. "I could rip a board apart right now," Fitch said. "No one can tell me you've got your head in the ballgame if you let people rebound like that."

Three days later Boston won the battle of the boards, outmuscling the Bullets, 92-83, at Landover in a game that would give the duration of the series a physical flavor.

The war of elbows, shoves and bumping, spearheaded on the Boston side by Parish (25 points, 13 rebounds), led to the inevitable in the closing minutes. Washington's Rick Mahorn fired the ball at the back of Gerald Henderson's head, igniting a near-brawl that included Robey grabbing Jim Chones by the throat, Kevin McHale and Parish confronting Mahorn, and Charles Bradley exchanging threats with fellow rookie Jeff Ruland.

"All that scene reminded me of was a hockey game," Johnson said.

Game 4 at the Capital Centre was no-less hard fought, but this time the intensity was prevented from boiling over during a simmering 103-99 Boston overtime victory.

Trailing 60-50 midway through the third period, the Celtics rallied to catch up, 75-75, in the fourth quarter, the first of seven deadlocks during the period.

With 39 seconds left in regulation and Boston down 91-89, McHale missed two free throws and on the ensuing rebound scramble Parish (28 points, 15 rebounds) fouled out. But Mahorn missed the subsequent free throw, teammate Greg Ballard grabbed the rebound, fell, and gave the ball back to the Celtics. Cedric Maxwell sank two free throws 14 seconds later, and when Spencer Haywood missed a runner with three seconds to go, the game went into overtime.

That overtime belonged to McHale, who scored six points, and to Maxwell, who controlled the boards. The Celtics went ahead to stay, 98-97, on a Maxwell foul shot at 1:15.

The Celts clinched the series in Game 5 back in Boston—but needed two overtimes to do it.

Gerald Henderson proved an invaluable third guard, and along with Kevin McHale was the only Celtics to play in all 82 regular-season games. Henderson started 31 of them, a key replacement when injuries sidelined Nate Archibald and Chris Ford during the season's second half.

Tiny Archibald dealt a career-high 23 assists during a February game against Denver and the 12-season veteran passed the 15,000-point career mark at midseason. But the playmaker dislocated a shoulder during Game 3 of the Eastern finals and was lost the remainder of the series.

Kevin McHale signalled Boston Garden fans that the Celtics were still No. 1 after eliminating Washington from the playoffs in a double-overtime thriller. But the Celts would soon tumble from their No. 1 perch, dethroned by Philadelphia in the next round of the playoffs.

The Celtics owned an 18-point lead late in the third quarter and still had the momentum and an 11-point edge with 4:52 left in regulation. Then Robey and Johnson became embroiled in an argument, the benches emptied and the game was delayed five minutes. After that, the remainder of regulation belonged to the Bullets. "We lost all our momentum after the fight," Fitch said.

Ruland's relentless play (33 points, 13 rebounds) inside and three three-point bombs by Johnson in the final 2:52 of regulation tied it, 106-106.

Washington maintained control in the first overtime, Mahorn's foul-line jumper with 28 seconds left giving the Bullets a 119-116 edge. "I thought we had them put away," said coach Gene Shue.

An Archibald foul shot got it down by one seven seconds later, and the Celtics were forced to foul. Ruland was selected, but it was a non-shooting foul, giving the Bullets an inbounds pass.

Ballard inbounded to Johnson, and he was smothered by Bird, who forced a jump ball. Bird batted the tap to Archibald, who drove for a wild, off-balance shot. The ball ricocheted off the glass, but McHale was there to gently lay it in to force the second OT. "Quite a clever pass by Tiny," Fitch would say. "Really fooled them."

In the second overtime, the Celtics were hit with four quick foul calls as the Bullets built a 125-121 lead. Fitch then replaced Bird and Archibald in the backcourt with Henderson and M. L. Carr.

Maxwell (26 points) hit a leaner, and McHale connected on a jump hook to tie. And after a Johnson foul shot, Henderson drove for a layup that put Boston up to stay, 127-126, en route to a 131-126 victory. "I don't call these the playoffs," Fitch said. "I call this survival."

The next test of survival would come in what was seemingly becoming a rite of spring—an Eastern Conference final pitting the Celtics against the Philadelphia 76ers, the ninth time in 18 seasons, the fourth in six, that the rivals had met in the playoffs.

The prospects of another classic series seemed remote, however, after Game 1 in Boston as the Celtics shamed the Sixers, 121-81.

Led by Bird (24 points, 15 rebounds, 10 assists), the Celtics broke out of the slowdown game predominant during the Washington series and gleefully ran over Philadelphia in what would become known as the Mother's Day Massacre.

Down by 17 at the half, the Sixers unraveled in the third quarter, shooting 5-for-27. The Boston shelling continued into the fourth period, the Celtics at one time flaunting a 110-62 cushion to the delight of Garden fans.

"You have two choices," Philadelphia coach Billy Cunningham said. "You can cry or you can laugh. And I cried out there on the court."

The defeat included the 76ers' lowest playoff point total ever and was their most lopsided loss to Boston ever.

"It's a game Bill Fitch would like to get into a bottle and save," Cunningham said. "We'd just like to throw the bottle away."

"Mama said there'd be days like this," Earl Cureton said. "But not on Mother's Day. It felt disgusting just to be out there."

If the game lacked drama, it was replete with controversy, the Sixers charging that the Celtics had run up the score. Particularly galling to Philadelphia was Chris Ford's cross-court alley-oop pass to Bradley, who slammed home a dunk with 1:06 remaining.

"They're lucky nobody took them apart for pulling that stuff," Steve Mix said.

"I've known Steve Mix since 1968, when he was playing for Toledo," Fitch responded. "I had a 5-10 player who could clean his clock then, so I'm not worried about him taking us apart now."

"The only 5-10 guy in Toledo was Bill Fitch," Mix countered.

Philadelphia turned its anger into results in Game 2, avenging the humiliation with a 121-113 reprisal at the Garden.

Despite early mental mistakes and a flurry of turnovers, the Celtics trailed by just three points with six minutes to play. Then the Sixers' quiet man, Caldwell Jones, hit seven of his last eight shots for a 113-108 lead. Andrew Toney (30 points) sealed the triumph with two more baskets, and the teams were even at 1-1.

"It is going to be a hell of a series," Cunningham said.

A minute into Game 3 in Philadelphia, Boston suffered another setback—Archibald hitting the floor hard while diving for a loose ball, dislocating a shoulder and ultimately being sidelined for the remainder of the series. (Other Game 3 casualties were Ainge with six stitches in his mouth, Robey with four in an elbow.)

Without Archibald the Celtic attack sputtered, Philadelphia holding a 14-point lead early in the fourth quarter. The Celts rallied, though, coming close enough to have four chances to tie in the final 20 seconds.

Bird drove the right side but tossed his 22-footer long. Maxwell grabbed the rebound and arched a shot over Caldwell Jones from three feet out. The ball rolled in and out, Cornbread grabbed the rebound for another shot but was blocked by Julius Erving. Maxwell got the ball yet again and was ready to shoot when Maurice Cheeks stepped in, stripped the ball from Maxwell and dribbled out of the pack as the buzzer sounded—Philadelphia 99, Boston 97.

"I just closed my eyes when Maxwell got the ball," Cunningham said.

An astonished Fitch remained kneeling on a towel in front of the bench for nearly a minute while Maxwell stayed stretched out under the basket.

"Either you're a hero or you're Charlie Brown," Maxwell said, "and I played the Charlie Brown role today. At that moment I felt death, like there was a death in the family. It felt like death."

Still suffering without Archibald, the Celtics died a little more in Game 4 at the Spectrum as Toney overran the Boston backcourt for 39 points to spark the 76ers to a 119-94 victory—and their third 3-1 playoff advantage over the Celtics in three years. "I've never seen anyone his size dominate a game the way he did," Ainge said of the 6-3 Toney.

And now the Celtics had to try to be the fifth team in NBA history to overcome a 3-1 series deficit—and repeat the 1980-81 Celtics' feat against the Sixers.

"Well, one thing we have going for us is we know it can be done," Chris Ford said. "Because we did it."

"We're back in the coffin again," Kevin McHale said. "But at least we know it isn't shut."

Boston took a step toward recovery with a convincing 114-85 victory in Game 5 at the Garden.

Using the two days between games to regroup from Archibald's loss, the Celtics swarmed defensively, forcing the Sixers to shoot just .295 from the field in the first half and double-teaming (chiefly by Ainge and Carr) limited Toney to 18 points for the game.

Offensively, Boston varied its game inside and outside, Parish netting 26, Bird 20 and Maxwell 15.

Danny Ainge joined the Celtics in late November, giving up major league baseball for a pro basketball career.

CELTICS LOSE GAME 7 SHOWDOWN—AND TITLE

May 23, 1982, at Boston

CELTICS (106)

	Min.	FGA	FGM	FTA	FTM	Reb.	Ast.	PF	Pts.
Maxwell	26	6	3	3	1	5	0	4	7
Bird	44	18	7	8	6	11	9	4	20
Parish	42	21	8	8	7	14	0	2	23
Carr	19	8	3	1	1	2	3	2	7
Henderson	37	12*	5	3	1	4	7	5	11
McHale	31	15	9	5	2	6	2	5	20
Ainge	28	7*	4	8	7	2	2	5	17
Ford	7	1	0	0	0	1	0	0	0
Robey	4	1	0	0	0	0	0	1	0
Bradley	1	0	0	0	0	0	0	0	0
Fernsten	1	0	0	2	1	1	0	0	1
Totals	240	89	39	38	26	46	23	28	106

PHILADELPHIA 76ERS (120)

	Min.	FGA	FGM	FTA	FTM	Reb.	Ast.	PF	Pts.
Erving	42	21	10	9	9	4	5	4	29
B. Jones	31	11	4	10	9	4	2	4	17
C. Jones	38	7	3	0	0	10	0	4	6
Cheeks	33	15	8	4	3	2	11	5	19
Toney	43	23*	14	8	6	3	6	4	34
Dawkins	13	4	3	0	0	4	0	5	6
Bantom	19	3	1	0	0	6	0	5	2
Richardson	19	4	1	0	0	2	0	1	2
Edwards	1	1*	1	2	2	0	0	0	5
Cureton	1	1	0	0	0	0	1	1	0
Totals	240	90	45	33	29	35	25	33	120

Score by periods:	1	2	3	4
Celtics	28	21	22	35—106
76ers	30	22	31	37—120

**3-Point Shots:* Ainge 2-3, Henderson 0-1, Edwards 1-1, Toney 0-1.
Team Rebounds: Celtics 15, 76ers 15.
Turnovers: Celtics 22, 76ers 15.
Field Goal Percentage: Celtics .438, 76ers .500.
Free Throw Percentage: Celtics .684, 76ers .879.
Referees: Darell Garretson and Jack Madden.
Attendance: 15,320.

An NBA first team All-Star for the second straight season, Larry Bird led Celtic scorers with a 21.2-point average during the regular season, 21.9 in the playoffs — including a fat 26.7 mark (plus a 13.4 rebound average) in the crucial seven-game Eastern finals against Philadelphia.

Jo Jo White's No. 10 joined the numerals of other Celtic greats in the Garden Rafters — his family and former teammates participating in the April ceremony.

Now the 76ers grappled with the ghosts of playoffs past—the Garden crowd's chant of "See you Sunday" (the day of Game 7 if needed) ringing in their ears.

"Last year?" Darryl Dawkins said. "I try not to remember that. Who wants to remember that?"

"Every member of this team who was here last year (10 of the 12) remembers what happened," Earl Cureton said. "You don't forget something like that."

The Celtics forced that seventh game with an 88-75 victory at the Spectrum.

The Sixers appeared headed for the NBA finals early in the game, their fast break delivering and their defense effective enough to weave a 15-point lead in the first quarter.

Led by Ford (4-for-4), Boston closed to 48-42 at halftime. And in the second half, Philadelphia played the lowest-scoring 24 minutes (27 points) in the history of the 24-second clock, including a final 12 minutes that tied the worst playoff fourth quarter (11 points) in NBA history.

With less than 10 minutes to play and trailing 67-61, Fitch had no choice but to put Parish, saddled with five fouls, back in the game. The 7-foot center responded by dominating the boards and leading the offense as Philadelphia's shots airballed and bounded everywhere but through the hoop. Parish's turnaround with 7:58 remaining gave Boston the lead for good, 69-67.

Meanwhile, in Boston, the 29,671 at Fenway Park to watch the Red Sox—many of the fans with radios, some with portable televisions—had been cheering every Celtic basket in the fourth period, the baseball game halted twice because of the noise.

When it was over in Philadelphia, the 76ers rushed off the court to the jeers, taunts and boos of the frustrated Spectrum crowd.

"And now," McHale said, "we've got both legs out of the coffin—and they're climbing in."

But the Sixers finally shed the "chokers" image in the Game 7 showdown at the Garden, pulling away from the Celtics and never looking back in their 120-106 victory.

This time it was the 76ers who played with ferocity. Toney (34 points) and Erving (29 points) soared as the Celtics ran out of comebacks in the final stretch. Boston had chipped a 64-54 deficit down to two points before the Sixers bolted to a 70-62 lead at 4:45 of the third quarter, simply taking charge thereafter.

"You wonder if we lost this one by using so much emotion in winning the fifth and sixth games," Maxwell submitted. "You win those, you're looking forward to coming home, the crowd's at the airport. Basically, I think we celebrated too soon."

"It hurts," explained Bird, 7-for-18 from the floor. "It hurts more than anything. It hasn't hit me yet. Tomorrow you wake up and get ready to go to practice. There won't be any practice. There will be no repeating."

Red Auerbach:

"I'm proud of this ballclub. I didn't lose sight of the fact that we won 63 games and that anything can happen in one game or one series. Anyway, nobody can say we lose the big one. We've won too many of them."

THE MEMORIES

"As far as basketball is concerned, the greatest thing you can say is that you played for the Boston Celtics."

—Easy Ed Macauley

"How bad were we that first season? Well, one of the more frustrating losses came in a game at St. Louis when we blew a six-point lead in the final 24 seconds.

"I called a timeout with 26 seconds left and said, 'OK, boys, you know the situation: We have the ball and a six-point lead. The only way we can lose is for Connors to get the ball.'

"Everyone in the huddle starts laughing, and I said I was serious. I then explained very clearly that Chuck Connors was not *to get the basketball.*

"So we take the ball out under the St. Louis basket, and what happens? All four of my men on the floor drop back and the pass-in is weak. It's intercepted for a quick basket.

"Now we're up by four points with 23 seconds left. We manage to put the ball in play to one of our own guys this time and pass it around a few times before it's stolen. Swish!

"Now we're ahead by two points with about 10 seconds left and no timeouts. We have the ball, but St. Louis is really pressing now and there's only one of our people open—Connors.

"So the pass goes to him and he starts dribbling with that high dribble of his. Then he trips, loses the ball, and grabs the leg of the St. Louis player who has recovered the ball and is throwing up a desperation shot to beat the clock.

"As the ball goes through the hoop to tie the game, the referee calls the foul on Connors. St. Louis makes the free throw and we lose by a point.

"Mad? I fined Connors $200 on the spot, but it wasn't his fault. He just did what came natural to him—he loused up."

John (Honey) Russell

KEVIN (CHUCK) CONNORS, 1946-47 and 1947-48:

"Anyone who knows anything about the Boston Celtics knows that when they started they were the strongest team in the league—in the cellar holding everyone else up. Yes, sir, we were the *worst*.

"Well, although we weren't good we were versatile. Some of us played baseball. I was a first baseman and played a little for the Dodgers and the Cubs, and Johnny Simmons later played some outfield for the Washington Senators. Al Brightman and Eddie Ehlers played triple-A ball, I believe—Ehlers for the Yankees' Newark farm, a powerhouse that many people felt was a better team than some clubs in the majors. And one day a couple of NFL players from the Boston Yanks (now the Baltimore Colts), Hal Crisler and Bob Eliason, dropped by practice and ended up playing a couple of games for us.

"So we had some baseball and football talent. It was *basketball* that gave us problems. We weren't much of a basketball team, and I wasn't much of a basketball player. In fact, I'm positive my greatest value to the Celtics was as an after-dinner speaker. It seems to me I did more public speaking for the team than playing that first season.

"The Celtics were trying to get established, so they sent me all over New England on speaking engagements. I'd pick up $25 or $50 an appearance, whatever the traffic would bear. Once I came back from an engagement and told the other players, 'If you guys would only win a few games I could get rich.' If we'd had a good team, I would have owned the town.

"Instead, I spent half the time apologizing for the team. When I wasn't apologizing, I was doing things like 'Casey at the Bat' and 'Face on the Bar Room Floor.' I did 'Casey' at the Boston Baseball Writers Dinner that first winter, and Ted Williams was there too after winning the 1946 American League MVP Award. Ted was very kind to me and laughed his head off at my rendition. Afterward, he said to me, 'Kid, I don't know what kind of a basketball player you are, but you ought to give it up and be an actor.'

"Ted always had a great eye for talent, didn't he? Seriously, I'll never forget that quote. I've always thought Ted was terrific, and one ambition I had was to make the story of Ted Williams' life. I wanted to play the lead role.

"So doing those after-dinner speeches was my raison d'etre. Howie McHugh was the Celtics' public relations man then, in fact their PR guy from the time I began until his recent retirement as senior man in NBA service—the only one with unbroken service with the same team since day one of the league. He's one of the really marvelous human beings in the world, totally unique in his character, totally unique in his dedication, and one hell of a guy.

"We got along great together. The team was having problems at the gate, so Howie and I contrived to spread some goodwill for the club. I was always thinking up stunts—I loved that sort of thing—and Howie guided me along.

"Mostly, there were speaking dates and radio appearances—there was no TV in Boston then. And if the team had been good I would have made my living in Boston. But the team was bad, and so like everyone else I got swept up and out eventually. I had to come to Hollywood to make it. You know, before Hollywood I thought Eggs Benedict was a baseball player some place.

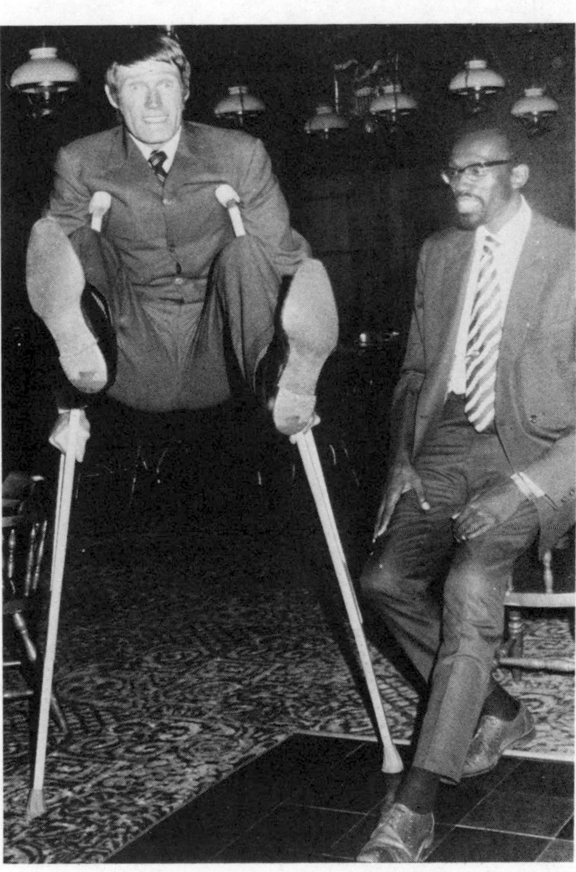

"But I miss Boston and the Celtics, and Boston Garden and Boston Arena. I have some great memories back there.

"Yes, like the first home game ever—at the old Arena against Chicago, I believe. During warmups I took a set shot—a harmless set shot—and *crash*, the glass backboard shattered. Glass backboards were just coming into prominence in those days, and these new ones at the Arena were made very poorly and just shattered.

"The Arena didn't have any replacements, so they had to send a pickup truck across town to get one at the Garden, where Gene Autry's Rodeo was packing them in. Well, Howie McHugh was there and tells how the Garden's backboards were stored behind the pen where the Brahma bulls were kept, and nobody was fool enough to challenge the bulls for them.

"Meanwhile, back at the Arena, my good friend John Kiley was wearing out the organ and we were having all sorts of shooting contests to keep what fans there were from walking out.

"Finally, at the Garden, Howie found two drunken cowboys and slipped them a couple of bucks to go into the pen, dodge the bulls, and get a glass backboard out. If he hadn't, we might still be waiting at the Arena. A Boston writer sent me some old clippings recently, and they indicate the game was delayed a little over an hour. But it seemed an eternity. Ask John Kiley. He played so long his fingers may still be numb.

"Those clippings also indicate we lost by two points that night, and that I scored eight points—the third high Celtic behind Johnny Simmons and Wyndol Gray, who both were in the low teens. And Jack Barry, bless him, wrote in his *Globe* story, 'Kevin Connors stood out for the Celtics.' Ahem.

"Eight points were an improvement. In our very first league game a few nights earlier on the road against Providence, I scored seven, according to the clips. Red Wallace was our top scorer with nine. A lot of games we didn't have anyone in double figures, but you have to remember that in those days you were a sensation if you scored 20 points in a game.

"The clippings also indicate it wasn't long before I started hitting double figures. In the Celtics' first victory ever—over Toronto at Boston Garden, after five or six losses—the box score indicates Kevin Joseph Connors scored 11 points, second high Celtic behind Wyndol Gray's 13. Now how about *that?*

"Honey Russell, our coach, probably wasn't impressed, though. After I broke that glass backboard opening night, from then on he hated me. He thought I ruined his career before the season started.

"Honey used to tell a story about how he spotted one of his players strolling through a hotel lobby that first season carrying a book. He asked the name of the book, and the player said it was Shakespeare. 'Shakespeare!' Honey roared. 'What kind of players are they giving me, anyway?'

"He was referring to me, and of course what Honey didn't add was that he was the guy who had sent me to himself. He'd been my college coach at Seton Hall. But, yes, I was interested in the theater and acting even as a Celtic.

"Actually, when you're playing professional sports, you're in show business, too. You're out there to please the crowd and a little showmanship doesn't hurt. And any time a batter is called out on strikes, he does plenty of acting. First he tries to convince the umpire he was wrong. And failing that, when he returns to the bench he does his best to convince his manager that the ump is a lunkhead and was dead wrong.

"So, sure, I always played to the crowd, whether it was basketball or baseball. Once, while playing baseball in Montreal, I got down on my hands and knees and prayed at bat.

"Well, the Celtics were a lot of fun, but we couldn't win many basketball games. So changes had to be made. And when I came back for the '47-'48 season, I played a few games and was unceremoniously dumped. Honey threw me out to pasture.

"Actually, baseball was my game; basketball was something I just lucked into. Besides my time with the Dodgers (1949) and Cubs (1951), I spent a lot of time in triple-A ball with the Dodgers' top farm at Montreal and the Cubs' top farm at Los Angeles, long before expansion made them National League towns. In fact, it was playing for the old Los Angeles Angels in the Pacific Coast League that put me near the Hollywood studios and got me started in movies.

"Well, baseball and basketball didn't mix. Definitely not. I had to leave the Celtics in late February or early March for spring training and figured I was in great shape because I had been running on the boards all winter. But because of that I found my legs actually were much tougher to get into condition. I think my baseball legs were bothered very much by basketball.

"Yes, they called me Chuck when I started playing baseball because they thought Kevin was effeminate. But when I got into the movies, I wanted to get back my real name. However, Warner Brothers studio wouldn't let me. They said, 'We bought the baseball hero Chuck Connors and we're not going to do anything to disguise him.'

"Yes, it was always my ambition to become an actor. Maybe that was the reason I never turned out to be a great basketball or baseball player. If I could have made it as big as a Bill Russell or a Carl Yastrzemski or a Bobby Orr, I would rather have become a sports star than a show business celebrity. It's more realistic to make it in sports. And in show business, they can make you or break you overnight.

"But I was no Yastrzemski or Orr—and certainly no Russell. Ask anyone who saw me play for the Celtics.

"Still, I often think back to my time with the Celtics and recall how much I enjoyed it—as bad as we were. I'm proud that I was a Celtic, that I was in on the ground floor of something that's become an institution. I still follow the Celtics with great interest. They'll always be my basketball team."

"Red Auerbach was the best coach in the history of professional sports."

Bill Russell

*ARNOLD (RED) AUERBACH, 1950-51 through—**

"When I came to Boston, it was hostile to basketball. Everything was hockey first—the Garden, the town, the whole region. Whatever interest there was in basketball was mostly for Holy Cross, which had won the NCAA Tourney a few years earlier, the only New England team ever to do it. Other than that it was a hockey area.

"So our biggest problem immediately was to educate the public about basketball in general and *professional* basketball in particular. I knocked myself out during the preseason. We played exhibition games throughout the region, giving clinics the morning of the game wherever we were playing.

"I also was having trouble with the press and fans about the Celtics using local college heroes. Most thought the pros were nothing, but that anyone who had played for Holy Cross was the greatest thing since 7-Up. The Celtics had signed some Holy Cross people in the seasons before I arrived—guys like George Kaftan, Dermie O'Connell and Joe Mullaney—and none had exactly set the league on fire. Neither had two or three hotshots from Harvard or an All-America from Yale who had been a Greater Boston schoolboy sensation, Tony Lavelli.

"That's how I got into hot water in my very first press conference in Boston. The writers and broadcasters, most of whom didn't know a basketball from a head of cabbage, were badgering me about why Lavelli didn't fit into my plans and why we hadn't drafted the great Bob Cousy a few days before. Finally, I turned to Walter Brown and said loud enough for all to hear: 'Walter, am I supposed to win or am I supposed to worry about the local yokels and please these guys?' I'm *still* hearing about that one.

"Well, we ended up getting Cooz soon thereafter, and the first thing I did was arrange for a scrimmage with Holy Cross. I was sick of hearing everyone say, 'Hey, Holy Cross would bury you.' I decided

*Coach, 1950-51 through 1965-66; general manager, 1964-65 through present; president, 1970-71 through present.

to put that to rest once and for all. We beat them by about 40 points in front of all writers, and that stopped all that nonsense.

"I did a similar thing throughout northern New England. We went on an exhibition tour and played all these local teams that the townies thought were so damn good—you know, the ones that had the old high school heroes and maybe one or two guys who had starred in small colleges. We'd go in and rip them by 50–60 points and they got the message. Afterward, guys in those towns—in New Hampshire, Maine and Vermont as well around Massachusetts—would say to me, 'Gee, we actually thought we could beat you guys.'

"Part of the reason for that was that in the past pro teams had come through those towns and kept the score down, beating the locals by only four or five points. They wanted to be invited back. Well, that wasn't my style. And I didn't give a damn about coming back. I just wanted to establish a fact and make a point about the superiority of the NBA, that it had the best basketball players in the world.

"But I liked New England and thought it could be a good basketball area with a lot of work, and I was determined.

"We made progress from the start on the court, too. We had a winning record and made the playoffs that first season I got there. But it took six seasons to win our first championship.

"Before Russell joined us for that first title, I had scorers—Cousy, Sharman, guys who could put the ball in the hole—but you can't win without the ball. I needed a guy to get me the ball, something Macauley couldn't do. Ed was a shooting center, weak on defense because he weighed only 180 pounds. He took a beating and would run out of gas.

"So I wanted somebody bigger—somebody who could get me the ball and also could get me the tap. We had jump balls in those days, and they were very important. If you got the four of them, you're talking about a potential—realistically—of say six points, and that's maybe the difference in the game. Russell was a great, great rebounder, and I knew he was the guy we desperately needed. And, of course, he turned out to be all I expected and more—the greatest of them all.

"The only reason Russ says he's the best basketball player who ever lived is because I've been saying it for so long he finally believes it. And it's true. I've known Wilt Chamberlain since he was a kid and have never knocked his ability. He was a great athlete and a great basketball player. But Russell was *better*. Russell was better because he played more with his head and was better motivated, and he had a bigger heart.

"Before key games, Russell would get a little uptight, and he'd vomit; he'd play the game in advance, over and over in his mind. Not that Wilt wasn't up for games; he was, but not to the point Russ was.

"Russell had the game down to a science. Not only was he the greatest rebounder ever, but he had this enormous ability to intimidate because of his uncanny skill to block shots. He had every shooter in the league psyched.

"Even considering the greatness of Russell, though, we never maintained two sets of standards like many clubs do when they're dealing with superstars. Sure, I tried to be understanding about some little things, but I did that with *all* the guys.

"Russell never missed a practice without asking in advance. And those stories of him loafing in practice have gotten out of hand. He never sat on the sidelines and read a newspaper—not while *I* was coach. I'd have gone bananas. Maybe he did that when he was coach, I don't know; but I wouldn't have stood for any player doing that, even the great Russell.

"Maybe he wasn't as intense about practice as some others were, but that was no different than, say, Heinsohn or some others. And I didn't mind that. I wanted Russell to have his batteries charged for the games. Remember, he clocked a lot more minutes than anyone—often the full 48.

"I'll never forget Russ in one practice at the Cambridge 'Y,' though. He was loafing, and so were some others. So I blew the whistle and said, 'So that's the way you people want it, huh? OK, I want a 20-minute scrimmage going *all-out*.'

"Well, the scrimmage starts and Russell is still loafing. And since he's the leader the other guys are taking the cue and it's becoming a joke, a waste of time. So I blow the whistle again and yell, 'Get out! All of you! Get the hell out!' And I went stomping off.

"Now they're all wondering what I'm going to do the next day. They know my philosophy is not to fine people but to take it out of their hides in practice, to bust their humps.

"So the next day I walk in and say, 'OK, I've got six cigars here and I'm going to take a seat and start enjoying them. It'll be a 25-minute scrimmage—or maybe longer; it's up to you. If you haven't performed up to your abilities, then we won't stop at 25. We can go for as long as it takes me to smoke these six cigars. I've got no place to go, so suit yourselves. I'm just going to sit here and relax with my cigars and watch you guys.

"Well, Russell must have had an appointment or something. He played like a man possessed. No opponent could get off a shot within 18 feet of the basket; he must have blocked 19 in five minutes. He was sensational.

"I got so excited I jumped up, blew my whistle and made the craziest statement of my coaching career. 'Hey, I didn't want you to practice *that* hard,' I said. 'Go home.'

"I shocked everyone with that statement, including me. But there was a basic involved there. I never wanted our guys leaving their best on the practice floor. I wanted them to save it for the game. A coach can take that you-play-as-you-practice stuff too far, particularly in pro ball where you have so many games.

"Another big mistake a coach can make—one of the biggest—is over-exposure of his voice; particularly if he's been coach over a long period with basically the same personnel, the players can get sick of that voice. Another big potential pitfall is overcoaching. You've got to keep it simple, because basketball is a simple game. Sometimes I see

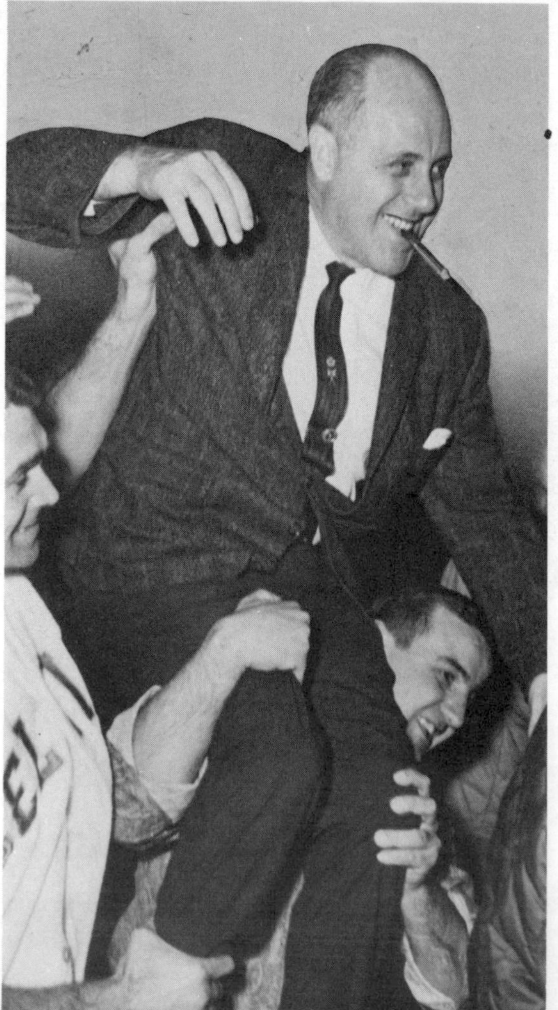

some coaches pull out a clipboard during a crucial timeout late in a game and work out a new play in the huddle. That's laughable, just crazy. You're going to design something in a matter of seconds—and execute it successfully—that you haven't put together in all the hours of practice all season?

"I'd just say basically two things at most in that situation. First, I'd sometimes ask, 'Do any of you have a fish out there?'—an opponent we could exploit in that situation. If not, then I just called one of our simple plays, one that we knew inside out and knew we could execute. That's the key to a play: *executing* it.

"And, of course, communication is vital. As I've said, you can't have two sets of standards; but that doesn't mean you don't communicate with each player a bit differently, depending on his personality. Some guys you whisper to, some you talk to, some you yell at—whatever it takes to get the message across to get the most out of that man's abilities.

"And you've got to give them leadership. My people knew, number one, that I'd go to bat for them on and off the court. They knew that in return all I wanted was their maximum effort. And I always explained to them, 'Hey, you don't win it for *me;* you win it for *you!*'

"But, yes, we accomplished things *together*. We succeeded *together*. Without being sloppy about it, it was a family.

"No, I have no regrets. None. If I had it all to do again, I wouldn't want it any different. Sure, if we'd done this in New York I'd be a multi-millionaire. Boston never fully appreciated that string of championships year after year after year. They just felt we should win automatically. In other towns our success was considered fantastic, just unbelievable. In Boston our success was taken for granted for a long time.

"No, I don't feel shortchanged about it. But I think the team was. And I wish Boston could have appreciated the club while Walter Brown was alive so he could have enjoyed it all more fully, so he could have seen the dream he created come true.

"Well, at last the town is appreciating the Boston Celtics. But it took a hell of a lot of championships before it happened, didn't it?"

"Chuck Cooper was a man of class, intelligence and sensitivity who blazed a trail that wasn't easy.

"He also was a pretty damn good basketball player."

Bob Cousy

CHUCK COOPER, 1950-51 through 1953-54:

"I'm convinced that no NBA team would have made the move on blacks in 1950 if the Celtics hadn't drafted me early, taking me on the second round. Seven rounds later the Washington Caps took Earl Lloyd, and a couple of months later the New York Knicks bought Sweetwater Clifton's contract from the Harlem Globetrotters. But it was a case of the Caps and Knicks following the Celtics' lead. Walter Brown was the man who put his neck on the line.

"It took a lot of guts to do what he did. He was defying the then very powerful Globetrotters. He also was incurring the displeasure of his fellow owners who didn't want to risk the wrath of the Trotters.

"The NBA was struggling to survive—something like a half-dozen teams were going out of business that spring—and all the clubs depended on the Globetrotters to help fill their buildings. Abe Saperstein had a monopoly on black players, and teams didn't want to anger him and risk a boycott by his Trotters.

"That didn't stop Mr. Brown, though, even though he was in an extremely vulnerable position financially—having mortgaged his home to keep the Celtics alive. I'm sure he knew the dangers when he drafted me, and I guess he was reminded of it immediately. As soon as he named me on the second round, the story goes, another owner said, 'Walter, don't you know he's a colored boy?' And they say Mr. Brown roared, 'I don't care if he's striped or polka dot or plaid; Boston takes Charles Cooper of Duquesne!'

"Well, I guess Saperstein got pretty upset, as everyone feared he would. From what I understand he raised all kinds of hell and said his team would never play in Boston Garden again. And Mr. Brown said in the newspapers that was fine with him because as far as he was concerned the Globetrotters were no longer welcome at Boston Garden.

"That was Walter Brown for you. The man wasn't afraid to stick out his neck all the way.

"No, I don't see myself as basketball's Jackie Robinson. There was only one Jackie. When he broke baseball's color line three years earlier he shouldered a terrific burden that helped all other sports. A lot of acceptance that he pioneered transferred over to all who followed in *all* sports.

"Yes, I may have helped carry on what Jackie started. But it was inevitable after he blazed the trail. Oh, I suppose if Sweetwater or Earl or I had robbed a bank or been picked up on drugs—that might have delayed things. So in the sense that we didn't blow it and had some success, yes, that contributed something.

"And, uh-huh, I do feel a sense of accomplishment in a very modest way and can't help but feel proud now. But when I was playing, I never thought about it like that. I was more preoccupied with just making the team.

"Red Auerbach has written that I had to 'go through hell' on the road. I wouldn't necessarily call it hell, but, yes, the worst part was traveling. It was those separate hotels and restaurants in some towns. Some hotels—like in Washington and St. Louis—said, 'OK, you can stay here but keep out of our dining room.' To soften the hurt, Red always told me I could eat in my room and charge my meals on room service if I wanted—and teammates always joined me.

"Later, with the Hawks, I wasn't allowed to stay with the team in Miami or Shreveport. I had to stay in a reform school in Shreveport. And I wasn't allowed to play in Baton Rouge.

"Red Holzman was our coach and asked me if I wanted him to take a stand. I got angry because I didn't think his offer was sincere—and told him so. I knew they weren't going to cancel with 7,000 people in the stands. So I went out and sat in the front row near the press row. When the teams came out, all the Hawks came over one by one and shook hands in a gesture to the crowd—all except one. Bob Pettit ignored me. Maybe I should be understanding. He was in his hometown and environment. But that's exactly why a gesture by him would have been the biggest gesture of all.

"With the Celtics, though, I always had good support in terms of acceptance by teammates and, of course, by Red and Mr. Brown. I felt a strong relationship with them all, including with Howie McHugh, who's still the team's publicity man and an institution himself. They all did what they could to make my road easier.

"No, I don't have strong recollections about something that's been written about quite a bit—circumstances surrounding a neutral-court game we played against the Rochester Royals at Raleigh, North Carolina.

"As the story goes, the Celtics were told that I had to sit out because no mixed team had ever played there, and that Auerbach then refused to play. So the ban was lifted, according to the story, but I wasn't permitted to stay at the hotel with the team after the game. So rather than stay elsewhere, it's been written, I took a train out of town in the middle of the night, and that Bob Cousy insisted on going with me, and that Red and Ed Macauley accompanied us to the train station.

"According to the story, they wouldn't serve the four of us together at the station's segregated lunch counter, so Red bought a bunch of sandwiches to go and we desegregated a baggage cart on the platform. I've also read that Cooz and I then walked the streets of Raleigh until the train came at 2 or 3 in the morning.

"Well, I'm not saying these things didn't happen, just that I don't recall some of them and what I do recall is hazy.

"The part about them not wanting to let me play could have happened without my knowledge, of course, with Red handling it privately and not bothering me about it. And I don't specifically recall being barred from the hotel, yet I do remember taking the train with a teammate; so there had to be a reason we were leaving without the rest of the team. And I do recall sitting on a railroad platform eating sandwiches with some of our people. But after nearly 30 years it's all pretty fuzzy and I can't even recall which guys for sure—or even which teammate I took the train with, although it probably was Cooz. We were very close. It also sounds like something Red and Easy Ed would have done.

"What does stick out about that night was something that happened in the locker room before the game when a white custodial type made it apparent that he was uncomfortable with my presence. It wasn't a big deal, and my teammates probably weren't even aware of it. Yet that's what I recall most about that night.

"That game was in 1952, I believe, and it's funny how one's memory functions over the years. Two people can be involved in something, yet years later one recalls it clearly and the other can't.

"Whatever, I always had good support from the team, as I've said. They did their best to keep incidents to a minimum.

"Of course I wasn't happy about some of the things that went on, but you made the best of it. If you fought every insult and every rebuff, you wouldn't have time to play basketball. And a lot of these things just didn't seem all that important anyway. Young people today might say that's backward. But if they stop and think about it, they'll see that even today there are a lot of things you don't start a revolution over.

"No, it wasn't so much that I was turning my cheek so as not to risk an incident that might jeopardize black progress. I can't claim that. No, it was mostly that things went relatively smoothly except for lodging and transportation—practices so deeply established at that time that blacks a lot bigger than Chuck Cooper acquiesced.

"There were things I wouldn't take, though—like name-calling. One night in Moline, Illinois, we were playing the Tri-Cities Blackhawks and one of their players called me a 'black bastard.' I asked him what he said and he repeated it. So I pushed him in the face as hard as I could. I wanted to fight him but wanted him to throw the first punch. He wouldn't fight—but everyone else did.

"Both benches cleared and everyone started pairing off. Bob Brannum and Mel Hutchins, a couple of muscle guys, squared off. Even the opposing coaches, Auerbach and Doxie Mooe, went at it. It was quite a sight, the worst fight I remember. I was thrown out and fined by the league. But when the commissioner, Maurice Podoloff, heard the full story he rescinded the fine.

"But that kind of name-calling was a rarity.

"There certainly was never any racial problem within the Celtics. Oh, once in a while somebody would get overanxious in letting me know he'd 'grown up with blacks and had been best friends,' the sort of stuff that gets stale after hearing it over again. But their intentions were good and, as I've said, everyone was very supportive.

"I felt a solid relationship with all the guys. I considered most friends as well as teammates, and certainly none were *un*friendly.

"My first season in Boston I shared a nice apartment in Back Bay with Macauley, Bob Donham and Ed Leede. We may have been the sloppiest housekeepers in Boston history. Brannum and Bob Harris were close, too, and Bill Sharman. And when Don Barksdale—our second black—joined the team my last season in Boston, we roomed together on the road. We had similar skin tone, size and looked a little alike, so had some fun passing ourselves off as brothers.

"For real communication and friendship, though, Leede and Cousy probably were closest to me. Cooz and I would go out a lot together, particularly on the road. We shared an enjoyment of music of all kinds, particularly jazz, and would hit those places. I had great respect for his attitudes and approach to life.

"There was a certain bond between us that went beyond being teammates; we were *friends*. And that almost got my block knocked off one day. I started a pretty good brawl in Boston one day by coming to Cousy's aid in a game against Philadelphia. This fight had nothing to do with racism; it was strictly a friendship and loyalty thing, a matter of going to the rescue of a friend and taking a few blows in the process if you have to.

"I was kneeling by the scorer's table waiting to check back into a game when Neil Johnston threw what I considered a football block at Cooz. Well, I didn't think that was quite right, especially since Johnston was quite a bit bigger than Bob. So I acted impulsively to seeing a friend getting clobbered only a few feet away. I sprang at Johnston and threw him across the scorer's table, with me leaning over him. As I recall he then took a half-punch at me, and I responded with a half-swing of my own.

"Both benches cleared, and it took quite a while to get things under control. It was a mess, with fans coming out of the stands to join in.

"Meanwhile, while I was involved with Johnston, I got whacked a couple of times on the back of the head and shoulders. Later, as order was being restored, I asked my teammates who had been hitting me from behind. They said Bob Zawoluk, so I went after him and ended up putting a kind of choke hold on him.

"Well, the next day there were pictures all over the newspapers,

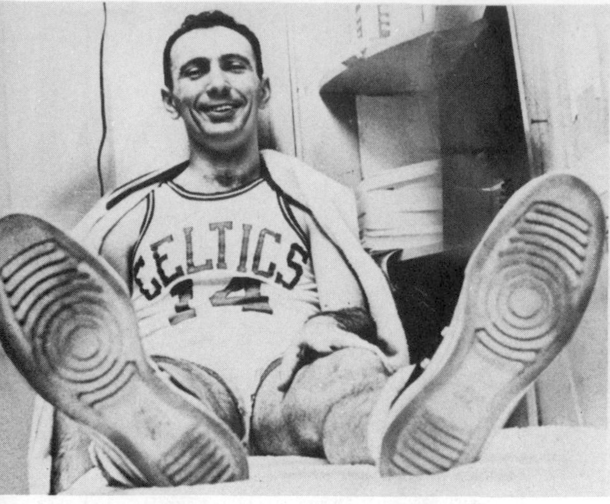

and there was one that caught my attention in particular. It showed Bob Harris airborne, throwing a flying tackle at a Philadelphia player—and there was my pal Cousy, standing by nonchalantly watching it all.

"Well, old Cooz was not a fighter by any stretch of the imagination. What he was was one hell of a basketball player and one hell of a person, the highest kind of individual. Bob is as free of racism as any white person I've ever known. He's just a beautiful person. And I'm not only basing that on our closeness as old mates but on some things in recent years that don't even involve me. He's done things that are—well—just beautiful, too personal to reveal.

"Red Auerbach? I love the guy—*now*. We had some strong words at times, though, some conflicts, and things were sour for awhile. And I finally asked to be traded because I wasn't playing much that last season in Boston. But I have good feelings about the man now. In fact, the last time I saw him, about 10 years ago here in Pittsburgh, we hugged each other.

"So I'll never forget any of those people. Most of all, of course, I'll never forget Walter Brown. He was a gentleman with backbone. Give all the credit to that man. He made it all possible when nobody else would."

"Bob Cousy is the Boston Celtics.

"He was the most spectacular, inspiring and greatest clutch performer I have ever seen in any sport.

"There will never be another Bob Cousy. Like Babe Ruth, he revolutionized a game. And like Babe Ruth, no one can ever take his place."

Walter Brown

BOB COUSY, 1950-51 through 1962-63:

"The lingering notion that there was friction between Bob Cousy and Red Auerbach when we both joined the Celtics in 1950 is vintage myth. Thirty years later I'm still hearing about a 'feud', people insisting, 'C'mon, you and Auerbach really hated each other's guts at first, didn't you?"

"Obviously, some rumors die hard. I've been denying that one for 30 years; yet it persists. Well, let's try straightening out the record once again.

"Arnold and I met for the first time in October 1950. Five minutes later I knew we were going to hit it off—and we did. I'll admit I had wondered if we could.

"The Boston newspapers had been harping for months that I'd been snubbed by the Celtics. I had played on the Cinderella Holy Cross basketball teams after World War II that had attracted sellout after sellout to Boston Garden. The 'Fancy Pants A.C.' had captured the imagination of New England, particularly after we won the NCAA championship. And I had won a certain ultra-loyal following; to them I could do no wrong.

"Everyone took it for granted the Celtics would draft me. Not only did they have territorial rights to me, but I believe they had first pick anyway after finishing with the worst record among the teams surviving from the previous season. It was a sure thing: Cousy would be the No. 1 choice.

"Only I wasn't. The Celtics chose 6-11 Bowling Green All-America

Charlie Share. Bob Cousy was the first-round pick of some place called Tri-Cities. The Boston press seethed. And a few days later it was furious. At a press conference to introduce Auerbach, he got sick of being cross-examined about me and snapped his instantly immortal line: 'Am I supposed to win or am I supposed to worry about local yokels?'

"That's Arnold—push him and he'll come back swinging. Here was a brash outsider not only downgrading my talent and their opinion but doing it in fairly insulting language. That was undoubtedly the start of the rumor that lives on 30 years later.

"The writers weren't the only ones unhappy that I hadn't been drafted by Boston. So was I—tremendously so. I was already engaged to Missy and planning to settle and go into business in Worcester. And, frankly, it never occurred to me the Celtics wouldn't take me.

"When I got the news they hadn't, I was very upset and said some things I shouldn't have—including, 'What the hell is a *Tri-Cities?'* But after cooling off within hours I had to admit—despite myself—that the Celtics had done the wisest thing. Besides having every bit the college reputation I had, Share also had about 10 more inches in height. And height was what the Celtics needed at the time. They had about a dozen guys who could play the backcourt. So if I had been Auerbach or Walter Brown, I would have made exactly the same decision.

"Well, no sooner had the writers finally simmered down from the Celtics ignoring me and Red's 'local yokels' crack than they were outraged a third time. The Celtics had tried to pass up another chance to get me, and made no bones about it.

"I had no intention of going to Tri-Cities, and was traded to Chicago that summer. And almost immediately the Chicago franchise folded. Its players were distributed around the league, except for the three most in demand: Max Zaslofsky, Andy Phillip and me. And when the owners couldn't agree on who should get whom, our names were put in a hat. Walter drew me—the last one he wanted.

"So neither Walter nor Arnold—men who always sacrificed tact for honesty—were saying things calculated to get them elected to the Bob Cousy Fan Club's Board of Directors.

"Naturally I was a little apprehensive of the reception I'd get when I was to meet Auerbach the first time. It had been made clear he wasn't crazy about having me. In fact, the very day of our meeting the newspapers had carried this quote from Red: 'Cousy is going to have to make this ball club.'

"Well, without being cocky about it, I had no thoughts about *not* being able to make the Celtics. Of course, the team didn't have the talent it had later. For instance, after Sam and K.C. Jones joined Bill Sharman and myself, I can appreciate a rookie guard coming in, looking at four established pros, and saying to himself, 'How the devil will I make this team?' But that wasn't the case in 1950, and I knew damn well I was going to play. And any concerns about the welcome mat were pretty much overshadowed by my being happy to be in Boston.

"So I met Auerbach in Boston with an open mind. Typically, Arnold was direct. 'It's a big man's game, and you're not a big man,' he said. 'You're going to work in the backcourt with Sonny Hertzberg; he knows this league and can teach you a lot. I hope you

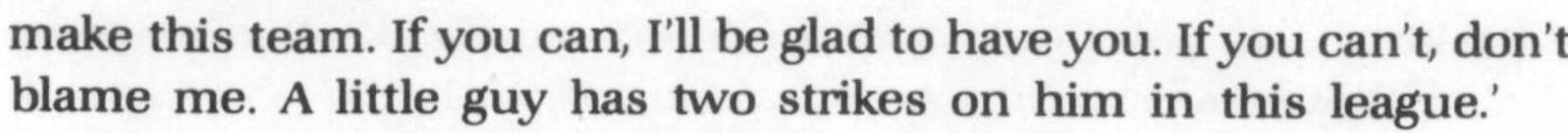

make this team. If you can, I'll be glad to have you. If you can't, don't blame me. A little guy has two strikes on him in this league.'

"I was impressed. His bluntness made sense. And the more I got to know Red, the more I realized everything he did in basketball made sense.

"The fact that Auerbach proceeded to needle me in the press the next few years made sense, too. He never failed to point to my rough edges. He made sort of a game out of damning me with faint praise when he talked with newsmen. If I had a good game and a writer pointed it out, he'd shrug: 'Yes, he scored a bundle. But he gave away more with lousy defense.' If someone complimented my passing, he'd say: 'Yeah, and his shooting was off.' And if a writer praised my shooting and defense, he'd snap: 'Uh-huh, and he was passing like a clown.'

"My reaction to this was exactly what Arnold figured. Each time I'd say to myself: 'I'll show this guy,' and the next game I'd try even harder.

"Auerbach knew my temperament better than I did. He knew I couldn't stand failure. He knew that while I rarely showed feelings on the surface I burned inside. And he knew I played best when angry.

" 'You sure know how to get Cooz mad,' someone once told him. And Red grinned: 'I sure do, don't I?'

"Arnold's quotes were accomplishing something else, too. One of the best needlers I know, he was happily feeding newsmen the last thing they wanted to hear. Usually he didn't mean it. He simply wanted to get on the writers' nerves.

"After a year or so he was conceding to them: 'Cousy's the greatest playmaker.' Later it was: 'Cousy's the best little man.' Finally it was: 'Cousy's one of the greatest.' But it wasn't until after we'd won our first championship in 1957 that he took off all the wraps.

"Through it all we were never enemies, though, nor did we ever reach the point of disliking each other. The worst things that happened were disagreeing on some of my passing theories the first season and over some public criticism of myself, Sharman and Ed Macauley a couple of seasons later. Both matters were quickly ironed out. I'll admit I didn't feel close to Red for a couple of years. But after that we became very close.

"Yes, we went through a lot of big games together during 13 seasons. There are so many memories, and none were bigger than my first and last championships.

"Winning for the first time in 1957 had to be the highlight. We won six NBA titles during my career, but you tend to remember the first most—particularly after suffering through the agony of six seasons of trying and failing. The longer you struggle to overcome adversity, the sweeter the success when it finally comes.

"And there was another dimension to '57. Without being overly sentimental, we all wanted the championship so much for Walter Brown, knowing how much he wanted it. Walter may have been the last of the true sportsmen, and the whole team had a unique relationship with him. He was a lot more than an owner to us.

"So it was a combination of those two factors that made that first title such a highlight. It certainly wasn't the money. I don't recall how much our playoff shares were, but it wasn't much. A lot of us would have been better off financially if we'd worked on an outside

job instead those six weeks. So money didn't enter into the thrill; it was truly the pride factor.

"My last game was memorable in a different way. I was playing one last season in '62-'63 and very much wanted to go out a winner with one more championship.

"We were leading the Lakers in the finals, three games to two, and hoping to wrap it up at Los Angeles in the sixth game. We were leading by about 10 points early in the last quarter when I tore a ligament in my left foot. The pain was excruciating for a while before Buddy LeRoux worked on it, packing it in ice.

"Meanwhile, our lead dropped to one point with less than five minutes remaining. It was important to me that I go back in. I hoped my presence might have some psychological impact—both ways, on my teammates and on the bad guys. I knew I'd have limitations with the foot, but my teammates and opponents wouldn't know that. So I hoped to give the Celtics a mental lift and the Lakers something more to think about. I also didn't want to end my career on the sidelines.

"Well, the way it worked out was like a Hollywood script—in Los Angeles, appropriately enough.

"After freezing the foot, Buddy strapped it and I had only slight discomfort. I don't know what effect I had. Maybe I helped psychologically, maybe I didn't. Who's to say we wouldn't have won by 10 if I had stayed on the bench? In any case, we won by five. And as the clock ran out, I heaved the ball to the rafters and jumped up and down—bad foot or no bad foot.

"And it's well for me that we did wrap it up that night. There's no way I could have played a seventh game. I couldn't walk the next day. In fact, I couldn't do any significant exercise on it for 6-8 weeks, and still feel it to this day.

"So it was quite a way to go out, with a touch of Hollywood and all."

"Ed Macauley was a Celtic and a great one. He was a key man in establishing our franchise.

"He left us before we started winning titles, and he even helped St. Louis beat us out of the '58 championship. But in my mind Ed Macauley will always be a Celtic, one of my guys."

Red Auerbach

ED MACAULEY, 1950-51 through 1955-56:

"My children were watching 'Happy Days' on television not long ago. The Fonz and Richie were fooling around with a basketball, and one of them said to the other, 'Hey, who did you think you are, The Cooz or Easy Ed?'

"Wow, that really impressed my kids—and their friends. The phone started ringing and didn't quit. Funny, I played basketball for 20 years and was a Boston Celtic, a team respected around the world, and that never impressed my kids. But one mention of 'Easy Ed' on 'Happy Days' made me a big man around the house—for awhile, anyway.

"That 'Easy Ed' nickname started at St. Louis University, during my first season there, I believe. Most people assume it stemmed from my style—that I was one of the first graceful tall men, *they* said.

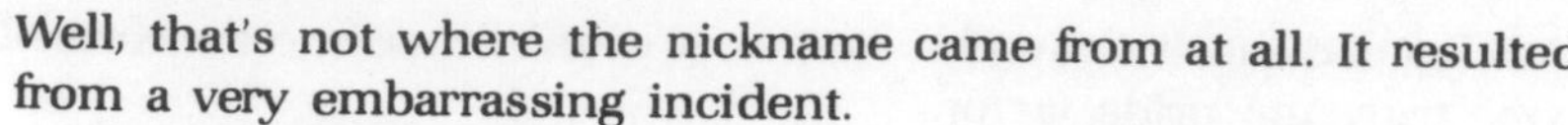

Well, that's not where the nickname came from at all. It resulted from a very embarrassing incident.

"Our homecourt was our gym. We dressed in the basement and came up an iron spiral staircase to a door that led out to the court. On game days, that door was kept shut until it was time for us to come out on the floor. When everyone was up from downstairs, the captain would open the door and we'd come running out behind him.

"Our coach, John Flanigan, rotated the captaincy, a different player each game. On this night, just before we went out, he handed me the ball and said, 'Ed, you be the captain tonight. You lead the team out.'

"It was the first time I'd been tapped for that honor and, wow, I was excited. I burst through the door, dribbled the ball smartly the length of the court and put up a smooth layup. As I landed after taking the shot and looked back up court, I saw I was alone. All my teammates were back in the doorway. Then I looked up in the stands and was *horrified.* Everyone was standing! Then I opened my ears and *heard* the National Anthem. It was almost half over, but I was so nervous I hadn't heard it. I could have crawled into the woodwork—my first big job and I blow it.

"When the anthem ended, the crowd burst out laughing, and a fan yelled: 'Hey, Ed, take it *easy!* The game hasn't even started yet. Take it *easy,* Ed!'

"Well, our sports publicist, Warren Boecklin, heard that and tagged me Easy Ed in all press released from that moment on. And it stuck. But understand that it came about by my act of stupidity, not grace.

"I carried that nickname from college into the pros, and from St. Louis to Boston after I joined the Celtics in a dispersal draft when the old St. Louis Bombers folded after my rookie year.

"That's the season—1950-51—when Boston's love affair with the Celtics began, with the coming of Bob Cousy along with Red Auerbach and myself all at the same time.

"We weren't the powerhouse that the Celtics later became. But we were a contender, an appealing club, a colorful team featuring great shooters and Cooz' fantastic ballhandling. We didn't win any titles—in fact, usually were knocked out of the playoffs in the first round—but we changed the Boston fans' image of pro basketball. They began to appreciate the sport in general and the team in particular. That's when the Celtics' winning tradition started, to be followed by the fantastic years that made the team an institution.

"The Celtics went through six seasons of frustration during my six years there—contending but not winning a title—and the fans worked as hard as the players for that championship.

"Yes, it was an odd feeling not to be around when that championship finally came. Well, actually I was *around*—ironically playing *against* the Celtics in that great seven-game series for the '57 title, including the double-overtime finale. I had been sent to St. Louis the previous spring with Cliff Hagan in the deal that brought the Celtics rights to Bill Russell. And my leaving was tied to the Celtics becoming champions because their dynasty was built around Russell.

"Those championships could have been achieved if you had taken away any of the other players—a Cousy, a Sharman, a Heinsohn, a Ramsey, either Jones, and so on. It would have been difficult, but the Celtics still would have succeeded. But if you took

away Russell the Celtics would not have done what they did. That's certain.

"Even more than Babe Ruth, Bill Russell was the most dominating athlete who ever played any team game. And I can say that as an *opponent*—first an opposing center, then an opposing coach.

"Among Russ' extraordinary abilities, of course, was his fantastic rebounding. And that's something I couldn't give the Celtics no matter how hard I tried. If you had come to me in 1953 and said I wasn't a very good rebounder, I would have said, 'Like hell I'm not. I'm breaking my butt out there.' And I was. But let's face it: I wasn't big enough to take the pounding on the boards.

"So that's all the Celtics lacked—the big strong rebounder. And Russell gave them that, and how.

"Now, here's what he did. To be a great shooter, you must concentrate; when you go up to shoot, you've got to have only one thing on your mind—the hoop. But when Russell was in the game against you, you had to concentrate on another thing besides shooting. You had to think, 'Where is he?' I mean literally. You know he could always get the ball. As a result, he stopped many shots he didn't lay a hand on, shots that hit the rim or went to the side, because as you went up you were distracted by *'Where is he?'*

"When you drive down the center, you usually go right up and shoot. With Russell, you had to look. You had to fake once, just to see where he was. Many times he wasn't even around you, but you lost the split-second advantage and then someone would catch you. That element of distraction was Russell's key asset as a defender.

"Again, his great abilities were all the more apparent to me as an opponent, after being traded to St. Louis. That was hard, leaving the Celtics, but St. Louis was my hometown and I felt the move would be better for my family and all concerned.

"I'll never forget the circumstances. The previous Spring, just before we went into the '56 playoffs, my one-year-old son Patrick contracted spinal meningitis. He had gone into convulsions and we'd rushed him to Children's Hospital in Boston. When the doctors told my wife Jackie and me the diagnosis, we were shook. So as soon as the playoffs ended we had Patrick transferred to specialists near our home in St. Louis. I wasn't even sure if I'd ever play again at that point. He was going to need constant care.

"So all these things were going through my mind one day when the phone rang. It was Walter Brown, and he sounded awful. 'Ed,' he said, 'I've got some bad news. Red has a chance to trade you to St. Louis for the rights to Bill Russell, but I don't want to make the deal because I just can't imagine your not being a Celtic.'

"That really touched me. But at the same time the move seemed like the best thing for me. I could continue playing ball and still be near Patrick. And I'd be playing in my hometown. So I told Walter to go ahead and make the deal.

"Are you sure?' he said. I told him I was. And then he did a very beautiful thing, something typical of Walter. 'You haven't signed your contract yet, have you?' he asked. I said no. 'Good,' he said. 'I'll give you a nice raise and they'll have to honor it.'

"But I told him not to do it. Do you know why? Because Walter would sit down, think about it, realize he wasn't being fair to Hawks owner Ben Kerner, and then reach into his own pocket and pay the difference. That's the kind of man Walter was, just a super individual. So I told him to leave it the way it was and I'd negotiate later with St. Louis.

"But I've always believed in the back of my mind that if I had ever said, 'Gee, Walter, how could I not be a Celtic?' he wouldn't have allowed Red to make that deal. And what might that have done to Celtic history—although it's possible that Red could have arranged a different deal for Russell, of course.

"Walter always saw me as part of the Celtic family, though, and proved it one day at the Garden. It was always a weird feeling coming back to that building as an opponent, but Boston fans treated me fine—usually. This particular game they got on me. The Celtics-Hawks rivalry had become intense—they met in the finals four out of five years, remember?—and the Garden fans were all over us, including me.

"Well, that upset Walter and he got on the p.a. system and told the fans they should lay off Easy Ed Macauley because 'he's one of our own.' So the fans stopped booing me—and booed Walter.

"That shows how rabid that rivalry was, because Walter Brown was probably the greatest sportsman who ever lived and was much beloved. But *nobody* messes with Celtic fans—not even Walter. I think God Himself would have problems if He walked into the Garden wearing the opposing team's uniform.

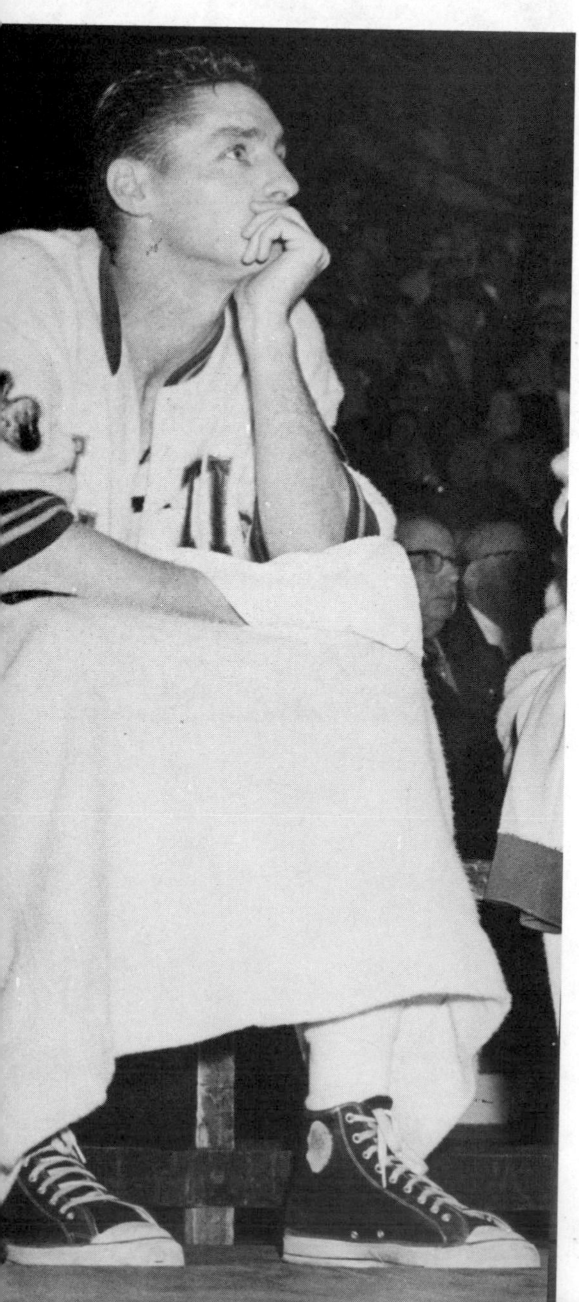

"Bostonians love those Celtics, and they're not alone. Not only do the Celts have fans around the country but around the world. I've made trips abroad for 7-Up—from England and Ireland to the Philippines—and I marvel at the Celtics' great, great reputation. As people would introduce me with a short bio, they'd invariably say:

"'St. Louis University.' No reaction.

"'St. Louis Hawks.' No reaction, not even a wrinkle.

"'Boston Celtics.' Super reaction. 'Really?' people would say in obvious awe. 'You played for the *Celtics?* The *Boston Celtics?*'

"So after awhile, even though I'd played on a Hawk championship team and never was on a Celtic championship edition, I told the people introducing me that we might just as well forget everything else and simply say *Celtics*. Period.

"As far as basketball is concerned, the greatest thing you can say is that you played for the Boston Celtics."

"Bill Sharman had ferocious pride. He was the fiercest competitor of all."

Frank Ramsey

BILL SHARMAN, 1951-52 through 1960-61:

"My ambition had always been to be a big leaguer—in baseball, not in basketball. I played pro basketball on the side only because I figured it would take me a couple of years to work myself up to the majors in baseball. Remember, that was long before baseball expanded, and there were only 16 teams.

"And I was with one of baseball's best organizations, signing out of USC with the Brooklyn Dodgers. Uh-huh, the 'Boys of Summer' Dodgers. They had Jackie Robinson, Pee Wee Reese and all the others, including a great outfield—Duke Snider, Carl Furillo and Andy Pafko. And I was an outfielder, naturally.

"So I'd go to spring training with the big club, then spend the season in Triple A. I thought I was getting my big chance in 1951. The Dodgers were running away with the pennant—ahead by 13½ games by mid-August and they called me up with a month to go. I was told, 'You'll play as soon as we clinch the pennant.' That didn't figure to be long, but you know what happened: the Dodgers blew the lead and then lost to the Giants in the playoff. You're talking to the guy who watched that collapse from the dugout—including the final blow: Bobby Thomson's historic homer.

"It took maybe the most famous nosedive in baseball history to do it, but I never got into a single major league baseball game. So after another couple of seasons I gave it up and concentrated on basketball. Now I look at baseball and it almost bores me it's so slow.

"Well, if I'd been unlucky in baseball, how lucky was I in basketball? I ended up with the greatest team in basketball history, part of the greatest dynasty in any sport at any time. Those years with the Celtics were 10 of the happiest years in my life. The championships were sweet, and in one sense may have been a bit sweeter for Auerbach, Cousy and Sharman than for the fellows who came along later and knew only success. I mean, the three of us knew the frustrations of losing in the earlier seasons, so by comparison could thoroughly enjoy success once it came with the arrival of Russell and Heinsohn.

"Before Russ, we were a bunch of guys who did a lot of things well. We had good ballhandlers, especially Cooz, the best who ever handled a basketball, and Ed Macauley, the best ballhandling and shooting center of that time. But we were weak rebounding, and that made us defensively weaker, too. We just didn't have the physical strength up front to battle teams like the Lakers, who had Mikan, Mikkelsen and Pollard. Even their subs were physically stronger.

"Still, we did have excellent speed and finesse, great passing, shooting and scoring. And Red was a master at manipulating what he had. What he *didn't* have was rebounding and better defense—until Russell came along to change all that. Then we really started rolling. And it's like a boxer or any other champion—as soon as you win, it gives you a little more confidence, makes you a little tougher. So the more we won, the better we got.

"I can recall only once when we ever got into any kind of disagreement, and it had Bob ripping mad at me. It happened my first or second season. During a timeout, something was said about passing. I don't even remember who said it now, but I hollered out, 'Pass the ball!' I didn't mean that Bob wasn't passing enough, but Bob interpreted it that way.

"Well, the next four or five times downcourt, Cooz fired the ball to me—always right to me, but hard. And I could tell from the look on his face that something was upsetting him. It was just a misunderstanding and we got it straightened out right after the game.

"Other than that, we've always had a great relationship and have been through a lot together. And, as I've said, winning that first championship in '57 meant a lot to both of us because we had been trying to win it for so long.

"Perhaps because we wanted to win that title so darn much—with a passion—neither of us had a great shooting game in that final double-overtime seventh game against St. Louis in Boston. Bob and I both were ice cold. I'm not sure what Cooz got, but I scored only 10 or 11 points in a game that lasted 58 minutes. But Tommy Heinsohn had a great shooting night, scoring 37 before fouling out midway through the second five-minute overtime.

"With one second to go, we led by two points and Alex Hannum took the ball out of bounds under his basket at the other end. The clock wouldn't start until someone in bounds touched it, of course, so Alex heaved it the length of the court off the backboard, and the ball bounced to Bob Pettit near the foul line. He put up a little shot, and it seemed to hang in midair for an eternity before hitting the rim and skidding off as the buzzer sounded.

"Another playoffs I'll never forget was 1959, when we won the title by sweeping the Minneapolis Lakers in four games. I made 56 free throws in a row and wanted the distinction of going through the entire playoffs without missing one. That was within my grasp late in the final game at Minneapolis when I went to the line—and *missed.*

"Three times in my career I had strings of making 50 or more consecutive free throws—50, 55 and 56. And each ended the exact same way—the ball hitting the front rim, then the back rim, then kicking out.

"Well, they were 10 beautiful years. And it wasn't only the championships. For a guy who wanted to be a baseball player, I certainly grew to love basketball. It's such a finesse game, almost like a ballet.

"Take a Bill Russell, like when he used to go up and shoot with that little flick of his wrist, remember? Or a Julius Erving doing some of his contortions today. Put those things on film, then slow it down in replay. God, it's beautiful."

"There was never anyone quite like Gene Conley. Not only would he go through a brick wall for you, but he was a truly remarkable athlete—the only one who ever won world championship rings in two sports. There's no telling how good Gino would have been if he had elected to stay in one sport or the other."

Red Auerbach

GENE CONLEY, 1952-53, 1958-59 through 1960-61:

"You know, it's funny when you look back on it all. When we were winning all those championships our locker room at Boston Garden consisted of one little old room. There were two toilets and a shower—and sometimes you were lucky to get hot water out of that one shower. There was a bench along the wall to put your shoes under and a nail to hang your clothes on. And that was it.

"But when we poured out of that room, John Kiley would bang that old Garden organ and the P.A. announcer would bellow, 'And here come the *world champion* Boston Celtics!' And we'd come running onto the court like a million dollars after hanging our clothes on 10 nails.

"Wow, those were great years. Just unforgettable.

"Uh-huh, I used to sign autographs 'Easy Ed Macauley' sometimes during my rookie season. Macauley was one of our big stars along with Bob Cousy and Bill Sharman, and everyone wanted Easy Ed's autograph. I guess we looked a little alike, so a lot of people thought I was him—*off* the court.

"So who was I to disappoint them? It made them happy. Besides, I thought I'd help old Ed out. Now I suppose there'll be a lot of people rushing up to the attic and wondering if they've got Easy Ed's autograph or mine.

"Well, it was a lot of fun. That's something I had a lot of as a Celtic. Uh-huh, a few scraps, too. Gee, I don't remember all the fights. One with Woody Sauldsberry comes to mind. Another with Ed Conlin. One of the best came away from the Celtics—in the ABL. I broke my right hand on the jaw of that guy; in fact, I knocked him out twice—once on the court, and later under the stands I had to do it again when he requested a rematch.

"Red always told us, 'If any punches are to be thrown, I don't want anybody on this team to punch second.' I never forgot that.

"What I had most as a Celtic, though, were thrills. And my biggest were playing on three world champions when I rejoined the team in 1958, combining two sports again after concentrating on baseball for five years.

"Disappointments? I can't really say I had any with the Celtics. Oh, sure, I would have loved to have played more minutes. But how could I realistically expect to with people like Russell, Heinsohn, Ramsey and the others up front? Heck, I was lucky to play as much as I did.

"I had the privilege of playing with the two greatest basketball players I ever saw. Cooz was the best little man, Russ the greatest big man. I saw Russ from both sides, first as a teammate and later as an opposing center. He was enormous; he had extraordinary timing and was a great competitor. He didn't score that much but wouldn't let you score either.

"Wilt Chamberlain was something, too—the strongest man I ever faced. Uh-huh, I scored 24 on him one time in Philly—and he got something like 48. And I thought I did a whale of a job on him! The man was a machine, a scoring machine. What did he average one season, 50?

"Wilt and I had some wars when Red put me on him, switching Russ to covering a forward. You know, a lot of people's memories are playing tricks; they recall me as Russell's backup. That wasn't really the case because that was when Russ was in his prime, playing 47 minutes a game and almost never missing a game. So while I'd fill in for Russ when necessary, it was rarely necessary. Instead, my role was to combine with him on the boards against certain teams.

"What a pleasure it was teaming with that man. You knew if you did your job blocking out, Russ would get you the ball—guaranteed. I remember one night against Cincinnati, with me working on Wayne Embry, Russ vacuumed something like 17 rebounds in one quarter, a record, and at least 40 for the game. He looked like a human windshield wiper, sweeping those boards clean.

"So I enjoyed my Celtic years tremendously. My only regret was that they came to an end. A new Chicago franchise came into the league in '61-'62 and they drafted Sharman from us. But Bill wouldn't report, jumping to the new ABL. So Chicago was entitled to another Celtic and took me. I didn't go, either, taking an excellent offer from the Tuck Tapers in the ABL. That league lasted only one season, and I came back to the NBA and finished up with two seasons at New York with the Knicks.

"Yes, between basketball and baseball I had quite a career—11 seasons in major league baseball, seven more in big league basketball. You've got to be a sports rat to do that. Sure that grind took a toll, and over the years the pressure of going both summer and

winter—no breaks—got to me. Man, you couldn't stay alive like that unless you hit the booze.

"And as I got older, I began to wonder, 'Where am I going?' I had been through the whole bit: Celtics' championships, Braves' championships, the whole ball of wax. But my pitching arm had been killing me for years and I knew I was near the end of my career. The world was closing in on me, and it was getting to me. I was just about to crack.

"That's when Pumpsie Green and I jumped the Red Sox bus on a hot day in July 1962 after a very bad day at Yankee Stadium, and took a little 'vacation.'

"Some guys want to lick the world when they get half-loaded. Not me. I'd start thinking and get all bogged down in my mind. And this time I kind of flipped out—almost.

"I had started reading the Bible around that time. And the more I got tanked, the more an idea made sense to me. 'Hey,' I thought, 'I'm going to go to Bethlehem and Jerusalem and get all my problems straightened out.' So at one point I said, 'C'mon, Pumps, let's head for Israel. You'll come back a .400 hitter and I'll win 20.' I thought I had him just about convinced, but then he said, 'Hey, man, you're crazy. I'm going back.'

"I was gone three days in all—even bought a plane ticket for Tel Aviv, but couldn't go without a passport—and all the newspapers made quite a fuss about it. I got fined $1500, but Mr. Yawkey gave it back to me at season's end.

"Incidentally, that's another area where I was blessed in my career. I played for two of the greatest owners in sports history—Tom Yawkey of the Red Sox and Walter Brown of the Celtics.

"Anyway, I still hear about that AWOL incident all the time: 'Oh, yes, Gene Conley. You're the guy who wanted to go to Israel.' At first I thought, 'Hey, what is this? I broke my butt in two sports and all people remember is that one mistake.' It was kind of embarrassing, but I'm used to it now and have learned to accept it. Now I think it's interesting that it's what people recall first about me—one incident. I'll admit it was an incident that almost went too far, though. It sure was a pip, wasn't it?

"I used to take that 100 percent stuff a little too far. I always gave 100 percent on the field, and that's the way it should be. But I also gave 100 percent off the field, and that sometimes got me into trouble.

"Well, that's all in the past. My drinking was getting so bad I was on the way to becoming a first-class drunk and would have blown everything. I don't think I was an alcoholic, but I had a real problem. Who knows? Maybe I *was* an alcoholic and didn't realize it. But religion saved me and I haven't had a drink in about 15 years. Isn't that *awful?*

"Meanwhile, Katie and I have had our own business all those years, selling coarse paper products around New England. And I think of the Celtics every day I step into my office. There's a framed photograph of Red Auerbach over my desk, and the old coach keeps me company. He's always scowling down at me, pushing me along and telling me to keep hustling."

"Frank Ramsey was by far the greatest sixth man in basketball history. He had a dramatic impact on any game within 15 seconds after coming off the bench.

"Rams never played in an NBA All-Star Game because of the rule restricting a maximum of three players from any team. But the guy belongs in the Hall of Fame for ability that wasn't fully recognized through no fault of his own."

Tom Heinsohn

FRANK RAMSEY, 1954-55 through 1963-64*:

"Not starting didn't bother me. I enjoyed the sixth-man role and felt it was comparatively easy.

"When a game started, you could see how the tempo was going and get a feel for it. And you knew the man you'd be guarding would be a little tired after trying to cope with a Heinsohn or a Loscutoff. So as sixth man I was resting while the people I'd be covering were getting tired. Also, it's a psychological fact that you're going to relax a little when a substitute comes in against you.

"So all those things were in my favor. I know one year I had to start for awhile and I don't feel I was nearly as effective.

"Either way, I was surrounded by a galaxy of talent that was unique. I doubt there will ever again be the concentration of talent on one basketball team. With expansion, there's no way.

"And the first thing all those guys wanted to do was win. No one went out for personal glory. Nobody was looking for anything except to be the best team. We went out to win, and usually did. I wasn't looking for anything but the playoff check and to come back as world champions.

"And we *liked* each other. There was no jealousy. Unlike some clubs, on our team nobody ever criticized anybody else. There never was any friction.

"Oh, in the locker room we might say, 'Hey, look, you're turning your head, or you're not doing this or that.' But it was said constructively and taken that way. Oh, once in a while somebody might get in a little argument here or there, saying, 'Why in hell didn't you throw me the ball?' But we were close enough that you could ask somebody that rather than let it build up and fester.

"And anything like that was said in private, never in print. It was a great bunch of guys who *cared* for each other. We had a good time together. We kidded a lot. You couldn't be sensitive about anything or you'd get eaten alive. And if you got mad, that certainly didn't do any good. And *no one* was excluded, veteran or rookie.

"I remember Satch really getting the business about something that happened late in his rookie year. He didn't have a driver's license, and all season he'd been bumming rides or getting cabs. Then, all of a sudden, Satch saw the playoff money ahead and went to an auto dealer near where we practiced at the Cambridge 'Y' and ordered a car. Then he went to driving school but didn't let anyone know. The day he got his license he told Russ and K.C. so when he picked up the car that afternoon they could drive him home. He was that nervous about it all.

"They left him outside his place, and Satch just sat in his car and admired it like a big toy. Then he noticed the clock didn't work, and that bothered him. So he headed for the dealer, driving back across

*Spent entire 1955-56 season and part of 1956-57 season in the Army "guarding the gold" at Fort Knox, Kentucky.

the bridge and down Massachusetts Avenue, which was getting busy with late-afternoon traffic.

"The traffic got really heavy by MIT—one car crowding Satch on the left, a big trailer truck on his tail. So it was like Satch was watching a tennis match, his attention bouncing back and forth between side window and rear-view mirror—looking everywhere except where he was going.

"Well, the cop directing traffic put his hand up. But Satch never saw him until it was too late—*bang*—and the guy is spread-eagled across Satch's hood, looking at him nose-to-nose through the windshield and holding on for dear life. He finally slid off to one side, but Satch was *still* frozen and so the car kept rolling with the cop chasing it and blowing his whistle. When he finally caught up with Satch—who now resembled Don Knotts, sweat popping out all over—the cop saw the ink was still wet on the license, only a few hours old, and then really blew his top.

"Believe it or not, Satch didn't get a ticket. The cop just called him a menace and told him to get out of Cambridge pronto and to never come back—just like in the old West.

"When we found out, Satch didn't have a peaceful minute the rest of the season. Neither did Gene Conley after what happened to him one night in Philadelphia.

"We'd been in a fight in Syracuse the previous night and Gino hurt his little finger. When we got to the hotel in Philly, Buddy LeRoux gave Gene some Epsom salts in a glass. Buddy told him to put it in the john and during the night mix it with hot water and soak the finger.

"I was Gino's roommate, and he was a very considerate guy, and never wanted to bother anyone. So when he woke up during the night for a drink of water, he didn't put on the light, not wanting to disturb me. He groped for a glass in the bathroom, filled it and chuggalugged it down in the dark—the one filled with the Epsom salts!

"The next night during warmups, Gino is saying, 'Boy, I've got a bad boiler.' And before he finished warming up he had to dash to the bathroom. We're playing at big old Convention Hall, and our locker room was at the opposite end of the building from the visiting team bench. You had to go down an aisle through the crowd, up some stairs to the stage, across the stage and up a flight of stairs to the locker room on the second floor.

"Well, Red put Conley into the game in the second quarter, Gino went up and down the floor twice, then got the urge again. The poor guy sprinted for the locker room but didn't come close to making it in time. He literally left a trail from midcourt, down the aisle, across the stage and up the stairs and into the locker room. Some of us went up to see if he was all right, and there was Gino, sitting on the john moaning, 'Oh, wow, I got a bad boiler.'

"We didn't let Gene forget about that for awhile. But he was a great guy—a genuinely nice person—and he laughed along with us.

"It's well Gene was so good natured, because he was one of the strongest guys I ever met. And he knew how to fight. When a brawl started, I always got behind Conley or Loscutoff.

"Loscy, Heinie, Red and myself went into a business deal one time involving 16,000 laying chickens back in my home area of Kentucky. We ended up losing money when the price of eggs dropped off. Then a darned wind came along and blew the thing through town.

It was a mess. I sent a picture of some of the dead chickens to Red and told him mine had all survived and these dead ones were all his.

"Red still talks about that. And I like to remind him about the time we were within one of a winning-streak record and flew into Detroit on New Year's Eve. The next day we were to play the opening game of a doubleheader against Cincinnati, which had the worst record in the league.

"Instead of letting us go off to a movie or whatever we normally did, Red said, 'Nobody's going out to celebrate New Year's Eve. You're all coming up to my room.' So we all go to Red's room, and there was Coca-Cola and sandwiches. We sat around looking at each other and playing a little cards and went to bed around 1 o'clock. The next day we got blown out by about 20 points.

"Yes, it's true, I used to sign a blank contract and let Walter Brown fill it in every year. Let me tell you about Walter. We loved that man. If you could do business with all Walter Browns in this world, there wouldn't be any need for lawyers. He was always very fair and I always felt I was overpaid compared to what I could be making in industry. I was doing what I loved and I was a Celtic, and was very proud of that.

"And I still am. When people talk about great basketball teams they generally agree that those Celtic teams were the best of all. It was great to be a part of all that, because that's something you can take to your grave."

"Loscy was considered super villain around the league. Fans called him 'Jungle Jim'—and a lot worse—and thought he was some kind of animal.

"Hey, listen, the guy was no animal; he just resented anyone trying to push us around and did one hell of a job keeping opponents in line. He was extremely conscientious about that.

"So, deep down, when all those people were screaming at Loscy they were wishing he was on their team. And if he had been on their team, they would have been cheering like hell for him.

"And let me tell you something else about Jim Loscutoff: He was a much, much better basketball player than most people gave him credit for."

Red Auerbach

JIM LOSCUTOFF, 1955-56 through 1963-64:

"When we went into the various cities, as soon as my name was announced, people would start booing like hell. Like I was a monster or something. I was what fans considered a hatchetman or a policeman. Fans became very emotional when they saw me.

"Once, an old lady—a real grandmotherly type—rushed up to our bench and started waving her cane under my nose and giving me what-for, calling me a brute and a bully among other things. Another time, during a timeout in Syracuse, some character sprinted the length of the court, leaped up and rabbit punched me behind the ear while we were in a huddle listening to Red.

"Yes, old Loscy was very popular around the NBA. When No. 18 went into a game, the people went bananas. They knew *something* was going to happen. And it usually did. Things just seemed to happen when I was around.

"Take the time in St. Louis during the 1957 playoff finals. It was one hell of a series before we finally beat the Hawks by two points in double-overtime of the seventh game for our first world championship.

"Well, early in the series, Slater Martin passed the ball to Bob Pettit under the basket, and I accidentally rolled under Pettit as he laid the ball up. Unfortunately, Bob came down with a broken wrist. A few minutes later, I blocked Martin as he drove by for a shot and he ricocheted into the stands. The St. Louis fans got a little upset.

"Later that week, we returned to St. Louis for the sixth game, and Pettit was playing with a cast on his wrist. I was guarding him when he faked one way, faked the other, then knocked himself cold as he cracked his head on the backboard attempting a layup. I needed a police escort to the locker room after that game.

"Take a time in Syracuse. Now there was a snakepit, a zoo. It was a party every time you went into that building. But this time was the worst ever, and I ended up popping a cop.

"It started with my skirmishing Lee Shaffer. Lee started moving back a bit, and I pursued. That's when Syracuse coach Alex Hannum bolted off the bench and levelled me with a flying tackle, and both benches emptied. Later, nearly the identical thing happened. This time Tommy Heinsohn jammed with Joe Roberts, and Hannum went into his flying-tackle act again.

"Now the stands emptied as well as both benches. By the time the police got to the floor, the thing had grown into a riot. About a dozen of the cops were wearing those white helmets and black leather jackets. Well, one lost his helmet in the scuffle, and it's this guy I spotted tugging away at one of our players. I figured he was a clown—one of those leather jacket phonies—and spun him around. As I threw my Sunday best, I caught a glimpse of the badge on the front of his jacket. But it was too late—*whack,* flush on the guy's kisser. I immediately held up both hands to let him know I'd made an error.

"A fellow cop, meanwhile, had seen his buddy get walloped and tackled me from behind, knocking me between two rows of seats. Both began to work me over until I explained. Both were pretty upset but didn't lock me up.

"I was lucky. I also was lucky that I never was seriously hurt in any scuffle while a Celtic. The worst was a cut lip that required a stitch or two my rookie year. That's when I underestimated the reach of Ray Felix one night at Madison Square Garden. He's 6-11 and has one hell of a reach. He was standing at least 10 feet from me when he threw a left. I didn't think it could reach me—until I was flat on my back.

"I nearly lost a finger once, too. I was wresting a Detroit Piston when he got my finger in his mouth and started chewing. I had to whack him on the back of the head a couple of times before he finally coughed it up. I still have the scar.

"Other than those two incidents, I held my own. Not that I was in that many brawls—an average of maybe four a year. There were guys who had just as many, but since I had the reputation I attracted the headlines. And although I didn't duck any brawls, I didn't look for them. Some guys tempted me, though—a couple of dirty players I can think of.

"Like Walter Dukes. He was a wiry seven-footer with elbows and knees like razor blades. We used to fight every year. I remember one night he was pushing his weight around in a game at Fort Wayne. I went around a pick when Dukes stuck out his knee. So I belted him in the puss, then jumped on top of him and beat the daylights out of him.

"And it didn't end there. After we both got kicked out, I'm in the locker room alone with our trainer, Buddy LeRoux. And in comes Dukes, saying, 'Let's get this straightened out right now.' And I said, 'OK, you son of a bitch. Let's go.'

"There were other tough guys, too. Everybody had a strong man, but I can honestly say I wasn't afraid of anybody. If there was any guy I would have been afraid of, it was Gene Conley. He was a wild man when he got mad. Luckily, we were teammates most of his years in the league.

"No, we never tangled when Gene played for the Knicks. I did go at it with a Knick who was a very close friend, though. No two opponents were closer friends than Kenny Sears and I. We played against each other in college and were teammates in AAU ball.

"Kenny had four inches in height on me, so I compensated by pushing and grabbing him at times. One night it really bugged him, and he threw a roundhouser. I ducked, and my counter punch knocked him cold. The next night we had a few brews together. No grudges. You realize tempers will flare. You get it out of your system, then forget about it.

"The only rule I had in fighting was to get in the first punch whenever possible. Basketball fights rarely go beyond two or three blows, and the player who scores first usually wins. Yes, I could handle myself. Rocky Marciano once wanted me to quit basketball for boxing and offered to be my manager. Although Rocky was convincing, I said no thanks. My face isn't much to look at, but I like what I've got.

"No, I didn't mind my policeman's role. Or my defensive role. I had both jobs from the start. I'm sure Red drafted me No. 1 with both in mind.

"Auerbach always had a policeman on his team. When he came to Boston, one of the first things he did was get Bob Brannum from Sheboygan. Bob fit the role perfectly. And when he retired, Red got the word out to his scouts that he needed a replacement. Bob Donham, the former Celtic who was freshman coach at the University of Washington, recommended me, adding: 'He's fast, can shoot, and is meaner than Brannum.' The newspapers got wind of the report and had a field day. The Celtics gave me Brannum's No. 18 to further create the image. So I was dubbed from the start.

"My defensive role came about almost as simply. The Celtics had scorers like Cousy, Sharman and Macauley my rookie year. The next season Ramsey came out of the service and we added Russell and Heinsohn. Although I'd been a 20-point man and had set some scoring records in college, I knew I wasn't in that class. Instead, what the Celtics needed was a good defensive man, one who could cover the opposition's big-scoring forwards—the Baylors, Arizins, Twymans, Pettits, Naulls, and so on.

"My defensive theories were simple. I usually wasted a foul or two on my man right away to soften him up. I wanted him to know that every time we went up for a shot he was going to get hit. The next time I could fake a hip or a jab, and he'd go for it. It wasn't that he lacked guts; it's just a natural reaction, a reflex. And if he tried to adjust, it usually threw off his game just enough. Basketball is

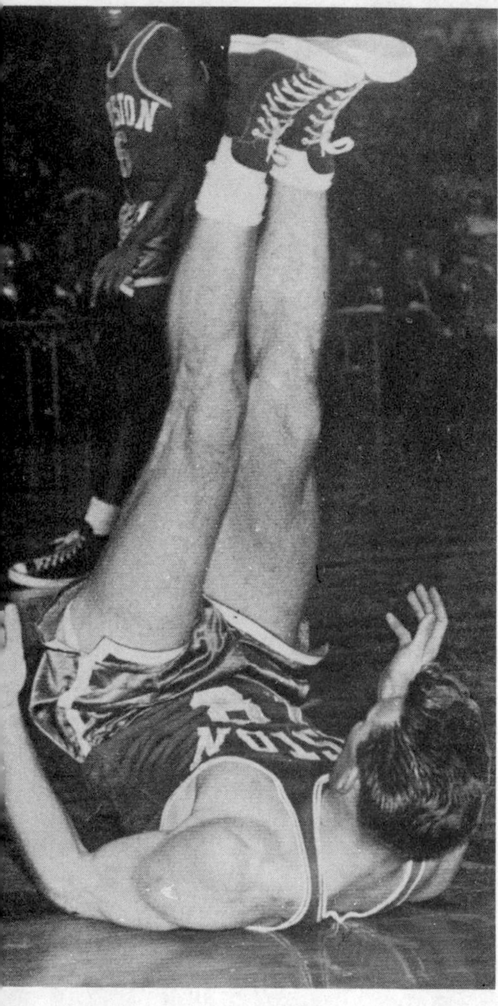

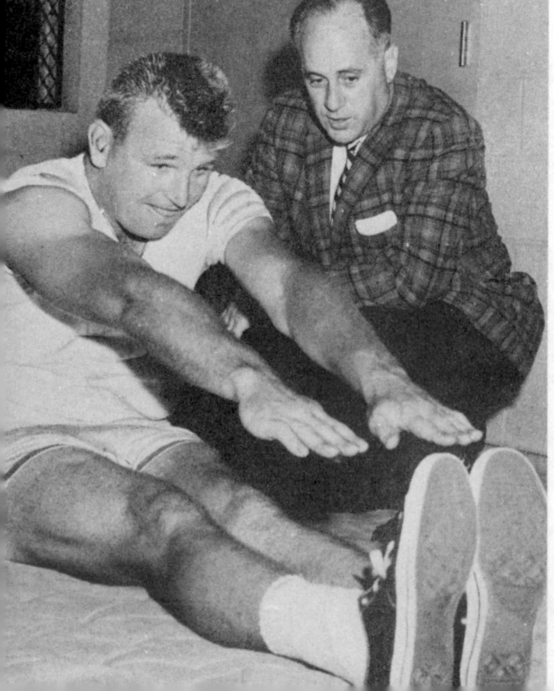

precision, and just a fraction of a change in shooting can throw you off completely.

"I also over-played my man, keeping my hands all over him and holding him as much as I could without getting caught. I was caught plenty, of course, but never so red-handed as once against the Pistons. On an out-of-bounds play, I had a tendency to hold a guy's pants as he lined up, taking the guy who figured to be the shooter—in this case, George Yardley. I grabbed his pants, and damned if he didn't get the ball. As he broke for the basket I held a bit too long, and *rip*—George's pants tore down the side from top to bottom. It was the easiest call a ref ever had to make.

"After making the transition from offense, it was fine with me to concentrate on defense and leave the scoring to the others. Being a Celtic brought out the best in a player, absorbing him. And what players we had.

"Bill Russell was the greatest player I ever saw. He instilled so much pride and desire. He hated to lose so much you knew he'd go out and play his heart out. When he was puking and burping and breaking wind before each game, we knew nobody would touch us that night. If he wasn't doing those things we worried.

"Bob Cousy was the greatest backcourt man I've ever seen. Bill Sharman was a great competitor and a self-made athlete; anything he did, he attempted to create perfection. Frank Ramsey was an old mother hen—and so mercenary. Everything was related to dollars in his mind. Before the playoffs started Frank could tell you to the penny how much each share would be worth if we went this far, or that far, or whatever. He also gave 120 percent, busting his butt every second.

"And Tommy Heinsohn was a great player, but he had no conscience. He'd throw up shots from everywhere. One night at an All-Star Game, Dick Hemric and I were sitting in the stands and figured out that Tommy touched the ball 23 times that night and shot it *21*. And the only reason he didn't shoot it the other two times was that once he got stuck with it at midcourt and had to dribble it around, and the other time he bounced the ball off his foot out of bounds.

"There was certainly a hell of a lot of pride on that team, and we had a lot of success. And when you're riding high, people fill the seats to see you every town you play in. It was that way with the Yankees and it was that way with us. Even towns that drew lousy, like Detroit, would have crowds pouring out to see us because we were the champions. It's the sweetest thing in the world to be on top and be a part of all that.

"It was quite a career. Sure I played rough and mean, but never dirty or vicious. There's a big difference. So I have nothing to be ashamed of. I had a job to do and I did it."

"Tom Heinsohn was a tough kid and the ideal forward.

"He could do it all: great offensive rebounding, great moves, great shots—including a beautiful soft hook—even great defense when he felt like playing it.

"And as Frank Ramsey used to say, Tommy would knock down his grandmother for two points.

"Tom Heinsohn was a winner. Period."

Red Auerbach

TOM HEINSOHN, 1956-57 through 1964-65; 1969-70 through 1977-78:*

"Not only was I Red Auerbach's favorite whipping boy, but he damn near got me killed. By Wilt Chamberlain. Red had me pester Wilt in a way that was just about guaranteed to infuriate Chamberlain, basically a mild-mannered giant. And it *did* infuriate him. And when it did, Wilt threatened to tear me apart—and damn near did.

"First you've got to understand that Wilt Chamberlain was the world's strongest man—King Kong in sneakers. He claimed to be 7-1, 250, but he looked a hell of a lot bigger than that to me. And he was powerful. The man was capable of dribbling me—and stuffing me through the hoop.

"So everyone was in awe of Chamberlain when he came into the league, and it didn't take long for us to have a few confrontations. The strategy around the league was to foul him when he got the ball inside. Wilt was deadly around the basket, but he was a poor foul shooter, his biggest weakness. I was the lucky Celtic grabbing him most often, and so Wilt and I got to know each other quite well that first season.

"A fight started one night in Philadelphia, and for some reason Chamberlain went after me. He grabbed me by my shoulder straps and ripped himself a handful of uniform like nothing at all. Do you know how strong you have to be to do that? That's like tearing a phonebook in half, because those straps are reinforced. Well, that gave me a hint that Wilt's patience was wearing thin.

"Another tactic the Celtics used against Wilt that season was something to exploit his slowness in making the transition from offense to defense. After Philly foul shots, we were getting a lot of fast-break baskets by Russell outhustling Chamberlain back up the floor, taking a long pass from Cousy, and stuffing the ball for two easy points.

"We'd get as many as 10 points a game doing this, and we did it all season. Wilt started catching on, of course, so Auerbach decided to add an extra wrinkle in the playoffs. He wanted someone to get in Wilt's way—a human stumbling block to impede Chamberlain as he started up court. The idea was to step in front of Chamberlain and cut him off while Russell took off with a nice head start.

"There were no volunteers for the job, of course. Who in his right mind wants to step in front of a subway train? So when nobody stepped forward, naturally Red made me take two paces forward. 'You're it, Heinsohn.' Of course.

"Wilt was delighted by this maneuver. He'd start to get a head of steam going, and I'd get in his way and he'd run into me. Oops.

*Player, 1956-57 through 1964-65; head coach, 1969-70 through first part of 1977-78.

There were some pretty awesome collisions the first game of the playoffs.

"When the second game became a repeat of the first one, Wilt finally exploded. 'Hey, he yelled, 'do that one more time and I'm going to knock you right on your ass!'

"I told him to go ahead and try it—and so he did the next time I cut him off. He hit me a shot from behind so hard that I ended up on my butt at midcourt. And as I scrambled to my feet, he came charging at me to let me have it. But one of his teammates, Tom Gola, ran in between us as a peacemaker just as Chamberlain unloaded—hitting Gola on the back of the head and breaking Wilt's right hand, his shooting hand.

"Well, they wrapped the hand in a heavy bandage for the third game. And during that game, Wilt caught a lob pass behind Russell, and my only hope was to *punch* the ball out of his hands. Chamberlain was so strong that you couldn't wrench it away from him, no way, so I punched at the ball—and punched him right on the bandaged hand.

"That sent the poor guy into a dance. When he calmed down, he started glaring at me, and I glared right back—like if you want to come at me, big guy, here I am. We just kept staring at each other. Finally, we just walked away from each other and Wilt went to the line for a well-deserved free throw.

"And that was the last time we had any problem. Wilt probably thought I was crazy and that he'd better leave me alone. So I escaped with my life, no thanks to Auerbach.

"Red was beautiful. As I've said, I was his favorite whipping boy. To him I could do no right. One night in Cincinnati I'd had a pretty fair first half, getting something like 25 points and 14 rebounds. Yet at intermission Red started in on me. But I was ready.

"'Heinsohn!' he started, and never got out another word.

"'Yeah, Red, I know,' I said. 'I didn't shoot, I didn't rebound and I didn't block out. What else didn't I do?

"Auerbach just glowered at me—then busted out laughing.

"Red knew my temperament. When he yelled, it didn't bother me—usually. Maybe three or four times a year it did, and I'd explode. I'd tell him, 'Listen, if you're serious about what you say, I shouldn't be starting. But if you're *not* serious, and you're doing what I *think* you're doing, it's gotten to a point where the rookies are starting to steal my socks and give me some heat. If I deserve to start, I deserve some respect.'

"And Red would look me in the eye and say, 'You're absolutely right.' And he'd get off my fanny for awhile. That was another Auerbach coaching quality; he usually was big enough to admit a mistake. He'd make a dumb move or a poor substitution and tell us afterward: 'You guys didn't lose it—I did.'

"Red used to be on me for two reasons: to push me to my maximum ability and to incite the team. You see, he couldn't yell at people like Cousy, Sharman or Ramsey because of their temperaments. Or Russell, either, although Red and Russ would have tete-a-tetes. Something would happen and Auerbach would say: 'Russell, you and I are going to have a little talk.' They'd go into the little equipment room off the locker room and straighten out the matter.

"Sophomores also got a come-uppance. Red never knocked a rookie, but the second year was something else. And it always was a revelation to the sophomore. I'll never forget the case of John Havlicek. He had a marvelous rookie season. Then came the next year. At halftime of our very first game, Auerbach climbed all over John something fierce for some little thing. I can still see Havlicek sitting there, mouth open. He couldn't believe Auerbach was chewing him out like that. As we left the locker room for the second half, I whispered to John: 'Welcome to the club, baby. The honeymoon is over.'

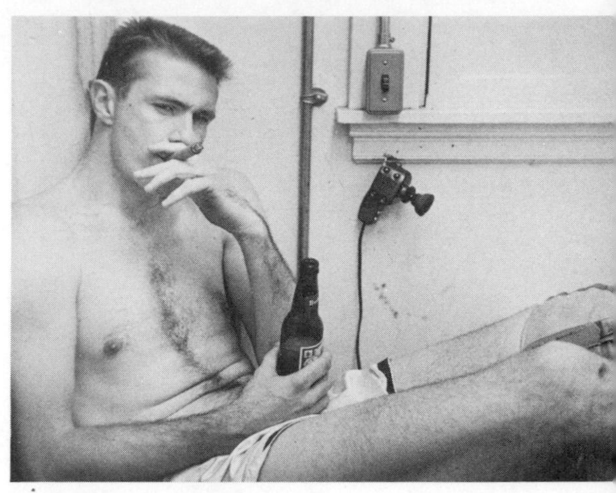

"Havlicek hadn't deserved the chewing-out. It was Red's way of letting John know he wasn't a rookie anymore. It was part of Auerbach's psychology, and the man was a master psychologist in motivating players. As such, he needed a sounding board because he couldn't yell at the other guys. And I was it—and Loscutoff, too, to some extent. Red knew I'd usually let it roll off my back. I could have said, 'Hey, Red, get off my back,' but it didn't make any difference to me—usually. There's nobody who could have taken the stuff I did. Sure he infuriated me at times, but I realized what was going on.

"Look, Red and I understood each other. I understood him perhaps better than anybody else on our team. Better than Russell, better than Cousy, better than any of them.

"In fact, Auerbach offered me the coaching job before Russell got it in 1966. But I told him, 'I don't think I could handle Russell. I think you're the only one who can. I'd be the wrong guy to coach the team with him on it. I think it'd be a good idea if Russell coached. He'd get more out of himself than Cousy, Ramsey, me or anybody else would get out of him.'

"Three years later I said to Red, 'I'm thinking about getting out of the insurance business. If Russell ever quits and you still want me, I'd really like to be involved in rebuilding this ballclub. I think it would be a lot of fun.'

"And Red said, 'I was thinking about another guy, but if you want the job, you've got it. When Russ retires, you'll be the coach.' Then Russell resigned after winning the '69 title, and I knew he was leaving before he announced it. He made a lot of statements in the newspapers after the Celtics beat the Lakers in the finals about Chamberlain sitting down in the last game, and Russell never did that. I knew that was his parting shot at Wilt, that he wouldn't be back.

"So I went on to work with Auerbach in a coach-general manager relationship after our player-coach relationship. And what people may have forgotten—except how could they?—is that Red and I also teamed on Celtic telecasts for a couple of years before I became coach. I did the play-by-play, he did the color, and we were the Frick and Frack of the Boston airwaves.

"Red didn't let his love for peanuts get in the way of his broadcasting, eating them during the telecasts. One night he dropped the bag on the floor while we were doing a game in Philadelphia. And as Red went head first under the table for them, Larry Siegfried decked Chet Walker who was driving for the hoop.

"Everyone had seen it—everyone at the arena, everyone watching the telecast—everyone except Auerbach. When Red finally looked up after finding the peanuts, he saw Walker horizontal. 'Hey, what's he doing?' he snarled into the mike. 'Is he pulling that same old jazz about 20 seconds?' Red was referring to automatic emergency timeouts for injuries that teams often faked for one reason or another.

"I knew Red hadn't seen the play because of the peanuts, but I couldn't let his comment go by because all the viewers had seen Walker get leveled. So I said, 'Red, he was driving toward the basket and Siegfried hit him.'

"Auerbach was at his stubborn best and wouldn't quit. 'He wasn't involved in the play,' he argued, putting me in a nice position. 'Siggy knocked him down,' I said, dropping my voice and hoping Red would take the hint. But he persisted, his voice rising an octave, 'He was *not* in the play!' Beautiful.

" 'OK, Red, have it your way,' I said finally. 'He was not in the *play*. But would you settle for this: he was in the *movie?* ' "

"Many opponents used to tell me they had nightmares about Bill Russell. 'God,' they'd say, 'I wake up in a sweat and see this big black hand over me.'

"And they were absolutely serious. Russ had an entire league psyched.

"He revolutionized basketball. He changed the patterns of play, both for individuals and for teams.

"And first and foremost, Bill Russell was a team man, the one who made us go. Without him we wouldn't have won a championship."

Bob Cousy

BILL RUSSELL, 1956-57 through 1968-69*:

"The key to being a true Celtic, if there's any one thing, is you have to be a man and accept responsibility for your actions. That's the way Walter Brown was, that's the way Red Auerbach was, that's the way Bob Cousy was, and that's the way I was.

"There were key people—Walter Brown, Red Auerbach, Bob Cousy, Bill Russell, John Havlicek—but there were no stars. We were in this to accomplish things *together*, and we really looked out for each other.

"I happen to have great affection for many of my Celtic teammates, great affection. I guess *love* is the proper word. They're friends of mine, and I'm a friend to them. It will be that way until one of us dies.

"Every one of those guys was a man, and I don't mean just a male over 21. We took care of each other; that's the way we were. And it started at the top.

"Walter Brown was essential to the whole thing. The first season I was there we lost the last game of the regular schedule to Syracuse, a team that had eliminated the Celtics in the playoffs just about every year and a team we'd probably be meeting later in that year's playoffs. So Walter stormed in after the game and said, 'You're a bunch of chokers. I can lose with a cheap team just as easily as I can with you guys. I'll never come into this dressing room again.'

"The next game he came in and kicked the floor and said, 'I'm sorry. I'm just a fan and was so scared that we were going to lose again that I got frustrated. I was upset. I didn't mean it. I apologize.' Well, this man owned the team. He didn't have to do that, you know? Walter Brown was just a very decent human being.

"So it started from the top and became a family thing. We were the *Celtics*. It wasn't Boston, it wasn't the NBA; it was the *Celtics*. And that was the only thing that really counted: the Celtics ... the Celtic

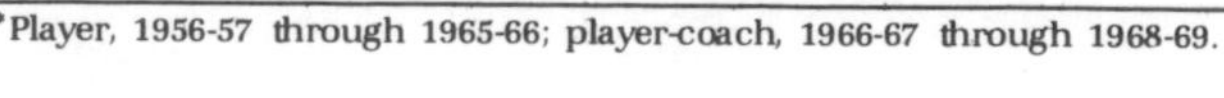

*Player, 1956-57 through 1965-66; player-coach, 1966-67 through 1968-69.

family. I couldn't imagine ever wanting to play anyplace else. I probably could have made another million dollars in my playing career—easily—but it wasn't worth it to me.

"Yes, in the beginning there was doubt that I could do the job in the pros. I was aware of that feeling in the East. Red went out on a limb and made quite a move, giving up Macauley and Hagan to get this player that there was doubt about.

"Well, when I went there I fit right in with a group of players. That means, for me, it was a tailor-made situation, and Auerbach was the tailor. And he maintained it, getting players who fit into the team concept psychologically as well as physically.

"We were part of a team, and it's a team sport. That's why we were so good. The Celtics played together because we knew it was the best way to win. We always recognized that and understood it. You quickly realize all the other things aren't that important. But it takes a man to be that way. A man doesn't need false praise and a pat on the back all the time to say I'm OK. I *know* I'm OK.

"With a coach other than Red, I would have been the same player, but the question is whether the results would have been the same. I have serious doubts. Again, it's a team game. I played with very intelligent players. I played with highly motivated players. I was a contributor, you see. I don't think what was accomplished could have been accomplished without these specific surroundings.

"So Auerbach's presence was necessary. There's no doubt about it. Having players with talent is one thing, but how do you get the most out of them? How do you turn that into winning consistently? That's the difficult thing.

"How many coaches have you noticed who have a good year—maybe Coach of the Year—but two years later he's losing and they're talking about firing him? It's very easy to lose control of a team, especially if you're keeping the same people. You know, guys can get into power positions—or think they do—and there can be problems that way. A coach has to have a system or a method to keep control of the team, and Auerbach did.

"I can think of no other coach who could have made me feel as comfortable or work as hard. And our rapport came from the most important place of all: mutual respect. Red always knew I was a man and I always knew he was a man, and we treated each other that way.

"Red and I had things that happened that none of the other guys knew about. For example, the day before training camp started my third year he called me in to see him and said, 'If I can't yell at you, I can't yell at anybody. So I'm going to yell like hell at you tomorrow and the rest of the week, but don't pay any attention to it. You know you're going to make the team, and I know you're going to make the team. We've got to work together.'

"I had no problem with that. I wanted to be on a winning team. He was the coach. If he thought that would help him win, then that's what I'd do. It wasn't a question of being submissive. In order to lead, you must know how to follow. And if your ego is intact, those things are not that important.

"Red and I always exchanged favors. He never made any demands on me and I didn't make any demands of him. We exchanged favors. And we worked very, very well together, and that's important. He coached and I played, and I don't think any player ever played any better than me. I never wanted to run the team. That was Red's

function, and he's the best coach in the history of professional sports. Period.

"What most people don't know is that he and I spent a lot of time together. After Cousy retired, I roomed by myself. So Red and I would get together a lot—sometimes in my room, sometimes in his room. We'd sit around and play cards—gin, mostly—and talked. We talked a lot.

"Those were my formative years and Auerbach was of great assistance to me, right from the start. He did a lot of things that were extraordinarily important to me. For example, my first contract.

"I never signed until I came back from the Olympics in Melbourne. Red said to me, 'You're probably worried about scoring, because everyone says you can't shoot well enough to play pro ball. Are you worried about that?' I told him, 'Well, yeah, I am a little bit concerned.' And he said, 'I'll make a deal with you today. I promise as long as you play here, when we talk contracts we'll never discuss statistics.' And we never did discuss statistics.

"I liked Red, in spite of him. Oh, yeah, he could be annoying at times. But I'd just look at him. When I look at people that way, they understand.

"Mostly, though, it was the opposition that Red annoyed. His victory cigar infuriated a lot of people, but I thought it was funny, funny as hell. Of course it wasn't gracious, but what's that got to do with it?

"And I was waiting. One of these days, I kept telling myself, one of these days he's going to light that cigar and we're going to completely fold and lose the game—and he's going to swallow that thing *lit!* It never did happen, though. Damn it."

"Sam Jones had a champion's heart. When the pressure was greatest, he was eager for the ball. In the seventh game of a championship series, I'll take Sam over anyone who ever stepped onto a basketball court."

Bill Russell

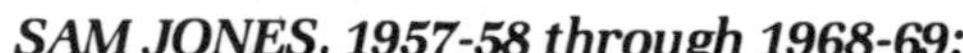

SAM JONES, 1957-58 through 1968-69:

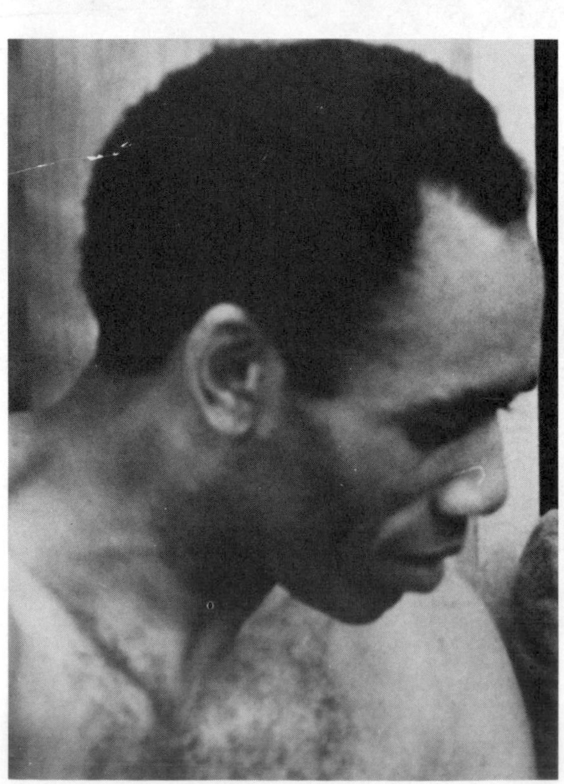

"Yes, I was one of the very few guys ever fined by Red Auerbach. He hit me for five dollars, and I still say he was wrong. Every time we get together I remind him about it, but he just laughs.

"And do you know what he nailed me for? Eating pancakes. We had a team rule against eating them on the day of a game and he caught me.

"We played Syracuse on a Saturday night in Boston, and after the game flew to Syracuse for a return game Sunday. As soon as we landed, Russ, K.C. and I went looking for a place to eat and ended up in a greasy spoon.

"We all ordered pancakes, but I got my order in first while they were gabbing. So naturally mine arrived first. I took a bite and heard a voice yell, 'That will be five dollars!'

"I look around and who's standing there but Auerbach. So I say, OK, I might as well pay the five and enjoy my meal. I dig for another forkful and Red says, 'Take another bite and it'll cost you another five dollars.'

"Meanwhile, Russ and K.C. are yelling to the cook: 'Cancel those orders!'

"So I was the only one who had to pay. And it was unfair. Why? It was 2 o'clock in the morning. The game wasn't for another 12 hours!

"I'll never forget that. I'll also never forget my first game with the Celtics. It was against the Knicks at old Madison Square Garden in 1957, and I was scared to death.

"Just before the game, they put out the lights and introduced the Celtics under a spotlight. They gave me a little extra flourish: *'And the only rookie to make the world champion Boston Celtics, Sam Jones!'*

"Then it was the Knicks' turn, and they came exploding through a paper hoop—Richie Guerin, Kenny Sears, Willie Naulls, Mel Hutchins, Ray Felix and all the others. The place went wild.

"Then they put the lights back on, and that's when the size of the crowd hit me. I couldn't believe my eyes. I'd never seen so many people in one building; they were hanging from the rafters.

"I'd come out of small North Carolina College, which had less than 2,000 students. Our biggest basketball crowd was maybe 4,000 tops. This was almost *five times* that, and the place was jumping. Celtics-Knicks games were always big. Man, I could feel king-sized chill bumps all over.

"The first time I got the ball that night, the Knicks doubled up on me. 'Oh, oh,' I said—and froze. So they tied me up for a jump ball. I can still see Red jumping up off the bench and shaking his head.

"I don't think I scored a point that game. You can't score if you don't shoot, and I was too scared to shoot. In fact, Russ quickly nicknamed me 'Right Back' because as soon as someone passed me the ball I passed it right back.

"I was like that for awhile, just trying to work myself in gently and not appear hoggish. Remember, you had some pretty fair shooters on that team named Cousy and Sharman, not to mention a couple of sophomores named Heinsohn and Russell. I was just a rookie.

"Yes, I was old for a rookie—24—having been in the Army already. Instead of my age being a disadvantage, though, being a vet probably helped me. The Celtics knew I couldn't be drafted into the service again.

"Still, I was doubtful I could make the team. Everyone was back from the team that had won the Celtics' first championship the previous season, so there were no openings. Luckily, I made it, bumping Dick Hemric. And there was a little irony there. The man who had advised Red to draft me No. 1 was Bones McKinney, and he had coached Hemric at Wake Forest.

"The toughest player I ever covered? There were two: Oscar Robertson and Jerry West. They had different styles—West was quick, Oscar deceptive. There was no joy in Mudville when you had to go against either of those two.

"K.C. did a lot more guarding of them than I did, thank goodness. K.C. was a wonder defensively and took on all the tough shooters. Thank the Lord for K.C. Jones. He was my man. And you know, some people still think we're brothers. I still hear that in my travels.

"I always felt bad that K.C. retired on the one year in the sixties that we didn't win the title. So he was one of the few Celtics of that era who didn't go out a winner. Luckily, I did.

"I had planned to retire in '66, the same year that Red did. But when Russ was made coach, he and I had a talk and I decided to play one more year. When we lost the title in '67, I didn't want to leave a loser. So I played another season—and then one more.

"We had won back the title in '68 and I said that '69 would be my last time around no matter what. And we won it again in '69, but it went down to the very end—the last minute of the seventh game in the NBA finals.

"That last game at Los Angeles stands out from all the others of my career. It was a great thrill for a number of reasons.

"One, of course, is that it was my *last* championship. Most say the first title is sweetest, but I say the last one is best—when you're retiring and know it's your last time around. The first one is nice, but you know you'll have chances at more. When you're retiring, you know it's your *last* chance at a title.

"And making it extra special was *how* we won it and the many circumstances involved.

"We'd finished fourth that season, and nobody expected us to do much in the playoffs. But what people didn't realize was *why* we were fourth. We had one injury after another and were missing key players all season. I was out most of December, another time a Bailey Howell would be out or a Larry Siegfried and so on. We never had the same cast—until the playoffs, when everything came together.

"In the finals we were playing an outstanding Laker team that was much younger than we were. It also had three of the greatest players in basketball history—Wilt Chamberlain, Elgin Baylor and Jerry West.

"The Lakers won the first two games and later had a 3-2 advantage before we tied the series to set up the seventh-game showdown at L.A.

"Most people didn't give us much chance—not only because of all the other factors, but because they felt we couldn't win the seventh game away from home. We'd had homecourt advantage in most seventh-game situations over the years. Now the Lakers had that edge.

"I'll never forget reading in an L.A. newspaper before the last game: 'The USC band will play *Happy Days Are Here Again* when the Lakers win the world title, and hundreds of balloons will be released from the Forum rafters.'

"And when we came out of the locker room for warmups, sure enough, there was the band fiddling with their instruments. And I looked up at the ceiling and there were all the balloons clustered in nets, all set to be released.

"They were still there three hours later when we ran off the court with another world championship, my last. How sweet it was."

"K.C. Jones was the best defensive man in basketball. Over the years I saw 'Case' do superhuman things and make them look natural. He was a marvel.

"I've never had a better friend or a greater inspiration."

Bill Russell

*K.C. JONES, 1958-59 through 1966-67; 1977-78 through—**

"You had to have been there to appreciate the feeling of being a Celtic during our string of championships. It's impossible to describe that feeling because it was so super special. We were doing

*Player, 1958-59 through 1966-67; assistant coach, 1977-78 through present.

something that had never been done before—and hasn't been done since.

"We had such great ties on the court, such togetherness. With some other club I probably would have been sitting down, or maybe not even been in the league. But the Celtics were different. There was Sam the shooter, Satch the rebounder, Russ the passer and blocker and rebounder, me on defense, and so forth. We each had our job and were part of a unit, and that unit made each of us stronger.

"And everybody—Satch, Russell, Havlicek, Nelson, *everyone*—was for everybody else. I remember when Nelson joined the club, Satch was quick to go over and say, 'Keep doing this and that and you can take my starting job.' We pulled for each other and understood each other.

"That closeness helped immensely. For example, Heinie loved to shoot the ball. If he'd been with some other club he might have heard, 'Man, that's a lousy shot' if he wasn't hitting. With the Celtics, whatever you did you had the other guys' blessings.

"Things mattered to the Celtics that didn't matter to other teams. Lots of things, some of them seemingly small but things that add up to winning. It built up a psychology. Points might be important to another team, but what was important to us was loose balls, getting shooters open, beating a guy on the break, knowing a team's weakness and working together to chop away at it.

"What we had was total concentration and total hustle. Most teams don't have that.

"Concentration and psyching a guy out has a lot to do with your success. You can't be scared. Say a guy zips by you on one side, then zips by you on the other side. Then, the next time, he stops short and throws up a jumper. Well, if you're standing there and thinking, 'Uh-oh, this is bad'—well, then you're scared. And you can't run scared. If I had, guys like West and Oscar would have devoured me. Sometimes they did anyway.

"Like one playoff game I'll never forget against the Lakers—a very *embarrassing* playoff game for me.

"It was the championship series, and the first two games were in Boston. I had a good game covering West in the opener, holding him to something like 16 points. Afterward, the press crowded around my locker—something I wasn't used to—and it seemed like every newspaper writer in the country was there. They were asking, 'What did you do to him? How did you stop him?' So I held court. I lost my head and told them *everything*: 'I did this and that, and that and this, and so forth and so on.' Man, I really poured it on.

"The next night Jerry scored 43. I had forgotten that besides knowing what to do with a basketball, Jerry West also knew how to read. It taught me a very big lesson: Be ever so humble when you're covering a superscorer.

"But things like that were OK with the Celtics. The air of that team was completely unselfish. No one ever criticized. Everyone wanted to help. We were in this thing *together*.

"And when you're successful time and time again at something—like winning championships—there's a built-in psychology right there. Another team comes to play you and they're a little shaky. That gives you added confidence, and a feeling of pride in being a Celtic.

"And because of this psychology thing, the other team can't really use all its thinking tools out there. Maybe I'm bringing the ball down

the floor and the play is set for Heinsohn. All of a sudden, one of the other guys jumps into the middle leaving, say, Satch on the weak side.

"All of a sudden—*boom*—Satch starts wheeling. See, the play is not automatic. You're always checking as you're going through your pattern and adjusting when the situation is ripe. When you've got this confidence, that means you can think clearly all the time.

"And no one was more confident than Bill Russell. Hell, he was damn near the whole thing.

"Let's say an opponent gets a breakaway layup. Russ may have little chance of stopping him, but he's still going to put everything he has into it. If he's chasing him and sees he can't catch up, Russ might start making a lot of noise with his feet and yelling, 'I got him, Case, I got him!' And, all of a sudden, the guy's looking around. A lot of guys missed layups that way.

"Russell was incredible. How would we have done against Kareem? How did he do against Wilt?

"Russ also was extraordinary off the court, a super nice guy although somewhat detached. He'd go out of his way to help you. If you needed money and he didn't have it, he'd go out and borrow it for you. Or if you were moping around the locker room, down about something, he'd slip over and say, 'Feel like going out after the game?' The public didn't see much of that Mr. Nice Guy side of Russ, a very private person.

"Russell wasn't alone in that nice guy department, of course. Everyone on that team was, really. There was such an unselfish attitude. For example, if Sharman thought Sam should be getting more playing time, he might go to Red and suggest that Sam start in his place. I did that once with Siegfried. We all knew that a guy who hustled like hell but wasn't getting much playing time can get down; so you say, why not start him in my place and maybe he can get himself together.

"That was the type attitude we had. We weren't afraid of losing our jobs. It was the success of the team that was important.

"The whole closeness thing helped a lot. It made you enjoy the game all the more. The fun things, things we did in the dressing room—yes, like goosing one another. Every time someone bent over, it seemed someone would be standing right there—*oops, pardon me!* It got to be so bad that when you were at home, and you bent over to pick up a shoe or something and your wife walked by, you'd snap to attention out of habit.

"You had to be there to appreciate that horseplay, and there was a lot of it to appreciate—a lot of good-natured fun. We enjoyed being together off the court as well as on. And it didn't hurt our great teamwork.

"A good example of how we worked together was my second year, when Maurice King arrived. I knew the way he could play. I had played with him in the service and I figured, 'This guy is going to take my job.'

"He was a better player than I was. Yet when he'd be out there going one-on-one with me I'd be showing him different things. It was automatic to help people on that team. The thought was never that the man is going to take my place so I'd better not help. Instead, you just felt like giving to the other person. It was a part of being a Celtic."

"Satch hardly got any recognition as a player. But he did more to help our team than anyone ever realized—except the players. We knew."

Tom Heinsohn

TOM (SATCH) SANDERS, 1960-61 through 1972-73; 1977-78 through 1978-79*:

"My biggest embarrassment as a Celtic? How could I possibly forget it? It lasted 48 minutes—48 very embarrassing, extremely uncomfortable minutes.

"It happened early in my career during a period when I was in love with barbequed ribs—ribs and a couple of beers to wash them down. I began enjoying them so much that I decided to indulge myself the morning of a game. I figured if I finished before noon, that would allow plenty of time for both the ribs and beer to be out of my system by gametime.

"It didn't work out that way. Any alcohol in your system results in immediate perspiration when coupled with physical exertion, and I have always perspired easily anyway. So that night I was soaked by the time I tried my first layup—and missed.

"Also, the pork had not digested well. So I was one ill dude. I was down on all fours at midcourt fighting off nausea more than once. But Simon Legree Auerbach wouldn't take me out. He left me in the entire game, and all the guys were laughing while I was dying.

"I ended up with no rebounds and no points despite playing the

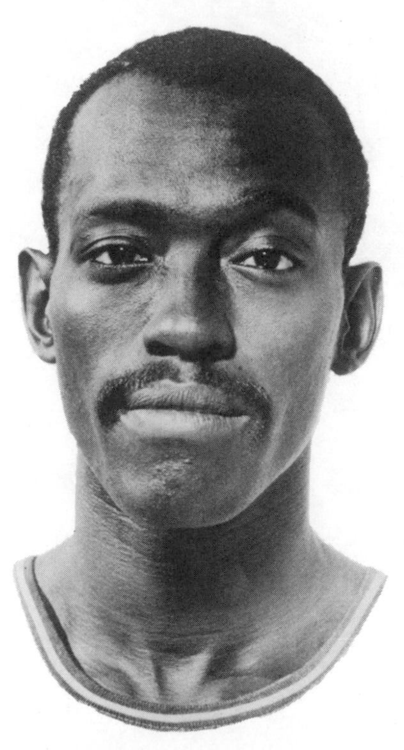

*Player, 1960-61 through 1972-73; assistant coach, first half of 1977-78; head coach, last half of 1977-78 and first part of 1978-79.

full 48 minutes. Fortunately, the Celtics could win without me. And Red never said a word about it to me, then or ever. He didn't have to. I got the message—eloquently.

"Yes, I was a No. 1 draft choice, the eighth player taken in the entire 1960 draft. A bonus? You must be joking. From Scrooge Auerbach? Wait, I may have gotten a bonus at that. Maybe a set of Celtic souvenir drinking glasses. Or perhaps a Celtic keychain or a Celtic ashtray. Red was big on those things then, but not with money.

"Basketball salaries weren't anywhere near what they are today. The top Celtic players were making in the teens. The *top* Celtics. The *world champions*. And you had to battle for every dollar if you were dealing with Red. Salary sessions with him were real workouts every season. So in my early years, if Red called me during the offseason and invited me to Boston for a Tuesday contract talk, I'd race up from New York on Monday to deal with Walter Brown. Then the next day I'd stroll into Auerbach's office and say, 'Gee, Red, I got in a little early yesterday and bumped into Walter. There was no problem, so I signed.'

"That made Red sizzle. He knew what was going on, that Walter was a lot easier to deal with. That's why all the guys wanted to deal with Walter instead. But after Walter died in 1964, we no longer had a choice; we had to negotiate with Red, and it was a battle every time. So each year I'd try something new, like walking into his office carrying a picket sign, or wearing rags and telling him I couldn't afford any better on what he was paying me.

"That first year, though, Red talked to me like a father after drafting me. Believe it or not, I hadn't been all that enthusiastic about being drafted by the Celtics, for a couple of reasons.

"One was that I was from New York City. So I was a Knicks' fan and had scrimmaged against them while at NYU. Sweetwater Clifton and Mel Hutchins were my favorites, and I was hoping to play with the Knicks and stay in my hometown. Also, it was a team that had finished last the previous season and needed help. In contrast, the Celtics were at the top of the heap—the best team in basketball—and making their squad would be an uphill battle, No. 1 draft choice or not.

"Also, I was tempted by an offer from the Tuck Tape Company to be in its management training program and play on its AAU team. Red said a job was something I could always get, but that a chance to play pro ball comes once in a lifetime—especially with the world champions. He also said Conley was getting tired of playing two big league sports and that Loscy's back was hurting, and kept stressing there was room for me.

"By the time he got through with me I envisioned myself rushing to the rescue of the world champions. Then I got to training camp and found about 25 forwards fighting for *my* position!

"Well, two things soon happened that still rank as my happiest memories as a Celtic. The first came at the end of camp when Red told me I'd made the team. The second followed a short time later when I flunked an Army physical; I was a little over the height limit and had an eye problem. That was a break because if I'd gone into the service, I'd probably have been forgotten. It was an eight-team league then, and slots weren't held open for rookies. You had to take advantage of an opportunity when it was there.

"Sure I remember my first game. It was against the Pistons at the Garden. I played about three minutes, got into a fight with Shellie

McMillon, carried the ball and put up a couple of shots that nearly broke the backboard because I was so nervous. It wasn't exactly the greatest presentation of a new talent in Celtic history.

"No, I didn't mind the conversion to the role of defensive forward as a pro. I hadn't been just a scorer in college; although averaging 22–23 points a game, I'd also enjoyed playing defense. Besides, I had no choice in my new role. Red already had clearly decided the Celtics had enough people shooting the ball and told me to concentrate on doing what he felt I did best—play defense.

"Oh, sure I would have appreciated the honors and glories, as they say, that go along with being a scorer. I would have appreciated the publicity like anyone else. But I really didn't miss the scoring part. I soon came to appreciate defense all the more, having so much fun going head-to-head against some of the greatest offensive forwards of all time. It was a super challenge and very satisfying when you shut down those people.

"K.C. and I would have little competitions between us, making little bets—Cokes, frappes, beers, even dinner sometimes—on which of us would contain his man better. We'd have our hands full against a team like the Lakers, for instance—K.C. covering West, me Baylor, the toughest man I ever covered.

"Afterward, it was easy to measure our contributions. K.C. and I would check the statistic sheets and could see it in the numbers. 'If so-and-so had gotten his average tonight,' we'd say, 'we'd have lost.' There's serious satisfaction in that, a very personal satisfaction.

"And if I wasn't fully convinced of that from the start, I got one final lesson early in my career. I began thinking about All-Star teams and all that jazz, so started shooting more and soon was averaging nearly 16 points a game. No one said anything. Not Red. Not Cooz. Not Russell or Heinie or any of the other guys.

"Then one night I scored something like 22 or 24 and we lost. While driving home I thought about it and began to realize what we had going for us. Each man was a specialist, and it only took one man crossing over into another man's specialty to spoil the balance of that beautiful machine. That's when I realized the overall picture was far more important than my own little picture.

"It taught me a lesson: Do what you do best. All the extras—the headlines, the ovation—don't count as much as winning. It was a much bigger claim to say I was part of the world champion Celtics than to say I averaged 35 points for an also-ran. I had what a lot of All-Stars wanted but couldn't have—*championships*. And cashing the checks that go with them covers a lot, too.

"So I never worried about headlines again. And I never bemoaned the fact that I never had a chance to play on an All-Star team—not with all those household names on our team. It didn't matter. I knew I had contributed."

"Havlicek is Havlicek. Will there ever be another?"
Tom (Satch) Sanders

JOHN HAVLICEK, 1962-63 through 1977-78:

"I graduated from Ohio State in June, went to football training camp with the Cleveland Browns in July, got cut in August, and started in pro basketball in September when I reported to the Celtics.

"Pro football was something I had to try, even though I hadn't

played that sport since high school. There were a lot of reasons. Yes, I suppose part of it was the challenge. But there were more practical reasons, too. Salaries were similar, but the schedule was much more in favor of football—14 games compared to 80-some in basketball. Also, by staying in Ohio, I wouldn't have to pick up my roots and start in another place; I could avoid that hassle. And the Browns were my favorite football team, too. So I thought I'd give pro football a shot. Even if I didn't make it, I wouldn't spend the rest of my life wondering if I could have.

"Well, I was with the Browns as a receiver about six weeks and played in a few exhibition games. There were a lot of veterans on that team, including a pretty fair receiver named Ray Renfro. And, yes, one of the Browns' two first-round picks that year was a receiver named Gary Collins. I was the last receiver cut, so I must have had some ability.

"I moved on to Boston and the Celtics, and that opened my eyes a little.

"I arrived in Boston around 11 o'clock one night with Jack (The Shot) Foley from the East-West Shrine Game in Kansas City and checked into the old Madison Hotel next to the Garden. There wasn't anything to eat there, so I went to the cafeteria on the corner with all the derelicts. It was a gloomy kind of night, raining, and the water was dripping down from the 'T' elevated tracks overhead.

"So it was a bleak first impression of Boston, and I wasn't impressed at all.

"The next day I went to the Celtic clubhouse and was shocked. It wasn't anything like I expecıed. Coming from Ohio State, where the locker room was just so, I thought it would be very open and spacious; what I saw was a dungeon. There were no lockers, just hooks and nails in the wall where you could hang your clothes above a long bench, which you sat on and put your shoes under. There was one coat rack where everybody including some of the sports writers hung their overcoats.

"The training room was big enough for three people—the trainer, one person being taped, and one person waiting. The shower consisted of two nozzles. There was one john, one urinal, one sink, and the fixtures dated back to when the Garden was built in the twenties.

"It was fairly clean, but Red smoked those cigars. And most of the players smoked; that was before the Surgeon General came out and said that cigarettes were harmful. So between the cigars and cigarettes, that smoke odor would never get out of that room.

"The uniforms were not the caliber I thought a world champion team's would be like, either. It was a mix 'n match sort of thing as compared to Ohio State, where everything was new. And in college there were equipment people, laundry people, a person for everything. Here it seemed like one man—Buddy LeRoux, the trainer—was running the whole thing.

"I did like the Garden's parquet floor, though.

"What stood out most in my mind, really, was the Celtics' togetherness. You could see that immediately. The first Celtic to come over and say hello was Frank Ramsey; he always went out of his way to make rookies feel welcome. I met everyone, but I seemed to end up talking most to Frank—yes, the guy I would succeed as sixth man.

"Red never took me aside and said, 'This'll be your job.' He said, 'We're probably going to play you a lot in the same manner that we play Ramsey.' That is, as a swingman between forward and guard, coming off the bench. They'd seen me play in the Milk Fund Game at Madison Square Garden, where the rookies used to play an exhibition game against the Knicks. There weren't many guards on that team, so that's where I was used instead of my usual forward position. And that's how the Celtics realized I could play guard defensively, which is probably the hardest thing to do.

"Red looked for defensive players, and I don't think most other pro coaches did. And I had been defense oriented right from the start in college When I arrived at Ohio State, I realized everyone there had averaged 30 points a game in high school. Even though I'd been a scorer in high school, I knew I wasn't going to be a scorer there, not with Jerry Lucas, Larry Siegfried, Mel Nowell, Bobby Knight and those people. I felt if I was going to play early in my career at Ohio State, I was going to have to show something other than scoring. So I pretty much abandoned my offense, and my job as a collegian became defense.

"And that's a big reason I was happy to be drafted by the Celtics. Red appreciated defense, and the Celtics played my style and my system.

"And Red brought me along offensively to the point where he gave me a lot of confidence. 'Don't let them insult you,' he'd say about opponents. 'When they give you the opportunity, you've got to shoot the ball.' Nobody had said that to me before. He gave me the green light.

"That lifted a big burden off my back because I'd always been looking to pass, to start a play. I'd always been saying to myself, 'Well, I've got the shot, but should I take it? There are the other shooters.' But Red wanted you to take those shots. He wanted to attack the other side's weakness, and if you happened to be in the spot to do so, then he wanted you to shoot the ball.

"So Red brought me along in a manner where I could feel comfortable.

"I can remember sitting on the bench and just itching. I was always ready. That's one thing I tried to get across to our younger players in my later years: you've always got to be ready to go. What good is having your sweatsuit on, your jacket buttoned up, and your arms through the sleeves? When the man wants you, he wants you *now*—not after you've had to do a striptease. I've seen guys waste a lot of time, even a timeout, getting into the game; they didn't get to the scorer's table in time, and then the foul shot was taken and the ball was put into play and the guy didn't get into the game until three or four minutes later.

"So being ready is really a big thing. Right from the start of the game, I'd have my sweatpants off and my jacket just draped over my shoulders. Then, as soon as the coach called me, all I had to do was bounce up, the jacket would fall off and I was on my way. That way I didn't miss out on anything.

"Red was a motivator on the bench, too. Sometimes he'd look down the bench at you, and you'd start to pop up; then he'd just look the other way. He was playing little games with you; he wanted to find out if you were ready.

"Early in my career I'd usually go into the game after six-seven-eight minutes; but sometimes Red would keep me out a quarter and a half, and that really ticked me off. Then, when you finally got in there, you played like a demon.

"I moved into a starting role later in the sixties. Actually, my Celtics career had three cycles.

"From 1962 until '65 I was really a newcomer. From 1965 to '69 I felt I was a veteran, a real part of the team. And then I became the old man in one year because of all the retirements. I became sort of the last link, and maybe a leader with more dimensions, once Russell retired after the '69 season. Then, from 1974 to '76, I was a person who had been the leader but had started to relinquish that role to others, like Dave Cowens and Jo Jo White. And my last two years you can call whatever you want. Maybe the bottom of my career—the turn of events, the way the team disintegrated, although I never lost my enthusiasm or hope.

"I don't think there's any question that I could have played another season or two. People say, well, you wouldn't have had to play that much. I could have played 20 minutes a night, but I don't think that would have agreed with me. I was used to 30-35 minutes, that kind of thing. Psychologically, 20-25 would have been bad for me.

"So I didn't stretch it out. Even so, I played in more NBA games that any other player, and that's one of the things that I'm proudest of now. It's a nice feeling because no one had ever done that before. I remember when I signed my first contract I figured if I played 10 years and reached a $25,000 plateau it would be a great career.

"Yes, there were a lot of thrills along the way. Everybody remembers the 'Havlicek stole the ball' game, when I deflected Hal Greer's pass-in for Chet Walker in the final seconds of the 1965 Eastern finale against Philadelphia. That was a great thrill, no question. But to me an even bigger play was the shot I made over Jabbar to put us ahead of Milwaukee by a point with eight seconds left in the second overtime of the sixth game in the '74 finals.

"It was one of the toughest plays I ever made, especially considering the circumstances. I was in the corner and had to shoot it so high, on such an exaggerated arc over Jabbar. When he came at me, the basket disappeared. And I was fouled on the play; Jabbar just crashed into me. I saw a picture of it later and everybody, including referee Mendy Rudolph, had his head turned watching the ball. So nobody saw the foul. It wouldn't have fouled Jabbar out, but it would have given us a chance at a two-point lead and a different set of circumstances going into the final seconds. Instead, Jabbar hit that great hook shot from the corner with three seconds to go to win the game.

"It's the 'Havlicek stole the ball' game that most people still talk about, though. What I'll never forget is what happened when the buzzer sounded. All hell broke loose at the Garden.

"Bill Russell was the first to get to me. He had been wearing goat horns about 10 feet long after hitting the guy wire with the ball while in-bounding it, giving Philadelphia one last chance. Then the fans started to claw away at me. They started tearing at my jersey and ended up ripping the stirrups right off my shoulders. I actually got a rope burn from each one and was bleeding from the collarbone.

"They got the jersey off by the time I'd reached the exit sign, and by the time I got to the corridor they'd pulled my pants down around my knees. That's how wild it got.

"And four years later, at Sam Jones' retirement party, a woman came up to me. She was wearing something that looked like a brooch attached to her dress.

" 'Do you know what this is?' she asked.

" 'Looks like a piece of rag,' I told her.

"And she said, 'That's part of your jersey from the night you stole the ball.' "

"His first day in training camp, Willie had himself a big lunch between double sessions. I tried to warn him, but he didn't know Auerbach.

"That afternoon Red had us running and jumping all over the place, then made us get down and start doing pushups.

"That was too much for Willie. He threw up and then passed out, landing in his own mess. A couple of players dragged him off the court, then went back to their pushups. Poor Willie was laying over there with puke all over him.

"We laughed all day about that."

Frank Ramsey

WILLIE NAULIS, 1963-64 through 1965-66:

"Yes, I passed out that first day. I thought Red was crazy. I couldn't believe the kind of running they were doing because, hell, we'd never done that kind of running for at least three or four weeks when I was with the Knicks.

"I thought to myself, 'What am I doing here? What have I gotten myself into?'

"You see, I was really coming out of what amounted to retirement. I had been traded from New York to San Francisco during the previous season after six years with the Knicks, and finished up playing half a year with Wilt, Attles and those guys on the Warriors. So after seven pro seasons, I wasn't going to play any more; I was just very tired of basketball. I was going to forget about basketball and go back to UCLA, do some studying and get into the private business world.

"Then I was contacted by Bill Russell about joining the Celtics. I had always greatly admired Russ, the greatest basketball player I'd ever seen. More than any other player, he dominated basketball. I used to tease him that I didn't see how one man could do so much with so little. He couldn't pass, he couldn't dribble, he couldn't run, but he always made the foul shot at the end of the game that won it, or blocked the shot, or got the rebound or whatever. I respected the great confidence he had in himself.

"Although I didn't want to play basketball again, I had to give this opportunity a lot of thought. I had always wanted to play with the Celtics because they played the type of ball—running, strong defense, all those kinds of things—that I had learned at UCLA. And they always won all the marbles.

"The Celtics were world champions. And not only were they world champs, but in my head they were the best because they had Bill Russell, because they had a great coach in Red Auerbach, because they played a certain style of basketball and because they had pride. Their guys weren't so concerned with egos and all that; they were concerned with winning basketball games.

"They did everything they could to win a game. They *lived* basketball. They were *thinking* players who outsnookered you all the time. I would learn more about professional basketball in my first year with them than I had learned in my first seven years in the league, and I was a damned good player when I joined them.

"And the Celtics had something else. In any sport the most important thing is self-respect, and when that grows into a team self-respect—with every individual respecting himself and the other guys on the team—it grows into something like the Celtics had. That's something that's not prevalent for any length of time anymore. You

find a team that comes up with it for a year or two, then it disintegrates. But the Celtics were able to carry that over year after year.

"So I told Russ I'd think about it. And while I was, I talked to Red once. I was really kind of wooed back into basketball. And what turned my head around was that chance to play with the Celtics—to play with that man I respected, for that man I respected and with that group of guys I enjoyed. The guys on the Celtics were literally my best friends in basketball.

"In life, we have our family and our friends, and those are our teams in life. When you don't feel well, or when you have a victory of some sort, you want to share those things. UCLA had that united feeling when I'd played there, but I hadn't found it in professional basketball; that's why I'd disliked it so much.

"But the Celtics were different. They *were* a family, complete with Red as the father and parent image. And the players—John Havlicek, K.C. Jones, Bill Russell—were like brothers, and still are. All those guys are like family members, and that was the biggest difference between the Celtics and other teams. The Celtics had *soul*.

"There's a lot said in the world about all for one and one for all, but on the Celtics those weren't empty words. We *lived* that. Russell was like a big brother. When I went to Boston, he just took over my life. Russ picked me up and took me everyplace, including his home. I took his bed, ate his food. And he did that to everybody. It was all part of Celtic life. All the ideals we have about what family is all about and what friends are—they were actually living within the Boston Celtics.

"Red was a dictator, of course. He called himself one—a *benevolent* dictator. You did what he said. Period. He put certain perimeters on the team, certain limitations, but he also utilized individual strengths better than anyone I've ever seen. He had a knowledge of the game second to none. He was ahead of his time with the fast break, and he was a very astute judge of talent.

"Havlicek, Cowens, Chaney, Russell—none were first picks in the country. Yet all had certain capacities that Red saw. He picked Russell and K.C. Jones when everyone in the media—especially in the East, because we were farmboys from out West, weren't we?—never thought Russell would make professional basketball. When I was with the Knicks, guys in New York used to ask me about Russ while he was in college. They thought he was a stiff. I told them that he was going to revolutionize basketball, and that Neil Johnston and all those guys with the sweeping hook shots had better find themselves another line of work because Russell was going to take the game away from them.

"There was great rapport and great understanding between Russell and Auerbach. Several times they had words, but Russ never went too far out of line—except at practice. He was awful in practice. *Awful*. Guys would complain and complain, especially Sam Jones. Sam would get hysterical and say, 'Look at Russell! Look at Russell!' And Red would say, 'Listen, Sam, I'm going to tell you, and I'm going to tell all the rest of you guys, there are two sets of rules on this team: one for all you guys and one for Russell—and I want you to know that.'

"We laughed and laughed and laughed, but we all knew it was the truth. Russell performed, he did things in the games, but he just did not practice. Red would stop practice and say, 'OK, Russell, go sit up in the stands,' and Russ would be up there reading the newspaper while we were running our tongues out. But there were times when Red would put his foot down, and Russ would respond immediately. He knew what limits to push Red to and when to stop.

"The two knew how to handle each other. If things got out of hand, nobody ever knew about it because Red would pull Russ off into a corner or they'd go to another room and talk. You had to understand Russell. He wanted to win as much as anybody, and he knew what he had to do. Practice he hated; he just didn't feel he needed it, and obviously he didn't. The man was one of a kind—the greatest ever, with a tremendous heart and spirit. He inspired us, he carried us. Without him there'd have been no string of championships.

"And Auerbach was behind it all, the man who put it together.

"Yes, that cigar of his ticked off a lot of the opposition. A lot of guys—Earl Lloyd and Johnny Kerr, to name a couple—hated him for it. When I see Lloyd today he *still* talks about it. If those guys had their way they'd take Red's cigar and crumble it right up his nose. But you know something? If Red Auerbach hadn't been successful, nobody would have given a damn about his cigar."

"Siggy was a flake, all right. He also had one of the best basketball minds in the game."

Bill Russell

LARRY SIEGFRIED, 1963-64–1969-70:

"Do they still recall me in Boston as the first contract holdout in Celtic history? I guess they're going to put that on my gravestone. Well, I hope my seven years in Boston are remembered for a lot more than that distinction.

"It's true, though. I did hold out before my last season in Boston and sent in my attorney, Bob Woolf, to deal with Red. That sort of thing wasn't done much in those days. Especially not on the Celtics, not with Auerbach. And Red hit the roof, going clean through the ceiling.

"Listen, I didn't hold out because I had any ax to grind. Or because I was trying to stir things up. Or because I was a troublemaker. I did it out of desperation. We'd had a coaching change—Russell had retired and Heinsohn was taking his place—and I guess I just didn't fit into the new plans. I had found out that once I signed I would be traded to Atlanta. I knew what was going on and didn't know how to handle it.

"I felt lost. And scared. I didn't have a no-cut contract, so I had no leverage. I wanted to play for the Celtics, but that was out of my hands if they wanted to trade me. I had no say in the matter. I would have played for less money in Boston than I would in Atlanta. So I figured if I was going to Atlanta, I'd hold out for every penny.

"So Woolf told me, 'Go get lost, stay in shape, and I'll take care of it.' Then he went in to see Auerbach, and Red blew up. He figured it was illegal or something. Before that, a player would just go in by himself, talk with Red and kind of herky-jerky a figure. Now this lawyer business was something altogether new to Red. It was unheard of. And so I was the bad guy. Well, if I was a troublemaker, what are these guys today?

"I always enjoyed playing for Red, though. He always said your offense is a derivative of your defense, and it is. He proved that with

Russell, didn't he? The man was a master whose record speaks for itself. He put together a lot of talent and got the most out of it. It takes more than talent, though. It's a *team* game and you've got to play *together*. And Red made sure we did. He has to rank as one of the greatest coaches of all time in any sport, and it was a thrill to play for him.

"Of course I hated leaving Boston. It was a big disappointment. There was a sense of loss after those seven seasons and five world championships. I wish I'd been able to bridge the gap from Russell to Cowens and finish my career as a Celtic.

"On the other hand, that last year in Boston was a bad, bad year for me.

"First there was all that talk about trade. And that hurt. We had just come off a championship year in '69 and then you read in the newspapers that they're trading you. All our championships had been made because a lot of people were loyal to a team cause. It made the Celtics one of the greatest sports organizations that will ever be. Suddenly that cause was destroyed. It's difficult to think loyalty when you're reading that you're going to be traded.

"Well, it turned out that I didn't get traded that year. But it turned out to be a terrible season anyway—for everybody. I don't think anyone enjoyed it.

"So, under the circumstances, being let go in the expansion draft at season's end wasn't the worst thing in the world. One of the reasons I was let go was that they and I had some disagreements about the fast break. Everyone knows you can't fast break without a big man. Now, as I look back, it's sadder because the Celtics got Cowens the season after I left and could run again.

"Still, except for the last year, I enjoyed my years with the Celtics overall. Tremendously. How could you *not* enjoy being part of all those championship years? There's never been anything like it in basketball history, and what are the odds on it ever happening again?

"In the process, I played in an awful lot of very big ball games. I enjoyed that, especially the playoffs. I enjoyed the challenge. It's very difficult to get up for 82 games, a long schedule. But the playoffs are something else; that's when the money is on the line. And it's not just the money; it's the championship. You can really get some emotion into it and get yourself revved up.

"I was a tough man to beat in the trenches when that money was on the line. I couldn't get 50 points or 30 rebounds, but what I could do I did well. Yes, that includes diving after those loose balls.

"A loose ball was *my* ball. It's as simple as that. Every free ball you get is a big plus for your team, a matter of four potential points—two your team can get, two the other team can't get. Diving for loose basketballs is the way I learned basketball. If that stands out as an abnormality in pro basketball it's because most guys won't bend over to pick up the ball. But that's what the game is all about. And that's the way I played it. You've got to hustle, I mean *really* hustle.

"Take a John Havlicek. As great a player as he was, John was a bona fide digger and scratcher. There were many guys who had more pure basketball ability than John. But John was a digger and a scratcher, and that lifted him above the others.

"So I did whatever I could to win. I *cared*. I really *wanted* to win and played that way. That was my way of getting recognition.

"Many of my assets were overlooked in Boston. Hey, there was a lot of talent on those teams. I can remember Russ saying in the locker room one day, 'Siggy, you always got to remember that some guys are always going to get press.'

"But I don't care what the press wrote—or didn't write. I knew I contributed. I feel my years in Boston were productive. I know I was there. I just feel very fortunate—tickled to death—that I was part of it.

"A lot of championships. And as I've said, a lot of big games—some *great* games. And some great playoff series: Celtics-Lakers, Celtics-Philly. That rivalry between Boston and Philadelphia was just awesome. Those games were *wars.*

"Yes, Boston versus Philly and later Boston versus L.A. meant Russell versus Chamberlain. And, yes, Wilt was awesome. But Russ was the greatest athlete who ever lived in terms of his value to the team. He always rose to the occasion and would do superhuman things when he had to. The man was, well, superhuman.

"It was live-or-die basketball then. Winning was everything to us. And it was a lot more than that, too. Talent was part of it, but just *part* of it. There was also the *inner man.* It was what we were made of, and that's what I'm most proud of.

"You know, there isn't a franchise in NBA history that more teams tried to imitate than the Celtics. Everybody wanted to be like the Celtics. They've tried to imitate the Celtics with outward ability, but the thing they can't imitate is the man *inside.* Tell me how you can duplicate the heart of a K.C. Jones or a Tom Sanders. You can't.

"Take any one of those guys, suck out his intensity and put it in a bottle, and do you know what you've got? You've got something that'll make you a multimillionaire. You've got what the Celtics were all about."

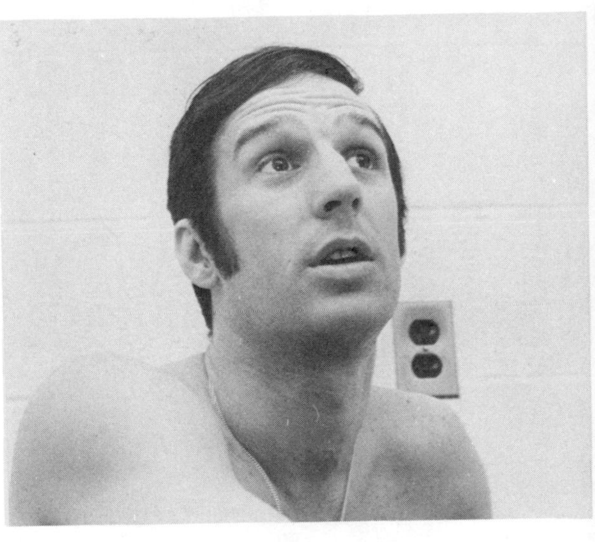

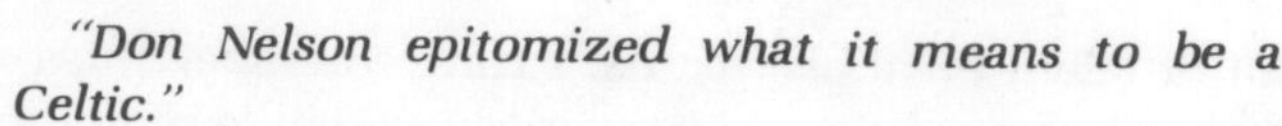

> *"Don Nelson epitomized what it means to be a Celtic."*
>
> Bill Russell

DON NELSON, 1965-66 through 1975-76:

"My happiest memory as a player? That's easy: Being picked up as a free agent by the Celtics five games into the '65-'66 season—and then making the team.

"I'd thought my career was over. Let's face it, when you clear waivers you're usually all done. So I couldn't believe it when Red Auerbach called and invited me to Boston—especially since there were other forwards available who had better statistics.

"I had to beat out Ronnie Watts, and Red had us battling head to head for two or three days. Red liked that kind of competition. Besides, he felt if Ronnie's job was at stake he deserved a chance to fight for it.

"When I got the contract I was sitting on top of the world. In less than a week I'd gone from the pits to the heights, from a down-and-out free agent to a job with the greatest team in basketball history.

"If I hadn't made it, I probably would have returned to my alma mater, Iowa, as coach of the freshman team. And, hopefully, I would have worked my way up to a varsity berth somewhere.

"So Red changed the whole course of my life by picking me up. And the question is *why* he picked me. He could have had Jackie Moreland instead; he was bigger, had much better stats and had been around the league longer. Yet Red picked me.

"I believe he sees things in certain players that no one else sees, or maybe no one else bothers to look for. It's something inside a player, something other than talent alone. Look at the people Auerbach has picked up late in their careers: Bailey Howell, Wayne Embry, guys like that. Look at a player like Paul Silas. What do you see when you look at men like that? You see dedication. You see someone who wants to win very badly. I'd like to think that's what Red saw in me, too.

"Whatever, like I've said, the man changed the course of my life. Not only did I go on to 11 seasons and five championships with the Celtics, but that helped me go directly into coaching at the pro level as an assistant at Milwaukee. And, as it turned out, I became head coach there after a month or so. Now I'm passing on to my players so many of the things I learned from Auerbach and the Celtics.

"I have a lot of happy Celtic memories. One concerns something that happened not long after I'd joined the team. Russ came up to me the day before Christmas and said, 'Where are you going tomorrow?' I had no place to go, really, because my family was back in Illinois. 'Come over and spend the day with me and my family,' he said. I felt funny, like I would be intruding, so I said no. But Russ insisted, and I went to his home and had a beautiful day.

"I'll never forget Bill Russell for that. Nobody can ever tell me a bad thing about that man.

"As far as memorable games go, for openers, I'll always remember everything about my first game as a Celtic. It was at Boston and we beat Cincinnati—Oscar Robertson, Wayne Embry, Jerry Lucas. Red put me in early and I did pretty well—blocking a shot or two, scoring seven points or so, and making some pretty good plays.

"I also have some vivid playoff memories. All five world championships were great thrills, but the '66 and '69 titles were super special.

"The '66 championship was especially important to me because it was my first one—and extra sweet because we beat the Lakers, the team that had cut me eight months earlier. And '69 was the most satisfying. We had finished fourth in the regular season, and lost the first two games in the finals against the Lakers. But we bounced back to beat the finest team in basketball that season—and on their home court in the final game.

"Yes, it was in that seventh game at Los Angeles that I scored the deciding basket on that lucky shot that everyone seems to remember.

"The Lakers had cut our lead from 17 points to one point, and there were about 80 seconds left. Our 24-second clock was expiring when I picked up a loose ball to the right of the key and put up a 15-footer to at least get the ball up there and beat the clock.

"The shot didn't *feel* good and I didn't think it would go in. I was just hoping it'd hit the rim in time so we'd have a chance at the rebound. It was a high, arching shot and hit the back of the rim. The ball bounced straight up, about as high as the top of the backboard—it was agony watching it come back down—and it dropped straight through, *swish!*

"Of every 100 of those bounces, 99 will go astray. This was the one in 100—plain lucky. But it counted—we won by two points—and I didn't give it back. And when I tell about it now, I say the shot hit nothing but string—which it did, on the way back *down*. I neglect to mention that the ball took one very big and very lucky bounce along the way.

"It was my biggest basket ever, helping win a world championship.

"Another playoff thrill that ranks high was coming back to beat Philadelphia in the '68 Eastern finals. We had a two-game deficit in that series, too, and that also went the full seven games. We were down 1-3 and on the brink of elimination to a team that had finished eight games ahead of us during the season—Chamberlain, Green, Cunningham, Walker, Jackson, Jones. But then we won three straight, two of them at Philly including the deciding seventh game.

"My most frustrating loss was what proved my longest game—when I played 53 of the 58 minutes of our double-overtime loss at New York, the controversial fourth game of the '73 playoffs. We lost on some very questionable calls, and I still feel that if we'd won that game we'd have gone all the way. After eliminating us, 4-3, the Knicks went on to easily beat the Lakers, 4-1, for the title. So that's one championship that got away, because I still feel we had the best team that season.

"Yes, my last season was terribly frustrating, the toughest I spent as a Celtic. I didn't play much, so I wasn't able to contribute much. And contributing is what basketball is all about. So I decided to retire.

"Yes, there was some interest by other clubs, but I wasn't interested. I wanted to end my playing career as a Celtic. I had too many fond memories in Boston. It just wouldn't have been the same playing anywhere else. Once a Celtic, always a Celtic. If I couldn't play there, then it was nowhere. It was time to move on and find a new gig.

"I certainly didn't leave with any bitterness. Not at all. Instead, I was appreciative of all the good years, of having had the chance to be a *Celtic*. You know, I've really been fortunate. A lot of very good players have spent entire NBA careers with losing teams. They'd have given anything for the opportunity I had."

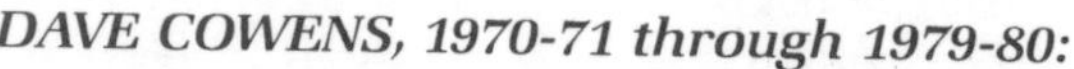
"Dave Cowens was the rock of the Celtics."

Bill Fitch

DAVE COWENS, 1970-71 through 1979-80:

(This text was written by Cowens as a farewell to Celtic fans upon his surprise retirement on October 1, 1980.)

Why is it that athletes who retire always allow other people to write their career obituary? Isn't it important for the fans to realize firsthand the factors and thoughts behind the decision to hang 'em up? How could an athlete possibly sever the emotional bond between him and his loyal supporters without giving an explanation for his actions?

I always took pride in my performance and thought that I gave a little extra something to the game. I never identified myself as a great player, only as one who set high standards regarding his performance. I worked diligently to live up to those standards so as to make my mark on the world of basketball. I wanted to offer something different. Perhaps it was just a certain flair or wildness or unexpected behavior on the court, but something critically different. I was given a fairly sound body to develop and train, and I worked it long and hard so that I would be asked to play a major role in the outcome of games.

I used to treasure the individual confrontations with Kareem Abdul-Jabbar or Bob McAdoo and relished the fact that we were playing against teams like the Knicks of the early '70s and the old Chicago Sloan-Love-Walker quintets, who made you reach for everything you had in order to compete with their type of team play. These challenges were exciting and real; they were invigorating and exhausting.

However, I can no longer play that caliber of basketball, and it is unbelievably frustrating to remain in a rugged occupation with waning skills.

Enter here the fact that I have been playing basketball for 16 years on two feet which can best be described by the observations that a team of foot and bone specialists made a couple of years ago. They were amazed I had been able to play up to that point in time without any radical, serious injuries, at which time I pointed out that I had sprained my ankles at least 30 times over the duration of my career, broken both legs and fractured a foot. Now I am not explaining this for you to extend sympathy to me, or use it as a crutch, but only to explain that there is something fundamentally wrong with my feet and ankles that would make me more susceptible to injury. Just last year I sustained a different type of foot injury when I severely stretched all the tendons around my big toe. This joint is now twice its normal size, and possibly always will be.

The primary reason that I will not remain on the active roster of the Celtics or any other professional ballclub is the fact that I have a highly weakened and worn out set of feet and ankles. Knowing this about my feet, and the fact that I have not been able to play a full season since 1976, I'd say my chances of getting hurt and not being able to contribute in all the games this year were highly probable.

So now I must assess my situation. I have given my feet a valid test to see if they were able to make the grade after three weeks of training sessions and exhibition games. The result is that I am basically playing on one leg. My right ankle is so weak that I can best describe it by saying that I have a sponge for an ankle. My left leg and ankle are therefore taking an extraordinary amount of abuse and they would no doubt give out before the year was over.

Accompanying all of these injuries is a notable amount of pain which I have been able to tolerate during each season, but which is progressively getting worse. I do not believe in taking medication which many others utilize to mask the pain and allow them to play more years and earn more income.

I considered all the issues concerning the 1980-81 Celtic season-ticket-holder and the possible fraudulent act done to them on both an investment level and emotional scale while analyzing all this, and finally wondered if it wouldn't be more unjust to ask them to witness a deteriorated performance. I decided that even though there would be a small group of fans that would get bent out of shape, the majority of the folks who are serious viewers would recognize the tremendous talent of the players who are continuing to demonstrate their skills and would see I am not able to perform against these players in the manner I would want to and in the manner the fan expects me to. I hope I am correct in my assumption because I would not want anyone to get even remotely upset.

So I asked myself, "Why should I play?" To take up a slot that another man could fill? To jeopardize the success of the club? To risk injuring my ankles? To embarrass myself by not playing up to the expectations of the fans?

I'll tell you why it is such a difficult decision to make—because of the financial reward.

I have climbed the ladder of success in the NBA to the point where I command top dollar for my services. But the last time I negotiated a contract was five years ago. The only reason I am getting paid top dollar now is not because I am a top talent; it is because I negotiated from a point of strength five years ago. I have one year remaining in my contract, and part of the pressure to play comes from the commitment I have to live up to my obligations with the Celtics.

I wouldn't feel guilty about the amount of money I would earn under these conditions if I thought I could play even as well as I did last year. But I can't. I have made an extraordinary living from basketball and feel that the Celtics and Dave Cowens have been equally fair to one another over the past 10 years. In addition, I don't want preferential treatment from the coach due to my status as a seasoned veteran, because then I wouldn't be able to expect maximum effort from my teammates. Fairness goes hand-in-hand with dedication, especially when one is involved in a group participation sport.

I do not want anyone to suspect that I was only going through the motions as a player. My whole reputation has been one of giving maximum effort, and I want to be remembered as just such a player. Now, don't get me wrong, I'm not perfect. I've dogged it in practices, performed extremely poorly in games, and done my share of complaining. But I've always had the desire to work hard and do my part, more, if necessary. I think every one of my teammates enjoyed playing ball with me. I think one of the basic characteristics of a quality player is being able to complement his teammates, increasing their worth along with his.

So after all this deliberation and soul-searching over the past five months, and, taking into consideration the combination of positive

and negative factors such as the exceptional talent the Celtics have in their front line, the camaraderie among players, the rigors of traveling, etc., I have decided to retire.

I have enjoyed performing for you over the past 10 years while hopefully engraving myself into the history of the Celtic organization.

> *"Jo Jo White was a complete basketball player. He ran the offense, called the plays, pushed the ball up the floor on the break, scored and played the good defense. You couldn't ask for more than that.*
> *"Jo Jo was a superstar."*
>
> Tom Heinsohn

JO JO WHITE, 1969-70 through 1978-79:

"Yes, it was a strange feeling coming back to Boston Garden in 1980 wearing a different color uniform. Really strange. I had put my heart into that building too many years not to feel something. So it hit me kind of hard when I walked into the Garden as a *Golden State Warrior*, then into the *visiting team* locker room, then onto the floor wearing a *blue* uniform. And, yes, a lot went through my mind when the fans gave me that standing ovation, which was nice. I appreciated that.

"I took a lot of pride in being a Celtic—a *lot* of pride—and wanted to finish my career as a Celtic. And being traded from Boston was definitely a jolt, one of the biggest disappointments of my life. But I asked to be traded, feeling I had run out my string in Boston and that a change was needed. That wasn't an easy thing to do, but it had been a bad couple of years for me, the most frustrating of my life.

"First, in '77-'78, there was the heel injury that would require surgery and also the contract squabble. Between the two, I was really discouraged.

"For a long time I felt I was letting down the team and my teammates because I couldn't play the way I was capable of playing because of the heel. I kept trying and hoping, but it became very frustrating. Then, when the controversy over my contract developed, I felt I had been let down by the Celtics. I felt that I had been getting the run-around and that I was double-crossed. I never had any problem with Red. I wasn't referring to him when I made those statements about management's disloyalty. He knew I meant the other guy (then owner Irv Levin).

"Well, the following summer I signed a nice contract, and I thought the bad dream was over. But another was starting. Everything went wrong for everyone; there were a lot of problems for everybody, some things fans didn't know anything about. Personally, the way I was treated was wrong. I didn't like the BS that people were giving me. I thought I deserved better than that. Management—again, not Auerbach—was screwing up the franchise and playing games with my head, and I said so.

"I'd had it. Under the circumstances, I thought it was best just to get out. So, with very mixed feelings, I asked to be traded.

"Well, that's history now and I like to feel I'm past all that. I have too many great feelings and memories about my Celtic years to let them be spoiled by what happened at the end.

"That first championship in '74 was a thrill, a great moment in my career because it was my first. And it was a great final series with the Bucks, particularly that double-overtime sixth game—with so many people making so many great plays—and then going on to Milwaukee to win the seventh game.

"The second championship in '76 meant much more to me, though. I felt I was a lot more involved and contributed a lot more. Everything seemed to fall into place. The finals against Phoenix just seemed like my series.

"My greatest moment had to be the fifth game, the triple-overtime game. You know that saying about when it's your day, everything goes right. Well, that was *my* day. Everything I put up went in, everything I did was right.

"And it certainly wasn't only me doing the job. One of us was always making the big play, so we were able to hold on and had a little bit more when we needed it. That's what the Celtics are all about, that's what they're predicated on—giving that little extra.

"Yes, I was named MVP of those playoffs, and that was a thrill, too. It's always nice to have your work recognized, to get a pat on the back once in a while.

"No, for the most part I don't think I was fully recognized by the media as a Celtic. I don't think I'm very egotistical, but sure it bothered me that I was never picked all-league—not first-team, although I guess I was second-team twice. No matter how well I played, I never seemed to get the type media coverage some others got. In Boston, too. Some players could make bad plays and that rarely was written about. But if I made a bad shot or poor pass—boom—I'd sure read about it in the papers. But I got used to it after awhile and didn't worry about it anymore.

"Yes, I thought the Boston media could be vicious at times. But it could also be good. Overall, more often than not, I believe they say it like it is, and that's the way it should be.

"Well, the Celtics are back now and playing together again as we did in those good years. Auerbach has done it, and that doesn't surprise me because he's done it before a couple of times—like when I first got there and, of course, 'way back before that, too.

"The same with the Boston fans. For the most part they were very good. I've always felt they had a lot to do with the way the Celtics performed because they were behind the players 100 percent. But I think they're also very, very spoiled because they've always seen basketball at its very best. But they were a little cruel when the team was going through its process of changing and learning before I left, and that put a lot of pressure on the players.

"Red is like a father figure to me. We'll always be close even though we're not working together now, even though there's not the communication like there was when I was with the Celtics. But he'll always be someone very special to me. Do you remember during all that turmoil when Red was thinking of leaving and going to New York? I told the press then that if Red quit, I wanted to go too, that I'd demand a trade. I said that wherever he went, I wanted to go too. He's my man.

"And Tom Heinsohn belongs in the same breath as Auerbach. They both were there when I came along and both taught me a lot about the game. We went on to win—what?—five division titles and two NBA championships? During that time Tom and I didn't always agree, but I'll always admire him as a coach and respect him for his position on things he wanted to do.

"Auerbach, Heinsohn—they're all so much of the Celtic tradition that's still a part of me. I remember when I was drafted by the Celtics

out of Kansas. I was very honored and proud to be chosen by an organization like the *Boston Celtics,* a team with a great tradition.

"Pro basketball was something I wanted to play since I was a little guy back in St. Louis. I thought a lot about it my senior year in college and remember figuring that if I ever earned $20,000 a year I'd really be doing something. I expected the NBA to be very demanding, a very tough league, and it was everything I expected.

"Players like John Havlicek, Don Nelson and Paul Silas were very helpful. They were veterans and the type of unselfish players that young players coming into the league need. That's a problem with the NBA now. You have some great young talent coming into the league, but you don't have as many veterans guiding them around in their first years.

"So I had help in making the adjustment. And there was an adjustment from college to pros for me, just as there had been from high school to college. Not just in the level of basketball, but in my role.

"Actually, I considered football my main sport when I started high school. All my friends were playing it and I played half a year—before my mother found out and I had to quit. She said there weren't as many injuries in basketball.

"In high school my role was the big scorer. In college, at Kansas, I was used primarily as a playmaker for a possession team and as a defensive specialist. I was taught the ball was a gem.

"I've seen my college coach, Ted Owens, a lot over the years, and he says he regrets not using me more in his offense. But he had always built his team around big men and defense, and you can't argue with his success. And, actually, my role at Kansas made me a better pro because it taught me all phases of the game.

"People have a tendency to measure performances strictly by how many points you scored. Scoring is fine, but you can make a contribution even if you don't score a point. In fact, as I look back over my career, a lot of my better games were when I didn't score a lot of points but contributed in other key ways. It might be ball-handling or defense, and those were two important aspects I came to enjoy in college.

"And then I came to Boston and there was the adjustment to the fastbreak and to the Celtics wanting me to be a shooter again. And actually that was ideal for me because I was better shooting on the run, which was their game.

"So, all considered, I was very fortunate to be chosen by the Celtics. Even though they had lost a lot of good players and were rebuilding, they still had some good ones to uphold the Celtic tradition, to carry it over. And I like to think I helped carry on that tradition, too. To me, being a Celtic is putting all you have into a game and caring about your teammates. I always did that. Celtic pride is self pride.

"As I've said, even though I'm no longer in the organization, the Celtic tradition is still in me—and always will be. I'll *always* be a Celtic."

THE RECORDS

"... Some day in the far-off future, there'll be other great teams, no doubt. But they'll have no stature in Boston, where people will sneer: 'Aw, you shoulda seen the Celtics.'"

—*Boston Globe* editorial
May 7, 1969

CAREER RECORDS

HEAD COACHES

Arnold (Red) Auerbach

Born: September 20, 1917 College: George Washington '40

Season	Team	Regular Season Won	Regular Season Lost	Playoffs Won	Playoffs Lost
1950-51	Celtics	39	30	0	2
1951-52	Celtics	39	27	1	2
1952-53	Celtics	46	25	3	3
1953-54	Celtics	42	30	2	4
1954-55	Celtics	36	36	3	4
1955-56	Celtics	39	33	1	2
1956-57*	Celtics	44	28	7	3
1957-58	Celtics	49	23	6	5
1958-59*	Celtics	52	20	8	3
1959-60*	Celtics	59	16	8	5
1960-61*	Celtics	57	22	8	2
1961-62*	Celtics	60	20	8	6
1962-63*	Celtics	58	22	8	5
1963-64*	Celtics	59	21	8	2
1964-65*	Celtics	62	18	8	4
1965-66*	Celtics	54	26	11	6
Totals		795	397	90	58

*Won NBA championship.

Note: Auerbach also coached Washington, 1946-47 through 1948-49 (115-53 during regular season, 8-9 in playoffs), and Tri-Cities, 1949-50 (28-29 during regular season, 1-2 in playoffs). So Auerbach's overall NBA record is 938-479 during regular season and 99-69 in playoffs—by far the best regular-season winning percentage (.662) in NBA history as well as most regular-season and playoff victories.

Dave Cowens

Born: October 25, 1948 College: Florida State '70

Season	Team	Regular Season Won	Regular Season Lost	Playoffs Won	Playoffs Lost
1978-79	Celtics	27	41	—	—

Note: Cowens was player-coach.

Bill Fitch

Born: May 19, 1933 College: Coe '54

Season	Team	Regular Season Won	Regular Season Lost	Playoffs Won	Playoffs Lost
1979-80	Celtics	61	21	5	4
1980-81	Celtics	62	20	12	5
1981-82	Celtics	63	19	7	5
Totals		186	60	24	14

Note: Fitch also coached Cleveland. 1970-71 through 1978-79 (304-434 during regular season, 7-11 in playoffs). So Fitch's overall NBA record is 490-494 during regular season and 31-25 in playoffs.

Tom Heinsohn

Born: August 26, 1934 College: Holy Cross '56

Season	Team	Regular Season Won	Regular Season Lost	Playoffs Won	Playoffs Lost
1969-70	Celtics	34	48	—	—
1970-71	Celtics	44	38	—	—
1971-72	Celtics	56	26	5	6
1972-73	Celtics	68	14	7	6
1973-74*	Celtics	56	26	12	6
1974-75	Celtics	60	22	6	5
1975-76*	Celtics	54	28	12	6
1976-77	Celtics	44	38	5	4
1977-78	Celtics	11	23	—	—
Totals		427	263	47	33

*Won NBA championship.

Alvin (Doggie) Julian

Born: April 5, 1901 College: Bucknell '23

Season	Team	Regular Season Won	Regular Season Lost	Playoffs Won	Playoffs Lost
1948-49	Celtics	25	35	—	—
1949-50	Celtics	22	46	—	—
Total		47	81	—	—

Bill Russell

Born: February 12, 1934 College: San Francisco '56

Season	Team	Regular Season Won	Regular Season Lost	Playoffs Won	Playoffs Lost
1966-67	Celtics	60	21	4	5
1967-68*	Celtics	54	28	12	7
1968-69*	Celtics	48	34	12	6
Totals		162	83	28	18

*Won NBA championship.

Notes: (1) Russell was player-coach with Celtics. (2) Russell also coached Seattle. 1973-74 through 1976-77 (162-166 during regular season, 6-9 in playoffs). So Russell's overall NBA record is 324-249 during regular season and 34-27 in playoffs.

John (Honey) Russell

Born: May 31, 1903 College: Seton Hall '23

Season	Team	Regular Season Won	Regular Season Lost	Playoffs Won	Playoffs Lost
1946-47	Celtics	22	38	—	—
1947-48	Celtics	20	28	1	2
Totals		42	66	1	2

Tom (Satch) Sanders

Born: November 8, 1938 College: New York University '60

Season	Team	Regular Season Won	Regular Season Lost	Playoffs Won	Playoffs Lost
1977-78	Celtics	21	27	—	—
1978-79	Celtics	2	12	—	—
Totals		23	39	—	—

Flinty Red Auerbach fires another cigar.

ASSISTANT COACHES

K.C. Jones

Born: May 25, 1932 College: San Francisco '56

Assistant coach since 1977-78 under Celtic head coaches Tom Sanders, Dave Cowens and Bill Fitch.

Note: Jones was head coach of Washington, 1973-74 through 1975-76 (155-91 record), and was assistant coach with Los Angeles, 1971-72.

John Killilea

Born: June 29, 1928 College: Boston University '52

Assistant coach 1972-73 through 1976-77 under Celtic head coach Tom Heinsohn.

Note: Killilea had been the Celtics' chief scout since 1971 before adding assistant coach duties in 1972. He has been assistant coach with Milwaukee since 1977-78.

Bob MacKinnon

Born: December 5, 1927 College: Canisius '50

Assistant coach 1978-79 with K.C. Jones under Celtic head coaches Tom Sanders and Dave Cowens.

Note: MacKinnon was with Buffalo staff five seasons before joining Celtics—general manager 1976-77, personnel director 1975-76, assistant coach 1972-73, 1973-74 and 1977-78. He was assistant coach with New Jersey, 1979-80.

Note: Before joining Celtics, MacKinnon was with Buffalo staff five seasons—general manager 1976-77, personnel director 1975-76, assistant coach 1972-73, 1973-74 and 1977-78. He was assistant coach with New Jersey, 1979-80 and part of 1980-81, before becoming head coach of the Nets.

Henry McCarthy

Born: September 11, 1889

Assistant coach 1948-49 and 1949-50 under Celtic head coach Alvin (Doggie) Julian.

Jimmy Rodgers

Born: March 12, 1943 College: Iowa '65

Assistant coach 1980-81 and 1981-82 under Celtic head coach Bill Fitch.

Tom (Satch) Sanders

Born: November 8, 1938 College: New York University '60

Assistant coach 1977-78 under Celtic head coach Tom Heinsohn.

Note: Sanders succeeded Heinsohn during season, serving as head coach remainder of 1977-78 season and beginning of 1978-79 season.

Danny Silva

Born: October 5, 1896 College: Muhlenberg

Assistant coach 1946-47 and 1947-48 under Celtic head coach John (Honey) Russell.

Art Spector

Born: October 17, 1920 College: Villanova '44

Assistant coach and scout (also played in 7 games) 1949-50 under head coach Alvin (Doggie) Julian.

PLAYERS

Danny Ainge

No. 44 College: Brigham Young '80
Born: March 17, 1959 Height: 6-5 Weight: 188

Regular Season

Season	Team	G.	Min.	FGA	FGM	Pct.	FTA	FTM	Pct.	—Rebounds— Off.	Def.	Tot.	Ast.	PF	DQ	Stl.	Blk.	Pts.	Ave.
1981-82	Celtics	53	564	221*	79	.357	65	56	.862	25	31	56	87	86	1	37	3	219	4.1

*Converted 5 of 17 (.294) 3-point field-goal attempts.

Playoffs

Season	Team	G.	Min.	FGA	FGM	Pct.	FTA	FTM	Pct.	—Rebounds— Off.	Def.	Tot.	Ast.	PF	DQ	Stl.	Blk.	Pts.	Ave.
1981-82	Celtics	10	129	45*	19	.422	13	10	.769	6	7	13	11	21	0	2	2	50	5.0

*Converted 2 of 4 (.500) 3-point field-goal attempts.

Jerome Anderson

No. 42 College: West Virginia '75
Born: October 9, 1953 Height: 6-5 Weight: 195

Regular Season

Season	Team	G.	Min.	FGA	FGM	Pct.	FTA	FTM	Pct.	—Rebounds— Off.	Def.	Tot.	Ast.	PF	DQ	Stl.	Blk.	Pts.	Ave.
1975-76	Celtics	22	126	45	25	.556	16	11	.688	4	9	13	6	0	3	3	3	61	2.8

Playoffs

Season	Team	G.	Min.	FGA	FGM	Pct.	FTA	FTM	Pct.	—Rebounds— Off.	Def.	Tot.	Ast.	PF	DQ	Stl.	Blk.	Pts.	Ave.
1975-76	Celtics	4	5	3	1	.333	0	0	.000	1	0	1	1	1	0	0	0	2	0.5

Anderson also played in 27 regular-season games for Indiana, 1976-77.

Zaid Abdul-Aziz (Don Smith)

No. 54 College: Iowa State '68
Born: April 7, 1946 Height: 6-9 Weight: 235

Regular Season

Season	Team	G.	Min.	FGA	FGM	Pct.	FTA	FTM	Pct.	Reb.	Ast.	PF	DQ	Pts.	Ave.
1977-78	Celtics	2	24	13	3	.231	3	2	.667	15	3	4	0	8	4.0

Abdul-Aziz also played in 503 regular-season games for Cincinnati, Milwaukee, Seattle, Houston and Buffalo, 1968-69 through 1977-78.

A Celtic fan named John Fitzgerald Kennedy lunched with his hometown team at the White House in January 1963. President Kennedy's guests were (left to right): John Havlicek, trainer Buddy LeRoux, Clyde Lovellette, K.C. Jones, Bob Cousy, Red Auerbach, Jim Loscutoff, Sam Jones, Frank Ramsey, Tom Heinsohn and Tom (Satch) Sanders. As the Celtics were leaving, Sanders shook hands with the President and advised, "Take it easy, baby."

Nate (Tiny) Archibald

No. 7
Born: April 18, 1948

College: Texas El Paso '70
Height: 6-1 Weight: 165

Regular Season

										—Rebounds—									
Season	*Team*	*G.*	*Min.*	*FGA*	*FGM*	*Pct.*	*FTA*	*FTM*	*Pct.*	*Off.*	*Def.*	*Tot.*	*Ast.*	*PF*	*DQ*	*Stl.*	*Blk.*	*Pts.*	*Ave.*
1978-79	Celtics	69	1662	573	259	.452	307	242	.788	25	78	103	324	132	2	55	6	760	11.0
1979-80	Celtics	80	2864	794*	383	.482	435	361	.830	59	138	197	671	218	2	106	10	1131	14.1
1980-81	Celtics	80	2820	766*	382	.499	419	342	.816	36	140	176	618	201	1	75	18	1106	13.8
1981-82	Celtics	60	2167	652*	308	.472	316	236	.747	25	91	116	541	131	1	52	3	858	12.6
Totals		289	9513	2785	1332	.478	1477	1181	.800	145	447	592	2154	682	6	288	37	3855	13.0

*Converted 4 of 18 (.222) 3-point field-goal attempts in 1979-80, none of 9 (.000) in 1980-81 and 6 of 16 (.375) in 1981-82 for a total of 10 of 43 (.233).

Playoffs

										—Rebounds—									
Season	*Team*	*G.*	*Min.*	*FGA*	*FGM*	*Pct.*	*FTA*	*FTM*	*Pct.*	*Off.*	*Def.*	*Tot.*	*Ast.*	*PF*	*DQ*	*Stl.*	*Blk.*	*Pts.*	*Ave.*
1979-80	Celtics	9	332	89*	45	.506	42	37	.881	3	8	11	71	28	1	10	0	128	14.2
1980-81	Celtics	17	630	211*	95	.450	94	76	.809	6	22	28	107	39	0	13	0	266	15.6
1981-82	Celtics	8	277	70*	30	.429	28	25	.893	1	16	17	52	21	0	5	2	85	10.6
Totals		34	1239	370	170	.459	164	138	.841	10	46	56	230	88	1	28	2	479	14.1

*Converted 1 of 2 (.500) 3-point field-goal attempts in 1979-80, none of 5 (.000) in 1980-81 and none of 4 (.000) in 1981-82 for a total of 1 of 11 (.091).

Archibald also played in 467 regular-season games for Cincinnati, Kansas City-Omaha, Kansas City and New York Nets, 1970-71 through 1976-77, and was sidelined by injury the entire 1977-78 season with Buffalo.

Jim Ard

No. 34
Born: September 19, 1948

College: Cincinnati '70
Height: 6-9 Weight: 230

Regular Season

										—Rebounds—									
Season	*Team*	*G.*	*Min.*	*FGA*	*FGM*	*Pct.*	*FTA*	*FTM*	*Pct.*	*Off.*	*Def.*	*Tot.*	*Ast.*	*PF*	*DQ*	*Stl.*	*Blk.*	*Pts.*	*Ave.*
1974-75	Celtics	59	719	266	89	.335	65	48	.738	59	140	199	40	96	2	13	32	226	3.8
1975-76	Celtics	81	853	294	107	.364	100	71	.710	96	193	289	48	141	2	12	36	285	3.5
1976-77	Celtics	63	969	254	96	.378	76	49	.645	77	219	296	53	128	1	18	28	241	3.8
1977-78	Celtics	1	9	1	0	.000	2	1	.500	1	3	4	1	1	0	0	0	1	1.0
Totals		204	2550	815	292	.358	243	169	.695	233	555	788	142	366	5	43	96	753	00.0

Playoffs

										—Rebounds—									
Season	*Team*	*G.*	*Min.*	*FGA*	*FGM*	*Pct.*	*FTA*	*FTM*	*Pct.*	*Off.*	*Def.*	*Tot.*	*Ast.*	*PF*	*DQ*	*Stl.*	*Blk.*	*Pts.*	*Ave.*
1974-75	Celtics	5	14	8	1	.125	0	0	.000	2	0	2	1	5	0	0	1	2	0.4
1975-76	Celtics	16	110	29	13	.448	14	11	.786	10	16	26	8	29	0	1	3	37	2.3
Totals		21	124	37	14	.378	14	11	.786	12	16	28	9	34	0	1	4	39	1.9

Ard also played in 14 regular-season games for Chicago, 1977-78.

Bill Sharman gave his teammates a ride one day (left to right): Tom Heinsohn, Andy Phillip, Jim Loscutoff, Arnie Risen (mostly hidden behind Sharman) and Frank Ramsey.

Dennis Awtrey

No. 34 — College: Santa Clara '70
Born: February 22, 1948 — Height: 6-10 Weight: 240

Regular Season

Season	Team	G.	Min.	FGA	FGM	Pct.	FTA	FTM	Pct.	Reb.	Ast.	PF	DQ	Pts.	Ave.
1978-79	Celtics	23*	247	44	17	.368	20	16	.800	47	20	37	0	50	2.2

*Played in 40 games for Seattle later that season.

Awtrey also played in 587 regular-season games for Philadelphia, Chicago and Phoenix, 1970-71 through 1977-78, and in 73 for Chicago and Seattle, 1980-81 through 1981-82.

John Bach

No. 17 — College: Fordham '48
Born: July 10, 1924 — Height: 6-2 Weight: 180

Regular Season

Season	Team	G.	FGA	FGM	Pct.	FTA	FTM	Pct.	Ast.	PF	Pts.	Ave.
1948-49	Celtics	34	119	34	.286	75	51	.680	25	24	119	3.5

Tom Barker

No. 35 — College: Hawaii '76
Born: March 11, 1955 — Height: 6-11 Weight: 230

Regular Season

Season	Team	G.	Min.	FGA	FGM	Pct.	FTA	FTM	Pct.	Reb.	Ast.	PF	DQ	Pts.	Ave.
1978-79	Celtics	12*	131	48	21	.438	15	11	.733	30	6	26	0	53	4.4

*Played in 5 games for Houston earlier that season and 22 games for New York Knicks later that season.

Barker also played in 59 regular-season games for Atlanta, 1976-77.

Don Barksdale

No. 17 — College: UCLA '49
Born: March 31, 1923 — Height: 6-6 Weight: 200

Regular Season

Season	Team	G.	Min.	FGA	FGM	Pct.	FTA	FTM	Pct.	Reb.	Ast.	PF	DQ	Pts.	Ave.
1953-54	Celtics	63	1358	415	156	.376	225	149	.662	345	117	213	4	461	7.3
1954-55	Celtics	72	1790	699	267	.382	338	220	.651	545	129	225	7	754	10.5
Totals		135	3148	1114	423	.380	563	369	.655	890	246	438	11	1215	9.0

Playoffs

Season	Team	G.	Min.	FGA	FGM	Pct.	FTA	FTM	Pct.	Reb.	Ast.	PF	DQ	Pts.	Ave.
1953-54	Celtics	6	106	36	11	.306	11	8	.727	27	7	23	2	30	5.0
1954-55	Celtics	7	122	40	18	.450	21	18	.857	35	10	17	1	54	7.7
Totals		13	228	76	29	.382	32	26	.813	62	17	40	3	84	6.4

Barksdale also played in 127 regular-season games for Baltimore, 1951-52 through 1952-53.

Jim (Bad News) Barnes

No. 28 — College: Texas Western '64
Born: April 13, 1941 — Height: 6-8 Weight: 240

Regular Season

Season	Team	G.	Min.	FGA	FGM	Pct.	FTA	FTM	Pct.	Reb.	Ast.	PF	DQ	Pts.	Ave.
1968-69*	Celtics	49	595	202	92	.455	92	65	.707	194	27	107	2	249	5.1
1969-70	Celtics	77	1049	434	178	.410	128	95	.742	350	52	229	4	451	5.9
Totals		126	1644	636	270	.425	220	160	.727	544	79	336	6	700	5.6

*Played in 10 games for Chicago earlier that season.

Barnes also played in 307 regular season games for New York Knicks, Baltimore and Chicago, 1964-65 through 1967-68, and in 11 for Baltimore, 1970-71.

Marvin Barnes

No. 27 — College: Providence '74
Born: July 27, 1952 — Height: 6-9 Weight: 225

Regular Season

Season	Team	G.	Min.	FGA	FGM	Pct.	FTA	FTM	Pct.	Reb.	Ast.	PF	DQ	Pts.	Ave.
1978-79	Celtics	38	796	271	133	.491	66	43	.652	177	43	144	3	309	8.1

Barnes also played in 113 regular-season games for Detroit and Buffalo, 1976-77 and 1977-78, and in 20 for San Diego in 1979-80.

Jim Barnett

No. 11 — College: Oregon '66
Born: July 7, 1944 — Height: 6-4 Weight: 180

Regular Season

Season	Team	G.	Min.	FGA	FGM	Pct.	FTA	FTM	Pct.	Reb.	Ast.	PF	DQ	Pts.	Ave.
1966-67	Celtics	48	383	211	78	.370	62	42	.677	53	41	61	0	198	4.1

Playoffs

Season	Team	G.	Min.	FGA	FGM	Pct.	FTA	FTM	Pct.	Reb.	Ast.	PF	DQ	Pts.	Ave.
1966-67	Celtics	5	26	21	6	.286	2	2	1.000	4	1	5	0	14	2.8

Barnett also played in 648 regular-season games for San Diego, Portland, Golden State, New Orleans, New York Knicks and Philadelphia, 1967-68 through 1976-77.

Ernie Barrett

No. 23 — College: Kansas State '51
Born: December 27, 1929 — Height: 6-3 Weight: 180

Regular Season

Season	Team	G.	Min.	FGA	FGM	Pct.	FTA	FTM	Pct.	Reb.	Ast.	PF	DQ	Pts.	Ave.
1953-54	Celtics	59	641	191	60	.314	25	14	.560	100	55	116	2	134	2.3
1955-56*	Celtics	72	1451	533	207	.388	118	93	.788	243	174	184	4	507	7.0
Totals		131	2092	724	267	.369	143	107	.748	343	229	300	6	641	4.9

Playoffs

Season	Team	G.	Min.	FGA	FGM	Pct.	FTA	FTM	Pct.	Reb.	Ast.	PF	DQ	Pts.	Ave.
1953-54	Celtics	6	63	20	3	.150	2	2	1.000	6	4	14	0	8	1.3
1955-56*	Celtics	3	43	13	4	.308	3	3	1.00	7	4	7	0	11	3.7
Totals		9	106	33	7	.212	5	5	1.000	13	8	21	0	19	2.1

*Missed 1954-55 while serving in Air Force.

Moe Becker

No. 5 — College: Duquesne '41
Born: February 24, 1917 — Height: 6-1 Weight: 185

Regular Season

Season	Team	G.	FGA	FGM	Pct.	FTA	FTM	Pct.	Ast.	PF	Pts.	Ave.
1946-47	Pit-Det-Boston	43*	358	70	.196	44	22	.500	30	98	162	3.8

*6 games Boston, 17 Pittsburgh, 20 Detroit.

Hank Beenders

No. 6 — College: Long Island University
Born: June 2, 1916 — Height: 6-6 Weight: 185

Regular Season

Season	Team	G.	FGA	FGM	Pct.	FTA	FTM	Pct.	Ast.	PF	Pts.	Ave.
1946-47	Celtics	8	28	6	.214	9	7	.778	3	9	19	2.4

Beenders also played in 103 regular-season games for Providence and Philadelphia, 1946-47 through 1947-48.

Bob Bigelow

No. 34 College: Penn '75
Born: December 26, 1953 Height: 6-7 Weight: 215

Regular Season

Season	Team	G.	Min.	FGA	FGM	Pct.	FTA	FTM	Pct.	Reb.	Ast.	PF	DQ	Pts.	Ave.
1977-78	Celtics	4	17	12	3	.250	0	0	.000	4	0	1	0	6	1.5

Bigelow also played in 90 regular-season games for Kansas City and San Diego, 1975-76 through 1978-79.

Dave Bing

No. 44 College: Syracuse '66
Born: November 24, 1943 Height: 6-3 Weight: 180

Regular Season

Season	Team	G.	Min.	FGA	FGM	Pct.	FTA	FTM	Pct.	Reb.	Ast.	PF	DQ	Pts.	Ave.
1977-78	Celtics	80	2256	940	422	.449	296	244	.824	212	300	247	2	1088	13.6

Bing also played in 821 regular-season games with Detroit and Washington, 1966-67 through 1976-77.

Larry Bird

No. 33 College: Indiana State '79
Born: December 7, 1956 Height: 6-9 Weight: 220

Regular Season

										—Rebounds—									
Season	Team	G.	Min.	FGA	FGM	Pct.	FTA	FTM	Pct.	Off.	Def.	Tot.	Ast.	PF	DQ	Stl.	Blk.	Pts.	Ave.
1979-80	Celtics	82	2955	1463*	693	.474	360	301	.836	216	636	852	370	279	4	143	53	1745	21.3
1980-81	Celtics	82	3239	1503*	719	.478	328	283	.863	191	704	895	451	239	2	161	63	1741	21.2
1981-82	Celtics	77	2923	1414*	711	.503	380	328	.863	200	637	837	447	244	0	143	66	1761	22.9
Totals		241	9117	4380	2123	.485	1068	912	.854	607	1977	2584	1268	762	6	447	182	5247	21.8

*Converted 58 of 143 (.406) 3-point field-goal attempts in 1979-80, 20 of 74 (.270) in 1980-81 and 11 of 52 (.212) in 1981-82 for a total of 89 of 269 (.331).

Playoffs

										—Rebounds—									
Season	Team	G.	Min.	FGA	FGM	Pct.	FTA	FTM	Pct.	Off.	Def.	Tot.	Ast.	PF	DQ	Stl.	Blk.	Pts.	Ave.
1979-80	Celtics	9	372	177*	83	.469	25	22	.880	22	79	101	42	30	0	14	8	192	21.3
1980-81	Celtics	17	750	313*	147	.470	85	76	.894	49	189	238	103	53	0	39	17	373	21.9
1981-82	Celtics	12	490	206*	88	.427	45	37	.822	33	117	150	68	43	0	23	17	214	17.8
Totals		38	1612	696	318	.457	155	135	.871	104	385	489	213	126	0	76	42	779	20.5

*Converted 4 of 15 (.267) 3-point field-goal attempts in 1979-80, 3 of 8 (.375) in 1980-81 and 1 of 6 (.167) in 1981-82 for a total of 8 of 29 (.276).

Meyer (Mike) Bloom

No. 10 College: Temple
Born: January 14, 1915 Height: 6-6 Weight: 190

Regular Season

Season	Team	G.	FGA	FGM	Pct.	FTA	FTM	Pct.	Ast.	PF	Pts.	Ave.
1947-48	Balt-Bos	48*	640	174	.272	229	160	.699	38	116	508	10.6

*14 games Boston, 34 Baltimore.

Playoffs

Season	Team	G.	FGA	FGM	Pct.	FTA	FTM	Pct.	Ast.	PF	Pts.	Ave.
1947-48	Celtics	3	42	11	.262	19	14	.737	2	10	36	12.0

Bloom also played in 45 regular-season games for Minneapolis and Chicago, 1948-49.

Ron Bonham

No. 21
Born: May 31, 1942

College: Cincinnati '64
Height: 6-5 Weight: 200

Regular Season

Season	Team	G.	Min.	FGA	FGM	Pct.	FTA	FTM	Pct.	Reb.	Ast.	PF	DQ	Pts.	Ave.
1964-65	Celtics	37	369	220	91	.414	112	92	.821	78	19	33	0	274	7.4
1965-66	Celtics	39	312	207	76	.367	61	52	.852	35	11	29	0	204	5.2
Totals		76	681	427	167	.390	173	144	.836	113	30	62	0	478	6.3

Playoffs

Season	Team	G.	Min.	FGA	FGM	Pct.	FTA	FTM	Pct.	Reb.	Ast.	PF	DQ	Pts.	Ave.
1964-65	Celtics	4	13	12	5	.417	5	4	.800	1	0	1	0	14	3.5
1965-66	Celtics	5	16	11	7	.636	9	3	.333	3	0	2	0	17	3.4
Totals		9	29	23	12	.522	14	7	.500	4	0	3	0	31	3.4

Tom Boswell

No. 31
Born: October 2, 1953

College: South Carolina '75
Height: 6-9 Weight: 225

Regular Season

										—Rebounds—									
Season	Team	G.	Min.	FGA	FGM	Pct.	FTA	FTM	Pct.	Off.	Def.	Tot.	Ast.	PF	DQ	Stl.	Blk.	Pts.	Ave.
1975-76	Celtics	35	275	93	41	.441	24	14	.583	26	45	71	16	70	1	2	1	96	2.7
1976-77	Celtics	70	1083	340	175	.515	135	96	.711	111	195	306	85	237	9	27	8	446	6.4
1977-78	Celtics	65	1149	357	185	.518	123	93	.756	117	171	288	71	204	5	25	14	463	7.1
Totals		170	2507	790	401	.508	282	203	.720	254	411	665	172	511	15	54	23	1005	5.9

Playoffs

										—Rebounds—									
Season	Team	G.	Min.	FGA	FGM	Pct.	FTA	FTM	Pct.	Off.	Def.	Tot.	Ast.	PF	DQ	Stl.	Blk.	Pts.	Ave.
1975-76	Celtics	3	3	2	1	.500	0	0	.000	0	1	1	0	2	0	0	0	2	0.7
1976-77	Celtics	9	81	18	8	.444	6	4	.667	10	10	20	7	18	0	1	0	20	2.2
Totals		12	84	20	9	.450	6	4	.667	10	11	21	7	20	0	1	0	22	1.8

Boswell also played in 158 regular-season games for Denver and Utah, 1978-79 through 1979-80.

Harry Boykoff

No. 24
Born: July 24, 1922

College: St. John's '47
Height: 6-10 Weight: 227

Regular Season

Season	Team	G.	Min.	FGA	FGM	Pct.	FTA	FTM	Pct.	Reb.	Ast.	PF	DQ	Pts.	Ave.
1950-51	Bos-Tri C	48*	—	336	126	.375	100	74	.740	220	60	197	12	326	6.8

*(32 games Boston, 16 Tri-Cities)

Boykoff also played in 61 regular-season games for Waterloo, 1949-50.

Charles Bradley

No. 35
Born: May 16, 1959

College: Wyoming '81
Height: 6-5 Weight: 215

Regular Season

										—Rebounds—									
Season	Team	G.	Min.	FGA	FGM	Pct.	FTA	FTM	Pct.	Off.	Def.	Tot.	Ast.	PF	DQ	Stl.	Blk.	Pts.	Ave.
1981-82	Celtics	51	339	122*	55	.451	62	42	.667	12	26	38	22	61	0	14	6	152	3.0

*Converted none of 1 (.000) 3-point field-goal attempts.

Playoffs

										—Rebounds—									
Season	Team	G.	Min.	FGA	FGM	Pct.	FTA	FTM	Pct.	Off.	Def.	Tot.	Ast.	PF	DQ	Stl.	Blk.	Pts.	Ave.
1981-82	Celtics	7	18	8*	2	.250	2	0	.000	1	4	5	1	6	0	1	0	4	0.7

*Bradley attempted no 3-point field goals during the playoffs.

Bob Brannum

No. 18
May 28, 1925

Colleges: Kentucky, Michigan State
Height: 6-5 Weight: 215

Regular Season

Season	*Team*	*G.*	*Min.*	*FGA*	*FGM*	*Pct.*	*FTA*	*FTM*	*Pct.*	*Reb.*	*Ast.*	*PF*	*DQ*	*Pts.*	*Ave.*
1951-52	Celtics	66	1324	404	149	.369	171	107	.626	406	76	235	9	405	6.1
1952-53	Celtics	71	1900	541	188	.348	185	110	.595	537	147	287	17	486	6.8
1953-54	Celtics	71	1729	453	140	.309	206	129	.626	509	144	280	10	409	5.8
1954-55	Celtics	71	1623	465	176	.378	127	90	.709	492	127	232	6	442	6.2
Totals		279	6576	1863	653	.351	689	436	.633	1944	494	1034	42	1742	6.2

Playoffs

Season	*Team*	*G.*	*Min.*	*FGA*	*FGM*	*Pct.*	*FTA*	*FTM*	*Pct.*	*Reb.*	*Ast.*	*PF*	*DQ*	*Pts.*	*Ave.*
1951-52	Celtics	3	48	12	4	.333	6	1	.167	10	3	16	2	9	3.0
1952-53	Celtics	6	83	23	12	.522	11	7	.636	21	10	23	2	31	5.2
1953-54	Celtics	6	136	38	11	.289	11	6	.545	45	10	29	2	28	4.7
1954-55	Celtics	7	225	61	26	.426	19	11	.579	79	13	32	2	63	9.0
Totals		22	492	134	53	.396	47	25	.532	155	36	100	8	131	5.6

Brannum also played in 59 regular-season games for Sheboygan, 1949-50.

Carl Braun

No. 4
Born: September 25, 1927

College: Colgate '49
Height: 6-5 Weight: 180

Regular Season

Season	*Team*	*G.*	*Min.*	*FGA*	*FGM*	*Pct.*	*FTA*	*FTM*	*Pct.*	*Reb.*	*Ast.*	*PF*	*DQ*	*Pts.*	*Ave.*
1961-62	Celtics	49	414	207	78	.377	27	20	.741	50	71	49	0	176	3.6

Playoffs

Season	*Team*	*G.*	*Min.*	*FGA*	*FGM*	*Pct.*	*FTA*	*FTM*	*Pct.*	*Reb.*	*Ast.*	*PF*	*DQ*	*Pts.*	*Ave.*
1961-62	Celtics	6	42	28	110	.393	4	3	.750	7	2	3	0	25	4.2

Braun also played in 740 regular-season games for New York Knicks, 1947-48 through 1960-61.

Al Brightman

No. 8
Born: 1922

Colleges: Morris Harvey, Southern Cal
Height: 6-2 Weight: 195

Regular Season

Season	*Team*	*G.*	*FGA*	*FGM*	*Pct.*	*FTA*	*FTM*	*Pct.*	*Ast.*	*PF*	*Pts.*	*Ave.*
1946-47	Celtics	58	870	223	.256	193	121	.627	60	115	567	9.8

Bob Cousy was a magician with a basketball.

Henry Finkel gets word from Red Auerbach in November 1975 that he's been put on waivers. It concluded the popular 7-footer's career after 6 Boston seasons during which Finkel needed only to doff his sweatsuit to stir the Garden crowd into cheers.

Emmette Bryant

No. 7 College: DePaul '64
Born: November 4, 1938 Height: 6-1 Weight: 175

Regular Season

Season	Team	G.	Min.	FGA	FGM	Pct.	FTA	FTM	Pct.	Reb.	Ast.	PF	DQ	Pts.	Ave.
1968-69	Celtics	80	1388	488	197	.404	100	65	.650	192	176	264	9	459	5.7
1969-70	Celtics	71	1617	520	210	.404	181	135	.746	269	231	201	5	555	7.8
Totals		151	3005	1008	407	.404	281	200	.712	461	407	465	14	1014	6.7

Playoffs

Season	Team	G.	Min.	FGA	FGM	Pct.	FTA	FTM	Pct.	Reb.	Ast.	PF	DQ	Pts.	Ave.
1968-69	Celtics	18	607	193	79	.409	53	40	.755	88	54	75	0	198	11.0

Bryant also played in 288 regular-season games with New York Knicks, 1964-65 through 1967-68, and in 127 for Buffalo, 1970-71 and 1971-72.

Elbert (Al) Butler

No. 9 College: Niagara '61
Born: July 9, 1938 Height: 6-2 Weight: 175

Regular Season

Season	Team	G.	Min.	FGA	FGM	Pct.	FTA	FTM	Pct.	Reb.	Ast.	PF	DQ	Pts.	Ave.
1961-62	Bos-NY	59*	2008	756	350	.463	183	131	.716	342	203	154	0	831	14.1

*5 games Boston, 54 New York.

M. L. Carr

No. 30 College: Guilford '73
Born: July 9, 1951 Height: 6-6 Weight: 210

Regular Season

										—Rebounds—									
Season	Team	G.	Min.	FGA	FGM	Pct.	FTA	FTM	Pct.	Off.	Def.	Tot.	Ast.	PF	DQ	Stl.	Blk.	Pts.	Ave.
1979-80	Celtics	82	1994	763*	362	.474	241	178	.739	106	224	330	156	214	1	120	36	914	11.1
1980-81	Celtics	41	655	216*	97	.449	67	53	.791	26	57	83	56	74	0	30	18	248	6.0
1981-82	Celtics	56	1296	409*	184	.450	116	82	.707	56	94	150	128	136	2	67	21	455	8.1
Totals		179	3945	1388	643	.463	424	313	.738	188	375	563	340	424	3	217	75	1617	9.0

*Converted 12 of 41 (.293) 3-point field-goal attempts in 1979-80, 1 of 14 (.071) in 1980-81 and 5 of 17 (.294) in 1981-82 for a total of 18 of 72 (.250).

Playoffs

										—Rebounds—									
Season	Team	G.	Min.	FGA	FGM	Pct.	FTA	FTM	Pct.	Off.	Def.	Tot.	Ast.	PF	DQ	Stl.	Blk.	Pts.	Ave.
1979-80	Celtics	9	172	80*	32	.400	24	16	.667	14	19	33	11	20	0	6	1	82	9.1
1980-81	Celtics	17	288	101*	42	.416	24	18	.750	8	17	25	14	32	0	10	6	102	6.0
1981-82	Celtics	12	305	105*	37	.352	23	15	.652	21	22	43	28	30	0	11	0	89	7.4
Totals		38	765	286	111	.388	71	49	.690	43	58	101	53	82	0	27	7	273	7.2

*Converted 2 of 5 (.400) 3-point field-goal attempts in 1979-80, none of 4 (.000) in 1980-81 and none of 4 (.000) in 1981-82 for a total of 2 of 13 (.154).

Carr also played in 241 regular-season games for Detroit, 1976-77 through 1978-79.

Howie McHugh, a Celtic institution who helped name the club in 1946, retired as team publicist in 1981-82. But the former Dartmouth hockey star remained a courtside fixture as club historian and consultant—still the only NBA veteran with unbroken service with the same team since the league's start.

Don Chaney

Nos. 12 & 42
Born: March 22, 1946

College: Houston '68
Height: 6-5 Weight: 210

Regular Season

Season	Team	G.	Min.	FGA	FGM	Pct.	FTA	FTM	Pct.	Rebounds— Off.	Def.	Tot.	Ast.	PF	DQ	Stl.	Blk.	Pts.	Ave.
1968-69	Celtics	20	209	113	36	.319	20	8	.400	—	—	46	19	32	0	—	—	80	4.0
1969-70	Celtics	63	839	320	115	.359	109	82	.752	—	—	152	72	118	0	—	—	312	5.0
1970-71	Celtics	81	2289	766	348	.454	313	234	.748	—	—	463	235	288	11	—	—	930	11.5
1971-72	Celtics	79	2275	786	373	.475	255	197	.773	—	—	395	202	295	7	—	—	943	11.9
1972-73	Celtics	79	2488	859	414	.482	267	210	.787	—	—	449	221	276	6	—	—	1038	13.1
1973-74	Celtics	81	2258	750	348	.464	180	149	.828	210	168	378	176	247	7	83	62	845	10.4
1974-75	Celtics	82	2208	750	321	.428	165	133	.806	171	199	370	181	244	5	122	66	775	9.5
1977-78*	Celtics	42	702	233	91	.391	39	33	.846	36	69	105	49	93	0	36	10	215	5.1
1978-79	Celtics	65	1074	414	174	.420	42	36	.857	63	78	141	75	167	3	72	11	384	5.9
1979-80	Celtics	60	523	189**	67	.354	42	32	.762	31	42	73	38	80	1	31	11	167	2.8
Totals		652	14,865	5180	2287	.442	1432	1114	.778	—	—	2572	1268	1840	40	—	—	5689	8.7

*Played in 9 games for Los Angeles earlier that season.

**Converted 1 of 6 (.167) 3-point field-goal attempts.

Playoffs

Season	Team	G.	Min.	FGA	FGM	Pct.	FTA	FTM	Pct.	Rebounds— Off.	Def.	Tot.	Ast.	PF	DQ	Stl.	Blk.	Pts.	Ave.
1968-69	Celtics	7	25	6	1	.167	4	3	.750	—	—	4	0	7	0	—	—	5	0.7
1971-72	Celtics	11	271	81	41	.506	20	15	.750	—	—	39	22	39	0	—	—	97	8.8
1972-73	Celtics	12	288	82	39	.476	17	12	.706	—	—	40	25	41	1	—	—	90	7.5
1973-74	Celtics	18	545	141	65	.461	50	41	.820	37	40	77	40	64	0	24	9	171	9.5
1974-75	Celtics	11	294	105	48	.457	29	23	.793	24	14	38	21	46	2	21	5	119	10.8
Totals		59	1423	415	194	.467	120	94	.783	—	—	198	108	197	3	—	—	482	8.2

Chaney also played in 90 regular-season games for Los Angeles, 1976-77 through 1977-78.

Ben Clyde

No. 33
Born: June 10, 1951

College: Florida State '74
Height: 6-7 Weight: 198

Regular Season

Season	Team	G.	Min.	FGA	FGM	Pct.	FTA	FTM	Pct.	Reb.	Ast.	PF	DQ	Pts.	Ave.
1974-75	Celtics	25	157	72	31	.431	9	7	.778	41	5	34	1	69	2.8

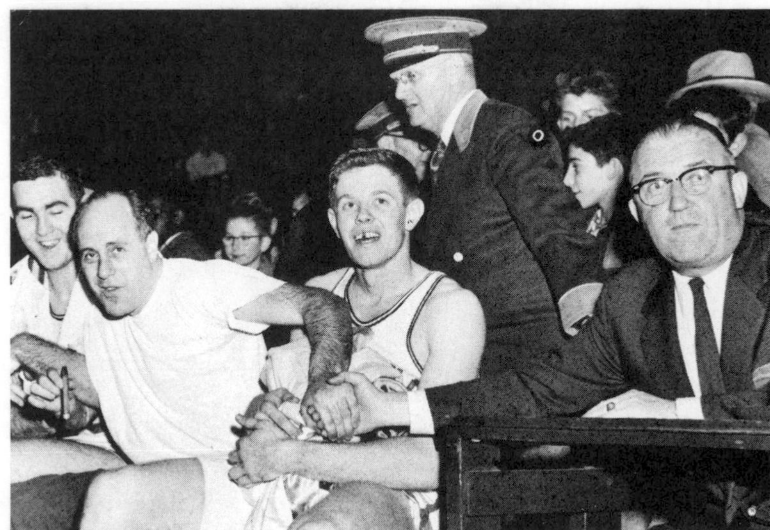

Anticipating a victory shower, Red Auerbach starts a striptease on the Boston bench as the clock runs on the Celtics clinching their first division title ever in March 1957. Team founder Walter Brown (right) helps hold Auerbach, assisted by players Dick Hemric (left) and Frank Ramsey.

Gene Conley

No. 17
Born: November 10, 1930

College: Washington State '52
Height: 6-9 Weight: 230

Regular Season

Season	Team	G.	Min.	FGA	FGM	Pct.	FTA	FTM	Pct.	Reb.	Ast.	PF	DQ	Pts.	Ave.
1952-53	Celtics	39	461	108	35	.324	31	18	.581	171	19	74	1	88	2.3
1958-59	Celtics	50	663	262	86	.328	64	37	.578	276	19	117	2	209	4.2
1959-60	Celtics	71	1330	539	201	.373	114	76	.667	590	32	270	10	478	6.7
1960-61	Celtics	75	1342	495	183	.370	153	106	.693	550	40	275	15	472	6.3
Totals		235	3796	1404	505	.360	362	237	.655	1587	110	736	28	1247	5.3

Playoffs

Season	Team	G.	Min.	FGA	FGM	Pct.	FTA	FTM	Pct.	Reb.	Ast.	PF	DQ	Pts.	Ave.
1958-59	Celtics	11	157	66	24	.364	13	6	.462	75	7	40	2	54	4.9
1959-60	Celtics	13	269	88	34	.386	22	16	.727	116	3	59	2	84	6.5
1960-61	Celtics	9	56	33	12	.364	12	7	.583	31	1	20	0	31	3.4
Totals		33	482	187	70	.374	47	29	.617	222	11	119	4	169	5.1

Conley also played in 116 regular-season games for New Yock Knicks, 1962-63 through 1963-64.

Kevin (Chuck) Connors

No. 11
Born: April 10, 1921

College: Seton Hall
Height: 6-7 Weight: 205

Regular Season

Season	Team	G.	FGA	FGM	Pct.	FTA	FTM	Pct.	Ast.	PF	Pts.	Ave.
1946-47	Celtics	49	380	94	.247	84	39	.464	40	129	227	4.6
1947-48	Celtics	4	13	5	.385	3	2	.667	1	5	12	3.0
Totals		53	393	99	.252	87	41	.471	41	134	239	4.5

Norm Cook

No. 52
Born: March 21, 1955

College: Kansas '77
Height: 6-9 Weight: 210

Regular Season

Season	Team	G.	Min.	FGA	FGM	Pct.	FTA	FTM	Pct.	Reb.	Ast.	PF	DQ	Pts.	Ave.
1976-77	Celtics	25	138	72	27	.375	17	9	.529	27	5	27	0	63	2.5

Playoffs

Season	Team	G.	Min.	FGA	FGM	Pct.	FTA	FTM	Pct.	Reb.	Ast.	PF	DQ	Pts.	Ave.
1976-77	Celtics	1	3	0	0	.000	2	2	1.000	0	0	0	0	4	4.0

Cook also played in 2 regular-season games for Denver, 1977-78.

Chuck Cooper

No. 11
Born: September 29, 1926

College: Duquesne '50
Height: 6-5 Weight: 220

Regular Season

Season	Team	G.	Min.	FGA	FGM	Pct.	FTA	FTM	Pct.	Reb.	Ast.	PF	DQ	Pts.	Ave.
1950-51	Celtics	66	—	601	207	.344	267	201	.753	562	174	219	7	615	9.3
1951-52	Celtics	66	1976	545	197	.361	201	149	.741	502	134	219	8	543	8.2
1952-53	Celtics	70	1994	466	157	.337	190	144	.758	439	112	258	11	458	6.5
1953-54	Celtics	70	1101	261	78	.299	116	78	.672	304	74	150	1	234	3.3
Totals		272	—	1873	639	.341	774	572	.739	1807	494	846	27	1850	6.8

Playoffs

Season	Team	G.	Min.	FGA	FGM	Pct.	FTA	FTM	Pct.	Reb.	Ast.	PF	DQ	Pts.	Ave.
1950-51	Celtics	2	—	12	4	.333	5	2	.400	13	3	8	—	10	5.0
1951-52	Celtics	3	128	25	8	.320	19	17	.895	16	4	17	2	33	11.0
1952-53	Celtics	6	195	48	19	.396	27	22	.815	39	14	27	2	60	10.0
1953-54	Celtics	6	108	16	8	.500	11	8	.727	31	4	21	1	24	4.0
Totals		17	—	101	39	.386	62	49	.790	99	25	73	—	127	7.5

Cooper also played in 137 regular-season games for Milwaukee, St. Louis and Fort Wayne, 1954-55 through 1955-56.

Mel Counts

No. 11
Born: October 16, 1941

College: Oregon State '64
Height: 7-0 Weight: 230

Regular Season

Season	Team	G.	Min.	FGA	FGM	Pct.	FTA	FTM	Pct.	Reb.	Ast.	PF	DQ	Pts.	Ave.
1964-65	Celtics	55	572	272	100	.368	74	58	.784	265	19	134	1	258	4.7
1965-66	Celtics	67	1021	549	221	.403	145	120	.826	432	50	207	5	562	8.4
Totals		122	1593	821	321	.391	219	178	.813	697	69	341	6	820	6.7

Playoffs

Season	Team	G.	Min.	FGA	FGM	Pct.	FTA	FTM	Pct.	Reb.	Ast.	PF	DQ	Pts.	Ave.
1964-65	Celtics	4	30	15	4	.267	1	1	1.000	11	1	10	0	9	2.3
1965-66	Celtics	10	82	39	14	.359	17	15	.882	40	3	26	0	43	4.3
Totals		14	112	54	18	.333	18	16	.889	51	4	36	0	52	3.7

Counts also played in 667 regular-season games for Baltimore, Los Angeles, Phoenix, Philadelphia and New Orleans, 1966-67 through 1975-76.

Bob Cousy

No. 14
Born: August 9, 1928

College: Holy Cross '50
Height: 6-1 Weight: 175

Regular Season

Season	Team	G.	Min.	FGA	FGM	Pct.	FTA	FTM	Pct.	Reb.	Ast.	PF	DQ	Pts.	Ave.
1950-51	Celtics	69	—	1138	401	.352	365	276	.756	474	341	185	2	1078	15.6
1951-52	Celtics	66	2681	1388	512	.369	506	409	.808	421	441	190	5	1433	21.7
1952-53	Celtics	71	2945	1320	464	.352	587	479	.816	449	547	227	4	1407	19.8
1953-54	Celtics	72	2857	1262	486	.385	522	411	.787	394	518	201	3	1383	19.2
1954-55	Celtics	71	2747	1316	522	.397	570	460	.807	424	557	165	1	1504	21.2
1955-56	Celtics	72	2767	1223	440	.360	564	476	.844	492	642	206	2	1356	18.8
1956-57	Celtics	64	2364	1264	478	.378	442	363	.821	309	478	134	0	1319	20.6
1957-58	Celtics	65	2222	1262	445	.353	326	277	.850	322	463	136	1	1167	18.0
1958-59	Celtics	65	2403	1260	484	.384	385	329	.855	359	557	135	0	1297	20.0
1959-60	Celtics	75	2588	1481	568	.383	403	319	.791	352	715	146	2	1455	19.4
1960-61	Celtics	76	2564	1382	513	.371	452	352	.779	331	591	196	0	1378	18.1
1961-62	Celtics	75	2116	1181	462	.391	333	251	.754	261	584	135	0	1175	15.7
1962-63	Celtics	76	1976	988	392	.397	298	219	.735	201	515	175	0	1033	13.2
Totals		917	—	16,465	6167	.375	5753	4621	.803	4789	6949	2231	20	16,955	18.5

Playoffs

Season	Team	G.	Min.	FGA	FGM	Pct.	FTA	FTM	Pct.	Reb.	Ast.	PF	DQ	Pts.	Ave.
1950-51	Celtics	2	—	42	9	.214	12	10	.833	15	12	8	—	28	14.0
1951-52	Celtics	3	138	65	26	.400	44	41	.932	12	19	13	1	93	31.0
1952-53	Celtics	6	270	120	46	.383	73	61	.836	25	37	21	0	153	25.5
1953-54	Celtics	6	260	116	33	.284	75	60	.800	32	38	20	0	126	21.0
1954-55	Celtics	7	299	139	53	.381	48	46	.958	43	65	26	0	152	21.7
1955-56	Celtics	3	124	56	28	.500	25	23	.920	24	26	4	0	79	26.3
1956-57	Celtics	10	440	207	67	.324	91	68	.747	61	93	27	0	202	20.2
1957-58	Celtics	11	457	196	67	.342	75	64	.853	71	82	20	0	198	18.0
1958-59	Celtics	11	460	221	72	.326	94	70	.745	76	119	28	0	214	19.5
1959-60	Celtics	13	468	262	80	.305	51	39	.765	48	116	27	0	199	15.3
1960-61	Celtics	10	337	147	50	.340	88	67	.761	43	91	33	1	167	16.7
1961-62	Celtics	14	474	241	86	.357	76	52	.684	64	123	43	0	224	16.0
1962-63	Celtics	13	413	204	72	.353	47	39	.830	32	116	44	2	183	14.1
Totals		109	—	2116	689	.326	799	640	.801	546	937	314	—	2018	18.5

Cousy also played in 7 games as player-coach for Cincinnati, 1969-70.

Why is future Celtic Bailey Howell laughing as Tom Heinsohn puts up a shot?

Dave Cowens

No. 18 — College: Florida State '70
Born: October 25, 1948 — Height: 6-8½ Weight: 230

Regular Season

Season	Team	G.	Min.	FGA	FGM	Pct.	FTA	FTM	Pct.	Reb.	Ast.	PF	DQ	Pts.	Ave.
1970-71	Celtics	81	3076	1302	550	.422	373	273	.732	1216	228	350	15	1373	17.0
1971-72	Celtics	79	3186	1357	657	.484	243	175	.720	1203	245	314	10	1489	18.8
1972-73	Celtics	82	3425	1637	740	.452	262	204	.779	1329	333	311	7	1684	20.5

										—Rebounds—									
Season	Team	G.	Min.	FGA	FGM	Pct.	FTA	FTM	Pct.	Off.	Def.	Tot.	Ast.	PF	DQ	Stl.	Blk.	Pts.	Ave.
1973-74	Celtics	80	3352	1475	645	.437	274	228	.832	264	993	1257	354	294	7	95	101	1518	19.0
1974-75	Celtics	65	2632	1199	569	.475	244	191	.783	229	729	958	296	243	7	87	73	1329	20.4
1975-76	Celtics	78	3101	1305	611	.468	340	257	.756	335	911	1246	325	314	10	94	71	1479	19.0
1976-77	Celtics	50	1888	756	328	.434	198	162	.818	147	550	697	248	181	7	46	49	818	16.4
1977-78	Celtics	77	3215	1220	598	.490	284	239	.842	248	830	1078	351	297	5	102	67	1435	18.6
1978-79	Celtics	68	2517	1010	488	.483	187	151	.807	152	500	652	242	263	16	76	51	1127	16.6
1979-80	Celtics	66	2159	932*	422	.453	122	95	.779	126	408	534	206	216	2	69	61	940	14.2
Totals		726	28,551	12,193	5608	.460	2527	1975	.782	—	—	10,170	2828	2783	86	—	—	13,192	18.2

*Converted 1 of 12 (.083) 3-point field-goal attempts.

Playoffs

Season	Team	G.	Min.	FGA	FGM	Pct.	FTA	FTM	Pct.	Reb.	Ast.	PF	DQ	Pts.	Ave.
1971-72	Celtics	11	441	156	71	.455	47	28	.596	152	33	50	2	170	15.5
1972-73	Celtics	13	598	273	129	.473	41	27	.659	216	48	54	2	285	21.9

										—Rebounds—									
Season	Team	G.	Min.	FGA	FGM	Pct.	FTA	FTM	Pct.	Off.	Def.	Tot.	Ast.	PF	DQ	Stl.	Blk.	Pts.	Ave.
1973-74	Celtics	18	772	370	161	.435	59	47	.797	60	180	240	66	85	2	21	17	369	20.5
1974-75	Celtics	11	479	236	101	.428	26	23	.885	49	132	181	46	50	2	18	6	225	20.5
1975-76	Celtics	18	798	341	156	.457	87	66	.759	87	209	296	83	85	4	22	13	378	21.0
1976-77	Celtics	9	379	148	66	.446	22	17	.773	29	105	134	36	37	3	8	13	149	16.6
1979-80	Celtics	9	301	103*	49	.476	11	10	.909	18	48	66	21	37	0	9	7	108	12.0
Totals		89	3768	1627	733	.432	293	218	.744	—	—	1285	333	398	15	—	—	1684	18.9

*Converted none of 2 (.000) 3-point field-goal attempts.

Hal Crisler

No. 15 — College: San Jose State
Height: 6-3 Weight: 215

Regular Season

Season	Team	G.	FGA	FGM	Pct.	FTA	FTM	Pct.	Ast.	PF	Pts.	Ave.
1946-47	Celtics	4	6	2	.333	2	2	1.000	0	6	6	1.5

Dick Dickey

No. 23 — College: North Carolina State '50
Born: October 26, 1926 — Height: 6-1 Weight: 175

Regular Season

Season	Team	G.	Min.	FGA	FGM	Pct.	FTA	FTM	Pct.	Reb.	Ast.	PF	DQ	Pts.	Ave.
1951-52	Celtics	45	440	136	40	.294	69	47	.681	81	50	79	2	127	2.8

Playoffs

Season	Team	G.	Min.	FGA	FGM	Pct.	FTA	FTM	Pct.	Reb.	Ast.	PF	DQ	Pts.	Ave.
1951-52	Celtics	3	31	8	1	.125	7	6	.857	3	5	7	0	8	2.7

Ernie DiGregorio

No. 7 — College: Providence '73
Born: January 15, 1951 — Height: 6-0 Weight: 180

Regular Season

Season	Team	G.	Min.	FGA	FGM	Pct.	FTA	FTM	Pct.	Reb.	Ast.	PF	DQ	Stl.	Blk.	Pts.	Ave.
1977-78	Celtics	27	274	109	47	.431	13	12	.923	27	66	22	0	12	1	106	3.9

*Played in 25 games for Los Angeles earlier that season.

DiGregorio also played in 260 regular-season games with Buffalo, 1973-74 through 1976-77.

Bill Dinwiddie

No. 27
Born: July 15, 1943

College: New Mexico Highlands '66
Height: 6-7 Weight: 200

Regular Season

Season	Team	G.	Min.	FGA	FGM	Pct.	FTA	FTM	Pct.	Reb.	Ast.	PF	DQ	Pts.	Ave.
1969-70	Cin-Bos	(Missed season with injury)													
1970-71	Celtics	61	717	328	123	.375	74	54	.730	209	34	90	1	300	4.9

Dinwiddie also played 136 regular-season games for Cincinnati, 1967-68 through 1968-69, and in 23 for Milwaukee, 1971-72.

Bob Doll

No. 19
Born: August 10, 1919

College: Colorado '42
Height: 6-5 Weight: 195

Regular Season

Season	Team	G.	FGA	FGM	Pct.	FTA	FTM	Pct.	Ast.	PF	Pts.	Ave.
1948-49	Celtics	47	438	145	.331	117	80	.684	117	118	370	7.9
1949-50	Celtics	47	347	120	.346	114	75	.658	108	117	315	6.7
Totals		94	785	265	.338	231	155	.671	225	235	685	7.3

Doll also played 102 regular-season games for St. Louis, 1946-47 through 1947-48.

Bob Donham

No. 12
Born: October 11, 1926

College: Ohio State '50
Height: 6-2 Weight: 190

Regular Season

Season	Team	G.	Min.	FGA	FGM	Pct.	FTA	FTM	Pct.	Reb.	Ast.	PF	DQ	Pts.	Ave.
1950-51	Celtics	68	—	298	151	.507	229	114	.498	235	139	179	3	416	6.1
1951-52	Celtics	66	1980	413	201	.487	293	149	.509	330	228	223	9	551	8.3
1952-53	Celtics	71	1435	353	169	.479	240	113	.471	239	153	213	8	451	6.4
1953-54	Celtics	68	1451	315	141	.448	213	118	.554	267	186	235	11	400	5.9
Totals		273	—	1379	662	.480	975	494	.507	1071	706	850	31	1818	6.7

Playoffs

Season	Team	G.	Min.	FGA	FGM	Pct.	FTA	FTM	Pct.	Reb.	Ast.	PF	DQ	Pts.	Ave.
1950-51	Celtics	2	—	9	4	.444	12	5	.417	8	2	9	1	13	6.5
1951-52	Celtics	3	112	19	9	.474	18	9	.500	13	17	16	1	27	9.0
1952-53	Celtics	6	138	38	11	.289	27	11	.407	21	13	24	3	33	5.5
1953-54	Celtics	6	98	15	7	.467	19	6	.316	12	6	32	4	20	3.3
Totals		17	—	81	31	.383	76	31	.408	54	38	81	9	93	5.5

Steve Downing

No. 32
Born: September 9, 1950

College: Indiana '73
Height: 6-8 Weight: 225

Regular Season

Season	Team	G.	Min.	FGA	FGM	Pct.	FTA	FTM	Pct.	Reb.	Ast.	PF	DQ	Pts.	Ave.
1973-74	Celtics	24	137	64	21	.328	38	22	.579	39	11	33	0	64	2.7
1974-75	Celtics	3	9	2	0	.000	2	0	.000	2	0	0	0	0	0.0
Totals		27	146	66	21	.318	40	22	.550	41	11	33	0	64	2.4

Playoffs

Season	Team	G.	Min.	FGA	FGM	Pct.	FTA	FTM	Pct.	Reb.	Ast.	PF	DQ	Pts.	Ave.
1973-74	Celtics	1	4	2	1	.500	0	0	.000	2	0	1	0	2	2.0

Terry Duerod

No. 40
Born: July 29, 1956

College: Detroit '79
Height: 6-2 Weight: 180

Regular Season

Season	Team	G.	Min.	FGA	FGM	Pct.	FTA	FTM	Pct.	—Rebounds— Off.	Def.	Tot.	Ast.	PF	DQ	Stl.	Blk.	Pts.	Ave.
1980-81**	Celtics	32	114	73*	30	.411	14	13	.929	2	3	5	6	8	0	5	0	79	2.5
1981-82	Celtics	21	146	77*	34	.442	12	4	.333	6	9	15	12	9	0	3	1	72	3.4
Totals		53	260	150	64	.427	26	17	.654	8	12	20	18	17	0	8	1	151	2.8

*Converted 6 of 10 (.600) 3-point field-goal attempts in 1980-81, none of 1 (.000) in 1981-82 for a total of 6 of 11 (.545).
**Also played in 18 games for Dallas earlier that season.

Playoffs

Season	Team	G.	Min.	FGA	FGM	Pct.	FTA	FTM	Pct.	—Rebounds— Off.	Def.	Tot.	Ast.	PF	DQ	Stl.	Blk.	Pts.	Ave.
1980-81	Celtics	10	12	10*	4	.400	0	0	.000	0	0	0	0	0	0	1	0	8	0.8

*Converted none of 2 (.000) 3-point field-goal attempts.

Duerod also played in 67 regular-season games for Detroit in 1979-80 and 18 for Dallas early in 1980-81 season before being signed as a free agent by Boston on December 4, 1980.

Bob Duffy

No. 17
Born: July 5, 1922

College: Tulane
Height: 6-4 Weight: 175

Regular Season

Season	Team	G.	FGA	FGM	Pct.	FTA	FTM	Pct.	Ast.	PF	Pts.	Ave.
1946-47	Chi-Bos	17*	32	7	.219	7	5	.714	0	17	19	1.1

*6 Boston, 11 Chicago.

Andy Duncan

No. 21
Born: 1923

College: William & Mary
Height: 6-6 Weight: 195

Regular Season

Season	Team	G.	Min.	FGA	FGM	Pct.	FTA	FTM	Pct.	Reb.	Ast.	PF	DQ	Pts.	Ave.
1950-51	Celtics	14	—	40	7	.175	22	15	.682	30	8	27	0	29	2.1

Duncan also played in 122 regular-season games for Rochester, 1948-49 through 1949-50.

Ed Ehlers

No. 14
Born: 1924

College: Purdue '47
Height: 6-3 Weight: 198

Regular Season

Season	Team	G.	FGA	FGM	Pct.	FTA	FTM	Pct.	Ast.	PF	Pts.	Ave.
1947-48	Celtics	40	417	104	.249	144	78	.542	44	92	286	7.2
1948-49	Celtics	59	583	182	.312	225	150	.667	133	119	514	8.7
Totals		99	1000	286	.286	369	228	.618	177	211	800	8.1

Bob Eliason

No. 14

College: Hamline '42
Height: 6-2 Weight: 200

Regular Season

Season	Team	G.	FGA	FGM	Pct.	FTA	FTM	Pct.	Ast.	PF	Pts.	Ave.
1946-47	Celtics	1	0	0	.000	0	0	.000	0	1	0	0.0

Wayne Embry

No. 28 College: Miami (Ohio) '58
Born: March 26, 1937 Height: 6-8 Weight: 255

Regular Season

Season	Team	G.	Min.	FGA	FGM	Pct.	FTA	FTM	Pct.	Reb.	Ast.	PF	DQ	Pts.	Ave.
1966-67	Celtics	72	729	359	147	.409	144	82	.569	294	42	137	0	376	5.2
1967-68	Celtics	78	1088	483	193	.400	185	109	.589	321	52	174	1	495	6.3
Totals		150	1817	842	340	.404	329	191	.581	615	94	311	1	871	5.8

Playoffs

Season	Team	G.	Min.	FGA	FGM	Pct.	FTA	FTM	Pct.	Reb.	Ast.	PF	DQ	Pts.	Ave.
1966-67	Celtics	5	38	31	12	.387	4	2	.500	13	3	9	0	26	5.2
1967-68	Celtics	16	162	59	23	.390	29	13	.448	45	6	36	0	59	3.7
Totals		21	200	90	35	.389	33	15	.455	58	9	45	0	85	4.1

Embry also played in 603 regular-season games for Cincinnati, 1958-59 through 1965-66, and in 78 for Milwaukee, 1968-69.

Gene Englund

No. 10 College: Wisconsin '41
Born: October 21, 1917 Height: 6-5 Weight: 205

Regular Season

Season	Team	G.	FGA	FGM	Pct.	FTA	FTM	Pct.	Ast.	PF	Pts.	Ave.
1949-50	Bos-Tri C	46	274	104	.380	192	152	.792	41	816	360	7.8

John Ezersky

Nos. 16 & 10 College: St. John's
Born: 1921 Height: 6-3 Weight: 175

Regular Season

Season	Team	G.	FGA	FGM	Pct.	FTA	FTM	Pct.	Ast.	PF	Pts.	Ave.
1948-49	Prov-Balt-Boston*	56	407	128	.314	160	109	.681	67	98	365	6.5
1949-50	Balt-Bos**	54	487	143	.294	183	127	.694	86	139	413	7.6
Totals		110	894	271	.303	343	236	.688	153	237	778	7.0

*18 games Boston, 11 Providence, 27 Baltimore.

**16 games Boston, 38 Baltimore.

Ezersky also played in 25 regular-season games for Providence, 1947-48.

Phil Farbman

No. 8 College: CCNY '48
Born: 1924 Height: 6-2 Weight: 185

Regular Season

Season	Team	G.	FGA	FGM	Pct.	FTA	FTM	Pct.	Ast.	PF	Pts.	Ave.
1948-49	Phil-Bos	48*	163	50	.307	81	55	.679	36	86	155	3.2

*21 games Boston, 27 Philadelphia.

Rookie Jack (The Shot) Foley is welcomed in 1962 by fellow Holy Cross graduates Bob Cousy and Tom Heinsohn. Foley, a frail sharpshooter drafted No. 2 behind John Havlicek, played only 5 games for the Celtics before moving on to New York, where he ended his abbreviated NBA career after just 6 games with the Knicks.

Warren Fenley

No. 7 College: Manhattan
Born: February 8, 1922 Height: 6-3 Weight: 190

Regular Season

Season	Team	G.	FGA	FGM	Pct.	FTA	FTM	Pct.	Ast.	PF	Pts.	Ave.
1946-47	Celtics	23	138	31	.225	45	23	.511	16	59	85	3.7

Eric Fernsten

No. 45 College: San Francisco '75
Born: November 1, 1953 Height: 6-10 Weight: 205

Regular Season

										—Rebounds—									
Season	Team	G.	Min.	FGA	FGM	Pct.	FTA	FTM	Pct.	Off.	Def.	Tot.	Ast.	PF	DQ	Stl.	Blk.	Pts.	Ave.
1979-80	Celtics	56	431	153*	71	.464	52	33	.635	40	56	96	28	48	0	17	12	175	3.1
1980-81	Celtics	45	279	79*	38	.481	30	20	.667	29	33	62	10	29	0	6	7	96	2.1
1981-82	Celtics	43	202	49*	19	.388	30	19	.633	12	30	42	8	23	0	5	7	57	1.3
Totals		144	912	281	128	.456	112	72	.643	81	119	200	46	100	0	28	26	328	2.3

Playoffs

										—Rebounds—									
Season	Team	G.	Min.	FGA	FGM	Pct.	FTA	FTM	Pct.	Off.	Def.	Tot.	Ast.	PF	DQ	Stl.	Blk.	Pts.	Ave.
1979-80	Celtics	5	18	6*	2	.333	3	2	.667	3	2	5	0	1	0	0	3	6	1.2
1980-81	Celtics	8	14	3*	0	.000	3	2	.667	1	3	4	1	3	0	1	0	2	0.3
1981-82	Celtics	5	11	2*	1	.500	2	1	.500	2	0	2	0	0	0	0	0	3	0.6
Totals		18	43	11	3	.273	8	5	.625	6	5	11	1	4	0	1	3	11	0.6

*Fernsten attempted no 3-point field goals during his 3 Celtic seasons, either during the regular season or the playoffs.

Fernsten also played in 42 regular-season games for Cleveland and Chicago, 1975-76 through 1976-77.

Henry (Hank) Finkel

No. 29 College: Dayton '66
Born: April 20, 1942 Height: 7-0 Weight: 245

Regular Season

Season	Team	G.	Min.	FGA	FGM	Pct.	FTA	FTM	Pct.	Reb.	Ast.	PF	DQ	Pts.	Ave.
1969-70	Celtics	80	1866	683	310	.454	233	156	.670	613	103	292	13	776	9.7
1970-71	Celtics	80	1234	489	214	.438	127	93	.732	343	79	196	5	521	6.5
1971-72	Celtics	78	736	254	103	.406	74	43	.581	251	61	118	4	249	3.2
1972-73	Celtics	76	496	173	78	.451	52	28	.538	151	26	83	0	184	2.4

										—Rebounds—									
Season	Team	G.	Min.	FGA	FGM	Pct.	FTA	FTM	Pct.	Off.	Def.	Tot.	Ast.	PF	DQ	Stl.	Blk.	Pts.	Ave.
1973-74	Celtics	60	427	130	60	.462	43	28	.651	41	94	135	27	62	1	3	7	148	2.5
1974-75	Celtics	62	518	129	52	.403	43	23	.535	33	79	112	32	72	0	7	3	127	2.0
Totals		436	5277	1858	817	.440	572	371	.649	—	—	1605	328	823	23	—	—	2005	4.6

Playoffs

Season	Team	G.	Min.	FGA	FGM	Pct.	FTA	FTM	Pct.	Reb.	Ast.	PF	DQ	Pts.	Ave.
1971-72	Celtics	8	68	22	10	.455	0	0	.000	24	3	11	0	20	2.5
1972-73	Celtics	7	23	9	6	.667	0	0	.000	6	3	4	0	12	1.7

										—Rebounds—									
Season	Team	G.	Min.	FGA	FGM	Pct.	FTA	FTM	Pct.	Off.	Def.	Tot.	Ast.	PF	DQ	Stl.	Blk.	Pts.	Ave.
1973-74	Celtics	8	46	18	8	.444	1	1	1.000	5	5	10	3	9	0	1	0	17	2.1
1974-75	Celtics	7	25	7	3	.429	5	3	.600	3	3	6	4	2	0	0	0	9	1.3
Totals		30	162	56	27	.482	6	4	.667	—	—	46	13	26	0	—	—	58	1.9

Finkel also played in 115 regular-season games for Los Angeles and San Diego, 1966-67 through 1968-69.

Jack (The Shot) Foley

No. 21 College: Holy Cross '62
Born: November 17, 1940 Height: 6-3 Weight: 185

Regular Season

Season	Team	G.	Min.	FGA	FGM	Pct.	FTA	FTM	Pct.	Reb.	Ast.	PF	DQ	Pts.	Ave.
1962-63	Bos-NY	11*	86	52	20	.385	15	13	.867	16	5	8	0	53	4.8

*5 games Boston, 6 New York.

Chris Ford

No. 42
Born: January 11, 1949

College: Villanova '72
Height: 6-5 Weight: 190

Regular Season

Season	Team	G.	Min.	FGA	FGM	Pct.	FTA	FTM	Pct.	—Rebounds— Off.	Def.	Tot.	Ast.	PF	DQ	Stl.	Blk.	Pts.	Ave.
1978-79	Celtics	81	2737	1142	538	.471	227	172	.758	124	150	274	374	209	3	115	20	1284	15.0
1979-80	Celtics	73	2115	709*	330	.465	114	86	.754	77	104	181	215	178	0	111	27	815	11.2
1980-81	Celtics	82	2723	707*	314	.444	87	64	.736	72	91	163	295	212	2	100	23	728	8.9
1981-82	Celtics	76	1591	450*	188	.418	56	39	.696	52	56	108	142	143	0	42	10	435	5.7
Totals		312	9166	3008	1370	.455	484	361	.746	325	401	726	1026	742	5	368	80	3262	10.5

*Converted 70 of 164 (.427) 3-point field-goal attempts in 1979-80, 36 of 109 (.330) in 1980-81 and 20 of 61 (.328) in 1981-82 for a total of 126 of 334 (.377).

Playoffs

Season	Team	G.	Min.	FGA	FGM	Pct.	FTA	FTM	Pct.	—Rebounds— Off.	Def.	Tot.	Ast.	PF	DQ	Stl.	Blk.	Pts.	Ave.
1979-80	Celtics	9	279	79*	34	.430	15	12	.800	9	16	25	21	35	1	14	6	82	9.1
1980-81	Celtics	17	507	146*	66	.452	25	15	.600	13	32	45	46	47	0	14	1	154	9.1
1981-82	Celtics	12	138	42*	20	.476	7	5	.714	6	9	15	15	15	0	3	1	47	3.9
Totals		38	924	267	120	.449	47	32	.681	28	57	85	82	97	1	31	8	283	7.4

*Converted 2 of 13 (.154) 3-point field-goal attempts in 1979-80, 7 of 25 (.280) in 1980-81 and 2 of 7 (.286) in 1981-82 for a total of 11 of 45 (.244).

Ford also played in 482 regular-season games for Detroit, 1972-73 through 1977-78.

Jack (Dutch) Garfinkel

Nos. 15 & 21
Born: June 13, 1918

College: St. John's
Height: 6-0 Weight: 190

Regular Season

Season	Team	G.	FGA	FGM	Pct.	FTA	FTM	Pct.	Ast.	PF	Pts.	Ave.
1946-47	Celtics	40	304	81	.266	28	17	.607	58	62	179	4.5
1947-48	Celtics	43	380	114	.300	46	35	.761	59	78	263	6.1
1948-49	Celtics	9	70	12	.171	14	10	.714	17	19	34	3.8
Totals		92	754	207	.275	88	62	.705	134	159	476	5.2

Playoffs

Season	Team	G.	FGA	FGM	Pct.	FTA	FTM	Pct.	Ast.	PF	Pts.	Ave.
1947-48	Celtics	3	23	7	.304	10	8	.800	7	15	22	7.3

Following his Celtic retirement in 1963, Bob Cousy came back as a network broadcaster and interviewed former teammate and car-pool copilot Tom Heinsohn.

Ward Gibson

No. —
Born: December 6, 1921

College: Creighton '47
Height: 6-5 Weight: 198

Regular Season

Season	Team	G.	FGA	FGM	Pct.	FTA	FTM	Pct.	Ast.	PF	Pts.	Ave.
1949-50	Bos-Wat	32*	195	67	.344	64	42	.656	37	106	176	5.5

*2 games Boston, 30 Waterloo.

Clarence Glover

No. 28
Born: November 1, 1947

College: Western Kentucky '71
Height: 6-8 Weight: 210

Regular Season

Season	Team	G.	Min.	FGA	FGM	Pct.	FTA	FTM	Pct.	Reb.	Ast.	PF	DQ	Pts.	Ave.
1971-72	Celtics	25	119	55	25	.455	32	15	.469	46	4	26	0	65	2.6

Playoffs

Season	Team	G.	Min.	FGA	FGM	Pct.	FTA	FTM	Pct.	Reb.	Ast.	PF	DQ	Pts.	Ave.
1971-72	Celtics	3	10	6	2	.333	2	2	1.000	3	0	1	0	6	2.0

Mal Graham

No. 11
Born: February 23, 1945

College: New York University '67
Height: 6-1 Weight: 185

Regular Season

Season	Team	G.	Min.	FGA	FGM	Pct.	FTA	FTM	Pct.	Reb.	Ast.	PF	DQ	Pts.	Ave.
1967-68	Celtics	48	786	272	117	.430	88	56	.636	94	61	123	0	290	6.0
1968-69	Celtics	22	103	55	13	.236	14	11	.786	24	14	27	0	37	1.7
Totals		70	889	327	130	.398	102	67	.657	118	75	150	0	327	4.7

Playoffs

Season	Team	G.	Min.	FGA	FGM	Pct.	FTA	FTM	Pct.	Reb.	Ast.	PF	DQ	Pts.	Ave.
1967-68	Celtics	5	22	5	2	.400	3	1	.333	4	1	3	0	5	1.0
1968-69	Celtics	2	3	2	0	.000	0	0	.000	0	1	0	0	0	0.0
Totals		7	25	7	2	.286	3	1	.333	4	2	3	0	5	0.7

Wyndol Gray

No. 4
Born: March 20, 1922

Colleges: Harvard, Bowling Green
Height: 6-1 Weight: 175

Regular Season

Season	Team	G.	FGA	FGM	Pct.	FTA	FTM	Pct.	Ast.	PF	Pts.	Ave.
1946-47	Celtics	55	476	139	.292	124	72	.581	47	105	350	6.4

Gary also played in 12 regular-season games for Providence and St. Louis in 1947-48.

Tom Heinsohn took a great fall.

Sihugo Green

No. 28 — College: Duquesne '56
Born: August 20, 1934 — Height: 6-2 Weight: 185

Regular Season

Season	Team	G.	Min.	FGA	FGM	Pct.	FTA	FTM	Pct.	Reb.	Ast.	PF	DQ	Pts.	Ave.
1965-66	Celtics	10	92	31	12	.387	16	8	.500	11	9	16	0	32	3.2

Green also played in 494 regular-season games for Rochester, Cincinnati, St. Louis, Chicago and Baltimore, 1956-57 through 1964-65.

Gene Guarilia

No. 20 — College: George Washington '59
Born: September 13, 1927 — Height: 6-5 Weight: 220

Regular Season

Season	Team	G.	Min.	FGA	FGM	Pct.	FTA	FTM	Pct.	Reb.	Ast.	PF	DQ	Pts.	Ave.
1959-60	Celtics	48	423	154	58	.377	41	29	.707	85	18	57	1	145	3.0
1960-61	Celtics	25	199	94	38	.404	10	3	.300	61	5	28	0	79	3.2
1961-62	Celtics	46	367	161	61	.379	64	41	.641	124	11	56	0	163	3.5
1962-63	Celtics	11	83	38	11	.289	11	4	.364	14	2	5	0	26	2.4
Totals		130	1072	447	168	.376	126	77	.611	284	36	146	1	413	3.2

Playoffs

Season	Team	G.	Min.	FGA	FGM	Pct.	FTA	FTM	Pct.	Reb.	Ast.	PF	DQ	Pts.	Ave.
1959-60	Celtics	7	41	18	4	.222	6	6	1.000	19	3	4	0	14	2.0
1961-62	Celtics	5	26	8	2	.250	5	2	.400	4	1	6	0	6	1.2
Totals		12	67	26	6	.231	11	8	.727	23	4	10	0	20	1.7

Charles (Chick) Halbert

No. 11 — College: West Texas '42
Born: February 27, 1919 — Height: 6-9 Weight: 225

Regular Season

Season	Team	G.	FGA	FGM	Pct.	FTA	FTM	Pct.	Ast.	PF	Pts.	Ave.
1948-49	Bos-Pro	60*	647	202	.312	345	214	.620	113	175	618	10.3

*33 games Boston, 27 Providence.

Halbert also played in 107 games for Chicago and Philadelphia, 1946-47 through 1947-48, and in 136 for Washington and Baltimore, 1949-50 through 1950-51.

Cecil Hankins

No. 5 — College: Oklahoma State '46
Born: January 6, 1922 — Height: 6-1 Weight: 175

Regular Season

Season	Team	G.	FGA	FGM	Pct.	FTA	FTM	Pct.	Ast.	PF	Pts.	Ave.
1947-48	Celtics	25	116	23	.198	35	24	.686	8	28	70	2.8

Phil Hankinson

No. 20 — College: Penn '73
Born: July 26, 1951 — Height: 6-8 Weight: 195

Regular Season

Season	Team	G.	Min.	FGA	FGM	Pct.	FTA	FTM	Pct.	Reb.	Ast.	PF	DQ	Pts.	Ave.
1973-74	Celtics	28	163	103	50	.485	13	10	.769	50	4	18	0	110	3.9
1974-75	Celtics	3	24	11	6	.545	0	0	.000	7	2	3	0	12	4.0
Totals		31	187	114	56	.491	13	10	.769	57	6	21	0	122	3.9

Playoffs

Season	Team	G.	Min.	FGA	FGM	Pct.	FTA	FTM	Pct.	Reb.	Ast.	PF	DQ	Pts.	Ave.
1973-74	Celtics	2	5	4	2	.500	2	2	1.000	1	0	0	0	6	3.0
1974-75	Celtics	2	3	3	1	.333	0	0	.000	2	0	0	0	2	1.0
Totals		4	8	7	3	.429	2	2	1.000	3	0	0	0	8	2.0

Bob (Gabby) Harris

Nos. 13 & 18
Born: March 16, 1927

College: Oklahoma State '49
Height: 6-7 Weight: 195

Regular Season

Season	*Team*	*G.*	*Min.*	*FGA*	*FGM*	*Pct.*	*FTA*	*FTM*	*Pct.*	*Reb.*	*Ast.*	*PF*	*DQ*	*Pts.*	*Ave.*
1950-51	FtW-Bos	56*	—	295	98	.332	127	86	.677	291	64	157	4	282	5.0
1951-52	Celtics	66	1899	463	190	.410	209	134	.641	531	120	194	5	514	7.8
1952-53	Celtics	70	1971	459	192	.418	226	133	.588	485	95	238	6	517	7.4
1953-54	Celtics	71	1898	409	156	.381	172	108	.628	517	94	224	8	420	5.9
Totals		263	—	1626	636	.391	734	461	.628	1824	373	813	23	1733	6.6

*12 games Fort Wayne, 44 Boston.

Playoffs

Season	*Team*	*G.*	*Min.*	*FGA*	*FGM*	*Pct.*	*FTA*	*FTM*	*Pct.*	*Reb.*	*Ast.*	*PF*	*DQ*	*Pts.*	*Ave.*
1950-51	Celtics	2	—	10	1	.100	7	5	.714	4	2	4	0	7	3.5
1951-52	Celtics	3	87	21	9	.429	5	5	1.000	25	4	16	1	23	7.7
1952-53	Celtics	6	193	35	16	.457	24	18	.750	56	12	28	3	50	8.3
1953-54	Celtics	6	150	25	16	.640	23	16	.696	35	3	25	1	48	8.0
Totals		17	—	91	42	.462	59	44	.746	120	21	73	5	128	7.5

Harris also played in 62 regular-season games for Fort Wayne, 1949-50.

John Havlicek

No. 17
Born: April 8, 1940

College: Ohio State '62
Height: 6-5 Weight: 205

Regular Season

Season	*Team*	*G.*	*Min.*	*FGA*	*FGM*	*Pct.*	*FTA*	*FTM*	*Pct.*	*Reb.*	*Ast.*	*PF*	*DQ*	*Pts.*	*Ave.*
1962-63	Celtics	80	2200	1085	483	.445	239	174	.728	534	179	189	2	1140	14.3
1963-64	Celtics	80	2587	1535	640	.417	422	315	.746	428	238	227	1	1595	19.9
1964-65	Celtics	75	2169	1420	570	.401	316	235	.744	371	199	200	2	1375	18.3
1965-66	Celtics	71	2175	1328	530	.399	349	274	.785	423	210	158	1	1334	18.8
1966-67	Celtics	81	2602	1540	684	.444	441	365	.828	532	278	210	0	1733	21.4
1967-68	Celtics	82	2921	1551	666	.429	453	368	.812	546	384	237	2	1700	20.7
1968-69	Celtics	82	3174	1709	692	.405	496	387	.780	570	441	247	0	1771	21.6
1969-70	Celtics	81	3369	1585	736	.464	578	488	.844	635	530	211	1	1960	24.2
1970-71	Celtics	81	3678	1982	892	.450	677	554	.818	730	607	200	0	2338	28.9
1971-72	Celtics	82	3698	1957	897	.458	549	458	.834	672	614	183	1	2252	27.5
1972-73	Celtics	80	3367	1704	766	.450	431	370	.858	567	529	195	1	1902	23.8

										—Rebounds—									
Season	*Team*	*G.*	*Min.*	*FGA*	*FGM*	*Pct.*	*FTA*	*FTM*	*Pct.*	*Off.*	*Def.*	*Tot.*	*Ast.*	*PF*	*DQ*	*Stl.*	*Blk.*	*Pts.*	*Ave.*
1973-74	Celtics	76	3091	1502	685	.456	416	346	.832	138	349	487	447	196	1	95	32	1716	22.6
1974-75	Celtics	82	3132	1411	642	.455	332	289	.870	154	330	484	432	231	2	110	16	1573	19.2
1975-76	Celtics	76	2598	1121	504	.450	333	281	.844	116	198	314	278	204	1	97	29	1289	17.0
1976-77	Celtics	79	2193	1283	580	.452	288	235	.816	109	273	382	400	208	4	84	18	1395	17.7
1977-78	Celtics	82	2797	1217	546	.449	269	230	.855	93	239	332	328	185	2	90	22	1322	16.1
Totals		1270	45,751	23,930	10,513	.439	6589	5369	.815	—	—	8007	6114	3281	21	476	117	26,395	20.8

Playoffs

Season	*Team*	*G.*	*Min.*	*FGA*	*FGM*	*Pct.*	*FTA*	*FTM*	*Pct.*	*Reb.*	*Ast.*	*PF*	*DQ*	*Pts.*	*Ave.*
1962-63	Celtics	11	254	125	56	.448	27	18	.667	53	17	28	1	130	11.8
1963-64	Celtics	10	289	159	61	.384	44	35	.795	43	32	26	0	157	15.7
1964-65	Celtics	12	405	250	88	.352	55	46	.836	88	29	44	1	222	18.5
1965-66	Celtics	17	719	374	153	.409	113	95	.841	154	70	69	2	401	23.6
1966-67	Celtics	9	330	212	95	.448	71	57	.803	73	28	30	0	247	27.4
1967-68	Celtics	19	862	407	184	.452	151	125	.828	164	142	67	1	493	25.9
1968-69	Celtics	18	850	382	170	.445	138	118	.855	179	100	58	2	458	25.4
1971-72	Celtics	11	517	235	108	.460	99	85	.859	92	70	35	1	301	27.4
1972-73	Celtics	12	479	235	112	.477	74	61	.824	62	65	24	0	285	23.8

										—Rebounds—									
Season	*Team*	*G.*	*Min.*	*FGA*	*FGM*	*Pct.*	*FTA*	*FTM*	*Pct.*	*Off.*	*Def.*	*Tot.*	*Ast.*	*PF*	*DQ*	*Stl.*	*Blk.*	*Pts.*	*Ave.*
1973-74	Celtics	18	811	411	199	.484	101	89	.881	28	88	116	108	43	0	24	6	487	27.1
1974-75	Celtics	11	464	192	83	.432	76	66	.868	18	39	57	51	38	1	16	1	232	21.1
1975-76	Celtics	15	505	180	80	.444	47	38	.809	18	38	56	51	22	0	12	5	198	13.2
1976-77	Celtics	9	375	167	62	.371	50	41	.820	15	34	49	62	33	0	8	4	165	18.3
Totals		172	6860	3329	1451	.436	1046	874	.836	—	—	1186	825	517	9	60	16	3776	22.0

John Hazen

Nos. 3 & 10
Born: 1927

College: Indiana State
Height: 6-2 Weight: 172

Regular Season

Season	Team	G.	FGA	FGM	Pct.	FTA	FTM	Pct.	Ast.	PF	Pts.	Ave.
1948-49	Celtics	6	17	6	.353	7	6	.857	3	10	18	3.0

Tom Heinsohn

No. 15
Born: August 26, 1934

College: Holy Cross '56
Height: 6-7 Weight: 218

Regular Season

Season	Team	G.	Min.	FGA	FGM	Pct.	FTA	FTM	Pct.	Reb.	Ast.	PF	DQ	Pts.	Ave.
1956-57	Celtics	72	2150	1123	446	.397	343	271	.790	705	117	304	12	1163	16.2
1957-58	Celtics	69	2206	1226	468	.382	394	294	.746	705	125	274	6	1230	17.8
1958-59	Celtics	66	2089	1192	465	.390	391	312	.798	638	164	271	11	1242	18.8
1959-60	Celtics	75	2420	1590	673	.423	386	283	.734	794	171	275	8	1629	21.7
1960-61	Celtics	74	2306	1660	627	.376	424	325	.766	732	141	260	5	1579	21.3
1961-62	Celtics	78	2382	1613	692	.429	437	358	.819	747	165	280	2	1742	22.3
1962-63	Celtics	77	2004	1290	550	.426	407	340	.835	569	95	267	4	1440	18.7
1963-64	Celtics	76	2040	1223	487	.398	342	283	.827	460	183	268	3	1257	16.5
1964-65	Celtics	67	1706	954	365	.383	229	182	.795	399	157	252	5	912	13.6
Totals		654	19,303	11,871	4773	.402	3353	2648	.790	5749	1318	2451	56	12,194	18.6

Playoffs

Season	Team	G.	Min.	FGA	FGM	Pct.	FTA	FTM	Pct.	Reb.	Ast.	PF	DQ	Pts.	Ave.
1956-57	Celtics	10	370	231	90	.390	69	49	.710	117	20	40	1	229	22.9
1957-58	Celtics	11	349	194	68	.351	72	56	.778	119	18	52	3	192	17.5
1958-59	Celtics	11	348	220	91	.414	56	37	.661	98	32	41	0	219	19.9
1959-60	Celtics	13	423	267	112	.419	80	60	.750	126	27	53	2	284	21.8
1960-61	Celtics	10	291	201	82	.408	43	33	.767	99	20	36	1	197	19.7
1961-62	Celtics	14	445	291	116	.399	76	58	.763	115	34	58	4	290	20.7
1962-63	Celtics	13	413	270	123	.456	98	75	.765	116	15	55	2	321	24.7
1963-64	Celtics	10	308	180	70	.412	42	34	.810	80	26	36	0	174	17.4
1964-65	Celtics	12	276	181	66	.365	32	20	.625	84	23	46	1	152	12.7
Totals		104	3223	2035	818	.402	568	422	.743	954	215	417	14	2058	19.8

Dixon (Dick) Hemric

No. 20
Born: August 29, 1933

College: Wake Forest '55
Height: 6-6 Weight: 220

Regular Season

Season	Team	G.	Min.	FGA	FGM	Pct.	FTA	FTM	Pct.	Reb.	Ast.	PF	DQ	Pts.	Ave.
1950-51	TriC-Bos	71*	—	644	189	.294	237	155	.654	448	92	261	8	533	7.5
1952-53	Bos-Ind	10**	62	31	4	.129	5	3	.600	19	4	18	0	11	1.0
Totals		81	—	675	193	.286	242	158	.653	467	96	279	8	544	6.7

*48 games Tri-Cities, 23 Boston.

**4 games Boston, 6 Indianapolis.

Playoffs

Season	Team	G.	Min.	FGA	FGM	Pct.	FTA	FTM	Pct.	Reb.	Ast.	PF	DQ	Pts.	Ave.
1955-56	Celtics	3	54	24	5	.208	16	9	.563	22	1	7	0	19	6.3
1956-57	Celtics	2	19	7	1	.143	0	0	.000	9	1	1	0	2	1.0
Totals		5	73	31	6	.194	16	9	.563	31	2	8	0	21	4.2

Gerald Henderson

No. 43
Born: January 16, 1956

College: Virginia Commonwealth '78
Height: 6-2 Weight: 175

Regular Season

Season	Team	G.	Min.	FGA	FGM	Pct.	FTA	FTM	Pct.	—Rebounds— Off.	Def.	Tot.	Ast.	PF	DQ	Stl.	Blk.	Pts.	Ave.
1979-80	Celtics	76	1061	382*	191	.500	129	89	.690	37	46	83	147	96	0	45	15	473	6.2
1980-81	Celtics	82	1608	579*	261	.451	157	113	.720	43	89	132	213	177	0	79	12	636	7.8
1981-82	Celtics	82	1844	705*	353	.501	172	125	.727	47	105	152	252	199	3	82	11	833	10.2
Totals		240	4513	1666	805	.483	458	327	.714	127	240	367	612	472	3	206	38	1942	8.1

*Converted 2 of 6 (.333) 3-point field-goal attempts in 1979-80, 1 of 16 (.063) in 1980-81 and 2 of 12 (.167) in 1981-82 for a total of 5 of 34 (.147).

Playoffs

Season	Team	G.	Min.	FGA	FGM	Pct.	FTA	FTM	Pct.	—Rebounds— Off.	Def.	Tot.	Ast.	PF	DQ	Stl.	Blk.	Pts.	Ave.
1979-80	Celtics	9	101	37*	15	.405	20	12	.600	4	6	10	12	8	0	4	0	42	4.7
1980-81	Celtics	16	228	86*	41	.477	12	10	.833	10	15	25	26	24	0	10	3	92	5.8
1981-82	Celtics	12	310	93*	38	.409	35	24	.686	12	13	25	48	30	0	14	2	100	8.3
Totals		37	639	216	94	.435	67	46	.687	26	34	60	86	62	0	28	5	234	6.3

*Converted none of 2 (.000) 3-point field-goal attempts in 1979-80, none of 1 (.000) in 1980-81 and none of 2 (.000) in 1981-82 for a total of none of 5 (.000).

Clarence (Kleggie) Hermsen

No. 10
Born: March 12, 1923

College: Minnesota '48
Height: 6-9 Weight: 235

Regular Season

Season	Team	G.	Min.	FGA	FGM	Pct.	FTA	FTM	Pct.	Reb.	Ast.	PF	DQ	Pts.	Ave.
1950-51	TriC-Bos	71	—	644	189	.294	237	155	.654	448	92	261	8	533	7.5
1951-52	Bos-Ind	10	62	31	4	.129	5	3	.600	19	4	18	0	11	1.0
Totals		81	—	675	193	.286	242	158	.653	467	96	279	8	544	6.7

Playoffs

Season	Team	G.	Min.	FGA	FGM	Pct.	FTA	FTM	Pct.	Reb.	Ast.	PF	DQ	Pts.	Ave.
1950-51	Celtics	2	—	6	1	.167	0	0	.000	3	0	6	—	2	1.0

Hermsen also played in 207 regular-season games for Cleveland, Toronto, Baltimore, Washington and Chicago, 1946-47 through 1949-50.

Red Auerbach's pupils appear unimpressed with their coach's shooting technique.

Sidney (Sonny) Hertzberg

No. 4
Born: July 29, 1922

College: CCNY
Height: 6-0 Weight: 176

Regular Season

Season	*Team*	*G.*	*Min.*	*FGA*	*FGM*	*Pct.*	*FTA*	*FTM*	*Pct.*	*Reb.*	*Ast.*	*PF*	*DQ*	*Pts.*	*Ave.*
1949-50	Celtics	68	—	865	275	.318	191	143	.749	—	200	153	—	693	10.2
1950-51	Celtics	65	—	651	206	.316	270	223	.826	260	244	156	4	635	9.8
Totals		133	—	1516	481	.317	461	366	.794	—	444	309	—	1328	10.0

Playoffs

Season	*Team*	*G.*	*Min.*	*FGA*	*FGM*	*Pct.*	*FTA*	*FTM*	*Pct.*	*Reb.*	*Ast.*	*PF*	*DQ*	*Pts.*	*Ave.*
1950-51	Celtics	2	—	13	3	.231	5	4	.800	2	3	8	—	10	5.0

Hertzberg also played in 160 regular-season games for New York Knicks and Washington, 1946-47 through 1948-49.

Jack Hewson

No. 17
Born: September 7, 1924

College: Temple '48
Height: 6-6 Weight: 195

Regular Season

Season	*Team*	*G.*	*FGA*	*FGM*	*Pct.*	*FTA*	*FTM*	*Pct.*	*Ast.*	*PF*	*Pts.*	*Ave.*
1947-48	Celtics	24	89	22	.247	30	21	.700	1	39	65	2.7

Mel Hirsch

No. 3
Born: July 31, 1921

College: Brooklyn '43
Height: 5-6 Weight: 165

Regular Season

Season	*Team*	*G.*	*FGA*	*FGM*	*Pct.*	*FTA*	*FTM*	*Pct.*	*Ast.*	*PF*	*Pts.*	*Ave.*
1946-47	Celtics	13	45	9	.200	2	1	.500	10	18	19	1.5

Chuck Hoefer

No. 3
Born: July 12, 1922

College: Hofstra
Height: 5-9 Weight: 158

Regular Season

Season	*Team*	*G.*	*FGA*	*FGM*	*Pct.*	*FTA*	*FTM*	*Pct.*	*Ast.*	*PF*	*Pts.*	*Ave.*
1946-47	Tor-Bos	58*	514	130	.253	139	91	.655	33	142	351	6.1
1947-48	Celtics	7	19	3	.158	8	4	.500	3	17	10	1.4
Totals		65	533	133	.250	147	95	.646	36	159	361	5.6

*35 games Boston, 23 Toronto.

Bob Houbregs

No. —
Born: March 12, 1932

College: Washington '53
Height: 6-8 Weight: 225

Regular Season

Season	*Team*	*G.*	*Min.*	*FGA*	*FGM*	*Pct.*	*FTA*	*FTM*	*Pct.*	*Reb.*	*Ast.*	*PF*	*DQ*	*Pts.*	*Ave.*
1954-55	Bal-Bos-Ft. Wayne	64*	1326	386	148	.383	182	129	.709	297	86	180	5	425	6.6

*Includes 2 games Boston.

Bailey Howell

No. 18
Born: January 20, 1937

College: Mississippi State '59
Height: 6-7 Weight: 220

Regular Season

Season	Team	G.	Min.	FGA	FGM	Pct.	FTA	FTM	Pct.	Reb.	Ast.	PF	DQ	Pts.	Ave.
1966-67	Celtics	81	2503	1242	636	.512	471	349	.741	677	103	296	4	1621	20.0
1967-68	Celtics	82	2801	1336	643	.481	461	335	.727	805	133	285	4	1621	19.8
1968-69	Celtics	78	2527	1257	612	.487	426	313	.735	685	137	285	3	1537	19.7
1969-70	Celtics	82	2078	931	399	.429	308	235	.763	550	120	261	4	1033	12.6
Totals		323	9909	4766	2290	.480	1666	1232	.739	2717	493	1127	15	5812	18.0

Playoffs

Season	Team	G.	Min.	FGA	FGM	Pct.	FTA	FTM	Pct.	Reb.	Ast.	PF	DQ	Pts.	Ave.
1966-67	Celtics	9	241	122	59	.484	30	20	.667	66	5	35	2	138	15.3
1967-68	Celtics	19	597	264	135	.511	107	74	.692	146	22	84	6	344	18.1
1968-69	Celtics	18	551	229	112	.489	64	46	.719	118	19	84	3	270	15.0
Totals		46	1389	615	306	.498	201	140	.697	330	46	203	11	752	16.3

Howell also played in 546 regular-season games for Detroit and Baltimore, 1959-60 through 1965-66, and in 82 with Philadelphia, 1970-71.

Tracy Jackson

No. 11
Born: April 21, 1959

College: Notre Dame '81
Height: 6-6 Weight: 215

Regular Season

Season	Team	G.	Min.	FGA	FGM	Pct.	FTA	FTM	Pct.	—Rebounds— Off.	Def.	Tot.	Ast.	PF	DQ	Stl.	Blk.	Pts.	Ave.
1981-82	Celtics	11	66	26*	10	.385	10	6	.600	7	5	12	5	5	0	3	0	26	2.4

*Jackson attempted no 3-point field goals.

John Janisch

No. 17
Born: March 15, 1920

College: Valparaiso '46
Height: 6-3 Weight: 200

Regular Season

Season	Team	G.	FGA	FGM	Pct.	FTA	FTM	Pct.	Ast.	PF	Pts.	Ave.
1947-48	Bos-Pro	10*	50	14	.280	16	9	.563	2	5	37	3.7

*3 games Boston, 7 Providence.

Janisch also played in 60 regular-season games for Detroit, 1946-47.

Rich Johnson

No. 26
Born: December 18, 1946

College: Grambling '68
Height: 6-9 Weight: 210

Regular Season

Season	Team	G.	Min.	FGA	FGM	Pct.	FTA	FTM	Pct.	Reb.	Ast.	PF	DQ	Pts.	Ave.
1968-69	Celtics	31	163	76	29	.382	23	11	.478	52	7	40	0	69	2.2
1969-70	Celtics	65	898	361	167	.463	70	46	.657	208	32	155	3	380	5.8
1970-71	Celtics	1	13	5	4	.800	0	0	.000	5	0	3	0	8	8.0
Totals		97	1074	442	200	.452	93	57	.613	265	39	198	3	457	4.7

Playoffs

Season	Team	G.	Min.	FGA	FGM	Pct.	FTA	FTM	Pct.	Reb.	Ast.	PF	DQ	Pts.	Ave.
1968-69	Celtics	2	4	1	1	1.000	0	0	.000	2	0	0	0	2	1.0

Johnny Jones

No. 27
Born: March 12, 1943

College: Los Angeles State '67
Height: 6-7 Weight: 210

Regular Season

Season	Team	G.	Min.	FGA	FGM	Pct.	FTA	FTM	Pct.	Reb.	Ast.	PF	DQ	Pts.	Ave.
1967-68	Celtics	51	475	253	86	.340	68	42	.618	114	26	60	0	214	4.2

Playoffs

Season	Team	G.	Min.	FGA	FGM	Pct.	FTA	FTM	Pct.	Reb.	Ast.	PF	DQ	Pts.	Ave.
1967-68	Celtics	5	10	6	3	.500	0	0	.000	4	0	2	0	6	1.2

K.C. Jones

Nos. 25 & 27
Born: May 25, 1932

College: San Francisco '56
Height: 6-1 Weight: 200

Regular Season

Season	Team	G.	Min.	FGA	FGM	Pct.	FTA	FTM	Pct.	Reb.	Ast.	PF	DQ	Pts.	Ave.
1958-59	Celtics	49	609	192	65	.339	68	41	.603	127	70	58	0	171	3.5
1959-60	Celtics	74	1274	414	169	.408	170	128	.752	199	189	109	1	466	6.3
1960-61	Celtics	78	1607	601	203	.337	320	186	.581	279	253	200	3	592	7.6
1961-62	Celtics	79	2023	707	289	.409	231	145	.628	291	339	204	2	723	9.1
1962-63	Celtics	79	1945	591	230	.389	177	112	.633	263	317	221	3	572	7.2
1963-64	Celtics	80	2424	722	283	.392	168	88	.524	372	407	253	0	654	8.2
1964-65	Celtics	78	2434	639	253	.396	227	143	.630	318	437	263	5	649	8.3
1965-66	Celtics	80	2710	619	240	.388	303	209	.690	304	503	243	4	689	8.6
1966-67	Celtics	78	2446	459	182	.397	189	119	.630	239	389	273	7	483	6.2
Totals		675	17,472	4944	1914	.387	1853	1171	.632	2392	2904	1824	25	4999	7.4

Playoffs

Season	Team	G.	Min.	FGA	FGM	Pct.	FTA	FTM	Pct.	Reb.	Ast.	PF	DQ	Pts.	Ave.
1958-59	Celtics	8	75	20	5	.250	5	5	1.000	12	10	8	0	15	1.9
1959-60	Celtics	13	232	80	27	.337	22	17	.773	45	14	28	0	71	5.5
1960-61	Celtics	9	103	30	9	.300	14	7	.500	19	15	17	0	25	2.8
1961-62	Celtics	14	329	102	44	.431	53	38	.717	56	55	50	1	126	9.0
1962-63	Celtics	13	250	64	19	.297	30	21	.700	36	37	42	1	59	4.5
1963-64	Celtics	10	312	72	25	.347	25	13	.520	37	68	40	0	63	6.3
1964-65	Celtics	12	396	104	43	.413	45	35	.778	39	74	49	1	121	10.1
1965-66	Celtics	17	543	109	45	.413	57	39	.684	52	75	65	0	129	7.6
1966-67	Celtics	9	254	75	24	.320	18	11	.611	24	48	36	1	59	6.6
Totals		105	2494	656	241	.367	269	186	.691	320	396	335	4	668	6.4

K. C. Jones (left) and John Havlicek tasted pro football before joining the Celtics, both playing in NFL preseason games — K. C. as a defensive back for the Los Angeles Rams, Hondo as a wide receiver for the Cleveland Browns.

Sam Jones

No. 24
Born: June 24, 1933

College: North Carolina College '57
Height: 6-4 Weight: 205

Regular Season

Season	Team	G.	Min.	FGA	FGM	Pct.	FTA	FTM	Pct.	Reb.	Ast.	PF	DQ	Pts.	Ave.
1957-58	Celtics	56	594	233	100	.429	84	60	.714	160	37	42	0	260	4.6
1958-59	Celtics	71	1466	703	305	.434	196	151	.770	428	101	102	0	761	10.7
1959-60	Celtics	74	1512	782	355	.454	220	168	.764	375	125	101	1	878	11.9
1960-61	Celtics	78	2126	1062	474	.446	267	210	.786	423	209	149	1	1158	14.8
1961-62	Celtics	78	2384	1283	589	.459	297	239	.805	470	234	150	0	1417	18.2
1962-63	Celtics	76	2323	1305	621	.476	324	257	.793	396	241	162	1	1499	19.7
1963-64	Celtics	76	2389	1359	612	.450	314	249	.792	349	202	192	1	1473	19.4
1964-65	Celtics	80	2885	1818	821	.452	522	428	.820	411	223	176	0	2070	25.9
1965-66	Celtics	68	2155	1335	626	.469	407	325	.799	347	216	170	0	1577	23.2
1966-67	Celtics	72	2325	1406	638	.454	371	318	.857	338	217	191	1	1594	22.1
1967-68	Celtics	73	2408	1348	621	.461	376	311	.827	357	216	181	0	1553	21.3
1968-69	Celtics	70	1820	1103	496	.450	189	148	.783	265	182	121	0	1140	16.3
Totals		872	24,387	13,737	6258	.456	3567	2864	.803	4319	2203	1737	5	15,380	17.6

Playoffs

Season	Team	G.	Min.	FGA	FGM	Pct.	FTA	FTM	Pct.	Reb.	Ast.	PF	DQ	Pts.	Ave.
1957-58	Celtics	8	75	22	10	.455	16	11	.688	24	4	7	0	31	3.9
1958-59	Celtics	11	192	108	40	.370	39	33	.846	63	17	14	0	113	10.3
1959-60	Celtics	13	197	117	45	.385	21	17	.809	41	18	17	0	107	8.2
1960-61	Celtics	10	258	112	50	.446	35	31	.886	54	22	24	0	131	13.1
1961-62	Celtics	14	504	277	123	.444	60	42	.700	101	44	30	0	288	20.6
1962-63	Celtics	13	450	248	120	.484	83	69	.831	81	32	42	1	309	23.8
1963-64	Celtics	10	356	181	91	.503	68	50	.735	47	23	24	0	232	23.2
1964-65	Celtics	12	495	294	135	.459	84	73	.869	55	30	39	1	343	28.6
1965-66	Celtics	17	602	343	154	.449	136	114	.838	86	53	65	1	422	24.8
1966-67	Celtics	9	326	207	95	.459	58	50	.862	46	28	30	1	240	26.7
1967-68	Celtics	19	685	367	162	.441	84	66	.786	64	50	58	0	390	20.5
1968-69	Celtics	18	514	296	124	.419	69	55	.797	58	37	45	1	303	16.8
Totals		154	4654	2572	1149	.447	753	611	.811	720	358	395	5	2909	18.9

Jeff Judkins

No. 32
Born: March 23, 1956

College: Utah '78
Height: 6-6 Weight: 185

Regular Season

										—Rebounds—									
Season	Team	G.	Min.	FGA	FGM	Pct.	FTA	FTM	Pct.	Off.	Def.	Tot.	Ast.	PF	DQ	Stl.	Blk.	Pts.	Ave.
1978-79	Celtics	81	1521	587	295	.503	146	119	.815	70	121	191	145	184	1	81	12	709	8.8
1979-80	Celtics	65	674	276*	139	.504	76	62	.816	32	34	66	47	91	0	29	5	351	5.4
Totals		146	2195	863	434	.503	222	181	.816	102	155	257	192	275	1	110	17	1060	7.3

*Converted 11 of 27 (.407) 3-point field-goal attempts.

Playoffs

										—Rebounds—									
Season	Team	G.	Min.	FGA	FGM	Pct.	FTA	FTM	Pct.	Off.	Def.	Tot.	Ast.	PF	DQ	Stl.	Blk.	Pts.	Ave.
1979-80	Celtics	7	10	8*	4	.500	0	0	.000	3	1	4	0	0	0	1	0	9	1.3

*Converted 1 of 3 (.333) 3-point field-goal attempts.

Judkins also played in 92 regular-season games for Utah and Detroit, 1980-81 through 1981-82.

George Kaftan

No. 9
Born: February 22, 1928

College: Holy Cross '49
Height: 6-3 Weight: 190

Regular Season

Season	Team	G.	FGA	FGM	Pct.	FTA	FTM	Pct.	Ast.	PF	Pts.	Ave.
1948-49	Celtics	21	315	116	.368	115	72	.626	61	28	304	14.5
1949-50	Celtics	55	535	199	.372	208	136	.654	145	92	534	9.7
Totals		76	850	315	.371	323	208	.644	206	120	838	11.0

Kaftan also played in 136 games for New York Knicks and Baltimore, 1950-51 through 1952-53.

Tony Kappen

No. 5
Born: April 13, 1919

College: Did not attend college
Height: 5-10 Weight: 165

Regular Season

Season	Team	G.	FGA	FGM	Pct.	FTA	FTM	Pct.	Ast.	PF	Pts.	Ave.
1946-47	Pitt-Bos	59*	537	128	.238	161	128	.795	28	78	384	6.5

*18 games Boston, 41 Pittsburgh.

Gerard (Jerry) Kelly

Nos. 14 & 24
Born: 1922

College: Marshall
Height: 6-2 Weight: 180

Regular Season

Season	Team	G.	FGA	FGM	Pct.	FTA	FTM	Pct.	Ast.	PF	Pts.	Ave.
1946-47	Celtics	43	313	91	.291	111	74	.667	21	128	256	6.0

Kelly also played in 3 regular-season games for Providence, 1947-48.

Tom Kelly

No. 6
Born: March 5, 1924

College: New York University '48
Height: 6-2 Weight: 172

Regular Season

Season	Team	G.	FGA	FGM	Pct.	FTA	FTM	Pct.	Ast.	PF	Pts.	Ave.
1948-49	Celtics	27	218	73	.335	73	45	.616	38	73	191	7.1

Thomas (Toby) Kimball

No. 26
Born: September 23, 1942

College: Connecticut '65
Height: 6-8 Weight: 220

Regular Season

Season	Team	G.	Min.	FGA	FGM	Pct.	FTA	FTM	Pct.	Reb.	Ast.	PF	DQ	Pts.	Ave.
1966-67	Celtics	38	222	97	36	.361	40	27	.675	146	13	42	0	97	2.6

Playoffs

Season	Team	G.	Min.	FGA	FGM	Pct.	FTA	FTM	Pct.	Reb.	Ast.	PF	DQ	Pts.	Ave.
1966-67	Celtics	1	4	2	0	.000	0	0	.000	3	0	1	0	0	0.0

Kimball also played in 533 regular-season games for San Diego, Milwaukee, Kansas City-Omaha, Philadelphia and New Orleans, 1967-68 through 1974-75.

Maurice King

No. 19
Born: March 12, 1935

College: Kansas '57
Height: 6-3 Weight: 195

Regular Season

Season	Team	G.	Min.	FGA	FGM	Pct.	FTA	FTM	Pct.	Reb.	Ast.	PF	DQ	Pts.	Ave.
1959-60	Celtics	1	19	8	5	.625	1	0	.000	4	2	3	0	10	10.0

King also played in 37 regular-season games for Chicago, 1962-63.

Bob Kinney

No. 22
Born: September 16, 1920

College: Rice '42
Height: 6-6 Weight: 205

Regular Season

Season	Team	G.	FGA	FGM	Pct.	FTA	FTM	Pct.	Ast.	PF	Pts.	Ave.
1948-49	FtW-Bos	58*	495	161	.325	234	136	.581	77	224	458	7.9
1949-50	Celtics	60	621	233	.375	320	201	.628	100	251	667	11.1
Totals		118	1116	394	.353	554	337	.608	177	475	1125	9.5

*21 games Boston, 37 Fort Wayne.

Billy Knight

No. 35
Born: June 9, 1952

College: Pittsburgh '74
Height: 6-6 Weight: 195

Regular Season

Season	*Team*	*G.*	*Min.*	*FGA*	*FGM*	*Pct.*	*FTA*	*FTM*	*Pct.*	*Reb.*	*Ast.*	*PF*	*DQ*	*Pts.*	*Ave.*
1978-79*	Celtics	40	1119	436	219	.502	146	118	.808	173	66	86	1	556	13.9

*Played in 39 regular-season games for Indiana later that season.

Knight also played in 131 regular-season games for Indiana and Buffalo, 1976-77 through 1977-78, and in 238 more for Indiana, 1979-80 through 1981-82.

Harold Kottman

No. 9
Born: August 22, 1922

College: Culver-Stockton '46
Height: 6-8 Weight: 220

Regular Season

Season	*Team*	*G.*	*FGA*	*FGM*	*Pct.*	*FTA*	*FTM*	*Pct.*	*Ast.*	*PF*	*Pts.*	*Ave.*
1946-47	Celtics	53	188	59	.314	101	47	.465	17	58	165	3.1

Wayne Kreklow

No. 20
Born: January 4, 1957

College: Drake '79
Height: 6-4 Weight: 182

Regular Season

										—Rebounds—									
Season	*Team*	*G.*	*Min.*	*FGA*	*FGM*	*Pct.*	*FTA*	*FTM*	*Pct.*	*Off.*	*Def.*	*Tot.*	*Ast.*	*PF*	*DQ*	*Stl.*	*Blk.*	*Pts.*	*Ave.*
1980-81	Celtics	25	100	47*	11	.234	10	7	.700	2	10	12	9	20	0	2	1	30	1.2

*Converted 1 of 4 (.250) 3-point field-goal attempts.

Steve Kuberski

Nos. 11 & 33
Born: November 6, 1947

College: Bradley '69
Height: 6-8 Weight: 215

Regular Season

Season	*Team*	*G.*	*Min.*	*FGA*	*FGM*	*Pct.*	*FTA*	*FTM*	*Pct.*	*Reb.*	*Ast.*	*PF*	*DQ*	*Pts.*	*Ave.*
1969-70	Celtics	51	797	335	130	.388	92	64	.696	257	29	87	0	324	6.4
1970-71	Celtics	82	1867	745	313	.420	183	133	.727	538	78	198	1	759	9.3
1971-72	Celtics	71	1128	444	185	.417	102	80	.784	320	46	130	1	450	6.3
1972-73	Celtics	78	762	347	140	.403	84	65	.774	197	26	92	0	345	4.4

										—Rebounds—									
Season	*Team*	*G.*	*Min.*	*FGA*	*FGM*	*Pct.*	*FTA*	*FTM*	*Pct.*	*Off.*	*Def.*	*Tot.*	*Ast.*	*PF*	*DQ*	*Stl.*	*Blk.*	*Pts.*	*Ave.*
1973-74	Celtics	78	985	368	157	.427	111	86	.775	96	141	237	38	125	0	7	7	400	5.1
1975-76*	Celtics	60	882	274	128	.467	76	68	.895	86	148	234	44	123	1	11	11	324	5.4
1976-77	Celtics	76	860	312	131	.420	83	63	.759	76	133	209	39	89	0	7	5	325	4.3
1977-78	Celtics	3	14	4	1	.250	0	0	.000	1	5	6	0	2	0	1	0	2	0.7
Totals		499	7295	2829	1185	.419	731	559	.765	—	—	1998	300	846	3	—	—	2929	5.9

*Played in 10 games for Buffalo earlier that season.

Kuberski also played in 59 regular-season games for Milwaukee, 1974-75.

Playoffs

Season	*Team*	*G.*	*Min.*	*FGA*	*FGM*	*Pct.*	*FTA*	*FTM*	*Pct.*	*Reb.*	*Ast.*	*PF*	*DQ*	*Pts.*	*Ave.*
1971-72	Celtics	11	218	87	48	.552	38	32	.842	63	3	23	0	128	11.6
1972-73	Celtics	12	95	46	19	.413	10	7	.700	14	3	15	0	45	3.8

										—Rebounds—									
Season	*Team*	*G.*	*Min.*	*FGA*	*FGM*	*Pct.*	*FTA*	*FTM*	*Pct.*	*Off.*	*Def.*	*Tot.*	*Ast.*	*PF*	*DQ*	*Stl.*	*Blk.*	*Pts.*	*Ave.*
1973-74	Celtics	9	69	25	5	.200	10	5	.500	8	12	20	2	9	0	1	1	15	1.7
1975-76	Celtics	18	232	81	38	.469	26	21	.808	16	35	51	16	38	0	0	3	97	5.4
Totals		50	614	239	110	.460	84	65	.774	—	—	148	24	85	0	1	4	285	5.7

Frank (Apples) Kudelka

No. 21
Born: 1925

College: St. Mary's (Calif.)
Height: 6-2 Weight: 193

Regular Season

Season	Team	G.	Min.	FGA	FGM	Pct.	FTA	FTM	Pct.	Reb.	Ast.	PF	DQ	Pts.	Ave.
1950-51	Wash-Bos	62*	—	518	179	.346	119	83	.697	158	105	211	8	441	7.1

*35 games Washington, 27 Boston.

Playoffs

Season	Team	G.	Min.	FGA	FGM	Pct.	FTA	FTM	Pct.	Reb.	Ast.	PF	DQ	Pts.	Ave.
1950-51	Celtics	1	—	4	2	.500	3	0	.000	5	2	3	0	4	4.0

Kudelka also played in 65 regular-season games for Chicago, 1949-50, and in 101 for Baltimore and Philadelphia, 1951-52 through 1952-53.

Tony Lavelli

Nos. 4 & 11
Born: July 11, 1926

College: Yale '49
Height: 6-3 Weight: 185

Regular Season

Season	Team	G.	FGA	FGM	Pct.	FTA	FTM	Pct.	Ast.	PF	Pts.	Ave.
1949-50	Celtics	56	436	162	.372	197	168	.853	40	107	492	8.8

Lavelli also played in 30 regular-season games for New York Knicks, 1950-51.

Ed Leede

No. 5
Born: July 17, 1927

College: Dartmouth '48
Height: 6-3 Weight: 185

Regular Season

Season	Team	G.	Min.	FGA	FGM	Pct.	FTA	FTM	Pct.	Reb.	Ast.	PF	DQ	Pts.	Ave.
1949-50	Celtics	64	—	507	174	.343	316	223	.706	—	130	167	—	571	8.9
1950-51	Celtics	57	—	370	119	.322	189	140	.741	118	95	144	3	378	6.6
Totals		121	—	877	293	.335	505	363	.719	—	225	311	3	949	7.8

Playoffs

Season	Team	G.	Min.	FGA	FGM	Pct.	FTA	FTM	Pct.	Reb.	Ast.	PF	DQ	Pts.	Ave.
1950-51	Celtics	2	—	7	1	.143	1	1	1.000	0	2	3	—	3	1.5

Jim Loscutoff

No. 18
Born: February 4, 1930

College: Oregon '55
Height: 6-5 Weight: 230

Regular Season

Season	Team	G.	Min.	FGA	FGM	Pct.	FTA	FTM	Pct.	Reb.	Ast.	PF	DQ	Pts.	Ave.
1955-56	Celtics	71	1582	628	226	.360	207	139	.671	622	65	213	4	591	8.3
1956-57	Celtics	70	2220	888	306	.345	187	132	.706	730	89	244	5	744	10.6
1957-58	Celtics	5	56	31	11	.355	3	1	.333	20	1	8	0	23	4.6
1958-59	Celtics	66	1680	686	242	.353	84	62	.738	420	60	285	15	546	8.3
1959-60	Celtics	28	536	205	66	.322	36	22	.611	108	12	108	6	154	5.5
1960-61	Celtics	76	1180	497	154	.310	79	50	.633	295	29	240	4	358	4.7
1961-62	Celtics	79	1046	519	188	.362	84	45	.536	329	51	185	3	421	5.3
1962-63	Celtics	64	607	251	94	.375	42	22	.524	157	25	126	1	210	3.3
1963-64	Celtics	53	451	182	56	.308	31	18	.581	131	25	90	1	130	2.5
Totals		512	9358	3887	1343	.346	753	491	.652	2812	357	1499	39	3177	6.2

Playoffs

Season	Team	G.	Min.	FGA	FGM	Pct.	FTA	FTM	Pct.	Reb.	Ast.	PF	DQ	Pts.	Ave.
1955-56	Celtics	3	89	31	11	.355	9	7	.778	26	4	8	0	29	9.7
1956-57	Celtics	10	259	109	31	.284	28	18	.643	83	5	46	2	80	8.0
1958-59	Celtics	11	260	113	39	.345	21	11	.524	73	13	49	1	89	8.1
1960-61	Celtics	10	116	54	15	.278	9	7	.778	35	3	34	0	37	3.7
1961-62	Celtics	14	212	86	31	.360	10	4	.400	59	6	59	5	66	4.1
1962-63	Celtics	9	56	25	7	.280	2	1	.500	21	1	20	0	15	1.7
1963-64	Celtics	1	5	2	2	1.000	0	0	.000	2	0	3	0	4	4.0
Totals		58	997	420	136	.324	79	48	.608	299	32	219	8	320	5.5

Clyde Lovellette

Nos. 4 & 34
Born: September 7, 1929

College: Kansas '52
Height: 6-9 Weight: 235

Regular Season

Season	Team	G.	Min.	FGA	FGM	Pct.	FTA	FTM	Pct.	Reb.	Ast.	PF	DQ	Pts.	Ave.
1962-63	Celtics	61	568	366	161	.440	98	73	.745	177	29	137	0	395	6.5
1963-64	Celtics	45	437	305	128	.420	57	45	.789	126	24	100	0	301	6.7
Totals		106	1005	671	289	.431	155	118	.761	303	53	237	0	696	6.6

Playoffs

Season	Team	G.	Min.	FGA	FGM	Pct.	FTA	FTM	Pct.	Reb.	Ast.	PF	DQ	Pts.	Ave.
1962-63	Celtics	6	40	26	7	.269	6	4	.667	5	1	13	0	18	3.0
1963-64	Celtics	5	40	34	8	.235	4	4	1.000	7	2	8	0	20	4.0
Totals		11	80	60	15	.250	10	8	.800	12	3	21	0	38	3.5

Lovellette also played in 598 regular-season games for Minneapolis, Cincinnati and St. Louis, 1953-54 through 1961-62. 70

Al Lucas

No. 20
Born: July 4, 1922

College: Fordham
Height: 6-3 Weight: 195

Regular Season

Season	Team	G.	FGA	FGM	Pct.	FTA	FTM	Pct.	Ast.	PF	Pts.	Ave.
1948-49	Celtics	2	3	1	.333	0	0	.000	2	0	2	1.0

Ed (Easy Ed) Macauley

No. 22
Born: March 22, 1928

College: St. Louis '49
Height: 6-8 Weight: 190

Regular Season

Season	Team	G.	Min.	FGA	FGM	Pct.	FTA	FTM	Pct.	Reb.	Ast.	PF	DQ	Pts.	Ave.
1950-51	Celtics	68	—	985	459	.466	614	466	.759	616	252	205	4	1384	20.4
1951-52	Celtics	66	2631	888	384	.432	621	496	.799	529	292	174	0	1264	19.2
1952-53	Celtics	69	2902	997	451	.452	667	500	.750	629	280	188	0	1402	20.3
1953-54	Celtics	71	2792	950	462	.486	554	420	.758	571	271	168	1	1344	18.9
1954-55	Celtics	71	2706	951	403	.424	558	442	.792	600	275	171	0	1248	17.6
1955-56	Celtics	71	2354	995	420	.422	504	400	.794	422	211	158	2	1240	17.5
Totals		416	—	5766	2579	.447	3518	2724	.774	3367	1581	1064	7	7882	18.9

Playoffs

Season	Team	G.	Min.	FGA	FGM	Pct.	FTA	FTM	Pct.	Reb.	Ast.	PF	DQ	Pts.	Ave.
1950-51	Celtics	2	—	36	17	.472	16	10	.625	18	8	4	0	44	22.0
1951-52	Celtics	3	129	49	27	.551	19	16	.842	33	11	11	1	70	23.3
1952-53	Celtics	6	278	71	31	.437	54	39	.722	58	21	23	2	101	16.8
1953-54	Celtics	5	127	22	8	.364	13	9	.692	21	21	14	0	25	5.0
1954-55	Celtics	7	283	93	43	.462	54	41	.759	52	32	21	0	127	18.1
1955-56	Celtics	3	73	30	12	.400	11	7	.636	15	5	6	0	31	10.3
Totals		26	—	301	138	.458	167	122	.731	197	98	79	3	398	15.0

Macauley also played in 67 regular-season games for St. Louis Bombers, 1949-50, and in 158 for St. Louis Hawks, 1956-57 through 1958-59.

John Mahnken

No. 16
Born: June 16, 1922

College: Georgetown '45
Height: 6-8 Weight: 220

Regular Season

Season	*Team*	*G.*	*Min.*	*FGA*	*FGM*	*Pct.*	*FTA*	*FTM*	*Pct.*	*Reb.*	*Ast.*	*PF*	*DQ*	*Pts.*	*Ave.*
1949-50	FtW-TriC-Boston	62*	—	495	132	.267	115	77	.658	—	108	231	—	341	5.5
1950-51	Bos-Ind	58**	—	351	111	.316	70	45	.643	219	77	164	6	267	4.6
1951-52	Celtics	60	581	227	78	.344	43	26	.605	132	63	91	2	182	3.0
1952-53	Celtics	69	771	252	76	.302	56	39	.696	182	75	110	1	191	2.8
Totals		249	—	1325	397	.224	284	187	.658	—	323	596	—	981	3.9

*2 games Fort Wayne, 36 Tri-Cities, 24 Boston.

**46 games Boston, 12 Indianapolis.

Playoffs

Season	*Team*	*G.*	*Min.*	*FGA*	*FGM*	*Pct.*	*FTA*	*FTM*	*Pct.*	*Reb.*	*Ast.*	*PF*	*DQ*	*Pts.*	*Ave.*
1951-52	Celtics	3	50	7	2	.286	6	3	.500	10	3	11	1	7	2.3
1952-53	Celtics	6	72	10	0	.000	5	5	1.000	19	6	16	0	5	0.8
Totals		9	122	17	2	.118	11	8	.727	29	9	27	1	12	1.3

Mahnken also played in 165 regular-season games for Washington, Baltimore, Fort Wayne and Indianapolis, 1946-47 through 1948-49.

Francis (Mo) Mahoney

No. 19
Born: November 20, 1927

College: Brown '50
Height: 6-0 Weight: 205

Regular Season

Season	*Team*	*G.*	*Min.*	*FGA*	*FGM*	*Pct.*	*FTA*	*FTM*	*Pct.*	*Reb.*	*Ast.*	*PF*	*DQ*	*Pts.*	*Ave.*
1952-53	Celtics	6	34	10	4	.400	5	4	.800	7	1	7	0	12	2.0

Playoffs

Season	*Team*	*G.*	*Min.*	*FGA*	*FGM*	*Pct.*	*FTA*	*FTM*	*Pct.*	*Reb.*	*Ast.*	*PF*	*DQ*	*Pts.*	*Ave.*
1952-53	Celtics	4	45	14	3	.214	5	3	.600	7	2	14	0	9	2.3

Mahoney also played in 2 regular-season games for Baltimore, 1953-54.

Tom Heinsohn was left for dead by both friend and foe, but what hurt him most was being called for charging.

Pete (Pistol Pete) Maravich

No. 44
Born: June 22, 1948

College: Louisiana State '70
Height: 6-5 Weight: 200

Regular Season

										—Rebounds—									
Season	*Team*	*G.*	*Min.*	*FGA*	*FGM*	*Pct.*	*FTA*	*FTM*	*Pct.*	*Off.*	*Def.*	*Tot.*	*Ast.*	*PF*	*DQ*	*Stl.*	*Blk.*	*Pts.*	*Ave.*
1979-80*	Celtics	26	442	249**	123	.494	55	50	.909	10	28	38	29	49	1	9	3	299	11.5

*Played in 17 games for Utah early in season.

**Converted 3 of 4 (.750) 3-point field-goal attempts.

Playoffs

										—Rebounds—									
Season	*Team*	*G.*	*Min.*	*FGA*	*FGM*	*Pct.*	*FTA*	*FTM*	*Pct.*	*Off.*	*Def.*	*Tot.*	*Ast.*	*PF*	*DQ*	*Stl.*	*Blk.*	*Pts.*	*Ave.*
1979-80	Celtics	9	104	51*	25	.490	3	2	.667	0	8	8	6	12	0	3	0	54	6.0

*Converted 2 of 6 (.333) 3-point field-goal attempts.

Maravich also played in 615 regular-season games for Atlanta and New Orleans, 1970-71 through 1978-79.

Saul Mariaschin

No. 4
Born: September 1, 1924

College: Harvard '47
Height: 5-11 Weight: 165

Regular Season

Season	*Team*	*G.*	*FGA*	*FGM*	*Pct.*	*FTA*	*FTM*	*Pct.*	*Ast.*	*PF*	*Pts.*	*Ave.*
1947-48	Celtics	43	463	125	.270	117	83	.709	60	121	333	7.7

Playoffs

Season	*Team*	*G.*	*FGA*	*FGM*	*Pct.*	*FTA*	*FTM*	*Pct.*	*Ast.*	*PF*	*Pts.*	*Ave.*
1947-48	Celtics	3	42	10	.238	14	9	.643	1	12	29	9.7

Cedric (Cornbread) Maxwell

Nos. 30 & 31
Born: November 21, 1955

College: North Carolina Charlotte '77
Height: 6-8 Weight: 217

Regular Season

										—Rebounds—									
Season	*Team*	*G.*	*Min.*	*FGA*	*FGM*	*Pct.*	*FTA*	*FTM*	*Pct.*	*Off.*	*Def.*	*Tot.*	*Ast.*	*PF*	*DQ*	*Stl.*	*Blk.*	*Pts.*	*Ave.*
1977-78	Celtics	72	1213	316	170	.538	250	188	.752	138	241	379	68	151	2	53	48	528	7.3
1978-79	Celtics	80	2969	808	472	.584	716	574	.802	272	519	791	228	266	4	98	74	1518	19.0
1979-80	Celtics	80	2744	750*	457	.609	554	436	.787	284	420	704	199	266	6	76	60	1350	16.9
1980-81	Celtics	81	2730	750*	441	.588	450	352	.782	222	303	525	219	256	5	79	68	1234	15.2
1981-82	Celtics	78	2590	724*	397	.548	478	357	.747	218	281	499	183	263	6	79	49	1151	14.8
Totals		391	12,246	3348	1937	.579	2448	1907	.779	1134	1764	2898	897	1202	23	385	299	5781	14.8

*Maxwell attempted no 3-point field goals in 1979-80, completed none of 1 (.000) in 1980-81 and none of 3 (.000) in 1981-82 for a total of none of 4 (.000).

Playoffs

										—Rebounds—									
Season	*Team*	*G.*	*Min.*	*FGA*	*FGM*	*Pct.*	*FTA*	*FTM*	*Pct.*	*Off.*	*Def.*	*Tot.*	*Ast.*	*PF*	*DQ*	*Stl.*	*Blk.*	*Pts.*	*Ave.*
1979-80	Celtics	9	320	93*	59	.634	61	46	.754	31	59	90	19	25	0	5	10	164	18.2
1980-81	Celtics	17	598	174*	101	.580	88	72	.818	61	64	125	46	53	0	12	16	274	16.1
1981-82	Celtics	12	385	120*	62	.517	70	50	.714	37	50	87	26	40	0	18	11	174	14.5
Totals		38	1303	387	222	.574	219	168	.767	129	173	302	91	118	0	35	37	612	16.1

*Maxwell has attempted no 3-point field goals during the playoffs.

Bob McAdoo

No. 11
Born: September 25, 1951

College: North Carolina '73
Height: 6-9 Weight: 210

Regular Season

										—Rebounds—									
Season	*Team*	*G.*	*Min.*	*FGA*	*FGM*	*Pct.*	*FTA*	*FTM*	*Pct.*	*Off.*	*Def.*	*Tot.*	*Ast.*	*PF*	*DQ*	*Stl.*	*Blk.*	*Pts.*	*Ave.*
1978-79*	Celtics	20	637	334	167	.500	115	77	.670	36	105	141	40	55	1	12	20	411	20.6

*Played in 40 games for New York Knicks earlier that season.

McAdoo also played in 465 regular-season games for Buffalo and New York Knicks, 1972-73 through 1977-78, and in 115 for Detroit, New Jersey and Los Angeles, 1979-80 through 1981-82.

John McCarthy

No. 21
Born: April 25, 1934

College: Canisius '56
Height: 6-1 Weight: 185

Regular Season

Season	Team	G.	Min.	FGA	FGM	Pct.	FTA	FTM	Pct.	Reb.	Ast.	PF	DQ	Pts.	Ave.
1963-64	Celtics	28	206	48	16	.333	13	5	.385	35	24	42	0	37	1.3

Playoffs

Season	Team	G.	Min.	FGA	FGM	Pct.	FTA	FTM	Pct.	Reb.	Ast.	PF	DQ	Pts.	Ave.
1963-64	Celtics	1	8	1	1	1.000	0	0	.000	1	1	0	0	2	2.0

McCarthy also played in 288 regular-season games for Rochester, Cincinnati and St. Louis, 1956-57 through 1961-62.

Glenn McDonald

No. 30
Born: March 18, 1952

College: Long Beach State '74
Height: 6-6 Weight: 198

Regular Season

										—Rebounds—									
Season	Team	G.	Min.	FGA	FGM	Pct.	FTA	FTM	Pct.	Off.	Def.	Tot.	Ast.	PF	DQ	Stl.	Blk.	Pts.	Ave.
1974-75	Celtics	62	395	182	70	.385	37	28	.757	20	48	68	24	58	0	8	5	168	2.7
1975-76	Celtics	75	1019	456	191	.419	56	40	.714	56	79	135	68	123	0	39	20	422	5.6
Totals		137	1414	638	261	.409	93	68	.731	76	127	203	92	181	0	47	25	590	4.3

Playoffs

										—Rebounds—									
Season	Team	G.	Min.	FGA	FGM	Pct.	FTA	FTM	Pct.	Off.	Def.	Tot.	Ast.	PF	DQ	Stl.	Blk.	Pts.	Ave.
1974-75	Celtics	6	30	12	2	.167	3	1	.333	1	5	6	2	4	0	1	0	5	0.8
1975-76	Celtics	13	68	26	8	.308	6	5	.833	1	7	8	4	12	0	1	0	21	1.6
Totals		19	98	38	10	.263	9	6	.667	2	12	14	6	16	0	2	0	26	1.4

McDonald also played in 9 regular-season games for Milwaukee, 1976-77.

Kevin McHale

No. 32
Born: December 19, 1957

College: Minnesota '80
Height: 6-10 Weight: 230

Regular Season

										—Rebounds—									
Season	Team	G.	Min.	FGA	FGM	Pct.	FTA	FTM	Pct.	Off.	Def.	Tot.	Ast.	PF	DQ	Stl.	Blk.	Pts.	Ave.
1980-81	Celtics	82	1645	666*	355	.533	159	108	.679	155	204	359	55	260	3	27	151	818	10.0
1981-82	Celtics	82	2332	875*	465	.531	248	187	.754	191	365	556	91	264	1	30	185	1117	13.6
Totals		164	3977	1541	820	.532	407	295	.725	346	569	915	146	524	4	57	336	1935	11.8

*Converted none of 2 (.000) 3-point field-goal attempts in 1980-81, attempted none in 1981-82 for a total of none of 2 (.000).

Playoffs

										—Rebounds—									
Season	Team	G.	Min.	FGA	FGM	Pct.	FTA	FTM	Pct.	Off.	Def.	Tot.	Ast.	PF	DQ	Stl.	Blk.	Pts.	Ave.
1980-81	Celtics	17	296	113*	61	.540	36	23	.639	29	30	59	14	51	1	4	24	145	8.5
1981-82	Celtics	12	344	134*	77	.575	53	40	.755	41	44	85	11	44	0	5	27	194	16.2
Totals		29	640	247	138	.559	89	63	.708	70	74	144	25	95	1	9	51	339	11.7

*McHale has attempted no 3-point field goals during the playoffs.

Horace (Bones) McKinney

No. 17
Born: January 1, 1919

College: North Carolina '46
Height: 6-6 Weight: 187

Regular Season

Season	Team	G.	Min.	FGA	FGM	Pct.	FTA	FTM	Pct.	Reb.	Ast.	PF	DQ	Pts.	Ave.
1950-51	Wash-Bos	44*	—	327	102	.312	81	58	.716	198	85	136	6	262	6.0
1951-52	Celtics	63	1083	418	136	.325	80	65	.813	175	111	148	4	337	5.3
Totals		107	—	745	238	.319	161	123	.764	373	196	284	10	599	5.6

*10 games Washington, 34 Boston.

Playoffs

Season	Team	G.	Min.	FGA	FGM	Pct.	FTA	FTM	Pct.	Reb.	Ast.	PF	DQ	Pts.	Ave.
1950-51	Celtics	2	—	25	11	.440	5	4	.800	10	8	9	0	26	13.0
1951-52	Celtics	3	20	9	2	.222	0	0	.000	6	2	9	0	4	1.3
Totals		5	—	34	13	.382	5	4	.800	16	10	18	0	30	6.0

McKinney also played in 211 regular-season games for Washington, 1946-47 through 1949-50.

Dick Mehen

No. 13
Born: May 20, 1922

College: Tennessee '47
Height: 6-6 Weight: 195

Regular Season

Season	Team	G.	Min.	FGA	FGM	Pct.	FTA	FTM	Pct.	Reb.	Ast.	PF	DQ	Pts.	Ave.
1950-51	Bal-Bos-Ft. Wayne	66*	—	532	192	.361	123	90	.532	223	188	149	4	474	7.2

*Including 6 games Boston.

Mehen also played in 62 regular-season games for Waterloo, 1949-50, and in 65 for Milwaukee, 1951-52.

Ed Mikan

No. 16
Born: October 20, 1925

College: DePaul '48
Height: 6-8 Weight: 230

Regular Season

Season	Team	G.	Min.	FGA	FGM	Pct.	FTA	FTM	Pct.	Reb.	Ast.	PF	DQ	Pts.	Ave.
1953-54	Celtics	9	71	24	8	.333	9	5	.556	20	3	15	0	21	2.3

Mikan also played in 314 regular-season games for Chicago, Rochester, Washington, Philadelphia and Indianapolis, 1948-49 through 1952-53.

Young Bill Russell indulges in his electric trains hobby in the basement of his Greater Boston home.

Mark Minor

No. 27 — College: Ohio State '72
Born: May 14, 1950 — Height: 6-5 Weight: 210

Regular Season

Season	Team	G.	Min.	FGA	FGM	Pct.	FTA	FTM	Pct.	Reb.	Ast.	PF	DQ	Pts.	Ave.
1972-73	Celtics	4	20	4	1	.250	4	3	.750	4	2	5	0	5	1.3

Rex Morgan

No. 20 — College: Jacksonville '70
Born: October 27, 1948 — Height: 6-5 Weight: 190

Regular Season

Season	Team	G.	Min.	FGA	FGM	Pct.	FTA	FTM	Pct.	Reb.	Ast.	PF	DQ	Pts.	Ave.
1970-71	Celtics	34	266	102	41	.402	54	35	.648	61	22	58	2	117	3.4
1971-72	Celtics	28	150	50	16	.320	31	23	.742	30	17	34	0	55	2.0
Totals		62	416	152	57	.375	85	58	.682	91	39	92	2	172	2.8

Playoffs

Season	Team	G.	Min.	FGA	FGM	Pct.	FTA	FTM	Pct.	Reb.	Ast.	PF	DQ	Pts.	Ave.
1971-72	Celtics	4	10	7	1	.143	3	1	.333	6	0	6	0	3	0.8

Dwight (Red) Morrison

No. 15 — College: Idaho '54
Born: 1931 — Height: 6-8 Weight: 220

Regular Season

Season	Team	G.	Min.	FGA	FGM	Pct.	FTA	FTM	Pct.	Reb.	Ast.	PF	DQ	Pts.	Ave.
1954-55	Celtics	71	1227	284	120	.423	115	72	.626	451	82	222	10	312	4.4
1955-56	Celtics	71	910	240	89	.371	89	44	.494	345	53	159	5	222	3.1
Totals		142	2137	524	209	.399	204	116	.569	796	135	381	15	534	3.8

Playoffs

Season	Team	G.	Min.	FGA	FGM	Pct.	FTA	FTM	Pct.	Reb.	Ast.	PF	DQ	Pts.	Ave.
1954-55	Celtics	7	42	8	3	.375	3	1	.333	14	1	22	1	7	1.0
1955-56	Celtics	3	23	7	2	.286	4	0	.000	11	0	5	0	4	1.3
Totals		10	65	15	5	.333	7	1	.143	25	1	27	1	11	1.1

Morrison also played in 13 regular-season games for St. Louis, 1957-58.

Joe Mullaney

No. 17 — College: Holy Cross '49
Born: November 17, 1925 — Height: 6-0 Weight: 165

Regular Season

Season	Team	G.	FGA	FGM	Pct.	FTA	FTM	Pct.	Ast.	PF	Pts.	Ave.
1949-50	Celtics	37	70	9	.129	15	12	.800	52	30	30	0.8

George Munroe

No. 6 — College: Dartmouth '43
Born: January 5, 1922 — Height: 5-11 Weight: 175

Regular Season

Season	Team	G.	FGA	FGM	Pct.	FTA	FTM	Pct.	Ast.	PF	Pts.	Ave.
1947-48	Celtics	21	91	27	.297	26	17	.654	3	20	71	3.4

Playoffs

Season	Team	G.	FGA	FGM	Pct.	FTA	FTM	Pct.	Ast.	PF	Pts.	Ave.
1947-48	Celtics	3	5	1	.200	2	2	1.000	1	2	4	1.3

Munroe also played in 59 regular-season games for St. Louis, 1946-47.

Dick Murphy

No. 5
Born: 1921

College: Manhattan
Height: 6-1 Weight: 180

Regular Season

Season	Team	G.	FGA	FGM	Pct.	FTA	FTM	Pct.	Ast.	PF	Pts.	Ave.
1946-47	NY-Bos	31*	75	15	.200	9	4	.444	8	15	34	1.1

*7 games Boston, 24 New York.

Willie Naulls

No. 12
Born: October 7, 1934

College: UCLA '56
Height: 6-6 Weight: 225

Regular Season

Season	Team	G.	Min.	FGA	FGM	Pct.	FTA	FTM	Pct.	Reb.	Ast.	PF	DQ	Pts.	Ave.
1963-64	Celtics	78	1409	769	321	.417	157	125	.796	355	65	200	0	767	9.8
1964-65	Celtics	71	1465	786	302	.384	176	143	.813	336	72	225	5	747	10.5
1965-66	Celtics	71	1433	815	328	.402	131	104	.794	319	72	197	4	760	10.7
Totals		220	4307	2370	951	.401	464	372	.802	1010	209	622	9	2274	10.3

Playoffs

Season	Team	G.	Min.	FGA	FGM	Pct.	FTA	FTM	Pct.	Reb.	Ast.	PF	DQ	Pts.	Ave.
1963-64	Celtics	10	177	95	37	.389	23	17	.739	46	8	31	1	91	9.1
1964-65	Celtics	12	180	95	39	.411	15	10	.666	51	9	27	0	88	7.3
1965-66	Celtics	11	75	35	9	.257	21	17	.810	16	1	23	0	38	3.2
Totals		33	432	225	85	.378	59	44	.746	113	18	81	1	217	6.6

Naulls also played in 496 regular-season games for St. Louis, New York Knicks and San Francisco, 1956-57 through 1962-63.

Don Nelson

No. 19
Born: May 15, 1940

College: Iowa '62
Height: 6-6 Weight: 210

Regular Season

Season	Team	G.	Min.	FGA	FGM	Pct.	FTA	FTM	Pct.	Reb.	Ast.	PF	DQ	Pts.	Ave.
1965-66	Celtics	75	1765	618	271	.439	326	223	.684	403	79	187	1	765	10.2
1966-67	Celtics	79	1202	509	227	.446	190	141	.742	295	65	143	0	595	7.5
1967-68	Celtics	82	1498	632	312	.494	268	195	.728	431	103	178	1	819	10.0
1968-69	Celtics	82	1773	771	374	.485	259	201	.776	458	92	198	2	949	11.6
1969-70	Celtics	82	2224	920	461	.501	435	337	.775	601	148	238	3	1259	15.4
1970-71	Celtics	82	2254	881	412	.468	426	317	.744	565	153	232	2	1141	13.9
1971-72	Celtics	82	2086	811	389	.480	452	356	.788	453	192	220	3	1134	13.8
1972-73	Celtics	72	1425	649	309	.476	188	159	.846	315	102	155	1	777	10.8

										—Rebounds—									
Season	Team	G.	Min.	FGA	FGM	Pct.	FTA	FTM	Pct.	Off.	Def.	Tot.	Ast.	PF	DQ	Stl.	Blk.	Pts.	Ave.
1973-74	Celtics	82	1748	717	364	.508	273	215	.788	90	255	345	162	189	1	10	13	943	11.5
1974-75	Celtics	79	2052	785	423	.539	318	263	.827	127	342	469	181	239	2	32	15	1109	14.0
1975-76	Celtics	75	943	379	175	.462	161	127	.789	56	126	182	77	115	0	14	7	477	6.4
Totals		872	18,970	7672	3717	.484	3296	2534	.769	—	—	4517	1354	2094	16	—	—	9968	11.4

Playoffs

Season	Team	G.	Min.	FGA	FGM	Pct.	FTA	FTM	Pct.	Reb.	Ast.	PF	DQ	Pts.	Ave.
1965-66	Celtics	17	316	118	50	.424	52	42	.808	85	13	50	0	142	8.4
1966-67	Celtics	9	142	59	27	.458	17	10	.588	42	9	12	0	64	7.1
1967-68	Celtics	19	468	175	91	.520	74	55	.743	143	32	49	0	237	12.5
1968-69	Celtics	18	348	168	87	.518	60	50	.833	83	21	51	0	224	12.4
1971-72	Celtics	11	308	99	52	.525	48	41	.854	61	21	30	0	145	13.2
1972-73	Celtics	13	303	101	47	.465	56	49	.875	38	15	29	0	143	11.0

										—Rebounds—									
Season	Team	G.	Min.	FGA	FGM	Pct.	FTA	FTM	Pct.	Off.	Def.	Tot.	Ast.	PF	DQ	Stl.	Blk.	Pts.	Ave.
1973-74	Celtics	18	467	164	82	.500	53	41	.774	25	72	97	35	54	2	8	3	205	11.4
1974-75	Celtics	11	274	117	66	.564	41	37	.902	18	27	45	26	36	1	2	2	169	15.4
1975-76	Celtics	18	315	108	52	.481	69	60	.870	17	36	53	17	46	1	3	2	164	9.1
Totals		134	2941	1109	554	.500	470	385	.819	—	—	647	189	357	4	—	—	1493	11.1

Nelson also played in 182 regular-season games for Chicago and Los Angeles, 1962-63 through 1964-65.

Jack Nichols

No. 16
Born: April 9, 1926

College: Washington '48
Height: 6-7 Weight: 230

Regular Season

Season	Team	G.	Min.	FGA	FGM	Pct.	FTA	FTM	Pct.	Reb.	Ast.	PF	DQ	Pts.	Ave.
1953-54	Mil-Bos	75*	1607	528	163	.309	152	113	.743	363	104	187	2	439	5.9
1954-55	Celtics	64	1910	656	249	.380	177	138	.780	533	144	238	10	636	9.9
1955-56	Celtics	60	1964	799	330	.413	253	200	.791	625	160	228	7	860	14.3
1956-57	Celtics	61	1372	537	195	.363	136	108	.794	374	85	185	4	498	8.2
1957-58	Celtics	69	1224	484	170	.351	80	59	.738	302	63	123	1	399	5.8
Totals		329	8077	3004	1107	.369	798	618	.774	2197	556	961	24	2832	8.6

*15 games Milwaukee, 60 Boston.

Playoffs

Season	Team	G.	Min.	FGA	FGM	Pct.	FTA	FTM	Pct.	Reb.	Ast.	PF	DQ	Pts.	Ave.
1953-54	Celtics	6	211	72	35	.486	38	30	.789	62	31	24	0	100	16.7
1954-55	Celtics	7	231	81	30	.370	16	13	.813	49	23	28	1	73	10.4
1955-56	Celtics	3	100	43	16	.372	10	9	.900	36	10	13	0	41	13.7
1956-57	Celtics	10	117	40	16	.400	5	3	.600	17	7	23	0	35	3.5
1957-58	Celtics	11	148	66	23	.348	10	7	.700	45	8	21	1	53	4.8
Totals		37	807	302	120	.397	79	62	.785	209	79	109	2	302	8.2

Nichols also played in 175 regular-season games for Washington, Tri-Cities and Milwaukee, 1948-49 through 1952-53.

Rich Niemann

No. 27
Born: July 2, 1946

College: St. Louis '68
Height: 7-0 Weight: 252

Regular Season

Season	Team	G.	Min.	FGA	FGM	Pct.	FTA	FTM	Pct.	Reb.	Ast.	PF	DQ	Pts.	Ave.
1969-70	Celtics	6	18	5	2	.400	2	2	1.000	6	2	10	0	6	1.0

Niemann also played in 34 regular-season games for Detroit and Milwaukee, 1968-69.

Bob Nordmann

No. 34
Born: December 11, 1939

College: St. Louis '61
Height: 6-10 Weight: 262

Regular Season

Season	Team	G.	Min.	FGA	FGM	Pct.	FTA	FTM	Pct.	Reb.	Ast.	PF	DQ	Pts.	Ave.
1964-65	Celtics	3	25	5	3	.600	0	0	.000	8	3	5	0	6	2.0

Nordmann also played in 130 regular-season games for Cincinnati, St. Louis and New York Knicks, 1961-62 through 1963-64.

George Nostrand

No. 3
Born: April 5, 1924

College: Wyoming '46
Height: 6-8 Weight: 197

Regular Season

Season	Team	G.	FGA	FGM	Pct.	FTA	FTM	Pct.	Ast.	PF	Pts.	Ave.
1948-49	Pro-Bos	60*	651	212	.326	284	165	.581	94	164	589	9.8
1949-50	Bos-Chi-TriC	55**	255	78	.306	99	56	.566	29	118	212	3.9
Totals		115	906	290	.320	383	221	.577	123	282	801	7.0

*27 games Boston, 33 Providence.

**18 games Boston, 36 Chicago, 1 Tri-Cities.

Nostrand also played in 106 regular-season games for Chicago, Toronto and Providence, 1946-47 through 1947-48.

Stan Noszka

No. Nos. 10 & 11
September 19, 1920

College: Duquesne '43
Height: 6-1 Weight: 185

Regular Season

Season	Team	G.	FGA	FGM	Pct.	FTA	FTM	Pct.	Ast.	PF	Pts.	Ave.
1947-48	Celtics	22	97	27	.278	35	24	.686	4	52	78	3.5
1948-49	Celtics	30	123	30	.244	30	15	.500	25	56	75	2.5
Totals		52	220	57	.259	65	39	.600	29	108	153	2.9

Playoffs

Season	Team	G.	FGA	FGM	Pct.	FTA	FTM	Pct.	Ast.	PF	Pts.	Ave.
1947-48	Celtics	3	30	10	.333	8	5	.625	2	11	25	8.3

Noszka also played in 58 regular-season games for Pittsburgh, 1946-47.

Dermott (Dermie) O'Connell

No. 7
Born: April 13, 1928

College: Holy Cross '49
Height: 6-0 Weight: 174

Regular Season

Season	Team	G.	FGA	FGM	Pct.	FTA	FTM	Pct.	Ast.	PF	Pts.	Ave.
1948-49	Celtics	21	315	87	.276	56	30	.536	65	40	204	9.7
1949-50	Bos-StL	61*	425	111	.261	89	47	.528	91	91	269	4.4
Totals		82	740	198	.268	145	77	.531	156	131	473	5.8

*37 games Boston, 24 St. Louis.

Enoch (Bud) Olsen

No. 25
Born: July 25, 1940

College: Louisville '62
Height: 6-8 Weight: 230

Regular Season

Season	Team	G.	Min.	FGA	FGM	Pct.	FTA	FTM	Pct.	Reb.	Ast.	PF	DQ	Pts.	Ave.
1968-69	Celtics	7*	43	19	7	.368	6	0	.000	14	4	6	—	14	2.0

*Played in 10 games for Detroit later that season.

Olsen also played in 352 regular-season games for Cincinnati, San Francisco and Seattle, 1962-63 through 1967-68.

Togo Palazzi

No. 12
Born: August 8, 1932

College: Holy Cross '54
Height: 6-4 Weight: 205

Regular Season

Season	Team	G.	Min.	FGA	FGM	Pct.	FTA	FTM	Pct.	Reb.	Ast.	PF	DQ	Pts.	Ave.
1954-55	Celtics	53	504	253	101	.399	60	45	.750	146	30	60	1	247	4.7
1955-56	Celtics	63	703	373	145	.389	124	85	.685	182	42	87	0	375	6.0
1956-57	Bos-Syr	63*	1013	571	210	.368	175	136	.777	262	49	117	1	556	8.8
Totals		179	2220	1197	456	.381	359	266	.741	590	121	264	2	1178	6.6

*20 games Boston, 43 Syracuse.

Playoffs

Season	Team	G.	Min.	FGA	FGM	Pct.	FTA	FTM	Pct.	Reb.	Ast.	PF	DQ	Pts.	Ave.
1954-55	Celtics	5	30	24	12	.500	10	5	.500	14	1	7	0	29	5.8
1955-56	Celtics	2	7	5	1	.200	0	0	.000	2	0	1	0	2	1.0
Totals		7	37	29	13	.448	10	5	.500	16	1	8	0	31	4.4

Palazzi also played in 145 regular-season games for Syracuse, 1957-58 through 1959-60.

Robert Parish

No. 00
Born: August 30, 1953

College: Centenary '76
Height: 7-0½ Weight: 230

Regular Season

Season	Team	G.	Min.	FGA	FGM	Pct.	FTA	FTM	Pct.	Rebounds Off.	Def.	Tot.	Ast.	PF	DQ	Stl.	Blk.	Pts.	Ave.
1980-81	Celtics	82	2298	1166*	635	.545	397	282	.710	245	532	777	144	310	9	81	214	1552	18.9
1981-82	Celtics	80	2534	1235*	669	.542	355	252	.710	288	578	866	140	267	5	68	192	1590	19.9
Totals		162	4832	2401	1304	.543	752	534	.710	533	1110	1643	284	577	14	149	406	3142	19.4

*Converted none of 1 (.000) 3-point field-goal attempts in 1980-81, attempted none in 1981-82 for a total of none of 1 (.000).

Playoffs

Season	Team	G.	Min.	FGA	FGM	Pct.	FTA	FTM	Pct.	Rebounds Off.	Def.	Tot.	Ast.	PF	DQ	Stl.	Blk.	Pts.	Ave.
1980-81	Celtics	17	492	219*	108	.493	58	39	.672	50	96	146	19	116	3	21	39	255	15.0
1981-82	Celtics	12	426	209*	102	.488	75	51	.680	43	92	135	18	47	1	6	48	255	21.3
Totals		29	918	428	210	.491	133	90	.677	93	188	281	37	163	4	27	87	510	17.6

*Parish has attempted no 3-point field goals during the playoffs.

Parish also played in 307 regular-season games for Golden State, 1976-77 through 1979-80.

Andy Phillip

No. 17
Born: March 7, 1922

College: Illinois '47
Height: 6-2 Weight: 195

Regular Season

Season	Team	G.	Min.	FGA	FGM	Pct.	FTA	FTM	Pct.	Reb.	Ast.	PF	DQ	Pts.	Ave.
1956-57	Celtics	67	1476	277	105	.379	137	88	.642	181	168	121	1	298	4.4
1957-58	Celtics	70	1164	273	97	.355	71	42	.592	158	121	121	0	236	3.4
Totals		137	2640	550	202	.367	208	130	.625	339	289	242	1	534	3.9

Playoffs

Season	Team	G.	Min.	FGA	FGM	Pct.	FTA	FTM	Pct.	Reb.	Ast.	PF	DQ	Pts.	Ave.
1956-57	Celtics	10	128	22	8	.364	15	6	.400	20	17	18	0	22	2.2
1957-58	Celtics	10	91	21	5	.238	9	7	.778	14	7	20	0	17	1.7
Totals		20	219	43	13	.302	24	13	.542	34	24	38	0	39	2.0

Phillip also played in 564 regular-season games for Chicago, Philadelphia and Fort Wayne, 1947-48 through 1955-56.

Gary Phillips

No. 21
Born: December 7, 1939

College: Houston '61
Height: 6-3 Weight: 189

Regular Season

Season	Team	G.	Min.	FGA	FGM	Pct.	FTA	FTM	Pct.	Reb.	Ast.	PF	DQ	Pts.	Ave.
1961-62	Celtics	72	693	320	110	.344	86	50	.581	107	63	109	0	270	3.7

Playoffs

Season	Team	G.	Min.	FGA	FGM	Pct.	FTA	FTM	Pct.	Reb.	Ast.	PF	DQ	Pts.	Ave.
1961-62	Celtics	6	32	16	1	.062	11	8	.727	3	1	6	0	10	1.7

Phillips also played in 281 regular-season games for San Francisco, 1962-63 through 1965-66.

Frank Ramsey

No. 23 College: Kentucky '53
Born: July 13, 1931 Height: 6-3 Weight: 190

Regular Season

Season	*Team*	*G.*	*Min.*	*FGA*	*FGM*	*Pct.*	*FTA*	*FTM*	*Pct.*	*Reb.*	*Ast.*	*PF*	*DQ*	*Pts.*	*Ave.*
1954-55	Celtics	64	1754	592	236	.399	322	243	.755	402	185	250	11	715	11.2
1956-57*	Celtics	35	807	349	137	.393	182	144	.791	178	67	113	3	418	11.9
1957-58	Celtics	69	2047	900	377	.419	472	383	.811	504	167	245	8	1137	16.5
1958-59	Celtics	72	2013	1013	383	.378	436	341	.782	491	147	266	11	1107	15.4
1959-60	Celtics	73	2009	1062	422	.397	347	273	.787	506	137	251	10	1117	15.3
1960-61	Celtics	79	2019	1100	448	.407	354	295	.833	431	148	284	13	1191	15.1
1961-62	Celtics	79	1913	979	436	.445	405	334	.825	387	109	245	9	1206	15.3
1962-63	Celtics	77	1541	743	284	.382	332	271	.816	288	95	259	13	839	10.9
1963-64	Celtics	75	1227	604	226	.374	233	196	.841	233	81	245	7	648	8.6
Totals		623	15,330	7342	2949	.402	3083	2480	.804	3420	1136	2158	85	8378	13.4

Playoffs

Season	*Team*	*G.*	*Min.*	*FGA*	*FGM*	*Pct.*	*FTA*	*FTM*	*Pct.*	*Reb.*	*Ast.*	*PF*	*DQ*	*Pts.*	*Ave.*
1954-55	Celtics	7	154	54	28	.519	26	19	.731	35	16	27	0	75	10.7
1956-57*	Celtics	10	229	82	38	.463	59	46	.780	43	17	36	1	122	12.2
1957-58	Celtics	11	352	174	74	.425	59	54	.915	90	16	50	3	202	13.4
1958-59	Celtics	11	303	192	95	.495	81	65	.802	68	20	52	4	255	23.2
1959-60	Celtics	13	459	196	81	.413	63	55	.873	100	27	51	1	217	16.7
1960-61	Celtics	10	300	136	55	.407	75	61	.813	64	23	40	0	171	17.1
1961-62	Celtics	13	210	104	39	.375	45	41	.911	38	10	38	3	119	9.1
1962-63	Celtics	13	251	104	37	.356	47	34	.723	35	12	43	1	108	8.3
1963-64	Celtics	10	138	63	22	.349	21	18	.857	21	10	25	0	62	6.2
Totals		98	2396	1105	469	.424	476	393	.826	494	151	362	13	1331	13.6

*Missed all of 1955-56 and part of 1956-57 while serving in Army.

John Richter

No. 16 College: North Carolina State
Born: March 12, 1937 Height: 6-9 Weight: 225

Regular Season

Season	*Team*	*G.*	*Min.*	*FGA*	*FGM*	*Pct.*	*FTA*	*FTM*	*Pct.*	*Reb.*	*Ast.*	*PF*	*DQ*	*Pts.*	*Ave.*
1959-60	Celtics	66	808	332	113	.340	117	59	.504	312	27	158	1	285	4.3

Playoffs

Season	*Team*	*G.*	*Min.*	*FGA*	*FGM*	*Pct.*	*FTA*	*FTM*	*Pct.*	*Reb.*	*Ast.*	*PF*	*DQ*	*Pts.*	*Ave.*
1959-60	Celtics	8	95	38	15	.395	14	5	.357	29	2	18	1	35	4.4

Mel Riebe

Nos. 7 & 9 College: Ohio University
Born: July 12, 1916 Height: 5-11 Weight: 180

Playoffs

Season	*Team*	*G.*	*FGA*	*FGM*	*Pct.*	*FTA*	*FTM*	*Pct.*	*Ast.*	*PF*	*Pts.*	*Ave.*
1947-48	Celtics	48	653	202	.309	137	85	.620	41	137	489	10.2
1948-49	Bos-Prov	43*	589	172	.292	133	79	.594	104	110	423	9.8
Totals		91	1242	374	.301	270	164	.607	145	247	912	10.0

*33 games Boston, 10 Providence.

Playoffs

Season	*Team*	*G.*	*FGA*	*FGM*	*Pct.*	*FTA*	*FTM*	*Pct.*	*Ast.*	*PF*	*Pts.*	*Ave.*
1947-48	Celtics	3	43	14	.326	20	14	.700	3	10	42	14.0

Arnie Risen

No. 19 — College: Ohio State
Born: October 9, 1924 — Height: 6-9 Weight: 200

Regular Season

Season	Team	G.	Min.	FGA	FGM	Pct.	FTA	FTM	Pct.	Reb.	Ast.	PF	DQ	Pts.	Ave.
1955-56	Celtics	68	1597	493	189	.383	240	170	.708	553	88	300	17	548	8.1
1956-57	Celtics	43	935	307	119	.388	156	106	.679	286	53	163	4	344	8.0
1957-58	Celtics	63	1119	397	134	.338	167	114	.683	360	50	195	5	382	6.1
Totals		174	3651	1197	442	.369	563	390	.693	1199	191	658	26	1274	7.3

Playoffs

Season	Team	G.	Min.	FGA	FGM	Pct.	FTA	FTM	Pct.	Reb.	Ast.	PF	DQ	Pts.	Ave.
1955-56	Celtics	3	88	34	12	.353	18	13	.722	44	2	15	0	37	12.3
1956-57	Celtics	10	152	63	28	.444	29	19	.655	58	8	48	5	75	7.5
1957-58	Celtics	10	168	52	12	.231	33	22	.667	62	9	32	1	46	4.6
Totals		23	408	149	52	.349	80	54	.675	164	19	95	6	158	6.9

Risen also played in 463 regular-season games for Rochester, 1948-49 through 1954-55.

Bill Roberts

No. 5 — College: Wyoming
Born: 1925 — Height: 6-9 Weight: 210

Regular Season

Season	Team	G.	FGA	FGM	Pct.	FTA	FTM	Pct.	Ast.	PF	Pts.	Ave.
1948-49	Chi-Bos-St. Louis	50*	267	89	.333	63	44	.698	41	113	222	4.4

*26 games Boston, 22 St. Louis, 2 Chicago.

Roberts also played in 67 regular-season games for St. Louis, 1949-50.

Rick Robey

No. 53 — College: Kentucky '78
Born: January 30, 1956 — Height: 6-11 Weight: 230

Regular Season

										—Rebounds—									
Season	Team	G.	Min.	FGA	FGM	Pct.	FTA	FTM	Pct.	Off.	Def.	Tot.	Ast.	PF	DQ	Stl.	Blk.	Pts.	Ave.
1978-79**	Celtics	36	914	378	182	.481	103	84	.816	88	171	259	79	121	3	23	3	448	12.4
1979-80	Celtics	82	1918	727*	379	.521	269	184	.684	209	321	530	92	244	2	53	15	942	11.5
1980-81	Celtics	82	1569	547*	298	.545	251	144	.574	132	258	390	126	204	0	38	19	740	9.0
1981-82	Celtics	80	1186	375*	185	.493	157	84	.535	114	181	295	68	183	2	27	14	454	5.7
Totals		280	5587	2027	1044	.515	780	496	.636	543	931	1474	365	752	7	141	51	2584	9.2

*Converted none of 1 (.000) 3-point field-goal attempts in 1979-80, none of 1 (.000) in 1980-81 and none of 2 (.000) in 1981-82 for a total of none of 4 (.000).

**Also played in 43 games for Indiana earlier that season.

Playoffs

										—Rebounds—									
Season	Team	G.	Min.	FGA	FGM	Pct.	FTA	FTM	Pct.	Off.	Def.	Tot.	Ast.	PF	DQ	Stl.	Blk.	Pts.	Ave.
1979-80	Celtics	9	151	53*	24	.453	14	7	.500	13	19	32	10	27	0	7	3	55	6.1
1980-81	Celtics	17	265	81*	35	.432	35	16	.457	19	41	60	12	44	0	2	5	86	5.1
1981-82	Celtics	12	122	40*	21	.525	17	13	.765	13	16	29	4	27	0	2	2	55	4.6
Totals		38	538	174	80	.460	66	36	.545	45	76	121	26	98	0	11	10	196	5.2

*Converted none of 1 (.000) 3-point field-goal attempts in 1979-80, tried none in 1980-81 and converted none of 2 in 1981-82 for a total of none of 3 (.000).

Ken Rollins

No. 4 — College: Kentucky '48
Born: September 14, 1923 — Height: 6-0 Weight: 168

Regular Season

Season	Team	G.	Min.	FGA	FGM	Pct.	FTA	FTM	Pct.	Reb.	Ast.	PF	DQ	Pts.	Ave.
1952-53	Celtics	43	426	115	38	.330	27	22	.815	45	46	63	1	98	2.3

Playoffs

Season	Team	G.	Min.	FGA	FGM	Pct.	FTA	FTM	Pct.	Reb.	Ast.	PF	DQ	Pts.	Ave.
1952-53	Celtics	6	65	15	6	.400	8	8	1.000	8	7	14	0	20	3.3

Rollins also played in 125 regular-season games for Chicago, 1948-49 through 1949-50.

Curtis Rowe

No. 41 — College: UCLA '71
Born: July 2, 1949 — Height: 6-7 Weight: 225

Regular Season

										—Rebounds—									
Season	Team	G.	Min.	FGA	FGM	Pct.	FTA	FTM	Pct.	Off.	Def.	Tot.	Ast.	PF	DQ	Stl.	Blk.	Pts.	Ave.
1976-77	Celtics	79	2190	632	315	.498	240	170	.708	188	375	563	107	215	3	24	47	800	11.6
1977-78	Celtics	51	911	273	123	.451	89	66	.742	74	129	203	45	94	1	14	8	312	6.1
1978-79	Celtics	53	1222	346	151	.436	75	52	.693	79	163	242	69	105	2	15	13	354	6.7
Totals		183	4323	1251	589	.471	404	288	.714	341	667	1008	221	414	6	53	68	1466	8.0

Playoffs

										—Rebounds—									
Season	Team	G.	Min.	FGA	FGM	Pct.	FTA	FTM	Pct.	Off.	Def.	Tot.	Ast.	PF	DQ	Stl.	Blk.	Pts.	Ave.
1976-77	Celtics	9	237	68	32	.471	29	22	.759	29	43	72	10	29	1	1	4	86	9.9

Rowe also played in 407 regular-season games for Detroit, 1971-72 through 1975-76.

Bill Russell

No. 6 — College: San Francisco '56
Born: February 12, 1934 — Height: 6-10* Weight: 220

Regular Season

Season	Team	G.	Min.	FGA	FGM	Pct.	FTA	FTM	Pct.	Reb.	Ast.	PF	DQ	Pts.	Ave.
1956-57	Celtics	48	1695	649	277	.427	309	152	.492	943	88	143	2	706	14.7
1957-58	Celtics	69	2640	1032	456	.442	443	230	.519	1564	202	181	2	1142	16.6
1958-59	Celtics	70	2979	997	456	.457	428	256	.598	1612	222	161	3	1168	16.7
1959-60	Celtics	74	3146	1189	555	.467	392	240	.612	1778	277	210	0	1350	18.2
1960-61	Celtics	78	3458	1250	532	.426	469	258	.550	1868	264	164	0	1322	16.9
1961-62	Celtics	76	3433	1258	575	.457	481	286	.594	1891	341	207	3	1436	18.9
1962-63	Celtics	78	3500	1182	511	.432	517	287	.555	1843	348	189	1	1309	16.8
1963-64	Celtics	78	3482	1077	466	.433	429	236	.550	1930	370	190	0	1168	15.0
1964-65	Celtics	78	3466	980	429	.438	426	244	.573	1878	410	204	1	1102	14.1
1965-66	Celtics	78	3386	943	391	.415	405	223	.551	1779	371	221	4	1005	12.9
1966-67	Celtics	81	3297	870	395	.454	467	285	.610	1700	472	258	4	1075	13.4
1967-68	Celtics	78	2953	858	365	.425	460	247	.537	1451	357	242	2	977	12.5
1968-69	Celtics	77	3291	645	279	.433	388	204	.526	1484	374	231	2	762	9.9
Totals		963	40,726	12,930	5687	.440	5614	3148	.561	21,721	4096	2601	24	14,522	15.1

Playoffs

Season	Team	G.	Min.	FGA	FGM	Pct.	FTA	FTM	Pct.	Reb.	Ast.	PF	DQ	Pts.	Ave.
1956-57	Celtics	10	409	148	54	.365	61	31	.508	244	32	41	1	139	13.9
1957-58	Celtics	9	355	133	48	.361	66	40	.606	221	24	24	0	136	15.1
1958-59	Celtics	11	496	159	65	.409	67	41	.612	305	40	28	1	171	15.5
1959-60	Celtics	13	572	206	94	.456	75	53	.707	336	38	38	1	241	18.5
1960-61	Celtics	10	462	171	73	.427	86	45	.523	299	48	24	0	191	19.1
1961-62	Celtics	14	672	253	116	.458	113	82	.726	370	70	49	0	314	22.4
1962-63	Celtics	13	617	212	96	.453	109	72	.661	326	66	36	0	264	20.3
1963-64	Celtics	10	451	132	47	.356	67	37	.552	272	44	23	0	131	13.1
1964-65	Celtics	12	561	150	79	.527	76	40	.526	302	76	43	2	198	16.5
1965-66	Celtics	17	814	261	124	.475	123	76	.618	428	85	60	0	324	19.1
1966-67	Celtics	9	390	86	31	.360	52	33	.635	198	50	32	1	95	10.6
1967-68	Celtics	19	869	242	99	.409	130	76	.585	434	99	73	1	274	14.4
1968-69	Celtics	18	829	182	77	.423	81	41	.506	369	98	65	1	195	10.8
Totals		165	7497	2335	1003	.430	1106	667	.603	4104	770	536	8	2673	16.2

*Russell always took delight in claiming his height was "6-9 13/16ths."

Ed Sadowski

No. 22
Born: July 11, 1917

College: Seton Hall
Height: 6-5 Weight: 240

Regular Season

Season	Team	G.	FGA	FGM	Pct.	FTA	FTM	Pct.	Ast.	PF	Pts.	Ave.
1947-48	Celtics	47	953	308	.323	422	294	.697	74	182	910	19.4

Playoffs

Season	Team	G.	FGA	FGM	Pct.	FTA	FTM	Pct.	Ast.	PF	Pts.	Ave.
1947-48	Celtics	3	55	19	.345	38	23	.605	6	17	61	20.3

Sadowski also played in 53 regular-season games for Toronto and Cleveland, 1946-47, and in 129 for Philadelphia and Baltimore, 1948-49 through 1949-50.

Kenny Sailors

No. 13
Born: January 14, 1922

College: Wyoming '46
Height: 5-10 Weight: 176

Regular Season

Season	Team	G.	Min.	FGA	FGM	Pct.	FTA	FTM	Pct.	Reb.	Ast.	PF	DQ	Pts.	Ave.
1950-51	Bos-Bal	60*	—	533	181	.340	180	131	.728	120	150	196	8	493	8.2

*10 games Boston, 50 Baltimore.

Sailors also played in 216 regular-season games for Cleveland, Chicago, Philadelphia, Providence and Denver, 1946-47 through 1949-50.

Frankie Sanders

No. 45
Born: January 23, 1957

College: Southern '78
Height: 6-6 Weight: 200

Regular Season

Season	Team	G.	Min.	FGA	FGM	Pct.	FTA	FTM	Pct.	Reb.	Ast.	PF	DQ	Pts.	Ave.
1978-79*	Celtics	24	216	119	55	.462	27	22	.815	51	17	25	0	132	5.5

*Played in 22 games for San Antonio earlier that season.

Sanders also played in 23 regular-season games for Kansas City, 1980-81.

Tom (Satch) Sanders

No. 16
Born: November 8, 1938

College: New York University '60
Height: 6-6 Weight: 210

Regular Season

Season	Team	G.	Min.	FGA	FGM	Pct.	FTA	FTM	Pct.	Reb.	Ast.	PF	DQ	Pts.	Ave.
1960-61	Celtics	68	1084	352	148	.420	100	67	.670	385	44	131	1	363	5.3
1961-62	Celtics	80	2325	804	350	.435	263	197	.749	762	74	279	9	897	11.2
1962-63	Celtics	80	2148	744	339	.456	252	186	.738	576	95	262	5	864	10.8
1963-64	Celtics	80	2370	836	349	.417	280	213	.761	667	102	277	6	911	11.4
1964-65	Celtics	80	2459	871	374	.429	259	193	.745	661	92	318	15	941	11.8
1965-66	Celtics	72	1896	816	349	.428	276	211	.764	508	90	317	19	909	12.6
1966-67	Celtics	81	1926	755	323	.428	218	178	.817	439	91	304	6	824	10.2
1967-68	Celtics	78	1981	691	296	.428	255	200	.784	454	100	300	12	792	10.2
1968-69	Celtics	82	2184	847	364	.430	255	187	.733	574	110	293	9	915	11.2
1969-70	Celtics	57	1616	555	246	.443	183	161	.880	314	92	199	5	653	11.5
1970-71	Celtics	17	121	44	16	.364	8	7	.875	17	11	25	0	39	2.3
1971-72	Celtics	82	1631	524	215	.410	136	111	.816	353	98	257	7	541	6.6
1972-73	Celtics	59	423	149	47	.315	35	23	.657	88	27	82	0	117	2.0
Totals		916	22,164	7988	3416	.428	2520	1934	.767	5798	1026	3044	94	8766	9.6

Playoffs

Season	Team	G.	Min.	FGA	FGM	Pct.	FTA	FTM	Pct.	Reb.	Ast.	PF	DQ	Pts.	Ave.
1960-61	Celtics	10	216	75	37	.493	24	15	.625	84	7	42	2	89	8.9
1961-62	Celtics	14	439	130	56	.431	36	29	.806	115	14	65	4	141	10.1
1962-63	Celtics	13	387	119	52	.437	31	24	.774	96	19	61	4	128	9.8
1963-64	Celtics	10	292	94	34	.362	34	23	.676	71	6	45	5	91	9.1
1964-65	Celtics	12	365	152	64	.421	43	31	.721	102	19	58	4	159	13.3
1965-66	Celtics	17	500	201	97	.483	48	36	.750	110	27	70	2	230	13.5
1966-67	Celtics	9	144	61	21	.344	5	2	.400	43	5	31	1	44	4.9
1967-68	Celtics	14	289	99	50	.505	21	16	.762	63	12	53	4	116	8.3
1968-69	Celtics	15	197	73	32	.438	31	23	.742	48	7	40	0	87	5.8
1971-72	Celtics	11	186	53	17	.321	21	13	.619	26	10	36	0	47	4.3
1972-73	Celtics	5	24	9	5	.556	2	0	.000	5	1	7	0	10	2.0
Totals		130	3039	1066	465	.436	296	212	.716	763	127	508	26	1142	8.8

Woodrow (Woody) Sauldsberry

No. 18
Born: July 11, 1934

College: Texas Southern '57
Height: 6-7 Weight: 230

Regular Season

Season	Team	G.	Min.	FGA	FGM	Pct.	FTA	FTM	Pct.	Reb.	Ast.	PF	DQ	Pts.	Ave.
1965-66	Celtics	39	530	249	80	.321	22	11	.500	142	15	94	0	171	4.4

Sauldsberry also played in 442 regular-season games for Philadelphia, St. Louis and Chicago, 1957-58 through 1962-63.

Fred Saunders

No. 20
Born: June 13, 1951

College: Syracuse '74
Height: 6-7 Weight: 210

Regular Season

Season	Team	G.	Min.	FGA	FGM	Pct.	FTA	FTM	Pct.	Reb.	Ast.	PF	DQ	Pts.	Ave.
1976-77	Celtics	68	1051	395	184	.466	53	35	.660	223	85	191	3	403	5.9
1977-78	Celtics	26	243	91	30	.330	17	14	.824	37	11	34	0	74	2.8
Totals		94	1294	486	214	.440	70	49	.700	260	96	225	3	477	5.1

Playoffs

Season	Team	G.	Min.	FGA	FGM	Pct.	FTA	FTM	Pct.	Reb.	Ast.	PF	DQ	Stl.	Blk.	Pts.	Ave.
1976-77	Celtics	9	66	33	12	.364	6	5	.833	9	5	21	0	1	0	29	3.2

Saunders also played in 86 regular-season games for Phoenix, 1974-75 through 1975-76, and 30 for New Orleans, 1977-78.

Fred Scolari

No. 24
Born: March 1, 1922

College: San Francisco '43
Height: 5-10 Weight: 180

Regular Season

Season	Team	G.	Min.	FGA	FGM	Pct.	FTA	FTM	Pct.	Reb.	Ast.	PF	DQ	Pts.	Ave.
1954-55	Celtics	59	619	249	76	.305	49	39	.796	77	93	76	0	191	3.2

Playoffs

Season	Team	G.	Min.	FGA	FGM	Pct.	FTA	FTM	Pct.	Reb.	Ast.	PF	DQ	Pts.	Ave.
1954-55	Celtics	5	29	15	4	.267	5	4	.800	5	3	7	0	12	2.4

Scolari also played in 475 regular-season games for Washington, Syracuse, Baltimore and Fort Wayne, 1946-47 through 1953-54.

Charlie Scott

No. 11
Born: December 15, 1948

College: North Carolina '70
Height: 6-6 Weight: 175

Regular Season

										—Rebounds—									
Season	Team	G.	Min.	FGA	FGM	Pct.	FTA	FTM	Pct.	Off.	Def.	Tot.	Ast.	PF	DQ	Stl.	Blk.	Pts.	Ave.
1975-76	Celtics	82	2913	1309	588	.449	335	267	.797	106	252	358	341	356	17	103	24	1443	17.6
1976-77	Celtics	43	1581	734	326	.444	173	129	.746	52	139	191	196	155	3	60	12	781	18.2
1977-78*	Celtics	31	1080	485	210	.433	118	84	.712	24	77	101	143	97	2	51	6	504	16.3
Totals		156	5574	2528	1124	.445	626	480	.767	182	468	650	680	608	22	214	42	2728	17.5

*Played in 48 games for Los Angeles that season.

Playoffs

										—Rebounds—									
Season	Team	G.	Min.	FGA	FGM	Pct.	FTA	FTM	Pct.	Off.	Def.	Tot.	Ast.	PF	DQ	Stl.	Blk.	Pts.	Ave.
1975-76	Celtics	18	632	284	111	.391	72	55	.764	23	53	76	71	97	11	21	8	277	15.4
1976-77	Celtics	9	338	128	52	.406	52	44	.846	15	23	38	38	41	3	13	2	148	16.4
Totals		27	970	412	163	.396	124	99	.798	38	76	114	109	138	14	34	10	425	15.7

Scott also played in 208 regular-season games for Phoenix, 1971-72 through 1974-75, and in 148 for Denver, 1978-79 through 1979-80.

Ed Searcy

No. 36
Born: April 17, 1952

College: St. John's '74
Height: 6-6 Weight: 210

Regular Season

										—Rebounds—									
Season	*Team*	*G.*	*Min.*	*FGA*	*FGM*	*Pct.*	*FTA*	*FTM*	*Pct.*	*Off.*	*Def.*	*Tot.*	*Ast.*	*PF*	*DQ*	*Stl.*	*Blk.*	*Pts.*	*Ave.*
1975-76	Celtics	4	12	6	2	.333	2	2	1.000	0	0	0	1	4	0	0	0	6	1.5

Jim Seminoff

No. 15
Born: 1920

College: Southern California
Height: 6-2 Weight: 210

Regular Season

Season	*Team*	*G.*	*FGA*	*FGM*	*Pct.*	*FTA*	*FTM*	*Pct.*	*Ast.*	*PF*	*Pts.*	*Ave.*
1948-49	Celtics	58	487	153	.314	219	151	.689	229	195	457	7.9
1949-50	Celtics	65	283	85	.300	188	142	.755	249	154	312	4.8
Totals		123	770	238	.309	407	293	.720	478	349	769	6.3

Seminoff also played in 108 regular-season games for Chicago, 1946-47 through 1947-48.

Earl (River) Shannon

No. —
Born: November 23, 1923

College: Rhode Island
Height: 5-11 Weight: 170

Regular Season

Season	*Team*	*G.*	*FGA*	*FGM*	*Pct.*	*FTA*	*FTM*	*Pct.*	*Ast.*	*PF*	*Pts.*	*Ave.*
1948-49	Pro-Bos	32*	127	34	.268	58	39	.672	44	33	107	3.3

*5 games Boston, 27 Providence.

Shannon also played in 102 regular-season games for Providence, 1946-47 through 1947-48.

Howard Shannon

No. 8
Born: June 10, 1923

College: Kansas State '48
Height: 6-3 Weight: 185

Regular Season

Season	*Team*	*G.*	*FGA*	*FGM*	*Pct.*	*FTA*	*FTM*	*Pct.*	*Ast.*	*PF*	*Pts.*	*Ave.*
1949-50	Celtics	67	646	222	.344	182	143	.786	174	148	587	8.8

Shannon also played in 55 regular-season games for Providence, 1948-49.

Celtics past and present were honored by the B'nai Brith Sports Lodge in the early-sixties: Front row (left to right): Bill Russell, Andy Phillip, Sam Jones, Dan Swartz, Tom Heinsohn, K.C. Jones, Gene Guarilia and Chuck Cooper. Middle row: Sonny Hertzberg, Red Auerbach, Celtic President Walter Brown, guest senator Ted Kennedy, Celtic Vice President Lou Pieri, Celtic Treasurer Eddie Powers, Bob Cousy, Bill Sharman, trainer Buddy LeRoux and Voice of Celtics Johnny Most. Back row: Tom (Satch) Sanders, Jack Nichols, Bob Brannum, Lou Tsioropoulos, Ed Macauley, Arnie Risen, Gene Conley, Frank Ramsey, Carl Braun, John Havlicek, Dick Hemric, Jim Loscutoff and Clyde Lovellette.

Bill Sharman

No. 21
Born: May 25, 1926

College: Southern California '50
Height: 6-1 Weight: 190

Regular Season

Season	*Team*	*G.*	*Min.*	*FGA*	*FGM*	*Pct.*	*FTA*	*FTM*	*Pct.*	*Reb.*	*Ast.*	*PF*	*DQ*	*Pts.*	*Ave.*
1951-52	Celtics	63	1389	628	244	.389	213	183	.859	221	151	181	3	671	10.7
1952-53	Celtics	71	2333	925	403	.436	401	341	.850	288	191	240	7	1147	16.2
1953-54	Celtics	72	2467	915	412	.450	392	331	.844	255	229	211	4	1155	16.0
1954-55	Celtics	68	2453	1062	453	.427	387	347	.897	302	280	212	2	1253	18.4
1955-56	Celtics	72	2698	1229	538	.438	413	358	.867	259	339	197	1	1434	19.9
1956-57	Celtics	67	2403	1241	516	.416	421	381	.905	286	236	188	1	1413	21.1
1957-58	Celtics	63	2214	1297	550	.424	338	302	.893	295	167	156	3	1402	22.3
1958-59	Celtics	72	2382	1377	562	.408	367	342	.932	292	179	173	1	1466	20.4
1959-60	Celtics	71	1916	1225	559	.456	291	252	.866	262	144	154	2	1370	19.3
1960-61	Celtics	60	1538	908	383	.422	228	210	.921	223	156	127	0	976	16.3
Totals		679	21,793	10,807	4620	.428	3451	3047	.883	2683	2072	1839	24	12,287	18.1

Playoffs

Season	*Team*	*G.*	*Min.*	*FGA*	*FGM*	*Pct.*	*FTA*	*FTM*	*Pct.*	*Reb.*	*Ast.*	*PF*	*DQ*	*Pts.*	*Ave.*
1951-52	Celtics	1	27	12	7	.583	1	1	1.000	3	7	4	0	15	15.0
1952-53	Celtics	6	201	60	20	.333	32	30	.938	15	15	26	1	70	11.7
1953-54	Celtics	6	206	81	35	.432	50	43	.860	25	10	29	2	113	18.8
1954-55	Celtics	7	290	110	55	.500	38	35	.921	38	38	24	1	145	20.7
1955-56	Celtics	3	119	46	18	.391	17	16	.941	7	12	7	0	52	17.3
1956-57	Celtics	10	377	197	75	.381	64	61	.953	35	29	23	1	211	21.1
1957-58	Celtics	11	406	221	90	.407	56	52	.929	54	25	28	0	232	21.1
1958-59	Celtics	11	322	193	82	.425	59	57	.966	36	28	35	0	221	20.1
1959-60	Celtics	13	364	209	88	.421	53	43	.811	45	20	22	1	219	16.8
1960-61	Celtics	10	261	133	68	.511	36	32	.889	27	17	22	0	168	16.8
Totals		78	2573	1262	538	.426	406	370	.911	285	201	220	6	1446	18.5

Sharman also played in 31 regular-season games for Washington, 1950-51.

The Celtics score against the California Angels on "Sports Challenge."

Tom Heinsohn kicks over the water bucket and heads quickly and quietly back to his seat.

Larry Siegfried

No. 20
Born: May 22, 1939

College: Ohio State '61
Height: 6-3 Weight: 192

Regular Season

Season	*Team*	*G.*	*Min.*	*FGA*	*FGM*	*Pct.*	*FTA*	*FTM*	*Pct.*	*Reb.*	*Ast.*	*PF*	*DQ*	*Pts.*	*Ave.*
1963-64	Celtics	31	261	110	35	.318	39	31	.795	51	40	33	0	101	3.3
1964-65	Celtics	72	996	417	173	.415	140	109	.779	134	119	108	1	455	6.3
1965-66	Celtics	71	1675	825	349	.423	311	274	.881	196	165	157	1	972	13.7
1966-67	Celtics	73	1891	833	368	.442	347	294	.847	228	250	207	1	1030	14.1
1967-68	Celtics	62	1937	629	261	.415	272	236	.868	215	289	194	2	758	12.2
1968-69	Celtics	79	2560	1031	392	.380	389	336	.864	282	370	222	0	1120	14.2
1969-70	Celtics	78	2081	902	382	.424	257	220	.856	212	299	187	2	984	12.6
Totals		466	11,401	4747	1960	.413	1755	1500	.855	1318	1532	1108	7	5420	11.6

Playoffs

Season	*Team*	*G.*	*Min.*	*FGA*	*FGM*	*Pct.*	*FTA*	*FTM*	*Pct.*	*Reb.*	*Ast.*	*PF*	*DQ*	*Pts.*	*Ave.*
1963-64	Celtics	4	24	6	2	.333	6	3	.500	4	1	4	0	7	1.8
1964-65	Celtics	12	163	79	30	.380	28	24	.857	25	21	25	0	84	7.0
1965-66	Celtics	17	452	193	81	.420	75	62	.827	42	41	52	0	224	13.2
1966-67	Celtics	9	260	102	38	.373	43	35	.814	40	44	33	1	111	12.3
1967-68	Celtics	19	535	201	78	.388	85	77	.906	50	56	75	3	233	12.2
1968-69	Celtics	18	392	172	72	.419	70	55	.786	38	46	60	1	199	11.1
Totals		79	1826	753	301	.400	307	256	.834	199	209	249	5	858	10.9

Siegfried also played in 84 regular-season games for San Diego, Houston and Atlanta, 1970-71 through 1971-72.

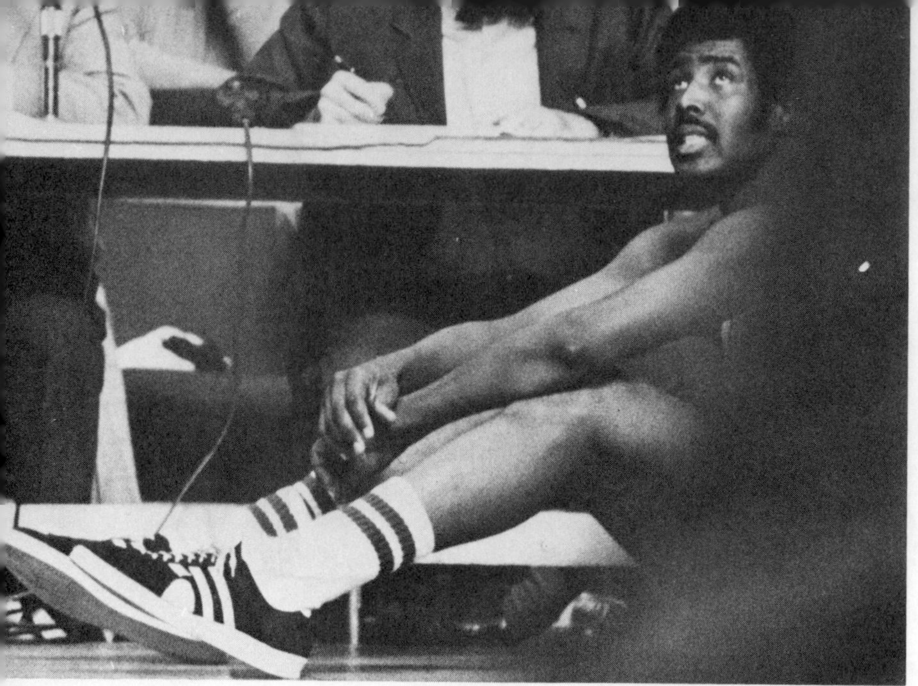

Paul Silas

No. 35
Born: July 12, 1943

College: Creighton '64
Height: 6-7 Weight: 220

Regular Season

Season	*Team*	*G.*	*Min.*	*FGA*	*FGM*	*Pct.*	*FTA*	*FTM*	*Pct.*	*Reb.*	*Ast.*	*PF*	*DQ*	*Pts.*	*Ave.*
1972-73	Celtics	80	2618	851	400	.470	380	266	.700	1039	251	197	1	1066	13.3

Season	*Team*	*G.*	*Min.*	*FGA*	*FGM*	*Pct.*	*FTA*	*FTM*	*Pct.*	—Rebounds— *Off.*	*Def.*	*Tot.*	*Ast.*	*PF*	*DQ*	*Stl.*	*Blk.*	*Pts.*	*Ave.*
1973-74	Celtics	82	2599	772	340	.440	337	264	.783	334	581	915	186	246	3	63	20	944	11.5
1974-75	Celtics	82	2661	749	312	.417	344	244	.709	348	677	1025	224	229	3	60	22	868	10.6
1975-76	Celtics	81	2662	740	315	.426	333	236	.709	365	660	1025	203	227	3	56	33	866	10.7
Totals		325	10,540	3112	1367	.439	1394	1010	.725	—	—	4004	864	899	10	—	—	3744	11.5

Playoffs

Season	*Team*	*G.*	*Min.*	*FGA*	*FGM*	*Pct.*	*FTA*	*FTM*	*Pct.*	*Reb.*	*Ast.*	*PF*	*DQ*	*Pts.*	*Ave.*
1972-73	Celtics	13	512	120	47	.392	50	31	.620	196	39	39	0	125	9.6

Season	*Team*	*G.*	*Min.*	*FGA*	*FGM*	*Pct.*	*FTA*	*FTM*	*Pct.*	—Rebounds— *Off.*	*Def.*	*Tot.*	*Ast.*	*PF*	*DQ*	*Stl.*	*Blk.*	*Pts.*	*Ave.*
1973-74	Celtics	18	574	126	50	.397	53	44	.830	53	138	191	47	51	2	13	9	144	8.0
1974-75	Celtics	11	405	92	42	.457	25	16	.640	46	84	130	40	45	1	12	2	100	9.1
1975-76	Celtics	18	741	154	69	.448	69	56	.812	78	168	246	42	67	1	24	6	194	10.8
Totals		60	2232	492	208	.423	197	147	.746	—	—	763	168	202	4	—	—	563	9.4

Silas also played in 601 regular-season games for St. Louis, Atlanta and Phoenix, 1964-65 through 1971-72, and in 327 for Denver and Seattle, 1976-77 through 1979-80.

Connie Simmons

No. 10
Born: March 15, 1925

College: Did not attend college
Height: 6-8 Weight: 225

Regular Season

Season	*Team*	*G.*	*FGA*	*FGM*	*Pct.*	*FTA*	*FTM*	*Pct.*	*Ast.*	*PF*	*Pts.*	*Ave.*
1946-47	Celtics	60	768	246	.320	189	128	.667	62	130	620	10.3
1947-48	Bos-Balt	45*	545	162	.297	108	62	.608	24	122	386	8.6
Totals		105	1313	408	.311	297	190	.640	86	252	1006	9.6

*32 games Boston, 13 Baltimore.

Simmons also played in 493 regular-season games for Baltimore, New York Knicks, Syracuse and Rochester, 1948-49 through 1955-56.

Connie (left) and Johnny (right) Simmons were the only brothers to ever play for the Celtics, teaming under coach Honey Russell (center in 1946-47.

John Simmons

No. 6
Born: 1922

College: New York University
Height: 6-1 Weight: 184

Regular Season

Season	*Team*	*G.*	*FGA*	*FGM*	*Pct.*	*FTA*	*FTM*	*Pct.*	*Ast.*	*PF*	*Pts.*	*Ave.*
1946-47	Celtics	60	429	120	.280	127	78	.614	29	78	318	5.3

Garfield Smith

No. 33
Born: November 18, 1945

College: Eastern Kentucky '68
Height: 6-9 Weight: 235

Regular Season

Season	*Team*	*G.*	*Min.*	*FGA*	*FGM*	*Pct.*	*FTA*	*FTM*	*Pct.*	*Reb.*	*Ast.*	*PF*	*DQ*	*Pts.*	*Ave.*
1970-71	Celtics	37	281	116	42	.362	56	22	.393	95	9	53	—	106	2.9
1971-72	Celtics	26	134	66	28	.424	31	6	.194	37	8	22	—	62	2.4
Totals		63	415	182	70	.390	87	28	.322	132	17	75	—	168	2.7

Playoffs

Season	*Team*	*G.*	*Min.*	*FGA*	*FGM*	*Pct.*	*FTA*	*FTM*	*Pct.*	*Reb.*	*Ast.*	*PF*	*DQ*	*Pts.*	*Ave.*
1971-72	Celtics	4	6	5	1	.200	3	0	.000	1	0	1	0	2	0.5

Art Spector

No. 12
Born: October 17, 1920

College: Villanova '44
Height: 6-4 Weight: 200

Regular Season

Season	*Team*	*G.*	*FGA*	*FGM*	*Pct.*	*FTA*	*FTM*	*Pct.*	*Ast.*	*PF*	*Pts.*	*Ave.*
1946-47	Celtics	55	460	123	.267	150	83	.553	46	130	329	6.0
1947-48	Celtics	48	243	67	.276	92	60	.652	17	106	194	4.0
1948-49	Celtics	59	434	130	.300	116	64	.552	77	111	324	5.5
1949-50	Celtics	7	12	2	.167	4	1	.250	3	4	5	0.7
Totals		169	1149	322	.280	362	208	.575	143	351	852	5.0

Playoffs

Season	*Team*	*G.*	*FGA*	*FGM*	*Pct.*	*FTA*	*FTM*	*Pct.*	*Ast.*	*PF*	*Pts.*	*Ave.*
1947-48	Celtics	3	9	2	.222	4	2	.500	0	9	6	2.0

Kevin Stacom

No. 27 College: Providence '74
Born: September 4, 1951 Height: 6-4 Weight: 185

Regular Season

										—Rebounds—									
Season	*Team*	*G.*	*Min.*	*FGA*	*FGM*	*Pct.*	*FTA*	*FTM*	*Pct.*	*Off.*	*Def.*	*Tot.*	*Ast.*	*PF*	*DQ*	*Stl.*	*Blk.*	*Pts.*	*Ave.*
1974-75	Celtics	61	447	159	72	.453	33	29	.879	30	25	55	49	65	0	11	3	173	2.8
1975-76	Celtics	77	1114	387	170	.439	91	68	.747	62	99	161	128	117	0	23	5	408	5.3
1976-77	Celtics	79	1051	438	179	.409	58	46	.793	40	57	97	117	65	0	19	3	404	5.1
1977-78	Celtics	55	1006	484	206	.426	71	54	.761	26	80	106	111	60	0	28	3	466	8.5
1978-79*	Celtics	24	260	133	52	.391	19	13	.684	10	14	24	35	18	0	15	0	117	4.9
Totals		296	3878	1601	679	.424	272	210	.772	168	275	443	440	325	0	96	14	1568	5.3

*Played in 44 games for Indiana early that season.

Besides appearing in 44 games for Indiana in 1978-79, Stacom also played in 7 regular-season games for Milwaukee in 1981-82.

Playoffs

										—Rebounds—									
Season	*Team*	*G.*	*Min.*	*FGA*	*FGM*	*Pct.*	*FTA*	*FTM*	*Pct.*	*Off.*	*Def.*	*Tot.*	*Ast.*	*PF*	*DQ*	*Stl.*	*Blk.*	*Pts.*	*Ave.*
1974-75	Celtics	4	7	2	0	.000	0	0	.000	0	0	0	0	0	0	0	0	0	0.0
1975-76	Celtics	17	195	45	13	.289	11	8	.727	9	8	17	16	21	0	5	0	34	2.0
1976-77	Celtics	5	25	6	3	.500	1	1	1.000	0	2	2	4	3	0	0	0	7	1.4
Totals		26	227	533	16	.302	12	9	.750	9	10	19	20	24	0	5	0	41	1.6

Ed (Moose) Stanczak

Nos. 19 & 21 College: Did not attend college
Born: August 15, 1921 Height: 6-1 Weight: 185

Regular Season

Season	*Team*	*G.*	*Min.*	*FGA*	*FGM*	*Pct.*	*FTA*	*FTM*	*Pct.*	*Reb.*	*Ast.*	*PF*	*DQ*	*Pts.*	*Ave.*
1950-51	Celtics	17	—	48	11	.229	43	35	.814	34	6	6	0	57	3.4

Stanczak also played in 57 regular-season games for Anderson, 1949-50.

Gene Stump

No. 13 College: DePaul '47
Born: November 13, 1923 Height: 6-2 Weight: 185

Regular Season

Season	*Team*	*G.*	*FGA*	*FGM*	*Pct.*	*FTA*	*FTM*	*Pct.*	*Ast.*	*PF*	*Pts.*	*Ave.*
1947-48	Celtics	43	247	59	.239	38	24	.632	18	66	142	3.3
1948-49	Celtics	56	580	193	.333	129	92	.713	56	102	478	8.5
Totals		99	827	252	.305	167	116	.695	74	168	620	6.3

Playoffs

Season	*Team*	*G.*	*FGA*	*FGM*	*Pct.*	*FTA*	*FTM*	*Pct.*	*Ast.*	*PF*	*Pts.*	*Ave.*
1947-48	Celtics	3	3	1	.333	0	0	.000	0	2	2	0.7

Stump also played in 49 regular-season games for Minneapolis and Waterloo, 1949-50.

Ben Swain

No. 16 College: Texas Southern '58
Born: December 16, 1933 Height: 6-8 Weight: 222

Regular Season

Season	*Team*	*G.*	*Min.*	*FGA*	*FGM*	*Pct.*	*FTA*	*FTM*	*Pct.*	*Reb.*	*Ast.*	*PF*	*DQ*	*Pts.*	*Ave.*
1958-59	Celtics	58	708	244	99	.406	110	67	.609	262	29	127	3	265	4.6

Playoffs

Season	*Team*	*G.*	*Min.*	*FGA*	*FGM*	*Pct.*	*FTA*	*FTM*	*Pct.*	*Reb.*	*Ast.*	*PF*	*DQ*	*Pts.*	*Ave.*
1958-59	Celtics	5	27	6	2	.333	2	1	.500	14	1	4	0	5	1.0

Dan Swartz

No. 12
Born: December 23, 1934

College: Morehead State '56
Height: 6-4 Weight: 215

Regular Season

Season	*Team*	*G.*	*Min.*	*FGA*	*FGM*	*Pct.*	*FTA*	*FTM*	*Pct.*	*Reb.*	*Ast.*	*PF*	*DQ*	*Pts.*	*Ave.*
1962-63	Celtics	39	335	142	57	.401	72	61	.847	88	21	92	0	175	4.5

Playoffs

Season	*Team*	*G.*	*Min.*	*FGA*	*FGM*	*Pct.*	*FTA*	*FTM*	*Pct.*	*Reb.*	*Ast.*	*PF*	*DQ*	*Pts.*	*Ave.*
1962-63	Celtics	1	4	0	0	.000	0	0	.000	0	0	0	0	0	0.0

Earl Tatum

No. 43
Born: July 26, 1953

College: Marquette '76
Height: 6-5 Weight: 185

Regular Season

Season	*Team*	*G.*	*Min.*	*FGA*	*FGM*	*Pct.*	*FTA*	*FTM*	*Pct.*	*Reb.*	*Ast.*	*PF*	*DQ*	*Pts.*	*Ave.*
1978-79*	Celtics	3	38	20	8	.400	5	4	.800	4	1	7	0	20	6.7

*Played in 76 games for Detroit later that season.

Tatum also played in 150 regular-season games for Los Angeles and Indiana, 1976-77 through 1977-78, and in 33 for Cleveland, 1979-80.

Tom Thacker

No. 11
Born: November 2, 1941

College: Cincinnati '63
Height: 6-3 Weight: 190

Regular Season

Season	*Team*	*G.*	*Min.*	*FGA*	*FGM*	*Pct.*	*FTA*	*FTM*	*Pct.*	*Reb.*	*Ast.*	*PF*	*DQ*	*Pts.*	*Ave.*
1967-68	Celtics	65	782	272	114	.419	84	43	.512	161	69	165	2	271	4.2

Playoffs

Season	*Team*	*G.*	*Min.*	*FGA*	*FGM*	*Pct.*	*FTA*	*FTM*	*Pct.*	*Reb.*	*Ast.*	*PF*	*DQ*	*Pts.*	*Ave.*
1967-68	Celtics	17	81	24	7	.292	7	2	.286	17	8	23	0	16	0.9

Thacker also played in 153 regular-season games for Cincinnati, 1963-64 through 1965-66.

John Thompson

Nos. 5 & 18
Born: September 2, 1941

College: Providence '64
Height: 6-10 Weight: 230

Regular Season

Season	*Team*	*G.*	*Min.*	*FGA*	*FGM*	*Pct.*	*FTA*	*FTM*	*Pct.*	*Reb.*	*Ast.*	*PF*	*DQ*	*Pts.*	*Ave.*
1964-65	Celtics	64	699	209	84	.402	105	62	.590	230	16	141	1	230	3.6
1965-66	Celtics	10	72	30	14	.467	6	4	.667	30	3	15	0	32	3.2
Totals		74	771	239	98	.410	111	66	.595	260	19	156	1	262	3.5

Playoffs

Season	*Team*	*G.*	*Min.*	*FGA*	*FGM*	*Pct.*	*FTA*	*FTM*	*Pct.*	*Reb.*	*Ast.*	*PF*	*DQ*	*Pts.*	*Ave.*
1964-65	Celtics	3	21	7	2	.286	7	7	1.000	12	1	2	0	11	3.7
1965-66	Celtics	3	11	7	1	.143	0	0	.000	4	0	2	0	2	0.7
Totals		6	32	14	3	.214	7	7	1.000	15	1	4	0	13	2.2

Lou Tsioropoulos

Nos. 20 & 29
Born: August 31, 1930

College: Kentucky '53
Height: 6-5 Weight: 195

Regular Season

Season	*Team*	*G.*	*Min.*	*FGA*	*FGM*	*Pct.*	*FTA*	*FTM*	*Pct.*	*Reb.*	*Ast.*	*PF*	*DQ*	*Pts.*	*Ave.*
1956-57	Celtics	52	670	256	79	.309	89	69	.775	207	33	135	6	227	4.4
1957-58	Celtics	70	1819	624	198	.317	207	142	.686	434	112	242	8	538	7.7
1958-59	Celtics	35	488	190	60	.316	33	25	.758	110	20	74	0	145	4.1
Totals		157	2977	1070	337	.315	329	236	.717	751	165	451	14	910	5.8

Playoffs

Season	*Team*	*G.*	*Min.*	*FGA*	*FGM*	*Pct.*	*FTA*	*FTM*	*Pct.*	*Reb.*	*Ast.*	*PF*	*DQ*	*Pts.*	*Ave.*
1957-58	Celtics	11	239	85	25	.294	29	19	.655	64	14	40	4	69	6.3

Virgil Vaughn

No. 17

College: Kentucky Wesleyan
Height: 6-4 Weight: 205

Regular Season

Season	Team	G.	FGA	FGM	Pct.	FTA	FTM	Pct.	Ast.	PF	Pts.	Ave.
1946-47	Celtics	17	78	15	.192	28	15	.536	10	18	45	2.6

Brady Walker

No. 13
Born: March 15, 1921

College: Brigham Young '48
Height: 6-6 Weight: 205

Regular Season

Season	Team	G.	Min.	FGA	FGM	Pct.	FTA	FTM	Pct.	Reb.	Ast.	PF	DQ	Pts.	Ave.
1949-50	Celtics	68	—	583	218	.374	114	72	.632	—	109	100	—	508	7.5
1950-51	Bos-Bal	66*	—	416	164	.394	103	72	.699	354	111	83	2	400	6.1
Totals		134	—	999	382	.382	217	144	.664	—	220	183	—	908	6.8

*16 games Boston, 50 Baltimore.

Walker also played in 59 regular-season games for Providence, 1948-49, and in 35 for Baltimore, 1951-52.

Mike (Red) Wallace

No. 13
Born: July 12, 1918

College: Scranton
Height: 6-1 Weight: 185

Regular Season

Season	Team	G.	FGA	FGM	Pct.	FTA	FTM	Pct.	Ast.	PF	Pts.	Ave.
1946-47	Bos-Tor	61*	809	225	.278	196	106	.541	58	167	556	9.1

*24 games Boston, 37 Toronto.

Gerry Ward

No. 4
Born: September 6, 1941

College: Boston College '63
Height: 6-4 Weight: 200

Regular Season

Season	Team	G.	Min.	FGA	FGM	Pct.	FTA	FTM	Pct.	Reb.	Ast.	PF	DQ	Pts.	Ave.
1964-65	Celtics	3	30	18	2	.111	1	1	1.000	5	6	6	0	5	1.7

Ward also played in 24 regular-season games for St. Louis, 1963-64, and in 142 for Philadelphia and Chicago, 1965-66 through 1966-67.

Kermit Washington

No. 26
Born: September 17, 1951

College: American '73
Height: 6-8 Weight: 230

Regular Season

Season	Team	G.	Min.	FGA	FGM	Pct.	FTA	FTM	Pct.	Reb.	Ast.	PF	DQ	Pts.	Ave.
1977-78*	Celtics	32	866	263	137	.521	136	102	.750	335	42	114	2	376	11.8

*Played in 25 games for Los Angeles earlier that season.

Washington also played in 189 regular-season games for Los Angeles, 1973-74 through 1976-77, and in 255 for San Diego and Portland, 1978-79 through 1981-82.

Ron Watts

No. 12
Born: May 21, 1943

College: Wake Forest '65
Height: 6-6 Weight: 210

Regular Season

Season	Team	G.	Min.	FGA	FGM	Pct.	FTA	FTM	Pct.	Reb.	Ast.	PF	DQ	Pts.	Ave.
1965-66	Celtics	1	3	2	1	.500	0	0	.000	1	1	1	0	2	2.0
1966-67	Celtics	27	89	44	11	.250	23	16	.696	38	1	16	0	38	1.4
Totals		28	92	46	12	.261	23	16	.696	39	2	17	0	40	1.4

Playoffs

Season	Team	G.	Min.	FGA	FGM	Pct.	FTA	FTM	Pct.	Reb.	Ast.	PF	DQ	Pts.	Ave.
1966-67	Celtics	1	5	6	1	.167	2	1	.500	2	0	3	0	3	3.0

Rick Weitzman

No. 26
Born: April 30, 1946

College: Northeastern '67
Height: 6-2 Weight: 175

Regular Season

Season	Team	G.	Min.	FGA	FGM	Pct.	FTA	FTM	Pct.	Reb.	Ast.	PF	DQ	Pts.	Ave.
1967-68	Celtics	25	75	46	12	.261	13	9	.692	10	8	8	0	33	1.3

Playoffs

Season	Team	G.	Min.	FGA	FGM	Pct.	FTA	FTM	Pct.	Reb.	Ast.	PF	DQ	Pts.	Ave.
1967-68	Celtics	3	5	3	2	.667	0	0	.000	1	1	0	0	4	1.3

Paul Westphal

No. 44
Born: November 30, 1950

College: Southern California '72
Height: 6-4 Weight: 195

Regular Season

										—Rebounds—									
Season	Team	G.	Min.	FGA	FGM	Pct.	FTA	FTM	Pct.	Off.	Def.	Tot.	Ast.	PF	DQ	Stl.	Blk.	Pts.	Ave.
1972-73	Celtics	60	482	212	89	.420	86	67	.779	—	—	67	69	88	0	—	—	245	4.1
1973-74	Celtics	82	1165	475	238	.501	153	112	.732	49	94	143	171	173	1	39	34	588	7.2
1974-75	Celtics	82	1581	670	342	.510	156	119	.763	44	119	163	235	192	0	78	33	803	9.8
Totals		224	3228	1357	669	.493	395	298	.754	—	—	373	475	453	1	—	—	1636	7.3

Playoffs

Season	Team	G.	Min.	FGA	FGM	Pct.	FTA	FTM	Pct.	Off.	Def.	Tot.	Ast.	PF	DQ	Stl.	Blk.	Pts.	Ave.
1972-73	Celtics	11	109	39	19	.487	7	5	.714	—	—	7	0	0	0	0	0	0	0
1973-74	Celtics	18	241	100	46	.460	15	11	.733	6	15	21	0	0	0	0	0	0	0
1974-75	Celtics	11	183	81	38	.469	18	12	.667	5	8	13	0	0	0	0	0	0	0
Totals		40	533	220	103	.468	40	28	.700	—	—	41	0	0	0	—	—	0	0

Westphal also played in 460 regular-season games for Phoenix, Seattle and New York, 1975-76 through 1981-82.

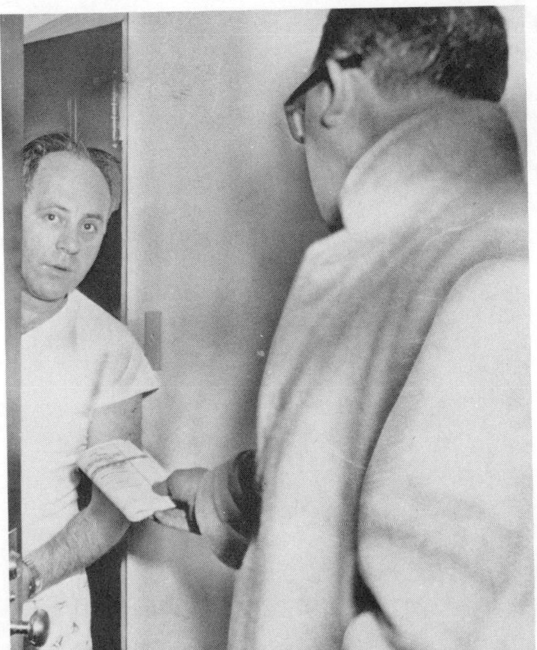

Red Auerbach was served a summons in his underwear when awakened in a Syracuse hotel. The coach and eight of his Celtic players were sued for a 1962 brawl with Syracuse fans.

Jo Jo White

No. 10
Born: November 16, 1946

College: Kansas '69
Height: 6-3 Weight: 197

Regular Season

Season	Team	G.	Min.	FGA	FGM	Pct.	FTA	FTM	Pct.	Reb.	Ast.	PF	DQ	Pts.	Ave.
1969-70	Celtics	60	1328	684	309	.452	135	111	.822	169	145	132	1	729	12.2
1970-71	Celtics	75	2787	1494	693	.464	269	215	.799	376	361	255	5	1601	21.3
1971-72	Celtics	79	3261	1788	770	.431	343	285	.831	446	416	227	1	1825	23.1
1972-73	Celtics	82	3250	1665	717	.431	228	178	.781	414	498	185	2	1612	19.7

										—Rebounds—									
Season	Team	G.	Min.	FGA	FGM	Pct.	FTA	FTM	Pct.	Off.	Def.	Tot.	Ast.	PF	DQ	Stl.	Blk.	Pts.	Ave.
1973-74	Celtics	82	3238	1445	649	.449	227	190	.837	100	251	351	448	185	1	105	25	1488	18.1
1974-75	Celtics	82	3220	1440	658	.457	223	186	.834	84	227	311	458	207	1	128	17	1502	18.3
1975-76	Celtics	82	3257	1492	670	.449	253	212	.838	61	252	313	445	183	2	107	20	1552	18.9
1976-77	Celtics	82	3333	1488	638	.429	383	333	.869	87	296	383	492	193	5	118	22	1609	19.6
1977-78	Celtics	46	1641	690	289	.419	120	103	.858	53	127	180	209	109	2	49	7	681	14.8
1978-79*	Celtics	47	1455	596	255	.428	89	79	.888	22	106	128	214	100	1	54	4	589	12.5
Totals		717	26,770	12,782	5648	.442	2270	1892	.833	—	—	3071	3686	1776	21	—	—	13,188	18.4

*Played in 29 games for Golden State later that season.

Playoffs

Season	Team	G.	Min.	FGA	FGM	Pct.	FTA	FTM	Pct.	Reb.	Ast.	PF	DQ	Pts.	Ave.
1971-72	Celtics	11	432	220	109	.495	48	40	.833	59	58	31	0	258	23.5
1972-73	Celtics	13	583	300	135	.450	54	49	.907	54	83	44	2	319	24.5

										—Rebounds—									
Season	Team	G.	Min.	FGA	FGM	Pct.	FTA	FTM	Pct.	Off.	Def.	Tot.	Ast.	PF	DQ	Stl.	Blk.	Pts.	Ave.
1973-74	Celtics	18	765	310	132	.426	46	34	.739	17	58	75	98	56	1	15	2	298	16.6
1974-75	Celtics	11	462	227	100	.441	33	27	.818	18	32	50	63	32	0	11	4	227	20.6
1975-76	Celtics	18	791	371	165	.445	95	78	.821	12	59	71	98	51	0	23	1	408	22.7
1976-77	Celtics	9	395	201	91	.453	33	28	.848	10	29	39	52	27	0	14	0	210	23.3
Totals		80	3428	1629	732	.449	309	256	.828	—	—	348	452	241	3	63	7	1720	21.5

White also played in 91 regular-season games for Golden State and Kansas City, 1979-80 through 1980-81.

Lucian (Skippy) Whittaker

No. —

College: Kentucky '52
Height: 6-1 Weight: 180

Regular Season

Season	Team	G.	Min.	FGA	FGM	Pct.	FTA	FTM	Pct.	Reb.	Ast.	PF	DQ	Pts.	Ave.
1954-55	Celtics	3	15	6	1	.167	0	0	.000	1	1	4	0	2	0.7

Sidney Wicks

No. 12
Born: September 19, 1949

College: UCLA '71
Height: 6-9 Weight: 225

Regular Season

Season	Team	G.	Min.	FGA	FGM	Pct.	FTA	FTM	Pct.	Reb.	Ast.	PF	DQ	Pts.	Ave.
1976-77	Celtics	82	2642	1012	464	.458	464	310	.668	824	169	331	14	1238	15.1
1977-78	Celtics	81	2413	927	433	.467	329	217	.660	673	171	318	9	1083	13.4
Totals		163	5055	1939	897	.463	793	527	.665	1497	340	649	23	2321	14.2

Playoffs

Season	Team	G.	Min.	FGA	FGM	Pct.	FTA	FTM	Pct.	Reb.	Ast.	PF	DQ	Pts.	Ave.
1976-77	Celtics	9	261	81	42	.519	47	34	.723	83	16	37	2	118	13.1

Wicks also played in 398 regular-season games for Portland, 1971-72 through 1975-76, and in 199 for San Diego, 1978-79 through 1980-81.

Art (Hambone) Williams

No. 7
Born: September 29, 1939

College: California Poly '63
Height: 6-1 Weight: 185

Regular Season

Season	Team	G.	Min.	FGA	FGM	Pct.	FTA	FTM	Pct.	Reb.	Ast.	PF	DQ	Pts.	Ave.
1970-71	Celtics	74	1141	330	150	.455	83	60	.723	205	233	182	1	360	4.9
1971-72	Celtics	81	1326	339	161	.475	119	90	.756	256	327	204	2	412	5.1
1972-73	Celtics	81	974	261	110	.421	56	43	.768	182	236	136	1	263	3.2
1973-74	Celtics	67	616	168	73	.435	32	27	.844	115	163	100	0	173	2.6
Totals		303	4057	1098	494	.450	290	220	.759	758	959	622	4	1208	4.0

Playoffs

Season	Team	G.	Min.	FGA	FGM	Pct.	FTA	FTM	Pct.	Reb.	Ast.	PF	DQ	Pts.	Ave.
1971-72	Celtics	11	173	64	25	.391	20	15	.750	28	33	30	0	65	5.9
1972-73	Celtics	10	156	47	21	.447	8	6	.750	27	41	31	1	48	4.8
1973-74	Celtics	12	96	27	10	.370	8	7	.875	23	29	14	0	27	2.3
Totals		33	425	138	56	.406	36	28	.778	78	103	75	1	140	4.2

Williams also played in 238 regular-season games for San Diego, 1967-68 through 1969-70.

Earl Williams

No. 52
Born: March 24, 1951

College: Winston-Salem '74
Height: 6-7 Weight: 230

Regular Season

										—Rebounds—									
Season	Team	G.	Min.	FGA	FGM	Pct.	FTA	FTM	Pct.	Off.	Def.	Tot.	Ast.	PF	DQ	Stl.	Blk.	Pts.	Ave.
1978-79	Celtics	20	273	123	54	.439	24	14	.583	41	64	105	12	41	0	12	9	122	6.1

Williams also played in 126 regular-season games for Phoenix, Detroit and New York Nets, 1974-75 through 1976-77.

Willie Williams

No. 28
Born: July 28, 1946

College: Florida State '70
Height: 6-7 Weight: 200

Regular Season

Season	Team	G.	Min.	FGA	FGM	Pct.	FTA	FTM	Pct.	Reb.	Ast.	PF	DQ	Pts.	Ave.
1970-71*	Celtics	16	56	32	6	.188	5	3	.600	10	2	8	—	15	0.9

*Played in 9 games for Cincinnati later that season.

Bobby Wilson

No. 42
Born: January 15, 1951

College: Wichita '74
Height: 6-1 Weight: 180

Regular Season

Season	Team	G.	Min.	FGA	FGM	Pct.	FTA	FTM	Pct.	Reb.	Ast.	PF	DQ	Pts.	Ave.
1976-77	Celtics	25	131	59	19	.322	13	11	.846	9	14	19	0	49	2.0

THE NUMBERS GAME

RETIRED CELTICS NUMBERS

1—Walter Brown
6—Bill Russell
10—Jo Jo White
14—Bob Cousy
15—Tom Heinsohn
16—Tom (Satch) Sanders
17—John Havlicek
18—Dave Cowens & Jim Loscutoff
19—Don Nelson
21—Bill Sharman
22—Ed Macauley
23—Frank Ramsey
24—Sam Jones
25—K.C. Jones

CELTICS NUMBERS OVER THE YEARS

No. 00

Robert Parish (1980-81—1981-82)

No. 1*

Never worn by a Celtic player.
*Retired in honor of Celtic founder Walter Brown.

No. 3

Mel Hirsch (1946-47)
Chuck Hoefer (1946-47—1947-48)
George Nostrand (1948-49—1949-50)
John Hazen (1948-49)
(also wore No. 10)

No. 4

Wyndol Gray (1946-47)
Saul Mariaschin (1947-48)
Tony Lavelli (1949-50)
(also wore No. 11)
Sonny Hertzberg (1949-50—1950-51)
Ken Rollins (1952-53)
Carl Braun (1961-62)
Clyde Lovellette (1962-63—1963-64)
(also wore No. 34)
Gerry Ward (1964-65)

No. 5

Tony Kappen (1946-47)
Moe Becker (1946-47)
Dick Murphy (1946-47)
Cecil Hankins (1947-48)
Bill Roberts (1948-49)
Ed Leede (1949-50—1950-51)
Lucian (Skip) Whittaker (1954-55)
John Thompson (1964-65—1965-66)
(also wore No. 18)

No. 6*

John Simmons (1946-47)
George Munroe (1947-48)
Hank Beenders (1948-49)
Tom Kelly (1948-49)
*Bill Russell (1956-57—1968-69)

No. 7

Bill Fenley (1946-47)
Mel Riebe (1947-48—1948-49)
Dermie O'Connell (1948-49—1949-50)
Emmette Bryant (1968-69—1969-70)
Art (Hambone) Williams (1970-71—1973-74)
Ernie DiGregorio (1977-78)
Nate (Tiny) Archibald (1978-79—1981-82)

No. 8

Al Brightman (1946-47)
Phil Farbman (1948-49)
Howie Shannon (1949-50)

No. 9

Harold Kottman (1946-47)
Mel Riebe (1947-48—1948-49)
(also wore No. 7)
George Kaftan (1948-49)
Al Butler (1961-62)

No. 10*

Connie Simmons (1946-47—1947-48)
Meyer (Mike) Bloom (1947-48)
Stan Noszka (1947-48—1948-49)
(also wore No. 11)
John Hazen (1948-49)
(also wore No. 3)
John Ezersky (1948-49—1949-50)
(also wore No. 16)
Gene Englund (1949-50)
Clarence (Kleggie) Hermsen (1950-51—1951-52)
*Jo Jo White (1969-70—1978-79)

No. 11

Kevin (Chuck) Connors (1946-47—1947-48)
Stan Noszka (1947-48—1948-49)
(also wore No. 10)
Chick Halbert (1948-49)
Tony Lavelli (1949-50)
(also wore No. 4)
Chuck Cooper (1950-51—1953-54)
Mel Counts (1964-65—1965-66)
Jim Barnett (1966-67)
Mal Graham (1967-68—1968-69)
Steve Kuberski (1969-70—1973-74; 1975-76—1977-78)
(also wore No. 33)
Charlie Scott (1975-76—1977-78)
Bob McAdoo (1978-79)
Tracy Jackson (1981-82)

No. 12

Art Spector (1946-47—1949-50)
Bob Donham (1950-51—1953-54)
Togo Palazzi (1954-55—1956-57)
Dan Swartz (1962-63)
Willie Naulls (1963-64—1965-66)
Ron Watts (1965-66—1966-67)
Tom Thacker (1967-68)
Don Chaney (1968-69—1974-75; 1977-78—1979-80)
(also wore No. 42)
Sidney Wicks (1976-77—1977-78)

No. 13

Mike (Red) Wallace (1946-47)
Gene Stump (1947-48—1948-49)
Brady Walker (1949-50—1950-51)
Kenny Sailors (1950-51)
Dick Mehen (1950-51)
Bob (Gabby) Harris (1950-51—1953-54)
(also wore No. 18)

No. 14*

Bob Eliason (1946-47)
Gerard Kelly (1946-47)
(also wore No. 24)
Ed Ehlers (1947-48—1948-49)
*Bob Cousy (1950-51—1962-63)

No. 15*

Hal Crisler (1946-47)
Jack (Dutch) Garfinkel (1946-47—1948-49)
(also wore No. 21)
Jim Seminoff (1948-49—1949-50)
Dwight (Red) Morrison (1954-55—1955-56)
*Tom Heinsohn (1956-57—1964-65)

No. 16*

John Ezersky (1948-49—1949-50)
(also wore No. 10)
John Mahnken (1949-50—1952-53)
Ed Mikan (1953-54)
Jack Nichols (1953-54—1957-58)
Ben Swain (1958-59)
John Richter (1959-60)
*Tom Sanders (1960-61—1972-73)

No. 17*

Virgil Vaughn (1946-47)
Bob Duffy (1946-47)
Jack Hewson (1947-48)
John Janisch (1947-48)
John Bach (1948-49)
Joe Mullaney (1949-50)
Horace (Bones) McKinney (1950-51—1951-52)
Gene Conley (1952-53; 1958-59—1960-61)
Don Barksdale (1953-54—1954-55)
Andy Phillip (1956-57—1957-58)
*John Havlicek (1962-63—1977-78)

No. 18*

Bob Harris (1950-51—1953-54)
(also wore No. 13)
Bob Brannum (1951-52—1954-55)
*Jim Loscutoff (1955-56—1963-64)
John Thompson (1964-65—1965-66)
(also wore No. 5)
Woody Sauldsberry (1965-66)
Bailey Howell (1966-67—1969-70)
*Dave Cowens (1970-71—1979-80)

No. 19*

Bob Doll (1948-49—1949-50)
Ed (Moose) Stanczak (1950-51)
Francis (Mo) Mahoney (1952-53)
Arnie Risen (1955-56—1957-58)
Maurice King (1959-60)
*Don Nelson (1965-66—1975-76)

No. 20

Al Lucas (1948-49)
Dick Hemric (1955-56—1956-57)
Lou Tsioropoulos (1956-57—1958-59)
(also wore No. 29)
Gene Guarilia (1959-60—1962-63)
Larry Siegfried (1963-64—1969-70)
Rex Morgan (1970-71—1971-72)
Phil Hankinson (1973-74—1974-75)
Fred Saunders (1976-77—1977-78)
Wayne Kreklow (1980-81)

No. 21*

Jack (Dutch) Garfinkel (1946-47—1948-49)
(also wore No. 15)
Frank (Apples) Kudelka (1950-51)
Ed (Moose) Stanczak (1950-51)
(also wore No. 19)
Andy Duncan (1950-51)
*Bill Sharman (1951-52—1960-61)
Gary Phillips (1961-62)
Jack (The Shot) Foley (1962-63)
John McCarthy (1963-64)
Ron Bonham (1964-65—1965-66)

No. 22*

Ed Sadowski (1947-48)
Bob Kinney (1948-49—1949-50)
*Ed Macauley (1950-51—1955-56)

No. 23*

Dick Dickey (1951-52)
Ernie Barrett (1953-54—1955-56)
*Frank Ramsey (1954-55; 1956-57—1963-64)

No. 24*

Gerard Kelly (1946-47)
(also wore No. 14)
Harry Boykoff (1950-51)
Fred Scolari (1954-55)
*Sam Jones (1957-58—1968-69)

No. 25*

*K.C. Jones (1958-59—1966-67)
(also wore No. 27)
Enoch (Bud) Olsen (1968-69)

No. 26

Toby Kimball (1966-67)
Rick Weitzman (1967-68)
Rich Johnson (1968-69—1970-71)
Kermit Washington (1977-78)

No. 27

K.C. Jones (1958-59—1966-67)
(also wore No. 25)
Johnny Jones (1967-68)
Rich Niemann (1969-70)
Bill Dinwiddie (1969-70—1970-71)
Mark Minor (1972-73)
Kevin Stacom (1974-75—1977-78; 1978-79)
Marvin Barnes (1978-79)

No. 28

Sihugo Green (1965-66)
Wayne Embry (1966-67—1967-68)
Jim (Bad News) Barnes (1968-69—1969-70)
Willie Williams (1970-71)
Clarence Glover (1971-72)

No. 29

Lou Tsioropoulos (1956-57—1958-59)
(also wore No. 20)
Henry Finkel (1969-70—1974-75)

No. 30

Glenn McDonald (1974-75—1975-76)
Cedric (Cornbread) Maxwell (1977-78—1981-82)
(also wore No. 31)
M. L. Carr (1979-80—1981-82)

No. 31

Tom Boswell (1975-76—1977-78)
Cedric (Cornbread) Maxwell (1977-78—1981-82)
(also wore No. 30)

No. 32

Steve Downing (1973-74—1974-75)
Jeff Judkins (1978-79—1979-80)
Kevin McHale (1980-81—1981-82)

No. 33

Steve Kuberski (1969-70—1973-74; 1975-76—1977-78)
(also wore No. 11)
Garfield Smith (1970-71—1971-72)
Ben Clyde (1974-75)
Larry Bird (1979-80—1981-82)

No. 34

Clyde Lovellette (1962-63—1963-64)
(also wore No. 4)
Bob Nordmann (1964-65)
Jim Ard (1974-75—1976-77)
Bob Bigelow (1977-78)
Dennis Awtrey (1978-79)

No. 35

Paul Silas (1972-73—1975-76)
Tom Barker (1978-79)
Billy Knight (1978-79)
Charles Bradley (1981-82)

No. 36

Ed Searcy (1975-76)

No. 40

Terry Duerod (1980-81—1981-82)

No. 41

Curtis Rowe (1976-77—1978-79)

No. 42

Don Chaney (1968-69—1974-75; 1977-78—1979-80)
(also wore No. 12)
Jerome Anderson (1975-76)
Bobby Wilson (1976-77)
Chris Ford (1978-79—1981-82)

No. 43

Earl Tatum (1978-79)
Gerald Henderson (1979-80—1981-82)

No. 44

Paul Westphal (1972-73—1974-75)
Dave Bing (1977-78)
Pete Maravich (1979-80)
Danny Ainge (1981-82)

No. 45

Frankie Sanders (1978-79)
Eric Fernsten (1979-80—1981-82)

No. 52

Norm Cook (1976-77)
Earl Williams (1978-79)

No. 53

Rick Robey (1978-79—1981-82)

No. 54

Zaid Abdul Aziz (Don Smith) (1977-78)

*Number retired in his honor.

Of the 190 players to have worn a Celtic uniform during a regular-season or playoff game, each one's jersey number has been recorded here except the following (where research has failed):
In order of season:
Earl Shannon, 5 games, 1948-49
Ward Gibson, 2 games, 1949-50
Bob Houbregs, 2 games, 1954-55

Notes:
Sometimes the same number was worn by more than one player during a season.
Occasionally, for a variety of reasons including lost baggage, a player wore a different number for a game or two. No effort has been made to compile those exceptions.
Some photographs in this book show players wearing numbers not indicated here. The reason may be the one cited above. More often, particularly in the franchise's early days, a player often donned any handy jersey when posing for photos. For example, Chuck Cooper is shown wearing No. 5 but wore only No. 11 in games during his Celtic career.
Is No. 13 unlucky? Mike (Red) Wallace was the first Celtic to wear it, on the original 1946-47 squad—and became the first Celt to be traded (to Toronto for Chuck Hoefer after only 24 games in a Boston uniform).
No Celtic has worn No. 13 since Bob Harris in the early 1950s. There's no Celtic ban on that number, according to Red Auerbach. "Nobody has asked for it," he shrugs.
And why has no Celtic ever worn Nos. 1 or 2, nor any worn Nos. 3, 4, 5, 8 or 9 in more than a decade or two? "For some reason the league had a rule for many years prohibiting players from wearing single digits," Auerbach says, "although it wasn't always followed closely."

CELTICS DRAFT CHOICES

(Number listed next to draftee is the order in which that player was drafted by the Celtics. The number is not necessarily the number of the round that player was drafted, although it often is.)

1946

No draft.

1947

1. Ed Ehlers, Purdue
2. Gene Stump, DePaul
3. Saul Mariaschin, Harvard
(No record of later draft choices.)

1948

1. George Hauptfuehrer, Harvard
(No record of later draft choices.)

1949

1. Tony Lavelli, Yale
*1A. George Kaftan, Holy Cross
2. Joe Mullaney, Holy Cross
*2A. Dermie O'Connell, Holy Cross
3. Bill Tom, Rice
4. Ed Little, Denver Junior College
5. Jim Simpson, Bates
6. Bill Vandenburgh, Washington
7. Duane Klueh, Indiana State
8. Emerson Speicher, Bowling Green
9. Bill Weight, Brigham Young
10. Russ Washburn, Colby

*Retroactive choices. Both Kaftan and O'Connell had played the final 21 games of the previous season, 1948-49, for the Celtics after graduating at midyear.

1950

1. Charlie Share, Bowling Green
2. Chuck Cooper, Duquesne
3. Bob Donham, Ohio State
4. Ken Reeves, Louisville
5. Jack Shelton, Oklahoma A&M
6. Francis (Mo) Mahoney, Brown
7. Dale Barnstable, Kentucky
8. Frank Oftring, Holy Cross
9. Bob Cope, Montana State
10. Matt Forman, Holy Cross

1951

1. Ernie Barrett, Kansas State
2. John Furlong, Pepperdine
3. Bill Garrett, Indiana
4. John Azary, Columbia
5. Bob Barnett, Evansville
6. Rip Gish, Western Kentucky
7. Jim Luisi, St. Francis (Brooklyn)
8. Hugo Kappler, North Carolina State

1952

1. Bill Stauffer, Missouri
2. Jim Iverson, Kansas State
3. J. C. Maze, Southwest Texas
4. Bob Hedderick, Canisius
5. Don Johnson, Oklahoma A&M
6. Jim Buchanan, Nebraska
7. Frank Eydt, Cornell
8. Gordon Mungier, Spring Hill
9. Jim Dilling, Holy Cross
* Gene Conley, Washington State

*Selected after draft meeting.

1953

1. Frank Ramsey, Kentucky
2. Chet Noe, Oregon
3. Cliff Hagan, Kentucky
4. Earl Markey, Holy Cross
5. John Holup, George Washington
6. Vern Stokes, St. Francis (Brooklyn)
7. Lou Tsioropoulos, Kentucky
8. Ted Lallier, Colby
9. Lewis Gilcrease, Southwest Texas
10. Tom Lillis, St. Louis
11. Gil Reich, Kansas
12. Jim Doherty, Whitworth

1954

1. Tony Palazzi, Holy Cross
2. Dwight Morrison, Idaho
3. Henry Daubenschmidt, St. Francis (Brooklyn)
4. Ron Perry, Holy Cross
5. Troy Burrus, West Texas
6. Otto Krieghauser, Washington (Mo.)
7. Paul Estergaard, Bradley
8. Jim Young, Santa Clara
9. Tony Daukas, Boston College
10. Bill Johnson, Nebraska

1955

1. Jim Loscutoff, Oregon
2. Dick Hemric, Wake Forest
3. Buzz Wilkinson, Virginia
4. Bart Leach, Penn
5. Bob Patterson, Tulsa
6. John Mahoney, William & Mary
7. John Moore, UCLA
8. Dean Parsons, Washington
9. Nick Romanoff, College of Pacific
10. Jim Ahearn, Connecticut
11. Carl Hartman, Alderson-Broaddus
12. Mark Davis, Marietta
13. Henry Dooley, Wiley
14. Bob Scuddelari, Cooper Union

1956

*1. Bill Russell, San Francisco
**1A. Tom Heinsohn, Holy Cross
3. K.C. Jones, San Francisco
4. George Linn, Alabama
5. Dan Swartz, Morehead
6. Bill Logan, Iowa
7. Don Boldebuck, Houston
8. O'Neal Weaver, Houston
9. Vic Molodet, North Carolina State
10. Jim Houston, Brandeis

*Acquired second pick in draft by trading veteran Ed Macauley and rookie Cliff Hagan, just coming out of the Army, to St. Louis for the Hawks' No. 1 choice, which the Celtics used to select Russell. (The Rochester Royals had first pick in draft but felt they could not afford Russell, so instead selected Sihugo Green of Duquesne.)

**Heinsohn was a territorial choice.

1957

1. Sam Jones, North Carolina College
2. Dick O'Neal, Texas Christian
3. Chuck Schramm, Western Illinois
4. Jim Ashmore, Mississippi State
5. Grady Wallace, South Carolina
6. Maurice King, Kansas
7. Dick Grott, Denver
8. Bill Von Weghe, Rhode Island
9. Joe Gibbon, Mississippi
10. Jack Butcher, Memphis State

1958

1. Ben Swain, Texas Southern
2. Jim Smith, Steubenville
3. Jim Cunningham, Fordham
4. Dom Flora, Washington & Lee
5. Gene Brown, San Francisco
6. Dave Kelleher, Morehead
7. Rudy Finderson, Brandeis

1959

1. John Richter, North Carolina State
2. Gene Guarilia, George Washington
3. Ralph Crosthwaite, Eastern Kentucky
4. Ed Kazakavich, Scranton
5. Don Lange, William & Mary
6. Bob Cumings, Boston University

1960

1. Tom Sanders, New York University
2. Leroy Wright, College of Pacific
3. Mike Graney, Notre Dame
4. Sid Cohen, Kentucky
5. Wayne Lawrence, Texas A&M
6. George Newman, Kentucky

1961

1. Gary Phillips, Houston
2. Al Butler, Niagara
3. Bill Depp, Vanderbilt
4. Carl Cole, Eastern Kentucky
5. Bob DiStefano, North Carolina State
6. New Twyman, Duquesne
7. Mel Klein, Aberdeen State

1962

1. John Havlicek, Ohio State
2. Jack Foley, Holy Cross
3. Jim Hadnot, Providence
4. Roger Strickland, Jacksonville
5. Gary Daniels, Citadel
6. Jim Hooley, Boston College
7. Clyde Arnold, Duquesne
8. Chuck Chevalier, Boston College
9. Mike Cingiser, Brown

1963

1. Bill Green, Colorado State
2. Ken Saylors, Arkansas Tech
3. Connie McGuire, Southeast Oklahoma
4. W.D. Stroud, Mississippi State
5. Vinnie Ernst, Providence
6. Herb McGee, Philadelphia Textile

1964

1. Mel Counts, Oregon State
2. Ron Bonham, Cincinnati
3. John Thompson, Providence
4. Joe Strawder, Bradley
5. Nick Werkman, Seton Hall
6. Levern Tart, Bradley
7. Rich Falk, Northwestern
8. Jeff Blue, Butler
9. Charlie Kelley, West Virginia Tech
10. Duane Corriveau, Clark

1965

1. Ollie Johnson, San Francisco
2. Ron Watts, Wake Forest
3. Toby Kimball, Connecticut
4. Richie Tarrant, St. Michael's
5. Don Davidson, Davidson
6. Haskell Tison, Duke
7. George Deehan, Lenoir Rhyne

1966

1. Jim Barnett, Oregon
2. Leon Clark, Wyoming
3. Gary Turner, Texas Christian
4. John Austin, Boston College
5. Charlie Hunter, Oklahoma City
6. Gerry Ward, Maryland
7. Russ Gumina, San Francisco

1967

1. Mal Graham, New York University
2. Neville Shed, Texas El Paso
3. Mike Redd, Kentucky Wesleyan
4. Ed Hummer, Princeton
5. Edgar Lacey, UCLA
6. Andy Anderson, Canisius
7. Henry Brown, Lowell Tech
8. Rick Weitzman, Northeastern
9. Joe Harrington, Maryland

1968

1. Don Chaney, Houston
2. Garfield Smith, Eastern Kentucky
3. Rich Johnson, Grambling
4. Thad Jaracz, Kentucky
5. Jerry Newsome, Indiana State
6. Mike Lewis, Duke
7. Julius Keyes, Alcorn A&M
8. Bill Butler, St. Bonaventure
9. Ivan Leschinsky, Long Island

1969

1. Jo Jo White, Kansas
2. Julius Keyes, Alcorn A&M
3. Steve Kuberski, Bradley
4. George Thompson, Marquette
5. Dolph Puliam, Drake
6. Jim Johnson, Wisconsin
7. Bob Whitmore, Notre Dame
8. Gordon Smith, Cincinnati
9. Jim Picka, High Point

1970

1. Dave Cowens, Florida State
2. Rex Morgan, Jacksonville
3. Willie Williams, Florida State
4. John McKinney, Norfolk State
5. Tom Carter, Paul Quinn College
6. Rod McIntyre, Jacksonville
7. Charlie Scott, North Carolina
8. Bob Croft, Tennessee
9. Tom Little, Seattle
10. Mike Maloy, Davidson

1971

1. Clarence Glover, Western Kentucky
2. Jim Rose, Western Kentucky
3. Dave Robisch, Kansas
4. Randy Denton, Duke
5. Thorpe Webber, Vanderbilt
6. Skip Young, Florida State
7. John Ribock, South Carolina
8. Ray Green, California (Pa.) State
9. Dale Dover, Harvard

1972

1. Paul Westphal, Southern Cal
2. Dennis Wuyicik, North Carolina
3. Wayne Grabiec, Michigan
4. Nate Stephens, Long Beach
5. Bryan Adrian, Davidson
6. Doug Holcomb, Memphis State
7. Steve Previs, North Carolina
8. Sam McCamey, Oral Roberts
9. Mark Minor, Ohio State
10. Marty Hunt, Kenyon

1973

1. Steve Downing, Indiana
2. Phil Hankinson, Penn
3. Martinez Denmon, Iowa State
4. Richard Fuqua, Oral Roberts
5. Byron Jones, San Francisco
6. Joe Cafferky, No. Carolina State
7. Mike Stewart, Santa Clara
8. Robert White, Sam Houston
9. Corky Taylor, Minnesota
10. Steve Turner, Vanderbilt

1974

1. Glenn McDonald, Long Beach
2. Kevin Stacom, Providence
3. Cliff Pondexter, Long Beach
4. Lerman Battle, Fairmont State
5. Ben Clyde, Florida State
6. Gene Harmon, Creighton
7. Ron Brown, Penn State
8. Richard Wallace, Georgia Southern
9. Al Skinner, Massachusetts
10. Phil Rodgers, Fairchild

1975

1. Tom Boswell, South Carolina
2. Jerome Anderson, West Virginia
3. Cyrus Mann, Illinois State
4. Darrell Brown, Fordham
5. Rick Coleman, Jacksonville
6. Al Boswell, Oral Roberts
7. Roger Morningstar, Kansas
8. Robert Rhodes, Albany State
9. Bill Endicott, Massachusetts

1976

1. Norm Cook, Kansas
2. Jerrel Fort, Nebraska
3. Lewis Linder, Kentucky State
4. Louis McKinney, St. Louis
5. Art Collins, Biscayne
6. Ralph Drollinger, UCLA
7. John Clark, Northeastern
8. Bill Collins, Boston College
9. Otho Tucker, Illinois

1977

1. Cedric Maxwell, North Carolina-Charlotte
2. Skip Brown, Wake Forest
3. Jeff Cummings, Tulane
4. Bill Langloh, Virginia
5. Ray Pace, Rutgers-Camden
6. Dave Kyle, Cleveland State
7. Tom Harris, Bowling Green

1978

1. Larry Bird, Indiana State
2. Freeman Williams, Portland State
3. Jeff Judkins, Utah
4. Dana Skinner, Merrimack
5. Dave Nelson, Bloomfield (N.J.)
6. Greg Tynes, Seton Hall
7. Dave Winey, Minnesota
8. Steve Balkun, Fairfield
9. Kim Fisher, Fairfield
10. Les Anderson, George Washington
11. Walter Harrigan, Brandeis

1979

1. Wayne Kreklow, Drake
2. Ernesto Malcolm, Briarcliff
3. Nick Galis, Seton Hall
4. Jimmy Allen, New Haven
5. Marvin Delph, Arkansas
6. Steve Castellan, Virginia
7. Glen Sudhop, North Carolina State
8. Kevin Sinnett, Navy
9. Alton Byrd, Columbia

1980

*1. Kevin McHale, Minnesota
2. Arnette Hallman, Purdue
**3. Ronnie Perry Jr., Holy Cross
4. Donald Newman, Idaho
5. Kevin Hamilton, Iona
6. Rufus Harris, Maine
7. Ken Evans, Norfolk State
8. Les Henson, Virginia Tech
9. Steve Wright, Boston University
10. Brian Jung, Northwestern
11. John Nolan, Providence

1981

1. Charles Bradley, Wyoming
2. Tracy Jackson, Notre Dame
3. Danny Ainge, Brigham Young
4. John Johnson, Michigan
5. Stanley Williams, LaSalle
6. Glen Grunwald, Indiana
7. Steve Waite, Iowa
8. Tom Seaman, Holy Cross
9. George Morrow, Creighton
10. Grey McCray, Virginia Commonwealth
11. Ken Matthews, North Carolina State

1982

1. Darren Tillis, Cleveland State
2. Tony Guy, Kansas
3. Perry Moss, Northeastern
4. Greg Stewart, Tulsa
5. William Brown, St. Peter's (N.J.)
6. John Schweitz, Richmond
7. Phil Collins, West Virginia
8. Ed Spriggs, Georgetown
9. Panayoti Giannakis, Hellenic
10. Landon Turner, Indiana

*The Celtics traded their two first-round draft selections—first and 13th places—to Golden State. In exchange, they received four-year veteran center Robert Parish and third choice in the draft, on which they picked McHale.

**The Celtics thus completed drafting a father and son, having chosen Ron Perry Sr. as their fourth pick in the 1954 draft. Perry Sr. never reported to the Celtics, entering the Marine Corps instead to fulfill military obligation; Perry Jr. reported to Celtic training camp after playing a summer in the Chicago White Sox' farm system, was a late cut by the Celts, and stayed with baseball until an injury cut his career short the following season.

(The only other father-son duo in Celtic history: the Wrights. College of Pacific's Leroy Wright was a No. 2 choice behind top pick Tom Sanders in 1960; Rhode Island's Stan Wright was a free-agent candidate in both 1978 and 1979 training camps. Neither Wright appeared in a regular-season game.)

Incidentally, the Celtics have never drafted brothers. However, they signed the Simmons brothers—Connie and Johnny—in 1946, the league's first season when there was no college draft. The Simmonses are the only brothers ever to play for the Celtics.

John Thompson, now successful basketball coach at Georgetown, was a Celtic 1964-65 and 1965-66 out of Providence College.

CELTICS WORLD CHAMPIONS

1956-57
(44-28* regular season, 7-3 playoffs)
Coach: Red Auerbach

Bob Cousy (64 games), Tom Heinsohn (72), Dick Hemric (67), Jim Loscutoff (70), Jack Nichols (61), Togo Palazzi (20***), Andy Philip (67), Frank Ramsey (35), Arnie Risen (43), Bill Russell (48), Bill Sharman (67) and Lou Tsioropoulos (52). Trainer: Harvey Cohn.

***Palazzi sold on December 29 to Syracuse, where he played 43 more games. teams.

1958-59
(52-20* regular season, 8-3 playoffs)
Coach: Red Auerbach

Gene Conley (50 games), Bob Cousy (65), Tom Heinsohn (66), K.C. Jones (49), Sam Jones (71), Jim Loscutoff (66), Frank Ramsey (72), Bill Russell (70), Bill Sharman (72), Ben Swain (58) and Lou Tsioropoulos (35). Trainer: Buddy LeRoux.

1959-60
(59-16* regular season, 8-5 playoffs)
Coach: Red Auerbach

Gene Conley (71 games), Bob Cousy (75), Gene Guarilia (48), Tom Heinsohn (75), K.C. Jones (74), Sam Jones (74), Maurice King (1), Jim Loscutoff (28), Frank Ramsey (73), John Richter (66), Bill Russell (74) and Bill Sharman (71). Trainer: Buddy LeRoux.

1960-61
(57-22* regular season, 8-2 playoffs)
Coach: Red Auerbach

Gene Conley (75 games), Bob Cousy (76), Gene Guarilia (25), Tom Heinsohn (74), K.C. Jones (78), Sam Jones (78), Jim Loscutoff (76), Frank Ramsey (79), Bill Russell (78), Tom Sanders (68) and Bill Sharman (61). Trainer: Buddy LeRoux.

1961-62
(60-20* regular season, 8-6 playoffs)
Coach: Red Auerbach

Carl Braun (48 games), Bob Cousy (75), Gene Guarilia (45), Tom Heinsohn (79), K.C. Jones (80), Sam Jones (78), Jim Loscutoff (79), Gary Phillips (67), Frank Ramsey (79), Bill Russell (76) and Tom Sanders (80). Trainer: Buddy LeRoux.

1962-63
(58-22* regular season, 8-5 playoffs)
Coach: Red Auerbach

Bob Cousy (76 games), Gene Guarilia (11), John Havlicek (80), Tom Heinsohn (76), K.C. Jones (79), Sam Jones (76), Jim Loscutoff (63), Clyde Lovellette (61), Frank Ramsey (77), Bill Russell (78), Tom Sanders (80) and Dan Swartz (39). Trainer: Buddy LeRoux.

1963-64
(59-21* regular season, 8-2 playoffs)
Coach: Red Auerbach

John Havlicek (80 games), Tom Heinsohn (76), K.C. Jones (80), Sam Jones (76), Jim Loscutoff (53), Clyde Lovellette (45), Johnny McCarthy (28), Willie Naulls (78), Frank Ramsey (75), Bill Russell (78), Tom Sanders (80) and Larry Siegfried (31). Trainer: Buddy LeRoux.

1964-65
(62-18* regular season, 8-4 playoffs)
Coach: Red Auerbach

Ron Bonham (37 games), Mel Counts (54), John Havlicek (75), Tom Heinsohn (67), K.C. Jones (78), Sam Jones (80), Willie Naulls (71), Bob Nordmann (3), Bill Russell (78), Tom Sanders (80), Larry Siegfried (72), John Thompson (64) and Gerry Ward (3). Trainer: Buddy LeRoux.

1965-66
(54-26, 2d in East one game behind Philadelphia during regular season; 11-6 in playoffs)
Coach: Red Auerbach

Ron Bonham (39 games), Mel Counts (67), Sihugo Green (10), John Havlicek (71), K.C. Jones (80), Sam Jones (67), Willie Naulls (71), Don Nelson (75), Bill Russell (78), Tom Sanders (72), Woody Sauldsberry (39), Larry Siegfried (71), John Thompson (10) and Ron Watts (1). Trainer: Buddy LeRoux.

1967-68
(54-28, 2d in East eight games behind Philadelphia during regular season; 12-7 in playoffs)
Player-coach: Bill Russell

Wayne Embry (78 games), Mal Graham (78), John Havlicek (82), Bailey Howell (82), Johnny Jones (51), Sam Jones (73), Don Nelson (82), Bill Russell (78), Tom Sanders (78), Larry Siegfried (62), Tom Thacker (65) and Rick Weitzman (25). Trainer: Joe DeLauri.

1968-69
(48-34, 4th in East nine games behind first-place Baltimore during regular season; 12-6 in playoffs)
Player-coach: Bill Russell

Jim Barnes (49 games), Emmette Bryant (80), Don Chaney (20), Mal Graham (22), John Havlicek (82), Bailey Howell (78), Rich Johnson (31), Sam Jones (70), Don Nelson (82), Bud Olsen (7), Bill Russell (77), Tom Sanders (82) and Larry Siegfried (79). Trainer: Joe DeLauri.

1973-74
(56-26 regular season, 12-6 playoffs)
Coach: Tom Heinsohn
Assistant Coach: John Killilea

Don Chaney (81 games), Dave Cowens (80), Steve Downing (24), Henry Finkel (60), Phil Hankinson (28), John Havlicek (76), Steve Kuberski (78), Don Nelson (82), Paul Silas (82), Paul Westphal (82), Jo Jo White (82) and Art Williams (67). Trainer: Frank Challant. Assistant trainer: Mark Volk.

1975-76
(54-28 regular season, 12-6 playoffs)
Coach: Tom Heinsohn
Assistant Coach: John Killilea

Jerome Anderson (22 games), Jim Ard (81), Tom Boswell (35), Dave Cowens (78), John Havlicek (76), Steve Kuberski (60), Glenn McDonald (75), Don Nelson (75), Charlie Scott (82), Ed Searcy (4), Paul Silas (81), Kevin Stacom (77) and Jo Jo White (82). Trainer: Frank Challant. Assistant trainer: Mark Volk.

*Best record in NBA.

1980-81
(62-20** regular season, 12-5 playoffs)
Coach: Bill Fitch
Assistant Coaches: K.C. Jones and Jimmy Rodgers

Nate Archibald (80 games), Larry Bird (82), M. L. Carr (41), Terry Duerod (32***), Eric Fernsten (45), Chris Ford (82), Gerald Henderson (82), Wayne Kreklow (25***), Cedric Maxwell (81), Kevin McHale (82), Robert Parish (82) and Rick Robey (82). Trainer: Ray Melchiorre.

***Duerod started season with Dallas and was acquired by Boston as a free agent on December 4; Kreklow was waived by Celtics on January 21.

*Best record in NBA.
**Tied for best record in NBA.

CELTICS DIVISION CHAMPIONS

*1956-57	(44-28**)
1957-58	(49-23**)
*1958-59	(52-20**)
*1959-60	(59-16**)
*1960-61	(57-22**)
*1961-62	(60-20**)
*1962-63	(58-22**)
*1963-64	(59-21**)
*1964-65	(62-18**)
1971-72	(56-26)
1972-73	(68-14**)
*1973-74	(56-26)
1974-75	(60-22***)
*1975-76	(54-28)
1979-80	(61-21**)
*1980-81	(62-20***)
1981-82	(63-19**)

*Also won NBA championship.

**Best record in NBA.

***Tied for best record in NBA.

Notes:

Won 1965-66 NBA championship but finished second in NBA East with a 54-26 regular-season record, one game behind Philadelphia.

Won 67-68 NBA championship but finished second in NBA East with a 54-28 regular-season record, eight games behind Philadelphia.

Won 1968-69 NBA championship but finished fourth in NBA East with a 48-34 regular-season record, nine games behind Baltimore.

Officially speaking

Dave Cowens

Bob Cousy

Bill Russell

John Havlicek

John Havlicek, K.C. Jones, Bill Russell and Sam Jones

PLAYOFF RESULTS

1946-47

Did not qualify

1947-48

Eastern Semifinals

March 28—Chicago 79, Celtics 72 (H)*
March 31—Celtics 81, Chicago 77 (H)*
April 2—Chicago 81, Celtics 74 (H)*
(Celtics eliminated, 1-2)

*Chicago home court unavailable.

1948-49

Did not qualify.

1949-50

Did not qualify.

1950-51

Eastern Semifinals

March 20—New York 83, Celtics 69 (H)
March 22—New York 92, Celtics 78 (A)
(Celtics eliminated, 0-2)

1951-52

Eastern Semifinals

March 19—Celtics 105, New York 94 (H)
March 23—New York 101, Celtics 97 (A)
March 26—New York 88, Celtics 87 (2 OTs) (H)
(Celtics eliminated, 1-2)

1952-53

Eastern Semifinals

March 19—Celtics 87, Syracuse 81 (A)
March 21—Celtics 111, Syracuse 105 (4 OTs) (H)
(Celtics win series, 2-0)

Eastern Finals

March 25—New York 95, Celtics 91 (A)
March 26—Celtics 86, New York 70 (H)
March 28—New York 101, Celtics 82 (A)
March 29—New York 82, Celtics 75 (H)
(Celtics eliminated, 1-3)

1953-54

Eastern Semifinals

March 16—Celtics 93, New York 71 (A)
March 17—Syracuse 96, Celtics 95 (1 OT) (H)
March 20—Celtics 79, New York 78 (H)
March 22—Syracuse 98, Celtics 85 (A)
(Celtics advanced to Eastern Finals with 2-2 record after New York was eliminated in round robin after two losses each to Celtics and New York.)

Eastern Finals

March 25—Syracuse 109, Celtics 94 (A)
March 27—Syracuse 83, Celtics 76 (H)
(Celtics eliminated, 0-2)

1954-55

Eastern Semifinals

March 15—Celtics 122, New York 101 (H)
March 16—New York 102, Celtics 95 (A)
March 19—Celtics 116, New York 109 (A)
(Celtics won series, 2-1)

Eastern Finals

March 22—Syracuse 110, Celtics 100 (A)
March 24—Syracuse 116, Celtics 110 (A)
March 26—Celtics 100, Syracuse 97 (1 OT) (H)
March 27—Syracuse 110, Celtics 94 (H)
(Celtics eliminated, 1-3)

1955-56

Eastern Semifinals

March 17—Celtics 110, Syracuse 92 (H)
March 19—Syracuse 101, Celtics 98 (A)
March 21—Syracuse 102, Celtics 97 (H)
(Celtics eliminated, 1-2)

1956-57

Eastern Semifinals

Bye

Eastern Finals

March 21—Celtics 108, Syracuse 90 (H)
March 23—Celtics 120, Syracuse 105 (A)
March 24—Celtics 83, Syracuse 80 (H)
(Celtics won series, 3-0)

NBA Finals

March 30—St. Louis 125, Celtics 123 (1 OT) (H)
March 31—Celtics 119, St. Louis 99 (H)
April 6—St. Louis 100, Celtics 98 (A)
April 7—Celtics 123, St. Louis 118 (A)
April 9—Celtics 124, St. Louis 109 (H)
April 11—St. Louis 96, Celtics 94 (A)
April 13—Celtics 125, St. Louis 123 (2 OTs) (H)
(Celtics won series, 4-3, and NBA title)

1957-58

Eastern Semifinals

Bye

Eastern Finals

March 19—Celtics 107, Philadelphia 98 (H)
March 22—Celtics 109, Philadelphia 87 (A)
March 23—Celtics 106, Philadelphia 92 (H)
March 26—Philadelphia 111, Celtics 97 (A)
March 27—Celtics 93, Philadelphia 88 (H)
(Celtics won series, 4-1)

NBA Finals

March 29—St. Louis 104, Celtics 102 (H)
March 30—Celtics 136, St. Louis 112 (H)
April 2—St. Louis 111, Celtics 107 (A)
April 5—Celtics 109, St. Louis 98 (A)
April 9—St. Louis 102, Celtics 100 (H)
April 12—St. Louis 110, Celtics 109 (A)
(Celtics eliminated, 2-4)

1958-59

Eastern Semifinals

Bye

Eastern Finals

March 18—Celtics 131, Syracuse 109 (H)
March 21—Syracuse 120, Celtics 118 (A)
March 22—Celtics 133, Syracuse 111 (H)
March 25—Syracuse 119, Celtics 107 (A)
March 28—Celtics 129, Syracuse 108 (H)
March 29—Syracuse 133, Celtics 121 (A)
April 1—Celtics 130, Syracuse 125 (H)
(Celtics won series, 4-3)

NBA Finals

April 4—Celtics 118, Minneapolis 115 (H)
April 5—Celtics 128, Minneapolis 108 (H)
April 7—Celtics 123, Minneapolis 110 (A)*
April 9—Celtics 118, Minneapolis 113 (A)
(Celtics won series, 4-0, and NBA title)

*At St. Paul.

1959-60

Eastern Semifinals

Bye

Eastern Finals

March 16—Celtics 111, Philadelphia 105 (H)
March 18—Philadelphia 115, Celtics 110 (A)
March 19—Celtics 120, Philadelphia 90 (H)
March 20—Celtics 112, Philadelphia 104 (A)
March 22—Philadelphia 128, Celtics 107 (H)
March 24—Celtics 119, Philadelphia 117 (A)
(Celtics won series, 4-2)

NBA Finals

March 27—Celtics 140, St. Louis 122 (H)
March 29—St. Louis 113, Celtics 103 (H)
April 2—Celtics 102, St. Louis 86 (A)
April 3—St. Louis 106, Celtics 96 (A)
April 5—Celtics 127, St. Louis 102 (H)
April 7—St. Louis 105, Celtics 102 (A)
April 9—Celtics 122, St. Louis 103 (H)
(Celtics won series, 4-3, and NBA title)

1960-61

Eastern Semifinals

Bye

Eastern Finals

March 19—Celtics 128, Syracuse 115 (H)
March 21—Syracuse 115, Celtics 98 (A)
March 23—Celtics 133, Syracuse 110 (H)
March 25—Celtics 120, Syracuse 107 (A)
March 26—Celtics 123, Syracuse 101 (H)
(Celtics won series, 4-1)

NBA Finals

April 2—Celtics 129, St. Louis 95 (H)
April 5—Celtics 116, St. Louis 108 (H)
April 8—St. Louis 124, Celtics 120 (A)
April 9—Celtics 119, St. Louis 104 (A)
April 11—Celtics 121, St. Louis 112 (H)
(Celtics won series, 4-1, and NBA title)

Bill Russell naps between flights, travel the unseen and unglamorous side of pro basketball life—even for world champions.

1961-62

Eastern Semifinals

Bye

Eastern Finals

March 24—Celtics 117, Philadelphia 89 (H)
March 27—Philadelphia 113, Celtics 106 (A)
March 28—Celtics 129, Philadelphia 114 (H)
March 31—Philadelphia 110, Celtics 106 (A)
April 1—Celtics 119, Philadelphia 104 (H)
April 3—Philadelphia 109, Celtics 99 (A)
April 5—Celtics 109, Philadelphia 107 (H)
(Celtics won series, 4-3)

NBA Finals

April 7—Celtics 122, Los Angeles 108 (H)
April 8—Los Angeles 129, Celtics 122 (H)
April 10—Los Angeles 117, Celtics 115 (A)
April 11—Celtics 115, Los Angeles 103 (A)
April 14—Los Angeles 126, Celtics 121 (H)
April 16—Celtics 119, Los Angeles 105 (A)
April 18—Celtics 110, Los Angeles 107 (1 OT) (H)
(Celtics won series, 4-3, and NBA title)

1962-63

Eastern Semifinals

Bye

Eastern Finals

March 28—Cincinnati 135, Celtics 132 (H)
March 29—Celtics 125, Cincinnati 102 (A)
March 31—Cincinnati 121, Celtics 116 (H)
April 3—Celtics 128, Cincinnati 110 (A)
April 6—Celtics 125, Cincinnati 120 (H)
April 7—Cincinnati 109, Celtics 99 (A)
April 10—Celtics 142, Cincinnati 131 (H)
(Celtics won series, 4-3)

NBA Finals

April 14—Celtics 117, Los Angeles 114 (H)
April 16—Celtics 113, Los Angeles 106 (H)
April 17—Los Angeles 119, Celtics 99 (A)
April 19—Celtics 108, Los Angeles 105 (A)
April 21—Los Angeles 126, Celtics 119 (H)
April 24—Celtics 112, Los Angeles 109 (A)
(Celtics won series, 4-2, and NBA title)

1963-64

Eastern Semifinals

Bye

Eastern Finals

March 31—Celtics 103, Cincinnati 87 (H)
April 2—Celtics 101, Cincinnati 90 (H)
April 5—Celtics 102, Cincinnati 92 (A)
April 7—Cincinnati 102, Celtics 93 (A)
April 9—Celtics 109, Cincinnati 95 (H)
(Celtics won series, 4-1)

NBA Finals

April 18—Celtics 108, San Francisco 96 (H)
April 20—Celtics 124, San Francisco 101 (H)
April 22—San Francisco 115, Celtics 91 (A)
April 24—Celtics 98, San Francisco 95 (A)
April 26—Celtics 105, San Francisco 99 (H)
(Celtics won series, 4-1, and NBA title)

1964-65

Eastern Semifinals

Bye

Eastern Finals

April 4—Celtics 108, Philadelphia 98 (H)
April 6—Philadelphia 109, Celtics 103 (A)
April 8—Celtics 112, Philadelphia 94 (H)
April 9—Philadelphia 134, Celtics 131 (1 OT) (A)
April 11—Celtics 114, Philadelphia 108 (H)
April 13—Philadelphia 112, Celtics 106 (A)
April 15—Celtics 110, Philadelphia 109 (H)
(Celtics won series, 4-3)

NBA Finals

April 18—Celtics 142, Los Angeles 110 (H)
April 19—Celtics 129, Los Angeles 123 (H)
April 21—Los Angeles 126, Celtics 105 (A)
April 23—Celtics 112, Los Angeles 99 (A)
April 25—Celtics 129, Los Angeles 96 (H)
(Celtics won series, 4-1, and NBA title)

1965-66

Eastern Semifinals

March 23—Cincinnati 107, Celtics 103 (H)
March 26—Celtics 132, Cincinnati 125 (A)
March 27—Cincinnati 113, Celtics 107 (H)
March 30—Celtics 120, Cincinnati 103 (A)
April 1—Celtics 112, Cincinnati 103 (H)
(Celtics won series, 3-2)

Eastern Finals

April 3—Celtics 115, Philadelphia 96 (A)
April 6—Celtics 114, Philadelphia 93 (H)
April 7—Philadelphia 111, Celtics 105 (A)
April 10—Celtics 114, Philadelphia 108 (1 OT) (H)
April 12—Celtics 120, Philadelphia 112 (A)
(Celtics won series, 4-1)

NBA Finals

April 17—Los Angeles 133, Celtics 129 (1 OT) (H)
April 19—Celtics 129, Los Angeles 109 (H)
April 20—Celtics 120, Los Angeles 106 (A)
April 22—Celtics 122, Los Angeles 117 (A)
April 24—Los Angeles 121, Celtics 117 (H)
April 26—Los Angeles 123, Celtics 115 (A)
April 28—Celtics 95, Los Angeles 93 (H)
(Celtics won series, 4-3, and NBA title)

1966-67

Eastern Semifinals

March 21—Celtics 140, New York 110 (H)
March 25—Celtics 115, New York 108 (A)
March 26—New York 123, Celtics 112 (H)
March 28—Celtics 118, New York 109 (A)
(Celtics won series, 3-1)

Eastern Finals

March 31—Philadelphia 127, Celtics 113 (A)
April 2—Philadelphia 107, Celtics 102 (H)
April 5—Philadelphia 115, Celtics 104 (A)
April 9—Celtics 121, Philadelphia 117 (H)
April 11—Philadelphia 140, Celtics 116 (A)
(Celtics eliminated, 1-4)

1967-68

Eastern Semifinals

March 24—Celtics 123, Detroit 116 (H)
March 25—Detroit 126, Celtics 116 (A)
March 27—Detroit 109, Celtics 98 (H)
March 28—Celtics 135, Detroit 110 (A)
March 31—Celtics 110, Detroit 96 (H)
April 1—Celtics 111, Detroit 103 (A)
(Celtics won series, 4-2)

Eastern Finals

April 5—Celtics 127, Philadelphia 118 (A)
April 10—Philadelphia 115, Celtics 106 (H)
April 11—Philadelphia 122, Celtics 114 (A)
April 14—Philadelphia 110, Celtics 105 (H)
April 15—Celtics 122, Philadelphia 104 (A)
April 17—Celtics 114, Philadelphia 106 (H)
April 19—Celtics 100, Philadelphia 96 (A)
(Celtics won series, 4-3)

NBA Finals

April 21—Celtics 107, Los Angeles 101 (H)
April 24—Los Angeles 123, Celtics 113 (H)
April 26—Celtics 127, Los Angeles 119 (A)
April 28—Los Angeles 119, Celtics 105 (A)
April 30—Celtics 120, Los Angeles 117 (1 OT) (H)
May 2—Celtics 124, Los Angeles 109 (A)
(Celtics won series, 4-2, and NBA title)

1968-69

Eastern Semifinals

March 26—Celtics 114, Philadelphia 100 (A)
March 28—Celtics 134, Philadelphia 103 (H)
March 30—Celtics 125, Philadelphia 118 (A)
April 1—Philadelphia 119, Celtics 116 (H)
April 4—Celtics 93, Philadelphia 90 (A)
(Celtics won series, 4-1)

Eastern Finals

April 6—Celtics 108, New York 100 (A)
April 9—Celtics 112, New York 97 (H)
April 10—New York 101, Celtics 91 (A)
April 13—Celtics 97, New York 96 (H)
April 14—New York 112, Celtics 104 (A)
April 18—Celtics 106, New York 105 (H)
(Celtics won series, 4-2)

NBA Finals

April 23—Los Angeles 120, Celtics 118 (A)
April 25—Los Angeles 118, Celtics 112 (A)
April 27—Celtics 111, Los Angeles 105 (H)
April 29—Celtics 89, Los Angeles 88 (H)
May 1—Los Angeles 117, Celtics 104 (A)
May 3—Celtics 99, Los Angeles 90 (H)
May 5—Celtics 108, Los Angeles 106 (A)
(Celtics won series, 4-3, and NBA title)

1969-70

Did not qualify.

1970-71

Did not qualify.

1971-72

Eastern Semifinals

March 29—Celtics 126, Atlanta 108 (H)
March 31—Atlanta 113, Celtics 104 (A)
April 2—Celtics 136, Atlanta 113 (H)
April 4—Atlanta 112, Celtics 110 (A)
April 7—Celtics 124, Atlanta 114 (H)
April 9—Celtics 127, Atlanta 118 (A)
(Celtics won series, 4-2)

Eastern Finals

April 13—New York 116, Celtics 94 (H)
April 16—New York 106, Celtics 105 (A)
April 19—Celtics 115, New York 109 (H)
April 21—New York 116, Celtics 98 (A)
April 23—New York 111, Celtics 103 (H)
(Celtics eliminated, 1-4)

1972-73

Eastern Semifinals

April 1—Celtics 134, Atlanta 109 (H)
April 4—Celtics 126, Atlanta 113 (A)
April 6—Atlanta 118, Celtics 105 (H)
April 8—Atlanta 97, Celtics 94 (A)
April 11—Celtics 108, Atlanta 101 (H)
April 13—Celtics 121, Atlanta 103 (A)
(Celtics won series, 4-2)

Eastern Finals

April 15—Celtics 134, New York 108 (H)
April 18—New York 129, Celtics 96 (A)
April 20—New York 98, Celtics 91 (H)
April 22—New York 117, Celtics 110 (2 OTs) (A)
April 25—Celtics 98, New York 97 (H)
April 27—Celtics 110, New York 100 (A)
April 29—New York 94, Celtics 78 (H)
(Celtics eliminated, 3-4)

Referees often saw Red

1973-74

Eastern Semifinals

March 30—Celtics 107, Buffalo 97 (H)
April 2—Buffalo 115, Celtics 105 (A)
April 3—Celtics 120, Buffalo 107 (H)
April 6—Buffalo 104, Celtics 102 (A)
April 9—Celtics 100, Buffalo 97 (H)
April 12—Celtics 106, Buffalo 104 (A)
(Celtics won series, 4-2)

Eastern Finals

April 14—Celtics 113, New York 88 (H)
April 16—Celtics 111, New York 99 (A)
April 19—New York 103, Celtics 100 (H)
April 21—Celtics 98, New York 91 (A)
April 24—Celtics 105, New York 94 (H)
(Celtics won series, 4-1)

NBA Finals

April 28—Celtics 98, Milwaukee 83 (A)
April 30—Milwaukee 105, Celtics 96 (OT) (A)
May 3—Celtics 95, Milwaukee 83 (H)
May 5—Milwaukee 97, Celtics 89 (H)
May 7—Celtics 96, Milwaukee 87 (A)
May 10—Milwaukee 102, Celtics 101 (2 OTs) (H)
May 12—Celtics 102, Milwaukee 87 (A)
(Celtics won series, 4-3, and NBA title)

1974-75

Eastern Semifinals

April 14—Celtics 123, Houston 106 (H)
April 16—Celtics 112, Houston 100 (H)
April 19—Houston 117, Celtics 102 (A)
April 22—Celtics 122, Houston 117 (A)
April 24—Celtics 128, Houston 115 (H)
(Celtics won series, 4-1)

Eastern Finals

April 27—Washington 100, Celtics 95 (H)
April 30—Washington 117, Celtics 92 (A)
May 3—Celtics 101, Washington 90 (H)
May 7—Washington 119, Celtics 108 (A)
May 9—Celtics 103, Washington 99 (H)
May 11—Washington 98, Celtics 92 (A)
(Celtics eliminated, 2-4)

1975-76

Eastern Semifinals

April 21—Celtics 107, Buffalo 98 (H)
April 23—Celtics 101, Buffalo 96 (H)
April 25—Buffalo 98, Celtics 93 (A)
April 28—Buffalo 124, Celtics 122 (A)
April 30—Celtics 99, Buffalo 88 (H)
May 2—Celtics 104, Buffalo 100 (A)
(Celtics won series, 4-2)

Eastern Finals

May 6—Celtics 111, Cleveland 99 (H)
May 9—Celtics 94, Cleveland 89 (H)
May 11—Cleveland 83, Celtics 78 (A)
May 14—Cleveland 106, Celtics 87 (A)
May 16—Celtics 99, Cleveland 94 (H)
May 18—Celtics 94, Cleveland 87 (A)
(Celtics won series, 4-2)

NBA Finals

May 23—Celtics 98, Phoenix 87 (H)
May 27—Celtics 105, Phoenix 90 (H)
May 30—Phoenix 105, Celtics 98 (A)
June 2—Phoenix 109, Celtics 107 (A)
June 4—Celtics 128, Phoenix 126 (3 OTs) (H)
June 6—Celtics 87, Phoenix 80 (A)
(Celtics won series, 4-2, and NBA title)

1976-77

Eastern Quarterfinals

April 12—Celtics 104, San Antonio 94 (H)
April 15—Celtics 113, San Antonio 109 (A)
(Celtics won series, 2-0)

Eastern Semifinals

April 17—Celtics 113, Philadelphia 111 (A)
April 20—Philadelphia 113, Celtics 101 (A)
April 22—Philadelphia 109, Celtics 100 (H)
April 24—Celtics 124, Philadelphia 119 (H)
April 27—Philadelphia 110, Celtics 91 (A)
April 29—Celtics 113, Philadelphia 108 (H)
May 1—Philadelphia 83, Celtics 77 (A)
(Celtics eliminated, 3-4)

1977-78

Did not qualify.

1978-79

Did not qualify.

1979-80

Eastern Quarterfinals

Bye

Eastern Semifinals

April 9—Celtics 119, Houston 101 (H)
April 11—Celtics 95, Houston 75 (H)
April 13—Celtics 100, Houston 81 (A)
April 14—Celtics 138, Houston 121 (A)
(Celtics won series, 4-0)

Eastern Finals

April 18—Philadelphia 96, Celtics 93 (H)
April 20—Celtics 96, Philadelphia 90 (H)
April 23—Philadelphia 99, Celtics 97 (A)
April 25—Philadelphia 102, Celtics 90 (A)
April 27—Philadelphia 105, Celtics 94 (H)
(Celtics eliminated, 1-4)

1980-81

Eastern Quarterfinals

Bye

Eastern Semifinals

April 5—Celtics 121, Chicago 109 (H)
April 7—Celtics 106, Chicago 97 (H)
April 10—Celtics 113, Chicago 107 (A)
April 12—Celtics 109, Chicago 103 (A)
(Celtics won series, 4-0)

Eastern Finals

April 21—Philadelphia 105, Celtics 104 (H)
April 22—Celtics 118, Philadelphia 99 (H)
April 24—Philadelphia 110, Celtics 100 (A)
April 26—Philadelphia 107, Celtics 105 (A)
April 29—Celtics 111, Philadelphia 109 (H)
May 1—Celtics 100, Philadelphia 98 (A)
May 3—Celtics 91, Philadelphia 90 (H)
(Celtics won series, 4-3)

NBA Finals

May 5—Celtics 98, Houston 95 (H)
May 7—Houston 92, Celtics 90 (H)
May 9—Celtics 94, Houston 71 (A)
May 10—Houston 91, Celtics 86 (A)
May 12—Celtics 109, Houston 80 (H)
May 14—Celtics 102, Houston 91 (A)
(Celtics won series, 4-2, and NBA title)

1981-82

Eastern Quarterfinals

Bye

Eastern Semifinals

April 25—Celtics 109, Washington 91 (H)
April 28—Washington 103, Celtics 102 (H)
May 1—Celtics 92, Washington 83 (A)
May 2—Celtics 103, Washington 99 (A)
May 5—Celtics 131, Washington 126 (2 OTs) (H)
(Celtics won series, 4-1)

Eastern Finals

May 9—Celtics 121, Philadelphia 81 (H)
May 12—Philadelphia 121, Celtics 113 (H)
May 15—Philadelphia 99, Celtics 97 (A)
May 16—Philadelphia 119, Celtics 94 (A)
May 19—Celtics 114, Philadelphia 85 (H)
May 21—Celtics 88, Philadelphia 75 (A)
May 23—Philadelphia 120, Celtics 106 (H)
(Celtics eliminated, 3-4)

Red Auerbach was named coach of the NBA's Silver Anniversary team in 1971. Bill Russell, Bob Cousy, Bill Sharman and Sam Jones were other Celtics selected. The squad (left to right): Paul Arizin, Russell, Joe Fulks, George Mikan, Bob Davies, Dolph Schayes, Cousy, Bob Pettit, Sharman and Jones.

CELTICS ON NBA'S SILVER ANNIVERSARY TEAM

(Chosen in 1971 to honor the top performers in the league's first 25 seasons.)

Coach: *Arnold (Red) Auerbach*

Players: *Bob Cousy*

Bill Russell

Bill Sharman

Sam Jones

(In all, 10 players were chosen. The other six: George Mikan, Bob Pettit, Dolph Schayes, Paul Arizin, Bob Davies and Joe Fulks.)

CELTICS ON NBA'S 35TH ANNIVERSARY TEAM

(Chosen in 1980 to honor the top performers in the league's first 35 seasons.)

Coach: *Arnold (Red) Auerbach*

Players: *Bob Cousy*

John Havlicek

*Bill Russell**

*Russell voted the league's greatest all-time player.

(In all, 11 players were chosen. The other eight: Kareem Abdul-Jabbar, Elgin Baylor, Wilt Chamberlain, Julius Erving, George Mikan, Bob Pettit, Oscar Robertson and Jerry West.)

INDIVIDUAL AWARDS

NBA EXECUTIVE OF THE YEAR

(Originated in 1972-73; selected by the *Sporting News*)

1979-80 Red Auerbach

NBA COACH OF THE YEAR

(Originated in 1962-63; selected by the media)

1964-65 Red Auerbach
1972-73 Tom Heinsohn
1979-80 Bill Fitch

(Two other Celtic family members won the award coaching other teams —Bill Sharman with the Los Angeles Lakers in 1971-72, Bill Fitch with the Cleveland Cavaliers in 1975-76.)

NBA MOST VALUABLE PLAYER

(Originated in 1955-56; selected by NBA players)

1956-57 Bob Cousy
1957-58 Bill Russell
1960-61 Bill Russell
1961-62 Bill Russell
1962-63 Bill Russell
1964-65 Bill Russell
1972-73 Dave Cowens

PLAYOFFS' MOST VALUABLE PLAYER

(Originated in 1969; selected by Sport *magazine)*

1974 John Havlicek
1976 Jo Jo White
1981 Cedric Maxwell

NBA ROOKIE OF THE YEAR

(Originated in 1952-53; selected by the media)

1956-57 Tom Heinsohn
1970-71 Dave Cowens
(shared with Portland's Geoff Petrie)
1979-80 Larry Bird

NBA ALL-DEFENSIVE TEAM

(Originated in 1968-69; selected by the coaches)

1968-69 Bill Russell (1st team)
John Havlicek (2d team)
Tom Sanders (2d team)
1969-70 John Havlicek (2d team)
1970-71 John Havlicek (2d team)
1971-72 John Havlicek (1st team)
Don Chaney (2d team)
1972-73 John Havlicek (1st team)
Don Chaney (2d team)
Paul Silas (2d team)
1973-74 John Havlicek (1st team)
Don Chaney (2d team)
1974-75 John Havlicek (1st team)
Paul Silas (1st team)
Don Chaney (2d team)
Dave Cowens (2d team)
1975-76 Dave Cowens (1st team)
John Havlicek (1st team)
Paul Silas (1st team)
1981-82 Larry Bird

ALL-NBA TEAM

(Originated in 1946-47; selected by the media)

1947-48	Ed Sadowski (1st team)
1950-51	Ed Macauley (1st team)
1951-52	Bob Cousy (1st team) Ed Macauley (1st team)
1952-53	Bob Cousy (1st team) Ed Macauley (1st team) Bill Sharman (2d team)
1953-54	Bob Cousy (1st team) Ed Macauley (2d team)
1954-55	Bob Cousy (1st team) Bill Sharman (2d team)
1955-56	Bob Cousy (1st team) Bill Sharman (1st team)
1956-57	Bob Cousy (1st team) Bill Sharman (1st team)
1957-58	Bob Cousy (1st team) Bill Sharman (1st team) Bill Russell (2d team)
1958-59	Bob Cousy (1st team) Bill Russell (1st team) Bill Sharman (1st team)
1959-60	Bob Cousy (1st team) Bill Russell (2d team) Bill Sharman (2d team)
1960-61	Bob Cousy (1st team) Tom Heinsohn (2d team) Bill Russell (2d team)
1961-62	Bob Cousy (2d team) Tom Heinsohn (2d team) Bill Russell (2d team)
1962-63	Bill Russell (1st team) Bob Cousy (2d team) Tom Heinsohn (2d team)
1963-64	John Havlicek (2d team) Tom Heinsohn (2d team) Bill Russell (2d team)
1964-65	Bill Russell (1st team) Sam Jones (2d team)
1965-66	John Havlicek (2d team) Sam Jones (2d team) Bill Russell (2d team)
1966-67	Sam Jones (2d team) Bill Russell (2d team)
1967-68	John Havlicek (2d team) Bill Russell (2d team)
1968-69	John Havlicek (2d team)
1969-70	John Havlicek (2d team)
1970-71	John Havlicek (1st team)
1971-72	John Havlicek (1st team)
1972-73	John Havlicek (1st team) Dave Cowens (2d team)
1973-74	John Havlicek (1st team)
1974-75	Dave Cowens (2d team) John Havlicek (2d team) Jo Jo White (2d team)
1975-76	Dave Cowens (2d team) John Havlicek (2d team)
1976-77	Jo Jo White (2d team)
1979-80	Larry Bird (1st team)
1980-81	Larry Bird (1st team) Nate Archibald (2d team)
1981-82	Larry Bird (1st team) Robert Parish (2d team)

Red Auerbach finally was voted Coach of the Year in 1965, receiving the award from NBA Commissioner Walter Kennedy.

All-NBA Totals

Player	*1st team*	*2d team*	*Total*
Bob Cousy	10	2	12
John Havlicek	4	7	11
Bill Russell	3	8	11
Bill Sharman	4	3	7
Ed Macauley	3	1	4
Tom Heinsohn	0	4	4
Larry Bird	3	0	3
Dave Cowens	0	3	3
Sam Jones	0	3	3
Jo Jo White	0	2	2
Ed Sadowski	1	0	1
Nate Archibald	0	1	1
Robert Parish	0	1	1

NBA ALL-ROOKIE TEAM

(Originated in 1963-64; selected by the coaches)

1969-70	Jo Jo White
1970-71	Dave Cowens
1979-80	Larry Bird*
1980-81	Kevin McHale

*Also first-team all-NBA choice.

ALL-STAR GAMES

CELTICS IN NBA ALL-STAR GAMES

COACHES

RED AUERBACH—11 games (won 7, lost 4): '57*, '58*, '59, '60*, '61, '62, '63*, '64*, '65*, '66* and '67**.

TOM HEINSOHN—4 games (won 2, lost 2): '72, '73*, '74 and 76*

BILL FITCH—1 game (won 1): '82*.

*Winning coach.

**(1) Came out of retirement to coach '67 East squad, and (2) became first coach ever ejected from NBA All-Star Game.

Note: Celtic alumni Bill Sharman ('68, '72 and '73), Ed Macauley ('59 and '60) and K.C. Jones ('75) also coached in the NBA All-Star Game while representing other teams.

PLAYERS

BOB COUSY—13 games, 147 points, 13.8 average: '51* (8 points), '52* (9), '53* (15), '54* (20), '55* (20), '56* (7), '57* (10), '58* (20), '59* (13), '60* (2), '61* (4), '62* (11) and '63* (8).

JOHN HAVLICEK—13 games, 179 points, 13.8 average: '66* (18 points), '67 (14), '68 (26), '69* (14), '70* (17), '71* (12), '72* (15), '73* (14), '74* (10), '75* (16), '76* (9), '77 (4) and '78* (10).

BILL RUSSELL—12 games, 120 points, 10.0 average: '58* (11 points), '59* (7), '60 (6) '61 (24), '62 (12), '63* (19), '64* (13), '65* (17), '66 (2), '67 (2), '68 (4) and '69* (3).

BILL SHARMAN—8 games, 102 points, 12.8 average: '53* (11 points), '54* (14), '55* (15), '56* (7), '57* (12), '58* (15), '59* (11) and '60 (17).

JO JO WHITE—7 games, 64 points, 9.1 average: '71 (10 points), '72 (12), '73 (6), '74 (13), '75 (7), '76 (6) and '77 (10).

DAVE COWENS—**6 games, 76 points, 12.7 average: '72* (14 points), '73* (15), '74* (11), '75 (6), '76 (16) and '78* (15). (**Also selected to '80 East squad but didn't play because of injury.)

ED MACAULEY—***6 games, 76 points, 12.7 average: '51* (20 points), '52* (15), '53* (18), '54* (13), '55* (6) and '56* (4).

TOM HEINSOHN—**5 games, 51 points, 10.2 average: '57 (12 points), '61 (4), '62* (10), '63* (15) and '64* (10). (**Also selected to '65 East squad but didn't play because of injury.)

SAM JONES—5 games, 41 points, 8.2 average: '62 (2 points), '64 (16), '65* (6), '66* (12) and '68 (5).

NATE ARCHIBALD—***3 games, 17 points, 5.7 average: '80 (2 points), '81 (9) and '82* (6).

LARRY BIRD—3 games, 28 points, 9.3 average: '80 (7 points), '81* (2) and '82* (21).

ROBERT PARISH—2 games, 37 points, 18.5 average: '81 (16 points) and '82 (21).

DON BARKSDALE—1 game, 1 point, 1.0 average: '53 (1 point).

BAILEY HOWELL—***1 game, 4 points, 4.0 average: '67* (4 points).

PAUL SILAS—***1 game, 6 points, 6.0 average: '75 (6 points).

*Started.

**Selected to an additional NBA All-Star Game but didn't play because of injury.

***Played in NBA All-Star Game other years representing other team(s).

CELTIC MOST VALUABLE PLAYERS IN NBA ALL-STAR GAME

1951—Ed Macauley
1954—Bob Cousy
1955—Bill Sharman
1957—Bob Cousy
1963—Bill Russell
1973—Dave Cowens
1981—Nate Archibald
1982—Larry Bird

CELTICS AMONG ALL-TIME NBA ALL-STAR GAME LEADERS

Most Games

Player	*Place*	*Games*
Bob Cousy	1st*	13
John Havlicek	1st*	13
Bill Russell	4th*	12

*Tied

Most Minutes

Player	*Place*	*Minutes*
Bob Cousy	3d	368
Bill Russell	5th	343
John Havlicek	8th	303

Scoring

Player	*Place*	*Points*	*Games*	*Average*
John Havlicek	5th	179	13	13.8
Bob Cousy	7th	147	13	11.3
Bill Russell	11th	120	12	10.0

Assists

Player	*Place*	*Assists*	*Games*	*Average*
Bob Cousy	1st	86	13	6.6
Bill Russell	4th	39	12	3.3
John Havlicek	6th	31	13	2.4

Rebounds

Player	*Place*	*Rebounds*	*Games*	*Average*
Bill Russell	3d	139	12	11.6
Dave Cowens	8th	81	6	13.5
Bob Cousy	9th	78	13	6.0

Field Goals

Player	*Place*	*Games*	*FGs*	*FG Pct.*
John Havlicek	3d	13	74	.481

Free Throws (Number)

Player	*Place*	*Games*	*FTs*	*FT Pct.*
Bob Cousy	5th	13	43	.843
Ed Macauley	8th	7*	35	.854
John Havlicek	9th	13	31	.756

*Six games representing Celtics, one St. Louis Hawks.

Free-Throws (Percentage)

Player	*Place*	*Games*	*FT Pct.*	*FTA*	*FTM*
Tom Heinsohn	3d	5	.875	8	7
Ed Macauley	5th	7*	.854	41	35
Bob Cousy	7th	13	.843	51	43

*Six games representing Celtics, one St. Louis Hawks.

Personal Fouls

Player	*Place*	*Games*	*Fouls*	*Average*
Bill Russell	2d*	12	37	3.1
Bob Cousy	10th	13	27	2.1

Miscellaneous

Most points in one game by a Celtic:

John Havlicek, 26, in 1968*
Bill Russell, 24, in 1961*
Robert Parish, 21, 1982*
Ed Macauley, 20, in 1951
Bob Cousy, 20, in 1954
20, in 1955
20, in 1958

*Neither Havlicek, Russell nor Parish was a starter those years, each coming off the bench to be his team's high scorer.

Notes:

Bill Russell is tied with three others for most minutes played in an All-Star Game—42 (1964).

Bill Sharman has most field-goal attempts in a quarter—12 (1960).

Bob Cousy is tied for most assists in (a) a half, 8 (1952), and (b) a quarter, 6 (1952).

Cousy and Rick Barry are the only two players ever to foul out of two All-Star Games, Cousy doing it in '56 and '61.

Many more Celtics undoubtedly would have played in the All-Star Game during Boston's championship reign except for a rule that limited (usually to three) the number of players selected from any team.

NBA ALL-STAR GAMES AT BOSTON GARDEN

First Annual Game
March 2, 1951

East Coach—Joe Lapchick (New York) West Coach—John Kundla (Minneapolis)

EAST ALL-STARS (111)

Player and Team	FGA	FGM	FTA	FTM	Reb.	Ast.	PF	Pts.
Joe Fulks, Philadelphia	15	6	9	7	7	3	5	19
Paul Arizin, Philadelphia	12	7	2	1	7	0	2	15
Dolph Schayes, Syracuse	10	7	2	1	14	3	1	15
Vince Boryla, New York	6	4	1	1	2	2	3	9
Ed Macauley, Boston	12	7	7	6	6	1	3	20
Harry Gallatin, New York	4	2	1	1	5	2	4	5
Bob Cousy, Boston	12	2	5	4	9	8	3	8
Red Rocha, Baltimore	10	2	4	4	2	3	2	8
Dick McGuire, New York	4	3	0	0	5	10	2	6
Andy Phillip, Philadelphia	8	3	0	0	10	8	1	6
Totals	93	43	31	25	67	40	26	111

WEST ALL-STARS (94)

Player and Team	FGA	FGM	FTA	FTM	Reb.	Ast.	PF	Pts.
Alex Groza, Indianapolis	16	8	1	1	13	1	4	17
Dike Eddleman, Tri-Cities	9	2	5	3	0	3	3	7
Jim Pollard, Minneapolis	11	2	0	0	4	5	1	4
Vern Mikkelsen, Minneapolis	11	4	4	3	9	1	3	11
George Mikan, Minneapolis	17	4	6	4	11	3	2	12
Larry Foust, Fort Wayne	6	1	0	0	5	2	3	2
Bob Davies, Rochester	6	4	5	5	5	5	3	13
Frank Brian, Tri-Cities	14	5	5	4	6	3	2	14
Ralph Beard, Indianapolis	8	3	3	0	3	2	1	6
Fred Schaus, Fort Wayne	9	2	4	4	4	2	3	8
Totals	107	35	33	24	60	27	25	94

Score by Periods:	1st	2nd	3rd	4th	Totals
East	31	22	30	28	— 111
West	22	20	22	30	— 94

Referees—Pat Kennedy and Charley Eckman. Attendance—10,094.

Second Annual Game
February 11, 1952

East Coach—Al Cervi (Syracuse) West Coach—John Kundla (Minneapolis)

EAST ALL-STARS (108)

Player and Team	Min.	FGA	FGM	FTA	FTM	Reb.	Ast.	PF	Pts.
Paul Arizin, Philadelphia	32	13	9	8	8	6	0	1	26
Joe Fulks, Philadelphia	9	7	3	1	0	5	2	2	6
Red Rocha, Syracuse	28	11	5	2	2	5	2	4	12
Max Zaslofsky, New York	25	7	3	5	5	4	2	0	11
Ed Macauley, Boston	28	7	3	9	9	7	3	2	15
Harry Gallatin, New York	22	5	3	4	1	9	3	3	7
Bob Cousy, Boston	33	14	4	2	1	4	13	3	9
Dick McGuire, New York	18	0	0	3	1	1	4	0	1
Andy Phillip, Philadelphia	30	6	4	3	3	3	6	1	11
Fred Scolari, Baltimore	15	9	5	0	0	0	2	0	10
Dolph Schayes, Syracuse	Selected but did not play due to injury.								
Totals	240	79	39	37	30	53	37	16	108

WEST ALL-STARS (91)

Player and Team	Min.	FGA	FGM	FTA	FTM	Reb.	Ast.	PF	Pts.
Vern Mikkelsen, Minneapolis	23	8	5	2	2	10	0	2	12
Dike Eddleman, Milwaukee	26	3	1	0	0	2	2	2	2
Jim Pollard, Minneapolis	29	17	2	0	0	11	5	3	4
Leo Barnhorst, Indianapolis	23	16	7	1	0	2	2	4	14
George Mikan, Minneapolis	29	19	9	9	8	15	1	5	26
Arnie Risen, Rochester	19	7	3	1	0	5	1	3	6
Bob Davies, Rochester	27	11	4	0	0	0	5	4	8
Paul Walther, Indianapolis	17	4	1	0	0	2	2	1	2
Bobby Wanzer, Rochester	22	8	1	2	2	5	5	2	4
Frank Brian, Fort Wayne	25	10	4	6	5	7	4	2	13
Larry Foust, Fort Wayne	Selected but did not play due to injury.								
Totals	240	103	37	21	17	64	27	28	91

Score by Periods:	1st	2nd	3rd	4th	Totals
East	26	23	33	26	— 108
West	22	22	27	20	— 91

Referees—Sid Borgia and Stan Stutz. Attendance—10,211.

Seventh Annual Game
January 15, 1957

East Coach—Red Auerbach (Boston) West Coach—Bobby Wanzer (Rochester)

EAST ALL-STARS (109)

Player and Team	Min.	FGA	FGM	FTA	FTM	Reb.	Ast.	PF	Pts.
Paul Arizin, Philadelphia	26	13	6	2	1	5	0	2	13
Harry Gallatin, New York	24	7	4	2	0	11	1	3	8
Tom Heinsohn, Boston	23	17	5	2	2	7	0	3	12
Dolph Schayes, Syracuse	25	6	4	1	1	10	1	1	9
Neil Johnston, Philadelphia	23	12	8	3	3	9	1	2	19
Nat Clifton, New York	23	11	4	0	0	11	3	1	8
Bob Cousy, Boston	28	14	4	2	2	5	7	0	10
Jack George, Philadelphia	21	6	3	2	2	1	5	1	8
Bill Sharman, Boston	23	17	5	2	2	6	5	1	12
Carl Braun, New York	24	9	4	2	2	3	2	2	10
Totals	240	112	47	18	15	70	25	16	109

Team Rebounds—2.

WEST ALL-STARS (97)

Player and Team	Min.	FGA	FGM	FTA	FTM	Reb.	Ast.	PF	Pts.
George Yardley, Fort Wayne	25	10	4	1	1	9	0	2	9
Ed Macauley, St. Louis	19	6	3	2	1	5	3	0	7
Bob Pettit, St. Louis	31	18	8	6	5	11	2	2	21
Jack Twyman, Rochester	17	8	1	3	1	0	1	1	3
Mel Hutchins, Fort Wayne	26	12	4	3	2	7	0	0	10
Vern Mikkelsen, Minneapolis	21	10	3	4	0	9	1	3	6
Slater Martin, St. Louis	31	11	4	0	0	2	3	1	8
Maurice Stokes, Rochester	31	19	8	3	3	12	7	1	19
Richie Regan, Rochester	21	7	2	0	0	4	1	0	4
Dick Garmaker, Minneapolis	18	10	5	0	0	7	1	2	10
Totals	240	111	42	22	13	70	19	12	97

Team Rebounds—4.

Score by Periods:	1st	2nd	3rd	4th	Totals
East	18	23	33	35	— 109
West	26	17	23	31	— 97

Referees—Mendy Rudolph and Sid Borgia. Attendance—11,178.

Fourteenth Annual Game
January 14, 1964

East Coach—Red Auerbach (Boston) West Coach—Fred Schaus (Los Angeles)

EAST ALL-STARS (111)

Player and Team	Pos.	Min.	FGA	FGM	FTA	FTM	Reb.	Ast.	PF	Pts.
Jerry Lucas, Cincinnati	F	36	6	3	6	5	8	0	5	11
Len Chappell, New York		12	5	1	2	2	1	2	2	4
Tom Heinsohn, Boston	F	21	12	5	0	0	3	0	5	10
Tom Gola, New York		7	0	0	2	1	0	1	2	1
Bill Russell, Boston	C	42	13	6	2	1	21	2	4	13
Wayne Embry, Cincinnati		21	14	6	1	1	7	1	1	13
Oscar Robertson, Cincinnati	G	42	23	10	10	6	14	8	4	26
Chet Walker, Philadelphia		12	5	2	0	0	0	0	1	4
Hal Greer, Philadelphia	G	20	10	5	4	3	3	4	1	13
Sam Jones, Boston		27	20	8	0	0	4	3	2	16
Totals		240	108	46	27	19	77	21	27	111

Team Rebounds—16.

WEST ALL-STARS (107)

Player and Team	Pos.	Min.	FGA	FGM	FTA	FTM	Reb.	Ast.	PF	Pts.
Bob Pettit, St. Louis	F	36	15	6	9	7	17	2	3	19
Terry Dischinger, Baltimore		13	4	2	3	3	2	1	1	7
Elgin Baylor, Los Angeles	F	29	15	5	11	5	8	5	1	15
Bailey Howell, Detroit		6	3	1	0	0	2	0	0	2
Walt Bellamy, Baltimore	C	23	11	4	5	3	7	0	3	11
Wilt Chamberlain, San Francisco		37	14	4	14	11	20	1	2	19
Jerry West, Los Angeles	G	42	20	8	1	1	4	5	3	17
Don Ohl, Detroit		18	9	3	2	2	2	0	2	8
Guy Rodgers, San Francisco	G	22	6	3	0	0	2	2	4	6
Len Wilkens, St. Louis		14	5	1	1	1	0	0	3	3
Totals		240	102	37	46	33	75	16	22	107

Team Rebounds—11.

Score by Periods:	1st	2nd	3rd	4th	Totals
East	25	34	27	25	— 111
West	22	27	28	30	— 107

Referees—Sid Borgia and Mendy Rudolph. Attendance—13,464.

Ed Macauley, Walter Brown and Bob Cousy

Bill Sharman

A galaxy of All-Stars

Bob Cousy, Bill Russell and Tom Heinsohn

Bob Cousy makes entrance in early NBA All-Star game at Boston Garden.

Tom Heinsohn

Bob Cousy

Bill Russell

CELTICS VS. OPPONENTS OVER THE YEARS

Regular Season

	Atlanta Hawks	Chicago Bulls	Cleveland Cavaliers	Dallas Mavericks	Denver Nuggets	Detroit Pistons	Golden State Warriors	Houston Rockets	Indiana Pacers	Kansas City Kings	Los Angeles Lakers	Milwaukee Bucks	New Jersey Nets	New York Knicks	Philadelphia 76ers	Phoenix Suns	Portland Trailblazers	San Antonio Spurs	San Diego Clippers	Seattle SuperSonics	Utah Jazz	Washington Bullets	W-L
1946-47							1-5							4-2									22-38
1947-48							4-4							1-7									20-28
1948-49						4-1	3-3			1-4	2-3			3-3									25-35
1949-50	0-2					2-4	3-3			0-6	1-5			1-5	0-2								22-46
1950-51	4-2					5-1	4-4			2-4	3-3			4-4	3-5								39-30
1951-52	5-1					3-3	6-3			3-3	3-3			4-5	4-5								39-27
1952-53	5-1					4-2	9-1			4-2	1-5			6-4	5-6								46-25
1953-54	6-2					4-4	6-4			4-4	3-5			5-5	5-5								42-30
1954-55	6-3					4-5	7-5			4-5	3-6			6-6	6-6								36-36
1955-56	5-4					4-5	5-7			5-4	7-2			5-7	8-4								39-33
1956-57	7-2					6-3	8-4			6-3	5-4			7-5	5-7								44-28*
1957-58	5-4					8-1	6-6			7-2	9-0			7-5	7-5								49-23*
1958-59	4-5					8-1	9-3			8-1	9-0			7-5	7-5								52-20*
1959-60	6-3					9-0	8-5			8-1	8-1			12-1	8-5								59-16*
1960-61	6-4					8-2	8-5			7-3	8-2			10-3	10-3								57-22*
1961-62	7-2					5-3	8-4			7-1	6-3			8-4	10-2							9-1	60-20*
1962-63	5-3					8-0	8-1			9-3	4-5			10-2	6-6							8-2	58-22*
1963-64	7-2					7-1	5-3			5-7	6-3			10-2	10-2							9-1	59-21*
1964-65	9-1					10-0	9-1			8-2	7-3			7-3	5-5							7-3	62-18*
1965-66	7-3					6-4	8-2			5-5	7-3			10-0	4-6							7-3	54-26
1966-67	5-4	8-1				6-3	6-3			8-1	5-4			9-0	5-4							8-1	60-21
1967-68	4-3	5-2				6-2	4-3	7-0		3-5	4-3			6-2	4-4					6-1		5-3	54-28
1968-69	3-3	4-2				5-1	3-3	4-2		5-2	2-4	5-1		1-6	5-2	6-0				3-3		2-5	48-34
1969-70	0-6	3-3				4-3	2-4	4-2		3-3	3-3	1-6		4-3	2-4	2-4				5-1		2-5	34-48
1970-71	4-2	4-1	3-1			2-3	3-2	3-2		4-2	3-2	0-5		0-6	4-2	2-3	2-2		4-0	3-2		3-3	44-38
1971-72	4-0	3-2	5-1			5-0	2-3	5-0		4-2	1-4	2-3		3-3	6-0	2-3	4-0		6-0	2-3		2-2	56-26
1972-73	5-1	3-1	5-1			3-1	3-1	5-1		3-1	4-0	2-2		4-4	7-0	4-0	4-0		7-0	4-0		5-1	68-14*
1973-74	5-1	2-2	4-2			3-1	3-1	4-2		3-1	2-2	2-2		5-2	7-1	3-1	4-0		5-2	2-2		2-4	56-26
1974-75	4-0	3-1	3-1			3-1	1-3	4-0		2-2	4-0	4-0		7-2	5-3	3-1	4-0		5-4	2-2	4-0	2-2	60-22**
1975-76	3-2	2-2	3-2			4-0	2-2	4-1		2-2	4-0	2-2		5-2	4-3	4-0	2-2		4-3	2-2	4-1	3-2	54-28
1976-77	4-0	2-2	1-3		3-1	2-2	1-3	2-2	1-2	3-1	2-1	3-1	3-1	2-2	1-3	2-2	1-3	4-0	3-1	2-2	2-2	0-4	44-38
1977-78	2-2	1-3	1-3		1-3	1-3	2-2	2-2	2-1	2-2	1-2	3-1	3-1	2-2	0-4	2-2	1-3	0-4	3-1	0-4	2-2	1-3	32-50
1978-79	2-2	1-3	2-2		1-3	2-2	2-2	1-3	3-1	1-3	1-3	1-3	1-3	3-1	2-2	0-4	1-3	0-4	1-3	2-2	2-2	0-4	29-53
1979-80	4-2	2-0	4-2		2-0	6-0	2-0	6-0	4-2	1-1	0-2	2-0	5-1	5-1	3-3	1-1	2-0	4-2	2-0	0-2	2-0	4-2	61-21*
1980-81	4-2	5-1	4-1	2-0	2-0	4-1	1-1	2-0	3-3	1-1	2-0	3-3	6-0	5-1	3-3	2-0	2-0	2-0	2-0	1-1	1-1	5-1	62-20**
1981-82	5-1	4-2	5-0	2-0	1-1	6-0	1-1	1-1	4-1	2-0	1-1	3-3	5-1	5-1	4-2	1-1	1-1	2-0	2-0	0-2	2-0	6-0	63-19*
TOTALS	152-75	52-28	40-19	4-0	10-8	167-63	163-107	54-18	17-10	140-89	130-87	33-32	23-7	193-116	165-119	34-22	28-14	12-10	44-14	34-29	19-8	90-52	1709-1030

*Best record in NBA.
**Tied for best record in NBA.

Larry Siegfried always got his man—in this instance, Detroit's Dave Bing, a future Celtic.

Note: Both regular-season and playoff records trace back to the birth of each franchise, when some were located in other cities and, in some instances, had different nicknames.

The Atlanta Hawks were known as the Tri-Cities (Davenport, Iowa-Moline, Illinois-Rock Island, Illinois) Blackhawks (1949-50—1950-51) and Milwaukee Blackhawks (1951-52—1954-55) before becoming the St. Louis Hawks (1955-56—1968-69).

The Detroit Pistons were the Fort Wayne (Indiana) Pistons (1948-49—1956-57).

The Golden State Warriors were the Philadelphia Warriors (1946-47—1961-62).

The Houston Rockets were the San Diego Rockets (1967-68—1970-71).

The Kansas City Kings were the Rochester Royals (1948-49—1957-58) and Cincinnati Royals (1958-59—1971-72). They were also known as the Kansas City-Omaha Kings (1972-73—1974-75).

The Los Angeles Lakers were the Minneapolis Lakers (1948-49—1959-60).

The New Jersey Nets were the New York (Long Island) Nets (1976-77).

The Philadelphia 76ers were the Syracuse Nationals (1949-50—1962-63).

The San Diego Clippers were the Buffalo Braves (1970-71—1977-78).

The Utah Jazz was the New Orleans Jazz (1974-75—1978-79).

And the Washington Bullets were the Chicago Packers (1961-62), Chicago Zephyrs (1962-63), Baltimore Bullets (1963-64) before moving to Landover, Maryland, and becoming the Capital Bullets—changing their name to Washington Bullets a few years later.

Kevin McHale became the first No. 1 draftee to come to terms with the Celtics by transatlantic telephone from Italy. The Minnesotan was late reporting to 1981 training camp but proved worth the wait.

Robert Parish proved the Celtics' biggest surprise package of 1980-81 after being acquired from Golden State. He knew what to do at both ends of the floor, and was Boston's best shot blocker since Bill Russell.

Playoffs

	Atlanta Hawks	*Chicago Bulls*	*Cleveland Cavaliers*	*Dallas Mavericks*	*Denver Nuggets*	*Detroit Pistons*	*Golden State Warriors*	*Houston Rockets*	*Indiana Pacers*	*Kansas City Kings*	*Los Angeles Lakers*	*Milwaukee Bucks*	*New Jersey Nets*	*New York Knicks*	*Philadelphia 76ers*	*Phoenix Suns*	*Portland Trailblazers*	*San Antonio Spurs*	*San Diego Clippers*	*Seattle SuperSonics*	*Utah Jazz*	*Washington Bullets*	**W-L**
1946-47																							—
1947-48																							1-2**
1948-49																							—
1949-50																							—
1950-51														0-2									0-2
1951-52														1-2									1-2
1952-53														1-3	2-0								3-3
1953-54														2-0	0-4								2-4
1954-55														2-1	1-3								3-4
1955-56															1-2								1-2
1956-57	4-3														3-0								7-3*
1957-58	2-4						4-1																6-5
1958-59											4-0				4-3								8-3*
1959-60	4-3						4-2																8-5*
1960-61	4-1														4-1								8-2*
1961-62							4-3				4-3												8-6*
1962-63										4-3	4-2												8-5*
1963-64							4-1			4-1													8-2*
1964-65											4-1				4-3								8-4*
1965-66										3-2	4-3				4-1								11-6*
1966-67														3-1	1-4								4-5
1967-68						4-2					4-2				4-3								12-7*
1968-69											4-3			4-2	4-1								12-6*
1969-70																							—
1970-71																							—
1971-72	4-2													1-4									5-6
1972-73	4-2													3-4									7-6
1973-74												4-3		4-1					4-2				12-6*
1974-75								4-1														2-4	6-5
1975-76			4-2													4-2			4-2				12-6*
1976-77															3-4			2-0					5-4
1977-78																							—
1978-79																							—
1979-80								4-0							1-4								5-4
1980-81		4-0						4-2							4-3								12-5*
1981-82															3-4							4-1	7-5
TOTALS	22-15	4-0	4-2	—	—	4-2	16-7	12-3	—	11-6	28-14	4-3	—	21-20	43-40	4-2	—	2-0	8-4	—	—	6-5	190-125

*Won NBA championship.

**Lost 2 of 3 in 1947-48 playoffs to the now defunct Chicago Stags.

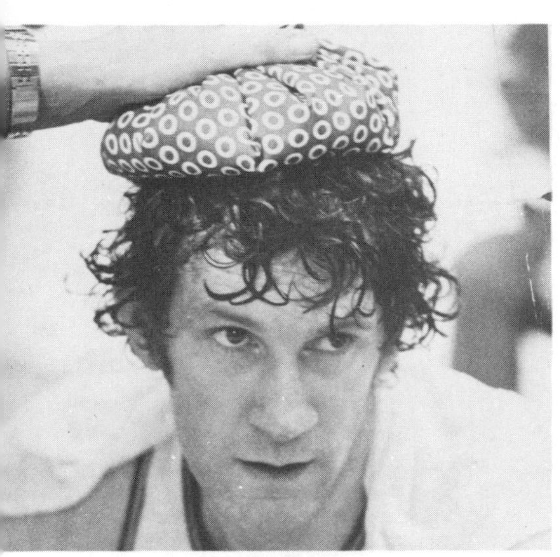

John Havlicek

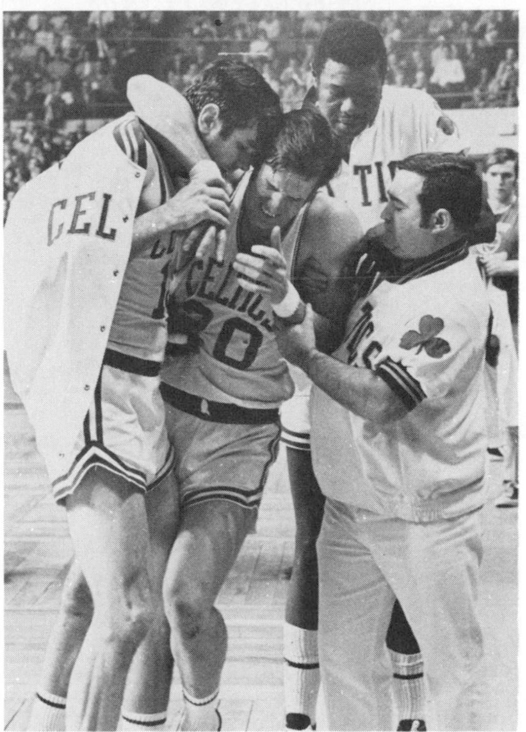

Larry Siegfried

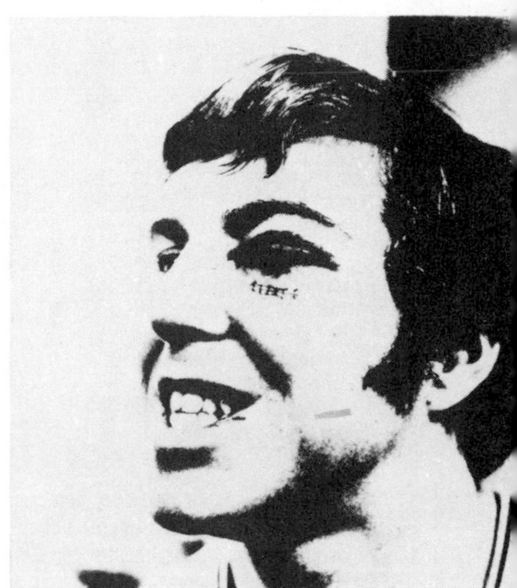

Dave Cowens

Who says basketball isn't a contact sport?

Tom Heinsohn

Bill Russell

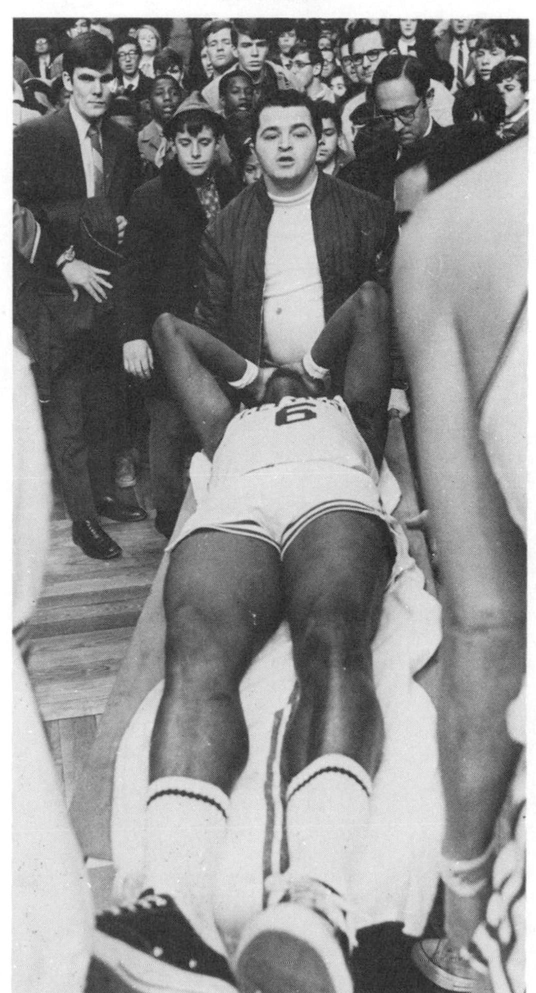

Sam Jones

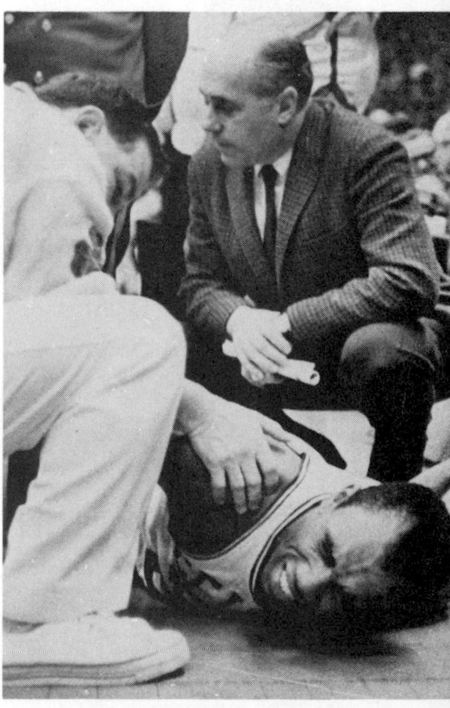

CELTICS CAREER LEADERS

REGULAR SEASON

Games

	Player	
1.	John Havlicek	1,270
2.	Bill Russell	963
3.	Bob Cousy	917
4.	Tom Sanders	916
5.	Sam Jones	872
5.	Don Nelson	872
7.	Dave Cowens	726
8.	Jo Jo White	717
9.	Bill Sharman	679
10.	K.C. Jones	675
11.	Tom Heinsohn	654
12.	Frank Ramsey	623

Minutes

	Player	
1.	John Havlicek	46,471
2.	Bill Russell	40,726
3.	Bob Cousy	30,230
4.	Dave Cowens	28,551
5.	Jo Jo White	26,770
6.	Sam Jones	24,387
7.	Tom Sanders	22,164
8.	Bill Sharman	21,793
9.	Tom Heinsohn	19,303
10.	Don Nelson	18,970

Points

	Player	
1.	John Havlicek	26,395
2.	Bob Cousy	16,955
3.	Sam Jones	15,380
4.	Bill Russell	14,522
5.	Dave Cowens	13,192
6.	Jo Jo White	13,188
7.	Bill Sharman	12,287
8.	Tom Heinsohn	12,194
9.	Don Nelson	9,968
10.	Tom Sanders	8,766

Average

	Player	
1.	Larry Bird	21.8
2.	John Havlicek	20.6
3.	Robert Parish	19.4
4.	Ed Macauley	18.9
5.	Tom Heinsohn	18.6
6.	Bob Cousy	18.5
7.	Jo Jo White	18.4
8.	Dave Cowens	18.2
9.	Bill Sharman	18.0
10.	Bailey Howell	18.0
11.	Sam Jones	17.6
12.	Charlie Scott	17.5

Field Goals Attempted

	Player	
1.	John Havlicek	23,930
2.	Bob Cousy	16,465
3.	Sam Jones	13,737
4.	Bill Russell	12,930
5.	Jo Jo White	12,782
6.	Dave Cowens	12,193
7.	Tom Heinsohn	11,871
8.	Bill Sharman	10,907
9.	Tom Sanders	7,988
10.	Don Nelson	7,672

Field Goals Made

	Player	
1.	John Havlicek	10,513
2.	Sam Jones	6,258
3.	Bob Cousy	6,167
4.	Bill Russell	5,687
5.	Jo Jo White	5,648
6.	Dave Cowens	5,608
7.	Tom Heinsohn	4,773
8.	Bill Sharman	4,620
9.	Don Nelson	3,717
10.	Tom Sanders	3,416

Field-Goal Percentage

	Player		
1.	Cedric Maxwell	.579	(3,348/1,937)
2.	Robert Parish	.543	(2,401/1,304)
3.	Rick Robey	.515	(2,027/1,044)
4.	Larry Bird	.485	(4,380/2,123)
5.	Don Nelson	.484	(7,672/3,717)
6.	Bailey Howell	.480	(4,766/2,990)
7.	Nate Archibald	.478	(2,785/1,332)
8.	Dave Cowens	.460	(12,193/5,608)
9.	Sam Jones	.456	(13,737/6,258)
10.	Chris Ford	.455	(3,008/1,370)
11.	Ed Macauley	.447	(5,766/2,570)
12.	Jo Jo White	.442	(12,782/5,648)
13.	Don Chaney	.442	(5,180/2,287)
14.	Bill Russell	.440	(12,930/5,687)
15.	John Havlicek	.439	(23,930/10,513)

Free Throws Attempted

	Player	
1.	John Havlicek	6,589
2.	Bob Cousy	5,753
3.	Bill Russell	5,614
4.	Sam Jones	3,567
5.	Ed Macauley	3,518
6.	Bill Sharman	3,451
7.	Tom Heinsohn	3,353
8.	Don Nelson	3,296
9.	Frank Ramsey	3,083
10.	Dave Cowens	2,527

Free Throws Made

	Player	
1.	John Havlicek	5,369
2.	Bob Cousy	4,621
3.	Bill Russell	3,148
4.	Bill Sharman	3.047
5.	Sam Jones	2,864
6.	Ed Macauley	2,724
7.	Tom Heinsohn	2,648
8.	Don Nelson	2,534
9.	Frank Ramsey	2,480
10.	Dave Cowens	1,975

Free-Throw Percentage

	Player		
1.	Bill Sharman	.883	(3,451/3,047)
2.	Larry Siegfried	.855	(1,755/1,500)
3.	Larry Bird	.854	(1,068/912)
4.	Jo Jo White	.833	(2,270/1,892)
5.	John Havlicek	.814	(6,589/5,369)
6.	Frank Ramsey	.804	(3,083/2,480)
7.	Bob Cousy	.803	(5,753/4,621)
8.	Sam Jones	.803	(3,567/2.864)
9.	Nate Archibald	.800	(1,477/1,181)

Assists

	Player	
1.	Bob Cousy	6,949
2.	John Havlicek	6,114
3.	Bill Russell	4,096
4.	Jo Jo White	3,686
5.	K.C. Jones	2,904
6.	Dave Cowens	2,828
7.	Sam Jones	2,203
8.	Nate Archibald	2,154
9.	Bill Sharman	2,072
10.	Ed Macauley	1,581

Rebounds

	Player	
1.	Bill Russell	21,721
2.	Dave Cowens	10,170
3.	John Havlicek	8,007
4.	Tom Sanders	5,798
5.	Tom Heinsohn	5,749
6.	Don Nelson	4,517
7.	Sam Jones	4,319
8.	Paul Silas	4,004
9.	Frank Ramsey	3,410
10.	Ed Macauley	3,367

Personal Fouls

	Player	
1.	John Havlicek	3,281
2.	Tom Sanders	3,044
3.	Dave Cowens	2,783
4.	Bill Russell	2,601
5.	Tom Heinsohn	2,451
6.	Bob Cousy	2,231
7.	Frank Ramsey	2,158
8.	Don Nelson	2,094
9.	Don Chaney	1,840
10.	Bill Sharman	1,839

Technical Fouls

	Player	
1.	Red Auerbach	*

Disqualifications

	Player	
1.	Tom Sanders	94
2.	Dave Cowens	86
3.	Frank Ramsey	85
4.	Tom Heinsohn	56
5.	Bob Brannum	42
6.	Don Chaney	40
7.	Jim Loscutoff	39
8.	Bob Donham	31
9.	Gene Conley	28
10.	Arnie Risen	26

Ejections

	Player	
1.	Red Auerbach	*

*No figures available. It's estimated that Auerbach paid $17,000 in NBA fines, the majority incurred during the regular season.

PLAYOFFS

Games

	Player	
1.	John Havlicek	172
2.	Bill Russell	165
3.	Sam Jones	154
4.	Don Nelson	134
5.	Tom Sanders	130
6.	Bob Cousy	109
7.	K.C. Jones	105
8.	Tom Heinsohn	104
9.	Frank Ramsey	98
10.	Dave Cowens	89
11.	Jo Jo White	80
12.	Larry Siegfried	79
13.	Bill Sharman	78

Minutes

	Player	
1.	Bill Russell	7497
2.	John Havlicek	6860
3.	Sam Jones	4654
4.	Bob Cousy	3940
5.	Dave Cowens	3768
6.	Jo Jo White	3428
7.	Tom Heinsohn	3223
8.	Tom Sanders	3039
9.	Don Nelson	2941
10.	Bill Sharman	2573
11.	K.C. Jones	2494
12.	Frank Ramsey	2396
13.	Paul Silas	2232

Points

	Player	
1.	John Havlicek	3776
2.	Sam Jones	2909
3.	Bill Russell	2673
4.	Tom Heinsohn	2058
5.	Bob Cousy	2018
6.	Jo Jo White	1720
7.	Dave Cowens	1684
8.	Don Nelson	1493
9.	Bill Sharman	1446
10.	Frank Ramsey	1331
11.	Tom Sanders	1142

Average

	Player	
1.	John Havlicek	22.0
2.	Jo Jo White	21.5
3.	Larry Bird	20.5
4.	Tom Heinsohn	19.8
5.	Dave Cowens	18.9
6.	Sam Jones	18.9
7.	Bill Sharman	18.5
8.	Bob Cousy	18.5
9.	Robert Parish	17.6
10.	Bailey Howell	16.3
11.	Bill Russell	16.2
12.	Cedric Maxwell	16.1
13.	Ed Macauley	15.3

Field Goals Attempted

	Player	
1.	John Havlicek	3329
2.	Sam Jones	2572
3.	Bill Russell	2335
4.	Bob Cousy	2116
5.	Tom Heinsohn	2035
6.	Jo Jo White	1629
7.	Dave Cowens	1627
8.	Bill Sharman	1262
9.	Don Nelson	1109
10.	Frank Ramsey	1105
11.	Tom Sanders	1066

Field Goals Made

	Player	
1.	John Havlicek	1451
2.	Sam Jones	1149
3.	Bill Russell	1003
4.	Tom Heinsohn	818
5.	Dave Cowens	733
6.	Jo Jo White	732
7.	Bob Cousy	689
8.	Don Nelson	554
9.	Bill Sharman	538
10.	Frank Ramsey	469

Field-Goal Percentage

	Player		
1.	Cedric Maxwell	.574	(387/222)
2.	Don Nelson	.500	(1,109/554)
3.	Bailey Howell	.498	(615/306)
4.	Robert Parish	.491	(428/210)
5.	Don Chaney	.467	(415/194)
6.	Nate Archibald	.459	(370/170)
7.	Larry Bird	.457	(696/318)
8.	Chris Ford	.449	(267/120)
9.	Jo Jo White	.447	(1,638/732)
10.	Sam Jones	.447	(2,572/1,149)
11.	Tom Sanders	.436	(1,066/465)
12.	John Havlicek	.436	(3,329/1,451)
13.	Dave Cowens	.432	(1,627/733)
14.	Bill Russell	.430	(2,335/1,003)
15.	Bill Sharman	.426	(1,262/538)

Free Throws Attempted

	Player	
1.	Bill Russell	1106
2.	John Havlicek	1046
3.	Bob Cousy	799
4.	Sam Jones	753
5.	Tom Heinsohn	568
6.	Frank Ramsey	476
7.	Don Nelson	470
8.	Bill Sharman	406
9.	Jo Jo White	309
10.	Larry Siegfried	307

Free Throws Made

	Player	
1.	John Havlicek	874
2.	Bill Russell	667
3.	Bob Cousy	644
4.	Sam Jones	611
5.	Tom Heinsohn	422
6.	Frank Ramsey	393
7.	Don Nelson	385
8.	Bill Sharman	370
9.	Jo Jo White	256
9.	Larry Siegfried	256

Free-Throw Percentage

	Player		
1.	Bill Sharman	.911	(406/370)
2.	Larry Bird	.871	(155/135)
3.	Nate Archibald	.841	(164/138)
4.	John Havlicek	.836	(1,046/874)
5.	Larry Siegfried	.834	(307/256)
6.	Jo Jo White	.828	(309/256)
7.	Frank Ramsey	.826	(476/393)
8.	Don Nelson	.819	(470/385)
9.	Sam Jones	.811	(753/611)
10.	Bob Cousy	.801	(799/640)
11.	Cedric Maxwell	.767	(219/168)
12.	Paul Silas	.746	(197/147)
13.	Dave Cowens	.744	(298/218)
14.	Tom Heinsohn	.743	(568/422)

Assists

	Player	
1.	Bob Cousy	937
2.	John Havlicek	825
3.	Bill Russell	770
4.	Jo Jo White	453
5.	K.C. Jones	396
6.	Sam Jones	358
7.	Dave Cowens	333
8.	Nate Archibald	230
9.	Tom Heinsohn	215
10.	Larry Bird	213
11.	Larry Siegfried	209
12.	Bill Sharman	201

Rebounds

	Player	
1.	Bill Russell	4104
2.	Dave Cowens	1285
3.	John Havlicek	1186
4.	Tom Heinsohn	954
5.	Tom Sanders	763
6.	Sam Jones	720
7.	Don Nelson	647
8.	Bob Cousy	546
9.	Frank Ramsey	494
10.	Larry Bird	489
11.	Bailey Howell	330

Personal Fouls

	Player	
1.	Bill Russell	536
2.	John Havlicek	517
3.	Tom Sanders	508
4.	Tom Heinsohn	417
5.	Dave Cowens	398
6.	Sam Jones	395
7.	Frank Ramsey	362
8.	Don Nelson	357
9.	Bob Cousy	314
10.	Larry Siegfried	249

Technical Fouls

	Player	
1.	Red Auerbach	*

Disqualifications

	Player	
1.	Tom Sanders	26
2.	Dave Cowens	15
3.	Charlie Scott	14
3.	Tom Heinsohn	14
5.	Frank Ramsey	13
6.	Bailey Howell	11
7.	John Havlicek	9
7.	Bob Donham	9
9.	Bill Russell	8
9.	Jim Loscutoff	8
9.	Bob Brannum	8

Ejections

	Player	
1.	Red Auerbach	*

*See both Technical Fouls and Ejections categories among regular-season leaders.

SEASON - BY - SEASON

Season	Scoring Average	Total Points	Team High	Minutes
1946-47	C. Simmons, 10.3	C. Simmons, 620	A. Brightman, 26	—
1947-48	E. Sadowski, 19.4	E. Sadowski, 910	C. Simmons, 26	—
1948-49	E. Ehlers, 8.7	E. Ehlers, 514	E. Sadowski, 34	—
1949-50	B. Kinney, 11.1	S. Hertzberg, 693	G. Stump, 28	—
1950-51	E. Macauley, 20.4	E. Macauley, 1,384	G. Kaftan, 34	—
1951-52	B. Cousy, 21.7	B. Cousy, 1,463	B. Cousy, 39	B. Cousy, 2,681
1952-53	E. Macauley, 20.3	B. Cousy, 1,407	E. Macauley, 35	B. Cousy, 2,945
1953-54	B. Cousy, 19.2	B. Cousy, 1,383	B. Cousy, 50	B. Cousy, 2,857
1954-55	B. Cousy, 21.2	B. Cousy, 1,504	B. Cousy, 42	B. Cousy, 2,747
1955-56	B. Sharman, 19.9	B. Sharman, 1,434	B. Cousy, 40	B. Cousy, 2,767
1956-57	B. Sharman, 21.2	B. Sharman, 1,413	B. Sharman, 35	B. Sharman, 2,403
1957-58	B. Sharman, 22.3	B. Sharman, 1,402	T. Heinsohn, 41	B. Russell, 2,640
1958-59	B. Sharman, 20.4	B. Sharman, 1,466	B. Sharman, 44	B. Russell, 2,979
1959-60	T. Heinsohn, 21.7	T. Heinsohn, 1,629	T. Heinsohn, 43	B. Russell, 3,146
1960-61	T. Heinsohn, 21.3	T. Heinsohn, 1,579	B. Cousy, 46	B. Russell, 3,458
1961-62	T. Heinsohn, 22.1	T. Heinsohn, 1,742	S. Jones, 44	B. Russell, 3,433
1962-63	S. Jones, 19.7	S. Jones, 1,499	T. Heinsohn, 45	B. Russell, 3,500
1963-64	J. Havlicek, 19.9	J. Havlicek, 1,595	S. Jones, 47	B. Russell, 3,482
1964-65	S. Jones, 25.9	S. Jones, 2,070	J. Havlicek, 43	B. Russell, 3,466
1965-66	S. Jones, 23.5	S. Jones, 1,577	S. Jones, 44	B. Russell, 3,386
1966-67	J. Havlicek, 21.4	J. Havlicek, 1,733	S. Jones, 51	B. Russell, 3,297
1967-68	J. Havlicek, 20.7	J. Havlicek, 1,700	S. Jones, 42	B. Russell, 2,953
1968-69	J. Havlicek, 21.6	J. Havlicek, 1,771	J. Havlicek, 41	B. Russell, 3,291
1969-70	J. Havlicek, 24.2	J. Havlicek, 1,960	J. Havlicek, 41	J. Havlicek, 3,369
1970-71	J. Havlicek, 28.9	J. Havlicek, 2,338	J. Havlicek, 43	J. Havlicek, 3,678
1971-72	J. Havlicek, 27.5	J. Havlicek, 2,252	J. Havlicek, 39	J. Havlicek, 3,698
1972-73	J. Havlicek, 23.8	J. Havlicek, 1,902	J. Havlicek, 42	D. Cowens, 3,425
1973-74	J. Havlicek, 22.6	J. Havlicek, 1,716	J. White, 37	D. Cowens, 3,352
1974-75	D. Cowens, 20.4	J. Havlicek, 1,573	J. Havlicek, 40	J. White, 3,220
1975-76	D. Cowens, 19.0	J. White, 1,552	D. Cowens, 39	J. White, 3,257
1976-77	J. White, 19.6	J. White, 1,609	J. White, 41	J. White, 3,333
1977-78	D. Cowens, 18.6	D. Cowens, 1,435	D. Cowens, 36	D. Cowens, 3,215
1978-79	C. Maxwell, 19.0	C. Maxwell, 1,518	B. McAdoo, 42	C. Maxwell, 2,969
1979-80	L. Bird, 21.3	L. Bird, 1,745	L. Bird, 45	L. Bird, 2,955
1980-81	L. Bird, 21.2	L. Bird, 1,741	R. Parish, 40	L. Bird, 3,239
1981-82	L. Bird, 22.9	L. Bird, 1,761	L. Bird, 40	L. Bird, 2,923

Celtic fans bid farewell to K.C. Jones and family in 1967. K.C. would return a decade later as an assistant coach.

Season	FG Attempted	FG Made	FG Pct.
1946-47	A. Brightman, 870	C. Simmons, 246	C. Simmons, .320
1947-48	E. Sadowski, 953	E. Sadowski, 308	E. Sadowski, .323
1948-49	E. Ehlers, 583	G. Stump, 193	G. Stump, .333
1949-50	S. Hertzberg, 865	S. Hertzberg, 275	B. Kinney, .375
1950-51	B. Cousy, 1,138	E. Macauley, 459	E. Macauley, .466
1951-52	B. Cousy, 1,388	B. Cousy, 512	B. Donham, .487
1952-53	B. Cousy, 1,320	B. Cousy, 464	B. Donham, .479
1953-54	B. Cousy, 1,262	B. Cousy, 486	E. Macauley, .486
1954-55	B. Cousy, 1,316	B. Cousy, 522	B. Sharman, .427
1955-56	B. Sharman, 1,229	B. Sharman, 538	B. Sharman, .438
1956-57	B. Cousy, 1,264	B. Sharman, 516	B. Russell, .427
1957-58	B. Sharman, 1,297	B. Sharman, 550	B. Russell, .442
1958-59	B. Sharman, 1,377	B. Sharman, 562	B. Russell, .457
1959-60	T. Heinsohn, 1,590	T. Heinsohn, 673	B. Russell, .467
1960-61	T. Heinsohn, 1,566	T. Heinsohn, 627	S. Jones, .449
1961-62	T. Heinsohn, 1,613	T. Heinsohn, 692	S. Jones, .464
1962-63	S. Jones, 1,305	S. Jones, 621	S. Jones, .476
1963-64	J. Havlicek, 1,535	J. Havlicek, 640	S. Jones, .450
1964-65	S. Jones, 1,818	S. Jones, 821	S. Jones, .452
1965-66	S. Jones, 1,335	S. Jones, 626	S. Jones, .469
1966-67	J. Havlicek, 1,540	J. Havlicek, 684	B. Howell, .512
1967-68	J. Havlicek, 1,551	J. Havlicek, 666	D. Nelson, .494
1968-69	J. Havlicek, 1,709	J. Havlicek, 692	B. Howell, .487
1969-70	J. Havlicek, 1,585	J. Havlicek, 736	D. Nelson, .501
1970-71	J. Havlicek, 1,982	J. Havlicek, 892	D. Nelson, .468
1971-72	J. Havlicek, 1,957	J. Havlicek, 897	D. Cowens, .484
1972-73	J. Havlicek, 1,704	J. Havlicek, 766	D. Chaney, .482
1973-74	J. Havlicek, 1,502	J. Havlicek, 685	D. Nelson, .508
1974-75	J. White, 1,440	J. White, 658	D. Nelson, .539
1975-76	J. White, 1,492	J. White, 670	D. Cowens, .468
1976-77	J. White, 1,488	J. White, 638	T. Boswell, .515
1977-78	D. Cowens, 1,220	D. Cowens, 598	C. Maxwell, .538
1978-79	C. Ford, 1,107	C. Ford, 525	C. Maxwell, .584
1979-80	L. Bird, 1,463	L. Bird, 693	C. Maxwell, .609
1980-81	L. Bird, 1,414	L. Bird, 711	C. Maxwell, .548
1981-82	L. Bird, 1,503	L. Bird, 719	C. Maxwell, .588

Season	FT Attempted	FT Made	FT Pct.
1946-47	A. Brightman, 193	C. Simmons, 128	C. Simmons, .677
1947-48	E. Sadowski, 422	E. Sadowski, 294	D. Garfinkle, .761
1948-49	E. Ehlers, 225	J. Seminoff, 151	G. Stump, .713
1949-50	B. Kinney, 320	B. Kinney, 201	T. Lavelli, .853
1950-51	E. Macauley, 614	E. Macauley, 466	S. Hertzberg, .826
1951-52	E. Macauley, 621	E. Macauley, 496	B. Sharman, .859
1952-53	E. Macauley, 667	E. Macauley, 500	B. Sharman, .850
1953-54	E. Macauley, 554	E. Macauley, 420	B. Sharman, .844
1954-55	B. Cousy, 570	B. Cousy, 460	B. Sharman, .897
1955-56	B. Cousy, 564	B. Cousy, 476	B. Sharman, .867
1956-57	B. Cousy, 442	B. Sharman, 381	B. Sharman, .905
1957-58	F. Ramsey, 472	F. Ramsey, 383	B. Sharman, .893
1958-59	F. Ramsey, 436	B. Sharman, 342	B. Sharman, .929
1959-60	B. Cousy, 403	B. Cousy, 319	B. Sharman, .866
1960-61	B. Russell, 469	B. Cousy, 352	B. Sharman, .921
1961-62	B. Russell, 481	T. Heinsohn, 358	F. Ramsey, .825
1962-63	B. Russell, 517	T. Heinsohn, 340	T. Heinsohn, .835
1963-64	B. Russell, 429	J. Havlicek, 315	T. Heinsohn, .827
1964-65	S. Jones, 522	S. Jones, 428	S. Jones, .820
1965-66	S. Jones, 407	S. Jones, 325	L. Siegfried, .881
1966-67	B. Howell, 471	J. Havlicek, 365	S. Jones, .857
1967-68	B. Howell, 461	J. Havlicek, 368	L. Siegfried, .868
1968-69	J. Havlicek, 496	J. Havlicek, 387	L. Siegfried, .864
1969-70	J. Havlicek, 578	J. Havlicek, 488	T. Sanders, .880
1970-71	J. Havlicek, 677	J. Havlicek, 554	J. Havlicek, .818
1971-72	J. Havlicek, 549	J. Havlicek, 458	J. Havlicek, .834
1972-73	J. Havlicek, 431	J. Havlicek, 370	J. Havlicek, .858
1973-74	J. Havlicek, 416	J. Havlicek, 346	J. White, .837
1974-75	P. Silas, 344	J. Havlicek, 289	J. Havlicek, .870
1975-76	D. Cowens, 340	J. Havlicek, 281	S. Kuberski, .895
1976-77	S. Wicks, 464	J. White, 333	J. White, .869
1977-78	S. Wicks, 329	D. Bing, 244	J. White, .858
1978-79	C. Maxwell, 716	C. Maxwell, 574	J. White, .888
1979-80	C. Maxwell, 554	C. Maxwell, 436	L. Bird, 836
1980-81	C. Maxwell, 450	C. Maxwell, 352	T. Duerod, .929
1981-82	C. Maxwell, 478	C. Maxwell, 357	L. Bird, .863

Young Bob Cousy said he'd rather keep pumping gas at his Worcester service station than play for Tri-Cities, which chose him when the Celtics ignored the Holy Cross hero in the 1950 draft.

Season	Assists	Rebounds	Personal Fouls	Disqualified
1946-47	C. Simmons, 62	—	C. Simmons, 130 A. Spector, 130	—
1947-48	E. Sadowski, 74	—	E. Sadowski, 182	—
1948-49	J. Seminoff, 229	—	J. Seminoff, 195	—
1949-50	J. Seminoff, 249	—	B. Kinney, 251	—
1950-51	B. Cousy, 341	E. Macauley, 616	C. Cooper, 219	C. Cooper, 7
1951-52	B. Cousy, 441	B. Harris, 531	B. Brannum, 235	B. Donham, 9 B. Brannum, 9
1952-53	B. Cousy, 547	E. Macauley, 629	B. Brannum, 287	B. Brannum, 17
1953-54	B. Cousy, 518	E. Macauley, 571	B. Brannum, 280	B. Donham, 11
1954-55	B. Cousy, 557	E. Macauley, 600	F. Ramsey, 250	F. Ramsey, 11
1955-56	B. Cousy, 642	J. Nichols, 625	A. Risen, 300	A. Risen, 17
1956-57	B. Cousy, 478	B. Russell, 943	T. Heinsohn, 304	T. Heinsohn, 12
1957-58	B. Cousy, 463	B. Russell, 1,564	T. Heinsohn, 274	F. Ramsey, 8 L. Tsioropoulos, 8
1958-59	B. Cousy, 557	B. Russell, 1,612	J. Loscutoff, 285	J. Loscutoff, 15
1959-60	B. Cousy, 715	B. Russell, 1,778	T. Heinsohn, 275	F. Ramsey, 10 G. Conley, 10
1960-61	B. Cousy, 587	B. Russell, 1,868	F. Ramsey, 284	G. Conley, 15
1961-62	B. Cousy, 584	B. Russell, 1,790	T. Heinsohn, 280	F. Ramsey, 10
1962-63	B. Cousy, 515	B. Russell, 1,843	T. Heinsohn, 270	F. Ramsey, 13
1963-64	K.C. Jones, 407	B. Russell, 1,930	T. Sanders, 277	F. Ramsey, 7
1964-65	K.C. Jones, 437	B. Russell, 1,878	T. Sanders, 318	T. Sanders, 15
1965-66	K.C. Jones, 503	B. Russell, 1,779	T. Sanders, 317	T. Sanders, 19
1966-67	B. Russell, 472	B. Russell, 1,700	T. Sanders, 304	K.C. Jones, 7
1967-68	J. Havlicek, 384	B. Russell, 1,451	T. Sanders, 300	T. Sanders, 12
1968-69	J. Havlicek, 441	B. Russell, 1,484	T. Sanders, 293	T. Sanders, 9 E. Bryant, 9
1969-70	J. Havlicek, 550	J. Havlicek, 635	H. Finkel, 292	H. Finkel, 13
1970-71	J. Havlicek, 607	D. Cowens, 1,216	D. Cowens, 350	D. Cowens, 15
1971-72	J. Havlicek, 614	D. Cowens, 1,203	D. Cowens, 314	D. Cowens, 10
1972-73	J. Havlicek, 529	D. Cowens, 1,329	D. Cowens, 311	D. Cowens, 7
1973-74	J. White, 448	D. Cowens, 1,257	D. Cowens, 294	D. Cowens, 7 D. Chaney, 7
1974-75	J. White, 458	P. Silas, 1,025	D. Chaney, 244	D. Cowens, 7
1975-76	J. White, 445	D. Cowens, 1,246	C. Scott, 356	C. Scott, 17
1976-77	J. White, 492	S. Wicks, 824	S. Wicks, 331	S. Wicks, 14
1977-78	D. Cowens, 351	D. Cowens, 1,078	S. Wicks, 318	S. Wicks, 9
1978-79	C. Ford, 369	C. Maxwell, 791	C. Maxwell, 266	D. Cowens, 16
1979-80	N. Archibald, 671	L. Bird, 852	L. Bird, 279	C. Maxwell, 6
1980-81	N. Archibald, 618	L. Bird, 895	R. Parish, 310	R. Parish, 9
1981-82	N. Archibald, 541	R. Parish, 866	R. Parish, 267	C. Maxwell, 6

Young Bill Russell knew his way around a hoop.

CELTICS AMONG NBA LEADERS (TOP 10) SEASON BY SEASON

SCORING

Season	Place	Player	Pts.	Ave.
1947-48	3d	Ed Sadowski	910	19.4
1950-51	3d	Ed Macauley	1,384	20.4
	9th	Bob Cousy	1,078	15.6
1951-52	3d	Bob Cousy	1,433	21.7
	4th	Ed Macauley	1,264	19.2
1952-53	3d	Bob Cousy	1,407	19.8
	4th	Ed Macauley	1,402	20.3
	6th	Bill Sharman	1,147	16.2
1953-54	2d	Bob Cousy	1,383	19.2
	3d	Ed Macauley	1,344	18.9
	7th	Bill Sharman	1,155	16.0
1954-55	3d	Bob Cousy	1,504	21.2
	9th	Bill Sharman	1,253	18.4
	10th	Ed Macauley	1,248	17.6
1955-56	6th	Bill Sharman	1,434	19.9
	7th	Bob Cousy	1,356	18.8
	8th	Ed Macauley	1,240	17.5
1956-57	7th	Bill Sharman	1,413	21.1
	8th	Bob Cousy	1,319	20.6
1957-58	6th	Bill Sharman	1,402	22.3
1958-59	8th	Bill Sharman	1,466	20.4
	9th	Bob Cousy	1,297	20.0
1959-60	8th	Tom Heinsohn	1,629	21.7
1963-64	10th	John Havlicek	1,595	19.9
1964-65	4th	Sam Jones	2,070	25.9
1965-66	10th	Sam Jones	1,577	23.5
1966-67	7th	John Havlicek	1,733	21.4
	9th	Bailey Howell	1,621	20.0
1969-70	8th	John Havlicek	1,960	24.2
1970-71	2d	John Havlicek	2,338	28.9
1971-72	3d	John Havlicek	2,252	27.5
1972-73	10th*	John Havlicek	1,902	23.8
1973-74	10th	John Havlicek	1,716	22.6
1978-79	4th**	Bob McAdoo	1.487	24.8
1981-82	10th	Larry Bird	1,761	22.9

*Tied.

**Played first 40 games with New York Knicks, last 20 games with Celtics.

FIELD-GOAL PERCENTAGE

Season	Place	Player	Pct.	Att.	Made
1946-47	7th	Connie Simmons	.320	768	246
1947-48	2d	Ed Sadowski	.323	953	308
	8th	Mel Riebe	.309	653	202
1950-51	2d	Ed Macauley	.466	985	459
1951-52	3d	Ed Macauley	.432	888	384
1952-53	2d	Ed Macauley	.452	997	451
	4th	Bill Sharman	.436	925	403
1953-54	1st	Ed Macauley	.486	950	462
	2d	Bill Sharman	.450	915	412
1954-55	6th	Bill Sharman	.427	1,062	453
	7th	Ed Macauley	.424	951	403
1955-56	4th*	Bill Sharman	.438	1,229	538
1956-57	5th	Bill Russell	.427	649	277
	10th*	Bill Sharman	.416	1,241	516
1957-58	3d	Bill Russell	.442	1,032	456
	10th	Bill Sharman	.424	1,297	550
1958-59	2d	Bill Russell	.457	997	456
	9th	Sam Jones	.434	703	305
1959-60	4th	Bill Russell	.467	1,189	555
	7th	Bill Sharman	.456	1,225	559
	9th	Sam Jones	.454	782	355
1962-63	9th	Sam Jones	.476	1,305	621
1966-67	3d	Bailey Howell	.512	1,242	636
1967-68	9th	Don Nelson	.494	632	312
1968-69	10th*	Bailey Howell	.487	1,257	612
1973-74	7th	Don Nelson	.508	717	364
1974-75	1st	Don Nelson	.539	785	423
	7th	Paul Westphal	.510	670	342
1978-79	1st	Cedric Maxwell	.584	808	472
1979-80	1st	Cedric Maxwell	.609	750	457
1980-81	3d	Cedric Maxwell	.588	750	441

*Tied.

THREE-POINT FIELD-GOAL PERCENTAGE

Season	Place	Player	Pct.	Att.	Made
1979-80	2d	Chris Ford	.427	164	70
	3d	Larry Bird	.406	143	58
1980-81	7th	Chris Ford	.330	109	36

FREE-THROW PERCENTAGE

Season	Place	Player	Pct.	Att.	Made
1946-47	2d	Tony Kappen**	.795	161	128
1950-51	7th	Sonny Hertzberg	.826	270	223
1951-52	3d	Bill Sharman	.859	213	183
	10th	Bob Cousy	.808	506	409
1952-53	1st	Bill Sharman	.850	401	341
	8th	Bob Cousy	.816	587	479
1953-54	1st	Bill Sharman	.844	392	331
	6th	Bob Cousy	.787	522	411
	10th	Ed Macauley	.758	554	420
1954-55	1st	Bill Sharman	.897	387	347
	9th	Bob Cousy	.807	560	460
1955-56	1st	Bill Sharman	.867	413	358
	4th	Bob Cousy	.844	564	476
1956-57	1st	Bill Sharman	.905	421	381
	6th	Bob Cousy	.821	442	363
1957-58	2d	Bill Sharman	.893	338	302
	3d	Bob Cousy	.850	326	277
1958-59	1st	Bill Sharman	.932	367	342
	4th	Bob Cousy	.855	385	329
1959-60	4th	Bill Sharman	.866	291	252
1960-61	1st	Bill Sharman	.921	228	210
	4th	Frank Ramsey	.833	354	295
1961-62	4th*	Frank Ramsey	.825	405	334
	8th*	Tom Heinsohn	.819	437	358
	10th	Sam Jones	.818	297	243
1962-63	4th	Tom Heinsohn	.835	407	340
	6th	Frank Ramsey	.816	332	271
1963-64	4th	Tom Heinsohn	.827	342	283
1964-65	6th	Sam Jones	.820	522	428
1965-66	1st	Larry Siegfried	.881	311	274
1966-67	5th	Sam Jones	.857	371	318
	6th	Larry Siegfried	.847	347	294
	8th	John Havlicek	.828	441	365
1967-68	2d	Larry Siegfried	.868	272	236
	6th	Sam Jones	.827	376	311
	8th	John Havlicek	.812	453	368
1968-69	1st	Larry Siegfried	.864	389	336
1969-70	4th	John Havlicek	.844	578	488
1971-72	7th	John Havlicek	.834	549	458
1972-73	9th	John Havlicek	.858	431	370
1974-75	6th	John Havlicek	.870	332	289
1976-77	7th	Jo Jo White	.869	383	333
1977-78	7th	John Havlicek	.855	269	230
1978-79	6th***	Jo Jo White	.880	158	139
1980-81	8th	Larry Bird	.863	328	283
1981-82	5th	Larry Bird	.863	380	328

*Tied.

**Played first 18 games with Celtics, last 44 games with Pittsburgh Ironmen.

***Played first 47 games with Celtics, last 29 games with Golden State Warriors.

Boston Garden fans have been known to question referees' eyesight.

ASSISTS

Season	Place	Player	No.	Ave.
1947-48	5th	Ed Sadowski	74	1.6
	10th	Saul Mariaschin	60	1.4
1948-49	6th	Jim Seminoff	229	3.9
1949-50	8th	Jim Seminoff	249	3.8
1950-51	4th	Bob Cousy	341	4.9
	10th*	Sonny Hertzberg	244	3.8
1951-52	2d	Bob Cousy	441	6.7
1952-53	1st	Bob Cousy	547	7.7
	6th	Ed Macauley	280	4.1
1953-54	1st	Bob Cousy	518	7.2
	9th	Ed Macauley	271	3.8
1954-55	1st	Bob Cousy	557	7.8
	10th	Bill Sharman	280	4.1
1955-56	1st	Bob Cousy	642	8.9
	7th	Bill Sharman	339	4.7
1956-57	1st	Bob Cousy	478	7.5
	8th	Bill Sharman	236	3.5
1957-58	1st	Bob Cousy	463	7.1
1958-58	1st	Bob Cousy	557	8.6
	8th	Bill Sharman	292	4.1
1959-60	1st	Bob Cousy	715	9.5
1960-61	3d	Bob Cousy	587	7.7
1961-62	3d	Bob Cousy	584	7.8
1962-63	3d	Bob Cousy	515	6.8
1963-64	3d	K.C. Jones	407	5.1
	8th	Bill Russell	370	4.7
1964-65	3d	K.C. Jones	437	5.6
	5th	Bill Russell	410	5.3
1965-66	3d	K.C. Jones	503	6.3
1966-67	4th	Bill Russell	472	5.8
	8th	K.C. Jones	389	5.0
1967-68	8th	John Havlicek	384	4.7
1968-69	9th	John Havlicek	441	5.4
1969-70	7th	John Havlicek	550	6.8
1970-71	4th	John Havlicek	607	7.5
1971-72	5th	John Havlicek	614	7.5
1972-73	7th	John Havlicek	529	6.6
	10th	Jo Jo White	498	6.1
1973-74	9th	John Havlicek	447	5.9
1976-77	7th	Jo Jo White	492	6.0
1979-80	2nd	Nate Archibald	671	8.4
1980-81	5th	Nate Archibald	618	
1981-82	4th	Nate Archibald	541	

*Tied.

REBOUNDS

Season	Place	Player	No.	Ave.
1950-51	9th	Ed Macauley	616	9.1
1956-57	4th	Bill Russell	943	19.6
	10th	Jim Loscutoff	730	10.4
1957-58	1st	Bill Russell	1,564	22.7
1958-59	1st	Bill Russell	1,612	23.0
1959-60	2d	Bill Russell	1,778	24.0
1960-61	2d	Bill Russell	1,868	23.9
1961-62	2d	Bill Russell	1,790	23.6
1962-63	2d	Bill Russell	1,843	23.0
1963-64	1st	Bill Russell	1,930	24.7
1964-65	1st	Bill Russell	1,878	24.1
1965-66	2d	Bill Russell	1,779	22.8
1966-67	2d	Bill Russell	1,700	21.0
1967-68	3d	Bill Russell	1,451	18.6
1968-69	3d	Bill Russell	1,484	19.3
1970-71	7th	Dave Cowens	1,216	15.0
1971-72	5th	Dave Cowens	1,203	15.2
1972-73	3d	Dave Cowens	1,329	16.2
	9th	Paul Silas	1,039	13.0
1973-74	2d	Dave Cowens	1,257	15.7
1974-75	2d	Dave Cowens	958	14.7
	7th	Paul Silas	1,025	12.5
1975-76	2d	Dave Cowens	1,246	16.0
	4th	Paul Silas	1,025	12.7
1977-78	3d	Dave Cowens	1,078	14.0
1979-80	10th	Larry Bird	852	10.4
1980-81	4th	Larry Bird	895	10.9
1981-82	7th	Larry Bird	837	10.9
	8th	Robert Parish	866	10.8

CELTIC CLUB RECORDS

REGULAR-SEASON RECORDS

Player in One Game

Points:	51	Sam Jones at Detroit, October 29, 1965 (21 FG, 9 FT)
	46	Bob Cousy vs. New York at Boston, February 7, 1960 (18 FG, 10 FT)
	46	Ed Macauley vs. Minneapolis at Boston, March 6, 1953 (18 FG, 10 FT)
	45	Tom Heinsohn at Syracuse, December 25, 1961 (19 FG, 7 FT)
	45	Larry Bird at Phoenix, February 13, 1980 (19 FG [including 3 3-pointers], 4 FT)
	44	Bill Sharman vs. New York at Boston, December 26, 1957 (17 FG, 10 FT)
	44	Sam Jones at Syracuse, March 12, 1960 (16 FG, 12 FT)
Field Goals Attempted:	42	John Havlicek vs. Baltimore at Boston, February 3, 1965
Field Goals Made:	21	Sam Jones at Detroit, October 29, 1965 (FGA 35)
Free Throws Attempted:	24	John Havlicek vs. Seattle at Boston, February 6, 1970
	20	Nate Archibald vs. Chicago at Boston, January 16, 1980
Free Throws Made:	19	Bill Sharman at Philadelphia, March 8, 1956
	19	Frank Ramsey at Detroit, December 3, 1957
	19	John Havlicek vs. Seattle at Boston, February 6, 1970
	19	Cedric Maxwell vs. New Jersey at Boston, January 14, 1979
Rebounds:	51	Bill Russell vs. Syracuse at Boston, February 8, 1960
	49	Bill Russell vs. Philadelphia at Boston, November 19, 1957
	49	Bill Russell vs. Detroit at Providence, March 11, 1965
Assists:	28	Bob Cousy vs. Minneapolis at Boston, February 27, 1959
	23	Nate Archibald vs. Denver at Boston, February 5, 1982

Player in One Half

Points:	32	Ed Macauley vs. Detroit at Boston, January 15, 1958
Field Goals Attempted:	23	Bob Cousy vs. New York at Boston, March 10, 1959
Field Goals Made:	13	Sam Jones at Detroit, October 29, 1965
Free Throws Attempted:	15	John Havlicek vs. Seattle at Boston, February 6, 1970
	15	Nate Archibald vs. Chicago at Boston, January 16, 1980
Free Throws Made:	13	Nate Archibald vs. Chicago at Boston, January 16, 1980
Rebounds:	32	Bill Russell vs. Philadelphia at Boston, November 11, 1957
Assists:	19	Bob Cousy vs. Minneapolis at Boston, February 27, 1959

Player in One Quarter

Points:	23	Tom Heinsohn vs. Cincinnati at Boston, February 8, 1959
	12	(overtime period) Bob Cousy at Syracuse, February 2, 1951
Field Goals Attempted:	17	Bob Cousy vs. New York at Boston, March 10, 1959
Field Goals Made:	10	Tom Heinsohn vs. Cincinnati at Boston, February 8, 1959
Free Throws Attempted:	13	Bill Russell at Philadelphia, February 9, 1959
Free Throws Made:	11	Frank Ramsey at Detroit, December 3, 1957
Rebounds:	17	Bill Russell vs. Philadelphia at Boston, November 16, 1957
	17	Bill Russell vs. Cincinnati at Boston, December 12, 1958
	17	Bill Russell at Syracuse, February 5, 1960
Assists:	12	Bob Cousy vs. Minneapolis at Boston, February 27, 1959
Personal Fouls:	5	Jim Loscutoff vs. Cincinnati at Boston, November 12, 1962

Team in One Game

Points:	173	vs. Minneapolis at Boston, February 27, 1959
Field Goals Attempted:	150	vs. Philadelphia at Boston, December 2, 1960
Field Goals Made:	72	vs. Minneapolis at Boston, February 27, 1959
Free Throws Attempted:	66	at Minneapolis, November 28, 1954
Free Throws Made:	56	at Minneapolis, November 28, 1954
Rebounds:	112	vs. Detroit at Boston, December 24, 1960
Assists:	43	vs. Baltimore at Boston, January 11, 1953
	43	vs. Minneapolis at Boston, February 27, 1959

Team in One Half

Points:	91	vs. Detroit at Providence, February 10, 1960
	91	at Cincinnati, November 11, 1959
Field Goals Attempted:	83	at Philadelphia, December 27, 1960
Field Goals Made:	40	vs. Minneapolis at Boston, February 27, 1959
Free Throws Attempted:	39	at Chicago, January 9, 1963
Free Throws Made:	32	vs. Syracuse at Boston, January 30, 1951
Rebounds:	65	vs. Cincinnati at Boston, January 12, 1962
Assists:	26	vs. Detroit at Boston, November 3, 1963

Team in One Quarter

Points:	54	vs. San Diego at Boston, February 25, 1970
	21	(overtime period) at San Francisco, January 2, 1963
Field Goals Attempted:	47	vs. Minneapolis at Boston, February 27, 1959
Field Goals Made:	23	vs. Minneapolis at Boston, February 27, 1959
Free Throws Attempted:	30	at Chicago, January 9, 1963
Free Throws Made:	23	at Chicago, January 9, 1963
Rebounds:	35	vs. Minneapolis at Boston, February 26, 1960
Assists:	16	vs. Minneapolis at Boston, February 27, 1959

PLAYOFF RECORDS

Player in One Game

Points:	54	John Havlicek vs. Atlanta at Boston, April 1, 1973
Field Goals Attempted:	36	John Havlicek vs. Atlanta at Boston, April 1, 1973
Field Goals Made:	24	John Havlicek vs. Atlanta at Boston, April 1, 1973
Free Throws Attempted:	32	Bob Cousy vs. Syracuse at Boston, March 21, 1953****
Free Throws Made:	23	Bob Cousy vs. Syracuse at Boston, March 21, 1953 (18 in a row)****
Rebounds:	40	Bill Russell vs. St. Louis at Boston, March 29, 1960
	40	Bill Russell vs. Los Angeles at Boston, April 18, 1962*
Assists:	19	Bob Cousy vs. St. Louis at Boston, April 9, 1958
	19	Bob Cousy vs. Minneapolis at St. Paul, April 7, 1959

Player in One Half

Points:	30	John Havlicek vs. Atlanta at Boston, April 1, 1973
Field Goals Attempted:	19	John Havlicek vs. Atlanta at Boston, April 1, 1973
Field Goals Made:	14	John Havlicek vs. Atlanta at Boston, April 1, 1973
Free Throws Attempted:	15	Bill Russell vs. St. Louis at Boston, April 11, 1961
Free Throws Made:	11	Frank Ramsey vs. Los Angeles at Boston, April 14, 1962
Rebounds:	25	Bill Russell vs. St. Louis at Boston, March 29, 1960
	25	Bill Russell vs. Los Angeles at Boston, April 18, 1962
Assists:	11	Bob Cousy vs. Cincinnati at Boston, April 10, 1963
	11	John Havlicek vs. Philadelphia at Boston, April 24, 1977
Personal Fouls:	6	Gene Conley vs. Syracuse at Boston, March 22, 1959
	6	Frank Ramsey vs. Syracuse at Boston, April 1, 1959

Player in One Quarter

Points:	20	Dave Cowens vs. Buffalo at Boston, March 30, 1974
	*12	(overtime period) Bob Cousy at Syracuse, March 17, 1954
Field Goals Attempted:	13	Dave Cowens vs. Buffalo at Boston, March 30, 1974
Field Goals Made:	9	Dave Cowens vs. Buffalo at Boston, March 30, 1974
	9	John Havlicek at New York, April 1974
Free Throws Attempted:	10	Frank Ramsey vs. Minneapolis at Boston, April 4, 1959
Free Throws Made:	9	Frank Ramsey vs. Minneapolis at Boston, April 4, 1959
Rebounds:	19	Bill Russell vs. Los Angeles at Boston, April 18, 1962
Assists:	8	Bob Cousy vs. Los Angeles at Boston, April 9, 1957
	8	John Havlicek vs. Philadelphia at Boston, April 24, 1977
Personal Fouls:	5	Arnie Risen vs. Syracuse at Boston, March 21, 1957

Team in One Game

Points:	142	vs. Los Angeles at Boston, April 18, 1965
Field Goals Attempted:	140	vs. Syracuse at Boston, March 18, 1959
Field Goals Made:	61	vs. St. Louis at Boston, March 27, 1960
Free Throws Attempted:	64	vs. Syracuse at Boston, March 21, 1953****
Free Throws Made:	57	vs. Syracuse at Boston, March 21, 1953****
Rebounds:	107	vs. Philadelphia at Boston, March 19, 1960
Assists:	38	at Los Angeles, April 21, 1965

Team in One Half

Points:	78	vs. Los Angeles at Boston, April 18, 1965
Field Goals Attempted:	77	vs. Philadelphia at Boston, March 22, 1960
Field Goals Made:	32	vs. St. Louis at Boston, March 27, 1960
	32	vs. Philadelphia at Boston, April 1, 1962
Free Throws Attempted:	30	vs. St. Louis at Boston, April 9, 1958
Free Throws Made:	20	vs. St. Louis at Boston, March 30, 1958
Rebounds:	60	vs. Philadelphia at Boston, March 19, 1960
Assists:	21	vs. St. Louis at Boston, April 9, 1957
Personal Fouls:	21	vs. Cincinnati at Boston, March 28, 1963

Team in One Quarter

Points:	46	vs. St. Louis at Boston, March 27, 1960
Field Goals Attempted:	42	vs. Philadelphia at Boston, March 22, 1960
Field Goals Made:	21	vs. Los Angeles at Boston, April 18, 1965
Free Throws Attempted:	18	vs. Los Angeles at Boston, April 18, 1962
Free Throws Made:	14	vs. Minneapolis at Boston, April 5, 1959
Rebounds:	31	vs. Philadelphia at Boston, March 19, 1960
	31	vs. Syracuse at Boston, March 23, 1961
Assists:	11	vs. St. Louis at Boston, April 9, 1957
Personal Fouls:	11	vs. Los Angeles at Boston, April 17, 1966
Disqualifications:	3	vs. Los Angeles at Boston, April 18, 1962

*Overtime Period.

ALL-TIME SEASON RECORDS

Individual

Most Points—2,338 by John Havlicek, 1970-71 (81 games)
Most Seasons over 1,000 Points—16 by John Havlicek
Highest Per Game Average—28.9 by John Havlicek, 1970-71
Longest Consecutive Games Streak—488 by Jo Jo White, January 21, 1972 to January 29, 1978
Most Field Goals Made—897 by John Havlicek, 1971-72
Most Field Goals Attempted—1,982 by John Havlicek, 1970-71
Highest Field Goal Average—.609 (457 of 750) by Cedric Maxwell, 1979-80
Most Free Throws Attempted—716 by Cedric Maxwell, 1978-79
Most Free Throws Made—574 by Cedric Maxwell, 1978-79
Highest Free Throw Percentage—.932 (342 of 367) by Bill Sharman, 1958-59
Most Consecutive Free Throws Made—55 by Bill Sharman, November 22, 1956-December 27, 1956
Most Consecutive Free Throws Made—56 (playoffs) by Bill Sharman, March 18, 1959-April 9, 1959
Most Rebounds—1,930 by Bill Russell, 1963-64
Most Assists—715 by Bob Cousy, 1959-60
Highest Assists Average—9.5 by Bob Cousy, 1959-60
Most Personals—356 on Charlie Scott, 1975-76
Most Minutes—3,698 by John Havlicek, 1971-72 (82 games)
Most Minutes Per Game—45.4 by John Havlicek, 1970-71
Most Disqualifications—19 by Tom Sanders, 1964-65

Team

Most Wins—68, 1972-73
Most Losses—53, 1978-79
Most Consecutive wins—18, February 24, 1982-March 28, 1982
Most Consecutive Losses—10, January 7, 1949-January 30, 1949
Highest Winning Percentage—.829 (68 wins, 14 losses), 1972-73
Lowest Winning Percentage—.324 (22 wins, 46 losses), 1949-50
Most Wins at Home—35 (6 losses), 1972-73, 1979-80, 1980-81, 1981-82
Fewest Wins at Home—12 (14 losses), 1949-50
Most Wins on Road—33 (8 losses), 1972-73
Most Points in Season—9,687 (80 games), 1961-62
Highest Average Points Per Game—124.5, 1959-60
Lowest Average Points Against Per Game—103.9, 1975-76
Highest Average Points Per Game at Home—128.6, 1959-60
Highest Average Points Per Game Away—122.4, 1959-60
Most Field Goals Attempted—9,295, 1960-61
Most Field Goals Made—3,855, 1961-62
Highest Free Throw Percentage—.800, 1973-74
Most Free Throws Attempted—2,983, 1967-68
Most Free Throws Made—2,216, 1966-67
Highest Field Goal Percentage—.504, 1980-81
Most Rebounds—6,131, 1960-61
Most Assists—2,310, 1972-73
Most Personals, 2,320, 1969-70
Most Disqualifications—56, 1952-53
Most Players Averaging Double Figures—8, 1979-80
Highest Total Season Attendance at Boston Garden—565,105, 1979-80
Highest Average Attendance at Boston Garden—14,490, 1979-80

Bill Russell, Larry Siegfried and Sam Jones boarded motorcycles during Summer 1967. Red Auerbach blew his top when he saw these photos in the next morning's *Boston Herald Traveler* and ordered his stars to quit cycling "before somebody gets killed."

BOSTON GARDEN HOME-COURT RECORDS

PLAYER
Full Game

Most Points—62 by Wilt Chamberlain, Philadelphia vs. Boston, January 14, 1962.
Most Field Goals Attempted—56 by Wilt Chamberlain, Philadelphia vs. Chicago, January 24, 1962.
Most Field Goals Scored—27 by Wilt Chamberlain, Philadelphia vs. Boston, January 14, 1962.
Most Consecutive Goals Scored—18 by Wilt Chamberlain, San Francisco vs. New York, November 27, 1963.
Most Free Throws Attempted—32 by Bob Cousy, Boston vs. Syracuse, March 21, 1953.****#
Most Free Throws Scored—30 by Bob Cousy, Boston vs. Syracuse, March 21, 1953.****#
Most Consecutive Free Throws Scored—19 by Bob Pettit, St. Louis vs. Boston, November 22, 1961.
Most Rebounds—51 by Bill Russell, Boston vs. Syracuse, February 5, 1960.
Most Assists—28 by Bob Cousy, Boston vs. Minneapolis, February 27, 1959.
Most Personals—7 on Alex Hannum, Syracuse vs. Boston, December 26, 1950; 7 on Al Cervi, Syracuse vs. Boston, March 21, 1953.****

PLAYER
One Half

Most Points—by Hal Greer, Syracuse vs. Boston, February 14, 1959.
Most Field Goals Attempted—32 by Wilt Chamberlain, Philadelphia vs. Chicago, January 24, 1962.
Most Field Goals Scored—18 by Hal Geer, Syracuse vs. Boston, February 14, 1959.
Most Free Throws Attempted—17 by Ken Sears, New York vs. Boston, November 3, 1956; 17 by Wilt Chamberlain, San Francisco vs. Boston, February 9, 1963.
Most Free Throws Scored—16 by Ken Sears, New York vs. Boston, November 3, 1956.
Most Rebounds—32 by Bill Russell, Boston vs. Philadelphia, November 16, 1957.
Most Assists—19 by Bob Cousy, Boston vs. Minneapolis, February 27, 1959.
Most Personals—6 on Howie Schultz, Minneapolis vs. Boston, November 18, 1951; 6 on Jack Twyman, Cincinnati vs. Boston, October 17, 1959; 6 on Jim Palmer, New York vs. St. Louis, February 3, 1960.

PLAYER
One Quarter

Most Points—23 by Tom Heinsohn, Boston vs. Cincinnati, February 4, 1959; 23 by Togo Palazzi, Syracuse vs. Philadelphia, February 20, 1958; 23 by George Yardley, Detroit vs. Boston, January 13, 1958.
Most Field Goals Attempted—20 by Wilt Chamberlain, Philadelphia vs. Chicago, January 24, 1962.
Most Field Goals Scored—10 by Tom Heinsohn, Boston, vs. Cincinnati, February 8, 1959; 10 by Wilt Chamberlain, Philadelphia vs. Syracuse, November 25, 1959.
Most Free Throws Attempted—14 by Ken Sears, New York vs. Boston, November 3, 1956, 14 by Art Spoelstra, Minneapolis vs. Boston, January 5, 1958. (Providence)
Most Free Throws Scored—12 by Ken Sears, New York vs. Boston, November 3, 1956
Most Rebounds—17 by Bill Russell, Boston vs. Philadelphia, November 16, 1957; 17 by Bill Russell, Boston vs. Cincinnati, December 12, 1958*; 17 by Bill Russell, Boston vs. Syracuse, February 5, 1960*.
Most Assists—12 by Bob Cousy, Boston vs. Minneapolis, February 27, 1959.
Most Personals—5 on Joe Hutton, Minneapolis vs. Boston, November 11, 1951; 5 on Jim Loscutoff, Boston vs. Cincinnati, November 12, 1962; 5 on Jim Krebs, Los Angeles vs. Boston, April 21, 1963#.

ONE TEAM
Full Game

Most Points—173 by Boston vs. Minneapolis, February 27, 1959.
Most Field Goals Attempted—150 by Boston vs. Philadelphia, March 2, 1960.
Most Field Goals Scored—72 by Boston vs. Minneapolis, February 27, 1959.
Most Free Throws Attempted—64 by Boston vs. Syracuse, March 21, 1953****#; 64 by Syracuse vs. Boston, March 21, 1953****#.
Most Free Throws Scored—57 by Boston vs. Syracuse, March 21, 1953****#.
Most Rebounds—112 by Boston vs. Detroit, December 24, 1960.
Most Assists—43 by Boston vs. Baltimore, January 11, 1953; 43 by Boston vs. Minneapolis, February 27, 1959.
Most Personals—55 on Syracuse vs. Boston, March 21, 1953****#.
Most Disqualifications—7 from Syracuse vs. Boston, March 21, 1953.****#

ONE TEAM
One Half

Most Points—91 by Boston vs. Detroit, February 10, 1960 (Providence); 91 by Boston vs. Cincinnati, November 11, 1959.
Most Field Goals Attempted—80 by Boston vs. Minneapolis, February 27, 1959.
Most Field Goals Scored—40 by Boston vs. Minneapolis, February 27, 1959.
Most Free Throws Attempted—43 by New York vs. Boston, November 3, 1956.
Most Free Throws Scored—32 by Boston vs. Syracuse, January 30, 1951.
Most Rebounds—65 by Boston vs. Cincinnati, January 12, 1962.
Most Assists—26 by Boston vs. Detroit, November 3, 1962.
Most Personals—28 on Syracuse vs. Boston, December 26, 1950.
Most Disqualifications—6 from Syracuse vs. Boston, December 26, 1950.

Bill Sharman

Bill Sharman shoots record 50th consecutive free throw during a January 1955 game against the Syracuse Nats at Boston Garden. The sharpshooting Sharman would improve his record to 55 in a 1956 streak, and to 56 in 1959—the latter still the NBA playoff record.

ONE TEAM
One Quarter

Most Points—54 by Boston vs. San Diego, February 25, 1970
Most Field Goals Attempted—47 by Boston vs. Minneapolis, February 27, 1959.
Most Field Goals Scored—23 by Boston vs. Minneapolis, February 27, 1959.
Most Free Throws Attempted—29 by New York vs. Boston, November 3, 1956.
Most Free Throws Scored—20 by Minneapolis vs. Boston, December 21, 1957.
Most Rebounds—35 by Boston vs. Minneapolis, February 26, 1960.
Most Assists—16 by Boston vs. Minneapolis, February 27, 1959.
Most Personals—16 by Syracuse vs. Boston, Dec. 26, 1950.
Most Disqualifications—6 from Syracuse vs. Boston, December 26, 1950.

TWO TEAMS
Full Game

Most Points—312 (Boston 173, Minneapolis 139), February 27, 1959.
Most Field Goals Attempted—274 (Boston 149, Detroit 125), January 27, 1961.
Most Field Goals Scored—119 (Boston 72, Minneapolis 47), February 27, 1959; 119 (Boston 64, New York 55), March 9, 1960
Most Free Throws Attempted—128 (Boston 64, Syracuse 51), March 21, 1953****#
Most Free Throws Scored—108 (Boston 57, Syracuse 64), March 21, 1953****#
Most Rebounds—196 (Boston 106, Detroit 90), January 27, 1961.
Most Assists—73 (Boston 37, Milwaukee 36), December 15, 1954.
Most Personals—106 (Boston 51, Syracuse 53), March 21, 1953****#.
Most Disqualifications—12 (Syracuse 7, Boston 5), March 21, 1953****#.

TWO TEAMS
One Half

Most Points—165 (Boston 90, Minneapolis 65), February 27, 1959.
Most Field Goals Attempted—153 (Boston 80, Minneapolis 73) February 27, 1959.
Most Field Goals Scored—70 (Boston 40, Minneapolis 30), February 27, 1959.
Most Free Throws Attempted—68 (New York 43, Boston 25), November 3, 1956.
Most Free Throws Scored—54 (Boston 32, Syracuse 22), December 26, 1950; 54 (Boston 31, Rochester 23), February 1, 1953.
Most Rebounds—103 (Boston 55, Detroit 48), January 27, 1961.
Most Assists—38 (Boston 24, Baltimore 14), January 11, 1953.
Most Personals—51 (Syracuse 28, Boston 23), December 26, 1950.
Most Disqualifications—11 (Syracuse 6, Boston 5), December 26, 1950.

TWO TEAMS
One Quarter

Most Points—96 (Boston 52, Minneapolis 44), February 27, 1959.
Most Field Goals Attempted—86 (Boston 47, Minneapolis 39), February 27, 1959.
Most Field Goals Scored—40 (Boston 23, Minneapolis 17), February 27, 1959.
Most Free Throws Attempted—49 (New York 29, Boston 20), November 3, 1956.
Most Free Throws Scored—37 (New York 19, Boston 18), November 3, 1956.
Most Rebounds—64 (Syracuse 34, Boston 30), March 11, 1961.
Most Assists—21 (Boston 13, Baltimore 8), January 11, 1952; 21 (Boston 13, Indianapolis 8), January 20, 1952; 21 (Boston 16, Minneapolis 5), February 27, 1959; 21 (Chicago 11, Boston 10), December 1, 1961; 21 (Boston 15, Detroit 6), November 3, 1962.
Most Personals—27 (Syracuse 16, Boston 11), December 26, 1950.
Most Disqualifications—7 (Syracuse 4, Boston 3), December 26, 1950.

#Playoff game. *Overtime period.

SEASON BY SEASON

Season	Position	W-L	Pct.	GA/GB	Playoffs	Coach
1946-47	6th East*	22-38	.367	-27	Didn't qualify	J. Russell
1947-48	4th East	20-28	.417	- 7	Elim. 1st round	J. Russell
1948-49	5th East	25-35	.417	-13	Didn't qualify	A. Julian
1949-50	6th East*	22-46	.324	-31	Didn't qualify	A. Julian
1950-51	2d East	39-30	.565	- 2½	Elim. 1st round	A. Auerbach
1951-52	2d East	39-27	.591	- 1	Elim. 1st round	A. Auerbach
1952-53	3d East	46-25	.648	- 1½	Elim. East finals	A. Auerbach
1953-54	2d East	42-30	.583	- 2	Elim. East finals	A. Auerbach
1954-55	3d East	36-36	.500	- 7	Elim. East finals	A. Auerbach
1955-56	2d East	39-33	.542	- 6	Elim. 1st round	A. Auerbach
1956-57	1st East	44-28	.611	+ 6	Won NBA title	A. Auerbach
1957-58	1st East	49-23	.681	+ 8	Elim. NBA finals	A. Auerbach
1958-59	1st East	52-20	.722	+12	Won NBA title	A. Auerbach
1959-60	1st East	59-16	.787	+10	Won NBA title	A. Auerbach
1960-61	1st East	57-22	.722	+11	Won NBA title	A. Auerbach
1961-62	1st East	60-20	.750	+11	Won NBA title	A. Auerbach
1962-63	1st East	58-22	.725	+10	Won NBA title	A. Auerbach
1963-64	1st East	59-21	.738	+ 4	Won NBA title	A. Auerbach
1964-65	1st East	62-18	.755	+14	Won NBA title	A. Auerbach
1965-66	2d East	54-26	.675	- 1	Won NBA title	A. Auerbach
1966-67	2d East	60-21	.741	- 8	Elim. East finals	B. Russell
1967-68	2d East	54-28	.659	- 8	Won NBA title	B. Russell
1968-69	4th East	48-34	.585	- 9	Won NBA title	B. Russell
1969-70	6th East	34-48	.415	-26	Didn't qualify	T. Heinsohn
1970-71	3d Atlantic	44-38	.537	- 8	Didn't qualify	T. Heinsohn
1971-72	1st Atlantic	56-26	.683	+ 8	Elim. East finals	T. Heinsohn
1972-73	1st Atlantic	68-14	.829	+11	Elim. East finals	T. Heinsohn
1973-74	1st Atlantic	56-26	.683	+ 7	Won NBA title	T. Heinsohn
1974-75	1st Atlantic	60-22	.732	+11	Elim. East finals	T. Heinsohn
1975-76	1st Atlantic	54-28	.659	+ 8	Won NBA title	T. Heinsohn
1976-77	2d Atlantic	44-38	.537	- 6	Elim. East finals	T. Heinsohn
1977-78	3d Atlantic	32-50	.390	-23	Didn't qualify	T. Heinsohn (34); T. Sanders (48)
1978-79	5th Atlantic*	29-53	.354	-25	Didn't qualify	T. Sanders (14); D. Cowens (68)
1979-80	1st Atlantic	61-21	.744	+ 2	Elim. East finals	B. Fitch
**1980-81	1st Atlantic	62-20	.756	**	Won NBA title	B. Fitch
1981-82	1st Atlantic	63-19	.768	+ 5	Elim. East finals	B. Fitch

*Last in division.
**Tied with Philadelphia with NBA's top record, and awarded 1st place in division via tiebreaker formula.

SEASON-BY-SEASON SCORING

Season	FG Pct.	FT Pct.	Ave. Pts.	Opponents Ave. Pts.	Differential
1946-47	.272	.590	60.1	65.0	-4.9
1947-48	.287	.659	68.8	72.7	-3.9
1948-49	.311	.636	76.6	79.5	-2.9
1949-50	.338	.707	79.7	82.2	-2.5
1950-51	.368	.725	85.2	85.5	-0.3
1951-52	.387	.734	91.3	87.3	+4.0
1952-53	.392	.728	88.1	85.8	+2.3
1953-54	.400	.726	87.7	85.4	+2.3
1954-55	.399	.776	101.4	101.5	-0.1
1955-56	.397	.769	106.0	105.4	+0.6
1956-57	.383	.750	105.5	100.2	+5.3
1957-58	.387	.737	109.9	104.4	+5.5
1958-59	.395	.766	116.4	109.9	+6.5
1959-60	.417	.734	124.5	116.2	+8.3
1960-61	.398	.735	119.7	114.1	+5.6
1961-62	.423	.728	121.1	111.9	+9.2
1962-63	.427	.725	118.8	111.6	+7.2
1963-64	.413	.725	113.0	105.1	+7.9
1964-65	.414	.731	112.8	104.5	+8.3
1965-66	.417	.739	112.7	107.8	+4.9
1966-67	.447	.748	119.3	111.3	+8.0
1967-68	.440	.721	116.1	112.0	+4.1
1968-69	.431	.729	111.0	105.4	+5.6
1969-70	.443	.786	114.9	116.8	-1.9
1970-71	.442	.755	117.2	115.1	+2.1
1971-72	.453	.777	115.6	110.8	+4.8
1972-73	.448	.780	112.7	104.5	+8.2
1973-74	.456	.800	109.0	105.1	+3.9
1974-75	.458	.791	106.5	100.8	+5.7
1975-76	.446	.780	106.2	103.9	+2.3
1976-77	.445	.756	104.5	106.5	-2.0
1977-78	.458	.779	105.7	107.7	-2.0
1978-79	.480	.784	108.2	113.3	-5.1
1979-80	.490	.779	113.5	105.7	+7.8
1980-81	.504	.752	109.9	104.0	+5.9
1981-82	.499	.740	112.0	105.6	+6.4

*Won NBA championship.

Tom Heinsohn: Basketball's man of a thousand faces

Beth Havlicek

Cindy Westphal

Kathy & Henry Finkel

. . . and Tom Sanders' mother, Luethel.

INDIVIDUAL STATISTICS SEASON BY SEASON

1946-47

Regular Season

	G.	FGA	FGM	Pct.	FTA	FTM	Pct.	Ast.	PF	Pts.	Ave.
Connie Simmons	—	768	246	.320	189	128	.677	62	130	620	10.3
Al Brightman	58	870	223	.256	193	121	.627	60	115	567	9.8
Tony Kappen (41 Pittsburgh; 18 Boston)	59	537	128	.238	161	128	.795	28	78	384	6.5
Wyndol Gray	55	476	139	.292	124	72	.581	47	105	350	6.4
Chuck Hoefer (23 Toronto; 35 Boston)	58	514	130	.253	139	91	.655	33	142	351	6.1
Art Spector	55	460	123	.267	150	83	.553	46	130	329	6.0
John Simmons	60	429	120	.280	127	78	.614	29	78	318	5.3
Gerard Kelly	43	313	91	.291	111	74	.667	21	128	256	6.0
Chuck Connors	49	380	94	.247	84	39	.464	40	129	227	4.6
Dutch Garfinkel	40	304	81	.266	28	17	.607	58	62	179	4.5
Harold Kottman	53	188	59	.314	101	47	.465	17	58	165	3.1
Bill Fenley	23	138	31	.225	45	23	.511	16	59	85	3.7
Virgil Vaughn	17	78	15	.192	28	15	.536	10	18	45	2.6
Richard Murphy (24 New York; 7 Boston)	31	75	15	.200	9	4	.444	8	15	34	1.1
Red Wallace (24 Boston; 37 Toronto)	61	809	225	.278	196	106	.541	58	167	556	9.1
Moe Becker (17 Pittsburgh; 6 Boston; 20 Detroit)	43	358	70	.196	44	22	.500	30	98	162	3.8
Bob Duffy (11 Chicago; 6 Boston)	17	32	7	.219	7	5	.714	0	17	19	1.1
Mel Hirsch	13	45	9	.200	2	1	.500	10	18	19	1.5
Hal Crisler	4	6	2	.333	2	2	1.000	0	6	6	1.5
Don Eliason	1	1	0	.000	0	0	.000	0	1	0	0.0

Playoffs

Celtics did not qualify.

1947-48

Regular Season

	G.	FGA	FGM	Pct.	FTA	FTM	Pct.	Ast.	PF	Pts.	Ave.
Ed Sadowski	47	953	308	.323	422	294	.697	74	182	910	19.4
Mike Bloom (34 Baltimore; 14 Boston)	48	640	174	.272	229	160	.699	38	116	508	10.6
Mel Riebe	48	653	202	.309	137	85	.620	41	137	489	10.2
Saul Mariaschin	43	463	125	.270	117	83	.709	60	121	333	7.7
Ed Ehlers	40	417	104	.249	144	78	.542	44	92	286	7.2
Dutch Garfinkel	43	380	114	.300	46	35	.761	59	78	263	6.1
Art Spector	48	243	67	.276	92	60	.652	17	106	194	4.0
Gene Stump	43	247	59	.239	38	24	.632	18	66	142	3.3
Stan Noszka	22	97	27	.278	35	24	.686	4	52	78	3.5
George Munroe	21	91	27	.297	26	17	.654	3	20	71	3.4
Cecil Hankins	25	116	23	.198	35	24	.686	8	28	70	2.8
Jack Hewson	24	89	22	.247	30	21	.700	1	9	65	2.7
Chuck Connors	4	13	5	.385	3	2	.667	1	5	12	3.0
Chuck Hoefer	7	19	3	.158	8	4	.500	3	17	10	1.4
Connie Simmons (32 Boston; 13 Baltimore)	45	545	162	.297	108	62	.574	24	122	386	8.6
John Janisch (3 Boston; 7 Providence)	10	50	14	.280	16	9	.563	2	5	37	3.7

Playoffs

	G.	FGA	FGM	Pct.	FTA	FTM	Pct.	Ast.	PF	Pts.	Ave.
Ed Sadowski	3	55	19	.345	38	23	.605	6	17	61	20.3
Mel Riebe	3	43	14	.326	20	14	.700	3	10	42	14.0
Mike Bloom	3	42	11	.262	19	14	.737	2	10	36	12.0
Saul Mariaschin	3	42	10	.238	14	9	.643	1	12	29	9.7
Stan Noszka	3	30	10	.333	8	5	.625	2	11	25	8.3
Dutch Garfinkel	3	23	7	.304	10	8	.800	7	15	22	7.3
Art Spector	3	9	2	.222	4	2	.500	0	9	6	2.0
George Munroe	3	5	1	.200	2	2	1.000	1	2	4	1.3
Gene Stump	3	3	1	.333	0	0	.000	0	2	2	0.7

Bob Cousy didn't have that many arms, it just seemed that way.

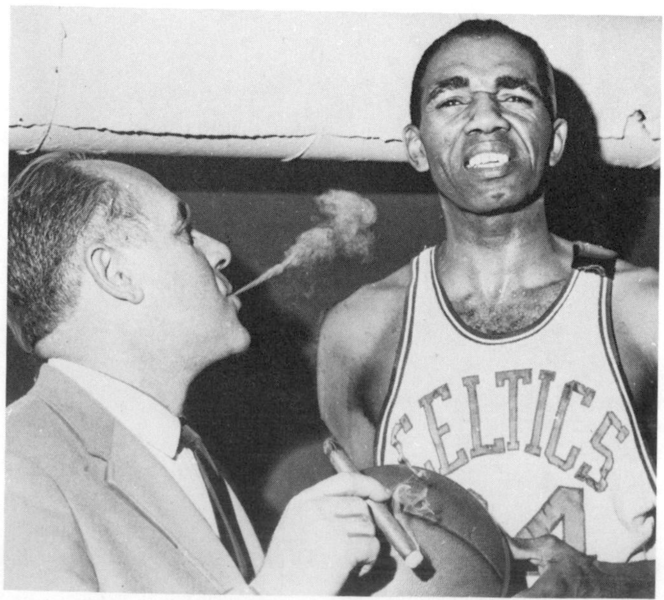

"Smoke gets in Your Eyes"

Heavyweight champion Rocky Marciano was a fan of his hometown Celtics and an admirer of Bill Sharman.

Rifleman Chuck Connors came home to Boston Garden 25 years later and hit some bullseyes with his old setshot.

1948-49

Regular Season

	G.	FGA	FGM	Pct.	FTA	FTM	Pct.	Ast.	PF	Pts.	Ave.
George Nostrand (33 Providence: 27 Boston)	60	651	212	.326	284	165	.581	94	164	589	9.8
Ed Ehlers	59	583	182	.312	225	150	.667	133	119	514	8.7
Gene Stump	56	580	193	.333	129	92	.713	56	102	478	8.5
Bob Kinney (37 Ft. Wayne: 21 Boston)	58	495	161	.325	234	136	.581	77	224	458	7.9
Jim Seminoff	58	487	153	.314	219	151	.689	229	195	457	7.9
Bob Doll	47	438	145	.331	117	80	.684	117	118	370	7.9
Art Spector	59	434	130	.300	116	64	.552	77	111	324	5.5
George Kaftan	21	315	116	.368	115	72	.626	61	28	304	14.5
Dermie O'Connell	21	315	87	.276	56	30	.536	65	40	204	9.7
Tom Kelly	27	218	73	.335	73	45	.616	38	73	191	7.1
Phil Farbman (27 Philadelphia: 21 Boston)	48	163	50	.307	81	55	.679	36	86	155	3.2
Earl Shannon (27 Providence: 5 Boston)	32	127	34	.268	58	39	.672	44	33	107	3.3
John Bach	34	119	34	.286	75	51	.680	25	24	119	3.5
Stan Noszka	30	123	30	.244	30	15	.500	25	56	75	2.5
Dutch Garfinkel	9	70	12	.171	14	10	.714	17	19	34	3.8
Hank Beenders	8	28	6	.214	9	7	.778	3	9	19	2.4
John Hazen	6	17	6	.353	7	6	.857	3	10	18	3.0
Al Lucas	2	3	1	.333	0	0	.000	2	0	2	1.0
Mel Riebe (33 Boston: 10 Providence)	43	589	172	.292	133	79	.594	104	110	324	9.8
Chick Halbert (33 Boston: 27 Providence)	60	647	202	.312	345	214	.620	113	175	618	10.3
Bill Roberts (26 Boston: 22 St. Loius: 2 Chicago)	50	267	89	.333	63	44	.698	41	113	222	4.4
John Ezersky (18 Boston: 27 Baltimore: 11 Providence)	56	407	128	.314	160	109	.681	67	98	365	6.5

Playoffs

Celtics did not qualify.

1949-50

Regular Season

	G.	FGA	FGM	Pct.	FTA	FTM	Pct.	Ast.	PF	Pts.	Ave.
Sonny Hertzberg	68	865	275	.318	191	143	.749	200	153	693	10.2
Bob Kinney	60	621	233	.375	320	201	.628	100	251	667	11.1
Howie Shannon	67	646	222	.344	182	143	.786	174	148	587	8.8
Ed Leede	64	507	174	.343	316	223	.706	130	167	571	8.9
George Kaftan	55	535	199	.372	208	136	.654	145	92	534	9.7
Brady Walker	68	583	218	.374	114	72	.632	109	100	508	7.5
Tony Lavelli	56	436	162	.372	197	168	.853	40	107	492	8.8
Jim Seminoff	65	283	85	.300	188	142	.755	249	154	312	4.8
John Mahnken (2 Tri-Cities: 24 Boston)	62	495	132	.267	115	77	.670	108	231	341	5.5
Bob Doll	47	347	120	.346	114	75	.658	108	117	315	6.7
John Ezersky (38 Baltimore: 16 Boston)	54	487	143	.294	183	127	.694	86	139	413	7.6
Joe Mullaney	37	70	9	.129	15	12	.800	52	30	30	0.8
Art Spector	7	12	2	.167	4	1	.250	3	4	5	0.7
Dermie O'Connell (37 Boston: 24 St. Louis)	61	425	111	.261	89	47	.528	91	91	269	4.4
George Nostrand (18 Boston: 36 Chicago: 1 Tri-Cities)	55	255	78	.306	99	56	.566	29	118	212	3.9
Ward Gibson	32	195	67	.344	64	42	.656	37	106	176	5.5
Gene Englund (24 Boston: 22 Tri-Cities)	46	274	104	.380	192	152	.792	41	167	360	7.8

Playoffs

Celtics did not qualify.

1950-51

Regular Season

	G.	FGA	FGM	Pct.	FTA	FTM	Pct.	Reb.	Ast.	PF	DQ	Pts.	Ave.
Ed Macauley	68	985	459	.466	614	466	.759	616	252	205	4	1384	20.4
Bob Cousy	69	1138	401	.352	365	276	.756	474	341	185	2	1078	15.6
Sonny Hertzberg	65	651	206	.316	270	223	.826	260	244	156	4	635	9.8
Chuck Cooper	66	601	207	.344	267	201	.753	562	174	219	7	615	9.3
Kleggie Hermsen (48 Tri-Cities: 23 Boston)	71	644	189	.293	237	155	.654	448	92	261	8	533	7.5
Frank Kudelka (35 Washington: 27 Boston)	62	518	179	.346	119	83	.697	158	105	211	8	441	7.1
Bob Donham	68	298	151	.507	229	114	.498	235	139	179	3	416	6.1
Ed Leede	57	370	119	.322	189	140	.741	118	95	144	3	378	6.6
Bob Harris (12 Ft. Wayne: 44 Boston)	56	295	98	.332	127	86	.677	291	64	157	4	282	5.0
Bones McKinney (10 Washington: 34 Boston)	44	327	102	.312	81	58	.716	198	85	136	6	262	6.0
Harry Boykoff (32 Boston: 16 Tri-Cities)	48	336	126	.375	100	74	.740	220	60	197	12	326	6.8
Ken Sailors (10 Boston: 50 Baltimore)	60	533	181	.340	180	131	.728	120	150	196	8	493	8.2
Richard Mehen) (Baltimore-Boston-Ft. Wayne: including 6 games with Celtics)	66	532	192	.361	123	90	.732	183	82	143	5	449	7.4
John Mahnken (46 Boston: 12 Indianapolis)	58	351	111	.316	70	45	.643	219	77	164	6	267	4.6
Brady Walker (16 Boston: 50 Baltimore)	66	416	164	.394	103	72	.699	354	111	82	2	400	6.1
Ed Stanczak	17	48	11	.229	43	35	.814	34	6	6	0	57	3.4
Andy Duncan	14	40	7	.175	22	15	.682	30	8	27	0	29	2.1

Playoffs

	G.	FGA	FGM	Pct.	FTA	FTM	Pct.	Reb.	Ast.	PF	DQ	Pts.	Ave.
Ed Macauley	2	36	17	.472	16	10	.625	18	8	4	0	44	22.0
Bob Cousy	2	42	9	.214	12	10	.833	15	12	8	0	28	14.0
Bones McKinney	2	25	11	.440	5	4	.800	10	8	9	0	26	13.0
Bob Donham	2	9	4	.444	12	5	.417	8	2	9	1	13	6.5
Chuck Cooper	2	12	4	.333	5	2	.400	13	3	8	0	10	5.0
Sonny Hertzberg	2	13	3	.231	5	4	.800	2	3	8	0	10	5.0
Bob Harris	2	10	1	.100	7	5	.714	4	2	4	0	7	3.5
Frank Kudelka	1	4	2	.500	3	0	.000	5	2	3	0	4	4.0
Ed Leede	2	7	1	.143	1	1	1.000	0	2	3	0	3	1.5
Kleggie Hermsen	2	6	1	.167	0	0	.000	3	0	6	0	2	1.0

1951-52

Regular Season

	G.	Min.	FGA	FGM	Pct.	FTA	FTM	Pct.	Reb.	Ast.	PF	DQ	Pts.	Ave.
Bob Cousy	66	2681	1388	512	.369	506	409	.808	421	441	190	5	1433	21.7
Ed Macauley	66	2631	888	384	.432	621	496	.799	529	232	174	0	1264	19.2
Bill Sharman	63	1389	628	244	.389	213	183	.859	221	151	181	3	671	10.7
Bob Donham	66	1980	413	201	.487	293	149	.509	330	228	223	9	551	8.3
Chuck Cooper	66	1976	545	197	.361	201	149	.741	502	134	219	8	543	8.2
Bob Harris	66	1899	463	190	.410	209	134	.641	531	120	194	5	514	7.8
Bob Brannum	66	1324	404	149	.369	171	107	.626	406	76	235	9	405	6.1
Bones McKinney	63	1083	418	136	.325	80	65	.813	175	111	148	4	337	5.3
John Mahnken	60	581	227	78	.344	43	26	.605	132	63	91	2	182	3.0
Dick Dickey	45	440	136	40	.294	69	47	.681	81	50	79	2	127	2.8

Playoffs

	G.	Min.	FGA	FGM	Pct.	FTA	FTM	Pct.	Reb.	Ast.	PF	DQ	Pts.	Ave.
Bob Cousy	3	138	65	26	.400	44	41	.932	12	19	13	1	93	31.0
Ed Macauley	3	129	49	27	.551	19	16	.842	33	11	11	1	70	23.3
Chuck Cooper	3	128	25	8	.320	19	17	.895	16	4	17	2	33	11.0
Bob Donham	3	112	19	9	.474	18	9	.500	13	17	16	1	27	9.0
Bob Harris	3	87	21	9	.429	5	5	.500	25	4	16	1	23	7.7
Bill Sharman	1	27	12	7	.583	1	1	1.000	3	7	4	0	15	15.0
Bob Brannum	3	48	12	4	.333	6	1	.167	10	3	16	2	9	3.0
Dick Dickey	3	31	8	1	.125	7	6	.857	3	5	7	0	8	2.7
John Mahnken	3	50	7	2	.286	6	3	.500	10	3	11	1	7	2.3
Bones McKinney	3	20	9	2	.222	0	0	.000	6	2	9	0	4	1.3

1952-53

Regular Season

	G.	Min.	FGA	FGM	Pct.	FTA	FTM	Pct.	Reb.	Ast.	PF	DQ	Pts.	Ave.
Bob Cousy	71	2945	1320	464	.352	587	479	.816	449	547	227	4	1407	19.8
Ed Macauley	69	2902	997	451	.452	667	500	.750	629	280	188	0	1402	20.3
Bill Sharman	71	2333	925	403	.436	401	341	.850	288	191	240	7	1147	16.2
Bob Harris	70	1971	459	192	.418	226	133	.588	485	95	238	6	517	7.4
Bob Brannum	71	1900	541	188	.348	185	110	.595	537	147	287	17	486	6.8
Chuck Cooper	70	1994	466	157	.337	190	144	.758	439	112	258	11	458	6.5
Bob Donham	71	1435	353	169	.479	240	113	.471	239	153	213	8	451	6.4
John Mahnken	69	771	252	76	.302	56	38	.696	182	75	110	1	191	2.8
Ken Rollins	43	426	115	38	.330	27	22	.815	45	46	63	1	98	2.3
Gene Conley	39	461	108	35	.324	31	18	.581	171	19	74	1	88	2.3
Frank Mahoney	6	34	10	4	.400	5	4	.800	7	1	7	0	12	2.0
Kleggie Hermsen (4 Boston: 6 Indianapolis)	10	62	31	4	.129	5	3	.600	19	4	18	0	10	1.1

Playoffs

	G.	Min.	FGA	FGM	Pct.	FTA	FTM	Pct.	Reb.	Ast.	PF	DQ	Pts.	Ave.
Bob Cousy	6	270	120	46	.383	73	61	.836	25	37	21	0	153	25.5
Ed Macauley	6	278	71	31	.437	54	39	.722	58	21	23	2	101	16.8
Bill Sharman	6	201	60	20	.333	32	30	.938	15	15	26	1	70	11.7
Chuck Cooper	6	195	48	19	.396	27	22	.815	39	14	27	2	60	10.0
Bob Harris	6	193	35	16	.457	24	18	.750	56	12	28	3	50	8.3
Bob Donham	6	138	38	11	.289	27	11	.407	21	13	24	3	33	5.5
Bob Brannum	6	83	23	12	.522	11	7	.636	21	10	23	2	31	5.2
Ken Rollins	6	65	15	6	.400	8	8	1.000	8	7	14	0	20	3.3
Frank Mahoney	4	45	14	3	.214	5	3	.600	7	2	14	0	9	2.3
John Mahnken	6	72	10	0	.000	5	5	1.000	19	6	16	0	5	0.8

Ed Macauley (right) and Bob Cousy weighed heavily on Celtic fortunes when they joined the team in Fall 1950, a potent 1-2 punch that helped make the Celtics instant winners.

John Havlicek and Philadelphia 76er Julius Erving got into the Mexican spirit during a 1977 vacation in Acapulco.

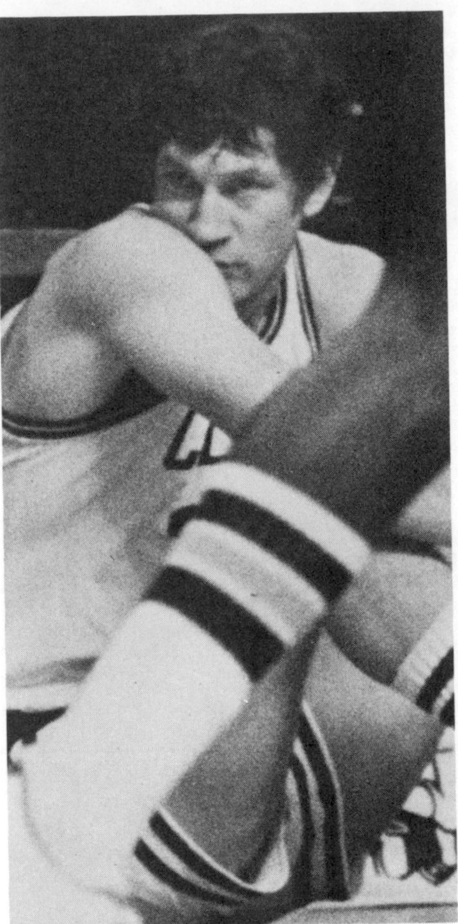

John Havlicek followed Frank Ramsey as basketball's "sixth man." Laker-turned-broadcaster Hot Rod Hundley once advised listeners: "Here comes Johnny Havlicek, the greatest substitute since cyclamate."

The Celtics had a candidate from Harvard among the 1968 rookies—George Plimpton. The author played in an exhibition game and wrote about it, and still plans to do a "Paper Lion"-type book on his Celtic experience.

1953-54

Regular Season

	G.	Min.	FGA	FGM	Pct.	FTA	FTM	Pct.	Reb.	Ast.	PF	DQ	Pts.	Ave.
Bob Cousy	72	2857	1262	486	.385	522	411	.787	394	518	201	3	1383	19.2
Ed Macauley	71	2792	950	462	.486	554	420	.758	571	271	168	1	1344	18.9
Bill Sharman	72	2467	915	412	.450	392	331	.844	255	229	211	4	1155	16.0
Don Barksdale	63	1358	415	156	.376	225	149	.662	345	117	213	4	461	7.3
Jack Nichols	75	1607	528	163	.309	152	113	.743	363	104	187	2	439	5.9
(15 Milwaukee: 60 Boston)														
Bob Harris	71	1898	409	156	.381	172	108	.628	517	94	224	8	420	5.9
Bob Brannum	71	1729	453	140	.309	206	129	.626	509	144	280	10	409	5.8
Bob Donham	68	1451	315	141	.448	213	118	.554	267	186	235	11	400	5.9
Chuck Cooper	70	1101	261	78	.299	116	78	.672	304	74	150	1	234	3.3
Ernie Barrett	59	641	191	60	.314	25	14	.560	100	55	116	2	134	2.3
Ed Mikan	9	71	24	8	.333	9	5	.556	20	3	15	0	21	2.3

Playoffs

	G.	Min.	FGA	FGM	Pct.	FTA	FTM	Pct.	Reb.	Ast.	PF	DQ	Pts.	Ave.
Bob Cousy	6	260	116	33	.284	75	60	.800	32	38	20	0	126	21.0
Bill Sharman	6	206	81	35	.432	50	43	.860	25	10	29	2	113	18.8
Jack Nichols	6	211	72	35	.486	38	30	.789	62	31	24	0	100	16.7
Bob Harris	6	150	25	16	.640	23	16	.696	35	3	25	1	48	8.0
Don Barksdale	6	106	36	11	.306	11	8	.727	27	7	23	2	30	5.0
Bob Brannum	6	136	38	11	.289	11	6	.545	45	10	29	2	28	4.7
Ed Macauley	6	127	22	8	.364	13	9	.692	21	21	14	0	25	5.0
Chuck Cooper	6	108	16	8	.500	11	8	.727	31	4	21	1	24	4.0
Bob Donham	6	98	15	7	.467	19	6	.316	12	6	32	4	20	3.3
Ernie Barrett	6	63	60	3	.150	2	2	1.000	6	4	14	0	8	1.3

1954-55

Regular Season

	G.	Min.	FGA	FGM	Pct.	FTA	FTM	Pct.	Reb.	Ast.	PF	DQ	Pts.	Ave.
Bob Cousy	71	2747	1316	522	.397	570	460	.807	424	557	165	1	1504	21.2
Bill Sharman	68	2453	1062	453	.427	387	347	.897	302	280	212	2	1253	18.4
Ed Macauley	71	2706	951	403	.424	558	442	.792	600	275	171	0	1248	17.6
Don Barksdale	72	1790	699	267	.382	338	220	.651	545	129	225	7	754	10.5
Frank Ramsey	64	1754	592	236	.399	322	243	.755	402	185	250	11	715	11.2
Jack Nichols	64	1910	656	249	.380	177	138	.780	533	144	238	10	636	9.9
Bob Brannum	71	1623	465	176	.378	127	90	.709	492	127	232	6	442	6.2
Dwight Morrison	71	1227	284	120	.423	115	72	.626	451	82	222	10	312	4.4
Togo Palazzi	53	504	253	101	.399	60	45	.750	146	30	60	1	247	4.7
Fred Scolari	59	619	249	76	.305	49	39	.796	77	93	76	0	191	3.2
Skippy Whittaker	3	15	6	1	.167	0	0	.000	1	1	4	0	2	0.7
Bob Houbregs (Baltimore-Boston-Ft. Wayne. including 2 games with Celtics)	64	1326	386	148	.383	182	129	.709	297	86	180	5	425	6.6

Playoffs

	G.	Min.	FGA	FGM	Pct.	FTA	FTM	Pct.	Reb.	Ast.	PF	DQ	Pts.	Ave.
Bob Cousy	7	299	139	53	.381	48	46	.958	43	65	26	0	152	21.7
Bill Sharman	7	290	110	55	.500	38	35	.921	38	38	24	1	145	20.7
Ed Macauley	7	283	93	43	.462	54	41	.759	52	32	21	0	127	18.1
Frank Ramsey	7	154	54	28	.519	26	19	.731	35	16	27	0	75	10.7
Jack Nichols	7	231	81	30	.370	16	13	.813	49	23	28	1	73	10.4
Bob Brannum	7	225	61	26	.426	19	11	.579	79	13	32	2	63	9.0
Don Barksdale	7	122	40	18	.450	21	18	.857	35	10	17	1	54	7.7
Togo Palazzi	5	30	24	12	500	10	5	.500	14	1	7	0	29	5.8
Fred Scolari	5	29	15	4	.267	5	4	.800	5	3	7	0	12	2.4
Dwight Morrison	7	42	8	3	.375	3	1	.333	14	1	22	1	7	1.0

1955-56

Regular Season

	G.	Min.	FGA	FGM	Pct.	FTA	FTM	Pct.	Reb.	Ast.	PF	DQ	Pts.	Ave.
Bill Sharman	72	2698	1229	538	.438	413	358	.867	259	339	197	1	1434	19.9
Bob Cousy	72	2767	1223	440	.360	564	476	.844	492	642	206	2	1356	18.8
Ed Macauley	71	2354	995	420	.422	504	400	.794	422	211	158	2	1240	17.5
Jack Nichols	60	1964	799	330	.413	253	200	.791	625	160	228	7	860	14.3
Jim Loscutoff	71	1582	628	226	.360	207	139	.671	622	65	213	4	591	8.3
Arnie Risen	68	1597	493	189	.383	240	170	.708	553	88	300	17	548	8.1
Ernie Barrett	72	1451	533	207	.388	118	93	.788	243	174	184	4	507	7.0
Dick Hemric	71	1329	400	161	.403	273	177	.648	399	60	142	2	499	7.0
Togo Palazzi	63	703	373	145	.389	124	85	.685	182	42	87	0	375	6.0
Dwight Morrison	71	910	240	89	.346	89	44	.494	345	53	159	5	222	3.1

Playoffs

	G.	Min.	FGA	FGM	Pct.	FTA	FTM	Pct.	Reb.	Ast.	PF	DQ	Pts.	Ave.
Bob Cousy	3	124	56	28	.500	25	23	.920	24	26	4	0	79	26.3
Bill Sharman	3	119	46	18	.391	17	16	.941	7	12	7	0	52	17.3
Jack Nichols	3	100	43	16	.372	10	9	.900	36	10	13	0	41	13.7
Arnie Risen	3	88	34	12	.353	18	13	.722	44	2	15	0	37	12.3
Ed Macauley	3	73	30	12	.400	11	7	.636	15	5	6	0	31	10.3
Jim Loscutoff	3	89	31	11	.355	9	7	.778	26	4	8	0	29	9.7
Dick Hemric	3	54	24	5	.208	16	9	.563	22	1	7	0	19	6.3
Ernie Barrett	3	43	13	4	.308	3	3	1.000	7	4	7	0	11	3.7
Dwight Morrison	3	23	7	2	.286	4	0	.000	11	0	5	0	4	1.3
Togo Palazzi	2	7	5	1	.200	0	0	.000	2	0	1	0	2	1.0

1956-57

Regular Season

	G.	Min.	FGA	FGM	Pct.	FTA	FTM	Pct.	Reb.	Ast.	PF	DQ	Pts.	Ave.
Bill Sharman	67	2403	1241	516	.416	421	381	.905	286	236	188	1	1413	21.1
Bob Cousy	64	2364	1264	478	.378	442	363	.821	309	478	134	0	1310	20.6
Tom Heinsohn	72	2150	1123	446	.397	343	271	.790	705	117	304	12	1163	16.2
Jim Loscutoff	70	2220	888	306	.345	187	132	.706	730	89	244	5	744	10.6
Bill Russell	48	1695	649	277	.427	309	152	.492	943	88	143	2	706	14.7
Jack Nichols	61	1372	537	195	.363	136	108	.794	374	85	185	4	498	8.2
Frank Ramsey	35	807	349	137	.393	182	144	.791	178	67	113	3	418	11.9
Dick Hemric	67	1055	317	109	.344	210	146	.695	304	42	98	0	364	5.4
Arnie Risen	43	935	307	119	.388	156	106	.679	286	53	163	4	344	8.0
Andy Phillip	67	1476	277	105	.379	137	88	.642	181	168	121	1	298	4.4
Lou Tsioropoulos	52	670	256	79	.309	89	69	.775	207	33	135	6	227	4.4
Togo Palazzi	63	1013	571	210	.368	175	136	.777	262	49	117	1	556	8.8

(20 Boston 43 Syracuse)

Playoffs

	G.	Min.	FGA	FGM	Pct.	FTA	FTM	Pct.	Reb.	Ast.	PF	DQ	Pts.	Ave.
Tom Heinsohn	10	370	231	90	.390	69	49	.710	117	20	40	1	229	22.9
Bill Sharman	10	377	197	75	.381	64	61	.953	35	29	23	1	211	21.1
Bob Cousy	10	440	207	67	.324	91	68	.747	61	93	27	0	202	20.2
Bill Russell	10	409	148	54	.365	61	31	.508	244	32	41	1	139	13.9
Frank Ramsey	10	229	82	38	.463	59	46	.780	43	17	36	1	122	12.2
Jim Loscutoff	10	259	109	31	.284	28	18	.643	83	5	46	2	80	8.0
Arnie Risen	10	152	63	28	.444	29	19	.655	58	8	48	5	75	7.5
Jack Nichols	10	117	40	16	.400	5	3	.600	17	7	23	0	35	3.5
Andy Phillip	10	128	22	8	.364	15	6	.400	20	17	18	0	22	2.2
Dick Hemric	2	19	7	1	.143	0	0	.000	9	1	1	0	2	1.0

1957-58

Regular Season

	G.	Min.	FGA	FGM	Pct.	FTA	FTM	Pct.	Reb.	Ast.	PF	DQ	Pts.	Ave.
Bill Sharman	63	2214	1297	550	.424	338	302	.893	295	167	156	3	1402	22.3
Tom Heinsohn	69	2206	1226	468	.382	394	294	.746	705	125	274	6	1230	17.8
Bob Cousy	65	2222	1262	445	.353	326	277	.850	322	463	136	1	1167	18.0
Bill Russell	69	2640	1032	456	.442	443	230	.519	1564	202	181	2	1142	16.6
Frank Ramsey	69	2047	900	377	.419	472	383	.811	504	167	245	8	1137	16.5
Lou Tsioropoulos	70	1819	624	198	.317	207	142	.686	434	112	242	8	538	7.7
Jack Nichols	69	1224	484	170	.351	80	59	.738	302	63	123	1	399	5.8
Arnie Risen	63	1119	397	134	.338	167	114	.683	360	50	195	5	382	6.1
Sam Jones	56	594	233	100	.429	84	60	.714	160	37	42	0	260	4.6
Andy Phillip	70	1164	273	97	.355	71	42	.592	158	121	121	0	236	3.4
Jim Loscutoff	5	56	31	11	.355	3	1	.333	20	1	8	0	23	4.6

Playoffs

	G.	Min.	FGA	FGM	Pct.	FTA	FTM	Pct.	Reb.	Ast.	PF	DQ	Pts.	Ave.
Bill Sharman	11	406	221	90	.407	56	52	.929	54	25	28	0	232	21.1
Frank Ramsey	11	352	174	74	.425	59	54	.919	90	16	50	3	202	18.4
Bob Cousy	11	457	196	67	.342	75	64	.853	71	82	20	0	198	18.0
Tom Heinsohn	11	349	194	68	.351	72	56	.778	119	18	52	3	192	17.5
Bill Russell	9	355	133	48	.361	66	40	.606	221	24	24	0	136	15.1
Lou Tsioropoulos	11	239	85	25	.294	29	19	.655	64	14	40	4	69	6.3
Jack Nichols	11	148	66	23	.348	10	7	.700	45	8	21	1	53	4.8
Arnie Risen	10	168	52	12	.231	33	22	.667	62	9	32	1	46	4.6
Sam Jones	8	75	22	10	.455	16	11	.688	24	4	7	0	31	3.9
Andy Phillip	10	91	21	5	.238	9	7	.778	14	7	20	0	17	1.7

Rarely steamed up, Bill Russell is restrained by Knicks rookie Willis Reed while hollering "coward" at New York coach Harry Gallatin. The January 1965 incident at Boston Garden followed a near fight between Gallatin and Red Auerbach, for which both coaches were fined by the NBA.

1958-59

Regular Season

	G.	Min.	FGA	FGM	Pct.	FTA	FTM	Pct.	Reb.	Ast.	PF	DQ	Pts.	Ave.
Bill Sharman	72	2382	1377	562	.408	368	342	.929	292	179	173	1	1466	20.4
Bob Cousy	65	2403	1260	484	.384	385	329	.855	359	557	135	0	1297	20.0
Tom Heinsohn	66	2089	1192	465	.390	391	312	.798	638	164	271	11	1242	18.8
Bill Russell	70	2979	997	456	.457	428	256	.598	1612	222	161	3	1168	16.7
Frank Ramsey	72	2013	1013	383	.378	436	341	.782	491	147	266	11	1107	15.4
Sam Jones	71	1466	703	305	.434	196	151	.770	428	101	102	0	761	10.7
Jim Loscutoff	66	1680	686	242	.353	84	62	.738	460	60	285	15	546	8.3
Ben Swain	58	708	244	99	.406	110	67	.609	262	29	127	3	265	4.6
Gene Conley	50	663	262	86	.328	64	37	.578	276	19	117	2	209	4.2
K.C. Jones	49	609	192	65	.339	68	41	.603	127	70	58	0	171	3.5
Lou Tsioropoulos	35	488	190	60	.316	33	25	.758	110	20	74	0	145	4.1

Playoffs

	G.	Min.	FGA	FGM	Pct.	FTA	FTM	Pct.	Reb.	Ast.	PF	DQ	Pts.	Ave.
Frank Ramsey	11	303	192	95	.495	81	65	.802	68	20	52	4	255	23.2
Bill Sharman	11	322	193	82	.425	59	57	.966	36	28	35	0	221	20.1
Tom Heinsohn	11	348	220	91	.414	56	37	.661	98	32	41	0	219	19.9
Bob Cousy	11	460	221	72	.326	94	70	.745	76	119	28	0	214	19.5
Bill Russell	11	496	159	65	.409	67	41	.612	305	40	28	1	171	15.5
Sam Jones	11	192	108	40	.370	39	33	.846	63	17	14	0	113	10.3
Jim Loscutoff	11	260	113	39	.345	21	11	.524	73	13	49	1	89	8.1
Gene Conley	11	157	66	24	.364	13	6	.462	75	7	40	2	54	4.9
K.C. Jones	8	75	20	5	.250	5	5	1.000	12	10	8	0	15	1.9
Ben Swain	5	27	6	2	.333	2	1	.500	14	1	4	0	5	1.0

1959-60

Regular Season

	G.	Min.	FGA	FGM	Pct.	FTA	FTM	Pct.	Reb.	Ast.	PF	DQ	Pts.	Ave.
Tom Heinsohn	75	2420	1590	673	.423	386	283	.734	794	171	275	8	1629	21.7
Bob Cousy	75	2588	1481	568	.383	403	319	.791	352	715	146	2	1455	19.4
Bill Sharman	71	1916	1225	559	.456	291	252	.866	262	144	154	2	1370	19.3
Bill Russell	74	3146	1189	555	.467	392	240	.612	1778	277	210	0	1350	18.2
Frank Ramsey	73	2009	1062	422	.397	347	273	.787	506	137	251	10	1117	15.3
Sam Jones	74	1512	782	355	.454	220	168	.764	375	125	101	1	878	11.9
Maurice King	1	19	8	5	.625	1	0	.000	4	2	3	0	10	10.0
Gene Conley	71	1330	539	201	.373	114	76	.667	590	32	270	10	478	6.7
K.C. Jones	74	1274	414	169	.408	170	128	.752	199	189	109	1	466	6.3
Jim Loscutoff	28	536	205	66	.322	36	22	.611	108	12	108	6	154	5.5
John Richter	66	808	332	113	.340	117	59	.504	312	27	158	1	285	4.3
Gene Guarilia	48	423	154	58	.377	41	29	.707	85	18	57	1	145	3.0

Playoffs

	G.	Min.	FGA	FGM	Pct.	FTA	FTM	Pct.	Reb.	Ast.	PF	DQ	Pts.	Ave.
Tom Heinsohn	13	423	267	112	.419	80	60	.750	126	27	53	2	284	21.8
Bill Russell	13	572	206	94	.456	75	53	.707	336	38	38	1	241	18.5
Frank Ramsey	13	459	196	81	.413	63	55	.873	100	27	51	1	217	18.1
Bill Sharman	13	364	209	88	.421	53	43	.811	45	20	22	1	219	16.8
Bob Cousy	13	468	262	80	.305	51	39	.765	48	116	27	0	199	15.3
Sam Jones	13	197	117	45	.385	21	17	.809	41	18	17	0	107	8.2
Gene Conley	13	269	88	34	.386	22	16	.727	116	3	59	2	84	6.5
K.C. Jones	13	232	80	27	.337	22	17	.773	45	14	28	0	71	5.5
John Richter	8	95	38	15	.395	14	5	.357	29	2	18	1	35	4.4
Gene Guarilia	7	41	19	4	.222	6	6	1.000	19	3	4	0	14	2.0

1960-61

Regular Season

	G.	Min.	FGA	FGM	Pct.	FTA	FTM	Pct.	Reb.	Ast.	PF	DQ	Pts.	Ave.
Tom Heinsohn	74	2306	1666	627	.376	424	325	.766	732	141	260	5	1579	21.3
Bob Cousy	76	2564	1382	513	.371	452	352	.779	331	591	196	0	1378	18.1
Bill Russell	78	3458	1250	532	.426	469	258	.550	1868	264	164	0	1322	16.9
Frank Ramsey	79	2019	1100	448	.407	354	295	.833	431	148	284	13	1191	15.1
Sam Jones	78	2126	1062	474	.446	267	210	.786	423	209	149	1	1158	14.8
Bill Sharman	60	1538	908	383	.422	228	210	.921	223	156	127	0	976	16.3
K.C. Jones	78	1607	601	203	.337	320	186	.581	279	253	200	3	592	7.6
Gene Conley	75	1342	495	183	.370	153	106	.693	550	40	275	15	472	6.3
Tom Sanders	68	1084	352	148	.420	100	67	.670	385	44	131	1	363	5.3
Jim Loscutoff	76	1180	497	154	.310	79	50	.633	295	29	240	4	358	4.7
Gene Guarilia	25	199	94	38	.404	10	3	.300	61	5	28	0	79	3.2

Playoffs

	G.	Min.	FGA	FGM	Pct.	FTA	FTM	Pct.	Reb.	Ast.	PF	DQ	Pts.	Ave.
Tom Heinsohn	10	291	201	82	.408	43	33	.767	99	20	36	1	197	19.7
Bill Russell	10	462	171	73	.427	86	45	.523	299	48	24	0	191	19.1
Frank Ramsey	10	300	136	55	.407	75	61	.813	64	23	40	0	171	17.1
Bill Sharman	10	261	133	68	.511	36	32	.889	27	17	22	0	168	16.8
Bob Cousy	10	337	147	50	.340	88	67	.761	43	91	33	1	167	16.7
Sam Jones	10	258	112	50	.446	35	31	.886	54	22	24	0	131	13.1
Tom Sanders	10	216	75	37	.493	24	15	.625	84	7	42	2	89	8.9
Jim Loscutoff	10	116	54	15	.278	9	7	.778	35	3	34	0	37	3.7
Gene Conley	9	56	33	12	.364	12	7	.583	31	1	20	0	31	3.4
K.C. Jones	9	103	30	9	.300	14	7	.500	19	15	17	0	25	2.8

1961-62

Regular Season

	G.	Min.	FGA	FGM	Pct.	FTA	FTM	Pct.	Reb.	Ast.	PF	DQ	Pts.	Ave.
Tom Heinsohn	78	2382	1613	692	.429	437	358	.819	747	165	280	2	1742	22.3
Bill Russell	76	3433	1258	575	.457	481	286	.594	1891	341	207	3	1436	18.9
Sam Jones	78	2384	1283	589	.459	297	239	.805	470	234	150	0	1417	13.2
Frank Ramsey	79	1913	979	436	.445	405	334	.825	387	109	245	9	1206	15.3
Bob Cousy	75	2116	1181	462	.391	333	251	.754	261	584	135	0	1175	15.7
Tom Sanders	80	2325	804	350	.435	262	197	.752	762	74	279	9	897	11.2
K.C. Jones	79	2023	707	289	.409	231	145	.628	291	339	204	2	723	9.1
Jim Loscutoff	79	1046	519	188	.362	84	45	.536	329	51	185	3	421	5.3
Gary Phillips	72	693	320	110	.344	86	50	.581	107	63	109	0	270	3.7
Carl Braun	49	414	207	78	.377	27	20	.741	50	71	49	0	176	3.6
Gene Guarilia	46	367	161	61	.379	64	41	.641	124	11	56	0	163	3.5
Al Butler	59	2008	756	350	.463	183	131	.716	342	203	154	0	831	14.1
(5 Boston; 54 New York)														

Playoffs

	G.	Min.	FGA	FGM	Pct.	FTA	FTM	Pct.	Reb.	Ast.	PF	DQ	Pts.	Ave.
Bill Russell	14	672	253	116	.458	113	82	.726	370	70	49	0	314	22.4
Tom Heinsohn	14	445	291	116	.399	76	58	.763	115	34	58	4	290	20.7
Sam Jones	14	504	277	123	.444	60	42	.700	101	44	30	0	288	20.6
Bob Cousy	14	474	241	86	.357	76	52	.684	64	123	43	0	224	16.0
Tom Sanders	14	439	130	56	.431	36	29	.805	115	14	65	4	141	10.1
K.C. Jones	14	329	102	44	.431	53	38	.717	56	55	50	1	126	9.0
Frank Ramsey	13	210	104	39	.375	45	41	.911	38	10	38	3	119	9.1
Jim Loscutoff	14	212	86	31	.360	10	4	.400	59	6	59	5	66	4.1
Carl Braun	6	42	28	11	.393	4	3	.750	7	2	3	0	25	4.2
Gary Phillips	6	32	16	1	.062	11	8	.727	3	1	6	0	10	1.7
Gene Guarilia	5	26	8	2	.250	5	2	.400	4	1	6	0	6	1.2

Charlie Scott wanted to fight Philadelphia's Doug Collins in the 1977 playoffs.

Pete Maravich ended his career as a Celtic. "I've been trying to get here for 10 years," the 31-year-old superstar said upon coming to Boston as a free agent in February 1980. Yet he retired during the following training camp.

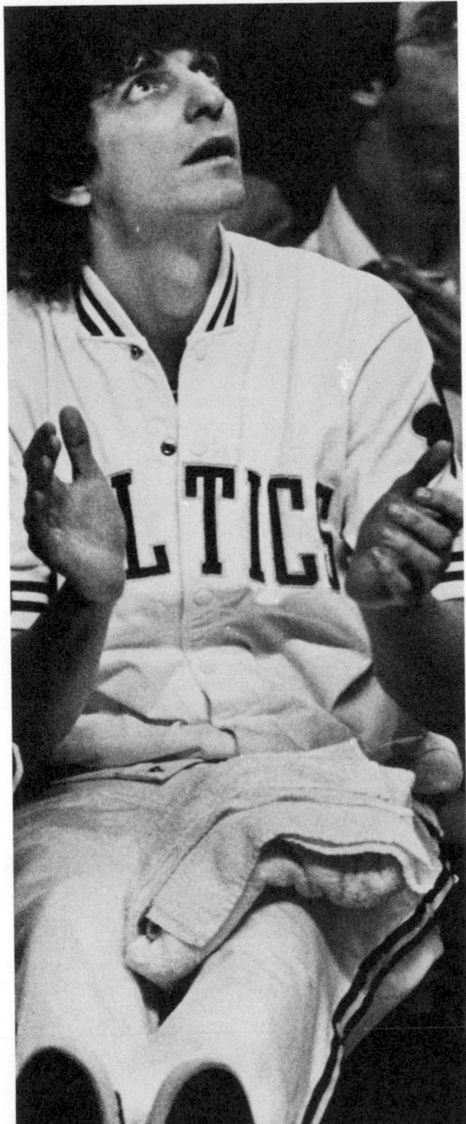

1962-63

Regular Season

	G.	Min.	FGA	FGM	Pct.	FTA	FTM	Pct.	Reb.	Ast.	PF	DQ	Pts.	Ave.
Sam Jones	76	2323	1305	621	.476	324	257	.793	396	241	162	1	1499	19.7
Tom Heinsohn	77	2004	1290	550	.426	407	340	.835	569	95	267	4	1440	18.7
Bill Russell	78	3500	1182	511	.432	517	287	.555	1843	348	189	1	1309	16.8
John Havlicek	80	2200	1085	483	.445	239	174	.728	534	179	190	1	1140	14.3
Bob Cousy	76	1976	988	392	.397	298	219	.735	201	515	175	0	1003	13.2
Tom Sanders	80	2148	744	339	.456	252	186	.738	576	100	262	5	864	10.8
Frank Ramsey	77	1541	743	284	.382	332	271	.816	288	95	259	13	839	10.9
K.C. Jones	79	1945	591	230	.389	177	112	.633	263	317	221	3	572	7.2
Clyde Lovellette	61	568	366	161	.440	98	73	.745	177	29	137	0	395	6.5
Jim Loscutoff	64	607	251	94	.375	42	22	.524	157	25	126	1	210	3.3
Dan Swartz	39	335	142	57	.401	72	61	.847	88	21	92	0	175	4.5
Gene Guarilia	11	83	38	11	.289	11	4	.364	14	2	5	0	26	2.4
Jack Foley	11	86	52	20	.385	15	13	.867	16	5	8	0	53	4.8
(5 Boston; 6 New York)														

Playoffs

	G.	Min.	FGA	FGM	Pct.	FTA	FTM	Pct.	Reb.	Ast.	PF	DQ	Pts.	Ave.
Tom Heinsohn	13	413	270	123	.456	98	75	.765	116	15	55	2	321	24.7
Sam Jones	13	450	248	120	.484	83	69	.831	81	32	42	1	309	23.8
Bill Russell	13	617	212	96	.453	109	72	.661	326	66	36	0	264	20.3
Bob Cousy	13	413	204	72	.353	47	39	.830	32	116	44	2	183	14.1
John Havlicek	11	254	125	56	.448	27	18	.667	53	17	28	1	130	11.8
Tom Sanders	13	387	119	52	.437	31	24	.774	96	19	61	4	128	9.8
Frank Ramsey	13	251	104	37	.356	47	34	.723	35	12	43	1	108	8.3
K.C. Jones	13	250	64	19	.297	30	21	.700	36	37	42	1	59	4.5
Clyde Lovellette	6	40	26	7	.269	6	4	.667	5	1	13	0	18	3.0
Jim Loscutoff	9	56	25	7	.280	2	1	.500	21	1	20	0	15	1.7
Dan Swartz	1	4	0	0	.000	0	0	.000	0	0	0	0	0	0.0

1963-64

Regular Season

	G.	Min.	FGA	FGM	Pct.	FTA	FTM	Pct.	Reb.	Ast.	PF	DQ	Pts.	Ave.
John Havlicek	80	2577	1535	640	.417	422	315	.746	428	238	227	1	1595	19.9
Sam Jones	76	2389	1359	612	.450	314	249	.792	349	202	192	1	1473	19.4
Tom Heinsohn	76	2040	1223	487	.398	342	283	.827	460	183	268	3	1257	16.5
Bill Russell	78	3482	1077	466	.433	429	236	.550	1930	370	190	0	1168	15.0
Tom Sanders	80	2370	836	349	.417	280	213	.761	667	102	277	6	911	11.4
Willie Naulls	78	1409	769	321	.417	157	125	.796	355	65	200	0	767	9.8
K.C. Jones	80	2424	722	283	.392	168	88	.524	372	407	253	0	654	8.2
Frank Ramsey	75	1227	604	226	.374	233	196	.841	223	81	245	7	648	8.6
Clyde Lovellette	45	437	305	128	.420	57	45	.789	126	24	100	0	201	6.7
Jim Loscutoff	53	451	182	56	.308	31	18	.581	131	25	90	1	130	2.5
Larry Siegfried	31	261	110	35	.318	39	31	.795	51	40	33	0	101	3.3
John McCarthy	28	206	48	16	.333	13	5	.385	35	24	42	0	37	1.3

Playoffs

	G.	Min.	FGA	FGM	Pct.	FTA	FTM	Pct.	Reb.	Ast.	PF	DQ	Pts.	Ave.
Sam Jones	10	356	181	91	.503	68	50	.735	47	23	24	0	232	23.2
Tom Heinsohn	10	308	180	70	.412	42	34	.810	80	26	36	0	174	17.4
John Havlicek	10	289	159	61	.384	44	35	.795	43	32	26	0	157	15.7
Bill Russell	10	451	132	47	.356	67	37	.552	272	44	23	0	131	13.1
Willie Naulls	10	177	95	37	.389	23	17	.739	46	8	31	1	91	9.1
Tom Sanders	10	302	94	34	.362	34	23	.676	71	6	45	5	91	9.1
K.C. Jones	10	312	72	25	.347	25	13	.520	37	68	40	0	63	6.3
Frank Ramsey	10	138	63	22	.349	21	18	.857	21	10	25	0	62	6.2
Clyde Lovellette	5	40	34	8	.235	4	4	1.000	7	2	8	0	20	4.0
Larry Siegfried	4	24	6	2	.333	6	3	.500	4	1	4	0	7	1.8
Jim Loscutoff	1	5	2	2	1.000	0	0	.000	2	0	3	0	4	4.0
John McCarthy	1	8	1	1	1.000	0	0	.000	1	1	0	0	2	2.0

1964-65

Regular Season

	G.	Min.	FGA	FGM	Pct.	FTA	FTM	Pct.	Reb.	Ast.	PF	DQ	Pts.	Ave.
Sam Jones	80	2885	1818	821	.452	522	428	.820	411	223	176	0	2070	25.9
John Havlicek	75	2169	1420	570	.401	316	235	.744	371	199	200	2	1375	18.3
Bill Russell	78	3466	980	429	.438	426	244	.573	1878	410	204	1	1102	14.1
Tom Sanders	80	2459	871	374	.429	259	193	.745	661	92	318	15	941	11.8
Tom Heinsohn	67	1706	954	365	.383	229	182	.795	399	157	252	5	912	13.6
Willie Naulls	71	1465	786	302	.384	176	143	.813	336	72	225	5	747	10.5
K.C. Jones	78	2434	639	253	.396	227	143	.630	318	437	263	5	649	8.3
Larry Siegfried	72	996	417	173	.415	140	109	.779	134	119	108	1	455	6.3
Ron Bonham	37	369	220	91	.414	112	92	.821	78	19	33	0	274	7.4
Mel Counts	55	572	272	100	.368	74	58	.784	265	19	134	1	258	4.7
John Thompson	64	699	209	84	.402	105	62	.590	230	16	141	1	230	3.6
Bob Nordmann	3	25	5	3	.600	0	0	.000	8	3	5	0	6	2.0
Gerry Ward	3	30	18	2	.111	1	1	1.000	5	6	6	0	5	1.7

Playoffs

	G.	Min.	FGA	FGM	Pct.	FTA	FTM	Pct.	Reb.	Ast.	PF	DQ	Pts.	Ave.
Sam Jones	12	495	294	135	.459	84	73	.869	55	30	39	1	343	28.6
John Havlicek	12	405	250	88	.352	55	46	.836	88	29	44	1	222	18.5
Bill Russell	12	561	150	79	.527	76	40	.526	302	76	43	2	198	16.5
Tom Sanders	12	365	152	64	.421	43	31	.721	102	19	58	4	159	13.3
Tom Heinsohn	12	276	181	66	.365	32	20	.625	84	23	46	1	152	12.7
K.C. Jones	12	396	104	43	.413	45	35	.778	39	74	49	1	121	10.1
Willie Naulls	12	180	95	39	.411	15	10	.666	51	9	27	0	88	7.3
Larry Siegfried	12	163	79	30	.380	28	24	.857	25	21	25	0	84	7.0
Ron Bonham	4	13	12	5	.417	5	4	.800	1	0	1	0	14	3.5
John Thompson	3	21	7	2	.286	7	7	1.000	12	1	2	0	11	3.7
Mel Counts	4	30	15	4	.267	1	1	1.000	11	1	10	0	9	2.3

Larry Bird wasn't caught with his pants down. He's just posing for a commercial before practice—from the waist up.

1965-66

Regular Season

	G.	Min.	FGA	FGM	Pct.	FTA	FTM	Pct.	Reb.	Ast.	PF	DQ	Pts.	Ave.
Sam Jones	67	2155	1335	626	.469	407	325	.799	347	216	170	0	1577	23.5
John Havlicek	71	2175	1328	530	.399	349	274	.785	423	210	158	1	1334	18.8
Bill Russell	78	3386	943	391	.415	405	223	.551	1779	371	221	4	1005	12.9
Larry Siegfried	71	1675	825	349	.423	311	274	.881	196	165	157	1	972	13.7
Tom Sanders	72	1896	816	349	.428	276	211	.764	508	90	317	19	909	12.6
Don Nelson	75	1765	618	271	.439	326	223	.684	403	79	187	1	765	10.2
Willie Naulls	71	1433	815	328	.402	131	104	.794	319	72	197	4	760	10.7
K.C. Jones	80	2710	619	240	.388	303	209	.690	304	503	243	4	689	8.6
Mel Counts	67	1021	549	221	.403	145	120	.828	432	50	207	5	562	8.4
Ron Bonham	39	312	207	76	.367	61	52	.852	35	11	29	0	204	5.2
Woody Sauldsberry	39	530	249	80	.321	22	11	.500	142	15	94	0	171	4.4
John Thompson	10	72	30	14	.467	6	4	.667	30	3	15	0	32	3.2
Sihugo Green	10	92	31	12	.387	16	8	.500	11	9	16	0	32	3.2
Ron Watts	1	3	2	1	.500	0	0	.000	1	1	1	0	2	2.0

Playoffs

	G.	Min.	FGA	FGM	Pct.	FTA	FTM	Pct.	Reb.	Ast.	PF	DQ	Pts.	Ave.
Sam Jones	17	602	343	154	.449	136	114	.838	86	53	63	1	422	24.8
John Havlicek	17	719	374	153	.409	113	95	.841	154	70	69	2	401	23.6
Bill Russell	17	814	261	124	.475	123	76	.618	428	85	60	0	324	19.1
Tom Sanders	17	500	201	97	.483	48	36	.750	110	27	70	2	230	13.5
Larry Siegfried	17	452	193	81	.420	75	62	.827	42	41	52	0	224	13.2
Don Nelson	17	316	118	50	.424	52	42	.808	85	13	50	0	142	8.4
K.C. Jones	17	543	109	45	.413	57	39	.684	52	75	65	0	129	7.6
Mel Counts	10	82	39	14	.359	17	15	.882	40	3	26	0	43	4.3
Willie Naulls	11	75	35	9	.257	21	17	.810	16	1	23	0	35	3.2
Ron Bonham	5	16	11	7	.636	9	3	.333	3	0	2	0	17	3.4
John Thompson	3	11	7	1	.143	0	0	.000	4	0	2	0	2	0.7

Larry Siegfried bows to referee after being tagged with a foul.

1966-67

Regular Season

	G.	Min.	FGA	FGM	Pct.	FTA	FTM	Pct.	Reb.	Ast.	PF	DQ	Pts.	Ave.
John Havlicek	81	2602	1540	684	.444	441	365	.828	532	278	210	0	1733	21.4
Bailey Howell	81	2503	1242	636	.512	471	349	.741	677	103	296	4	1621	20.0
Sam Jones	72	2325	1406	638	.454	371	318	.837	338	217	191	1	1594	22.1
Bill Russell	81	3297	870	395	.454	467	285	.610	1700	472	258	4	1075	13.4
Larry Siegfried	73	1891	833	368	.442	347	294	.847	228	250	207	1	1030	14.1
Tom Sanders	81	1926	755	323	.428	218	178	.817	439	91	304	6	824	10.2
Don Nelson	79	1202	509	227	.446	190	141	.742	295	65	143	0	595	7.5
K.C. Jones	78	2446	459	182	.397	189	119	.630	239	389	273	7	483	6.2
Wayne Embry	72	729	359	147	.409	144	82	.569	294	42	137	0	376	5.2
Jim Barnett	48	383	211	78	.370	62	42	.677	53	41	61	0	198	4.1
Toby Kimball	38	222	97	35	.361	40	27	.675	146	13	42	0	97	2.6
Ron Watts	27	89	44	11	.250	23	16	.696	38	1	16	0	38	1.4

Playoffs

	G.	Min.	FGA	FGM	Pct.	FTA	FTM	Pct.	Reb.	Ast.	PF	DQ	Pts.	Ave.
John Havlicek	9	330	212	95	.448	71	57	.803	73	28	30	0	247	27.4
Sam Jones	9	326	207	95	.459	58	50	.862	46	28	30	1	240	26.7
Bailey Howell	9	241	122	59	.484	30	20	.667	66	5	35	2	138	15.3
Larry Siegfried	9	260	102	38	.373	43	35	.814	40	44	33	1	111	12.3
Bill Russell	9	390	86	31	.360	52	33	.635	198	50	32	1	95	10.6
Don Nelson	9	142	59	27	.458	17	10	.588	42	9	12	0	64	7.1
K.C. Jones	9	254	75	24	.320	18	11	.611	24	48	36	1	59	6.6
Tom Sanders	9	144	61	21	.344	5	2	.400	43	5	31	1	44	4.8
Wayne Embry	5	38	31	12	.387	4	2	.500	13	3	9	0	26	5.2
Jim Barnett	5	26	21	6	.286	2	2	1.000	4	1	5	0	14	2.8
Ron Watts	1	5	6	1	.167	2	1	.500	2	0	3	0	3	3.0
Toby Kimball	1	4	2	0	.000	0	0	.000	3	0	1	0	0	0.0

1967-68

Regular Season

	G.	Min.	FGA	FGM	Pct.	FTA	FTM	Pct.	Reb.	Ast.	PF	DQ	Pts.	Ave.
John Havlicek	82	2921	1551	666	.429	453	368	.812	546	384	237	2	1700	20.7
Bailey Howell	82	2801	1336	643	.481	461	335	.727	805	133	285	4	1621	19.8
Sam Jones	73	2408	1348	621	.461	376	311	.827	357	216	181	0	1553	21.3
Bill Russell	78	2953	858	365	.425	460	247	.537	1451	357	242	2	977	12.5
Don Nelson	82	1498	632	312	.494	268	195	.728	431	103	178	1	819	10.0
Tom Sanders	78	1981	691	296	.428	255	200	.784	454	100	300	12	792	10.2
Larry Siegfried	62	1937	629	261	.415	272	236	.868	215	289	194	2	758	12.2
Wayne Embry	78	1088	483	193	.400	185	109	.589	321	52	174	1	495	6.3
Mal Graham	78	786	272	117	.430	88	56	.636	94	61	123	0	290	6.0
Tom Thacker	65	782	272	114	.419	84	43	.512	161	69	165	2	271	4.2
John Jones	51	475	253	86	.340	68	42	.618	114	26	60	0	214	4.2
Rick Weitzman	25	75	46	12	.261	13	9	.692	10	8	8	0	33	1.3

Playoffs

	G.	Min.	FGA	FGM	Pct.	FTA	FTM	Pct.	Reb.	Ast.	PF	DQ	Pts.	Ave.
John Havlicek	19	862	407	184	.452	151	125	.828	164	142	67	1	493	25.9
Sam Jones	19	685	367	162	.441	84	66	.786	64	50	58	0	390	20.5
Bailey Howell	19	597	264	135	.511	107	74	.692	146	22	84	6	344	18.1
Bill Russell	19	869	242	99	.409	130	76	.585	434	99	73	1	274	14.4
Don Nelson	19	468	175	91	.520	74	55	.743	143	32	49	0	237	12.5
Larry Siegfried	19	535	201	78	.388	85	77	.906	50	56	75	3	233	12.2
Tom Sanders	14	289	99	50	.505	21	16	.762	63	12	53	4	116	8.3
Wayne Embry	16	162	59	23	.383	29	13	.448	45	6	36	0	59	3.7
Tom Thacker	17	81	24	7	.292	7	2	.286	17	8	23	0	16	0.9
John Jones	5	10	6	3	.500	0	0	.000	4	0	2	0	6	1.2
Mal Graham	5	22	5	2	.400	3	1	.333	4	1	3	0	5	1.0
Rick Weitzman	3	5	3	2	.667	0	0	.000	1	1	0	0	4	1.3

Bill Russell is about to make his 1956 Celtic debut, watching the early action of a late-December game against the Hawks from the bench before entering to a standing ovation from the Boston Garden crowd.

A Celtic institution donned an enemy uniform briefly in 1969, when new Cincinnati Royals coach Bob Cousy activated superstar Bob Cousy. When Red Auerbach demanded a player (Bill Dinwiddie) and a draft choice for the 41-year-old Cousy's rights, it caused a rare rift in the close Cousy-Auerbach relationship. The fuss would prove much ado about nothing. Cousy would total only 1 basket, 3 free throws and 10 assists while clocking 34 minutes spread over 7 games before retiring again—this time for good.

1968-69

Regular Season

	G.	Min.	FGA	FGM	Pct.	FTA	FTM	Pct.	Reb.	Ast.	PF	DQ	Pts.	Ave.
John Havlicek	82	3174	1709	692	.405	496	387	.780	570	441	247	0	1771	21.6
Bailey Howell	78	2527	1257	612	.487	426	313	.735	685	137	285	3	1537	19.7
Sam Jones	70	1820	1103	496	.450	189	148	.783	265	182	121	0	1140	16.3
Larry Siegfried	79	2560	1031	392	.380	389	336	.864	282	370	222	0	1120	14.2
Don Nelson	82	1773	771	374	.485	259	201	.776	458	92	198	2	949	11.6
Tom Sanders	82	2184	847	364	.430	255	187	.733	574	110	293	9	915	11.2
Bill Russell	77	3291	645	279	.433	388	204	.526	1484	374	231	2	762	9.9
Emmette Bryant	80	1388	488	197	.404	100	65	.650	192	176	264	9	459	5.7
Jim Barnes (Total)	59	606	261	115	.441	111	75	.676	224	28	122	2	305	5.2
Jim Barnes (Boston)	49	595	202	92	.455	92	65	.707	194	27	107	2	249	5.1
Don Chaney	20	209	113	36	.319	20	8	.400	46	19	32	0	80	4.0
Rich Johnson	31	163	76	29	.382	23	11	.478	52	7	40	0	69	2.2
Mal Graham	22	103	55	13	.236	14	11	.786	24	14	27	0	37	1.7
Bud Olsen	7	43	19	7	.368	6	0	.000	14	4	6	0	14	2.0

Playoffs

	G.	Min.	FGA	FGM	Pct.	FTA	FTM	Pct.	Reb.	Ast.	PF	DQ	Pts.	Ave.
John Havlicek	18	850	382	170	.445	138	118	.855	179	100	58	2	458	25.4
Sam Jones	18	514	296	124	.419	69	55	.797	58	37	45	1	303	16.8
Bailey Howell	18	551	229	112	.489	64	46	.719	118	19	84	3	270	15.0
Don Nelson	18	348	168	87	.518	60	50	.833	83	21	51	0	224	12.4
Larry Siegfried	18	392	172	72	.419	70	55	.786	38	46	60	1	199	11.1
Emmette Bryant	18	607	193	79	.409	53	40	.755	88	54	75	0	198	11.0
Bill Russell	18	829	182	77	.423	81	41	.506	369	98	65	1	195	10.8
Tom Sanders	15	197	73	32	.438	31	23	.742	48	7	40	0	87	5.8
Don Chaney	7	25	6	1	.167	4	3	.750	4	0	7	0	5	0.7
Rich Johnson	2	4	1	1	1.000	0	0	.000	2	0	0	0	2	1.0
Mal Graham	2	3	2	0	.000	0	0	.000	0	1	0	0	0	0.0

1969-70

Regular Season

	G.	Min.	FGA	FGM	Pct.	FTA	FTM	Pct.	Reb.	Ast.	PF	DQ	Pts.	Ave.
John Havlicek	81	3369	1585	736	.464	578	488	.844	635	550	211	1	1960	24.2
Don Nelson	82	2224	920	461	.501	435	337	.775	601	148	238	3	1259	15.4
Larry Siegfried	78	2081	902	382	.424	257	220	.856	212	299	187	2	984	12.6
Bailey Howell	82	2078	931	399	.429	308	235	.763	550	120	261	4	1033	12.6
Jo Jo White	60	1328	684	309	.452	135	111	.822	169	145	132	1	729	12.2
Tom Sanders	57	1616	555	246	.443	183	161	.880	314	92	199	5	653	11.5
Henry Finkel	80	1866	683	310	.454	233	156	.670	613	103	292	13	776	9.7
Emmette Bryant	71	1617	520	210	.404	181	135	.746	269	231	201	5	555	7.8
Steve Kuberski	51	797	335	130	.388	92	64	.696	257	29	87	0	324	6.4
Jim Barnes	77	1049	434	178	.410	128	95	.742	350	52	229	4	451	5.9
Rich Johnson	65	898	361	167	.411	70	46	.657	208	32	155	3	380	5.8
Don Chaney	63	839	320	115	.359	109	82	.752	152	72	118	0	312	5.0
Rich Niemann	6	18	5	2	.400	2	2	1.000	6	2	10	0	6	1.0

Playoffs

Celtics did not qualify.

1970-71

Regular Season

	G.	Min.	FGA	FGM	Pct.	FTA	FTM	Pct.	Reb.	Ast.	PF	DQ	Pts.	Ave.
John Havlicek	81	3678	1982	892	.450	677	554	.818	730	607	200	0	2338	28.9
Jo Jo White	75	2787	1494	693	.464	269	215	.799	376	361	255	5	1601	21.3
Dave Cowens	81	3076	1302	550	.422	373	273	.732	1216	228	350	15	1373	17.0
Don Nelson	82	2254	881	412	.468	426	317	.744	565	153	232	2	1141	13.9
Don Chaney	81	2289	766	348	.454	313	234	.748	463	235	288	11	930	11.5
Steve Kuberski	82	1867	745	313	.420	183	133	.727	538	78	198	1	759	9.3
Rich Johnson	1	13	5	4	.800	0	0	.000	5	0	3	0	8	8.0
Henry Finkel	80	1234	489	214	.438	127	93	.732	343	79	196	5	521	6.5
Art Williams	74	1141	330	150	.455	83	60	.723	205	233	182	1	360	4.9
Bill Dinwiddie	61	717	328	123	.375	74	54	.730	209	34	90	1	300	4.9
Rex Morgan	34	266	102	41	.402	54	35	.648	61	22	58	2	117	3.4
Garfield Smith	37	281	116	42	.362	56	22	.393	95	9	53	0	106	2.9
Tom Sanders	17	121	44	16	.364	8	7	.875	17	11	25	0	39	2.3
Willie Williams	16	56	32	6	.188	5	3	.600	10	2	8	0	15	0.9

Playoffs

Celtics did not qualify.

Even 7-footer "High Henry" Finkel needs help to repair a 10-foot-tall basket.

1971-72

Regular Season

	G.	Min.	FGA	FGM	Pct.	FTA	FTM	Pct.	Reb.	Ast.	PF	DQ	Pts.	Ave.
John Havlicek	82	3698	1957	897	.458	549	458	.834	672	614	183	1	2252	27.5
Jo Jo White	79	3261	1788	770	.431	343	285	.831	446	416	227	1	1825	23.1
Dave Cowens	79	3186	1357	657	.484	243	175	.720	1203	245	314	10	1489	18.8
Don Nelson	82	2086	811	389	.480	452	356	.788	453	192	220	3	1134	13.8
Don Chaney	79	2275	786	373	.475	255	197	.773	395	202	295	7	943	11.9
Tom Sanders	82	1631	524	215	.410	136	111	.816	353	98	257	7	541	6.6
Steve Kuberski	71	1128	444	185	.417	102	80	.784	320	46	130	1	450	6.3
Art Williams	81	1326	339	161	.475	119	90	.756	256	327	204	2	412	5.1
Henry Finkel	78	736	254	103	.406	74	43	.581	251	61	118	4	249	3.2
Clarence Glover	25	119	55	25	.455	32	15	.469	46	4	26	0	65	2.6
Garfield Smith	26	134	66	28	.424	31	6	.194	37	8	22	0	62	2.4
Rex Morgan	28	150	50	16	.320	31	23	.742	30	17	34	0	55	2.0

Playoffs

	G.	Min.	FGA	FGM	Pct.	FTA	FTM	Pct.	Reb.	Ast.	PF	DQ	Pts.	Ave.
John Havlicek	11	517	235	108	.460	99	85	.859	92	70	35	1	301	27.4
Jo Jo White	11	432	220	109	.495	48	40	.833	59	58	31	0	258	23.5
Dave Cowens	11	441	156	71	.455	47	28	.596	152	33	50	2	170	15.5
Don Nelson	11	308	99	52	.525	48	41	.854	61	21	30	0	145	13.2
Steve Kuberski	11	218	87	48	.552	38	32	.842	63	3	23	0	128	11.6
Don Chaney	11	271	81	41	.506	20	15	.750	39	22	39	0	97	8.8
Art Williams	11	173	64	25	.391	20	15	.750	28	33	30	0	65	5.9
Tom Sanders	11	186	53	17	.321	21	13	.619	26	10	36	0	47	4.3
Henry Finkel	8	68	22	10	.455	0	0	.000	24	3	11	0	20	2.5
Clarence Glover	3	10	6	2	.333	2	2	1.000	3	0	1	0	6	2.0
Rex Morgan	4	10	7	1	.143	3	1	.333	5	0	6	0	3	0.8
Garfield Smith	4	6	5	1	.200	3	0	.000	1	0	1	0	2	0.5

"Voice of Celtics" Johnny Most is a Boston institution. "Johnny's broadcasts," Tom Heinsohn once cracked with affection, "have led some people to think the Celtics played a doubleheader—one game they saw and the game Most announced."

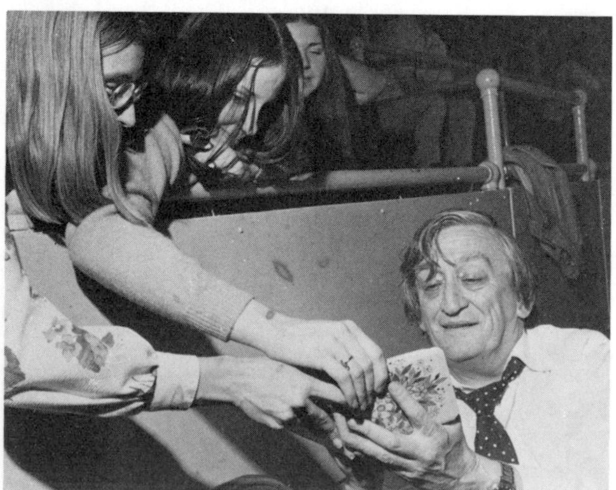

1972-73

Regular Season

	G.	Min.	FGA	FGM	Pct.	FTA	FTM	Pct.	Reb.	Ast.	PF	DQ	Pts.	Ave.
John Havlicek	80	3367	1704	766	.450	431	370	.858	567	529	195	1	1902	23.8
Dave Cowens	82	3425	1637	740	.452	262	204	.779	1329	333	311	7	1684	20.5
Jo Jo White	82	3250	1665	717	.431	228	178	.781	414	498	185	2	1612	19.7
Paul Silas	80	2618	851	400	.470	380	266	.700	1039	251	197	1	1066	13.3
Don Chaney	79	2488	859	414	.482	267	210	.787	449	221	276	6	1038	13.1
Don Nelson	72	1425	649	309	.476	188	159	.846	315	102	155	1	777	10.8
Steve Kuberski	78	762	347	140	.403	84	65	.774	197	26	92	0	345	4.4
Paul Westphal	60	482	212	89	.420	86	67	.779	67	69	88	0	245	4.1
Art Williams	81	974	261	110	.421	56	43	.768	182	236	136	1	263	3.2
Henry Finkel	76	496	173	78	.451	52	28	.538	151	26	83	0	184	2.4
Tom Sanders	59	423	149	47	.315	35	23	.657	88	27	82	0	117	2.0
Mark Minor	4	20	4	1	.250	4	3	.750	4	2	5	0	5	1.3

Playoffs

	G.	Min.	FGA	FGM	Pct.	FTA	FTM	Pct.	Reb.	Ast.	PF	DQ	Pts.	Ave.
Jo Jo White	13	583	300	135	.450	54	49	.907	54	83	44	2	319	24.5
John Havlicek	12	479	235	112	.477	74	61	.824	62	65	24	0	285	23.8
Dave Cowens	13	598	273	129	.473	41	27	.659	216	48	54	2	285	21.9
Don Nelson	13	303	101	47	.465	56	49	.875	38	15	29	0	143	11.0
Paul Silas	13	512	120	47	.392	50	31	.620	196	39	39	0	125	9.6
Don Chaney	12	288	82	39	.476	17	12	.706	40	25	41	1	90	7.5
Art Williams	10	156	47	21	.447	8	6	.750	27	41	31	1	48	4.8
Paul Westphal	11	109	39	19	.487	7	5	.714	7	9	24	1	43	3.9
Steve Kuberski	12	95	46	19	.413	10	7	.700	14	3	15	0	45	3.8
Tom Sanders	5	24	9	5	.556	2	0	.000	5	1	7	0	10	2.0
Henry Finkel	7	23	9	6	.667	0	0	.000	6	3	4	0	12	1.7

1973-74

Regular Season

	G.	Min.	FGA	FGM	Pct.	FTA	FTM	Pct.	Off. Reb.	Def. Reb.	Tot. Reb.	Ast.	PF	DQ	Stl.	Blk. Sh.	Pts.	Ave.	Hi
John Havlicek	76	3091	1502	685	.456	416	346	.832	138	349	487	447	196	1	95	32	1716	22.6	34
Dave Cowens	80	3352	1475	645	.437	274	228	.832	264	993	1257	354	294	7	95	101	1518	19.0	35
Jo Jo White	82	3238	1445	649	.449	227	190	.837	100	251	351	448	185	1	105	25	1488	18.1	37
Paul Silas	82	2599	772	340	.440	337	264	.783	334	581	915	186	246	3	63	20	944	11.5	31
Don Nelson	82	1748	717	364	.508	273	215	.788	90	255	345	162	189	1	19	13	943	11.5	29
Don Chaney	81	2258	750	348	.464	180	149	.828	210	168	378	176	247	7	83	62	845	10.4	26
Paul Westphal	82	1165	475	238	.501	153	112	.732	49	94	143	171	173	1	39	34	588	7.2	28
Steve Kuberski	78	985	368	157	.427	111	86	.775	96	141	237	38	125	0	7	7	400	5.1	21
Phil Hankinson	28	163	103	50	.485	13	10	.769	22	28	50	4	18	0	3	1	110	3.9	13
Steve Downing	24	137	64	21	.328	38	22	.579	14	25	39	11	33	0	5	0	64	2.7	4
Art Williams	67	617	168	73	.435	32	27	.844	20	95	115	163	100	0	44	3	173	2.6	14
Henry Finkel	60	427	130	60	.462	43	28	.651	41	94	135	27	62	1	3	7	148	2.5	14

Playoffs

	G.	Min.	FGA	FGM	Pct.	FTA	FTM	Pct.	Off. Reb.	Def. Reb.	Tot. Reb.	Ast.	PF	Stl.	Blk. Sh.	Pts.	Ave.	Hi
John Havlicek	18	811	411	199	.484	101	89	.881	28	88	116	108	43	24	6	487	27.1	43
Dave Cowens	18	772	370	161	.435	59	47	.797	60	180	240	66	85	21	17	369	20.5	30
Jo Jo White	18	765	310	132	.426	46	34	.739	17	58	75	98	56	15	2	298	16.6	27
Don Nelson	18	467	164	82	.500	53	41	.774	25	72	97	35	54	8	3	205	11.4	24
Don Chaney	18	545	141	65	.461	50	41	.820	37	40	77	40	64	24	9	171	9.5	19
Paul Silas	18	574	126	50	.397	53	44	.830	53	158	191	47	51	13	9	144	8.0	16
Paul Westphal	18	241	100	46	.460	15	11	.733	6	15	21	31	37	8	2	103	5.7	16
Phil Hankinson	2	5	4	2	.500	2	2	1.000	0	1	1	0	0	0	1	6	3.0	4
Art Williams	12	96	27	10	.370	8	7	.875	4	19	23	29	14	7	0	27	2.3	8
Henry Finkel	8	46	18	8	.444	1	1	1 000	5	5	10	3	9	1	0	17	2.1	8
Steve Downing	1	4	2	1	.500	0	0	.000	2	0	2	0	1	0	0	2	2.0	2
Steve Kuberski	9	69	25	5	.200	10	5	.500	8	12	20	2	9	1	1	15	1.7	8

. . . Reluctant to leave, Cowens sits at the press table—until Red Auerbach comes down from the stands to talk him out of it. That's Dr. Tom Silva, long-time team physician, with a hand on Cowens' shoulder . . .

Dave Cowens swings at Seattle's Tom Burleson, and is ejected from a November 1975 game . .

1974-75

Regular Season

	G.	Min.	FGA	FGM	Pct.	FTA	FTM	Pct.	Off. Reb.	Def. Reb.	Tot. Reb.	Ast.	PF	DQ	Stl.	Blk. Sh.	Pts.	Ave.	Hi
Dave Cowens	65	2632	1199	569	.475	244	191	.783	229	729	958	296	243	7	87	73	1329	20.4	38
John Havlicek	82	3132	1411	642	.455	332	289	.870	154	330	484	432	231	2	110	16	1573	19.2	40
Jo Jo White	82	3220	1440	658	.457	223	186	.834	84	227	311	458	207	1	128	17	1502	18.3	33
Don Nelson	79	2052	785	423	.539	318	263	.827	127	342	469	181	239	2	32	15	1109	14.0	35
Paul Silas	82	2661	749	312	.417	344	244	.709	348	677	1025	224	229	3	60	22	868	10.6	22
Paul Westphal	82	1581	670	342	.510	156	119	.763	44	119	163	235	192	0	78	33	803	9.8	27
Don Chaney	82	2208	750	321	.428	165	133	.806	171	199	370	181	244	5	122	66	775	9.5	28
Phil Hankinson	3	24	11	6	.545	0	0	.000	1	6	7	2	3	0	1	0	12	4.0	6
Jim Ard	59	719	266	89	.335	65	48	.738	59	140	199	40	96	2	13	32	226	3.8	19
Kevin Stacom	61	447	159	72	.453	33	29	.879	30	25	55	49	65	0	11	3	173	2.8	10
Ben Clyde	25	157	72	31	.431	9	7	.778	15	26	41	5	34	1	5	3	69	2.8	16
Glenn McDonald	62	395	182	70	.385	37	28	.757	20	48	68	24	58	0	8	5	168	2.7	14
Henry Finkel	62	518	129	52	.403	43	23	.535	33	79	112	32	72	0	7	3	127	2.0	10
Steve Downing	3	9	2	0	.000	2	0	.000	0	2	2	0	0	0	0	0	0	0.0	0

Playoffs

	G.	Min.	FGA	FGM	Pct.	FTA	FTM	Pct.	Off. Reb.	Def. Reb.	Tot. Reb.	Ast.	PF	DQ	Stl.	Blk. Sh.	Pts.	Ave.	Hi
John Havlicek	11	464	192	83	.432	76	66	.868	18	39	57	51	38	1	16	1	232	21.1	30
Jo Jo White	11	462	227	100	.441	33	27	.818	18	32	50	63	32	0	11	4	227	20.6	32
Dave Cowens	11	479	236	101	.428	26	23	.885	49	132	181	46	50	2	18	6	225	20.5	31
Don Nelson	11	274	117	66	.564	41	37	902	18	27	45	26	36	1	2	2	169	15.4	25
Don Chaney	11	294	105	48	.457	29	23	793	24	14	38	21	46	2	21	5	119	10.8	29
Paul Silas	11	405	92	42	.457	25	16	.640	46	84	130	40	45	1	12	2	100	9.1	13
Paul Westphal	11	183	81	38	.469	18	12	.667	5	8	13	32	21	0	6	2	88	8.0	14
Henry Finkel	7	25	7	3	.429	5	3	.600	3	3	6	4	2	0	0	0	9	1.3	4
Phil Hankinson	2	3	3	1	.333	0	0	.000	2	0	2	0	0	0	0	0	2	1.0	2
Glenn McDonald	6	30	12	2	.167	3	1	.333	1	5	6	2	4	0	1	0	5	0.8	2
Jim Ard	5	14	8	1	.125	0	0	.000	2	0	2	1	5	0	0	1	2	0.4	2
Kevin Stacom	4	7	2	0	.000	0	0	.000	0	0	0	1	0	0	0	0	0	0.0	0

1975-76

Regular Season

	G.	Min.	FGA	FGM	Pct.	FTA	FTM	Pct.	Off. Reb.	Def. Reb.	Tot. Reb.	Ast.	PF	DQ	Stl.	Blk. Sh.	Pts.	Ave.	Hi
Dave Cowens	78	3101	1305	611	.468	340	257	.756	335	911	1246	325	314	10	94	71	1479	19.0	39
Jo Jo White	82	3257	1492	670	.449	253	212	.838	61	252	313	445	183	2	107	20	1552	18.9	34
Charlie Scott	82	2913	1309	588	.449	335	267	.797	106	252	358	341	356	17	103	24	1443	17.6	32
John Havlicek	76	2598	1121	504	.450	333	281	.844	116	198	314	278	204	1	97	29	1289	17.0	38
Paul Silas	81	2662	740	315	.426	333	236	.709	365	660	1025	203	227	3	56	33	866	10.7	19
Don Nelson	75	943	379	175	.462	161	127	.789	56	126	182	77	115	0	14	7	477	6.4	27
Glenn McDonald	75	1019	456	191	.419	56	40	.714	56	79	135	68	123	0	39	20	422	5.6	18
Kevin Stacom	77	1114	387	170	.439	91	68	.747	62	99	161	128	117	0	23	5	408	5.3	16
Steve Kuberski (Total)	70	967	291	135	.464	79	71	.899	90	169	259	47	133	1	12	13	341	4.9	20
Steve Kuberski (Boston)	60	882	274	128	.467	76	68	.895	86	148	234	44	123	1	11	11	324	5.4	20
Jim Ard	81	853	294	107	.364	100	71	.710	96	193	289	48	141	2	12	36	285	3.5	18
Jerome Anderson	22	126	45	25	.556	16	11	.688	4	9	13	6	25	0	3	3	61	2.8	8
Tom Boswell	35	275	93	41	.441	24	14	.583	26	45	71	16	70	1	2	1	96	2.7	9
Ed Searcy	4	12	6	2	.333	2	2	1.000	0	0	0	1	4	0	0	0	6	1.5	2

Playoffs

	G.	Min.	FGA	FGM	Pct.	FTA	FTM	Pct.	Off. Reb.	Def. Reb.	Tot. Reb.	Ast.	PF	DQ	Stl.	Blk. Sh.	Pts.	Ave.	Hi
Jo Jo White	18	791	371	165	.445	95	78	.821	12	59	71	98	51	0	23	1	408	22.7	33
Dave Cowens	18	798	341	156	.457	87	66	.759	87	209	296	83	85	4	22	13	378	21.0	30
Charlie Scott	18	632	284	111	.391	72	55	.764	23	53	76	71	97	11	21	8	277	15.4	31
John Havlicek	15	505	180	80	.444	47	38	.809	18	38	56	51	32	0	12	5	198	13.2	26
Paul Silas	18	741	154	69	.448	69	56	.812	78	168	246	42	67	1	24	6	194	10.8	21
Don Nelson	18	315	108	52	.481	69	60	.870	17	36	53	17	46	1	3	2	164	9.1	27
Steve Kuberski	18	232	81	38	.469	26	21	.808	16	35	51	16	38	0	0	3	97	5.4	12
Jim Ard	16	110	29	13	.448	14	11	.786	10	16	26	8	29	0	1	3	37	2.3	9
Kevin Stacom	17	195	45	13	.289	11	8	.727	9	8	17	16	21	0	5	0	34	2.0	9
Glenn McDonald	13	68	26	8	.308	6	5	.833	1	7	8	4	12	0	1	0	21	1.6	8
Tom Boswell	3	3	2	1	.500	0	0	.000	0	1	1	0	2	0	0	0	2	0.7	2
Jerome Anderson	4	5	3	1	.333	0	0	.000	1	0	1	1	1	0	0	0	2	0.5	2

1976-77

Regular Season

	G.	Min.	FGA	FGM	Pct.	FTA	FTM	Pct.	Off. Reb.	Def. Reb.	Tot. Reb.	Ast.	PF	DQ	Stl.	Blk. Sh.	Pts.	Ave.	Hi
Jo Jo White	82	3333	1488	638	.429	383	333	.869	87	296	383	492	193	5	118	22	1609	19.6	41
Charlie Scott	43	1581	734	326	.444	173	129	.746	52	139	191	196	155	3	60	12	781	18.2	31
John Havlicek	79	2913	1283	580	.452	288	235	.816	109	273	382	400	208	4	84	18	1395	17.7	33
Dave Cowens	50	1888	756	328	.434	198	162	.818	147	550	697	248	181	7	46	49	818	16.4	33
Sidney Wicks	82	2642	1012	464	.458	464	310	.668	268	556	824	169	331	14	64	61	1238	15.1	25
Curtis Rowe	79	2190	632	315	.489	240	170	.708	188	375	563	107	215	3	24	47	800	10.1	22
Tom Boswell	70	1083	340	175	.515	135	96	.711	111	195	306	85	237	9	27	8	446	6.4	22
Fred Saunders	68	1051	395	184	.466	53	35	.660	73	150	223	85	191	3	26	7	403	5.9	21
Kevin Stacom	79	1051	438	179	.409	58	46	.793	40	57	97	117	65	0	19	3	404	5.1	16
Steve Kuberski	76	860	312	131	.420	83	63	.759	76	133	209	39	89	0	7	5	325	4.3	16
Jim Ard	63	969	254	96	.378	76	49	.645	77	219	296	53	128	1	18	28	241	3.8	14
Norm Cook	25	138	72	27	.375	17	9	.529	10	17	27	5	27	0	10	3	63	2.5	10
Bobby Wilson	25	131	59	19	.322	13	11	.846	3	6	9	14	19	0	3	0	49	2.0	10

Playoffs

	G.	Min.	FGA	FGM	Pct.	FTA	FTM	Pct.	Off. Reb.	Def. Reb.	Tot. Reb.	Ast.	PF	DQ	Stl.	Blk. Sh.	Pts.	Ave.	Hi
Jo Jo White	9	395	201	91	.453	33	28	.848	10	29	39	52	27	0	14	0	210	23.3	40
John Havlicek	9	375	167	62	.371	50	41	.820	15	34	49	62	33	0	8	4	165	18.3	31
Dave Cowens	9	379	148	66	.446	22	17	.773	29	105	134	36	37	3	8	13	149	16.6	37
Charlie Scott	9	338	128	52	.406	52	44	.846	15	23	38	38	41	3	13	2	148	16.4	22
Sidney Wicks	9	261	81	42	.519	47	34	.723	26	57	83	16	37	2	13	3	118	13.1	21
Curtis Rowe	9	237	68	32	.471	29	22	.759	29	43	72	10	29	1	1	4	86	9.6	15
Norm Cook	1	3	2	2	1.000	0	0	—	0	0	0	0	0	0	0	0	4	4.0	4
Fred Saunders	9	66	33	12	.364	6	5	.833	1	8	9	5	21	0	1	0	29	3.2	7
Tom Boswell	9	81	18	8	.444	6	4	.667	10	10	20	7	18	0	1	0	20	2.2	7
Kevin Stacom	5	25	6	3	.500	1	1	1.000	0	2	2	4	3	0	0	0	7	1.4	5

. . . After showering, Cowens watches the remainder of the Celtic loss from an exit area.

1977-78
Regular Season

	G.	Min.	FGA	FGM	Pct.	FTA	FTM	Pct.	Off. Reb.	Def. Reb.	Tot. Reb.	Ast.	PF	DQ	Stl.	Blk. Sh.	Pts.	Ave.	Hi
Dave Cowens	77	3215	1220	598	.490	284	239	.842	248	830	1078	351	297	5	102	67	1435	18.6	36
Charlie Scott	31	1080	485	210	.433	118	84	.712	24	77	101	143	97	2	51	6	504	16.3	30
John Havlicek	82	2797	1217	546	.449	269	230	.855	93	239	332	328	185	2	90	22	1322	16.1	32
Jo Jo White	46	1641	690	289	.419	120	103	.858	53	127	180	209	109	2	49	7	681	14.8	27
Dave Bing	80	2256	940	422	.449	296	244	.824	76	136	212	300	247	2	79	18	1088	13.6	30
Sidney Wicks	81	2413	927	433	.467	329	217	.660	223	450	673	171	318	9	67	46	1083	13.4	35
Kermit Washington (Total)	57	1617	507	247	.487	246	170	.691	215	399	614	72	188	3	47	64	664	11.6	22
Kermit Washington (Boston)	32	866	263	137	.521	136	102	.750	105	230	335	42	114	2	28	40	376	11.8	18
Kevin Stacom	55	1006	484	206	.426	71	54	.761	26	80	106	111	60	0	28	3	466	8.5	22
Cedric Maxwell	72	1213	316	170	.538	250	188	.752	138	241	379	68	151	2	53	48	528	7.3	21
Tom Boswell	65	1149	357	185	.518	123	93	.756	117	171	288	71	204	5	25	14	463	7.1	22
Curtis Rowe	51	911	273	123	.451	89	66	.742	74	129	203	45	94	1	14	8	312	6.1	20
Don Chaney (Total)	51	835	269	104	.387	45	38	.844	40	76	116	66	107	0	44	13	246	4.8	17
Don Chaney (Boston)	42	702	233	91	.391	39	33	.846	36	69	105	49	93	0	36	10	215	5.1	17
Zaid Abdul-Aziz	2	24	13	3	.231	3	2	667	6	9	15	3	4	0	1	1	8	4.0	6
Ernie DiGregorio (Total)	52	606	209	88	.421	33	28	.848	7	43	50	137	44	0	18	1	204	3.9	24
Ernie DiGregorio (Boston)	27	274	109	47	.431	13	12	.923	2	25	27	66	22	0	12	1	106	3.9	24
Fred Saunders	26	243	91	30	.330	17	14	.824	11	26	37	11	34	0	7	4	74	2.8	12
Bob Bigelow (Total)	5	24	13	4	.308	0	0	—	3	6	9	0	3	0	0	0	8	1.6	4
Bob Bigelow (Boston)	4	17	12	3	.250	0	0	—	1	3	4	0	1	0	0	0	6	1.5	4
Jim Ard	1	9	1	0	.000	2	1	.500	1	3	4	1	1	0	0	0	1	1.0	1
Steve Kuberski	3	14	4	1	.250	0	0	—	1	5	6	0	2	0	1	0	2	0.7	2

Playoffs
Celtics did not qualify.

Red Auerbach congratulates one of basketball's immortal players, Bob Cousy, upon his election to The Basketball Hall of Fame.

1978-79

Regular Season

	G	Min	FGA	FGM	Pct	FTA	FTM	Pct	Off Reb	Def Reb	Tot Reb	Ast	PF	DQ	Stl	Blk Sh	Pts	Ave	Hi
Bob McAdoo (Total)	60	2231	1127	596	529	450	295	656	130	390	520	168	189	3	74	67	1487	24.8	45
Bob McAdoo (Boston)	20	637	334	167	500	115	77	670	36	105	141	40	55	1	12	20	411	20.6	42
Cedric Maxwell	80	2969	808	472	584	716	574	802	272	519	791	228	266	4	98	74	1518	19.0	35
Dave Cowens	68	2517	1010	488	483	187	151	.807	.152	500	652	242	263	16	76	51	1127	16.6	32
Chris Ford (Total)	81	2737	1142	538	471	227	172	758	124	150	274	374	209	3	115	25	1248	15.4	34
Chris Ford (Boston)	78	2629	1107	525	474	219	165	753	115	141	256	369	200	2	114	24	1215	15.6	34
Billy Knight	40	1119	436	219	502	146	118	.808	41	132	173	66	86	1	31	3	556	13.9	37
Jo Jo White	47	1455	596	255	428	89	79	888	22	106	128	214	100	1	54	4	589	12.5	28
Nate Archibald	69	1662	573	259	452	307	242	788	25	78	103	324	132	2	55	6	760	11.0	25
Rick Robey (Total)	79	1763	673	322	478	224	174	777	168	345	513	132	232	4	48	15	818	10.4	28
Rick Robey (Boston)	36	914	378	182	481	103	84	816	88	171	259	79	121	3	23	3	448	12.4	27
Jeff Judkins	81	1521	587	295	503	146	119	815	70	121	191	145	184	1	81	12	709	8.8	29
Marvin Barnes	38	796	271	133	491	66	43	652	57	120	177	53	144	3	38	39	309	8.1	29
Curtis Rowe	53	1222	346	151	436	75	52	693	79	163	242	69	105	2	15	13	354	6.7	21
Earl Tatum	3	38	20	8	400	5	4	.800	1	3	4	1	7	0	0	1	20	6.7	11
Earl Williams	20	273	123	54	439	24	14	.583	41	64	105	12	41	0	12	9	122	6.7	27
Don Chaney	65	1074	414	174	420	42	36	.857	63	78	141	75	167	3	72	11	384	5.9	20
Frankie Sanders (Total)	46	479	246	105	427	68	54	.794	35	75	110	52	69	1	21	6	264	5.7	16
Frankie Sanders (Boston)	24	216	119	55	462	27	22	.815	22	29	51	17	25	0	7	3	132	5.5	14
Kevin Stacom (Total)	8	831	342	128	374	60	44	.733	30	55	85	112	47	0	29	1	300	4.4	16
Kevin Stacom (Boston)	24	260	133	52	391	19	13	.684	10	14	24	35	18	0	15	0	117	4.9	15
Tom Barker	14	131	48	21	438	15	11	.733	12	18	30	6	26	0	4	4	53	4.4	14
Dennis Awtrey	23	247	44	17	386	20	16	800	13	34	47	20	37	0	3	6	50	2.2	7

Playoffs

Celtics did not qualify.

1979-80

Regular Season

	G	Min.	FGA	FGM	Pct.	FTA	FTM	Pct.	Off. Reb.	Def. Reb.	Tot. Reb.	Ast.	PF	DQ	Stl.	Blk. Sh.	Pts.	Ave.	Hi
Larry Bird	82	2955	1463	693	.474	360	301	.836	216	636	852	370	279	4	143	53	1745	21.3	45
Cedric Maxwell	80	2744	750	457	.609	554	436	.787	284	420	704	199	266	6	76	60	1350	16.9	29
Dave Cowens	66	2159	932	422	.453	122	95	.779	126	408	534	206	216	2	69	61	940	14.2	32
Nate Archibald	80	2864	794	383	.482	435	361	.830	59	138	197	671	218	2	106	10	1131	14.1	29
Pete Maravich (Total)	43	964	543	244	.449	105	91	.867	17	61	78	83	79	1	24	7	589	13.7	31
Pete Maravich (Boston)	26	442	249	123	.494	55	50	.909	10	28	38	29	49	1	9	3	299	11.5	31
Rick Robey	82	1918	727	379	.521	269	184	.684	209	321	530	92	244	2	53	15	942	11.5	27
Chris Ford	73	2115	709	330	.465	114	86	.754	77	104	181	215	178	0	111	27	816	11.2	27
M.L. Carr	82	1994	763	362	.474	241	178	.739	106	224	330	156	214	1	120	36	914	11.1	25
Gerald Henderson	76	1061	382	191	.500	129	89	.690	37	46	83	147	96	0	45	15	473	6.2	17
Jeff Judkins	65	674	276	139	.504	76	62	.816	32	34	66	47	91	0	29	5	351	5.4	17
Eric Fernsten	56	431	153	71	.464	52	33	.635	40	56	96	28	43	0	17	12	175	3.1	11
Don Chaney	60	523	189	67	.354	42	32	.762	31	42	73	38	80	1	31	11	167	2.8	8

3-point field goals: Celtics 162-422 (.384); Bird 58-143 (.406); Cowens 1-12 (.083); Archibald 4-18 (.222); Maravich (Total) 10-15 (.667), (Boston) 3-4 (.750); Robey 0-1 (.000); Ford 70-164 (.427); Carr 12-41 (.293); Henderson 2-6 (.333); Judkins 11-27 (.407); Chaney 1-6 (.167). Opponents 74-259 (.286).

Playoffs

	G.	Min.	FGA	FGM	Pct.	FTA	FTM	Pct.	Off. Reb.	Def. Reb.	Tot. Reb.	Ast.	PF	DQ	Stl.	Blk. Sh.	Pts.	Ave.	Hi
Larry Bird	9	372	177	83	.469	25	22	.880	22	79	101	42	30	0	14	8	192	21.3	34
Cedric Maxwell	9	320	93	59	.634	61	46	.754	31	59	90	19	25	0	5	10	164	18.2	27
Nate Archibald	9	332	89	45	.506	42	37	.881	3	8	11	71	28	1	10	0	128	14.2	22
Dave Cowens	9	301	103	49	.476	11	10	.909	18	48	66	21	37	0	9	7	108	12.0	22
M.L. Carr	9	172	80	32	.400	24	16	.667	14	19	33	11	20	0	6	1	82	9.1	23
Chris Ford	9	279	79	34	.430	15	12	.800	9	16	25	21	35	1	14	6	82	9.1	19
Rick Robey	9	151	53	24	.453	14	7	.500	13	19	32	10	27	0	7	3	55	6.1	14
Pete Maravich	9	104	51	25	.490	3	2	.667	0	8	8	6	12	0	3	0	54	6.0	12
Gerald Henderson	9	101	37	15	.405	20	12	.600	4	6	10	12	8	0	4	0	42	4.7	9
Jeff Judkins	7	10	8	4	.500	0	0	—	3	1	4	0	0	0	1	0	9	1.3	3
Eric Fernsten	5	18	6	2	.333	3	2	.667	3	2	5	0	1	0	0	3	6	1.2	4

3-point field goals: Celtics 12-49 (.245); Archibald 1-2 (.500); Cowens 0-2 (.000); Carr 2-5 (.400); Ford 2-13 (.154); Robey 0-1 (.000); Maravich 2-6 (.333); Henderson 0-2 (.000); Judkins 1-3 (.333). Opponents 10-33 (.303).

Bob Cousy receives the annual Big Brother of the Year Award from President Johnson.

1980-81

Regular Season

	G	Min.	FGA	FGM	Pct.	FTA	FTM	Pct.	Off. Reb.	Def. Reb.	Tot. Reb.	Ast.	PF	DQ	Stl.	Blk. Sh.	Pts.	Ave.	Hi
Nate Archibald	80	2820	766	382	.499	419	342	.816	36	140	176	618	201	1	75	18	1106	13.8	26
Larry Bird	82	3239	1503	719	.478	328	283	.863	191	704	895	451	239	2	161	63	1741	21.2	36
M. L. Carr	41	655	216	97	.449	67	53	.791	26	57	83	56	74	0	30	18	248	6.0	25
Terry Duerod	32	114	73	30	.411	14	13	.929	2	3	5	6	8	0	5	0	79	2.5	12
Eric Fernsten	45	279	79	38	.481	30	20	.667	29	33	62	10	29	0	6	7	96	2.1	9
Chris Ford	82	2723	707	314	.444	87	64	.736	72	91	163	295	212	2	100	23	728	8.9	23
Gerald Henderson	82	1608	579	261	.451	157	113	.720	43	89	132	213	177	0	79	12	636	7.8	19
Wayne Kreklow	25	100	47	11	.234	10	7	.700	2	10	12	9	20	0	2	1	30	1.2	4
Cedric Maxwell	81	2730	750	441	.588	450	352	.782	222	303	525	219	256	5	79	68	1234	15.2	34
Kevin McHale	82	1645	666	355	.533	159	108	.679	155	204	359	55	260	3	27	151	818	10.0	23
Robert Parish	82	2298	1166	635	.545	397	282	.710	245	532	777	144	310	9	81	214	1552	18.9	40
Rick Robey	82	1569	547	298	.545	251	144	.574	132	258	390	126	204	0	38	19	740	9.0	24
CELTICS	82		7099	3581	.504	2369	1781	.752	1155	2424	3579	2202	1990	22	683	594	9008	109.9	136
OPPONENTS	82		7296	3372	.462	2277	1752	.769	1192	2174	3366	1890	2059	33	736	351	8526	104.0	128

3-point field goals: Celtics 65-241 (.270): Archibald 0-9 (.000); Bird 20-74 (.270); Carr 1-14 (.071); Duerod 6-10 (.600); Ford 36-109 (.330); Henderson 1-16 (.063); Kreklow 1-4 (.250); Maxwell 0-1 (.000); McHale 0-2 (.000); Parish 0-1 (.000); Robey 0-1 (.000). Opponents 30-139 (.216).

Playoffs

	G	Min.	FGA	FGM	Pct.	FTA	FTM	Pct.	Off. Reb.	Def. Reb.	Tot. Reb.	Ast.	PF	DQ	Stl.	Blk. Sh.	Pts.	Ave.	Hi
Nate Archibald	17	630	211	95	.450	94	76	.809	6	22	28	107	39	0	13	0	266	15.6	27
Larry Bird	17	750	313	147	.470	85	76	.894	49	189	238	103	53	0	39	17	373	21.9	35
M. L. Carr	17	288	101	42	.416	24	18	.750	8	17	25	14	32	0	10	6	102	6.0	11
Terry Duerod	10	12	10	4	.400	0	0	.000	0	0	0	0	0	0	1	0	8	0.8	4
Eric Fernsten	8	14	3	0	.000	3	2	.667	1	3	4	1	3	0	1	0	2	0.3	2
Chris Ford	17	507	146	66	.452	25	15	.600	13	32	45	46	47	0	14	1	154	9.1	17
Gerald Henderson	16	228	86	41	.477	12	10	.833	10	15	25	26	24	0	10	3	92	5.8	12
Cedric Maxwell	17	598	174	101	.580	88	72	.818	61	64	125	46	53	0	12	17	274	16.1	28
Kevin McHale	17	296	113	61	.540	36	23	.639	29	30	59	14	51	1	4	24	145	8.5	21
Robert Parish	17	492	219	108	.493	58	39	.672	50	96	146	19	74	2	21	39	255	15.0	27
Rick Robey	17	265	81	35	.432	35	16	.457	19	41	60	12	44	0	2	5	86	5.1	14
CELTICS	17		1457	700	.480	460	347	.754	246	509	755	388	420	3	127	112	1757	103.3	121
OPPONENTS	17		1471	645	.438	452	357	.790	261	457	718	356	412	2	122	103	1654	97.2	109

3-point field goals: Celtics 10-45 (.222): Archibald 0-5 (.000); Bird 3-8 (.375); Carr 0-4 (.000), Duerod 0-2 (.000); Ford 7-25 (.280); Henderson 0-1 (.000). Opponents 7-38 (.184).

1981-82

Regular Season

	G	Min.	FGA	FGM	Pct.	FTA	FTM	Pct.	Off. Reb.	Def. Reb.	Tot. Reb.	Ast.	PF	DQ	Stl.	Blk. Sh.	Pts.	Ave.	Hi
Danny Ainge	53	564	221	79	.357	65	56	.862	25	31	56	87	86	1	37	3	219	4.1	17
Nate Archibald	68	2167	652	308	.472	316	236	.747	25	91	116	541	131	1	52	3	858	12.6	26
Larry Bird	77	2923	1414	711	.503	380	328	.863	200	637	837	447	244	0	143	66	1761	22.9	40
Charles Bradley	51	339	122	55	.451	62	42	.677	12	26	38	22	61	0	14	6	152	3.0	10
M.L. Carr	56	1296	409	184	.450	116	82	.707	56	94	150	128	136	2	67	21	455	8.1	22
Terry Duerod	21	146	77	34	.442	12	4	.333	6	9	15	12	9	0	3	1	72	3.4	12
Eric Fernsten	43	202	49	19	.388	30	19	.633	12	30	42	8	23	0	5	7	57	1.3	6
Chris Ford	76	1591	450	188	.418	56	39	.696	52	56	108	142	143	0	42	10	435	5.7	15
Gerald Henderson	82	1844	705	353	.501	172	125	.727	47	105	152	252	199	3	82	11	833	10.2	27
Tracy Jackson	11	66	26	10	.385	10	6	.600	7	5	12	5	5	0	3	0	26	2.4	4
Cedric Maxwell	78	2590	724	397	.548	478	357	.747	218	281	499	183	263	6	79	49	1151	14.8	31
Kevin McHale	82	2332	875	465	.531	248	187	.754	191	365	556	91	264	1	30	185	1117	13.6	28
Robert Parish	80	2534	1235	669	.542	355	252	.710	288	578	866	140	267	5	68	192	1590	19.9	37
Rick Robey	80	1186	375	185	.493	157	84	.535	114	181	295	68	183	2	27	14	454	5.7	15
CELTICS	82		7334	3657	.499	2457	1817	.740	1253	2489	3742	2126	2014	21	652	568	9180	112.0	145
OPPONENTS	82		7429	3490	.470	2172	1638	.754	1193	2247	3440	1972	2240	28	681	367	8657	105.6	144

3-point field goals: Celtics 49-184 (.266): Ainge 5-17 (.294); Archibald 6-16 (.375); Bird 11-52 (.212): Bradley 0-1 (.000); Carr 5-17 (.294); Duerod 0-1 (.000); Ford 20-61 (.328); Henderson 2-12 (.167); Maxwell 0-3 (.000); Robey 0-2 (.000). Opponents 39-203 (.192).

Playoffs

	G	Min.	FGA	FGM	Pct.	FTA	FTM	Pct.	Off. Reb.	Def. Reb.	Tot. Reb.	Ast.	PF	DQ	Stl.	Blk. Sh.	Pts.	Ave.	Hi
Danny Ainge	10	129	45	19	.422	13	10	.769	6	7	13	11	21	0	2	2	50	5.0	17
Nate Archibald	8	277	70	30	.429	28	25	.893	1	16	17	52	21	0	5	2	85	10.6	24
Larry Bird	12	490	206	88	.427	45	37	.822	33	117	150	68	43	0	23	17	214	17.8	26
Charles Bradley	7	18	8	2	.250	2	0	.000	1	4	5	1	6	0	1	0	4	0.7	2
M.L. Carr	12	305	105	37	.352	23	15	.652	21	22	43	28	30	0	11	0	89	7.4	21
Eric Fernsten	5	11	2	1	.500	2	1	.500	2	0	2	0	0	0	0	0	3	0.6	2
Chris Ford	12	138	42	20	.476	7	5	.714	6	9	15	15	15	0	3	1	47	3.9	9
Gerald Henderson	12	310	93	38	.409	35	24	.686	12	13	25	48	30	0	14	2	100	8.3	16
Cedric Maxwell	12	385	120	62	.517	70	50	.714	37	50	87	26	40	0	18	11	174	14.5	26
Kevin McHale	12	344	134	77	.575	53	40	.755	41	44	85	11	44	0	5	27	194	16.2	25
Robert Parish	12	426	209	102	.488	75	51	.680	43	92	135	18	47	1	6	48	255	21.3	33
Rick Robey	12	122	40	21	.525	17	13	.765	13	16	29	4	27	0	2	2	55	4.6	19
CELTICS	12		1074	497	.463	370	271	.753	216	390	606	281	324	1	89	112	1270	105.8	131
OPPONENTS	12		1072	462	.431	354	270	.763	187	334	521	273	341	6	93	69	1202	100.2	126

3-point field goals: Celtics 5-27 (.185): Ainge 2-4 (.500); Archibald 0-4 (.000); Bird 1-6 (.167); Carr 0-4 (.000); Ford 2-7 (.286); Henderson 0-2 (.000). Opponents 8-33 (.242).

ATTENDANCE

YEAR-BY-YEAR ATTENDANCE AT BOSTON GARDEN

Year	Games	Attendance	Average
1946-47	30*	108,240	3,608
1947-48	24*	90,264	3,761
1948-49	29*	144,275	4,975
1949-50	26*	110,552	4,252
1950-51	32*	197,888	6,184
1951-52	29*	160,167	5,523
1952-53	24	161,808	6,742
1953-54	21	156,912	7,472
1954-55	25	175,675	7,027
1955-56	26	209,645	8,064
1956-57	25	262,918	10,517
1957-58	29	240,943	8,308
1958-59	30	244,642	8,165
1959-60	27	209,374	7,755
1960-61	28	201,569	7,199
1961-62	28	191,855	6,852
1962-63	30	262,581	8,753
1963-64	30	223,347	7,445
1964-65	30	246,529	8,318
1965-66	31	246,189	7,941
1966-67	31	322,690	10,409
1967-68	37	320,788	8,670
1968-69	36	322,130	8,948
1969-70	37	277,632	7,504
1970-71	39	313,768	8,045
1971-72	41	346,701	8,456
1972-73	39	423,234	10,852
1973-74	32	355,261	11,102
1974-75	34	452,421	13,307
1975-76	36	484,039	13,446
1976-77	35	453,672	12,962
1977-78	36	437,937	12,165
1978-79	41	407,926	10,193
1979-80	39	565,105**	14,490***
1980-81	36	536,883	14,913
1981-82	38	582,160	15,320

NOTE: Doesn't include "home" games at Providence and Hartford over the years.

*Includes games at Boston Arena.

**Includes a Celtic record 30 sellouts at the Garden (but doesn't include two more "home" sellouts of 15,622 each at Hartford Civic Center).

***91 percent of the Garden's 15,320 basketball capacity.

HOME OPENERS

Year	Game	Attendance
1946	Chicago 57, Celtics 55	4,329
1947	Philadelphia 79, Celtics 75 (OT)	4,665
1948	Celtics 85, Philadelphia 77	4,028
1949	Minneapolis 94, Celtics 84	6,024
1950	Celtics 76, Minneapolis 71	6,569
1951	Celtics 97, Indianapolis 65	3,012
1952	Celtics 106, Syracuse 83	5,873
1953	Minneapolis 84, Celtics 79	10,727
1954	Celtics 107, Syracuse 84	5,839
1955	Celtics 98, Philadelphia 87	9,594
1956	New York 113, Celtics 107	12,469
1957	Celtics 107, Syracuse 83	12,681
1958	Celtics 112, Detroit 98	8,813
1959	Celtics 129, Cincinnati 125	3,341
1960	Celtics 118, Detroit 116	8,660
1961	Celtics 137, Detroit 102	8,023
1962	Celtics 149, New York 116	10,705
1963	Celtics 123, Baltimore 108	10,333
1964	Celtics 112, Detroit 81	8,943
1965	Celtics 102, Cincinnati 98	12,044
1966	Celtics 121, San Francisco 113	13,909
1967	Celtics 105, Chicago 90	10,703
1968	Celtics 108, Cincinnati 101	10,035
1969	Cincinnati 110, Celtics 108	13,758
1970	Detroit 121, Celtics 118	9,606
1971	Golden State 97, Celtics 75	9,097
1972	Celtics 112, Los Angeles 104	15,316
1973	Celtics 118, Buffalo 112	15,320
1974	Buffalo 126, Celtics 119	15,320
1975	Celtics 109, Houston 94	13,082
1976	Washington 107, Celtics 104	15,040
1977	Cleveland 104, Celtics 101	11,562
1978	Cleveland 115, Celtics 101	15,547
1979	Celtics 114, Houston 108	15,320
1980	Celtics 130, Cleveland 103	15,320
1980	Celtics 130, Cleveland 103	15,320
1981	Celtics 124, Washington 100	15,320

Bill Russell had a gift of garb.

Hat trick

Dave Cowens

Don Nelson

Tom (Satch) Sanders

Bill Russell

CELTICS IN NAISMITH MEMORIAL BASKETBALL HALL OF FAME
at Springfield, Massachusetts

In order of election:

Ed Macauley (1960)
Andy Phillip (1961)
John (Honey) Russell (1964)
Walter Brown (1965)
Bill Mokray (1965)
Alvin (Doggie) Julian (1967)
Arnold (Red) Auerbach (1968)
Bob Cousy (1970)
Bill Russell (1974)
Bill Sharman (1975)
Frank Ramsey (1982)

Cousy, Macauley, Phillip, Ramsey, both Russells and Sharman were elected as players.

Auerbach and Julian were elected as coaches.

Brown and Mokray were elected as contributors to basketball. Brown founded the Celtics, co-founded the Basketball Association of America (later renamed the National Basketball Associaton) and originated the NBA All-Star Game. Mokray was a Celtic vice-president and promotions director during the Brown era; he also edited the *Official NBA Guide* for many years and was a league historian.

Note: (1) The individual's contribution to college basketball was a key factor in some selections. (2) The first Hall of Fame selections were in 1959, although the building didn't open until 1968 on the Springfield College campus where Dr. James Naismith invented basketball in 1891.

CELTICS OWNERSHIP

1946-47—1947-48: Walter Brown/ Boston Garden-Arena Corporation.

Brown founds and heads the Celtics as president of the Boston Garden-Arena Corporation.

1950-51—1963-64: Walter Brown/Lou Pieri.

After two years of heavy losses by the team, the Boston Garden-Arena Corporation wants to dump the Celtics. Brown buys the club to keep it alive, and mortgages his house and puts up his Garden-Arena and Ice Capades stock as collateral on loans to keep the franchise afloat.

After two more years of dark red ink, Brown sells half ownership to Pieri, who becomes vice president. Pieri, then owner of Rhode Island Auditorium in Providence, had been among original franchise owners in the league; but his Providence Steamrollers were scuttled after three seasons (during which they lost 122 while winning 46, including a 6-42 record in 1947-48).

1964-65: Lou Pieri/Marjorie Brown.

Upon Walter Brown's death on Labor Day 1964, his widow Marjorie takes over Celtic partnership with Pieri. Pieri becomes president, Mrs. Brown vice president. And Arnold (Red) Auerbach is brought into the partnership on March 22, 1965, as part-owner (of a percentage estimated at 10 percent).

1965-66: Jack Waldron/Ruppert Knickerbocker breweries.

The Pieri-Brown-Auerbach ownership sells Celtics to Ruppert Knickerbocker. Its president, Waldron, becomes Celtic president.

1965-66—1966-67: Jack Waldron/Marvin Kratter/National Equities.

A few months after buying the Celtics, Ruppert Knickerbocker is purchased by Kratter's National Equities. Waldron remains president of both the Celtics and Ruppert Knickerbocker.

1967-68: Marvin Kratter/National Equities.

National Equities sells Ruppert Knickerbocker but retains the Celtics. Waldron is succeeded as Celtic president by Clarence Adams, a Kratter aide.

1968-69: Jack Waldron/Ballantine brewery.

Waldron regains Celtic presidency when Ballantine, which he now heads, purchases the team from Kratter's National Equities.

1969-70—1971-72: E.E. (Woody) Erdman/Trans-National Communications.

Ballantine sells the Celtics to Trans-National Communications, headed by Erdman (and including among its investors former New York Yankee Whitey Ford and former New York football Giant Dick Lynch.).

1971-72: Jack Waldron/Ballantine/Investors Funding Corporation.

Waldron regains Celtic presidency a third time, briefly, when Trans-National goes bankrupt and the team reverts back to Ballantine, now under the corporate umbrella of Investors Funding Corporation.

1972-73—1973-74: Bob Schmertz/Leisure Technology.

Investors Funding Corporation sells the Celtics to Leisure Technology, headed by Schmertz.

1974-75: Bob Schmertz/Irv Levin.

Levin, a California businessman, claims that Schmertz reneged on a handshake agreement to allow him to buy 50 percent of the team. A California court agrees and awards Levin a $4,000,000 judgment based on the Celtics' appraised value of $8,000,000. When Schmertz is unable to come up with the $4,000,000, Levin becomes an equal partner in the Celtics.

1975-76—1977-78: Irv Levin.

Levin purchases Schmertz' stock upon the latter's death during Summer 1975. Levin's attorney, Harold Lipton, becomes a minority partner.

1978-79: John Y. Brown and Harry Mangurian.

Levin and Buffalo Braves co-owners Brown and Mangurian swap franchises. Levin promptly moves the Braves to San Diego in his Southern California home area. Brown, of Kentucky Fried Chicken fame, and Mangurian take over the Celtics—Brown as chairman, Mangurian as vice chairman.

1979-80—1981-82: Harry Mangurian.

Mangurian buys out Brown, who heads back to Kentucky to become governor.

Tom Heinsohn knew something about crowns. The Celtics won 10 of them with his help—8 as a player, 2 as their coach.

GENERAL MANAGERS (2)

Walter Brown, 1946-47—1949-50
Arnold (Red) Auerbach, 1964-65—1981-82

Note: Officially, the Celtics had no general manager 1950-51 through 1963-64. President Walter Brown and coach Red Auerbach collaborated in performing the GM duties, with Brown essentially leaving basketball matters to Auerbach while concentrating on the business side (as well as heading Boston Garden and the Boston Bruins hockey team). Upon Brown's death on Labor Day 1964, Auerbach assumed the full GM role.

HEAD COACHES (8)

John (Honey) Russell, 1946-47—1947-48
Alvin (Doggie) Julian, 1948-49—1949-50
Arnold (Red) Auerbach, 1950-51—1965-66
Bill Russell, 1966-67—1968-69
Tom Heinsohn, 1969-70—1977-78*
Tom (Satch) Sanders, 1977-78*—1978-79*
Dave Cowens, 1978-79*
Bill Fitch, 1979-80—1981-82

*Part of season.
Note: Bill Russell and Dave Cowens were player-coaches.

ASSISTANT COACHES (7)

Danny Silva, 1946-47—1947-48
Henry McCarthy, 1948-49—1949-50
Art Spector, 1949-50
John Killilea, 1972-73—1976-77
Tom (Satch) Sanders, 1977-78*
K.C. Jones, 1977-78*—1981-82
Bob MacKinnon, 1978-79
Jimmy Rodgers, 1980-81—1981-82

*Part of season.

TRAINERS (5)

Harvey Cohn, 1946-47—1957-58
Edward (Buddy) LeRoux, 1957-58*—1966-67*
Joe DeLauri, 1966-67*—1970-71
Frank Challant, 1971-72—1978-79
Ray Melchiorre, 1979-80—1981-82

*Part of season.

TRAINING CAMPS

The Celtics have had a variety of training camp locations dating back to 1946. The first Celtic squad reported on October 1 that year to the old Boston Arena Annex, where candidates worked out on a second-floor gym by day and slept on cots downstairs by night—a convenient arrangement born partly because of the post-World War II housing shortage and undoubtedly partly because of the new team's frail finances.

Celtics training camp sites over the years have been located within Greater Boston with two exceptions. One camp was held at Ellsworth, Maine, in the early 1950s, and camps through much of the 1970s were held at Massachusetts Maritime Academy on Buzzards Bay, Cape Cod.

Six Boston-area colleges have housed Celtic training camps: Babson, Boston State, Brandeis, Gordon, Hellenic and Northeastern. So has a Cambridge prep school, Browne & Nichols (now Buckingham, Browne & Nichols).

Other Celtic training bases have included an old Boston armory, the St. Botolph Street Armory . . . a Navy facility, the Fargo Building in South Boston . . . a Roxbury community center, the Maurice J. Tobin gym . . . the Cambridge YMCA . . . and both Boston Garden and Boston Arena (main building after the annex burned down).

At training sites where housing was not available, the team was often billeted at a hotel, usually the Hotel Lenox next to the Boston Public Library in Copley Square.

Bill Sharman and Red Auerbach

A different Celtic green

Bill Russell

Tom Heinsohn

Tom Heinsohn and Bob Cousy

NOTABLE ARRIVALS & DEPARTURES

(Beginning with the 1950-51 season, the start of the Auerbach era, when the Celtics put together their first winning record after being a consistent loser their first four years.)

	ENTER (at start or during season)	EXIT (during or after season)
1950-51	Auerbach (as coach), Cooper, Cousy, Donham, Harris, Macauley, McKinney.	Hertzberg, Leede.
1951-52	Brannum, Dickey, Mahnken, Sharman.	Dickey, McKinney.
1952-53	Conley, Rollins.	Conley, Mahnken, Rollins.
1953-54	Barrett, Barksdale, Nichols.	Cooper, Donham, Harris.
1954-55	Morrison, Palazzi, Ramsey, Scolari.	Barksdale, Brannum, Scolari.
1955-56	Hemric, Loscutoff, Risen.	Barrett, Macauley, Morrison.
1956-57	Heinsohn, Phillip, Russell, Tsioropoulos.	Hemric, Palazzi.
1957-58	S. Jones.	Nichols, Phillip, Risen.
1958-59	Conley*, K.C. Jones, Swain.	Tsioropoulos, Swain.
1959-60	Guarilia, Richter.	Guarilia, Richter.
1960-61	Sanders.	T. Sanders.
1961-62	Braun, Phillips.	Braun, Phillips.
1962-63	Havlicek, Lovellette, Swartz.	Cousy, Guarilia, Swartz.
1963-64	McCarthy, Naulls, Siegfried.	Loscutoff, Lovellette, McCarthy, Ramsey.
1964-65	Bonham, Counts, Thompson.	Heinsohn.
1965-66	Nelson, Sauldsberry, Watts.	Auerbach (as coach), Bonham, Counts, Naulls, Sauldsberry, Thompson.
1966-67	Russell (becoming coach as well as player), Barnett, Embry, Howell, Kimball.	Barnett, K.C. Jones, Kimball, Watts.
1967-68	Graham, J. Jones, Thacker, Weitzman.	Embry, J. Jones, Thacker, Weitzman.
1968-69	J. Barnes, Bryant, Chaney, Johnson.	Russell (as player-coach), Graham, S. Jones.
1969-70	Heinsohn (as coach), Finkel, Kuberski, White.	J. Barnes, Bryant, Howell, Siegfried.
1970-71	Cowens, Dinwiddie, Morgan, Smith, A. Williams.	Dinwiddie, Johnson.
1971-72	Glover.	Glover, Morgan, Smith.
1972-73	Silas, Westphal.	T. Sanders.
1973-74	Downing, Hankinson.	Kuberski, A. Williams.
1974-75	Ard, Clyde, McDonald, Stacom.	Chaney, Clyde, Downing, Finkel, Hankinson, Westphal.
1975-76	Anderson, Boswell, Kuberski*, Scott.	Anderson, McDonald, Nelson, Silas.
1976-77	Cook, Rowe, Saunders, Wicks, Wilson.	Cook, Wilson.
1977-78	T. Sanders (as coach last 48 games), Bing, Chaney*, DiGregorio, Maxwell, Washington.	Heinsohn (as coach after 34 games), Ard, Bing, Boswell, DiGregorio, Havlicek, Kuberski, Saunders, Scott, Stacom, Washington, Wicks.
1978-79	Cowens (becoming coach as well as player last 68 games), Archibald, Awtrey, M. Barnes, Ford, Judkins, Knight, McAdoo, Robey, Stacom*, F. Sanders, E. Williams.	T. Sanders (as coach after 14 games), Cowens (as coach after 68 games), Awtrey, M. Barnes, Knight, McAdoo, Rowe, F. Sanders, Stacom, White, E. Williams.
1979-80	Fitch (as coach), Bird, Carr, Fernsten, Henderson, Maravich.	Chaney, Judkins.
1980-81	Parish, McHale, Duerod.	Maravich**, Cowens**, Kreklow.
1981-82	Ainge, Bradley, Jackson.	Jackson.

*Second time with Celtics.
**Retired during preseason training.

Dave Cowens

Photo by John Fredrickson

A former sports columnist for the *Boston Herald Traveler,* George Sullivan is a contributing writer for the *Boston Globe.*

Sullivan has been following the Celtics since their birth in 1946, first as a teenage fan and soon afterward as a newsman. He has been writing about them since the 1955-56 season, when he covered his first Celtic game (vs. Rochester Royals at Boston Arena), and was on the Celtics' beat during their unparalleled reign of the 1960s.

A former journalism professor at Boston University, his alma mater, Sullivan's stories have been featured in the *New York Times* and *Washington Post* as well as in national magazines such as *Sport.* He has written four books.

Sullivan, wife Betty and their three children divide their time between homes in the Boston suburb of Belmont, Massachusetts, and the seaside town of Little Compton, Rhode Island.